W9-ARK-364

CONTENTS

INTRODUCTION

by Senator Robert Dole,
Senate Minority Leader

Throughout my years in public service, I have received literally thousands of letters from people who want help in allowing a relative or loved one to immigrate to America. I have yet to receive my first letter from someone who wants help in leaving America.

I believe this says a great deal about our political system. Despite its weaknesses ... despite the criticism it receives ... our American democracy is still better than any other form of government. And, as we have seen in recent years, it is a democracy that continues to inspire freedom-seeking men and women around the world.

And just as the people of Russia, Poland, and so many other Europen countries have reclaimed their government in recent years, the American people are also reclaiming theirs.

In 1992, the voters sent a loud and clear message—the days of business as usual are over. It's time for government to stop spending money we don't have, to do more with less, and to take meaningful steps to reduce the deficit which endangers the future of our children and grandchildren.

And I urge each American to keep holding our feet to the fire, and to keep sending those cards and letters to your elected representatives. Your opinion—as well as your vote—does count.

And to the young people who may be reading this, I would urge you to remain interested in the great issues of our time, and not to rule out a career in public or government service. There are many jobs that are more financially rewarding than those in public service, but I don't think there's any career that is as rewarding in terms of the difference you can make in improving your country and in helping others.

In his farewell address to the nation in January 1989, President Ronald Reagan said, "Ours was the first revolution in the history of mankind that truly reversed the course of government. And we did it with three little words—we, the people."

By working together, and by expecting the best out of their government, we, the people, can ensure that the American Revolution will survive, and that the best days of our country are truly yet to come.

INTRODUCTION

by Thomas S. Foley,
Speaker of the House

When historians look back on 1993, 1994, and the 103rd Congress, it is safe to predict that the words *change* and *reform* will be prominently featured. No matter what history's final judgment on these years may be, this era will be seen as an historic watershed in American politics. Most likely, the dramatic changes in official Washington will lead to a new and revitalized federal government. Certainly the American electorate will demand no less.

This is the first Congress to serve districts with the lines drawn under the 21st decennial census—the last census of the 20th century. While redistricting is a tumultuous and sometimes painful process that resulted in the loss of some valuable members of Congress, it is a constitutionally mandated procedure, assuring that the House of Representatives reflects the ever-changing demographics of our evolving nation.

In the House of Representatives, 110 new members have taken office along with 14 new Senators. There are now more African Americans, Hispanics, and women in Congress than ever before, providing a better reflection of the broad diversity of citizens who make up the American nation than at any time in the 28 years I have served in the House of Representatives.

This strikingly new Congress will serve under a new President. Bill Clinton is nearly 23 years younger than the outgoing President, the biggest age difference by far since John Kennedy succeeded Dwight Eisenhower. George Bush was the 10th consecutive president with a direct connection to World War II. Clinton is the first president born after World War II, and will be the first to serve his entire term in the post–cold-war world. He will serve during a time when the United States is the world's sole military superpower but must learn to share its role as an economic superpower.

It is impossible not to note that the most salient change of the past year has been the ascendancy of the Democratic party. Democrats now control the Presidency and both houses of Congress. Inherent in this opportunity, however, is the responsibility to govern. The Democratic party has gained considerable authority but has lost the ambiguity and shared responsibility that characterized divided government.

As President Clinton said in his inaugural address, the urgent question of our time is whether we can make change our friend and not our enemy.

The current climate in Washington is not unlike that of 1961 when the newly inaugurated President John F. Kennedy spoke of the torch being passed to a new generation of Americans; or of 1965, the year I entered Congress, when a large and energetic class of freshman members joined President Johnson to enact legislation that would bring into reality the unfulfilled goals of his predecessor. During the Johnson era, America put in place the Medicare and Medicaid programs, declared war on poverty, and enacted long overdue civil rights laws. Along with these laudable measures, however, came the gradual quagmire of Vietnam. Change is always accompanied by peril as well as opportunity.

In the mid-1970s, Congress experienced another dramatic influx of young, reform-minded members bent on effecting change. I was involved then, as a member and later chairman of the Democratic Study Group, in efforts to open up the House of Representatives to public scrutiny and to make it more accountable to those who send it to Washington. The results of those efforts included requirements that committees adopt written rules, conduct hearings in public, and open conference committees to the public.

Among the prime concerns of this newest generation of political leaders will be reform of the institutions of government. James Madison recognized the inherent problems when he wrote: "In framing a government which is to be administered by men over men, the great difficulty lies in this: you must first enable the government to control the governed; and in the next place oblige it to control itself."

Significant elements of the electorate, as measured in public opinion polls, demand changes in the way government operates. There will be limits, however, to how much reform government can undergo without threatening our constitutional traditions. The Judiciary, as we know, is designed *not* to respond to the current mode of popular opinion. Its task is to deliberate in secrecy and to deliver decisions insulated from the public clamor. The Executive branch, in all its bureaucracies, agencies and departments, functions at the direction of the President. The President's appointees owe him a duty of loyalty and coordinated action.

We in the Congress have been a frequent target of criticism that clearly will have to be addressed. But it is the nature of the Congress, the most responsive of the three branches, to have its divisions between parties and within parties. Our operations are never free of the controversy from which the Constitution seeks to insulate much of the operations of the other two branches. The Constitution provides for shared powers and counterbalancing forces, and it often serves to encourage delay, not efficiency.

The challenge faced by today's government is a formidable one. The nation suffers from a ballooning national debt and unacceptable annual deficits. During the two terms of the Reagan presidency, the budget deficit doubled; it doubled again in President Bush's single term. Both government and the American people appear to have reached agreement that this trend cannot be allowed to continue and that significant action must be taken to reverse it. Nonetheless, Congress and the Administration still have the obligation to meet the needs of economic expansion, job growth, and income growth. We in Congress, more than ever, must balance the needs of home districts, states, and regions with the long-term financial requirements of the nation.

The founding fathers foresaw these difficulties. In Federalist Paper No. 46, James Madison wrote that "the members of the federal legislature will be likely to attach themselves too much to local objects . . . Measures will too often be decided according to their probable effect, not on the national prosperity and happiness, but on the prejudices, interests, and pursuits of the governments and people of the individual States." Madison was warning that Congress could become a body more concerned with the interests of local states and districts than with the good of the nation at large.

It is crucial that the voices from home be taken into account. The Constitution requires Congress to meet at least once a year, and says nothing concerning a member's obligation to report back to constituents, tally their phone calls, and answer their mail. While the formal role of the legislator is to participate in the process of passing the laws that govern our nation, all members of Congress must take into careful account the interests and concerns of the men and women who elected them. The hundreds of millions of letters and phone calls that pour into Congress annually are vitally important. Congress is the most direct link the people have to their federal government. Elected officials who track down lost Social Security checks or listen to their local Chamber of Commerce's views on tax policy are doing the job voters expect them to do.

At this time, however, it is important to remember the words of Edmund Burke, the 18th-century British Member of Parliament and political theorist, who said that "your representative owes you, not his industry only, but his judgement; and he betrays instead of serving you if he sacrifices it to your opinion." While it is true that the duty of Congress under the Constitution is the representation of the people, not the guarantee of specific wisdom, this is clearly a time when our nation is looking to its leaders for wisdom and courage. It will be our job during the next few crucial years to channel the energy and ideas of this new generation of political leaders into policies which reflect the ideals of representative democracy, but most importantly, address the long-term needs of our nation as a whole.

THE 1992 ELECTION

THE PRESIDENT

Few elections in recent times have been as complex as 1992's. In it you had a incumbent president who had become highly unpopular, a principal challenger who was trying to significantly alter the liberal direction of his own party, and the first serious third party candidate in almost 30 years. This combination produced such confusion that six months after the election experts are not close to agreeing what actually happened.

Clearly Bill Clinton's victory was broad-based. He won every identifiable voter category—male–female, young–old, urban–suburban (Bush still captured the rural). But although they are loath to admit it, Clinton's brain trust actually thought he would do slightly better than he did, both in terms of the total number of electoral votes and the size of the popular vote.

As much as Bill Clinton won this election, George Bush lost it. In doing so, he broke apart the broad, but fragile, GOP coalition—begun by Richard Nixon in 1968 and then accelerated by Ronald Reagan in 1980—which was responsible for five successful GOP presidential campaigns out of six.

This somewhat unlikely combination of traditional conservatives, fundamentalists, moderate Republicans, both affluent and blue collar suburbanites, a broad spectrum of southern and border state Democrats, and younger voters were said to give the GOP an electoral college "lock" which made a Democratic White House victory seem impossible for years to come. But more than simply splitting apart, this GOP presidential dream shattered in the 1992 election.

Naturally, the key question in analyzing the 1992 contest is what effect did Perot have on the final outcome. In the end, Perot surprised the Clinton strategists. He did about three to four percent better overall than they predicted, and they believe that this cost them perhaps ten electoral votes, and a more comfortable victory margin in some other states—Georgia as a prime example.

But if Perot had not been in the contest, could George Bush have held the Oval Office? Despite reams of exit poll data, that is a question that may never be answered fully. But most analysts from both parties now seem to agree that Perot's presence in the race was not a deciding factor either for or against Bush and Clinton.

As these experts analyze the exit poll data, they believe that had Perot not been in the contest, those of his 18.8 million supporters who had gone to the polls (and how many would have is another interesting question) would have split their votes between Bush and Clinton in about the same way as the rest of the electorate voted. A few state results might have changed, but the overall outcome would almost surely have been little different.

With all the interest in the campaign, 104.5 million voters, almost 56 percent of the electorate, went to the polls to vote for a president in 1992. This was 13 million more than voted in 1988. The percentage of voters was the highest since 1960 (64 percent), and reversed a four election trend of declining turnout. But although the turnout was higher in 1992 than in the recent past, it was still well below what was normal before World War II. The record turnout was 82 percent in 1876.

Here are the final, official, vote totals for 1992 as compiled by the Federal Election Commission*:

Bill Clinton (D) 44,908,233—42.95 percent

George Bush (R) 39,102,282—37.40 percent

Ross Perot (I) 19,721,433—18.86 percent

Andrew Marrou (Lib) 291,612—0.28 percent

James "Bo" Gritz (Pop/Am First) 98,918—0.28 percent

Lenora Fulani (New Alliance) 73,248—0.07 percent

Howard Phillips (U.S. Tax) 42,960—0.04 percent

John Hagelin (Natural Law) 37,137—0.03 percent

Ron Daniels (I) 27,396—0.02 percent

1

Lyndon LaRouche (I) 25,863—0.02 percent

James Mac Warren (Soc. Workers) 22,883—0 percent

Drew Bradford (I) 4,749—0 percent

Jack Herer (Grass Rts.) 3,875—0 percent

Helen Halyard (Workers Leag.) 3,050—0 percent

J. Quinn Brisben (Soc.) 2,909—0 percent

None of The Above (Nevada) 2,537—0 percent

John Yiamouyiannis (I) 2,199—0 percent

Delbert Ehlers (I) 1,149—0 percent

Honest Jim Boren (Apathy) 956—0 percent

Earl Dodge (Prohibition) 935—0 percent

Eugene Hem (Third Pty.) 405—0 percent

Isabell Masters (Looking Bk.) 327—0 percent

Robert J. Smith (Amer.) 292—0 percent

Gloria La Riva (Workers Wrld.) 181—0 percent

Misc. Write Ins—177,207—0.17 percent

* Under various state laws, individuals trying to qualify for a place on the presidential ballot must list a party affiliation. As a result, various individuals ran in different states under different party names, even though they were registered with the federal Election Committee as "Independent." In some cases the same individual ran under different names in different states.

CONGRESS

This was supposed to be the election of change. The exit polls all said that the electorate had change on their minds, but that is tough to prove from the House results. Even with Bush trailing badly in the polls, what with the House bank and post office scandals, a record 66 retirements dominated by Democrats, and new district lines favoring the GOP, Republican prospects seemed bright. A big pickup was predicted, on the order of 25 seats. But in the end the swing of eight seats, was a bitter disappointment to the GOP and really good news to the Democrats.

The mood might have seemed, "throw the bums out," but by and large that did not happen. Ninety-three percent of the 349 incumbents seeking reelection were on their way back to Washington. This was down from the 95 percent or better averages of the recent past, but not significantly so.

As a way to gauge the race nationally, Democratic analysts chose 28 open seat House races across the country. Here there was no incumbent factor to cloud the results.

In the last Congress, 12 of the seats were held by Democrats, 10 by Republicans, and 6 were newly created. In the final results, Democrats captured 17, and Republicans 11. Give a slight edge to the Democrats.

Of the 12 seats formerly controlled by the Democrats six went Republican—a significant change. But surprisingly, half the former 10 Republican seats went Democratic. This showed no clear pattern.

STATE LEGISLATURES

In Campaign '92, Republicans made some gains but couldn't overcome the long-time Democratic dominance of state legislatures. The GOP made a net gain of five of the nation's 99 legislative chambers (Nebraska has but a single unicameral and nominally nonpartisan chamber). Democrats had a net loss of three in states where they control both chambers.

Democrats went into this election with majorities in 70 state chambers. Democrats controlled both in 29 states, the GOP controlled both in six states and 14 states were split.

On the state legislative level, 1992's big victory for the GOP came in Illinois where the Republicans, helped by redistricting, gained a majority in the State Senate for the first time in 18 years. Likewise, the GOP took control of a legislative chamber from the Democrats in both Iowa and Montana.

A big disappointment for the GOP was Florida where it fell one seat short of a majority. Party officials had hoped to make the chamber the first Republican-controlled legislative body in the South since Reconstruction. The GOP also lost chambers to the Democrats in Alaska and South Dakota.

As with members of Congress, generally speaking, state legislative incumbents of both parties who made it through the primaries fared well nationwide. One in five incumbents—about 1,500 of the nation's nearly 7,500 state lawmakers—retired or lost primaries. Of those who survived, some 93 percent won reelection.

In 1991, 31 states had divided government, where the same party didn't control the governor's office and both legislative chambers. That changed in November. Three states became solidly Democratic: Missouri and North Carolina where Democrats surprised in gubernatorial races while the party held control of both chambers of the legislatures, and the State of Washington where they kept the governor's office and the State Senate, while winning control of the State Assembly.

TERM LIMITATION

In the 1992 elections, the term limitation movement picked up real steam. In General Election balloting, voters in all 14 states in which they were proposed, approved some limits on the terms of state officials and/or members of Congress. These 14 join California, Colorado and Oklahoma which already have adopted measures limiting the terms of state office holders.

Over the past few years, poll after poll has shown that people have largely lost faith with Congress as an institution. By and large, they still like their own individual members—which is why most incumbents experience little difficulty being reelected. But when the question is asked if Congress should be reformed by limiting the length of service of members, those dissatisfied with the institution, even though they like their own congressman, are saying yes.

With poll after poll showing a clear majority of Americans supporting term limits, the battle is shifting away from the ballot box. Rather, as more constitutional challenges to term limits are being raised, the battle is turning to the courts and will ultimately be decided by the U.S. Supreme Court.

Few question the ability of voters in a state to approve an initiative setting the terms of office of state officials. In a key test, the California Supreme Court has upheld the California law passed in 1990, limiting California state assembly members to six years in office and state senators to eight years. It was challenged on the grounds that it violates the federal voting rights act because it limits the choice of minority voters as to whom they want to vote for.

But it is much less clear cut whether states can set term limits for members of the U.S. Congress. Term limit supporters rely on Article 1, Section 4 of the U.S. Constitution which reads: "The times, places and manner of holding elections for Senators and Representatives shall be prescribed in each state by the Legislature thereof; but the Congress may at any time by law make or alter such regulation." They are also relying on a 1982 Supreme Court decision, *Clements versus Fashing*, where the Court upheld a Texas law requiring a candidate to give up one state office in order to seek another.

But most other experts believe that a state law limiting congressional terms would be clearly unconstitutional. This is the conclusion of House of Representatives' legal counsel Steven Ross. In a memo to members, Ross noted that the Constitution sets only age and residency requirements for House and Senate service, while at the same time states (Article 1, Section 5) "Each House shall be the judge of the elections, returns, and qualifications of its own members."

In another widely circulated opinion, Paige Whittaker, a research lawyer for the Library of Congress reached the same conclusion. Whittaker believes a state law limiting congressional terms would be unconstitutional and says that proponents are totally misreading what the Supreme Court ruled in its Clements decision.

Colorado passed a limitation law in 1990 restricting U.S. House and Senate service to 12 years each. It has been challenged on constitutional grounds. Suits have also been filed against term limits passed in November 1992 in the states of Washington and Arkansas.

Proponents of term limits say that if state laws seeking to limit federal terms are struck down, they will attempt to win approval of state limits in a majority of states and then bring grass-roots pressure on Congress to adopt a constitutional amendment limiting service in the Senate to two 6-year terms and House service to six 2-year terms.

But would members of Congress, ever support an amendment limiting their own service? They very well might. Dozens of congressmen this year have come out in favor of the plan, and a limitation amendment will likely be introduced next year. If there is a groundswell of public opinion in favor of term limitation, Congress may not be able to resist.

And there is even the question of whether term limitation in Congress is necessary. The statistic usually cited is that in congressional election after congressional election, 95 plus percent of incumbents running for reelection win new terms. This percentage even held up this year in the face of the seeming anti-incumbent mood sweeping the country as only 13 of 405 incumbents were ousted.

While powerful committee chairman with 15 or 20 or more terms garner headlines, the fact is that because of retirements, deaths, and resignations to seek other offices more than 60 percent of House members have been elected since 1980. The same is true in the Senate where over 60 percent are in only their first or second terms.

TERM LIMITS APPROVED IN 1992

Arizona: U.S. House, three 2-year terms; state legislators, four terms. Approved by 73 to 27 percent.

Arkansas: U.S. House and state representatives, three terms; state senators, two terms; governor and other executive offices, two terms. Approved by 60 to 40 percent.

California: U.S. House, three terms. Approved by 63 to 37 percent.

Florida: U.S. House, four terms; state representative, four terms; state senator, two terms. Approved by 76 to 24 percent.

Michigan: U.S. House, three terms; state representative, three terms; state senator, two terms; governor and other executive offices, two terms. Approved by 60 to 40 percent.

Missouri: U.S. House, four terms (congressional term limits only take effect if half the states do the same.) Approved by 73 to 27 percent. State legislators, eight years. Approved by 75 to 25 percent.

Montana: U.S. House, three terms; state legislators, eight years; governor and other executive offices, eight years within 16-year period. Approved by 67 to 33 percent.

Nebraska: U.S. House, four terms; state legislators, two terms. Approved by 68 to 32 percent.

North Dakota: U.S. House, six terms. Approved by 55 to 45 percent.

Ohio: U.S. House, four terms. Approved by 66 to 34 percent. State representatives, eight years. Approved by 68 to 32 percent.

Oregon: U.S. House and state representatives, three terms; state senator, two terms; governor and other executive offices, two terms. Approved by 70 to 30 percent.

Rhode Island: Limit governor and other executive offices to four years. Approved by 60 to 40 percent.

South Dakota: U.S. House, six terms; state legislators, four terms. Approved by 63 to 37 percent.

Washington: U.S. House, three terms; state representative, six years; state senator, 12 years; governor, two terms. (Congressional term limits only take effect if nine other states do the same.) Approved by 52 to 48 percent.

Wyoming: U.S. House, three terms; state representative, six years; state senator, 12 years. Approved by 77 to 23 percent.

REAPPORTIONMENT and REDISTRICTING

Every ten years, as soon as they receive official population figures from the Census Bureau, every state must redraw their congressional district boundaries before the next election. Obviously those states gaining or losing House seats must redraw their districts, but also states which are neither gaining nor losing seats must also redraw district borders if population shifts within their states have caused current districts to vary significantly in population.

Based on the 1990 Census results, eight states gained new House seats and an equal number of additional electoral votes, while 13 states lost House seats and electoral votes.

Without a doubt the big winner in 1990s reapportionment was California which gained seven new House seats thanks to a massive shift west in population over the last ten years. California's gain in population accounts for fully one-quarter of all population gain in the U.S. between 1980 and 1990. Its gain was as if the entire state of Massachusetts, every man, woman and child, suddenly decided they wanted to live near the Pacific Ocean and called the moving van.

Where did these seven seats come from? The big states of the East and Midwest: New York (-3), Pennsylvania (-2) and Illinois (-2). The other big winners in the 1990 reapportionment were Florida (+4) and Texas (+3), the other big losers were Michigan (-2) and Ohio (-2).

Redistricting is first and always a political act (except in a very few states who have created nonpartisan commissions to do the job). It is done by the party in power with an eye on protecting its interests while dissipating (or perhaps concentrating in as few districts as possible) the strength of the opposing party. The most partisan of all the 1981 remaps was California's. The new district boundary map, which resembles nothing less than a crazed jigsaw puzzle, was the creation of the late Rep. Phil Burton. Each district was carefully crafted to give the maximum protection to Democratic incumbents while diluting the Republican strength in fast growing suburban areas by either spreading probable GOP votes over several districts, or by creating a district that was overwhelmingly Republican in order to safeguard adjoining Democratic districts. The plan has worked amazingly well. In 1980 the California congressional delegation stood at 22-21 Democratic. After redistricting, the margin grew to 28-17.

Redistricting is done by the two houses of the state legislatures (except those few who have established commissions) and must survive the possible veto of the governor. This is called the "redistricting triad." It is assumed that in any state where one party controls the triad it can pretty much have its way with redistricting.

More than ever before, state legislatures redrew their congressional district maps with the courts looking over their shoulders. For many years the Supreme Court and the lower courts treated redistricting as essentially a political matter. But in a series of court tests since the 1981 redrawing of district maps, the Supreme Court has taken a more active role.

In a famous 1963 decision (Reynolds versus Sims) the Supreme Court ruled based on one-man-one-vote that congressional districts and the districts of both state legislative chambers must have "substantially equal" populations. Critics led by Sen. Everett Dirksen, D.-Ill., were outraged. They saw the decision as an invasion

of state rights. So a constitutional amendment was proposed to allow every state to apportion one of its legislative chambers without regard to population and to allow for variances in congressional district size. While the amendment never received the required ⅔ vote to pass, the Supreme Court took notice and began to accept variances of up to 10 percent as being "substantially equal." But that attitude changed in the late 1960s. The Court rejected district maps from Missouri and Indiana with about a six percent variance. States got the message and after the 1971 remap, 386 of the 435 members of Congress came from almost identically sized districts. In the 93rd Congress (1973–75) the average difference in district size was one half of one percent as opposed to a difference approaching 20 percent just a decade earlier.

Finally in a 1983 decision (Karcher versus Daggett) by a 5-4 vote the Court struck down the New Jersey remap because the population size of the districts varied by seven-tenths of a percent. The Court ruled that the difference must be close to zero unless it can be shown that there is some overriding need to vary the size of the districts.

The Court's first gerrymandering verdict came in 1986 as part of a test of the 1982 Voting Rights Act. The Court ruled (Thornburg versus Gingles) that any gerrymander of congressional district lines that purposely dilutes minority voting strength—a common reason for gerrymandering in the past—is illegal. Then in reviewing the redrawn Indiana district map (Davis versus Bandemer) the Court held that a gerrymander was subject to legal challenge, but found that the Indiana map, admittedly a partisan Republican creation, was not sufficiently out of line to be considered illegal.

That leaves the question of how blatant a gerrymander has to be to be illegal. When the obviously gerrymandered California map finally made it to the Supreme Court on appeal in 1989 (Badham versus Eu) the Court by one vote (6-3) refused to hear the case and let stand a lower court ruling upholding the California district lines.

All this has left most observers to guess whether the Supreme Court will be tolerant of a gerrymander based on racial issues. That is being tested as this volume goes to print. In the 1992 remap, the North Carolina legislature created two very oddly shaped minority districts.

A group of white voters has challenged this remap on the grounds of reverse discrimination.

Still another lawsuit, could eventually result in the entire 1990 congressional remap being declared invalidated, and Congress being forced to start over again from scratch. This, in turn, could change the number of House seats in up to 21 states.

The suit was filed in Montana by state officials and members of Montana's congressional delegation angered over the loss of one of the state's two House seats in the new reapportionment.

Under a 50-year-old mathematical formula used by Congress to determine how the 435 House seats are divided among the states, it was decided that a model congressional district should have 572,000 residents. In the 1990 Census, Montana's population dropped to just over 800,000, meaning that it does not have the population to continue to support two congressional districts.

The result was the loss of one of its current two Congressional Districts, and the entire state of Montana becoming what amounts to the nation's largest and most widespread single congressional district.

The suit filed in federal district court in Helena alleged that the way Congress apportioned seats after the 1990 Census was unconstitutional for two reasons: that the 50-year-old mathematical formula is outdated and inaccurate and results in a violation of the Voting Rights Act guarantee of one-man, one-vote; and that the automatic way the formula is applied—without any Congressional vote—represents an unconstitutional delegation of Congress' power.

The suit was met with yawns in Washington. A low level cadre of Justice Department lawyers was sent out to oppose it. They argued that the plaintiffs had no standing to bring the suit and the court no right to hear it, since congressional apportionment deals with dividing seats among all states not within any one state.

They further argued that even if the plaintiffs did have a right to bring the suit, it was so transparently political that it should be summarily dismissed.

But a three judge panel headed by District Judge Charles C. Lovell has shocked Washington by not only agreeing with the state of Montana that Congress' apportionment system is illegal, but by issuing a permanent injunction forbidding elections to be held based on this apportionment.

District Judge James Battin joined in the opinion. Judge Diarmuid O'Scannlain, of the 9th Circuit Court of Appeals, sitting as the third judge on the panel, dissented.

Lovell ruled that whatever method of assigning seats the House employs, it must result in the smallest absolute difference in the size of districts. "While arguing that proportions and percentages are the proper criteria rather than absolute numbers," Lovell wrote, "(the House) ignores the fact that each number represents a person whose voting rights are potentially impacted."

Instead of simply applying a five-decades-old formula, Lovell ruled, Congress must examine various mathematical alternatives to determine which may be the most accurate.

It may take a number of years before this issue is finally resolved.

THE ELECTORAL COLLEGE

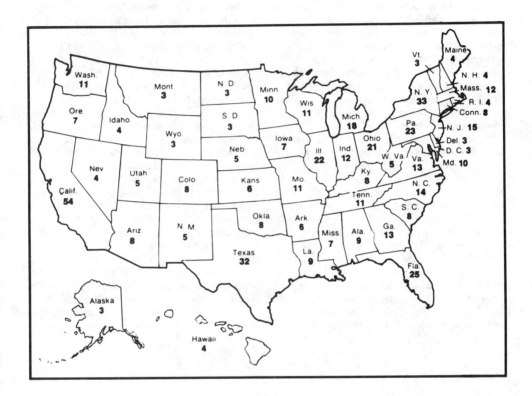

The president and the vice president of the United States are the only elective federal officials not elected by direct vote of the people. They are elected by the members of the Electoral College, an institution that has survived since the founding of the nation despite repeated attempts in Congress to alter or abolish it.

On presidential election day, the first Tuesday after the first Monday in November of every fourth year, each state chooses as many electors as it has senators and representatives in Congress. The chief reason the Constitution provided for a census of the population every 10 years was to give a basis for apportionment of representatives among the states. This apportionment largely determines the number of electoral votes allotted to each state.

The number of electors from each state is equivalent to the size of its Congressional delegation (number of Representatives plus senators).

Under provisions of a law that became effective November 15, 1941, apportionment of representatives is made by the method of equal proportions, i.e., so that the average population per representative has the least possible variation between one state and another. The first House of Representatives, in 1789, had 65 members, as provided by the Constitution. As the population grew, the number of representatives was increased, but the total membership has been fixed at 435 since the apportionment based on the 1910 census. In 1964, for the first time, as provided by the 23rd Amendment to the Constitution, the District of Columbia voted for

3 electors. Thus, with 100 senators and 435 representatives, the Electoral College has 538 members, with a majority of 270 electoral votes needed to elect the president and vice president.

The Founding Fathers never foresaw the rise of political parties that has occurred. They intended that the members of the Electoral College be independent voters exercising independent judgment. Today, political parties customarily nominate their lists of electors at their respective state conventions. An elector cannot be a member of Congress or any person holding federal office. Obviously, parties chose electors based on party loyalty.

Some states print the names of the candidates for president and vice president at the top of the November ballot; others list only the names and political party of the electors. In either case, the electors of the party receiving the highest vote are elected. It is winner-take-all, so if a party wins by just one vote in a state, it gets all the electors.

The electors meet on the first Monday after the second Wednesday in December in their respective state capitals, or in some other place prescribed by state legislatures. By long-established custom, they vote for their party nominees, although the Constitution does not require them to do so. The only Constitutional requirement is that at least one of the persons for whom each elector votes shall not be an inhabitant of that elector's home state (which means that a presidential and vice presidential candidate from the same party cannot come from the same state). In most elections one or two electors will not vote the way they are pledged, usually in the form of some kind of protest.

Certified and sealed lists of the votes of the electors in each state are mailed to the president of the U.S. Senate. He opens them in the presence of the members of the Senate and House of Representatives in a joint session held on January 6 (or the next day if that falls on a Sunday), and the electoral votes of all the states are then counted. If no candidate for president has a majority, the House chooses a president from among the top three candidates, with all representatives from each state combining to cast one vote for that state. That occurred in 1800, 1824, and 1876, and in 1888 the presidential candidate receiving the largest popular vote failed to win a majority of the electoral votes. If no candidate for vice president has a majority, the Senate chooses from the top two, with the senators voting as individuals. The new president and vice president officially take office on January 20, after they are sworn in.

THE POLITICAL PARTIES
THE DEMOCRATIC PARTY

The Democratic Party, the oldest political organization in the United States, traces its roots to one of the factions that emerged during the administration of George Washington. His shrewd and aggressive treasury secretary, Alexander Hamilton, assembled an entourage of cabinet members and congressmen who supported his provocative program for funding the federal government. In response, Virginia Congressman James Madison gathered a group that held opposing views. The Hamilton faction soon came to be known as the Federalists; the Madison faction as the Democratic Republicans. Effective leadership of the party fell almost immediately to Madison's good friend and fellow Virginian, Secretary of State Thomas Jefferson.

The lines were quickly drawn: the Federalists were pro-British, generally supported a strong central government and rule by the upper classes, and favored commerce and business interests. The Democratic Republicans were pro-French, believed in a decentralized government, were more inclined to popular rule, and advocated an agrarian-based society. Jefferson openly disdained Hamilton as a "monarchist" and the Federalists as a "mercenary phalanx."

In the election of 1796, Jefferson's electoral total placed him second to John Adams, and he became vice president in the new Federalist administration. As the country's top Democratic Republican, Jefferson was a lightning rod for the opposition; by 1800 his notoriety made him the obvious choice to head the Democratic Republican ticket. Thanks to a Hamilton feud with Adams, the Federalist vote split. The Democratic Republicans gained wide support among farmers, urban intellectuals, small traders, and artisans. An electoral tie between Jefferson and fellow Democratic Republican Aaron Burr ensued and, after much haggling, a lame-duck Federalist House of Representatives selected Jefferson as president, Burr as vice president.

For the next 40 years, the Democratic Republican Party, or variations thereof, dominated the political scene in the United States. The Federalists suffered a debilitating blow when Hamilton was shot dead by Burr in a duel in Weehawken, New Jersey, on July 11, 1804. By 1816 the party itself was nearly dead, and James Monroe won the presidency on the Democratic Republican ticket with token opposition. The fifth president paid little attention to party matters, however, and the Democratic Republicans disintegrated into bickering factions.

A national movement to select presidential electors by popular vote (rather than by state legislatures, as many states had done) revived public interest in presidential elections, and the contests of 1824 and 1828 were bitterly fought. Four candidates vied for the presidency in 1824, and none won a majority of the electoral vote. Thus the election was thrown into the House of Representatives, where John Quincy Adams, an independent-minded Democratic Republican, won in a controversial decision. Andrew Jackson, hero of the War of 1812, prevailed four years later. It was under Jackson, a fervent proponent of popular rule, that the Democratic Republicans became known simply as Democrats.

The opposition forces that coalesced in the vacuum left by the Federalists were a diverse lot who seemed united primarily in their distaste for Jackson's plebeian sympathies. The more conservative wing of the Democratic Republican Party became the National Republicans and joined with a third party, the Anti-Masons, and with Northern manufacturing and business groups to form the Whig Party in 1834. Over the next quarter century, however, the Whigs managed to elect only two war-hero presidents—William Henry Harrison in 1840 and Zachary Taylor in 1848, both of whom died in office and by 1852 the party had completely disintegrated.

The Democrats were finally dislodged from their seat of power by the great issue of the mid 19th century: slavery. As the nation was torn asunder by the question of whether slavery should be allowed in the Western territories, the party divided into Northern and Southern factions. But not even the Northern Democrats, led

9

by Illinois Senator Stephen A. Douglas, could bring themselves to champion absolute opposition to slavery. They favored the doctrine of *popular sovereignty*, by which the inhabitants of each territory would decide whether to allow slavery. At the Democratic convention of 1860, held in Charleston, South Carolina, the party formally split, the Northern Democrats nominating Douglas and the Southern Democrats nominating John C. Breckinridge of Kentucky. The division facilitated the election of Abraham Lincoln, standard bearer for the fledgling Republican Party.

The Democratic Party rose from its sickbed only twice during the next half-century, both times to send Grover Cleveland to the White House (1884 and 1892). But the Democrats periodically controlled one or both houses of Congress and remained popular on state and local levels. Thus they retained credibility as a viable opposition party, advocating reconciliation with the South, defending agrarian interests, supporting low interest rates and opposing tariffs and business trusts. At the 1896 convention in Chicago, radical elements seized control, nominated Populist William Jennings Bryan, and adopted a platform calling for free silver (the coinage of money without regard to a gold standard), income taxes, immigration restrictions, and railroad regulation. The party went down to its worst defeat since 1872.

With the Republican vote split in 1912 between regular party nominee William Taft and Bull Moose candidate Theodore Roosevelt, Democrat Woodrow Wilson emerged victorious. He remained in the White House until 1920, after which three Republicans held sway. With the nation in the throes of a devastating economic depression, liberal Democrat Franklin D. Roosevelt inaugurated the party's second golden age with a victory in 1932. He would be elected for an unprecedented four terms, restructure the nation's economic system, revamp the structure of government and guide the country through a world war before dying in office in 1945. Vice President Harry S. Truman succeeded him.

Truman survived yet another party split in 1948, when Southern Democrats opposed to civil rights reforms put forward their own ticket, and was narrowly reelected. In 1952 the party surrendered the White House to the popular Dwight D. Eisenhower, a World War II hero, for eight years, then recaptured it in 1960 with the election of the young and charismatic John F. Kennedy. Upon his tragic assassination in 1963, Lyndon Johnson took the reins and drove the country directly and deeply into the morass of the Vietnam War. Johnson chose not to run in 1968, and the party's nominee, Vice President Hubert Humphrey, could not overcome the stigma of the Vietnam conflict and a strong third-party movement led by Alabama conservative George C. Wallace.

That tumultuous year saw continued war in Asia, the assassinations of black leader Martin Luther King, Jr. and Senator Robert F. Kennedy, anti-war and race riots in the streets of American cities, and the election of Republican Richard Nixon. A victory of historic proportions carried Nixon past Democrat George McGovern in 1972, and until they were dislodged by Bill Clinton in 1992, Republicans held the White House, except for a four-year hiatus from 1976 until 1980, when Democrat Jimmy Carter occupied it. The technocratic Carter failed to excite the public's imagination and was turned out by Ronald Reagan in a landslide victory.

The 1992 contest may well be a turning point for the Democrats in national politics. While Democratic control of Congress grew in the late 1980s, the party could not break the coalition that had propelled first Reagan and then Bush to the Oval Office. With the breaking of that coalition in 1992, the Democrats could enjoy a long run in the White House if they can solve some of the nation's pressing problems.

THE REPUBLICAN PARTY

The relatively young Republican Party was formally organized in 1854, and although it shares half the name of Thomas Jefferson's Democratic Republicans, at least one of its major ideological bloodlines stems from Alexander Hamilton's Federalists: a favorable disposition toward business, commerce and finance. This particular baton was passed on to the contentious corps that called itself the Whig Party, elements of which became one of the main ingredients in the Republican blend.

However, the transcendent tenet that united all who came together to create the Republican Party was an abhorrence of slavery. Wounds that had been festering since the nation's founding were reopened in 1854 with the passage of the Kansas-Nebraska Act, which put into law Sen. Stephen Douglas's notion of popular sovereignty in those territories created from the lands of the Louisiana Purchase. It was a regrettable compromise that satisfied no one for long. As a result, the Whigs completely disintegrated, the Democrats split into Northern and Southern factions, and the Republican Party was born.

The party's formative meeting is a matter of mild dispute—some claim it was held in Ripon, Wisconsin, on February 28, 1854, others, that it was held in Jackson, Michigan, on July 6 of that year. The organization's name also has competing claimants: some credit newspaper magnate Joseph Medill, others, New York Tribune editor Horace Greeley. All agree, however, on the parties and factions that assembled under the new Republican roof: the anti-slavery Free-Soil Party and the anti-slavery defectors from the two major parties, known as "Conscience Whigs" and "Barnburner Democrats."

The first Republican convention was held in Philadelphia, and John C. Fremont—frontier explorer, soldier, senator and popular figure of the day—was selected as the party's presidential candidate. Fremont ran against seasoned politician and diplomat James Buchanan and former president Millard Fillmore, representing the American (Know-Nothing) Party. (The Know-Nothings evolved from two secret nativist organizations and got their nickname because they routinely denied knowing anything about the secret societies. See "Third Parties.") The Republican candidate polled more than one-third of the popular vote and an extraordinary 114 electoral votes. The Republicans were off to a rousing start.

Four years later, in Chicago, the party chose as its standard bearer a 51-year-old Illinois lawyer and former congressman with a reputation as a skillful orator and debater: Abraham Lincoln. The Democrats fielded two candidates, a Northerner (Stephen Douglas) and a Southerner (John Breckinridge), and a third party candidate (John Bell, Constitutional Union Party) drew off more than one-tenth of the popular vote. Lincoln won with 40 percent, and the slavery question was settled by the Civil War.

Lincoln's second vice president and successor upon his assassination, Andrew Johnson, was actually a dissident Democrat. But with that exception, and the two nonconsecutive terms of Grover Cleveland during the 1880s, the Republicans held the reins of political power in the White House and frequently in Congress for 52 years. For a decade after Lincoln's death, the party was sharply divided between Radical Republicans, who wanted the South severely punished, and the anti-radicals (who appeared as "Liberal Republicans" in the 1872 elections), who advocated reconciliation. Differences were settled by the 1876 election of Republican Rutherford B. Hayes, who lost the popular vote and was approved by the House of Representatives only after agreeing to a Democratic demand that he withdraw federal troops from the South.

Reconstruction aside, the two major parties exhibited few differences in issues during the postwar years. Generally, the Democrats advocated tariff reductions, regulation of business and income taxes. Republicans pushed high protective tariffs and tight money policies. Both parties periodically emphasized civil service reform. A severe economic depression in 1893 brought on a surge of support for the People's Party, more commonly referred to as the Populists. In 1896 both they and the Democrats nominated left-leaning William Jennings Bryan, and the Republicans raised the specter of inflation, factory closings and federal control of business. Republican candidate William McKinley won by a comfortable margin and achieved a landslide victory four years later.

McKinley's assassination in Buffalo, New York, in 1901 brought the vigorous and immensely popular Theodore Roosevelt to the presidency. As a progressive on domestic matters, Roosevelt pursued anti-trust suits against the giants of American business, pushed for the regulation of railroads and the food industry and forced the settlement of strikes in labor's favor. He stepped aside in 1908 in favor of his friend William Howard Taft but was disappointed by Taft's conservative turn. Rejected by the regular party in 1912, Roosevelt agreed to run as a candidate for the newly formed Progressive, or Bull Moose, Party. The Republican split resulted in the election of Democrat Woodrow Wilson, who held the White House for two terms.

The scandal-ridden administration of Republican Warren G. Harding followed, and his untimely death in 1923 resulted in the inauguration of Calvin Coolidge. "Silent Cal," a fervent follower of the less-is-best school of management, presided over the country during the raucous Roaring Twenties. His successor, Herbert Hoover, had the misfortune of being in office when the stock market crashed, bringing on the Great Depression and two decades of Democratic rule.

After Hoover's 1932 loss to Franklin D. Roosevelt, three other GOP candidates went down to defeat before the mighty FDR-Alfred M. Landon in 1936, Wendell Willkie in 1940, Thomas E. Dewey in 1944. Dewey lost again in 1948 to Harry S. Truman before Dwight D. Eisenhower put another Republican administration in the executive mansion. The popular Democrat John F. Kennedy succeeded "Ike," and Lyndon Johnson assumed the presidency upon Kennedy's death. Johnson won the office in his own right when he defeated staunch conservative Barry Goldwater by a landslide in 1964.

Four years later, Eisenhower's vice president and party stalwart Richard Nixon rose from the ashes of a 1960 defeat at the hands of Kennedy and a disastrous showing in the 1962 California gubernatorial race to gain the White House in a narrow victory over incumbent vice president Hubert Humphrey. Nixon retained the top job in 1972 with an easy win over liberal George McGovern, but seeds of dire scandal were sown when a team hired by Nixon's campaign officials burglarized the headquarters of the Democratic Party in the Watergate Hotel in Washington. High-level White House involvement in a coverup of the Watergate affair resulted in the president's ignominious resignation. Vice President Gerald Ford filled the vacancy admirably but lost the White House to Democrat Jimmy Carter in 1976.

The Carter interregnum ended four years later when a charismatic former governor of California, Ronald Reagan, led a Republican surge that resulted in his election and GOP control of the Senate. The upper chamber was returned to the Democrats in 1986, but the conservative Reagan retained his office and remained popular despite several scandals that swirled around his administration. In 1988 Reagan's Vice President, George Bush, won the GOP nomination in a contested primary over an initially crowded field and then went on to almost duplicate Reagan's winning margin in a landslide victory over the Democratic nominee, Massachusetts' Gov. Michael Dukakis. While the GOP continued to show its dominance in presidential politics, despite Bush's wide margin of victory (54-46 percent in the popular-vote translating into a 40-state electoral-vote runaway 426-112) the Democrats added to their majorities in both the House and Senate and made key state house gains. Then the GOP lost further ground both in Congress and in state legislative chambers in the 1990 off-year election.

Bush's loss in 1992 can only be seen as a major setback for the GOP. The coalition of blue collar workers, southern whites, suburban middle-class, traditional Republicans, conservatives and western voters that had been assembled by Ronald Reagan came apart. And unless the Democrats falter, and this fragile coalition can be reassembled, Republicans may not see the White House for some time to come.

THIRD PARTIES

The odds against getting to the White House on an independent or third-party ticket are cosmic. This was shown clearly by Ross Perot in 1992. No third party candidate in this century has been as well financed, or has as much popular support. Yet Perot was only able to finish second in two states—tiny Maine and Utah.

But optimism is obviously a characteristic of many would-be presidents. In the past 157 years of the nation's history, hundreds of third-party candidates have doggedly pursued the crown, but none has worn it. Only eight polled more than a million votes.

This is not to say that new parties have never been successful. But those that prospered were always second parties—opposition parties that sprang up to counter prevailing political attitudes and parties that were enjoying monopolies. The Democrats, for example, were organized to oppose strong central government and the Federalists who espoused it; the Republican Party was assembled in the wake of the Whig Party's demise to oppose slavery and the Southern-dominated Democratic Party that kept the institution alive.

Third parties are by no means superfluous props on the political stage. Their very creation is usually in response to problems that many citizens consider significant. Third parties frequently offer remedies to those problems and stimulate or intimidate politicians of the major parties into dealing with them.

There are any number of reasons why no third party has ever achieved a significant national victory. On most major issues, two broad positions can be taken, and before a third party can gain sufficient momentum, the two major parties have already made the tradeoffs, searched out the common denominators and seized the middle ground. Also working against third parties are the winner-take-all systems used in both popular and electoral contests, prohibitive advertising costs (particularly for television) and restrictive ballot access regulations in many states.

Still, there rarely seems to be a dearth of third-party candidates willing to make the sacrifices and bear the expense of going for the big prize. Many have enjoyed only local popularity or were on the national scene for such a brief moment that they warrant mere footnotes in history texts: the Workingmen's Party of the United States, the Honest Man's Party of Massachusetts, the Readjusters of Virginia, the Constitutional Union, the Anti-Monopolists. Others have had more widespread appeal. In the 1980 election, for example, 11 third-party or independent candidates ran in at least two states.

The first third party to appear on the national scene was the Anti-Masonic Party, which was opposed to elitism and privilege in American society and the secret organizations that seemed to symbolize and perpetuate those concepts. The party began in 1826, when a citizen of upstate New York published a book purporting to contain the secrets of the Masons. The author disappeared, and the Masons were blamed for it. The furor that resulted spread across the northern and mid-Atlantic states and into Ohio. By 1832 the spark of anti-Mason indignation had become a political party, which held the nation's first political convention and fielded a presidential candidate, William Wirt of Maryland. By the time the next election rolled around, however, the Anti-Masonic party had been engulfed by the Whigs.

Opposition to slavery ignited the next burst of third-party activity. Abolitionists formed the Liberty Party in 1849 and chose James G. Birney, a Kentuckian who had freed his own slaves, to head the ticket. He polled only 7,053 votes. Birney ran again in 1844, this time getting 62,197 votes. The party folded and the remnants joined with anti-slavery dissidents from the major parties to form the Free Soil Party. The Free-Soilers put former President Martin Van Buren at the head of their ticket in 1848 and managed to draw 10 percent of the popular vote but not a single electoral tally. With an ardent abolitionist, John P. Hale, as the Free Soil candidate in 1852, the party got less than 5 percent of the vote and merged into the ranks of the new Republican Party two years later. When the Republicans fielded a ticket headed by John C. Fremont, the Free Soil Party's name became incorporated into a battle cry: "Free Soil, Free Labor, Free Speech, Fremont!"

Just as the slavery issue was boiling over and political parties were being rearranged to deal with it, another issue erupted on the opposite end of the egalitarian continuum, and a peculiar political movement coalesced around it. At the midcentury point, Irish Catholic immigrants were pouring into the northeast and German immigrants were beginning to flood the Midwest. Two secret Native American organizations—the Supreme Order of the Star Spangled Banner and the National Council of the United States of North America—were organized to push for immigration restrictions. Eventually, their politically active members began running for office on the American Party ticket. When asked about the nativist societies they belonged to, they responded that they knew nothing about them. The American party thus became known as the "Know-Nothing Party."

The Know-Nothings enjoyed great regional success and elected governors in Connecticut, Rhode Island, Massachusetts and New Hampshire. They held their first and only political convention in Philadelphia in 1856 and immediately split into Northern and Southern factions. The latter prevailed, and former Whig president Millard Fillmore was chosen to head the ticket. He drew 21 percent of the popular vote and Maryland's eight electoral votes, then returned to retirement. The party fell apart, and the Northern Know-Nothing wings joined the Republican Party.

The issue that would dominate the last quarter of the 19th century—economic reform—had been heralded by the Greenback Party. The movement had peaked in 1878, when the party won 14 Congressional seats. Two years later, its presidential candidate, Rep. James B. Weaver of Iowa, had polled only 300,000 popular votes and the party had disappeared. But the corrupt Grant years had turned into the Gilded Age, an era dominated by business trusts, banks, manufacturing and railroad interests. Farmers, labor leaders and money reformers gathered in Cincinnati in 1891 and responded by forming the People's Party, commonly known as the Populists.

The party called for a host of reform measures, including the nationalization of railroads, telephones and the telegraph; free silver (the coinage of money without regard to a gold standard); a graduated income tax; and a one-term presidency.

Former Greenback nominee James Weaver polled more than a million votes as the Populist candidate in 1892. Two years later, the party elected six senators and seven members of the House of Representatives. In 1896 both the Democratic Party and the People's Party nominated celebrated orator William Jennings Bryan as their standard bearer, and he received nearly half the popular vote and 176 electoral votes. Since the Populists and the Democrats now shared many of the same interests, the minor party was absorbed into the major party, and Bryan unsuccessfully represented the Democrats on the national ticket in 1900 and 1908.

At the same time the economic reform parties were enjoying modest popularity, a more radical movement—this one calling for a total restructuring of the economic system—began attracting public notice. During the 1820s, a number of ephemeral "workingmen's" parties were organized on the East Coast. Spurred by the socialist and Marxist movements in Europe, American labor activists met in Philadelphia in 1876 and organized the Workingmen's Party of the United States. It was renamed the Socialist Labor Party a year later and fielded its first presidential candidate in 1892. Like most doctrinaire groups, it was highly fractionalized and suffered a number of secessions. One of the more moderate splinter groups was the Socialist Party, which ran one of its best-known leaders, Eugene Debs, in five different elections. He received nearly a million votes in 1912 and in 1920. The Communist Party peeled away from the Socialists in 1919 and promptly split into numerous factions. The Socialists have continued to nominate candidates to the present day, the best known of whom was Norman Thomas, who ran in every election from 1928 to 1944.

Meanwhile, the progressive movement within Republican Party ranks continued apace. Theodore Roosevelt, Republican president from 1901 until his friend and fellow Republican William Howard Taft took the oath in January 1909, tried and failed to gain the regular party nomination in 1912 and chose to run on the Progressive (Bull Moose) ticket instead. He lost the election, but the Progressive banner was picked up and carried by Wisconsin Senator Robert La Follette. In 1924, he ran for the presidency as a Progressive and garnered nearly five million votes. Franklin Roosevelt's third-term vice president, Henry A. Wallace, was nominated as the

Progressive Party candidate in 1948. He received more than a million votes.

There was yet another candidate on the ballot in that first postwar election. A group of southern Democrats, angry with Harry Truman's call for an end to poll taxes and a federal law against lynching, bolted party ranks and formed the States' Rights Democratic Party, also known as the Dixiecrats. The Democratic governor of South Carolina (and now the state's senior senator), J. Strom Thurmond, was selected as the new party's presidential candidate. He polled over a million popular votes and 39 electoral votes from 5 southern states.

The Dixiecrats disbanded after the 1948 election, but their conservative-Democratic credo only went into dormancy. It reemerged two decades later as the political philosophy of the American Independent Party, the political horse ridden by Alabama Governor George C. Wallace. As the protest party's 1968 presidential candidate, he opposed the civil rights activists in the Democratic Party, espoused law-and-order, be-

littled the antiwar movement and campaigned for the blue collar vote. And in that year of unsettling social upheaval, Wallace won 9,906,473 popular votes—the most ever by a third-party or independent candidate—and 46 electoral votes.

Prior to 1992, the most successful presidential candidate since 1968 who did not run as a Democrat or a Republican was Illinois congressman John B. Anderson. He ran as an independent in 1980 and won 5,720,060 popular votes, placing him second to George Wallace as the most successful third-party or independent candidate in the nation's history.

Now Wallace's feat has to some degree been eclipsed by the rather astounding showing of Ross Perot. Wallace was effectively a regional candidate, piling up the bulk of his votes and all his electoral votes in the South, Perot had significant levels of support in all regions. Perot is now trying to convert his popularity into a semipermanent national organization—United We Stand America—but it remains to be seen if it will be able to challenge the two major parties.

CAMPAIGN FINANCING

One of the big political stories of 1992 was that finally, after more than a decade, the Democrats managed to narrow the fundraising gap.

The Federal Election Commission keeps track of fundraising totals in two year election "cycles." Thus for Campaign '92 the cycle started on January 1, 1991 and actually ran through January 15, of 1993. For Campaign '90 it started on January 1, 1989 and ran through January of 1991. The parties each raise funds nationally under three separate entities: the national committee, a senatorial campaign committee, and a congressional campaign committee.

Under Ronald Reagan, and then George Bush, the GOP was a money raising (and spending) machine. In Ronald Reagan's reelection year of 1984 it set records that will likely never again be matched. In that election cycle, 1983–84, the Republican National Committee banked a staggering $105.9 million, the National Republican Senatorial Committee $81.6 million, and the National Republican Congressional Committee $58.3 million, a total of $245.8 million. By way of comparison, in the 1983–84 cycle, the Democratic National Committee raised $46.6 million, the Democratic Senatorial Committee $8.9 million, and the Democratic Congressional Campaign Committee $10.3 million, a total of $65.8.

Although 1984 was the high water mark for GOP fundraising, a startling disparity between Democratic fundraising and GOP fundraising continued for the balance of the decade. In the 1986 cycle, the GOP raised $208 million to the Democrats $42.9 million; in the 1988 election cycle the GOP banked $191 million to the Democrats $81 million; and in the 1990 election cycle, the Republicans raised $167 million to the Democrats $41.1 million.

And these figures relate only to the major central national campaign committees of the two parties. GOP state parties and individual candidates are also raising huge sums with the help of national party fund raisers.

To be sure, individual Democrats running for the House and Senate, especially incumbents running for reelection, have always been able to raise large sums; more than enough to mount campaigns that have held Democratic majorities in both bodies even as Republicans were capturing the White House. But the huge fundraising difference allowed the GOP to finance lavish national campaigns and to pour last minute money into toss-up contests.

But if 1992 is a guide, the Democrats have started to turn around this huge GOP money lead. Actually what happened, is that while GOP fundraising stayed about level with previous years, Democrats found significant new sources of revenue.

Combined totals show the Republicans raising $192 million, the Democrats $104 million. The Republican National Committee raised $85.4 million, down about $5 million from the last presidential election cycle. By contrast, the Democratic National Committee raised $65.7 million, up more than $13 million from 1987–88 levels and more than $50 million more than it raided in the 1990 election cycle.

Republicans still showed a significant edge in national fundraising for their Senate and House campaign committees. The NRSC raised $72.3 million, while its Democratic counterpart raised $25.4 million (a $10 million increase for the Democrats over 1988). In the House, the Republicans outraised the Democrats $34 million to $12.8 million.

Although the GOP's central fund raising arms far outstrip their Democratic counterparts, the GOP has not been able to take full advantage of the disparity because federal election law limits the amount of direct help that a party can give any of its candidates. A party organization can directly contribute only $17,500 to any of its senatorial candidates, and may pay bills for that candidate in amounts depending on the population of the state ($100,000 in Wyoming to $1.2 million in California).

And it has to be emphasized again that this represents only organized national fund raising by the parties. Individual Democrats still raise considerably more then their Republican counterparts on a race-by-race basis.

Overall, all Democratic candidates for the House and Senate, including those running in primaries raised $360 million in 1991–92. Republicans raised $293 million. More importantly, Democratic incumbents in the House, 227 of them, raised $126 million while 143 Republican incumbents raised $75 million.

Inflation has hit political campaigning in a big way. The use of expensive consultants, frequent polling, and heavy television advertising have pushed campaign costs through the roof. As recently as 1984, the $2 million senate campaign was unusual, and the $1 million House campaign almost unheard of. In 1992 every single winning Senate candidate spent more than $2 million and ten spent more than $5 million.

In 1992, by far, the most expensive campaigning was in California. In the state's two Senate contests Democrat Barbara Boxer spent $10.3 million to defeat Republican Bruce Herschensohn who spent $7.8 million, and Democrat Dianne Feinstein spent $8 million to defeat GOP incumbent Sen. John Seymour who spent $7.8 million.

In House campaigns, Republican businessman Michael Huffington spent more than $5 million of his own money to be elected from California's 22nd district, and Democratic businesswoman Jane Harman spent more than $2 million of her own money in winning California's 36th district.

FEDERAL ELECTION COMMISSION

By the elections of 1828, over a million Americans were eligible to vote, and this democratization of the political process brought with it unparalleled opportunities for corruption. Money and organizational talent were now needed to win, and cash contributions to national and local candidates, sometimes stuffed in bags or rolled up in bandannas, became routine.

For a century and a half, the country suffered Tammany Halls and Tweed Rings. National leaders like Theodore Roosevelt often called for reforms, and in 1925 Congress actually passed a law requiring the disclosure of campaign finances. But it was vague, noninclusive and difficult to enforce. When it became apparent, during the Watergate affair of the early 1970s, that wealthy contributors, corporations, and special-interest groups were exercising undue influence on the electoral process, Congress was finally shocked into writing a tough law to control the financing of federal elections.

The Federal Election Campaign Act of 1972 required all candidates for federal office and all national political committees to file detailed reports and designated three agencies—the Clerk of the House of Representatives, the Secretary of the Senate and the General Accounting Office—to collect and monitor them. The act also provided for public financing for presidential candidates in general elections.

Amendments to the law passed in 1974, 1976 and 1979 eliminated the GAOs role and established the Federal Election Commission to oversee the law and to serve as the repository of all campaign finance reports filed in connection with federal elections. The amendments also provided for the public financing of presidential primary elections, established limits on political contributions, and expanded the role of political parties in federal elections.

The FEC consists of six commissioners, appointed by the president. They serve staggered, six-year terms, and no more than three can be members of the same political party. A president and vice president from different parties are elected each year by their fellow commissioners. The Secretary of the Senate and the Clerk of the House serve as ex-officio members. The law requires the commission to assemble at least once a month, but it usually meets weekly, sometimes more often. Most proceedings are open to the public.

The FEC has three primary functions: It administers the public financing of presidential elections; receives, reviews, and maintains all reports on the campaign finance activities of candidates for federal office and the committees that support them; and monitors and enforces compliance with the law.

All candidates for federal office and the political committees that support them are required by the law to register with the Secretary of the Senate, the Clerk of the House, or the FEC and to file periodic reports disclosing their financial activities. The candidates and committees must also file with officials in the state or states where nomination or election is sought.

A candidate is defined as any individual who raises or spends more than $5,000 a year in pursuit of federal office. A political committee is any group of persons that receives or expends more than $1,000 on behalf of a federal candidate in any calendar year. Any organization authorized by a candidate to raise and spend money on the candidate's behalf is a political committee under the law, regardless of the amounts collected and expended. Political party organizations on the state and local levels that meet certain receiving and spending criteria also qualify as political committees.

The FEC's third major function—ensuring compliance with the Federal Election Campaign Act—is accomplished by reviewing and often auditing filed reports and advising candidates and committees of any violations of the rules. In general, the law prohibits:

• Contributions from the treasuries of corporations, labor unions or national banks.

• Contributions from government contractors.

• Contributions from foreign nationals who are not permanent residents of the United States.

• Cash contributions from one person totaling more than $100 per campaign period.

• Contributions made by a person in the name of another person.

• Contributions in excess of the limits prescribed by law (generally, $1,000 per person per candidate per election and $5,000 per committee per candidate per election).

The FEC first attempts enforcement through informal efforts. Candidates or committees who persist in bending the rules may have a civil penalty levied against them. The FEC can also file civil suits against suspected violators. If the commission encounters what it believes are "knowing and willful" violations of the law, the matter may be referred to the Justice Department for further investigation and prosecution.

PRESIDENTIAL ELECTIONS

Funds for the financing of presidential elections are provided by taxpayers, who voluntarily check off the appropriate box on their income tax forms. The money is retained in the Presidential Election Campaign Fund until the FEC certifies the candidates who are eligible to receive payments. The Treasury Department then disburses the public funds.

Presidential primary candidates are entitled to receive matching funds for small contributions received from private donors. To be eligible for the money, the candidates must first raise in excess of $5,000 in each of 20 different states in contributions of $250 or less. The candidates must agree to limit their expenditures to an inflation-adjusted amount (the maximum figure stood at slightly more than $23 million for each candidate in 1988, half of which would be federal funds).

After the major-party candidates are selected, they become eligible for outright grants of public monies to finance their general election campaigns. The amount was set at $20 million per candidate in 1974, but inflation had driven the figure to $46.1 million by 1988. All candidates who receive public funds must agree not to accept any private donations, except for a small amount determined by formula that political parties are permitted to expend on behalf of their nominees.

The major political parties are also eligible to receive public funds to finance their nominating conventions. In 1988 this inflation-adjusted amount stood at more than $9 million for each major party.

The FEC depends on the taxpayer check off for the funding of presidential campaigns. After the 1989 tax forms were tabulated the FEC warned that so many taxpayers had stopped checking the box to donate, the future solvency of the presidential election fund was in question. If that trend continues through 1991, the FEC warns, it will have to go to Congress for the first time to ask for a direct appropriation to pay for the 1992 presidential campaign.

POLITICAL ACTION COMMITTEES

All political committees that are not established or administered by a candidate for federal office, or by a political party, are commonly referred to as "political action committees," or PACs.

PACs were first created in the 1940s by labor unions, which were forbidden by federal law from using money collected as dues to support political candidates. But there were no restrictions on the collection of voluntary contributions from union members. Political action committees were set up to receive and disburse the funds. Most corporations were effectively prohibited from creating PACs by provisions of the Hatch Act, which bars federal contractors from contributing to the campaign of any candidate for national office. Most corporations do at least some business with the federal government and thus could not participate in the political process.

In the mid-70s, there were only about 600 PACs. Then labor leaders began to fear that because their organizations participated in manpower-training programs, they might also qualify as federal contractors. So labor and business began lobbying together to change the law. It was amended in 1974 to encourage the creation of PACs, which were seen as healthy and well-regulated vehicles that ordinary citizens could use to pool resources in support of candidates sharing their views.

PACs have proved popular beyond all expectations. The FECs most recent count, of PACs registered for the 1992 election cycle (1991–92), showed 4,585 PACs in existence. Virtually all of them are dedicated to special interests; the FEC breaks them down into corporate (1893), labor (365), nonconnected (1303), trade/member/health (818), cooperative (59), and corporation without stock (147). There are PACs for corporations, labor unions, trade associations, doctors, lawyers, farmers, realtors, machinists, carpenters, car dealers, letter carriers. Beer distributors have a committee called SixPAC. There is the pro-outdoors Back PAC, a Beef-PAC, a PeacePAC, an Ice Cream PAC.

By law, individual citizens can give only $1,000 to a candidate for each election. But PACs are allowed to donate $5,000 per candidate per election, primary and general. Since presidential elections are now financed with public funds, much PAC money is flowing into the campaign coffers of candidates for the House and Senate— mostly incumbents, according to FEC figures. Candidates have become so dependent on PAC money that they actually visit PAC offices and all but demand contributions. Putting it another way, the lobbyists used to lobby members of Congress. Now the lawmakers lobby the lobbyists.

CAMPAIGN FINANCING REFORM

In the 102nd Congress (1991–92) campaign finance reform was at the top of the agenda. It is still at the top of the agenda in the 103rd Congress as Democrats and Republicans remain far apart in their solutions.

So far, both sides are approaching the subject in a very partisan manner. Both say they want reform, but the reform they seek is the one that will do the most damage possible to the other side.

Republicans, with their huge overall fundraising advantage, do not want to limit how much candidates can spend and actually want to increase the amounts individuals can contribute to campaigns. But they want to limit who can give to campaigns, specifically they want to do away with collective giving through political action committees. PACs are the principal source of funds for Democratic congressional candidates, and PACs give much more to Democrats than to Republicans.

The Democrats answer is to limit the amount that candidates for House or Senate can spend on campaigning. They are pushing a voluntary state-by-state limit based on population, with the possible incentive of some amount of public financing for candidates who are willing to accept the spending limits. This is much the same way presidential campaigns are financed. Also included in the Democrats bill is a limit on the amounts PACs can give, both to individual campaigns and in the aggregate, and tax supported vouchers that will allow candidates to buy television time, which in turn will be price regulated.

There is a second kind of campaign reform in the air: regulated more closely on what campaign funds can be spent.

In a recent book, *Handbook of Campaign Spending* (CQ Press, $130), two experienced Los Angeles Times reporters—Sara Fritz and Dwight Morris—constructed a complex computer data base, and minutely analyzed the campaign spending reports of all Congressional candidates in the 1990 race. What they found was that millions of campaign dollars are being spent by candidates on things that seem to have little to do with attracting votes.

Cars are very popular. Many members of both the House and Senate buy or lease cars using campaign funds. A candidate must be well dressed, of course. Thus a significant number of candidates spend considerable amounts on new wardrobes. A candidate must also be well traveled, and informed on foreign affairs. Hundreds of thousands in campaign contributions went to finance foreign trips, usually for the candidate and his wife.

Sports tickets are a big item. Many members use campaign funds to buy season tickets for their home professional sports teams and then, they say, give the tickets away to constituents.

Constituent entertainment in general is a very big item. Virtually every candidate spends lavishly on what is lumped together as constituent entertainment. This might be buying lunch for a group of visitors to Capitol Hill from back home, or throwing a barbecue on a summer night for supporters.

The 1990 champion in this category appears to have been Rep. Bud Schuster, R.-Pa., who spent an average of $147 a day for constituent meals and entertainment.

Many members who need to spend little on campaigning, turn their campaign committees into mini-charities, doling out tens of thousands of dollars, or more, to favored causes. For Sen. Strom Thurmond, R.-S.C. in 1990 that favorite cause was the Strom Thurmond Foundation which received almost $400,000 in campaign funds.

What this book points out is that contrary to general belief, campaigns do not spend anywhere near as much as had been thought on traditional things like advertising and mailings and the like. Reform is needed because Congress has written campaign financing laws so loosely that almost any expenditure can be considered campaign related.

Even if campaign reform comes in 1993 or 1994, it will not take effect until at least the 1996 elections.

Any citizen who believes a candidate or committee has violated the Federal Election Campaign Act or any FEC regulation may file a complaint with the agency. The complaint should state the facts clearly and include available evidence of the alleged violation. The complaint must include the name, address and telephone number of the person making the complaint, and it must be sworn to, signed and notarized. All complaints should be addressed to the Office of the General Counsel of the FEC, whose address is:

Federal Election Commission
999 E Street, NW
Washington, D.C. 20463

Telephone:
In Washington, 376-3155
Toll Free, 800-424-9530

THE SIGHTS OF WASHINGTON: A CITIZEN'S TOUR

THE CAPITOL

Capitol Hill is Washington's political center, and most of what goes on there is open to the public. Generally speaking, Congress is in session from late January through November, except for what used to be called recesses but are now termed "Members' District Working Periods." They are usually grouped around holidays, include most of the month of August, and in the Senate are also every fourth week. Also, don't count on finding much going on in Congress on Fridays, or for that matter, many Mondays, especially in the summer.

The Hill is divided into the Senate side and the House side. Looking at the Capitol from the Mall, the Senate side is on the left and the House side on the right. Senators have their offices in either the Russell, Dirksen, or Hart Senate Office Buildings and representatives have their offices in either the Rayburn, Longworth, or Cannon House Office Buildings.

If you want to see the House or Senate in action from a visitor's gallery, you will have to join one of the guided tours (see below), or obtain passes from your senator's or representative's office. (Foreign visitors can enter the gallery by showing their passports.) Cameras and picture taking are not allowed. Much Congressional business is conducted in hearings, most of which are held in the various Senate and House office buildings. Except for the unusual executive session, all are open to the public. A list of hearings for a given day is published each morning in the Washington Post.

Once you have obtained a visitor's gallery pass, you can reach the Capitol either by walking across the plaza or by riding the private subway that runs from the basement of the office buildings into the basement of the Capitol. To enter the Capitol from the outside, go up the center steps directly under the dome (from the back; you cannot enter from the Mall side). This puts you in the Rotunda. To your left is Statuary Hall, which served as the original House chamber until 1857. Each state admitted to the Union before that date was asked to donate statues of two of its most prominent citizens. To the right, off the Rotunda, are both the original Senate chamber and the original Supreme Court chamber. Both have been restored and are open to visitors.

Free guided tours leave from the Rotunda constantly from 9:00 a.m. until 3:45 p.m. and are highly recommended. More extensive private tours can be arranged by writing in advance to a member of Congress. Restaurants in the Senate and House office buildings and one in the Capitol itself are open to the public from 8:00 a.m. to 11:15 a.m. and again from 1:15 p.m. until 2:30 p.m. The food, especially in the Capitol Refectory, is significantly better than you might expect and is relatively moderately priced compared to what you would expect to pay for the same quality food in a restaurant.

SUPREME COURT

Located directly across 1st Street, NE, from the Capitol, the court is open to the public from 9:00 a.m. to 4:30 p.m. Monday–Friday. The court is in session from the first Monday in October until June. The justices hear oral arguments on two successive Mondays, Tuesdays and Wednesdays and then take the next two weeks to decide cases. Oral argument sessions are open to the public. When the court is not in session, the only way to enter the court chamber itself is as part of a half–hour tour/lecture on the history and operation of the court, which begins every 30 minutes. The court building also contains a very good, small cafeteria that is open to the public except from 12:15 p.m. to 1:15 p.m., when it is reserved for court employees only.

LIBRARY OF CONGRESS

Located next to the Supreme Court on 1st Street, NE, the main building of the Library of Congress with its great hall and soaring main reading room is definitely worth a stop. (The only problem is that the building has been closed for almost two years for major renovations. Although scheduled to reopen in early 1991, the project is already far behind schedule.) On display throughout the main building are both permanent and changing exhibits, including very rare books (one of the three remaining Gutenberg Bibles among them), photos, maps and prints.

It should be remembered that the Library of Congress is a working research library. Anyone may use its facilities and obtain books from its 19-million-volume collection—the world's largest. But it is not a lending library. No book may leave the premises, nor may users browse through the collection. Except for some reference books and part of the Law Library collection, all books are kept in sections closed to the public (on 35 miles of shelves) and must be individually requested. A 60–90 minute wait for a requested book is not unusual.

THE WHITE HOUSE

Public tours lasting anywhere from 10-20 minutes (depending on how fast guards push you through) are available for five of the White House's 132 rooms from 10:00 a.m. to 2:00 p.m. (12:00 noon after Labor Day), Tuesday through Friday. People begin to line up early for these tours, and the wait can be lengthy. But everyone who is still in line at 2:00 p.m. will be admitted. In addition, slightly more extensive private VIP tours are given from 8:30 a.m. to 10:00 a.m. on most days; a limited number of tickets are available through members of Congress.

THE STATE DEPARTMENT

Slightly off the beaten tourist path at 22nd & C Streets, NW, the hour–long tours of the State Department's lavishly furnished and ornate Diplomatic Reception Rooms—given several times daily when the rooms are not in use—are worth the effort. Tours are available by advance reservation only (you can call at the last minute to inquire about cancellations: 202-647-3241).

THE NATIONAL ARCHIVES

Located on Constitution Ave. between 7th and 9th Streets, NW, the Archives are a combination repository, working research center, and museum. From 10:00 a.m. to 9:00 p.m. daily (4:30 p.m. after Labor Day), the Declaration of Independence, Constitution, and Bill of Rights are on public display, along with other historic documents.

THE SMITHSONIAN MUSEUMS

People tend to think of the Smithsonian as a single museum while actually the Smithsonian Institution system is a series of separate museums all grouped around the Mall. By far the most popular is the Air & Space which now includes a large, modern restaurant and cafeteria. Other museums include American History, Natural History, Arts and Industries, National Gallery of Art (East Wing and West Wing), the underground National Museum of African Art and the Sackler Gallery of Asian Art, Hirshhorn Museum & Sculpture Garden, Freer Gallery, the Main "Castle" administration building, and the National Zoo (some distance from the Mall on upper Connecticut Ave. NW). All are open every day (except Christmas Day) from 10:00 a.m. to 5:30 p.m. plus summer evenings. Not part of the Smithsonian system, but nearby and run on the same schedule is the new, privately funded, U.S. Holocaust Museum.

THE MEMORIALS

The Lincoln, Jefferson, and Vietnam War Memorials, and the Washington Monument, are all located on or adjacent to the Mall. They are stops on the tourmobile route and are open 24 hours a day, except the Washington Monument, which closes at midnight in the summer and at 4:30 p.m. the remainder of the year. Not well known, but not to be missed, is a huge cavern under the Lincoln Memorial that was created during its construction and now resembles a deep cave filled with stalactites. You can reach it by the stairs at the rear.

THE PENTAGON

Across the Potomac River, in Virginia, the 3.7–million–square–foot office building (the world's largest) is open to the public on an escorted one–hour tour every half–hour from 9:30 a.m. to 3:30 p.m. weekdays during the summer and six times daily for the rest of the year. The tours leave from the building entrance immediately above the Pentagon Metro (subway) stop.

ARLINGTON NATIONAL CEMETERY

Covering more than 1,000 acres in Virginia, across the Potomac, this is the final resting place of thousands of servicemen plus presidents, statesmen and national heroes. Major attractions include the Tomb of the Unknown Soldier, the graves of President Kennedy and his brother Robert, and the Custis–Lee Mansion built by George Washington's adopted son and occupied for many years by his daughter Mary, her husband Robert E. Lee and their seven children. Open daily 8:00 a.m. to 7:00 p.m. (5:00 p.m. after Labor Day). Trams, (for a $2.50 fee) carry guests from the Visitors' Center on a narrated tour including stops at the Tomb of the Unknown Soldier, the Kennedy grave site and the Mansion. Visitors may also walk throughout the cemetery for no charge. The changing of the guard ceremony takes place every hour at the Tomb of the Unknown Soldier (every 30 minutes in summer). The Visitors' Center is a Metro (subway) stop and on the tourmobile route.

OTHER POPULAR ATTRACTIONS

Two of Washington's most popular tours are of the FBI Building at 9th and Pennsylvania (75–minute tour leaving every half hour 9:00 a.m. to 4:00 p.m. Monday–Friday) and the Bureau of Printing and Engraving at 14th and C Streets, NW (continuous 9:00 a.m. to 2:00 p.m. Monday–Friday). Other popular attractions include Ford's Theater and the Lincoln Museum at 511 10th Street, NW (9:00 a.m. to 5:00 p.m. weekdays and till noon on weekends); Kennedy Center 2700 F Street (40–minute free tours 10:00 a.m. to 1:00 p.m. daily); U.S. Naval Observatory, 34th and Massachusetts Aves. (7:30 p.m. Monday nights only, limited to 120 ticket holders); the Washington Post, 1150 15th Street, NW (tours several times a day Monday–Friday; call for details).

GETTING AROUND

Parking: A word of warning. Street parking in and around Washington's tourist attractions, and on Capitol Hill is almost nonexistent. Commercial garages and parking lots are quite expensive. While the government of the District of Columbia is notoriously inefficient, it does one thing exceptionally well—issuing parking citations. If you overstay your time at a meter, you can almost count on having a ticket on your windshield when you return. If you park illegally, the chances are good that your car will be towed: In Washington, that is an experience that could ruin anyone's vacation. If you have driven to Washington, your best bet is to leave your car at your hotel and rely on taxis or public transportation.

Taxis: In Washington, despite several recent rate increases, taxis are relatively inexpensive compared to most other cities. Fares in District of Columbia cabs are determined not by meters, but by zones. If you take a cab from Virginia it will use a meter. The zone system is set by Congress, and it has been gerrymandered in such a way that everything from Capitol Hill to downtown is in the same zone. The result is a rather cheap ride. Go farther and you cross a zone line, which makes the ride a little more expensive. To compensate for the cheap zone fares, drivers get an additional 50 cents during rush hour, and they can pick up additional passengers along the way if they are going in the same direction as you are.

Subway: The Washington Metro subway system has a justifiable reputation as perhaps the cleanest, safest and most efficient in the nation. The system is extensive within the city, and there are stops near most of the major tourist attractions. Fares are based on distance and time of day (more expensive during rush hours). You must buy a fare card from a machine located in all subway station entrances and you must use it both to enter and exit the system. Your fare is automatically deducted from the card when you put it in the automated turnstile to exit the system. The card is returned if you have additional value remaining on it. Maps are located in all stations to tell you what the fare is from that station to any point in the system. The subway runs to and from National Airport but not Dulles Airport.

Tourmobiles: If you are going to spend the day sightseeing, the best way to get around is on the brightly painted tourmobiles, a concession of the National Park Service. They run between the White House, the Mall, the Kennedy Center, Capitol Hill, and Arlington National Cemetery. There is a narrated tour, and you can get off or on at any of the frequent stops. Tickets are sold for the day, and the service runs from 9:00 a.m. to 6:30 p.m. in the summer and 9:00 a.m. to 4:30 p.m. the rest of the year. Tickets bought after 2:00 p.m. are good for the entire next day. Tickets can be purchased at kiosks around the Mall, or from drivers.

THE EXECUTIVE BRANCH

THE PRESIDENT

Bill Clinton was born William Jefferson Blythe, IV, on August 19, 1946 in Hope, Arkansas. Three months before his birth, his father—a traveling autoparts salesman—was killed when he drove off a rain slicked road in Missouri. His mother, Virginia, began to raise him, but then left him with her parents when she left for New Orleans to study anesthesiology. His mother remarried Roger Clinton when "Little Billy" was seven, and he took his new stepfather's name. Roger Clinton was both an alcoholic and abusive father.

After his mother remarried, the Clintons moved to Hot Springs, Arkansas. It was at Hot Springs High that politics became an obsession for young Bill Clinton. He was elected from his school to attend the American Legion–sponsored "Boys State" conference in Little Rock, where he won a prize of representing Arkansas at a national Boys State conference in Washington, D.C. There, in perhaps the defining moment in his life, he met President John F. Kennedy and decided that he wanted to spend a life in politics.

Back in Hot Springs, he asked a guidance counselor where he should go to college if he wanted to be in public service. She suggested Georgetown University, where Clinton applied and was accepted, turning down a full music scholarship to Louisiana State University. While at college, Clinton worked in the office of Arkansas Sen. J. William Fulbright. In 1968 Clinton graduated with high honors, with a degree from the School of Foreign Service, and received a Rhodes scholarship to study at Oxford University in England.

He remained at Oxford for two years. During this period he legally avoided the draft, and possible service in Vietnam, through complicated maneuvering. He also participated in anti-war demonstrations. After the war he applied for, and was accepted at Yale Law School.

At Yale he was more interested in politics than in the law. He worked in several local and national campaigns, and had the ability to earn good grades without attending class very often. While at Yale, he met Hillary Rodham, a fellow student from Chicago, and the two were married a year after Clinton graduated in 1973.

Clinton returned to Little Rock after graduation and taught law at the University of Arkansas. In 1974, he made his first try for public office, running for the U.S. House in the Democratic primary. The then 27-year-old candidate lost badly. In 1976, Clinton ran for and was elected Attorney General of Arkansas. This launched his political career.

In 1978, Clinton was elected the youngest governor in Arkansas history, and at age 30 the youngest governor in the U.S. In those days governors served only 2-year terms. By most accounts Clinton was an aloof politician during his first term in office. Then in a second defining moment in his life, he was defeated for reelection in 1980. The defeat stung him, and while he practiced law in Little Rock, he traveled the state rebuilding grass roots support. He won the governor's mansion back in 1982 and served continuously until resigning after being elected President.

During this period he emerged as a national political personality. He became a leader of moderate Democrats, and a force in national Democratic politics. He toyed with entering the 1988 Democratic presidential sweepstakes, but decided against it saying his daughter was too young.

Bill and Hillary Clinton have one child, daughter Chelsea.

THE VICE-PRESIDENT

Albert Gore, Jr. was born in Washington, D.C. on March 31, 1948, the son of U.S. Rep. Albert Gore, Sr. and Pauline Gore. Albert Gore, Sr., a native of Carthage, Tennessee, served as a congressman from 1939 until 1952 and as a U.S. Senator from the state of Tennessee from 1952 until 1970 when he was defeated for reelection mainly because of his opposition to the Vietnam War.

Young Albert grew up in the Washington, D.C. area, going to private schools. He attended Harvard University, graduating cum laude in 1969 with a Bachelor of Arts degree. At the same time his father was losing his office over his opposition to the war, his son was joining the U.S. Army and serving in Vietnam from 1969 to 1971.

Gore returned from military service to Nashville, where he got a job as an investigative reporter and editorial writer for *The Tennessean* newspaper. He worked there until 1976, and was active as a home builder and land developer for Tanglewood Home Builders Company. During this time he also pursued graduate education at night. He attended Vanderbilt University in Nashville, receiving a Master's degree from The School of Religion in 1972, and a law degree (J.D.) from the Vanderbilt Law School in 1976.

When the man who succeeded his father in the House decided to retire in 1976, Al, Jr. quickly made the race. He won easily, and began to exactly follow in his father's footsteps. He served in the House from the 6th District of Tennessee from 1977 to 1985. He was a popular and hard working congressman who quickly made a name for himself on issues like the environment, arms control, and organ transplants. He served on both the Energy and the Intelligence Committees.

In 1984, Sen. Howard Baker announced he was retiring from the Senate. Gore easily won the contest to replace him and was just as easily reelected in 1990. In the Senate, Gore served on the Armed Services, Commerce Science & Transportation, and Rules committees. He was known for his strong support of environmental legislation, and as an expert on numerous scientific issues such as global warming. He also became the Senate's leading expert on what can be called the emerging technologies.

In 1988 Gore made a run for the Oval Office. He carried many southern states on Super Tuesday, and for awhile was the frontrunner. But his effort floundered when the campaign reached the major northern states and he ended up withdrawing in favor of Massachusetts Governor Michael Dukakis. Gore then became an early favorite for the Democrat's 1992 presidential nomination, but he decided not to enter the race after fellow southerner Bill Clinton jumped in.

On May 19, 1970 Gore married the former Mary Elizabeth ("Tipper") Aitcheson. They have three daughters and a son.

THE CABINET

SECRETARY OF STATE

Warren Christopher

Born October 27, 1925 in Scranton, N.Dak.; Univ. of S. Calif., B.A., 1945, Stanford Law School, LL.B., 1949; married (Marie Wyllis), 4 children.

Career: Clerk, U.S. Supreme Ct. Justice William O. Douglas 1949–50. Atty. O'Melveny & Myers, 1950–57, Ptrn. 1957–. Depty. U.S. Atty. Gen., 1967–69. Dpty. Secy. of State 1977–81.

SECRETARY OF DEFENSE

Les Aspin

Born July 21, 1938, Milwaukee, Wis.; Yale Univ., B.A. 1960, Oxford Univ. (England), M.A. 1962, M.I.T., Ph.D. 1965; religion: Episcopalian; divorced.

Career: Staff Asst. to U.S. Sen. William Proximire, 1960–63; Staff Asst. to Walter Heller, Pres. Cncl. of Econ. Advisers, 1963–66; Army, 1966–68; Asst. Prof. of Econ., Marquette U., 1969–70; Member, U.S. House of Reps. 1970–92.

SECRETARY OF THE TREASURY

Lloyd Bentsen

Born Feb. 11, 1921, Mission, Tex.; Univ. of Tex., LL.B. 1942; married (Beryl Ann), 3 children.

Career: Army Air Corps, WWII; Practicing atty., 1945–46, Judge, Hidalgo Cnty., 1946–48; U.S. House of Reps., 1949–55; Pres., Lincoln Consolidated, Inc., 1955–70. Member, U.S. Senate, 1971–92.

ATTORNEY GENERAL

Janet Reno

Born July 21, 1938, Miami, Fla.; Cornell, A.B. 1960, Harvard LL.B. 1963; single.

Career: Atty, Brigham & Brigham, 1963–67; Partner, Lewis & Reno, 1967–71; Fla. House Judiciary Comm. Staff Director, 1971–72; Admin. Asst. 11th Judicial Circuit of Fla., 1973–76; State's Attorney, Dade Cty. (Miami) Fla., 1978–92.

SECRETARY OF THE INTERIOR

Bruce E. Babbitt

Born June 27, 1938 in Flagstaff, Ariz.; Univ. of Notre Dame, B.A., 1961, Univ. of Newcastle (England), M.A., 1962, Harvard Univ. Law School, J.D., 1965; married (Hattie), 2 children.

Career: Atty., Brown & Bain (Phoenix) 1965–74. Arizona State Atty. Gen., 1975–78. Governor, State of Ariz., 1978-87. Presidential candidate, 1988. Atty. & ptrn., Steptoe & Johnson, 1989–92.

SECRETARY OF AGRICULTURE

Mike Espy

Born Nov. 30, 1953, in Yazoo City, Miss.; Howard Univ., B.A., 1975, Univ. of Santa Clara, J.D. 1978; religion, Baptist; married (Sheila), 2 children.

Career: Managing Atty., Mississippi Legal Services 1978–80. Asst. Secy. of State, Miss. 1980–84.

Asst. Atty. Gen. and Director of Miss. Dept. of Consumer Protection, 1984–85. Member, U.S. House of Reps. 1986–92.

SECRETARY OF COMMERCE

Ronald Harmon Brown

Born August 1, 1941 in Washington, D.C.; Middlebury Coll., B.A., 1962; St. John's Univ., J.D., 1970; married (Alma Arrington), 2 children.

Career: U.S. Army, 1963–67. Counsel, National Urban League, 1971–79. Counsel, Sen. Judiciary Comm., 1980–81. Atty. & ptrn., Patton, Boggs & Blow 1981–88. Chm., Dem. Nat. Comm, 1989–92.

SECRETARY OF LABOR

Robert Reich

Born: Born June 24, 1946 in Scranton, Pa.; Dartmouth Coll., A.B., 1968; Oxford Coll. (England), M.A., 1970; Yale Univ., J.D., 1973; married (Clare Dalton), 2 children.

Career: Asst. U.S. Solicitor General, 1974–76. Policy director, Federal Trade Comm., 1976–81. Prof. (Economics) Harvard Univ., 1981–92.

SECRETARY OF HEALTH AND HUMAN SERVICES

Donna E. Shalala

Born February 14, 1941 in Cleveland, Ohio; Western Coll. for Women, A.B., 1962, Syracuse Univ, M.S. 1968, Ph.D., 1970; single.

Career: Peace Corps volunteer, 1962–64; Asst. Prof. Pol Sci., Baruch Coll., 1970–72. Assoc. Prof. Politics & Ed., Columbia Univ., 1972–77. Asst. Sec. for Policy Develop., HUD, 1977–80. Pres. Hunter Coll., 1980–88. Chancellor, Univ. of Wisc., 1988–92.

SECRETARY OF HOUSING AND URBAN DEVELOPMENT

Henry Cisneros

Born June 11, 1947 in San Antonio, Tex.; Texas A&M Univ., B.A. 1969, Harvard Univ., M.A.

1973, Geo. Wash. Univ., Ph.D. (Public Admin.), 1975; married (Mary Alice Perez), 3 children.

Career: Staff, Nat. League of Cities, 1971–72. Teaching Asst., M.I.T, 1972–73. Mbr. Cty. Council of San Antonio 1975–81. Mayor of San Antonio, 1981–89. Pres. Cisneros Asset Mgm. Co., 1989–92. Radio Comm. 1989–92.

SECRETARY OF TRANSPORTATION

Federico Pena

Born March 15, 1947 in Laredo, Tex.; Univ. of Texas, B.A., 1968, J.D., 1971; married (Elen Mary Hart), 2 children.

Career: Counsel Mexican–American Legal Defense Fund. Member, Colo. Assembly. Mayor, City of Denver, 1983–91. Atty. and assoc. Brownstein, Hyatt, Farber & Strickland 1991–92.

SECRETARY OF ENERGY

Hazel R. O'Leary

Born May 17, 1937, in Newport News, Va.; Fisk Univ., B.S. 1959, Rutgers Univ. J.D., 1966; married (John F. O'Leary) 1 child.

Career: Partner, Coopers & Lybrand; Asst. Atty.

Gen. of New Jersey; Gen. Counsel, U.S. Community Serv. Adm.; Asst. Dir., Federal Energy Adm., 1974–76; Asst. Secy., U.S. Dept. of Energy, 1977–80; V.P., O'Leary Assoc., 1981–89. Ex. V.P., Northern States Power Co., 1989–1992.

SECRETARY OF EDUCATION

Richard W. Riley

Born January 2, 1933, in Greenville, S.C.; Furman Univ., B.A. 1954, Univ. of S.C. J.D., 1960; married (Ann Yarborough), 4 children.

Career: U.S. Navy, 1954–56. Counsel, U.S. Sen. Olin Johnson, 1961–62. Atty. & Member, S.C. House of Reps., 1963–67. Member, S.C. Sen., 1967–77. Gov. of S.C., 1979–87. Member, Nat. Ed. Assessment Gov. Bd., 1987–91. Atty. & ptrn, Nelson, Mullins, Riley & Scarborough, 1991–92.

SECRETARY OF VETERANS AFFAIRS

Jesse Brown

Born March 27, 1944, in Chicago, Ill.; Chi. Cty. Coll., B.A.; married (Sylvia), 2 children.

Career: U.S. Marine Corps, 1963–65. Staff, Disabled American Veterans, 1967–1992.

EXECUTIVE AGENCY HEADS

DIRECTOR, CENTRAL INTELLIGENCE AGENCY

R. James Woolsey

Born September 21, 1941 in Tulsa, Okla.; Stanford, B.A., 1963, Oxford Univ. (England) 1965; Yale Univ., J.D. 1968; married (Suzanne Hale), 3 children.

Career: Staff, Office of Secy. of Def., 1968–70. Staff, National Secy. Council, 1970. Counsel, Sen. Armed Serv. Comm, 1970–73. Atty. Shea & Gardner, 1973–77. Under Secy. of Navy, 1977–79. Prtn., Shea & Gardner, 1979–1992. Delegate-at-large, U.S.–Sov. Arms Negot., 1983–86. U.S. Rep. (ambassador) Disarm. Negot. 1989–91.

DIRECTOR - FEDERAL BUREAU OF INVESTIGATION

William S. Sessions

Born May 27, 1930 in Ft. Smith, Ark.; Baylor Univ., BA 1956, LL.B. 1958; married (Alice Lewis), 4 children.

Career: Air Force 1951–55; atty. & ptrn. McGregor & Sessions 1959-61; associate McLaughlin, Gorin, & McDonald, 1962–63; associate Haley, Koehne, Fulbright & Winniford, 1963–69; ptrn. Fulbright, Winniford, Sessions & Bice, 1969–71; U.S. Dept. of Justice 1971–74; U.S. Atty. So. Dist. of Tex., 1974–79. U.S. Dist. Judge 1979–80. Chief Judge West Dist. of Tex. 1980–87.

CHAIRMAN, FEDERAL RESERVE SYSTEM

Alan Greenspan

Born March 6, 1926 in New York City; New York Univ., B.S. 1948, M.A. 1950, Ph.D. 1970.

Career: Pres. & CEO Towsend & Greenspan 1954–74, 1977–87; Chm. Council of Ec. Ad. 1970–74, 1977–87. Appointed pres. pos. 1987.

CHAIRMAN, FEDERAL TRADE COMMISSION

Janet D. Steiger

Born June 10, 1939, Oshkosh, Wis.; Lawrence Col. B.A. 1961 (Phi Beta Kappa), Univ. of Reading (Eng.) Fulbright scholar.

Career: V.P. The Work Place 1975–80. U.S. Postal Rate Comm. 1980–88 (chm. 1982–88).

ADMINISTRATOR, ENVIRONMENTAL PROTECTION AGENCY

Carol M. Browner

Born December 16, 1955 in Miami, Fla.; Univ. of Fla., A.B. 1977, J.D., 1979; married (Michael Podhorzer), 1 child.

Career: Counsel, Comm. on Govt. Ops., Fla. State House, 1979–81. Assoc. Dir., Citizens Action, 1983–86. Leg. Asst., U.S. Sen. Lawton Chiles, 1986–89. Counsel, Energy Comm, U.S. Senate, 1989. Legs. Asst., U.S. Sen. Al Gore, 1989–91. Sec., Fla. Dept. of Envir. Regs., 1991–92.

CHAIRMAN, FEDERAL COMMUNICATIONS COMMISSION

Not yet appointed

ADMINISTRATOR, NATIONAL AERONAUTICS AND SPACE ADMINISTRATION

Daniel S. Goldin

Born Jul. 23, 1940 in New York City; City College (N.Y.), B.S. 1962; married (Judith), 2 children.

Career: NASA Research Scientist, Cleveland, 1962–67; Vice-President and General Manager TRW Space & Technology, Redondo Beach Calif., 1967–92.

CHAIRMAN, SECURITIES AND EXCHANGE COMMISSION

Arthur Levitt, Jr.

Born Feb. 3, 1931 in Brooklyn, N.Y.; Williams Coll. B.A., 1952; married (Marilyn), 2 children.

Career: U.S. Air Force, 1952–54. Asst. Prom. Dir., Time, Inc. 1954–59; ex. vice-president, Oppenheimer Ind., 1959–62; vice-president Shearson Lehman Bros., 1962–69, pres. 1969–78. Chm. & CEO, Am. Stock Exchange 1978–89; Chm., Levitt Media Co., 1989–; Chm., N.Y.C. Economic Develop. Corp., 1990–; White House Small Business Conference Comm., 1978–80; President's Task Force on Private Sector Incentives, 1981–82; (Military) Base Closure and Realignment Comm., 1991, 1993.

DIRECTOR, FEDERAL EMERGENCY MANAGEMENT AGENCY

James Lee Witt

Born Jan. 6, 1944, in Dardanelle, Ark.; Dardanelle High School; married (Lea), 2 children

Career: Owner, Witt Construction Co., 1968–79; Judge (Cty. Exec.), Yell Cty. (Arkansas), 1979–88; Dir. Ark. Off. of Emg. Serv., 1988–92.

PRINCIPAL ADVISERS
EXECUTIVE OFFICE OF THE PRESIDENT

WHITE HOUSE CHIEF OF STAFF

Thomas "Mack" McLarty

Born June 24, 1946 in Hope, Ark; Univ. of Ark, B.A., 1970; married (Donna Kay), 2 children.

Career: Member, Ark. State House 1970–72. Chm. Ark. Dem. Comm., 1972–76. Ark. Louisiana Gas Co., Mem. Bd. 1976–83, Pres. 1983, CEO, 1985–92.

DIRECTOR, OFFICE OF MANAGEMENT AND BUDGET

Leon E. Panetta

Born June 28, 1938, Monterey, Calif.; Univ. of Santa Clara, B.A. 1960, J.D. 1963; Roman Catholic; married (Sylvia), 3 children.

Career: Elected 1976. Army, 1963–65; Legis. Asst. to U.S. Sen. Thomas Kuchel, 1966–69; Dir., U.S. Office of Civil Rights, Dept. of H.E.W., 1969–70; Exec. Asst. to Mayor of New York City. 1970–71; Practicing atty., 1971–76. Member, U.S. House of Reps., 1976–1992.

NATIONAL SECURITY ADVISOR

Anthony Lake

Born April 2, 1939 in New York City; Harvard Coll., B.A., 1961, Trinity Coll. (England), M.A. 1964, Princeton Univ. Ph.D. 1974; married (Antonia), 3 children.

Career: Foreign Serv. Officer, U.S. Dept. of State, 1962–69. National Security Council staff, 1969–70. Academic and writer, 1970–76. Dir. Policy Planning, U.S. Dept. of State, 1976–81. Professor, Amherst Coll., 1981–84, Mount Holyoke Coll., 1984–92.

DIRECTOR, OFFICE OF DRUG CONTROL POLICY ("DRUG CZAR")

Lee P. Brown

Born Oct. 4, 1937 in Wewoka, Okla.; Calif. State Univ. (Fresno), B.S. (Criminology), 1960; San Jose State Univ., M.A. (Sociology), 1964; Univ. of Calif., M.A., Ph.D. (Criminology), 1968; widower (4 children).

Career: Police officer, San Jose, Calif., 1960–68; prof. Portland State Univ., 1968–72; Assoc. Dir. Howard Univ. Institute of Urban Affairs, 1972–75; Dir., Justice Services, Mulnomah Cty. (Oreg.), 1975–78; Pub. Safety Commissioner, Atlanta Ga., 1978–82; Chief of Police, Houston, Tex., 1982–89; Police Commissioner, New York City, 1989–92; Prof. Texas Southern Univ., 1992–93.

U.S. TRADE REPRESENTATIVE

Mickey Kantor

Born August 7, 1939 in Nashville, Tenn.; Vanderbilt Univ., B.A. 1961, Georgetown Univ. Law School, J.D., 1968; married (Heidi Schulman), 1 child.

Career: Atty. & prtnr., Manatt, Phelps, Phillips & Kantor.

CHAIRMAN, COUNCIL OF ECONOMIC ADVISERS

Laura D'Andrea Tyson

Born August 4, 1947, in Bayonne, N.J.; Smith Coll., A.B., MIT, Ph.D. (Economics), 1977; married (Erik Tarloff) 1 child.

Career: Univ. of Calif. at Berkeley, Asst. Prof. and Prof. 1978–92. Director of Berkeley Roundtable on the International Economy.

CHAIRMAN NATIONAL ECONOMIC COUNCIL ASSISTANT TO THE PRESIDENT FOR ECONOMIC POLICY (ECONOMIC SECURITY ADVISOR)

Robert E. Rubin

Born August 29, 1938 in New York City; Harvard Coll., B.A. 1960, London Sch. of Econ., M.A., 1961, Yale Univ. J.D., 1964; married (Judith Leah Oxenberg), 2 children.

Career: Atty. 1964–66. Goldman Sachs & Co., Assoc., 1966–70, Partner, 1971–80; Vice Chm. 1987–1992. Dir. Futures Exch., 1979–85.

U.S. AMBASSADOR TO THE UNITED NATIONS

Madeleine Albright

Born May 15, 1937 in Prague (Czechoslovakia); Wellesley Coll., B.A. 1959, Columbia Univ., M.A. 1968, Ph.D., 1976; divorced, 3 children.

Career: Staff, Sen. Ed Muskie, 1976–78. Staff, National Security Council, 1978–81. Prof. Georgetown Univ. 1982–1992.

U.S. SURGEON GENERAL (Designate)

Joycelyn Elders, M.D.

Born: March 15, 1937 in Laredo, Tex.; Philander Smith Coll., B.A., 1956, Univ. of Ark. Sch. of Med., M.D., 1961; married (Oliver Elders), 2 children.

Career: Prac. physician & Prof. of Pediatrics, Univ. of Ark. Med. School, 1961–87. Dir., Ark. Dept. of Health, 1987–92.

EXECUTIVE BRANCH DEPARTMENTS AND AGENCIES

NOTE: Unless otherwise indicated, all addresses are in Washington, D.C. Previous to the summer of 1990, all telephones in the Washington D.C. metropolitian area, whether in the District or in suburban Maryland or Virginia, could be reached by dialing area code 202. However, the phone company has now split the 202 (DC), 301 (Maryland) and 703 (Virginia) area codes. The correct area code must now be used to reach the number you are dialing if it is located outside the District. For instance, all Pentagon and CIA phones now must be dialed using the 703 area code where previously they were reached by dialing 202, even though they are in Virginia.

EXECUTIVE OFFICE OF THE PRESIDENT

Office of the President and Vice President
The White House 1600 Pennsylvania Ave. 20500. Phone 456-1414.

Office of Administration
Old Executive Office Building 20500. Phone 456-7052.

Domestic Policy Council
Old Executive Office Building 20500. Phone 456-6722

Economic Policy Council
Old Executive Office Building 20500. Phone 456-2705

Office of Management and Budget
New Executive Office Building 20503. Phone 395-7250.

Council of Economic Advisers
Old Executive Office Building 20500. Phone 395-5107.

National Security Council
Old Executive Office Building 20506. Phone 456-2255.

Council on Environmental Quality
722 Jackson Place 20503. Phone 395-3742.

Office of Policy Development
Old Executive Office Building 20506. Phone 456-6406.

Office of Science and Technology Policy
Old Executive Office Building 20506. Phone 456-7116.

Central Intelligence Agency
Washington, DC 20505. Phone 703-482-1100.

Office of the U.S. Trade Representative
600 17th St. 20506. Phone 395-3204.

Office of National Drug Control Policy
Old Executive Office Building 20500. Phone 467-9800.

CABINET DEPARTMENTS

DEPARTMENT OF AGRICULTURE

Independence Ave., between 12th and 14th Sts., SW 20250. General Locator Phone 202-720-2791. (All offices located at USDA Bldg., Independence between 12th and 14th Sts., SW 20250, unless otherwise indicated.)

Office of the Secretary
Room 200 A, Admin. Bldg, USDA, 14th St. and Independence Ave., SW Phone 720-3631.

Office of the Deputy Secretary
Room 200 A, Admin. Bldg. Phone 720-6158.

Under Secretary for International Affairs and Commodity Programs
Room 212 A, Admin. Bldg. Phone 720-3111.

Under Secretary for Small Community and Rural Development
Room 219 A, Admin. Bldg. Phone 720-4581.

Assistant Secretary for Administration/Chief Financial Officer
Room 240 W, Admin. Bldg. Phone 720-3291.

Assistant Secretary for Congressional Relations
Room 143 W, Admin. Bldg. Phone 720-7908.

Assistant Secretary for Economics
Room 227 E, Admin. Bldg. Phone 720-4164.

Assistant Secretary for Food and Consumer Services
Room 207 W, Admin. Bldg. Phone 720-7711.

Assistant Secretary for Marketing and Inspection Services
Room 228 W, Admin. Bldg. Phone 720-4256.

Assistant Secretary for Natural Resources and Environment
Room 217 E, Admin. Bldg. Phone 720-7173.

Assistant Secretary for Science and Education
Room 217 W, Admin. Bldg. Phone 720-5923.

Office of Public Affairs
Room 201 A, Admin. Bldg. Phone 720-4623.

Office of the General Counsel
Room 243 W, South Bldg. Phone 720-3351.

Office of the Inspector General
Room 248 E, Admin. Bldg. Phone 720-8001.

Judicial Officer
Room 510 A, Admin. Bldg. Phone 720-4764.

Agricultural Stabilization and Conservation Service
Room 3086, South Bldg. Phone 720-3467.

Foreign Agricultural Service
Room 5095, South Bldg. Phone 720-3935.

U.S. Forest Service
201 14th St SW 20250. Phone 205-1661.

Soil Conservation Service
Room 5015 A, South Bldg. Phone 720-4525.

Agricultural Research Service
Room 302 A, Admin. Bldg. Phone 720-3656.

USDA Extension Service
Room 338 A, Admin. Bldg. Phone 720-3377.

Cooperative State Research Service
Room 305 A, Admin. Bldg. Phone 720-4423.

National Agricultural Library
Rte. 1, Beltsville, MD 20705. Phone 301-504-5248.

Food and Nutrition Service
3101 Park Center Dr., Alexandria, VA 22302. Phone 703-756-3062.

Human Nutrition Information Services
6505 Belcrest Rd., Hyattsville, MD 20782. Phone 301-436-7725.

Economic Research Service
Room 1226, 1301 New York Ave. 20005. Phone 219-0300.

National Agricultural Statistics Service
Room 4117, South Bldg. Phone 720-2707.

Animal and Plant Health Inspection Service
Room 313 E, Admin. Bldg. Phone 720-3054.

Agricultural Marketing Service
Room 3071, South Bldg. Phone 720-5115.

Agricultural Cooperative Service
Room 4014, South Bldg. Phone 720-7558.

Food Safety and Inspection Service
Room 331 E, Admin. Bldg. Phone 720-7025.

Federal Grain Inspection Service
Room 1094, South Bldg. Phone 720-0219.

Farmers Home Administration
Room 5014, South Bldg. Phone 690-1533.

Federal Crop Insurance Corporation
2101 L St. NW 20037. Phone 720-6795.

Special Toll Free Information and Hotline Phone Numbers
Fraud & Waste Hotline 1-800-424-9121 202-690-1622
Grain Market News 202-720-7316
News Features 202-488-8358
Economic Statistics Hotline 202-219-0515

DEPARTMENT OF COMMERCE

Herbert C. Hoover Bldg., 14th St. and Constitution Ave. 20230. General locator phone 202-482-2000. (All offices located in the Herbert C. Hoover Bldg. unless otherwise indicated.)

Office of the Secretary
Room 5858. Phone 482-2112.

Under Secretary for Ecomomic Affairs
Room 4848. Phone 482-3727.

Under Secretary for Export Administration
Room 3898. Phone 482-1455.

Under Secretary for International Trade
Room 3850. Phone 482-2867.

Under Secretary for Oceans and Atmosphere
Room 5158. Phone 482-3436.

Under Secretary for Technology
Room 4824. Phone 482-1575.

Under Secretary for Travel and Tourism
Room 1863. Phone 482-0136.

Assistant Secretary for Administration/Chief Exec. Officer
Room 5830. Phone 482-4951.

Assistant Secretary for Communications and Information Policy
Room 4898. Phone 482-1840.

Assistant Secretary for Export Administration
Room 3886 C. Phone 482-5491.

Assistant Secretary for Export Enforcement
Room 3727. Phone 482-1561.

Assistant Secretary for Import Administration
Room 3099 B. Phone 482-1780.

Assistant Secretary for International Economic Policy
Room 3864. Phone 482-3022.

Assistant Secretary for Trade Development
Room 3832. Phone 482-1461.

Assistant Secretary/ Director General U.S. and Foreign Commercial Services
Room 3802. Phone 482-5777.

Assistant Secretary/ Deputy Administrator NOAA
Room 5804. Phone 482-3567.

Assistant Secretary for Technology Policy
Room 4814 C. Phone 482-1581.

Assistant Secretary for Tourism Marketing
Room 1860. Phone 482-4752.

Assistant Secretary for Economic Development
Room 7800 B. Phone 482-5081.

Assistant Secretary for Legislative and Intergovernmental Affairs
Room 5865. Phone 482-5485.

Assistant Secretary for Patents and Trademarks
Room 906 Crystal Park Bldg. 2, 2121 Crystal Dr., Arlington VA 22202. Phone 703-305-8600.

Office of Public Affairs
Room 5862. Phone 482-5151.

Office of the General Counsel
Room 5870 Phone 482-4772.

Office of Inspector General
Room 7898C. Phone 482-4661.

National Technical Information Service
5285 Port Royal Rd., Springfield, VA 22161 Phone 703-487-4681

National Institute of Standards and Technology (formerly National Bureau of Standards)
Gaithersburg, MD 20899. Locator phone 301-975-2000.

Bureau of Economic Analysis
1401 K St. 20230. Phone 523-0508.

Bureau of the Census
Federal Office Bldg. 3, Suitland, MD 20233. Phone 301-763-7662.

Economic Development Administration
Room 7800B. Phone 482-5081.

Minority Business Development Agency
Room 5053. Phone 482-5061.

International Trade Administration
Room 3850. Phone 482-2867.

U.S. Travel and Tourism Administration
Room 1855. Phone 482-0136.

National Oceanic and Atmospheric Administration
Bldg. 5, 6010 Executive Blvd. Rockville, MD 20852. Phone 301-443-8910.

National Weather Service
1335 East-West Hwy., Silver Spring, MD 20910 Phone 301-713-0610.

Patent and Trademark Office
Crystal City Park, Bldg. 2, 2121 Crystal Dr., Arlington, VA 22202. Phone 703-308-4455.

Bureau of Export Administration
Room 3898. Phone 482-2381.

National Telecommunications and Information Administration
Room 4898. Phone 482-1551.

Special Toll Free Information and Hotline Phone Numbers

Fraud, Waste & Abuse Hotline—800-424-5197
Census Information—301-763-7662
Business Liaison—202-482-3942
Consumer Liaison Hotline—202-482-2495
Consumer Information Center—202-482-2000
National Institute of Standards Hotline—301-975-2000
National Technical Information Service—301-975-4500
Bureau of Economic Analysis Information—202-523-0777

DEPARTMENT OF DEFENSE

The Pentagon 20301-1155. Phone 703-545-6700. (All offices located at the Pentagon unless otherwise indicated. All phone numbers use area code 703 unless otherwise indicated.)

Office of the Secretary
Room 3E880. Phone 695-5261.

Under Secretary for Acquisition
Room 3E933. Phone 695-2381

Under Secretary for Policy
Room 4E830. Phone 697-7200

Assistant Secretary for Force Management and Personnel
Room 3E764. Phone 695-5254

Assistant Secretary for Reserve Affairs
Room 2E520. Phone 697-6631

Assistant Secretary for Production and Logistics
Room 3E808. Phone 695-6639.

Assistant Secretary for International Security Affairs
Room 4E808. Phone 695-4351.

Assistant Secretary for International Security Policy
Room 4E838. Phone 695-0942.

Assistant Secretary for Special Operations and Low Intensity Conflict
Room 2E258. Phone 693-2895.

Assistant Secretary for Command, Control, Communications and Intelligence
Room 3E172. Phone 695-0348.

Assistant Secretary for Health Affairs
Room 3E346. Phone 697-2111.

Assistant Secretary for Legislative Affairs
Room 3E966. Phone 697-6210.

Assistant Secretary for Program Analysis and Evaluation
Room 3E836. Phone 695-0971.

Assistant Secretary for Public Affairs
Room 2E800. Phone 697-9312.

Office of Public Affairs
Room 2E800. Phone 697-9312.

Office of General Council
Room 3E980. Phone 695-3341.

Office of the Inspector General
Room 1000, 400 Army Navy Dr., Arlington, VA 22202. Phone 695-4249.

Defense Information Systems Agency
701 S. Courthouse Rd., Arlington, VA Phone 692-0018.

Defense Mapping Agency
8613 Lee Hwy., Fairfax, VA 22031 Phone 285-9290.

National Security Agency
Fort George G. Meade, MD 20755. Phone 301-686-7111.

Defense Intelligence Agency
Room 3E258. Phone 373-7353.

Defense Legal Services Agency
Room 3E980. Phone 697-3341.

Defense Nuclear Agency
6801 Telegraph Rd., Alexandria, VA 22310. Phone 325-7004.

Defense Security Assistance Agency
Room 4E841. Phone 695-3291.

Strategic Defense Initiative Organization
Room 1E1081. Phone 695-7060.

Defense Investigative Service
1900 Half St. SW, 20324. Phone 202-475-0966.

Defense Logistics Agency
Cameron Station, 5010 Duke St., Alexandria, VA 22304. Phone 274-7920.

Defense Advanced Research Projects Agency
8th Floor, 1400 Wilson Blvd., Arlington, VA 22209. Phone 694-5469

Defense Contract Audit Agency
3701 N. Fairfax Dr., Arlington, VA 22203. Phone 696-2444.

On-Site Inspection Agency
300 W. Service Rd., Fairchild Bldg. Dulles Airport, Chantilly, VA 20041. Phone 742-4480.

Office of the Joint Chiefs of Staff
Room 2E872. Phone 697-9121.

Specific Commands:
Aerospace
Strategic Air
Military Airlift

Unified Commands:
European
Atlantic
Central
Readiness
Pacific
Southern
Space

DEPARTMENT OF THE AIR FORCE

The Pentagon 20330-1000. Phone 697-7376. (All offices located at the Pentagon unless otherwise indicated. All phones use area code 703 unless otherwise indicated.)

Office of the Secretary
Room 4E871. Phone 697-7376.

Office of the Under Secretary
Room 4E886. Phone 697-1361.

Assistant Secretary for Acquisition
Room 4E964. Phone 697-6361.

Assistant Secretary for Financial Management
Room 4E984. Phone 693-6457.

Assistant Secretary for Manpower Reserve Affairs, Installations and Environment
Room 4E1020. Phone 697-2302

Assistant Secretary for Space
Room 4E998. Phone 693-5996

Office of the General Counsel
Room 4E998. Phone 697-0941.

Office of Public Affairs
Room 4D922. Phone 697-6061.

Office of the Inspector General
Room 4E1076. Phone 697-6733.

Office of the Judge Advocate General
Room 4E112. Phone 614-5732.

Office of the Air Force Chief of Staff
Room 4E925. Phone 697-9225.

DEPARTMENT OF THE ARMY

The Pentagon 20310-3070. Phone 703-695-5110. (All offices located at the Pentagon unless otherwise indicated. All phone numbers are area code 703 unless otherwise indicated.)

Office of the Secretary
Room 3E718. Phone 695-3211.

Office of the Under Secretary
Room 3E732. Phone 695-4311

Assistant Secretary for Civil Works
Room 2E570. Phone 697-8986.

Assistant Secretary for Financial Management
Room 3E606, Phone 697-8121.

Assistant Secretary for Installations and Logistics
Room 2E614. Phone 695-6527.

Assistant Secretary for Manpower and Reserve Affairs
Room 2E594. Phone 697-9253.

Assistant Secretary for Research, Development, and Acquisition
Room 2E673. Phone 695-6153.

Office of the General Counsel
Room 2E722. Phone 697-9235.

Office of Public Affairs
Room 2E636. Phone 694-5135.

Office of the Inspector General
Room 1E736. Phone 695-1500.

Office of the Judge Advocate General
Room 2E444. Phone 697-5151

Army Chief of Staff
Room 3E668. Phone 695-2077

DEPARTMENT OF THE NAVY

The Pentagon 20350-1000. Phone 614-3155. (All offices located at the Pentagon unless otherwise indicated. All phone numbers use area code 703 unless otherwise indicated.)

Office of the Secretary
Room 4E686. Phone 695-3131.

Office of the Undersecretary
Room 4E714. Phone 695-3141

Assistant Secretary for Installations & Environment
Room 266 Crystal Plaza Bldg. 5 2211 Jefferson Davis Hwy., Arlington, VA 20360. Phone 602-2239.

Assistant Secretary for Manpower and Reserve Affairs
Room 4E788. Phone 697-2179.

Assistant Secretary for Research, Engineering, and Systems
Room 4E732. Phone 695-6315.

Assistant Secretary for Financial Management
Room 4E768. Phone 697-2325.

Office of the General Counsel
Room 4E724. Phone 694-1994.

Office of Information
Room 2E340. Phone 697-7391

Naval Inspector General
Wash. Navy Yard, Bldg. 200, Washington, DC 20374. Phone 202-433-2000.

Office of the Judge Advocate General
Room 5D840, Hoffman Building No. 2, Alexandria, VA 22332. Phone 325-9820.

Chief of Naval Operations
Room 4E660. Phone 695-5664.

Commandant, U.S. Marine Corps
Columbia Pike & Southgate Road, Arlington, VA 22204. Phone 614-2500.

Special Toll Free Information and Hotline Phone Numbers

Fraud and Waste Hotline 800-424-9089; 202-693-5080
Veterans of Nuclear Tests Info—800-462-3683; 202-285-5610
Pentagon Tours—800-424-9080
U.S. Air Force Information—703-697-4100
Air Force Personnel Locator—202-695-4803
U.S. Army Personnel Locator—703-695-5110
Naval General Personnel Locator—703-694-3155
Naval Public Inquiries—703-695-0911
Marine Corps Specialized Information—703-614-1235

DEPARTMENT OF EDUCATION

400 Maryland Ave. SW 20202. Phone 202-708-5366. (All offices located at 400 Maryland Ave., SW, 20202, unless otherwise indicated.)

Office of the Secretary
Room 4181. Phone 401-3000.

Office of the Deputy Secretary
Room 4015. Phone 401-1000.

Assistant Secretary for Intergovernmental and Interagency Affairs
Room 4181. Phone 401-3414.

Assistant Secretary for Civil Rights
Room 5000, 330 C Street SW, 20202. Phone 205-5413.

Assistant Secretary for Educational Research and Improvement
Room 602, 555 New Jersey Ave., NW 20208 Phone 219-1385.

Assistant Secretary for Special Education and Rehabilitative Services
Room 3006, 330 C Street SW, 20202. Phone 205-5465.

Assistant Secretary for Elementary and Secondary Education
Room 2189. Phone 401-0113.

Assistant Secretary for Postsecondary Education
Room 4082, 7th and D Streets SW, 20202. Phone 708-5547.

Assistant Secretary for Vocational and Adult Education
Room 4090, 330 C Street SW, 20202. Phone 205-5451.

Assistant Secretary for Legislation and Congressional Affairs
Room 3153. Phone 401-0020.

Assistant Secretary for Human Resources and Administration
Room 3181. Phone 401-0470.

Assistant Secretary for Policy & Planning
Room 4155. Phone 401-3078.

Assistant Secretary for Management/Chief Financial Officer
Room 4079. Phone 401-1095.

Office of Public Affairs
Room 4181. Phone 401-1576

Office of the General Counsel
Room 4091. Phone 401-2600.

Office of Inspector General
Room 4006, 330 C Street SW 20202. Phone 453-4039.

Special Toll Free Information and Hotline Phone Numbers

Fraud and Waste Hotline—800-647-8733
Federal Student Aid—800-333-4636 202-708-8197
Clearinghouse on Handicapped Educational Services—800-424-8567
America 2000—800-872-5327; 202-401-2000

DEPARTMENT OF ENERGY

James Forrestal Bldg., 1000 Independence Ave. SW 20585. Phone 202-586-5000. (All offices located at the James Forrestal Bldg. unless otherwise indicated.)

Office of the Secretary
Room 7A-257. Phone 586-6210.

Office of the Deputy Secretary
Room 7B-252. Phone 586-5500.

Office of the Under Secretary
Room 7A-219. Phone 586-6479.

Assistant Secretary for Congressional and Intergovernmental Affairs
Room 7B-138. Phone 586-5450.

Assistant Secretary for Domestic and International Energy Policy
Room 7C-016. Phone 586-5800.

Assistant Secretary for Nuclear Energy
Room 5A-115. Phone 586-6450.

Assistant Secretary for Fossil Energy
Room 4G-084. Phone 586-6660.

Assistant Secretary for Conservation and Renewable Energy
Room 6C-016. Phone 586-9220.

Assistant Secretary for Defense Programs
Room 4A-014. Phone 586-2177.

Assistant Secretary for Environment, Safety, and Health
Room 7A-097. Phone 586-6151.

Assistant Secretary for Environmental Restoration and Waste Management
Room 7A-049. Phone 586-7710.

Office of Public Affairs
Room 8G-096. Phone 586-8325

Office of the General Counsel
Room 6A-245. Phone 586-5281.

Office of the Inspector General
Room 5D-039. Phone 586-4393.

Economic Regulatory Administration
Room 5B-148. Phone 586-6781.

Energy Information Administration
Room 2H-027 Phone 586-4361.

Federal Energy Regulatory Commission
825 N. Capitol Street NW 20426. Phone 357-0200.

Special Toll Free Information and Hotline Phone Numbers

Public Information—202-586-5575
Conservation and Renewable Energy—800-523-2929
Inspector General Hotline—800-541-1625
Alternative Fuels Hotline—800-423-1363

DEPARTMENT OF HEALTH AND HUMAN SERVICES

Hubert H. Humphrey Bldg., 200 Independence Ave. SW 20201. Phone 202-619-0257. (All offices located at the Hubert H. Humphrey Bldg. unless otherwise indicated.)

Office of the Secretary
Room 615 F. Phone 690-7000.

Office of the Deputy Secretary
Room 614 G. Phone 690-7431.

Assistant Secretary for Legislation
Room 416 G. Phone 690-7627.

Assistant Secretary for Public Affairs
Room 647 D. Phone 690-7850.

Assistant Secretary for Planning and Evaluation
Room 415 F. Phone 690-7858.

Assistant Secretary for Health
Room 716 G. Phone 690-7694

Assistant Secretary for Management and Budget
Room 514 G. Phone 690-6396.

Assistant Secretary for Administration for Children and Families
901 D St. SW Washington, DC 20447. Phone 401-9200.

Assistant Secretary for Personnel Administration
Room 522 A. Phone 690-7284.

Office of Public Affairs
Room 647 D. Phone 690-7850.

Office of the General Counsel
Room 722 A. Phone 690-7741.

Office of Inspector General
Room 5250, Cohen Bldg., 330 Independence Ave. SW 20201. Phone 619-3146.

Health Care Financing Administration
Room 314 G. Phone 245-6726.
Also: 6325 Security Blvd., Baltimore, MD 21207. Phone 410-966-3152

U.S. Public Health Service
Room 716 G. Phone 690-7694.

Office of the Surgeon General
Room 710 G. Phone 690-6467.

National AIDS Program Office
Room 729 H. Phone 690-5471.

Food and Drug Administration
Parklawn Bldg. 5600 Fishers Ln., Rockville, MD 20857. Phone 301-443-5315.

National Institutes of Health
9000 Rockville Pike, Bethesda, MD 20205. Phone 301-496-2433.

National Library of Medicine
Bldg. 38, NIH. Phone 301-496-6221.

National Cancer Institute
Bldg. 31, NIH. Phone 301-496-5615.

National Heart, Lung and Blood Institute
Bldg. 31, NIH. Phone 301-496-5166.

National Eye Institute
Bldg. 31, NIH. Phone 301-496-2234.

National Institute of Arthritis and Musculoskeletal and Skin Diseases
Bldg. 31, NIH. Phone 301-496-4353.

National Institute of Allergy and Infectious Diseases
Bldg. 31, NIH. Phone 301-496-2263.

National Institute of Diabetes and Kidney Diseases
Bldg. 31, NIH. Phone 301-496-5877.

National Institute of Child Health and Human Development
Bldg. 31, NIH. Phone 301-496-3454.

National Institute on Aging
Bldg. 31, NIH. Phone 301-496-0216.

National Institute of Neurological and Communicative Disorders and Stroke
Bldg. 31, NIH. Phone 301-496-9746.

Social Security Administration
6401 Security Boulevard, Baltimore, MD 21235. Phone 410-965-8882.

President's Council on Physical Fitness and Sports
Room 7103, 450 Fifth Street NW 20001. Phone 272-3430.

Special Toll Free Information and Hotline Phone Numbers

Whistle Blowers Hotline—800-368-5779
Fraud-Waste Hotline—800-368-5779
AIDS Information Hotline—800-342-2437 202-332-2437
Cancer Information Line—800-422-6237
Drug Abuse Information—800-638-2045
Civil Rights Information—800-368-1019
General Health Information—800-336-4797
Venereal Disease Hotline—800-227-8922
National Hotline for Missing or Exploited Children—800-843-5678
Runaway Children Hotline—800-621-4000
FDA Consumer Inquiries—301-443-3170
FDA Emergency Line (24 hrs)—301-857-8400
Social Security General Information—800-234-5772 800-325-0778 (TTY)

DEPARTMENT OF HOUSING AND URBAN DEVELOPMENT

HUD Bldg., 451 Seventh Street SW 20410. Phone 202-708-1112. (All offices located at the HUD Bldg. unless otherwise indicated.)

Office of the Secretary
Room 10000. Phone 708-6417.

Office of the Deputy Secretary
Room 10100. Phone 708-0123.

Assistant Secretary for Public Affairs
Room 10226. Phone 708-3161.

Assistant Secretary for Policy Development and Research
Room 8100. Phone 708-1600.

Assistant Secretary for Congressional and Intergovernmental Relations
Room 10120. Phone 708-0005.

Assistant Secretary for Administration
Room 10110. Phone 708-0940.

Assistant Secretary for Community Planning and Development
Room 7100. Phone 708-2690.

Assistant Secretary for Housing-Federal Housing Commissioner
Room 9100. Phone 708-3600.

Assistant Secretary for Fair Housing and Equal Opportunity
Room 5100. Phone 708-4252.

Assistant Secretary for Public and Indian Housing
Room 4100. Phone 708-0950.

Office of Public Affairs
Room 10226. Phone 708-3161.

Office of the Inspector General
Room 8256. Phone 708-0430.

Office of the General Counsel
Room 10214. Phone 708-2244.

Government National Mortgage Association (Ginnie Mae)
Room 6100. Phone 708-0926.

Special Toll Free Information and Hotline Phone Numbers

Grants Information—202-708-2690
Housing Discrimination Complaint Hotline—800-699-9777
Fraud and Waste Reports—202-347-3735

DEPARTMENT OF THE INTERIOR

Interior Bldg., 18th and C Sts. 20240. Phone 202-208-3100. (All offices located at the Interior Bldg., 18th and C Sts., 20240, unless otherwise indicated.)

Office of the Secretary
Room 6151. Phone 208-7351.

Office of the Deputy Secretary
Room 5100. Phone 208-4863.

Assistant Secretary for Policy, Budget and Administration
Room 6114. Phone 208-4123.

Assistant Secretary for Fish and Wildlife and Parks
Room 3156. Phone 208-4416.

Assistant Secretary for Indian Affairs
Room 4160. Phone 208-7163.

Assistant Secretary for Land and Minerals Management
Room 6608. Phone 208-5676

Assistant Secretary for Water and Science
Room 6654. Phone 208-3186.

Assistant Secretary for Territorial and International Affairs
Room 4310. Phone 208-4822.

Office of Public Affairs
Room 7214. Phone 208-6416.

Office of Congressional and Legislative Affairs
Room 6254. Phone 208-7693.

Office of the Inspector General
Room 5359. Phone 208-5745.

National Park Service
Room 3104. Phone 208-4621.

U.S. Fish and Wildlife Service
Room 3256. Phone 208-4717.

Minerals Management Service
Room 4212. Phone 208-3500.

U.S. Geological Survey
12201 Sunrise Valley Drive, Reston, VA 22092. Phone 703-648-4000.

Special Toll Free Information and Hotline Phone Numbers

Fraud-Waste Reports—800-424-5081
Abandoned Mine Reclamation Grants—202-208-7937

DEPARTMENT OF JUSTICE

10th St. & Constitution Ave., N.W. 20530. Phone 202-514-2000. (All offices are located in the Main Justice Bldg. unless otherwise indicated.)

Office of the Attorney General
Room 5111. Phone 514-2001.

Office of the Deputy Attorney General
Room 4111. Phone 514-2101.

Assistant Attorney General for Antitrust Division
Room 3101. Phone 514-2401.

Assistant Attorney General for Civil Division
Room 3143. Phone 514-3301.

Assistant Attorney General for Civil Rights Division
Room 5643. Phone 514-2151.

Assistant Attorney General for Criminal Division
Room 2107. Phone 514-2601.

Assistant Attorney General for Tax Division
Room 4143. Phone 514-2901.

Assistant Attorney General for Legal Counsel
Room 5214. Phone 514-2041.

Assistant Attorney General for Legislative Affairs
Room 1145. Phone 514-2141.

Assistant Attorney General for Justice Programs
633 Indiana Ave. 20530. Phone 307-5933.

Assistant Attorney General for Administration
Room 1111. Phone 514-3101.

Assistant Attorney General for Environment and Natural Resources
Room 2143. Phone 514-2701.

Office of Public Affairs
Room 1216. Phone 514-2007.

Executive Office for U.S. Attorneys
Room 1619. Phone 514-2121.

Office of the Solicitor General
Room 5143. Phone 514-2201.

Office of the Inspector General
Room 4706. Phone 514-3534.

Federal Bureau of Investigation
J. Edgar Hoover Bldg. 9th St. and Pennsylvania Ave. 20535. Phone 324-3000.

Drug Enforcement Administration
700 Army Navy Dr., Arlington, VA 22202 (mailing address: Washington, DC 20537) Phone 202-307-8000.

Immigration and Naturalization Services
425 I Street 20536. Phone 514-1900.

Executive Office for Immigration Review
Suite 1609, 5203 Leesburg Pike, Falls Church, VA 22041. Phone 703-756-6168.

Bureau of Prisons
HOLC Bldg. 320 First St. 20534. Phone 307-3250.

U.S. Marshals Service
600 Army Navy Dr., Arlington, VA 22202. Washington, DC Phone 202-307-9001.

International Criminal Police Organization (Interpol)—U.S. National Central Bureau
600 E. Street, NW 20530. Phone 272-8383.

Special Toll Free Information and Hotline Phone Numbers

Public Information—202-514-2007
INS Alien Information (English and Spanish)—800-255-7688
Amnesty Program—800-777-7700
Hate Crime Hotline—800-347-HATE
Alien Inquiries General Information—202-307-1501
Waste and Fraud Hotline—800-869-4499

DEPARTMENT OF LABOR

Frances Perkins Bldg., 200 Constitution Ave. NW 20210. Phone 219-6666. (All offices located at the Frances Perkins Bldg. unless otherwise indicated.)

Office of the Secretary
Room S2018. Phone 219-8274.

Office of the Deputy Secretary
Room S2018. Phone 219-6151.

Deputy Under Secretary for International Labor Affairs
Room S2235. Phone 219-6043.

Deputy Under Secretary for Labor-Management Relations and Cooperative Programs
Room S2235. Phone 219-6045.

Assistant Secretary for Policy
Room S2006. Phone 523-6181.

Assistant Secretary for Administration and Management
Room S2514. Phone 523-9086.

Assistant Secretary for Congressional and International Affairs
Room S2018. Phone 219-3629.

Assistant Secretary for Employment Standards
Room S2321. Phone 219-6191.

Assistant Secretary for Employment and Training
Room S2307. Phone 219-6050.

Assistant Secretary for Labor-Management Standards
Room S2203. Phone 219-9674.

Assistant Secretary for Mine Safety and Health
Ballston Tower #3, 4501 Wilson Blvd., Arlington, VA 22203. Phone 703-235-1385.

Assistant Secretary for Occupational Safety and Health
Room S1313. Phone 219-7162.

Assistant Secretary for Pension and Welfare Benefits Administration
Room S2524. Phone 523-8921.

Assistant Secretary for Policy
Room S2006. Phone 219-6181.

Assistant Secretary for Public Affairs
Room S1032. Phone 219-9711.

Assistant Secretary for Veterans' Employment and Training
Room S1313. Phone 219-9116.

Office of Public Affairs
Room S1032. Phone 523-9711.

Office of Inspector General
Room S1303. Phone 523-7296.

Employment Standards Administration
Room S2321. Phone 523-6191.

Employment and Training Administration
Room S2307. Phone 523-6050.

Bureau of Labor-Management Relations and Cooperative Programs
Room S2203. Phone 523-6045.

Bureau of Labor Statistics
GAO Bldg., Room 2106, 441 G Street 20212. Phone 523-1092.

Bureau of International Labor Affairs
Room S2235. Phone 523-6043.

Mine Safety and Health Administration
4015 Wilson Blvd., Arlington, VA 22203. Phone 703-235-1452.

Occupational Safety and Health Adminstration
Room S2315. Phone 523-8148.

Special Toll Free Information and Hotline Phone Numbers

Fraud-Waste Hotline—800-347-3756
General Information—202-219-7316

DEPARTMENT OF STATE

2201 C St. NW 20520. Phone 202-647-4000. (All offices located in the State Department Bldg., 2201 C St. 20520, unless otherwise indicated.)

Office of the Secretary
Room 7226 Phone 647-4910.

Under Secretary for Political Affairs
Room 7240. Phone 647-2471.

Under Secretary for Economic and Agricultural Affairs
Room 7250. Phone 647-6240.

Under Secretary for Management
Room 7207. Phone 647-1500.

Under Secretary for International Security Affairs
Room 7210. Phone 647-1049.

Assistant Secretary for Consular Affairs
Room 6811. Phone 647-9576.

Assistant Secretary for Economic and Business Affairs
Room 6828. Phone 647-7971.

Assistant Secretary for Public Affairs
Room 6800. Phone 647-5548.

Assistant Secretary for International Narcotics Matters
Room 7331. Phone 647-8464.

Assistant Secretary for Oceans and International, Environmental and Scientific Affairs
Room 7831. Phone 647-1554.

Assistant Secretary for Human Rights and Humanitarian Affairs
Room 7802. Phone 647-2264.

Assistant Secretary for European and Canadian Affairs
Room 6226. Phone 647-9626.

Assistant Secretary for African Affairs
Room 6234A. Phone 647-4440.

Assistant Secretary for East Asian and Pacific Affairs
Room 6205. Phone 647-9596.

Assistant Secretary for Inter-American Affairs
Room 6263. Phone 647-5780.

Assistant Secretary for Near Eastern and South Asian Affairs
Room 6242. Phone 647-7209.

Assistant Secretary for International Organization Affairs
Room 6323. Phone 647-9600.

Assistant Secretary for Legislative Affairs
Room 7261. Phone 647-4204.

Assistant Secretary for Diplomatic Security
Room 2509. Phone 647-6290

Assistant Secretary for Politico-Military Affairs
Room 7325A. Phone 647-9022.

Assistant Secretary for Intelligence and Research
Room 6533. Phone 647-2222.

Office of Public Affairs
Room 6800. Phone 647-6575.

Counselor of the Department
Room 7250. Phone 647-6240.

Legal Adviser
Room 6423. Phone 647-9598.

Office of the Inspector General
Room 6817. Phone 647-9450.

Special Toll Free Information and Hotline Phone Numbers
Passport Information—202-663-0518
Public Information—202-647-6575
Visa Information—202-663-1225

DEPARTMENT OF TRANSPORTATION

400 Seventh St. SW. 20590. Phone 202-366-4000. (All offices located at 400 Seventh St. SW, 20590, unless otherwise indicated.)

Office of the Secretary
Room 10200. Phone 366-1111.

Office of the Deputy Secretary
Room 10200. Phone 366-2222.

Assistant Secretary for Governmental Affairs
Room 10408. Phone 366-4573.

Assistant Secretary for Administration
Room 10314. Phone 366-2332.

Assistant Secretary for Public Affairs
Room 10414. Phone 366-4570.

Assistant Secretary for Budget and Programs
Room 10101. Phone 366-9191.

Assistant Secretary for Policy and International Affairs
Room 10228. Phone 366-4544.

Office of Public Affairs
Room 10414. Phone 366-4570.

Office of the General Counsel
Room 10428. Phone 366-4702.

Office of the Inspector General
Room 9210. Phone 366-1959.

U.S. Coast Guard
2100 Second St. SW 20593. Phone 267-2229.

Federal Aviation Administration (FAA)
800 Independence Ave. SW 20591. Phone 267-3484.

Federal Highway Administration
Room 4218. Phone 366-0660.

Maritime Administration
Room 7206. Phone 366-5812.

Federal Railroad Administration
Room 8206. Phone 366-0881.

National Highway Traffic Safety Administration
Room 5220. Phone 366-9550.

Research and Special Programs Administration
Room 8410. Phone 366-4000.

St. Lawrence Seaway Development Corporation
Room 5424. Phone 366-0091.

Special Toll Free Information and Hotline Phone Numbers
Public Information—202-366-5580
Fraud and Waste Hotline—800-424-9071
Coast Guard Hotline—800-424-8802
Auto Safety Hotline—800-424-9393
FAA Consumer Hotline—800-322-7873 202-267-8592
FAA Air Safety Hotline—800-255-1111
NHTSA Auto Defect and Recall Hotline—800-424-9393 202-366-0123
Hazardous Materials, Chemicals and Oil Spills —800-424-8002

DEPARTMENT OF THE TREASURY

1500 Pennsylvania Ave., NW 20220. Phone 202-622-2000. (All offices located in Main Treasury Bldg., 1500 Pennsylvania Ave., NW 20220, unless otherwise indicated.)

Office of the Secretary
Room 3330. Phone 622-1100.

Office of the Deputy Secretary
Room 3326. Phone 622-1070.

Under Secretary for International Affairs
Room 3432. Phone 622-1080.

Under Secretary for Finance
Room 3312. Phone 622-2800.

Assistant Secretary for Public Affairs and Public Liaison
Room 3442. Phone 622-2920.

Assistant Secretary for Management
Room 2426. Phone 622-0410.

Assistant Secretary for Domestic Finance
Room 2326. Phone 622-2600.

Assistant Secretary for Economic Policy
Room 3454. Phone 622-2200.

Fiscal Assistant Secretary
Room 2112. Phone 622-0550.

Assistant Secretary for International Affairs
Room 3430. Phone 622-0060.

Assistant Secretary for Tax Policy
Room 3120. Phone 622-0050.

Assistant Secretary for Enforcement
Room 4312. Phone 622-0200.

Assistant Secretary for Policy Management
Room 3414. Phone 622-0041.

Assistant Secretary for Legislative Affairs
Room 3134. Phone 622-1900.

Office of Public Affairs
Room 3442. Phone 622-2910.

Office of the General Counsel
Room 3000. Phone 622-0287.

Office of the Inspector General
Room 2412. Phone 622-1090.

Treasurer of the United States
Room 2124. Phone 622-0100.

Internal Revenue Service
IRS Bldg. 1111 Constitution Ave. 20224. Phone 800-829-1040.

Bureau of Alcohol, Tobacco and Firearms (ATF)
650 Massachusetts Ave. NW 20226. Phone 927-7777.

U.S. Customs Service
1301 Constitution Ave. NW 20229. Phone 566-5000.

U.S. Secret Service
Ste. 800, 1800 G St. NW 20223. Phone 435-5700.

Bureau of Engraving and Printing
14th and C Sts. SW, 20228. Phone 874-2485.

United States Mint
633 Third St. NW 20220. Phone 874-6000.

Financial Management Service
401 14th St., NW 20227. Phone 874-7000.

U.S. Savings Bonds Division
800 K St. NW 20226. Phone 377-7700.

Bureau of the Public Debt
Room 553, 999 E St. 20239-0001. Phone 219-3300.

Office of Thrift Supervision
5th Floor, 1700 G St., NW, 20552 Phone 906-6000.

Special Toll Free Information and Hotline Phone Numbers

Fraud-Waste Hotline—800-359-3898
Public Information—202-622-2960

Customs Service General Information—202-566-8195
IRS Taxpayer Assistance—800-424-1040
Savings Bond Info—202-447-1775
Treasury Bill Info—202-287-4091
USSS Presidential Protection Hotline—202-435-5721

DEPARTMENT OF VETERANS AFFAIRS

810 Vermont Ave. NW 20420. Phone 202-233-2300. (All offices located at 801 Eye St., NW 20001 unless otherwise indicated.)

Office of the Secretary
Room 1000. Phone 535-8900.

Office of the Deputy Secretary
Room 1121. Phone 535-8623.

Assistant Secretary for Acquisition and Facilities
Room 1209. Phone 535-8555.

Assistant Secretary for Congressional and Public Affairs
Room 618. Phone 535-8470.

Assistant Secretary for Finance and Information Resources Management
Room 931. Phone 535-8504.

Assistant Secretary for Public and Intergovernmental Affairs
Room 1019. Phone 535-8159.

Assistant Secretary for Policy and Planning
Room 751. Phone 535-8964.

Assistant Secretary for Human Resources and Administration
Room 1231. Phone 535-8535.

Office of Public Affairs
Room 1009. Phone 535-8165.

Office of the General Counsel
Room 1144. Phone 535-8111.

Office of the Inspector General
Room 1200, 1425 K. St. NW 20005. Phone 233-2636

Veterans Health Administration
Room 710. Phone 535-7010.

Veterans Benefits Administration
Room 811. Phone 535-7920.

National Cemetery System
Room 907. Phone 535-7810.

Special Toll Free Information and Hotline Phone Numbers

Complaint Center Hotline—800-368-5899 202-233-5394
Vietnam Veterans—800-424-7275 202-332-2700

INDEPENDENT AGENCIES

(All phone numbers use area code 202 unless otherwise indicated.)

Action
1100 Vermont Ave. NW 20525. Phone 606-5135.

Administrative Conference of the United States
Suite 500, 2120 L St. 20037. Phone 254-7020.

Advisory Commission on Intergovernmental Relations
800 K St. 20575. Phone 653-5640.

Advisory Council on Historic Preservation
1100 Pennsylvania Ave. 20004. Phone 606-8503.

African Development Foundation
1400 Eye St. NW 20005. Phone 673-3916.

Agency for International Development (AID)
Room 5942, Dept. of State 20523. Phone 647-4000.

American Battle Monuments Commission
Room 5127, 20 Massachusetts Ave. NW 20314. Phone 272-0533.

American Red Cross
National Headquarters, 17th & D Sts. NW 20006. Phone 737-8300.

AMTRAK (National Passenger Rail Corp.)
60 Massachusetts Ave. NE 20002. Phone 906-3000.

Appalachian Regional Commission
1666 Connecticut Ave. 20235. Phone 673-7856.

Board for International Broadcasting
Suite 400, 1201 Connecticut Ave. NW 20036. Phone 254-8040.

Commission on Civil Rights
Suite 800, 1121 Vermont Ave. NW 20425. Phone 523-5571.

Commission of Fine Arts
Suite 312, Pension Bldg., 441 F St., NW 20001. Phone 504-2200.

Commodity Futures Trading Commission
Suite 819, 2033 K St. NW 20581. Phone 254-6387.

Consumer Product Safety Commission
5401 Westbard Ave., Bethesda, MD 20207. Phone 301-504-0100. Hotline 800-638-2772 800-638-8270 (TTY).

Copyright Royalty Tribunal
Suite 450, 1111 20th St. NW 20036. Phone 653-5175.

Delaware River Basin Commission
1010 Massachusetts Ave. 20240. Phone 208-7351.

Environmental Protection Agency (EPA)
401 M St. SW 20460. Phone 260-2090. Emergency Response—800-424-8802.

Equal Employment Opportunity Commission (EEOC)
1801 L. St. NW 20507. Phone 663-4900.

Export-Import Bank of the United States
811 Vermont Ave. NW 20571. Phone 566-2117.

Farm Credit Administration
1501 Farm Credit Dr., McLean, VA 22102-5090. Phone 703-883-4056.

Federal Communications Commission
1919 M St. 20554. Phone 632-7000.

Federal Deposit Insurance Corporation
550 17th St. NW 20429. Phone 393-8400.

Federal Election Commission
999 E St. NW 20463. Phone 219-3420; 800-424-9530.

Federal Emergency Management Agency
500 C Street SW 20472. Phone 646-2500.

Federal Home Loan Mortgage Corp. (Freddie Mac)
8200 Jones Branch Dr., McLean, VA 22102. Phone 703-903-2000.

Federal Labor Relations Authority
500 C St. SW 20424. Phone 382-0751.

Federal Maritime Commission
800 N. Capitol St. NW 20573. Phone 523-5773.

Federal Mediation and Conciliation Service
2100 K St. NW 20427. Phone 653-5290.

Federal Mine Safety and Health Review Commission
6th Floor, 1730 K St. NW 20006. Phone 653-5633.

Federal National Mortgage Association (Fannie Mae)
3900 Wisconsin Ave. NW 20016. Phone 752-7000.

Federal Reserve System
20th & C Sts. NW 20551. Phone 452-3000.

Federal Trade Commission (FTC)
6th St. and Pennsylvania Ave. NW 20580. Phone 326-2000.

General Services Administration
GSA Bldg. 18th and F Sts. NW 20405. Phone 501-1231 (info); 702-5082 (locator).

Government Printing Office (GPO)
N. Capitol and G Sts., NW 20502. Phone 275-3648; 783-3238 (orders).

Harry S. Truman Scholarship Foundation
712 Jackson Pl. NW 20006. Phone 395-4831.

Inter-American Foundation
901 N. Stuart St., Arlington, VA 22203. Phone 703-841-3800.

Interstate Commerce Commission (ICC)
ICC Bldg., 12th St. and Constitution Ave. NW 20423. Phone 927-5885.

International Bank for Reconstruction and Development (World Bank)
1818 H St. NW 20433. Phone 477-1234.

International Monetary Fund (IMF)
700 19th St., NW 20431. Phone 566-7000.

Legal Services Corporation
750 First St. NE 20002. Phone 336-8800.

National Aeronautics and Space Administration (NASA)
Independence Square, 300 E St. SW, 20546. Phone 358-0000.

National Archives and Records Administration
8th St. and Pennsylvania Ave., NW 20408. Phone 501-5400.

National Commission on AIDS
1730 K St. NW 20006. Phone 254-5125.

National Historical Publications and Records Commission
National Archives Bldg. 20408. Phone 501-5400.

National Capital Planning Commission
801 Pennsylvania Ave. NW 20576. Phone 724-0174.

National Commission on Libraries and Information Science
1111 18th St., NW 20036. Phone 254-3100.

National Council on Disability
Ste. 814, 800 Independence Ave. SW, 20591. Phone 267-3846.

National Credit Union Administration
1776 G St. NW 20456. Phone 682-9650.

National Foundation of the Arts and the Humanities

National Endowment for the Arts
1100 Pennsylvania Ave. NW 20506. Phone 682-5400.

National Endowment For the Humanities
1100 Pennsylvania Ave. NW 20506. Phone 786-0443.

Institute of Museum Services
1100 Pennsylvania Ave. NW 20506. Phone 786-0536

National Labor Relations Board (NLRB)
1717 Pennsylvania Ave. NW 20570. Phone 632-4950.

National Mediation Board
Ste. 910, 1301 K St. NW 20005. Phone 523-5920.

National Research Council; National Academy of Sciences; National Academy of Engineering; Institute of Medicine
2101 Constitution Ave. NW 20418. Phone 334-2000.

National Science Foundation
1800 G St. NW 20550. Phone 357-9859.

National Transportation Safety Board (NTSB)
490 L'Enfant Plaza East SW 20594. Phone 382-6600.

Nuclear Regulatory Commission (NRC)
1 White Flint North Bldg. 11555 Rockville Pike, Rockville, MD 20852. Phone 301-492-7000.

Occupational Safety and Health Review Commission (OSHA)
1825 K St. NW 20006. Phone 634-7943.

Office of Personnel Management (OPM)
1900 E St. NW 20415. Phone 606-2424; 606-2700 (recording of job openings).

Overseas Private Investment Corporation
1100 New York Ave. NW 20527. Phone 336-8400.

Panama Canal Commission
Suite 550, 2000 L St. NW 20036. Phone 634-6441.

Peace Corps
1990 K Street NW 20526. Phone 606-3886; 800-424-8580, ext. 293.

Pennsylvania Avenue Development Corporation
Suite 1220 N, 1331 Pennsylvania Ave. NW 20004. Phone 724-9091.

Pension Benefit Guaranty Corporation (PBGC)
2020 K St. NW 20006. Phone 778-8808.

Postal Rate Commission
1333 H St. NW 20268. Phone 789-6000.

President's Commission on Executive Exchange
744 Jackson Pl. NW 20503. Phone 395-4616.

President's Commission on White House Fellowships
712 Jackson Pl. NW 20503. Phone 395-4522.

President's Committee on Employment of People with Disabilities
2100 M St. NW 20037. Phone 376-6200; 376-6205 (TDD).

Railroad Retirement Board
844 Rush St. Chicago, IL 60611. Phone 312-751-4777.

Resolution Trust Corp.
801 17th St. NW 20434. Phone 431-0600.

Securities and Exchange Commission (SEC)
450 Fifth St. NW 20549. Phone 272-3100; 272-7440 (complaints).

Selective Service System
National Headquarters, 1023 31st St., NW 20435. Phone 724-0820.

Small Business Administration
409 3rd Street SW 20416. Phone 205-6600.

Smithsonian Institution
1000 Jefferson Drive SW 20560. Phone 357-1300.

Susquehanna River Basin Commission
1010 Massachusetts Ave. NW 20240. Phone 343-4091.

Tennessee Valley Authority (TVA)
400 W. Summit Hill Dr., Knoxville, TN 37902. Phone (615) 632-8363.

U.S. Arms Control and Disarmament Agency
Dept. of State Bldg., 320 21st St. NW 20451. Phone 647-8677.

U.S. Holocaust Memorial Council
Suite 588 2000 L. St. NW 20036. Phone 653-9220.

U.S. Information Agency (USIA)
301 4th St. SW 20547. Phone 619-4700.

Voice of America (USIA)
330 Independence Ave. SW 20537. Phone 619-4700

U.S. Institute of Peace
Suite 700, 1550 M Street NW 20005. Phone 457-1700

U.S. International Trade Commission
500 E. Street SW 20436. Phone 205-2651.

U.S. Merit Systems Protection Board
1120 Vermont Ave. NW 20419. Phone 653-8898.

U.S. Postal Service
475 L'Enfant Plaza SW 20260-0010. Phone 268-2000.

Washington National Monument Association
740 Jackson Pl. NW 20503. Phone 842-0806.

WHERE TO WRITE AND WHOM TO CALL— FREQUENTLY CONTACTED DEPARTMENTS AND PROGRAMS

DEPARTMENT OF AGRICULTURE

Food and Nutrition Service

Food Donation Program: Food is made available to state agencies for distribution to qualifying individuals, programs, schools, charitable institutions, nutrition programs for the elderly and nonprofit summer camps. A household eligibility and distribution plan must be approved for each state; heads of households apply to local welfare authorities.

Food Stamps: Households receive a coupon allotment, which varies according to household size and income. The standard allotment is reduced by 30 percent of the net income. Coupons may be used in participating retail stores to buy food for human consumption and garden seeds and plants to produce food for personal consumption. Eligibility is determined by local welfare officials and is based on family size, income, and level of resources.

National School Lunch Program: Funds are available to each state agency to reimburse participating public and nonprofit private schools for lunches served to eligible students. All participating schools must agree to serve free and reduced-price meals to eligible students: Those who are determined by local authorities to have household income levels at or below 130 and 185 percent of the poverty line, respectively.

School Breakfast Program: Funds are available to reimburse participating public and nonprofit private schools for breakfasts served to eligible students. Breakfast is served free or at reduced prices to students who are determined by local school authorities to have household income levels at or below 130 and 185 percent of the income eligibility guidelines.

Special Milk Program for Children: Funds are made available to state agencies to encourage the consumption of milk by students in nonprofit schools.

Special Supplemental Food Program for Women, Infants and Children (WIC): Grants are made available to state health departments to supply, at no cost, supplemental nutritious foods and nutrition education to low-income pregnant and postpartum women, infants, and children up to five years of age. Funds are expended to purchase supplemental foods for participants or to redeem vouchers issued for that purpose.

Headquarters Office: Food and Nutrition Service, Department of Agriculture, 3101 Park Center Dr., Alexandria, VA 22302. Phone 703-305-2908.

Farmers Home Administration

Emergency Loans: Assists family farmers, ranchers and aquaculture operators with loans to cover losses resulting from major disasters.

Farm Operating Loans: Enables operators of not larger than family farms to make efficient use of their land, labor and other resources through the extension of credit and supervisory assistance.

Farm Ownership Loans: Assists eligible farmers, through the extension of credit and supervisory assistance, to become owner-operators of no larger than family farms, to make efficient use of land, labor and other resources, to carry on sound and successful farming operations; and to enable farm families to have a reasonable standard of living.

Very-Low-Income and Low-Income Housing Loans: Assists lower-income rural families to obtain decent, safe and sanitary dwellings and related facilities.

Headquarters Office: Farmers Home Administration, Department of Agriculture, 5014 South Bldg. Washington, DC 20250. Phone 202-690-1533.

HOUSING AND URBAN DEVELOPMENT

For information on all of the following programs, contact your local HUD field office.

Interest-Reduction Payment—Rental and Co-operative Housing for Lower-Income Families: Provides good-quality rental and cooperative housing for persons of low and moderate income by providing interest-reduction payments to lower their housing costs.

Headquarters Office: Director, Office of Multi-family Housing Programs, Department of Housing and Urban Development, Washington, DC 20410, 202-708-2495.

Rehabilitation Mortgage Insurance: Helps families repair or improve, purchase and improve, or refinance and improve existing residential structures more than one year old.

Mortgage Insurance—Homes: Insures lenders against loss on mortgage loans to help families undertake home ownership.

Mortgage Insurance—Homes for Low- and Moderate-Income Families: HUD insures lenders against loss on mortgage loans to make home ownership more readily available to low-income and moderate-income families.

Section 245 Graduated Payment Mortgage Program: Facilitates early home ownership for households that expect their income to rise. Program allows homeowners to make smaller monthly payments initially and to increase their size gradually over time.

Adjustable-Rate Mortgages: Provides mortgage insurance for an adjustable-rate mortgage.

Headquarters Office: Department of Housing and Urban Development, Washington, DC 20410. Phone 202-708-1420.

IMMIGRATION AND NATURALIZATION SERVICE

U.S. Immigration Law

The Immigration and Nationality Act, as amended (most recently in 1990, details follow), provides for the numerical limitation of annual immigration. Not subject to any numerical limitation are immigrants classified as immediate relatives (spouses, parents or natural children) of U.S. citizens; returning permanent resident aliens; certain former U.S. citizens; and certain long-term U.S. government employees. About 220,000 enter the U.S. annually in this classification.

The Refugee Act of 1980 (P.L. 96-212) calls for the special admission of persons who are of special humanitarian concern to the United States. The test is whether they possess a justified fear of persecution for political, racial, or religious reasons should they be forced to return to their native countries. The greatest difficulty is distinguishing between those who legitimately fear political prosecution and those seeking simply to better themselves economically. The number of refugees who may be admitted each year is determined by the President. In fiscal 1991, 131,000 refugees were admitted, most from East Asia and the Soviet Union. This number does not count against any numerical limitation category.

Numerical Limitation of Immigrants: As set by the new 1990 law, immigration to the United States is numerically limited to 700,000 annually in fiscal 1991-93. Thereafter it will be permanently set at 675,000.

Visa Categories: Of those immigrants subject to numerical limitations, applicants for immigration are classified as either preference or non-preference. The *preference* visa categories are based on certain relationships to persons in the United States, i.e., unmarried sons and daughters over 21 of U.S. citizens, spouses and unmarried sons and daughters of resident aliens, married sons and daughters of U.S. citizens, brothers and sisters of U.S. citizens 21 or over (first, 2d, 4th, and 5th preference, respectively); members of the professions or persons of exceptional ability in the sciences and arts whose services are sought by U.S. employers (3d preference); and skilled and unskilled workers in short supply (6th preference). Spouses and children of preference applicants are entitled to the same preference if accompanying or following to join such persons.

Preference status is based upon approved petitions, filed with the Immigration and Naturalization Service, by the appropriate relative or employer (or in the 3d preference by the alien himself).

Other immigrants not within one of these preference groups may qualify as *nonpreference* applicants and receive only those visa numbers not needed by preference applicants. The non-preference category has not been available since 1978 due to preferences using the allocation, but likely will be in the future because of the 1990 changes in the allocations.

Labor Certification: The Act of October 3, 1965, established controls to protect the U.S. labor market from an influx of skilled and unskilled foreign labor. Prior to the issuance of a visa, the potential 3d, 6th, and nonpreference immigrant must obtain the Secretary of Labor's certification, establishing that there are not sufficient workers in the U.S. at the alien's destination who are able, willing, and qualified to perform the job; and that the employment of the alien will not adversely affect the wages and working conditions of workers in the United States similarly employed; or that there is satisfactory evidence that the provisions of that section do not apply to the alien's case.

The Immigration Reform and Control Act of 1986 (PL 99-603): The first half of the 1980s saw Congress working on controlling illegal immigration. The result was this 1986 law which contains three major segments—legalization, employer sanctions, and temporary agricultural worker provisions. The law provided for a method for legalizing the status of many of the aliens who illegally entered the United States before 1982. The employer sanction section of the legislation, for the first time, imposed civil and criminal penalties on employers who knowingly hire, recruit, or refer aliens who are not authorized to work in the United States Civil fines range from $250 to $10,000 per alien and criminal penalties are possible for habitual violators. Finally, the temporary agricultural worker provisions of the act expand the existing temporary worker (H2) program. A grower wishing to hire H2 workers must file a petition with the Department of Labor. The Department will grant the petition provided there are insufficient workers who are able, willing, qualified, and available where and when needed to perform the labor, and there will be no adverse effect on the wages and working conditions of workers similarly employed in the United States.

The Legal Immigration Revision Act of 1990: This law, passed in the final days of the 101st Congress, is the most sweeping revision of legal immigration laws in the past 25 years. While generally keeping the established visa preference system, the new law calls for a sizable increase in the number of legal immigrants in all preference categories granted entry visas annually, allows significant increases in the number of immigrants from Europe (during the 1980s all but 10 percent of visas went to Asians and Latin Americans), gives increased preference to applicants possessing unusual talents or needed job skills, those willing to invest a significant amount in the United States and thereby create jobs, and creates a new class of preference (*diversity*) visas for those applying from countries currently "disadvantaged" under current and past immigration laws. (Ireland is a specific example.) In addition the new law eases or eliminates rules forbidding admission based on political convictions, religious beliefs, or sexual orientation. But admission can still be denied for possession of a "communicable disease of public health significance."

Headquarters Office: Immigration and Naturalization Service, 425 I Street NW 20536. Alien Information (English & Spanish)—800-777-7700; 202-514-4316.

Naturalization: How to Become an American Citizen

A person who desires to be naturalized as a citizen of the United States may obtain the necessary application form and detailed information from the nearest office of the Immigration and Naturalization Service, or from the clerk of a court handling naturalization cases.

An applicant must be at least 18 years old. He must have been a lawful resident of the United States continuously for five years. For husbands and wives of U.S. citizens, the period is three years in most instances. Special provisions apply to certain veterans of the armed forces.

An applicant must have been physically present in these United States for at least half of the required five-year residence period.

Every applicant for naturalization must:

(1) Demonstrate an understanding of the English language, including an ability to read, write, and speak words in ordinary usage in the English language (persons physically unable to do so, and persons who, on the date of their examinations, are over 50 years of age, and have been lawful permanent residents of the United States for 20 years or more, are exempt);

(2) Have been a person of good moral character, attached to the principles of the Constitution, and well-disposed to the good order and happiness of the United States, for the five years immediately preceding filing of the petition, or for whatever other period of residence

is required in his/her case, and continue to be such a person until admitted to citizenship; and

(3) Demonstrate a knowledge and understanding of the fundamentals of the history, principles and form of government of the United States.

When the applicant files his petition, he pays the court clerk $50. At the preliminary hearing, he may be represented by a lawyer or a social service agency. There is a 30-day waiting period. If action is favorable, there is a final hearing before a judge, who administers the following oath of allegiance:

I hereby declare, on oath, that I absolutely and entirely renounce and abjure all allegiance and fidelity to any foreign prince, potentate, state, or sovereignty, to whom or of which I have heretofore been a subject or citizen; that I will support and defend the Constitution and laws of the United States of America against all enemies, foreign and domestic; that I will bear true faith and allegiance to the same; that I will bear arms on behalf of the United States when required by the law; that I will perform noncombatant service in the armed forces of the United States when required by the law; that I will perform work of national importance under civilian direction when required by the law; and that I take this obligation freely, without any mental reservation or purpose of evasion; so help me God.

Related Programs

State Legalization Impact Assistance Grants: Offsets part of the costs state and local governments incur for providing public assistance and educational services to eligible legalized aliens.

Contact: Director, Division of State Legalization Assistance, Office of Refugee Resettlement, Family Support Administration,900 D Street SW, Washington, DC 20447. Phone (202) 401-9246.

Refugee Assistance—Voluntary Agency Programs: Assists refugees in becoming self-supporting and independent members of American society by providing grant funds to voluntary resettlement agencies currently resettling these refugees in the United States.

Contact: Director, Division of State Legalization Assistance, Office of Refugee Resettlement, Fam-

ily Support Administration, 900 D St. SW, Washington, DC 20447. Phone 202-401-9246.

Citizenship Education and Training: Promotes instruction and training in citizenship responsibilities for persons interested in becoming naturalized citizens. Public schools conducting citizenship education classes are qualified to receive free federal textbooks.

Headquarters Office: U.S. Justice Department, 425 I St., Washington, DC 20536. Phone (202) 514-2000.

INTERNAL REVENUE SERVICE

Free IRS Tax Services

Telephone Service: Toll free telephone assistance is available in all 50 states, the District of Columbia, Puerto Rico, and the Virgin Islands. The national toll free number is 1-800-829-1040. Under this system, taxpayers pay only local charges, with no long-distance charge for the call. Following are the toll-free numbers from your area. During periods of peak demand for telephone assistance, it may be difficult to get through. Generally, early in the morning and later in the week are the best times to call IRS.

Toll free telephone assistance for hearing-impaired taxpayers is available for those with access to TDD equipment or to TV-telephone-TTY equipment. The hearing-impaired everywhere in the United States, including Alaska, Hawaii, Puerto Rico, and the Virgin Islands, may call 1-800-829-4059. Hours of operation are 8:00 a.m. to 6:45 p.m. (EST) Jan. 1–April 15 and 8:00 a.m. to 4:30 p.m. (EST) April 16–Dec. 31 M-F.

Information for the Blind: Braille materials are available at Regional Libraries for the Blind and Physically Handicapped in conjunction with the Library of Congress. These materials include Publications 17 and 334; Forms 1040, 1040A, and 1040EZ; and Schedules A and B and instructions.

Walk-In Service: While the Internal Revenue Service will not prepare tax returns, assistors are available in most IRS offices throughout the country to help taxpayers prepare their own returns. Taxpayers will be expected to help themselves to the maximum extent possible. However, they will be provided assistance and, at the same time, provided the opportunity of learning how to research and prepare their own tax returns. An assistor will "walk through" a return with a number of taxpayers in a group setting.

In many IRS offices a walk-in counter is available to help with inquiries that do not involve preparation of a return, such as receipt of an IRS notice or bill. Certain technical information or publications may also be obtained at most IRS offices.

Taxpayers who wish assistance with their tax returns should bring in their tax package Forms W-2 and 1099, and any other information (such as a copy of last year's return), which will enable the IRS to help.

Taxpayer Education Programs: The Internal Revenue Service has a number of programs designed to educate the public about our nation's voluntary compliance tax system and each citizen's share in it, so that the system works as smoothly as possible. The more citizens understand about their role in this tax system, the better they will be able to carry out their responsibilities with a minimum of confusion. Most of these taxpayer education programs offer opportunity for citizen involvement through service as volunteers.

Understanding Taxes: This is a tax education program that begins in the schools, where young people are taught about their tax rights and responsibilities under our voluntary compliance tax system. They also learn how to fill out basic tax returns. Since many of them are working already, often at their first jobs, this learning has immediate practical value. They also learn about the history of taxes and current issues in taxation, such as tax reform. All materials that teachers need are available free of charge, including a series of video programs. These films were produced in cooperation with the states. Workshops are conducted during the year to help prepare teachers for course instruction.

Small Business Workshops: These workshops help people start small businesses by providing them with the information they need to carry out their tax responsibilities, including tax withholding, making correct and timely tax deposits, and filing a business return. Some sessions focus on the needs of the self-employed, minority entrepreneurs, and specialized business

groups. Active or retired businesspersons often volunteer their services and provide invaluable information.

Volunteer Income Tax Assistance: The Volunteer Income Tax Assistance program (VITA) provides free tax assistance to elderly, non-English–speaking, and handicapped people, and also to members of the military. Generally, those who receive these services can't afford professional tax assistance. After completing IRS training, volunteers provide free help at special locations.

Tax Counseling for the Elderly: Tax Counseling for the Elderly (TCE) provides free tax assistance to people 60 or older, especially those who are disabled or have other special needs. Nonprofit organizations under cooperative agreements with the IRS provide local assistance. Both VITA and TCE sites usually are located in neighborhood centers, libraries, churches and other places in the community.

Community Outreach Tax Assistance: This is a year-round program of assistance to groups who need help understanding tax laws, especially as they apply to members of their profession or group, such as teaching, business, or farming. Seminars are conducted at times and locations in the community that are convenient for members of the group.

MEDICAID AND MEDICARE

Medicaid

Medicaid provides financial assistance to states for payments of medical assistance to the categorically needy. States must provide in- and outpatient hospital services; rural health clinic services; other laboratory and X-ray services; skilled nursing home services; home health services for persons over age 21; family planning services; physicians' services; early and periodic screening, diagnosis and treatment for individuals under age 21; and services furnished by a nurse-midwife as licensed by the several states. Eligibility is determined by the state in accordance with federal regulations.

Contact: State or local welfare agency.

Headquarters Office: Director, Bureau of Quality Control, Health Care Financing Administration, Department of Health and Human Services,

Room 233, East High Rise Bldg., 6325 Security Blvd., Baltimore, MD 21207. Phone 410-966-3000.

Medicare

Hospital Insurance: Persons age 65 or over and certain disabled persons are eligible for hospital insurance protection. The program pays the cost of covered services for hospital and post-hospital care.

Contact: Local Social Security office.

Supplementary Medical Insurance: All persons age 65 and over, as well as those under 65 who are eligible for hospital insurance benefits, may voluntarily enroll for supplementary medical insurance at a monthly premium of $24.80. Some states and other third parties pay the premium on behalf of qualifying individuals. The program pays 80 percent of the reasonable charges (after a $75 deductible) for covered services.

Contact: Local Social Security office.

Headquarters Office: Director, Bureau of Program Operation Room 300, Meadows East Bldg., Health Care Financing Administration, Baltimore, MD 21207. Phone 410-965-8050.

PASSPORTS

Passports are issued by the U.S. Department of State to citizens and nationals of the United States for the purpose of documenting them for foreign travel and identifying them as Americans.

Headquarters Office: Passport Services, U.S. State Department, 2201 C St., Washington, DC 20520. Phone 202-647-0518.

How to Obtain a Passport

Applicants who have never previously been issued a passport in their own names must execute an application in person before (1) a passport agent; (2) a clerk of any federal court or state court of record or a judge or clerk of any probate court accepting applications; (3) a postal employee designated by the postmaster at a post office which has been selected to accept passport applications; or (4) a U.S. diplomatic or consular officer abroad. A DSP-11 is the correct form to use for applicants who must apply in person. Today, all persons are required to obtain individual passports in their own names, a change from the past when spouses and children could be included in a husband's passport. An applicant who is 13 years of age or older is required to appear in person before the clerk or agent executing the application. A parent or legal guardian may execute the application for children under 13.

If the applicant has no prior passport and was born in the United States, a certified copy of his or her birth certificate must be presented. To be acceptable, the certificate must show the given name and surname, the date and place of birth, and that the birth record was filed shortly after birth. A delayed birth certificate (a record filed more than one year after the date of birth) is acceptable provided that it shows that the report of birth was supported by acceptable secondary evidence of birth. If such primary evidence is not obtainable, a notice from the registrar shall be submitted stating that no birth record exists. The notice shall be accompanied by the best obtainable secondary evidence such as a baptismal certificate or a hospital birth record.

A naturalized citizen with no previous passport should present a naturalization certificate. A person born abroad claiming U.S. citizenship through either a native-born or naturalized citizen parent must submit a certificate of citizenship issued by the Immigration and Naturalization Service; or a Consular Report of Birth or Certification of Birth issued by the Department of State. If one of these documents has not been obtained, evidence of citizenship of the parent(s) through whom citizenship is claimed and evidence that would establish the parent/child relationship must be submitted. Additionally, if citizenship is derived through birth to citizen parent(s), the following documents will be required: parents' marriage certificate plus an affidavit from parent(s) showing periods and places of residence or physical presence in the United States and abroad, specifying periods spent abroad in the employment of the United States government, including the armed forces, or with certain international organizations. If citizenship is derived through naturalization of parents, evidence of admission to the United States for permanent residence also will be required.

Applicants must also establish their identity to the satisfaction of the person accepting the application. To establish identity, applicants may use a previous U.S. passport, a certificate of naturalization, a valid driver's license, or a government identification card. Applicants may not use a Social Security card, learner's or temporary driver's license, credit card, or expired identity card. Applicants unable to establish their identity must take the identification cards they have in their own name (i.e., Social Security card) and they must be accompanied by a person who has known them for at least two years and who is a U.S. citizen or legal U.S. permanent resident alien. That person must sign an affidavit before the individual who executes the passport application. The witness will be required to establish his or her own identity.

For those who have previously been issued a passport, or who were included on a spouse's or parent's, it will be accepted as proof of U.S. citizenship. Persons who have been issued a passport in their own names within the last 12 years may obtain new passports by filling out, signing and mailing a passport-by-mail application together with their previous passport, two recent identical photographs (photographs should be portrait-type prints, 2 × 2 inches in size, clear, front view, full face, with a plain light background), and the required fee to the nearest passport agency. Application forms are available at most post offices. As with persons applying for a passport for the first time, those whose prior passports were issued before their 16th birthday, must apply in person.

The loss or theft of a valid passport is a serious matter and should be reported in writing immediately to Passport Services, Department of State, Washington, DC 20524, or to the nearest Passport Agency or the nearest United States embassy or consular office of the United States when abroad.

Foreign Regulations

Many foreign countries require a visa before an American can enter their country. The visa is usually rubber stamped in a passport by a representative of the country to be visited, indicating that the holder is permitted to enter that country for a certain purpose and length of time. Visa information can be obtained by calling or writing the Washington embassy or nearest consular office of the country to be visited.

Aliens: An alien leaving the United States must request a passport from the embassy of the country of his or her nationality, must have a permit from his or her local Collector of Internal Revenue, and if he or she wishes to return, should request a reentry permit from the Immigration and Naturalization Service if it is required.

PATENT AND TRADEMARK OFFICE

Patent and Trademark Technical Information Dissemination

This office promotes the continued growth of American technology and commerce through the utilization and dissemination of technical information available through patents, and maintains public search centers containing patents and trademarks. The Patent and Trademark Office examines patent applications to determine the patentability of an invention and grants patents and registers trademarks which protect qualified inventions and discoveries when requirements of law are met. The office maintains detailed information on more than four million patents issued to date plus detailed documentation on more than one million trademarks protected. This information may be examined in person and is also available on microfilm at a number of Patent Depository Libraries across the nation (usually university libraries). Locations of such libraries can be obtained by calling 800-368-2532.

Headquarters Office: Patent and Trademark Office, U.S. Department of Commerce, Washington, DC 20231. Phone 703-557-3158.

SOCIAL SECURITY ADMINISTRATION

Headquarters Office: Office of Public Inquiries, Rm. 4100, Annex, Social Security Administration, Baltimore, MD 21235. Phone 800-772-1213.

Disability Insurance: A disabled worker under age 65 is eligible for Social Security disability benefits if he or she has worked for a sufficient period of time under Social Security to be insured. Certain family members of disabled workers are also eligible for benefits. Under the definition of disability in the Social Security Law, disability benefits are provided to a person who is unable to engage in any substantial gainful activity by reason of a medically determinable physical or mental impairment that has lasted or is expected to last at least 12 months, or to result in death.

Contact: Local Social Security office.

Retirement Insurance: Retired workers age 62 and over who have worked the required number of years under Social Security are eligible for monthly benefits. Also, certain family members can receive benefits. All benefits, other than benefits to disabled beneficiaries and beneficiaries age 70 and older, are subject to an earnings test, under which benefits are reduced by $1 for each $2 of earnings over certain limits (in 1988, $6,120 for people under age 65 and $8,400 for people ages 65 through 69).

Contact: Local Social Security office.

Special Benefits for Persons Aged 72 and Over: Individuals who reached age 72 before 1968, and those who reached age 72 after 1967 who have some Social Security work credits, are eligible for special payments.

Contact: Local Social Security office.

Survivors' Insurance: Monthly cash benefits are paid to eligible family members of deceased workers. Benefits are payable only if the deceased was insured for survivors insurance protection.

Contact: Local Social Security office.

Supplemental Security Income: Supplemental security income payments are made to eligible persons who have attained age 65 or who are blind or disabled. Eligibility is determined on the basis of an assessment of the individual's monthly income and resources.

Contact: Local Social Security office.

STUDENT FINANCIAL AID

Supplemental Educational Opportunity Grants: Grants are for undergraduate study and range from $100 to $4,000 per academic year, based on need.

Higher Education Act Insured Loans (Guaranteed Student Loans, Supplemental Loans for Students, and Consolidation Loans): Guaranteed loans are authorized for educational ex-

penses available to eligible students from eligible lenders such as banks, credit unions, savings and loan associations, pension funds, insurance companies and schools.

College Work-Study Program: The program pays up to 80 percent of the earnings of eligible students in eligible nonprofit jobs.

Perkins Loans: Provides eligible students, with demonstrated financial need, low-interest loan funds to help meet educational expenses.

Pell Grant Program: Provides eligible postsecondary students who demonstrate financial need with grant assistance to help meet educational expenses.

Robert C. Byrd Honors Scholarships: Provides scholarships to promote student excellence by making available grants to the states. The scholarships are for first-year study at institutions of higher education.

Harry S. Truman Scholarship Program: Provides scholarships for undergraduate sophomore college students preparing for a career in public service.

Headquarters Office: Division of Policy and Program Development, Office of Student Financial Assistance, Office of Postsecondary Education, Department of Education, 400 Maryland Ave. SW, Washington, DC 20202. Phone 202-708-8391.

DEPARTMENT OF VETERANS AFFAIRS

Employment

Disabled Veterans Outreach Program: This program provides funds to states to provide jobs and job training opportunities for disabled and other veterans, outreach to veterans through all community agencies and organizations, and job placement, counseling, testing, and referral to eligible veterans, especially disabled veterans of the Vietnam era.

Contact: Local Veterans' Employment and Training Service office.

Veterans Employment Program: Programs supported with these funds meet the employment and training needs of service-connected disabled veterans, veterans of the Vietnam era, and veterans who were recently separated from military service.

Contact: Local Veterans' Employment and Training Service office.

Headquarters Office: Veterans' Employment and Training Service, Office of the Assistant Secretary for Veterans' Employment and Training, Department of Labor Rm. S1313, 200 Constitution Ave. NW, Washington, DC 20210. Phone 202-219-9116.

Federal Employment Assistance for Veterans: To provide assistance to veterans in obtaining federal employment, certain veterans are eligible for preference in filling government positions.

Contact: Local federal Job Information Center.

Headquarters Office: Office of Affirmative Recruiting and Employment, Career Entry Group, Office of Personnel Management, 1900 E St., NW, Rm. 6355, Washington DC 20415. Phone 202-606-1059.

Medical Benefits

VA Domiciliary Care: Domiciliary care provides necessary inpatient medical care and physical, social and psychological support services in a therapeutic environment. Disabled veterans who meet certain requirements are eligible.

Contact: VA hospital or outpatient clinic.

Headquarters Office: Assistant Chief Medical Director for Geriatrics and Extended Care, Department of Veterans Affairs, Washington, DC 20420. Phone 202-535-7165.

VA Hospitalization: This program provides inpatient, medical, surgical, and neuropsychiatric care and related medical and dental services to eligible veterans.

Contact: VA Medical Center.

Headquarters Office: Veterans' Health Administration, Department of Veterans Affairs, Washington, DC 20420. Phone 202-535-7010.

Veterans Nursing Home Care: VA Nursing Home Care Units accommodate veterans who require skilled nursing care in a homelike atmosphere.

Contact: VA hospital.

Headquarters Office: Assistant Chief Medical Director for Geriatrics and Extended Care, De-

partment of Veterans Affairs, Washington, DC 20420. Phone 202-535-7165.

Veterans Outpatient Care: This program provides medical and dental services, medicines and medical supplies to eligible veterans on an outpatient basis.

Contact: VA medical center.

Headquarters Office: Office of the Chief Medical Director, Veterans' Health Administration, Department of Veterans Affairs, Washington, DC 20402. Phone 202-535-7010.

Veterans Prescription Service: Medicine for veterans provides eligible veterans and certain dependents and survivors of veterans with prescription drugs and expendable prosthetic devices from VA pharmacies.

Contact: VA Hospital.

Headquarters Office: Assistant Chief Medical Director for Clinical Programs, Veteran's Health Administration, Department of Veterans Affairs, Washington, DC 20420. Phone 202-535-7393.

Other Benefits

Headquarters Office: Department of Veterans Affairs, Washington, DC 20420

Burial Expenses Allowance for Veterans: Provides a monetary allowance not to exceed $150 toward the plot or interment expense for certain veterans not buried in a national cemetery.

Compensation for Service-Connected Deaths for Veterans' Dependents: Compensates surviving spouses, children and dependents for the death of any veteran who died before January 1, 1957, because of a service-connected disability.

Life Insurance for Veterans: Provides life insurance coverage for veterans of WWI, WWII, Korean conflict and service-disabled veterans separated from active duty on or after April 25, 1951.

Pension for Nonservice-Connected Disability for Veterans: Disability payments assist wartime veterans in need whose disabilities prevent them from following a substantially gainful occupation.

Pension to Veterans' Surviving Spouses and Children: Pension payments assist needy spouses and children of deceased wartime veterans whose deaths were not due to service.

Veterans Compensation for Service-Connected Disability: Compensates veterans for disabilities incurred or aggravated during military service.

Veterans Dependency and Indemnity Compensation for Service-Connected Death: Compensates surviving spouse, unmarried children and parents of deceased veterans who died on or after January 1, 1957, because of a service-connected disability.

Veterans Educational Assistance: Makes service in the armed forces more attractive by extending benefits of a higher education to veterans.

Veterans Housing—Guaranteed and Insured Loans: Program assists veterans, certain service personnel, and certain surviving spouses of veterans, in obtaining credit for the purchase, construction, or improvement of homes on more liberal terms than are generally available to nonveterans.

Dependents' Educational Assistance: Provides partial support to those seeking to advance their education who are qualifying spouses, surviving spouses or children of deceased or disabled veterans.

WELFARE AND SOCIAL SERVICES

Aid to Families with Dependent Children

State Aid: Cash payments are made directly to eligible needy families with dependent children deprived of parental support or care, and to families with children needing emergency welfare assistance. Federal funds go to a certified state welfare agency.

Contact: Local welfare agency.

Headquarters Office: Office of the Director, Office of Family Assistance, Administration for Children and Families, Department of Health and Human Services, 5th Floor, Aerospace Bldg. 370 L'Enfant Promenade SW Washington, DC 20201. Phone 202-401-9275.

Work Incentive Program: This program is directed to employable welfare recipients and applicants under the AFDC program who are required to register for work, training and

employment-related services, or who volunteer. Its objective is to move men, women and out-of-school youth from dependency on AFDC grants to economic independence through permanent productive employment by providing appropriate job training, job placement and other related services.

Contact: WIN demonstration authority, state employment security agencies and state welfare agencies.

Headquarters Office: Assistant secretary for Employment and Training Administration, Department of Labor, Washington, DC 20210. Phone 202-219-6050.

Job Training Partnership Act: This program provides job training and related assistance to economically disadvantaged individuals and others who face significant employment barriers.

Headquarters Office: Employment and Training Administration, Department of Labor, 200 Constitution Ave. NW, Washington, DC 20210. Phone 202-219-6050.

Employment Services: The employment service, through grant agreements with the states, supports the system to serve persons seeking or needing employment and employers seeking workers by providing a variety of placement-related services without charge to job seekers and employers.

Contact: State employment security agency.

Headquarters Office: Director, United States Employment Service, Employment and Training Administration, Department of Labor, Washington, DC 20210. Phone 202-535-0157.

Unemployment Insurance: The states have the direct responsibility for establishing and operating their own unemployment insurance programs, while the federal government finances the administration. Benefits are paid to workers whose employers contribute to state unemployment funds and who are involuntarily unemployed, able to work, available for work, meet the eligibility and qualifying requirements of the state law, and are free from disqualifications.

Contact: Local state unemployment insurance office.

Headquarters Office: Director, Unemployment Insurance Service, Employment and Training

Administration, Department of Labor, Washington, DC 20210. Phone 202-219-7831.

GOVERNMENT INFORMATION

The federal government and its hundreds of agencies stand ready to help citizens solve a myriad of problems or to provide information, often free, on an endless number of subjects. Some of the principle sources of that information follow.

Federal Information Centers

Every federal building in the United States has an Information Center. In larger cities these can be offices with large, multilingual staffs. In smaller cities it might only be a desk with a single staffer. They are designed to be a first stop for anyone with questions about the federal government, its agencies and programs. The centers can supply basic information and make referrals to specific agencies. They are a good place to start if you are in doubt about exactly what agency to contact with a question or problem.

Contact: Your local federal building or Federal Information Center, P.O. Box 600 Cumberland, MD 21501. Phone 301-722-9098; TDD 800-326-2996.

Consumer Information Center

The government distributes hundreds of publications prepared by various federal agencies at no cost to the public. Quarterly catalogs of available publications can be obtained.

Contact: Consumer Information Center, P.O. Box 100, Pueblo, CO 81002.

National Technical Information Service

This is the central source for information about U.S. government–sponsored research or foreign research done in cooperation with a U.S. agency. Some 75,000 new titles are published annually and over one million back titles are available. You can also identify new products and technology that have been developed by the government or any of its agencies and that are now available for licensing. For the latter, a monthly newsletter, *Government Inventions for Licensing,* is available by subscription. Also available is *The*

Small Business Guide to Federal Research and Development Opportunities.

Contact: National Technical Information Service (NTIS), 5285 Port Royal Road, Springfield VA 22161. Phone 703-487-4779 (information).

Health Information

The federal government has available a myriad of health information and publications. The Office of Disease Prevention—U.S. Public Health Service operates the National Health Information Center, which operates as a clearing house for government health information and as a referral service on where to obtain further information.

Contact: National Health Information Service, P.O. Box 1133, Washington, DC 20013-1133. Phone 800-336-4797; 301-565-4167 (Maryland).

In the area of cancer information, the NIH's National Cancer Institute operates the Cancer Information Service. CIS operates a series of regional information offices, which formulate personalized answers to individual's cancer questions and which publishes and distributes reference materials on cancer.

Contact: Cancer Information Service, NIH Bldg. 31, Bethesda MD 20505. Phone 1-800-4CANCER.

The National Institute of Health's National Library of Medicine publishes a short but valuable listing of toll free phone numbers of public and private organizations that provide health information on specific diseases and conditions. The publication is entitled *Health Hotlines* and is published annually.

Contact: National Library of Medicine, 8600 Rockville Pike, Bethesda, MD 20894.

Genealogy Research

The National Archives in Washington stands ready to assist individuals in tracing their roots. The best place to start in utilizing their help is by writing to obtain a free booklet, *Genealogy Records in the National Archives.* This booklet not only lists what records are available at the Archives, but gives tips on doing this kind of research and lists contact addresses and phone numbers.

Contact: Reference Service Office, National Archives, 8th St. and Pennsylvania Ave. NW 20408. Phone 202-501-5400 (recording).

THE JUDICIAL BRANCH

Article III of the Constitution states, "The judicial power of the United States shall be vested in one Supreme Court, and in such inferior courts as the Congress may from time to time ordain and establish." All federal judges, including Supreme Court justices, courts of appeals judges and district court judges ("inferior" judges), are appointed by the president and confirmed by the Senate to life terms. They can be removed only through passage of a bill of impeachment by the House of Representatives and after being found guilty in a formal trial by the Senate.

The federal court system has jurisdiction in all cases arising under the Constitution or federal law, in disputes between individuals and legal entities (corporations, partnerships, etc.) who are citizens of different states and where more than $25,000 is at issue, and in a variety of specialized matters including admiralty, maritime, bankruptcy, patent and copyright, postal, and the Internal Revenue Service.

THE SUPREME COURT

The Supreme Court, the nation's highest court, consists of the chief justice and eight associate justices. It has original jurisdiction in all cases involving "ambassadors, public ministers and counsels" and those arising from disputes between states. It can hear appeals from decisions of lower courts of appeal involving federal questions and to the final decisions of the highest courts of each state where constitutional issues are involved.

The court may choose which cases it wants to hear and limits its review to cases involving national questions. Appellants petition the court through writs of *certiorari* (review). If the court accepts the writ, the case is placed on the docket for argument. If the writ is rejected, the decision of the lower court is considered affirmed. Each year the court receives thousands of writs of which only a few hundred, at most, are accepted.

THE JUSTICES

In 1993, when Ruth Bader Ginsburg took the judicial oath to begin her service on the Supreme Court, she became the 107th person to do so. Actually, hers was the 112th time the oath was administered, because five associate justices—John Rutledge, Edward D. White, Charles Evan Hughes, Harlan F. Stone and William Rehnquist—were elevated from associate justice to chief justice, and were thus twice administered the oath.

Of the 107 who have served on the Court, 105 have been men. Associate Justices Sandra Day O'Connor and Ruth Bader Ginsburg are the only women ever to have served. Of the 107, 105 have been white. Only Associate Justice Thurgood Marshall, and the man who succeeded him, Clarence Thomas, have been black. Almost all the justices have been Protestant (92 of the 107). The first Catholic member of the Court was Chief Justice Roger B. Taney, who was nominated by President Andrew Jackson in 1835. But it was not until 30 years after Taney's death that the second Catholic was nominated, Edward D. White, in 1864. Other Catholic justices have been Joseph McKenna (1897), Pierce Butler (1922), Frank Murphy (1939), William Brennan (1956), Antonin Scalia (1987) and Anthony Kennedy (1988).

With Kennedy and Scalia sitting together, the Rehnquist Court is the first to have two Catholics sitting at the same time. The fear often expressed is that Catholic justices would allow their religious convictions to color their decisions, or that somehow they would be "controlled by Rome." In retrospect, this charge now seems almost silly. It is true that the two current Catholic justices are both personally opposed to abortion, but that opposition fits into the general conservative political philosophy both brought to the Court. In contrast, the Catholic justice who preceded them—William Brennan—was a champion of abortion rights during his tenure on the Court. That too fit into his generally liberal philosophy.

Including Ruth Bader Ginsburg, there have also been seven Jewish justices. The first, Louis Brandeis, was not nominated until 1916. His nomination was so controversial that his fellow justice, James McReynolds, refused to speak to him for the three years the two sat on the Court together. Actually, once Brandeis was seated, his became the "Jewish Chair." When Brandeis left the Court in 1932, President Hoover nominated Felix Frankfurter to replace him. Frankfurter was followed by Arthur Goldberg (1962), and he by Abe Fortas (1969). The practice of having a Jewish justice was broken when Harry Blackmun was nominated to replace Fortas.

Nominated justices have ranged in age from 32—William Johnson (1804) and Joseph Story (1812) with Story the youngest by three months, to age 65—Horace Lurton (1910) and Chief Justice Edward White (1910). Both Chief Justices Harlan Stone, at age 68, and Charles Evan Hughes, at age 67, were older when they were sworn in. But both had previously served on the Court as associate justices. Two other justices were under the age of 40 when appointed: Bushrod Washington (1799) and James Iredell (1790). Obviously these youthful appointments were made in the early days of the Republic when life expectancy was much shorter, and men were put into positions of trust at a much younger age. But even in modern time, a number of justices who went on to play significant roles on the Court received their nominations while still in their forties. These included William O. Douglas (1939), Potter Stewart (1958), Byron White (1962), Charles Evans Hughes (1910), John McLean (1830) and John Marshall Harlan (the first, 1877).

Eight justices have served past their 80th birthdays, with Justice Oliver Wendell Holmes the oldest ever to have served. Holmes finally retired at age 90. Chief Justice Taney died still in office at age 88. Justice Thurgood Marshall retired at age 83, Justices Louis Brandeis and Gabriel Duvall at age 82, Justices Joseph McKenna and Stephen Field at age 81, and Justice Samuel Nelson at age 80. By contrast, five justices left the Court before age 50. James Iredell, who had been appointed at age 38, died when only 48. Benjamin Curtis, Alfred Moore, John Jay and John Campbell, all retired from the Court to accept other positions while still in their forties.

The longest serving justice was William O. Douglas who had served 36 years, seven months when he retired in 1975. In all, eleven justices have served tenures longer than 30 years. After Douglas, the next longest serving justice was Stephen J. Field who served 34 years, nine months. Then in order come: William J. Brennan, 33 years, seven months; John Marshall, 34 years, five months; Hugo L. Black, 34 years, one month; John Marshall Harlan (the first), 33 years, one month; Joseph Story, 33 years; James Wayne, 32 years, four months; John McLean, 31 years, five months; William Johnson, 30 years, two months; Bushrod Washington, 30 years; and for good measure, Oliver Wendell Holmes, 29 years, 11 months, 11 days.

An appointment to the Supreme Court is for life, and for 50 of the 107 justices that has been exactly how long they served. The 50 died while still in office. Of the rest, the vast majority died within a few years of retirement. The two justices who lived the longest in retirement, George Shiras, who retired in 1903 at age 71 and lived another 20 years, and John H. Clarke, who retired in 1922 at age 65 and lived another 24 years, both enjoyed their retirements at leisure.

Historically, the two most prevalent reasons for selection to the Court have been politics, and personal friendship with the nominating president. With only a very few exceptions, presidents have chosen justices whose politics and political philosophies match their own. In many cases justiceships were given out as a reward for personal service to a president, or more often, as a reward for long service to the president's political party.

In the first century of the Court, geography played a major role in the selection of justices. When George Washington made his original six selections, he was very careful to ensure that there was one each from the four most important states of the time: New York, Massachusetts, Pennsylvania and Virginia; and that the south was represented in James Iredell from North Carolina and John Rutledge from South Carolina. For the next 100 years this pattern continued to the point that most presidents looked upon the Court as having a "New York" seat, a "New England" seat, and a "Maryland-Virginia" seat. Then too, when justices still road circuit, appointments had to be balanced to ensure that a justice lived in the judicial circuit over which he would be presiding.

The six men that George Washington selected for the first Supreme Court were lawyers. Although the Constitution or the Judicial Act of 1789 does not specify that a justice must be a lawyer, Washington thought it mandatory and made admission to a state bar a criteria for the six he selected. This established a precedent that has continued to this day. Every Supreme Court justice, and nominee, has been a lawyer.

But it is interesting to note that it was not until modern times—1957—that the Court, for the very first time, was composed entirely of law school graduates. In 1957, Charles Whittaker replaced Stanley Reed on the Court. Although Reed had studied law at the University of Virginia and Columbia University, he never graduated. The last justice to never have attended any law school was James Byrnes who served from 1941 to 1942.

It has to be remembered that what we understand today to be a law school did not exist before 1870 when the Harvard University Law School was established. Prior to that, a few colleges taught law courses and some even offered what they called a law degree. Benjamin Curtis, who was nominated in 1851, for instance, was the first justice to have received a university law degree—from Harvard College. It was not until 1902, when Oliver Wendell Holmes was sworn in, did any Supreme Court justice possess a modern law degree from what today we would recognize as a law school. Holmes had graduated from Harvard Law School, with an LL.B., in 1869.

Many Supreme Court appointees had held appointed or elected political office. Among the justices, 14 had served at some point as U.S. attorney generals or deputy attorney generals; four had served as Solicitor General; 23 others had served in various cabinet positions including Secretaries of State, Treasury, War, Commerce, Navy, Labor, and Interior. At some point in their careers, 28 had been congressmen and

seven had been U.S. senators. Five were still sitting in the Senate when nominated—John McKinley (1837), Levi Woodbury (1846), Edward White (1894), Hugo Black (1937), and Harold Burton (1945). One, James Wayne in 1835, went directly from the U.S. House to the Supreme Court. Six justices served previously as state governors, and three served as governors after leaving the Court.

Most every Supreme Court appointee was involved in the private practice of law at some point in their careers. But only 26 were in the private practice when selected for the Court. Almost two dozen justices taught in law schools at some point, but only three were either deans or law professors at the time of their nomination.

In their personal lives, justices have been the marrying kind. Of the 107 justices, only nine have been unmarried. The remaining have had 126 wives and two husbands. Justice William O. Douglas had four wives; while Henry Livingston, Benjamin Curtis and Samuel Chase each had three. But it must be noted that well into the 19th century, women tended to die young, often from child birth or complications. Many of the early justices were widowed two or even three times in their lifetimes.

Justices have also had a large number of children. Both John Marshall and John Rutledge had ten children, current Justice Antonin Scalia has nine, Justices William Johnson, Thomas Todd and Stanley Matthews each had eight, while six justices have each had seven children.

CURRENT MEMBERS OF THE SUPREME COURT

Chief Justice

William H. Rehnquist, 1971, 1987. Born Milwaukee, Wis., October 1, 1924. B.A., M.A. Stanford Univ. 1948, M.A. Harvard Univ. 1949, LL.B. Stanford Univ. 1952. Clerk to Justice Robert Jackson, 1953. Private law practice Phoenix, Ariz., 1953–69. Deputy Attorney General 1969–71. Appointed an Associate Justice by Richard Nixon, October 21, 1971; elevated to Chief Justice by Ronald Reagan, June 20, 1986.

Associate Justices

Ruth Bader Ginsburg, Nominated 1993. Born Brooklyn, N.Y., March 15, 1933. B.A. Cornell,

1954. Harvard Law School 1956–1958. LL.B., LL.M. Columbia Law School 1959. Clerk, U.S. District Court, 1959–61. Director, Project on Int'l Procedure, Columbia Law School 1961–63. Professor, Rutgers Law School 1963–1972. Professor, Columbia Univ. Law School 1972–1980. General Counsel, American Civil Liberties Union 1973–1980. Judge, U.S. Court of Appeals 1980–1993. Appointed to the court by Bill Clinton, 1993.

Harry A. Blackmun, 1970. Born Nashville, Ill., November 12, 1908. B.A. (1929) LL.B. (1932) Harvard Univ. Clerk U.S. Court of Appeals 1933. Private practice Minneapolis, Minn., 1934–50. Counsel, Mayo Clinic 1950–59. Judge, U.S. Court of Appeals 1959–70. Appointed to court by Richard Nixon, April 14, 1970.

John Paul Stevens, 1975. Born Chicago, Ill., April 20, 1920. A.B. Univ. of Chicago 1941, J.D. Northwestern Univ. 1947. Private practice Chicago, Ill., 1948–70. U.S. Circuit Judge 1970–75. Appointed to court by Gerald Ford, November 28, 1975.

Sandra Day O'Connor, 1981. Born El Paso, Tex., March 26, 1930. A.B. (1950), LL.B. (1952) Stanford Univ. Private law practice Phoenix, Ariz., 1959–65. Assistant Attorney General of Arizona 1965–69. Arizona state senator (Republican) 1969–75. County judge 1975–79. Arizona state appeals court judge 1979–81. Appointed to court by Ronald Reagan, August 19, 1981.

Antonin Scalia, 1986. Born Trenton, N.J., March 11, 1936. A.B. Georgetown Univ. 1957, LL.B. Harvard Univ. 1960. Private law practice Cleveland, Ohio, 1961–67. Law professor Univ. of Virginia 1967–74. Assistant Attorney General 1974–77. Law professor Georgetown, Stanford and Univ. of Chicago 1977–82. Judge, U.S. Court of Appeals 1982–87. Appointed to court by Ronald Reagan, June 24, 1986.

Anthony M. Kennedy, 1988. Born Sacramento, Calif., July 23, 1936. A.B. Stanford Univ. 1958, LL.B. Harvard Univ. 1961. Private law practice San Francisco, Calif., 1962–75. Judge, U.S. Court of Appeals 1975–88. Appointed to court by Ronald Reagan, November 30, 1987.

David H. Souter, 1990. Born Melrose, Mass., September 17, 1939. A.B. Harvard College, 1961. Rhodes Scholar Oxford Univ. 1961–63. LL.B. Harvard Univ. 1966. Private practice Concord, N.H., 1966–68. Assistant N.H. Attorney General 1968–71; Deputy Attorney General 1971–76;

Attorney General of N.H. 1976–78. Judge, N.H. Superior Court 1978–83; Justice, N.H. Supreme Court 1983–89. Judge, U.S. Court of Appeals 1990. Appointed to the court by George Bush, October 9, 1990.

Clarence Thomas, 1991. Born Savannah, Ga., June 23, 1948. A.B. Holy Cross College, 1971, J.D. Yale Law School, 1974. Assistant Attorney General of Missouri, 1974–77. Staff Attorney, Monsanto, Colo., 1977–79. Assistant to Senator John Danforth (Republican–Mo.), 1979–81. Counsel, Civil Rights Office, U.S. Department of Education, 1981–82. Chm. U.S. Equal Employment Opportunity Commission, 1982–90. Judge, U.S. Court of Appeals, 1990–91. Appointed to the court by George Bush, October 23, 1991.

THE COURT TODAY

With the appointments of Justices David H. Souter and Clarence Thomas to the already conservative court of Chief Justice Rehnquist, on paper at least, the Court became the most conservative since the Taft Court in the 1920s. But as became apparent in the 1991–92 term, the Chief Justice was still not able to fashion a dependable conservative majority to undo many of the liberal Warren Court's decisions.

What emerged during the 1991–92 term was what some Court observers have called a "cautious middle," comprised of justices Kennedy, Souter and O'Connor, all of whom often voted to go slow in overturning past precedents. In his second year on the Court, Souter emerged as the key swing vote. He began to establish himself in the role so long, and so well occupied by Justice Potter Stewart. At the same time Justice Kennedy appeared to become less conservative. If it can be used as a benchmark, in the 1988–89 term Kennedy voted with Justice Scalia, the conservative heart of the Court, 93 percent of the time. In the 1991–92 term, Kennedy agreed with Scalia only 75 percent of the time.

One result of this more cautious approach by the three justices in the middle was an unusual number of 5–4 votes in key decisions over the past two terms. In a majority of the fourteen such 5–4 votes in the 1991–92 term, the three justices in the middle, joined with the Court's two liberal justices—Blackmun and Stevens—to form a majority in opposition to Rehnquist and Scalia. That was the line–up in the most important decision of the term, Planned Parenthood of Southeastern Pennsylvania versus Casey, in which the Court upheld a Pennsylvania law restricting abortions in some ways while upholding the basic constitutional right of a woman to an abortion, a right established in Roe v. Wade.

With the election of Bill Clinton and appointment of Ruth Bader Ginsburg, the Court can now be expected to move if not left, at least more firmly to the middle. Justice Byron White, who announced his retirement at the end of the 1992–93 term, had always been a dependable conservative vote on most issues. His replacement by Justice Ginsburg will likely result in an evenly divided court: three relative liberals, three conservatives and the three justices in the middle. In this kind of a line-up, more and more David Souter will emerge as the intellectual heart of the Court and its critical swing vote.

MAJOR DECISIONS 1990–91, 1991–92

Civil Rights

Ruled (6–3) that the Voting Rights Act of 1965 applies to all elections, even those for judges (*Lawyers Association v. Attorney General of Texas*).

Voted (6–3) that U.S. antidiscrimination laws (specifically Title VII of the Civil Rights Act of 1964) do not apply to American workers, working abroad for American-owned companies (*EEOC v. Arabian American Oil Company*).

Voted (8–0) to free a school district from a court supervised antidiscrimination plan if it has achieved racial equality as best it can (*Freeman v. Pitts*).

Voted (7–2) that criminal defendants cannot exclude people from juries on the basis of race (*Georgia v. McCollum*).

Abortion/Reproductive Rights

Upheld (5–4) a state law (Pennsylvania) regulating abortions in the latter stages, ruling that such regulation is constitutional so long as it does not place an "undue burden" on a woman's ability to terminate her pregnancy. In so ruling, the majority upheld the basic constitutional right of a woman to an abortion (*Planned Parenthood of Southeastern Pennsylvania v. Casey*).

Upheld (5–4) the right of the federal government to ban abortion counseling at health clinics that receive federal funding (*Rust v. Sullivan*).

Ruled (5–4) that companies may not exclude women from some job categories that might harm a developing fetus (*United Auto Workers v. Johnson Controls, Inc.*)

Criminal Law

Ruled (5–4) that a coerced confession, introduced into evidence, does not automatically taint a conviction (*Arizona v. Fulimante*).

Ruled (6–3) that a death row prisoner may file only one habeas corpus petition in federal court unless there can be shown good reason why any new constitutional issues being raised were not raised in a previous petition (*McCleskey v. Zant*).

Ruled (6–3) that a death row prisoner may not file a habeas corpus petition in federal court if he failed to abide by all the state court procedural rules (*Coleman v. Thompson*).

Ruled (6–3) that the character of the defendant and the impact his or her crime had on the victim's family may be taken into consideration in determining the sentence, including the death penalty, of a convicted murderer (*Payne v. Tennessee*).

Ruled (5–4) that the imposition of a life sentence without parole against a first time drug offender was not cruel and unusual punishment (*Harmelin v. Michigan*).

Ruled (6–3) that the United States may kidnap a criminal defendant from a foreign country to bring him to the U.S. for trial even if a valid extradition treaty with that country exists (*U.S. v. Alvarez*).

Civil/Commercial Law

Upheld (7–1) a jury's right to assess punitive damages against defendants even in cases where the damages awarded are greatly disproportionate to the actual damage suffered (*Pacific Mutual Life Insurance v. Haslip*).

Ruled (8–1) that a state may not tax the sales of out-of-state mail order firms selling to customers in the state even though Congress passed a law allowing them to do so (*Quill Corp. v. North Dakota*).

Ruled (6–3) that property owners may be

entitled to compensation if a state ruling or regulation deprives their property of economic value (*Lucas v. S.Carolina Coastal Council*).

Free Speech

Upheld (5–4) a state law (Indiana) banning nude dancing. In so holding, ruled that free expression does not extend to nude dancing (*Barns v. Glen Theater*)

Ruled (5–4) that the First Amendment does not shield the news media from lawsuits if they break promises of confidentiality to their sources (*Cohen v. Cowles Media, Inc.*).

Struck down (8–0) a state crime victims' law (New York) prohibiting publishers from paying criminals for their stories (*Simon & Schuster v. Members of the New York State Crime Victims Board*).

Ruled (5–3) it is not a violation of the First Amendment to allow states to forbid electioneering near a polling place (*Burson v. Freeman*).

Struck down (9–0) a city ordinance (St. Paul, Minn.) outlawing hate crimes because the law also sought to ban constitutionally protected acts of free speech (*R.A.V. v. St. Paul*).

Freedom of Religion

Ruled (5–4) that an invitation to a clergyman to give an invocation at a public school graduation violates the First Amendment's prohibition against the establishment of religion (*Lee v. Weisman*).

U.S. COURTS OF APPEAL

The United States is divided into 11 geographical circuits (so named from the days when a judge used to ride a "circuit" on horseback), plus the District of Columbia and a roving "Federal Circuit." Each circuit court of appeals is headed by a chief judge and comprises between 6 and 26 judges. They meet, usually in three-judge panels to review decisions of lower courts. Occasionally, in important cases, larger panels may be formed; in rare cases all the judges of a circuit may join *en banc* to hear an appeal. (Salaries $141,700; *CJ* means Chief Judge.)

Federal Circuit. Helen W. Nies, CJ; Clerk's Office, Washington, DC 20439.

District of Columbia. Abner J. Mikva, CJ; Clerk's Office, Washington, DC 20001.

First Circuit. (Maine, Mass., N.H., R.I., P.R.). Stephan Breyer, CJ; Clerk's Office, Boston, MA 02109.

Second Circuit. (Conn., N.Y., Vt.). Thomas J. Meskill, CJ; Clerk's Office, New York, NY 10007.

Third Circuit. (Del., N.J., Pa., V.I.). Delores K. Sloviter, CJ; Clerk's Office, Philadelphia, PA 19106.

Fourth Circuit. (Md., N.C., S.C., Va., W.Va.). Sam J. Ervin III, CJ; Clerk's Office, Richmond, VA 23219.

Fifth Circuit. (La., Miss., Tex.). Henry A. Politz, CJ; Clerk's Office. New Orleans, LA 70130.

Sixth Circuit. (Ky., Mich., Ohio, Tenn.). Gilbert S. Merritt, CJ; Clerk's Office, Cincinnati, OH 45202.

Seventh Circuit. (Ill., Ind., Wis.). William J. Bauer, CJ; Clerk's Office, Chicago, IL 60604.

Eighth Circuit. (Ark., Ia., Minn., Mo., Nebr., N.Dak., S.Dak.). Richard Arnold, CJ; Clerk's Office, St. Louis, MO 63101.

Ninth Circuit. (Alaska, Ariz., Calif., Hawaii, Idaho, Mont., Nev., Oreg., Wash., Guam, N. Mariana Islands). J. Clifford Wallace, CJ; Clerk's Office, San Francisco, CA 94101.

Tenth Circuit. (Colo., Kans., N.Mex., Okla., Utah, Wyo.). Monroe G. McKay, CJ; Clerk's Office, Denver, CO 80294.

Eleventh Circuit. (Ala., Fla., Ga.). Gerald B. Tjoflat, CJ; Clerk's Office, Atlanta GA 30303.

Temporary Emergency Court of Appeals. Reynaldo G. Garza CJ; Clerk's Office, Washington, DC 20001.

DISTRICT COURTS

District courts have been established in every state and the District of Columbia plus the U.S. territories. Each state has at least one such court, and larger states are further subdivided into as many as four subdistricts. These courts are divided into civil and criminal divisions and are the basic trial courts in the federal system. (Salaries, $133,600; *CJ* means Chief Judge.)

Alabama—*Northern:* Sam C. Pointer, Jr., CJ; Clerk's Office, Birmingham 35203. *Middle:* Myron H. Thompson, CJ; Clerk's Office, Montgomery 36101. *Southern:* Alex T. Howard, Jr., CJ; Clerk's Office, Mobile 36652.

Alaska—H. Russell Holland, CJ; Clerk's Office, Anchorage 99513.

Arizona—William D. Browning, CJ; Clerk's Office, Phoenix 85025.

Arkansas—*Eastern:* Stephen M. Reasoner, CJ; Clerk's Office, Little Rock 72203. *Western:* H. Franklin Waters, CJ; Clerk's Office, Fort Smith 72902.

California—*Northern:* Thelton E. Henderson, CJ; Clerk's Office, San Francisco 94102. *Eastern:* Robert E. Coyle, CJ; Clerk's Office, Sacramento 95814. *Central:* Manuel L. Real, CJ; Clerk's Office, Los Angeles 90012. *Southern:* Judith N. Keep, CJ; Clerk's Office, San Diego 92189.

Colorado—Sherman G. Finesilver, CJ; Clerk's Office, Denver 80294.

Connecticut—Ellen B. Burns, CJ; Clerk's Office, New Haven 06510.

Delaware—Joseph J. Longobardi, CJ; Clerk's Office, Wilmington 19801.

District of Columbia—Aubrey E. Robinson, Jr., CJ; Clerk's Office, Washington DC 20001.

Florida—*Northern:* William H. Stafford, Jr. CJ; Clerk's Office, Tallahassee 32301. *Middle:* Vacant, CJ; Clerk's Office, Jacksonville 32201. *Southern:* Norman C. Roettger, Jr., CJ; Clerk's Office, Miami 33128.

Georgia—*Northern:* William C. O'Kelley, CJ; Clerk's Office, Atlanta 30335. *Middle:* Wilbur D. Owens, Jr., CJ; Clerk's Office, Macon 31202.

Southern: B. Avant Edenfield, CJ; Clerk's Office, Savannah 31412.

Hawaii—Alan C. Kay, CJ; Clerk's Office, Honolulu 96850.

Idaho—Edward J. Lodge, CJ; Clerk's Office, Boise 83724.

Illinois—*Northern:* James B. Moran, CJ; Clerk's Office, Chicago 60604. *Central:* Michael M. Mihm, CJ; Clerk's Office, Springfield 62705. *Southern:* William D. Stiehl, CJ; Clerk's Office, E. St. Louis 62202.

Indiana—*Northern:* Allen Sharp, CJ; Clerk's Office, South Bend 46601. *Southern:* Gene E. Brooks, CJ; Clerk's Office, Indianapolis 46204.

Iowa—*Northern:* Michael J. Malloy, CJ; Clerk's Office, Cedar Rapids 52401. *Southern:* Charles R. Wolle, CJ; Clerk's Office, Des Moines 50309.

Kansas—Patrick F. Kelly, CJ; Clerk's Office, Wichita 67202.

Kentucky—*Eastern:* William O. Bertlesman, CJ; Clerk's Office, Lexington 40586. *Western:* Ronald E. Meredith, CJ; Clerk's Office, Louisville 40202.

Louisiana—*Eastern:* Morey L. Sear, CJ; Clerk's Office, New Orleans 70130. *Middle:* John V. Parker, CJ; Clerk's Office, Baton Rouge 70821. *Western:* John M. Shaw, CJ; Clerk's Office, Shreveport 71101.

Maine—Gene Carter, CJ; Clerk's Office, Portland 04112.

Maryland—Walter E. Black, Jr., CJ; Clerk's Office, Baltimore 21201.

Massachusetts—Joseph L. Tauro, CJ; Clerk's Office, Boston 02109.

Michigan—*Eastern:* Julian A. Cook, Jr., CJ; Clerk's Office, Detroit 48226. *Western:* Benjamin F. Gibson, CJ; Clerk's Office, Grand Rapids 49503.

Minnesota—Diana E. Murphy, CJ; Clerk's Office, St. Paul 55101.

Mississippi—*Northern:* L. T. Senter, Jr., CJ; Clerk's Office, Oxford 38655. *Southern:* William H. Barbour, Jr., CJ; Clerk's Office, Jackson 39201.

Missouri—*Eastern:* Edward L. Filippine, CJ;

Clerk's Office, St. Louis 63101. *Western:* Joseph E. Stevens, Jr., CJ; Clerk's Office, Kansas City 64106.

Montana—Paul G. Hatfield, CJ; Clerk's Office, Billings 59101.

Nebraska—Lyle Strom, CJ; Clerk's Office, Omaha 68101.

Nevada—Lloyd D. George, CJ; Clerk's Office, Las Vegas 89101.

New Hampshire—Joseph A. DiClerico, CJ; Clerk's Office, Concord 03301.

New Jersey—John F. Gerry, CJ; Clerk's Office, Newark 07102.

New Mexico—Juan G. Burciaga, CJ; Clerk's Office, Albuquerque 87103.

New York—*Northern:* Neal P. McCurn, CJ; Clerk's Office, Syracuse 13261. *Eastern:* Thomas C. Platt, Jr., CJ; Clerk's Office, Brooklyn 11201. *Southern:* Thomas P. Griesa, CJ; Clerk's Office N.Y. City 10007. *Western:* Michael A. Telesca, CJ; Clerk's Office, Buffalo 14202.

North Carolina—*Eastern:* James C. Fox, CJ; Clerk's Office, Raleigh 27611. *Middle:* Frank W. Bullock, Jr., CJ; Clerk's Office, Greensboro 27402. *Western:* Richard L. Voorhees, CJ; Clerk's Office, Asheville 28802.

North Dakota—Rodney S. Webb, CJ; Clerk's Office, Bismarck 58502.

Ohio—*Northern:* Thomas D. Lambros, CJ; Clerk's Office, Cleveland 44114. *Southern:* John D. Holschuh, CJ; Clerk's Office, Columbus 43215.

Oklahoma—*Northern:* James O. Ellison, CJ; Clerk's Office, Tulsa 74103. *Eastern:* Frank H. Seay, CJ; Clerk's Office, Muskogee 74401. *Western:* Ralph G. Thompson, CJ; Clerk's Office, Oklahoma City 73102.

Oregon—James A. Redden, CJ; Clerk's Office, Portland 97205.

Pennsylvania—*Eastern:* Lewis C. Bechtle, CJ; Clerk's Office, Philadelphia 19106. *Middle:* Sylvia H. Rambo, CJ; Clerk's Office, Scranton 18501. *Western:* Maurice B. Cohill, Jr., CJ; Clerk's Office, Pittsburgh 15230.

Rhode Island—Ronald R. Lageux, CJ; Clerk's Office, Providence 02903.

South Carolina—Falcon B. Hawkins, CJ; Clerk's Office, Columbia 29202.

South Dakota—John B. Jones, CJ; Clerk's Office, Sioux Falls 57102.

Tennessee—*Eastern:* James H. Jarvis, CJ; Clerk's Office, Knoxville 37901. *Middle:* John T. Nixon, CJ; Clerk's Office, Nashville 37203. *Western:* Odell Horton, CJ; Clerk's Office, Memphis 38103.

Texas—*Northern:* Barefoot Sanders, CJ; Clerk's Office, Dallas 75242. *Southern:* Norman W. Black, CJ; Clerk's Office, Houston 77208. *Eastern:* Robert M. Parker, CJ; Clerk's Office, Tyler 75702. *Western:* Lucius D. Bunton, III, CJ; Clerk's Office, San Antonio 78206.

Utah—Bruce S. Jenkins, CJ; Clerk's Office, Salt Lake City 84101.

Vermont—Fred I. Parker, CJ; Clerk's Office, Burlington 05402.

Virginia—*Eastern:* James C. Cacheris, CJ; Clerk's Office, Alexandria 22320. *Western:* James C. Turk, CJ; Clerk's Office, Roanoke 24006.

Washington—*Eastern:* Justin L. Quackenbush, CJ; Clerk's Office, Spokane 99210. *Western:* Barbara J. Rothstein, CJ; Clerk's Office, Seattle 98104.

West Virginia—*Northern:* Robert Earl Maxwell, CJ; Clerk's Office, Elkins 26241. *Southern:* Charles H. Haden II, CJ; Clerk's Office, Charleston 25329.

Wisconsin—*Eastern:* Terence T. Evans, CJ; Clerk's Office, Milwaukee 53202. *Western:* Barbara B. Crabb, CJ; Clerk's Office, Madison 53701.

Wyoming—Alan B. Johnson, CJ; Clerk's Office, Cheyenne 82001.

U. S. Tax Court—Lapsley W. Hamblen, Jr., CJ; Clerk's Office, Washington DC 20217.

U.S. Court of Claims—Loren A. Smith, CJ; Clerk's Office, Washington, DC 20005

U.S. Court of International Trade—Dominick L. DeCarlo, CJ; Clerk's Office, New York 10007

In addition to the preceding, there are several specialized courts in the federal system whose jurisdiction is limited to narrow technical areas. These include Court of Claims (suits against the United States), U.S. Court of International Trade, and the U.S. Court of Customs and Patent Appeals.

THE STATE COURT SYSTEM

In addition to the federal system, each state has its own court system which deals with lawsuits brought under state law or with violations of state laws. Each state system differs, but all are set up on a basis of *inferior courts*, which are courts of original jurisdiction (trial courts) and appeals courts. Some states mirror the federal system in that their court system is divided into three levels: district trial courts usually divided by counties, intermediate appeals courts which review decisions from lower courts and state supreme courts which provide the ultimate review of decisions of appeals courts.

The names of these courts vary widely from state to state and can be very confusing, because the name of one level court in a given state can be the same as a very different level court in another. For example, in New York the *Supreme Court* is actually the lowest-level trial court; the highest court is called the *Court of Appeals.*

Many states further divide their lowest courts geographically by counties, cities, towns or villages. These courts usually have jurisdiction only within their own borders, or of violations of local ordinances or disputes involving limited dollar amounts. Some states also set up specialized local courts handling only certain narrow issues, such as probate courts, juvenile courts, domestic relations or family law courts (divorce and child custody cases), police courts (for the trial of minor offenses), and traffic courts. Many jurisdictions have set up small claims courts where a plaintiff can bring an action without a lawyer. These courts are usually limited to actions where less than $1,000 is in dispute, and some states require that all actions for less than a certain amount be taken to small claims courts.

HOW A CASE MOVES THROUGH COURT

CIVIL LAWSUITS

In both the federal system and most state systems, civil lawsuits follow a generally common path. The steps are, briefly:

1. A plaintiff (either an individual or a legal entity such as a corporation) files an action listing who is being sued, why, and for how much.

2. The defendant then files a response which can be a denial of the claim, the statement of an affirmative defense, or a counterclaim which is in effect a countersuit.

3. In the case of a small claims court action, a trial date might now be set. In more complex litigation, the case is assigned to a certain judge and lawyers from both sides are now allowed a period of pretrial discovery in which they can request documents from their opponents or question prospective witnesses under oath. When both sides say they are ready for trial (this can take months or even years), the case is placed on the court docket. Lawyers for both sides may now file and argue pretrial motions. This process, too, can be time-consuming.

4. After all motions are decided, the trial can begin. It may be decided solely by the judge (always true in small claims courts), or by a jury if either party so requests. If a jury trial, the jury is impaneled in a process (called *voir dire*) whereby each lawyer and the judge questions each juror to try to determine if they are unbiased and can reach a fair verdict. In most states each lawyer is given a certain number of challenges, whereby he can ask that a juror be excused for no stated reason, and usually an unlimited number of challenges for cause, with the judge deciding whether the cause is sufficient. In the federal system, most judges choose jurors themselves without the lawyers on both sides being directly involved. Although a 12-member jury is traditional in American jurisprudence, most jurisdictions, including the federal courts, now allow six-member civil court juries.

5. The trial then begins with each side presenting an opening argument in which it lays out its version of the case. Then the plaintiff presents the case. The burden is always on the plaintiff to prove the case by a "preponder-

ance" of the evidence. After each of the plaintiff's witnesses testifies, the defense gets to question the witnesses in cross-examination.

6. After the plaintiff completes his case, the defense will often ask the judge for a *directed verdict*. This means a decision by the judge that, as a matter of law, the plaintiff has not presented a case strong enough to allow the matter to go to the jury or, in a nonjury trial, for a judge to rule for the plaintiff. If the motion is denied, the defense then presents its case with the plaintiff given the right to cross-examine any witnesses.

7. After the defense has finished, both sides are usually given the right to present additional witnesses or information in a rebuttal phase of the trial. This right is usually limited to either newly discovered evidence or evidence to counter what has been brought up at trial.

8. In a nonjury trial the judge usually retires to make his decision. In more complex cases he often asks for written briefs from each side summing up their cases. The decision can be immediate, or it can take weeks or months.

In jury trials, each side sums up its case for the jury and the judge then instructs the jury on the law on which they must render their decision. Usually, both sides have submitted their own draft jury instructions to the judge, who decides exactly what instructions the jury hears.

9. The jury then retires to reach a verdict. Depending on the case, and the jurisdiction, it may not have to be a unanimous decision. In some jurisdictions, the jury only decides either for the plaintiff or the defendant and the judge sets any monetary award. In other jurisdictions, the jury both reaches a decision and sets an award amount. Usually, the judge can change the amount, but generally only to lower it.

10. Either or both parties can make post trial motions asking the judge to set aside the verdict or the awarded amount.

11. Once the trial court judge has affirmed the decision and the award, called a judgment, either side may appeal to the next higher level of court if it believes an error in law was made by the trial judge. It does so by filing and serving on its opponent a notice of appeal, and at the same time filing with the appropriate appeals court a memorandum of appeal, which sets out in detail the reason for the appeal with supporting arguments. The other side then has a number of days to file its own memorandum in opposition. In some cases the appeals court will reach a decision based solely on these written pleadings; in others, the lawyers will be allowed to argue their cases orally and be questioned by the appeals court judges.

12. The appeals court may decide to reverse the lower court's decision by simply deciding the case the opposite way. Or it may order a new trial because of some error. In still other cases, it may request the lower court judge to review the case, or the award, consistent with the appeals court's interpretation of the law.

13. If the losing side remains unhappy with the decision, it can ask the highest court in the state (or, in the federal system, the Supreme Court) to review the decision of the appeals court. In the federal system, and in most state systems, the high court does not have to review the lower court decision. In states that do not have an intermediate appeals court, the high court must review all appeals.

14. In the case of a decision by the highest court of a state, if the losing party feels that a constitutional issue is involved, he may file a writ of *certiorari* with the U.S. Supreme Court. If the court refuses to hear the matter—which is usually the case—the decision of the state court is affirmed.

CRIMINAL CASES

Many of the steps in a criminal case are similar to those in civil cases. As with civil suits, criminal cases can be tried in both the federal and state court systems. Criminal trials in the federal system are limited to violations of federal criminal statutes. Many crimes are violations of both state and federal statutes. Double jeopardy protections prevent a person from being tried for the same crime in both the state and federal systems once acquitted in either. But double jeopardy protections do not prevent a second prosecution for a different crime arising out of the same fact situation.

1. In a criminal action the plaintiff is the state or more properly, the "people." The criminal process usually begins with a person's arrest. Under the Supreme Court-mandated *Miranda Rule*, any person arrested or detained must be informed immediately of his/her right to a lawyer, including one appointed by the court if he or she cannot afford to retain one, and to an

absolute right to refuse to answer any questions, as well as the state's right to use anything he or she says against him in an eventual trial.

After being informed of these rights by the arresting officer, the defendant is usually taken to a local police station, or in the federal system to the nearest federal lock-up (usually a U.S. Marshal's office), where he/she is fingerprinted, photographed and *booked* (his name entered into an official arrest record).

2. Usually within 24 hours of an arrest, a defendant is taken into court for an *arraignment*—a hearing before a judge in which the charges against the defendant are detailed and, the defendant is asked if a lawyer has been retained; if not, the judge will appoint one. The defendant is then asked to enter a plea if he or she has had time to confer with the lawyer. A "not guilty" plea at an arraignment is almost proforma. Many judges will not accept guilty pleas at arraignments.

3. At the arraignment, the judge will usually set bail, an amount either in the form of cash or real property that the defendant or someone else will put up to guarantee that the defendant will appear at future proceedings. If the offense is minor enough, or the defendant well established in the community, the judge can release him or her without a bond being put up "on his own recognizance," or into the custody of a third party who personally guarantees the defendant's future appearances. If the state believes there is a possibility that the defendant might flee, or that he or she poses a danger to society, it can oppose the setting of bail or request an unusually high bail amount. In a complex case, a separate bail hearing is sometimes necessary.

4. The next step is usually a preliminary hearing in which a judge determines whether there is enough evidence to believe that a crime has taken place and that the defendant committed the crime. The prosecution is required to present enough evidence for the judge to make this determination, and the defendant may present exonerating evidence. The judge can dismiss the charges or order the defendant bound over for a trial. In some jurisdictions the judge can order the matter taken to the grand jury.

5. The *grand jury* is a group of citizens (the number varies from state to state and within the federal system) who are in session for a specified length of time and whose duty is to see that the state does not bring a criminal prosecution based on insufficient evidence. Prosecutors present their evidence in a case to the grand jury, who can then call its own witnesses. As opposed to a trial, a person does not have the right to have a lawyer present during a grand jury proceeding. But he or she has the constitutional right not to answer questions, and may leave the grand jury room to confer with an attorney before answering any question.

Often the grand jury is the starting point in the criminal process. If a person has not been arrested during the commission of a crime or shortly thereafter, the prosecution will often go to the grand jury to ask for an indictment, which will lead to the issuing of an arrest warrant and the start of the whole process. If the grand jury thinks that there is enough evidence to go forward with a trial, it will "return" what is called a *true bill*. If it does not believe there is enough evidence, it will return a *no true bill*. If additional evidence is obtained the prosecution can return to the grand jury on successive occasions to seek a true bill without violating the constitutional prohibition against double jeopardy.

6. Before the trial begins the defendant and his/her lawyer have a right to see all the evidence that will be used against him or her and to know what witnesses will be called by the prosecution. The defendant also has a right to obtain any evidence the state has that might help exonerate him or her. In some jurisdictions the defendant is also required to list all witnesses who will appear on his or her behalf.

At this point a defendant's lawyer may enter into plea bargaining negotiations with prosecutors. A plea bargain is an agreement between the state, the judge, and the defendant that if the defendant pleads guilty to the charge, he or she will receive a certain sentence, or, if he or she will plead guilty and save the state the cost and time of a full trial, the state will allow a plea of guilty to a lesser offense. Today plea bargaining occurs in a majority of criminal cases.

7. A criminal defendant has a right to a speedy trial. Many jurisdictions have specific statutes requiring a trial to begin within a certain period after the preliminary hearing or issuance of a true bill by a grand jury. Often the limit is 90 days, but it can be as long as six months.

The defendant also has an absolute right to a

trial by a jury of *peers.* Peers have long been considered a cross-section of the community—nothing more specific. But a defendant may waive this right and be tried only by the judge. Many states still require a 12-person jury in criminal cases, but the Supreme Court ruled in 1970 that a jury need only be large enough to guarantee group deliberation and a fair cross-section of the local community. Six members is considered the minimum number to guarantee this. As with civil cases, the jury is impaneled through the *voir dire* process.

8. Again as with civil cases, the trial begins with each side presenting an opening argument in which it lays out its version of the case. The state then presents its case. Whereas in a civil case the burden is on the plaintiff to prove his case by a preponderance of the evidence, in a criminal matter the state must prove its case *beyond a reasonable doubt.* After each of the state's witnesses testifies, the defense gets to question the witnesses in cross-examination.

9. After the state completes its case, the defense will usually ask the judge for a directed verdict, that is, a decision by the judge that, as a matter of law, the state has not presented a strong enough case to allow the matter to go to the jury. If the motion is denied, the defense then presents its case, with the state given the right to cross-examine any witnesses.

After the defense has finished, both sides are usually given the right to present additional witnesses or information in a rebuttal phase of the trial. As in civil trials, this right is usually limited to either newly discovered evidence or evidence to counter what has been brought up at trial.

10. Now each side sums up its case. In a jury trial, the judge then instructs the jury on the law and they retire to reach a verdict. In a criminal case, that verdict must be unanimous. In a nonjury criminal trial, the judge retires to reach a verdict, which is often a written decision.

11. The process now enters the sentencing phase. This varies widely from jurisdiction to jurisdiction. In some jurisdictions the jury sets the sentence during its deliberations of guilt or innocence. In others, it is up to the judge. In some a whole new minitrial with the same jury is held. Here the state presents evidence seeking one sentence and the defendant presents exonerating evidence seeking a lesser sentence. The jury then retires to make the determination. In most jurisdictions a presentencing investigation by the local probation office is conducted to guide the judge, or the judge and jury.

12. If a criminal defendant has been acquitted by judge or jury, that ends the proceeding. If he has been found guilty, the defense can file post trial motions asking the judge to set aside the verdict.

13. Once the trial court judge has affirmed the verdict, the defense may appeal to the next higher level of court if it believes an error in law was made by the trial judge. The process here is much the same as with a civil case, except that the higher court may also review the facts of the case, while in civil cases appeals courts usually accept findings of fact that have been established by lower courts.

In criminal matters, appeals courts do not reverse jury decisions unless they find that, as a matter of law, there was not enough evidence for the case to have been presented to the jury. Rather, if error is found, the appeals court will order a new trial.

14. Either side may appeal the decision of an appeals court to the next higher court. As with civil cases, the highest court of a state does not have to review a case and often will refuse to do so without a written decision (except in the case of a death penalty, where most states require automatic review by the highest court).

As with civil cases, in the case of a decision by the highest court of a state, if the losing party feels that a constitutional issue is involved, he may file a writ of *certiorari* with the U.S. Supreme Court. If the Court refuses to hear the matter—as it usually does—the decision of the state court is affirmed.

THE LEGISLATIVE BRANCH
CONGRESS

The Congress of the United States is unique among the legislative bodies of the world in that it has been given the power to both write its own legislation and to monitor, and largely control, the rest of the government. What makes the U.S. Congress so unusual is the dual role carried out by its members. They are legislators, passing laws for the nation as a whole, while at the same time they are elected to represent the specific interests of a particular portion of the country, and a particular number of citizens. There is often tension between these two roles.

As stated in Article I, Section I of the Constitution: "All legislative power herein granted shall be vested in a Congress of the United States, which shall consist of a Senate and a House of Representatives." This division of powers between two largely coequal chambers is what is known as the Great Compromise giving equal power to small states in the upper chamber which has two senators from each state regardless of size, and greater power to larger states in the lower chamber where membership is apportioned according to population.

Certainly the Founding Fathers, with their traditions as citizen-legislators, could not have dreamed of the present billion-dollars-plus-a-year Congress, many of whose members spend their entire careers and retire with generous pensions. But the legislative branch has grown to keep pace with the general growth of government. In 1947, the House and Senate combined had a total staff of 2,030. Within a decade that number had grown to 3,556. By 1970 the staff of the House and Senate exceeded 7,000. By the end of the 1970s it exceeded 10,000 and today stands at almost 12,000.

A TYPICAL DAY FOR
A MEMBER OF CONGRESS

The annual legislative calendar of the Congress is filled with frequent *Member's District Working Periods* (which used to be called *recesses*). During these many members can often be found on *fact finding missions* (which used to be called *junkets*) to someplace far off shore. Congress also works less than full time. The Senate has established a schedule of three weeks on, one week off. The House is considering adopting that same schedule. And when either body is in session, it is unusual for them to schedule a recorded vote on a Monday or a Friday (to give members the option of spending an additional day at home). But on those days that they do work, both senators and representatives typically work a very long day that will often start with an early breakfast meeting and end late at night following a "must-attend" reception and dinner. (Some younger members with families are campaigning to work more days with fewer hours so they will have some time with their families.) Add to this the fact that members are constantly running for reelection and constantly raising campaign funds, days are long and the work is surprisingly difficult.

A typical day for both congresspeople and senators often begins with an early morning breakfast speech or "issues briefing" for a trade association, interest group, or a group of constituents visiting from home. At times these sessions represent an exchange of ideas and views with key industry leaders. But often the session represents the chance to pick up a campaign donation on the way to work. Few members turn down such opportunities.

Much of the business of Congress is done in

committees and subcommittees. On any given day dozens of committee and subcommittee hearings are held. Most start at 9:30 a.m. and run through the lunch hour. This means members have to get to the office, go over their schedule and the day's mail, meet with the staff, and be in the appropriate hearing room on time. One area where congresspeople and senators differ is that with 435 representatives to only 100 senators, senators have double or triple the committee and subcommittee assignments of representatives. It is not unusual for senators to have two or three hearings going on simultaneously. Senators have considerably larger staffs than representatives, and most have separate staffers assigned to each committee or subcommittee to which they are assigned. In situations where senators are required to be in two or three places at once, there will be staffers in each hearing room monitoring the progress and briefing their senators when they arrive.

On a normal day both the House and the Senate convene at about 11:00 a.m. The first hour or so is given over to routine business such as the reading of messages from the White House and to members to make short speeches for the record. But usually starting at about noon, both the Senate and the House move into their main business of the day. Both bodies try not to schedule full roll call votes early in the day, because of the hearings likely still in progress. But very often all the members of committee or subcommittee will have to recess a hearing and rush the half mile or so to the floor for a vote. It is not unheard of for a hearing to be interrupted several times for floor votes, and afternoon hearings are often constantly interrupted (which is why afternoon hearings are avoided if possible).

Once finished with the hearing schedule, a member will spend the rest of the day going back and forth between the office and the floor trying to fit in meetings with staff on pending issues, meeting with constituents, meeting with lobbyists and meeting with representatives of agencies the member may have oversight jurisdiction over with business on the floor.

Another difference between the House and Senate is the amount of work actually done on the floor. In the House most of the work on legislation is done in committee, and by the time a bill reaches the floor it is pretty much in its final language. Much more shaping of final legislative language happens on the Senate floor, where unlimited debate is the rule, and any senator can attach a *rider* to any bill on any subject, as long as there is a second. What this means is that on many days a senator will have to spend considerably more time on the floor than does his or her House counterpart.

On a normal day both the House and Senate adjourn at anywhere from 5:00 p.m. to 7:00 p.m., although sessions lasting until midnight have become common. If there is an adjournment by dinner time, it's back to the office for more meetings, answering mail and returning phone calls, and preparing for the next day's hearings and expected floor votes. In this age of constant media attention, most members are required to fit in one or two interviews a day, often by satellite to a television station back home.

Then it's off for the evening's rounds. Most senators get an average of a dozen invitations a night for receptions, dinners, and parties. A congressperson will get four to six. They are nominally social events, but an awful lot of business in Washington gets done at these functions. Many members make a half-dozen stops in an evening. Then it's home to tackle a briefcase full of work, and then up at dawn to start again.

Realistically, many members coast, with their schedules only pale imitations of the preceding scenario. But a majority—a surprisingly large majority—regularly put in 18-hour days of running from hearing to floor to office and back again. The more conscientious the member, the harder they run.

WHAT A MEMBER OF CONGRESS CAN DO FOR YOU

A congressperson or senator simply could not function without a staff of aides. Senators, with their greater responsibilities, have much larger staffs. (The size of each senator's staff is dependent on the size of the state represented.) Staffers serve as the member's eyes and ears and are responsible for all facets of a representative's activities—including constituent service. How each office is set up varies, but generally a member will have a small personal staff consisting of an administrative assistant, a political aide and a press secretary. Then he or she will have a professional staff of persons with expertise in the areas of jurisdiction of the member's committees. Finally each office has a staff of specialists in constituent service, aides with great experience in dealing with the federal bureaucracy and twisting arms when and where necessary. If a member has enough seniority on a committee or subcommittee, they can also appoint committee staff members who deal only with committee business.

In addition, each representative has one or more offices back in the district with a separate staff, usually dealing solely in constituent service. About 50 percent of the workload in an average congressional office consists of constituent service. Much of the casework is handled in the district office. Members and their staffs are available to help constituents with Social Security, educational assistance, veterans' benefits, taxes and postal service problems. The congressional office often serves as a liaison between the constituent and such agencies as the Veterans' Administration, the Internal Revenue Service, and the Environmental Protection Agency.

By contacting a staff member in a member's home district, or in the Washington office, you can get help if you are experiencing delays in getting Social Security or disability benefits. Your member can also go to bat for you if you feel you've been denied veterans' benefits or Medicare reimbursements unfairly. The appropriate agency often finds it in their best interest to be responsive when a member of Congress calls. They want to get their fair share in the congressional budget process and to operate with minimal intervention from the lawmakers.

It should be understood, that much is written in members' names without their knowledge. Letters go out with their signatures even though they may never have seen them. Speeches and press releases on them are mailed out well in advance of delivery. Staff members make telephone calls on behalf of their bosses, although the members do not always know the calls have been made.

Local government officials also look to their congressional delegations to help acquire federal funding for projects. Congressional offices can provide information on available grants, and also help prepare the necessary paperwork and provide any other needed support. Senators, especially, have full-time assistants in charge of public casework. These people are assigned to ensure that the home state, its cities and its citizens get their fair share of federal projects and grants. They can help a scientist obtain a federal research grant. They also serve as information centers, ensuring that every business and community knows what it is entitled to and how to obtain it.

Members are central players in helping youths from their districts obtain appointments to U.S. military academies. The Army, Navy, Air Force, and Merchant Marines make their appointments based on nominations from members of Congress. Each member can nominate several young men and women each year for appointments to the academies. Information on how to be considered for a nomination can be obtained by writing or calling either your representative or senators.

If you need information on current laws, your member's office can be a valuable resource. Staff members can provide copies of legislative bills and reports, executive branch regulations and pictures and biographies of federal lawmakers. They even provide informational booklets on hundreds of subjects from cockroach control to infant care.

You can also request through your member an American flag, which has flown—at least for a few seconds—over the Capitol building.

If you are planning to visit Washington, members can help you obtain tickets for special tours of the White House and the Bureau of Engraving. He can also help you get passes to observe the House in session, and provide tourist information on Washington, D.C.

While your congressperson is likely to have more of a vested interest in problems unique to the district, your senator is often the best person to contact for problems that have statewide implications. For example, an erosion problem affecting a hundred miles of coastline in a Great Lakes state would be likely to draw a senator's attention, since he or she represents the entire state and the issue affects a large number of its residents.

Since you have two senators to choose from, you might become confused as to which one to approach about a given issue. Many lawmakers, over time, develop a reputation as experts in certain areas. Some become known for their stance on consumer affairs, while others may become experts on issues affecting the elderly. Researching each senator's area of expertise can help you decide which one is the best to call for help.

HOW A BILL BECOMES A LAW

Legislation is born in many ways. The Constitution directs the president to keep the Congress informed as to the *state of the union* and to "recommend to their Consideration such Measures as he shall judge necessary and expedient." The departments of government submit *executive communications* to Congress calling for legislative action. And organized groups and individual citizens barrage Capitol Hill with petitions and suggestions for new laws.

No matter what the origin of legislative proposals, they can be introduced officially in only one way: by senators and representatives. Every proposal takes the form of a *bill* or a *resolution*. Bills are more general in nature and may be *public bills*, which affect the general public, or *private bills*, which affect individuals or groups. Senate bills are given sequential numbers and the designation *S*. House bills are also sequentially numbered and carry the designation *HR*. *Simple* and *Concurrent Resolutions* are designed to express the "sense of Congress" to the president or other parties and to take care of "housekeeping" chores. *Joint resolutions* are designed to correct the language in previously passed legislation.

According to the rules, all bills must be "read" three times, twice before being assigned to a committee. By current practice, the first two readings are almost always accomplished simply by introducing, printing and distributing the proposed legislation. The bill is then cataloged, computerized and referred to the appropriate standing committee or committees of the House or Senate with jurisdiction over the subject matter of the proposed new law.

Usually, the full committee that gets a piece of proposed legislation immediately refers it to one of its standing subcommittees. The smaller panel holds hearings, studies the proposed legislation and then reports back to the parent committee. The full committee may adopt the report, reject it, amend it, or write an entirely different report. This final process is called *mark-up*, when the committee goes over the proposed legislation line by line, section by section. Mark-up at the full committee level is perhaps the most important step in the legislative process. The *marked-up bill* is then returned to the Senate or House and placed on the legislative calendar for floor action.

Every bill that goes to the floor must be accompanied by a *rule*, that is, a statement from the Rules Committee as to what the length and form of debate shall be, and in the House what types of amendments, if any, will be considered germane and will be accepted for debate.

Once the bill is on the floor in the House, amendments that are within the rule are debated and either accepted or rejected. In the Senate, amendments can be offered by the committee reporting it or by individual senators; under Senate rules they do not even have to pertain to the subject matter of the pending bill (nongermane amendments are known as *riders*) If the amendment has a second it will be debated and voted up or down.

The bill is then given a third reading—this time by title only—and is voted upon. A simple majority is all that is needed to approve it. After passage in one house, a measure is still generally referred to as a bill, but technically, it is an *Act*. It is then dispatched to the other chamber for its consideration.

Bills and resolutions are processed similarly in both legislative bodies. Each chamber can end up passing very different versions of the same bill. Each chamber can amend the other's bills. The differences are ironed out by appointed representatives of both chambers meeting in conference. The result, called a *conference report*, is sent back to both chambers for final approval on the floor. If the conference report is adopted by both, the legislative process is complete. The bill is *enrolled*—published in final form on parchment by the Government Printing Office—signed by the Speaker of the House and the Vice President (acting in his Constitutional role as the President of the Senate), or by the presiding officer of the Senate, and dispatched by messenger to the White House for the president's consideration.

Under the Constitution, the president has 10 days, excluding Sundays, in which to sign or veto a bill. If he does not sign the bill within 10 days, it becomes law automatically. If Congress adjourns during the 10-day period and the president signs the bill, it still becomes law. But if he does not sign it, and Congress has adjourned during the 10-day period, it fails to become a law. This is know as a *pocket veto*.

A vetoed bill can be enacted into law despite the president's objections if ⅔ of both houses vote to *override* the president's veto.

THE CONGRESSIONAL BUDGET PROCESS

Little that Congress does is as controversial and confusing as the way it decides how the federal government will tax citizens and spend the proceeds. Throughout the Nixon presidency, the White House and the Congress waged an almost continuous war over government spending. The Congress appropriated funds but the White House refused to spend them if it did not like what they were being spent on. At the same time, major turf battles raged within Congress, as powerful committee chairpersons with overlapping jurisdictions fought to control the purse strings of various federal agencies.

In an attempt to bring some kind of order to the federal budget process, Congress, in 1974, established an elaborate process for arriving at a new annual federal-spending plan. The process seems simple on paper, but in the 14 years that it has been in place (from fiscal 1976), it has proven anything but. In fact, in some years— the budget fiasco of the Summer of 1990 is a textbook example—it has proven to be all but unworkable.

The federal government operates on annual budgets, with a new fiscal year beginning each October 1. Therefore, Congress must have approved, and the president must sign into law, a plan detailing the spending for the coming year— down to the cent—by midnight on September 30. The Congressional budget planning process is built around a timetable whose purpose is to ensure that it is completed each year by that September 30 deadline.

Every other year a new Congress convenes on about the third Monday in January (or reconvenes if there has not been a new Congressional election the previous November). Fifteen days later the President must submit to both House and Senate his proposed detailed spending plan for the fiscal year to begin nine months later.

Immediately, the House and Senate break the budget up into its many component parts and send each part to the appropriate committee or subcommittee for hearings. Under the budget timetable, each committee is expected to complete action on its part of the budget, and to forward reports to the Senate and House Budget Committees, no later than March 15. At the same time, the Congressional Budget Office, a joint House–Senate body, reviews the entire budget with an eye to forecasting necessary levels of taxation and debt; and its report is due to both budget committees by April 1. With this information in hand, the two budget committees must report back to the House and Senate what is called the first budget resolution by April 15.

Now things become complicated. The budget resolution is really nothing more than a kind of statement of intent. It is not legislation, rather, it is a kind of "sense of the Congress"—a target—as to the appropriate levels of funding for each federal program during the coming year. Actually, spending is determined by a series of appropriations bills that must be passed separately by each body and then reconciled through House-Senate conferences. Under the budget timetable, final appropriations bills must be passed by seven days after Labor Day.

However, this is not the end of the process. Obviously, some needs have changed since the president first submitted his original budget nine months before. Therefore, each body now refines the budget via the *second budget resolution*. This fine tuning is then extended to the appropriations bills already passed, which are combined into what is called the budget reconciliation. This is the document that must be approved by September 25 and sent to the president for his signature, so that it will become law before the new fiscal year starts on October 1.

In some years, this process has worked; in others it has almost worked; and in some years it has failed miserably. On those occasions Congress has simply not met its target of having the final budget reconciliation on the president's desk by October 1. This has led to what is known as budgeting by continuous resolution (CR).

Technically, if the president has not signed a new federal budget into law by midnight on September 30, the federal government should grind to a halt. To prevent this, Congress tries to pass a law—a continuing resolution—which allows the government to continue operating at current levels for some period, usually a few days to a week, until the process can be finished. In some years, as the process has dragged on, a series of continuing resolutions has been necessary, and on three occasions (the most recent 1990), the government has actually shut down: all nonessential personnel have been told not to report for work, or sent home, until a continuing resolution could be passed and signed by the president.

Almost since the day it was approved, the entire Congressional budget process has been under fire. Calls for reform have been continuous. Besides the basic problem of inability to adhere to the schedule, critics charge that a major flaw in the entire system is the inherent inefficiency of budgeting on an annual basis. Many budget experts argue that the federal government should be budgeted over two fiscal years, or an even longer period, with some mechanism set up to make adjustments as they become necessary. This longer-term approach would give Congress additional time to complete its work and would allow federal managers to plan better, since they would know how much they had to spend over the next 24 months. This, experts argue, should result in long-term savings.

Then, too, every president who has operated under this system has been disturbed by the fact that he is faced ultimately with the choice of either approving or disapproving the entire budget. If he disagrees with the allocation approved by Congress for a specific department or program, his only option is to veto the entire measure and then watch the government shut down. This has led to a call for giving the President the *line item veto*, which would allow him to disapprove specific appropriations while still approving the overall budget. Needless to say, Congress, especially Congressional Democrats, are determined to prevent this, because the system as it now stands gives them a major check on a Republican in the Oval Office.

CONGRESSIONAL BUDGET TIMETABLE

15 days after Congress convenes—President's proposed budget submitted

March 15—Committees with jurisdictional responsibility over executive departments and agencies submit budget reports to their respective Budget Committees

April 1—Congressional Budget Office sends report to Budget Committees of both houses

April 15—Budget Committees report first budget resolution to House and Senate

May 15—Final action on first budget resolution and authorization bills

7 days after Labor Day—Final action on appropriations bills

September 15—Final action on second budget resolution

September 25—Final action on budget reconciliation

October 1—New fiscal year begins

HOW TO WRITE A MEMBER OF CONGRESS

A call or letter to your representative or senator can make a tremendous difference. Few members can afford to ignore mail from constituents; most are genuinely interested in the opinions of the people they represent. Even more important, most of them want to be reelected, and it is recognized in the halls of Congress that those who care enough to write, vote. A well-reasoned letter is certain to be noted.

Here are some ways to write letters your Congress members and their aides will find hard to ignore:

• Keep your letter short and focused on only one subject. If you want to get something other than a form letter in response, ask a specific question.

• If you are writing about a pending piece of legislation, explain the impact of the legislation on yourself.

• Try to show an understanding of how the legislation would affect the district or state on such things as the environment and local jobs.

• Don't assume your representative or senator has memorized every bill in the book. Refer to the legislation by its bill number or its title, or if you don't know, summarize it as best you know.

• It helps to show a familiarity with the representative's or senator's voting record: "I was glad to see you voted against synfuels development. Now I am hoping you will endorse the alternative and vote for a higher solar budget."

• Steer away from emotional outrage. And never threaten politicians. It will only make them angry; worse still, they may write you off.

• It's as important to thank congress members for voting the right way as it is to blast them for letting you down. Give thanks where they're due (and a token campaign contribution wouldn't hurt either).

Congress is being deluged with mail as never before. Much of it is coming as a result of organized letter writing campaigns. Congressional staffers take pride in being able to spot a letter writing campaign at work. Never use a sample letter form, such as those distributed by organized interest groups. The Congress member already knows the positions of these groups and has estimated the size and influence of their constituencies.

If time is of the essence, and you want to get your message to the Hill quickly, send a Western Union telegram. Immediate delivery to Congress over the wire in a "Public Opinion Message" telegram is $9.95 for 20 words plus signature or less and $3.50 for an additional 20 words. Or, for overnight delivery, a mailgram of up to 50 words can be sent for $16.95 ($5.95 for each additional 50 words). All messages can be charged to your home phone.

Other can't-lose tips for the citizen lobbyist:

• At times it may do you considerably more good contacting the staff person dealing with the issue you're interested in, than in contacting the member directly. You can call the member's office and inquire which staffer is dealing with a particular issue, and then write him or her directly. You can then later write the member directly, perhaps praising the staffer for his or her help and interest.

• A well thought out letter to the editor of your local newspaper explaining the impact of your representative's position on a certain issue is always effective. If it's published, it will be on his or her desk before lunchtime.

• Visit your representative when he or she is in the district. If you don't know where the field office is, write him or her in Washington and ask. Call the field office weeks ahead, if possible, to arrange an appointment.

• When you're in Washington, D.C., don't miss the chance to see your Congress members. Many legislators are less rushed and therefore more receptive in Washington than during their trips home. Write or phone ahead to ask for an appointment, but if you neglect to do so, you can still call the office when you get to Washington and probably get an appointment.

Your representative or senator can have his offices in any one of six buildings (three Senate and three House): DSOB—Dirksen Senate Office Bldg., HSOB—Hart Senate Office Bldg., RSOB—Russell Senate Office Bldg., CHOB—Cannon House Office Bldg., LHOB—Longworth House Office Bldg., or RHOB—Rayburn House Office Bldg. But to write, you only need address it as follows: The Honorable [representative], House Office Building, Washington, D.C. 20515; Senator [name], Senate Office Building, Washington, D.C. 20510. To telephone, simply dial the Capitol switchboard at (202) 224-3121 and ask for the member's office.

THE COMMITTEES OF CONGRESS

SENATE STANDING COMMITTEES

Committee on Agriculture, Nutrition and Forestry

328 A SROB 20510. Phone 202-224-2035 (Charles Riemenschneider, Staff Dir.)

Jurisdiction over agriculture, commodity, food, nutrition and hunger programs including agricultural exports, crop insurance, animal and forestry industries, Food for Peace program, food stamp program, school nutrition, many natural resources issues, including conservation, irrigation, soil conservation, stream channelization, watershed, and flood-control programs; oversees Agriculture Dept.; Interior Dept. and U.S. Forest Service.

Democrats
Patrick L. Leahy (Vt.), Chairman; David Pryor (Ark.), David Boren (Okla.), Howell Heflin (Ala.), Tom Harkin (Iowa), Kent Conrad (N. Dak.), Tom Daschle (S.Dak.), Max Baucus (Mont.), Bob Kerry (Nebr.) Russell D. Feingold (Wis.)

Republicans
Richard G. Lugar (Ind.), Ranking Member; Bob Dole (Kans.), Jesse Helms (N.C.), Thad Cochran (Miss.), Mitch McConnell (Ky.), Larry Craig (Idaho), Paul Coverdell (Ga.), Charles Grassley (Iowa)

Subcommittees
Agricultural Credit
(D) Conrad, Chm.; Boren and Daschle, Baucus
(R) Grassley, Craig, Coverdell

Agricultural Production and Stabilization of Prices
(D) Pryor, Chm.; Baucus, Kerrey, Feingold, Boren, Heflin, Harkin
(R) Helms, Dole, Grassley, Cochran, McConnell, Craig

Agricultural Research, Conservation, Forestry, and General Legislation
(D) Daschle, Chm.; Kerrey, Harkin
(R) Craig, Cochran

Domestic and Foreign Marketing and Product Promotion
(D) Boren, Chm.; Pryor, Baucus, Conrad, Fiengold, Heflin
(R) Cochran, Helms, Coverdell, Grassley, McConnell

Nutrition and Investigations
(D) Harkin, Chm.; Kerrey, Pryor, Feingold
(R) McConnell, Dole, Helms

Rural Development and Rural Electrification
(D) Heflin, Chm.; Conrad, Daschle
(R) Coverdell, Dole

Committee on Appropriations

S-128 The Capitol, 128 SDOB 20510. Phone 202-224-3471 (James English, Staff Dir.)

Jurisdiction over legislation to appropriate funds for all government programs; authorizes recissions of appropriated funds and transfer of surplus allocations; maintains data on congressional appropriating process and government spending.

Democrats
Robert Byrd (W.Va.), Chairman; Daniel Inouye, (Hawaii), Fritz Hollings (S.C.), J. Bennett Johnson (La.), Patrick Leahy (Vt.), Jim Sasser (Tenn.), Dennis DeConcini (Ariz.), Dale Bumpers (Ark.), Frank Lautenberg (N.J.), Tom Harkin (Iowa), Barbara Mikulski (Md.), Harry Reid (Nev.), Bob Kerry (Nebr.), Herb Kohl (Wis.), Patty Murray (Wash.), Dianne Feinstein (Calif.)

Republicans
Mark Hatfield (Oreg.), Ranking Member; Ted Stevens (Alaska), Thad Cochran (Miss.), Alfonse D'Amato (N.Y.), Arlen Specter (Pa.), Pete Domenici (N.Mex.), Don Nickles (Okla.), Phil Gramm (Tex.), Christopher Bond (Mo.), Slade Gorton (Wash.), Mitch McConnell (Ky.), Connie Mack (Fla.), Conrad Burns (Mont.)

Subcommittees
Agriculture, Rural Development, and Related Agencies

(D) Bumpers, Chm.; Harkin, Kerrey, Johnston, Kohl, Feinstein
(R) Cochran, Specter, Bond, Gramm, Gorton

Commerce, Justice, State, and Judiciary
(D) Hollings, Chm.; Inouye, Bumpers, Lautenberg, Sasser, Kerry
(R) Domenici, Stevens, Hatfield, Gramm, McConnell

Defense
(D) Inouye, Chm.; Hollings, Johnston, Byrd, Leahy, Sasser, DeConcini, Bumpers, Lautenberg, Harkin
(R) Stevens, D'Amato, Cochran, Specter, Domenici, Nickels, Gramm, Bond

District of Columbia
(D) Kohl, Chm.; Murray, Feinstein
(R) Burns, Mack

Energy and Water Development
(D) Johnston, Chm.; Byrd, Hollings, Sasser, DeConcini, Reid, Kerry
(R) Hatfield, Cochran, Domenici, Nickles, Gorton, McConnell

Foreign Operations
(D) Leahy, Chm.; Inouye, DeConcini, Lautenberg, Harkin, Mikulski, Feinstein
(R) McConnell, D'Amato, Specter, Nickles, Mack, Gramm

VA, HUD and Independent Agencies
(D) Mikulski, Chm.; Leahy, Johnston, Lautenberg, Kerrey, Feinstein
(R) Gramm, D'Amato, Nickles, Bond, Burns

Interior
(D) Byrd, Chm.; Johnston, Leahy, DeConcini, Bumpers, Hollings, Reid, Murray
(R) Nickles, Stevens, Cochran, Domenici, Gorton, Hatfield, Burns

Labor, Health and Human Services, and Education
(D) Harkin, Chm.; Byrd, Hollings, Inouye, Bumpers, Reid, Kohl, Murray
(R) Specter, Hatfield, Stevens, Cochran, Gorton, Mack, Bond

Legislative Branch
(D) Reid, Chm.; Mikulski, Murray
(R) Mack, Burns

Military Construction
(D) Sasser, Chm.; Inouye, Reid, Kohl
(R) Gorton, Stevens, McConnell

Transportation
(D) Lautenberg, Chm.; Byrd, Harkin, Sasser, Mikulski
(R) D'Amato, Domenici, Hatfield, Specter

Treasury, Postal Service, and General Government
(D) DeConcini, Chm.; Mikulski, Kerrey
(R) Bond, D'Amato

Committee on Armed Services

228 SROB 20510. Phone 202-224-3871 (Arnold Punaro, Staff Dir.)

Jurisdiction over legislation affecting defense; the Panama Canal (shared with Senate Commerce, Science and Transportation Committee); emergency preparedness, including civil defense, emergency mobilization of merchant fleets, emergency communications, and industrial planning and mobilization; national security matters, including military intelligence activities and aspects of nuclear energy; military personnel matters, including selective service, courts martial and appeals and military grievances, service clubs; military procurement (excluding construction) for all armed services; military contract services, research and development; naval petroleum reserves.

Democrats
Sam Nunn (Ga.), Chairman; James Exon (Nebr.), Carl Levin (Mich.), Edward Kennedy (Mass.), Jeff Bingaman (N.Mex.), John Glenn (Ohio), Richard Shelby (Ala.), Robert Byrd (W.Va.), Bob Graham (Fla.), Chuck Robb (Va.), Joe Lieberman (Conn.)

Republicans
Strom Thurmond (S.C.), Ranking Member; John Warner (Va.), William Cohen (Maine), John McCain (Ariz.), Trent Lott (Miss.), Dan Coats (Ind.), Bob Smith (N.H.), Dirk Kempthorne (Ind.), Launch Faircloth (N.C.), Kay Bailey Hutchison (Tex.)

Subcommittees
Coalition Defense and Reinforcing Forces
(D) Levin, Chm.; Exon, Glenn, Shelby, Byrd, Graham
(R) Warner, Cohen, Coats, Smith, Kempthorne

Defense Technology, Acquisition, and Industrial Base
(D) Bingaman, Chm.; Levin, Kennedy, Byrd, Graham, Robb, Lieberman

(R) Smith, Cohen, Lott, Coats, Kempthorne, Faircloth

Military Readiness and Defense Infrastructure
(D) Glenn, Chm.; Bingaman, Shelby, Robb
(R) McCain, Smith, Faircloth

Regional Defense and Contingency Forces
(D) Kennedy, Chm.; Exon, Graham, Robb, Lieberman
(R) Cohen, Warner, McCain, Lott

Force Requirements and Personnel
(D) Shelby, Chm.; Kennedy, Byrd, Lieberman
(R) Coats, McCain, Faircloth

Nuclear Deterrence, Arms Control, and Defense Intelligence
(D) Exon, Chm.; Levin, Bingaman, Glenn
(R) Lott, Warner, Kempthorne

Committee on Banking, Housing and Urban Affairs

534 SDOB 20510. Phone 202-224-7391 (Steve Harris, Staff Dir.)

Jurisdiction over legislation dealing with bank regulation, domestic monetary policy, financial aid to commerce and industry, the measurement of economic activity, federal loan guarantees, economic stabilization measures (including wage and price controls), gold and precious metals transactions, coins and currency, oversees the Federal Reserve System, public and private housing, urban development and mass transit and nursing home construction.

Democrats
Donald Riegle (Mich.), Chairman; Paul Sarbanes (Md.), Chris Dodd (Conn.), Jim Sasser (Tenn.), Richard Shelby (Ala.), John Kerry (Mass.), Richard Bryan (Nev.), Barbara Boxer (Calif.), Ben Nighthorse Campbell (Colo.), Carol Mosley-Braun (Ill.), Patty Murray (Wash.)

Republicans
Alfonse D'Amato (N.Y.), Ranking Member; Phil Gramm (Tex.), Kit Bond (Mo.), Connie Mack (Fla.), Bill Roth (Del.), Launch Faircloth (N.C.), Robert Bennett (Utah), Pete Domenici (N.Mex.)

Subcommittees
Economic Stabilization and Rural Development
(D) Shelby, Chm.; Campbell, Dodd, Kerry, Bryan
(R) Faircloth, Bennett, Gramm, Mack

Housing and Urban Affairs
(D) Sarbanes, Chm.; Dodd, Kerry, Bryan, Boxer, Mosley-Braun
(R) Bond, Domenici, Mack, Faircloth, Roth

International Finance and Monetary Policy
(D) Sasser, Chm.; Murray, Sarbanes, Kerry, Boxer, Campbell
(R) Gramm, Roth, Bennett, Bond, Mack

Securities
(D) Dodd, Chm.; Sasser, Shelby, Bryan, Moseley-Braun
(R) Gramm, Roth, Bond, Faircloth, Domenici

Committee on Budget

621 SDOB 20510. Phone 202-224-0642 (Larry Stein, Staff Dir.)

Jurisdiction over first budget resolution, which sets target totals for spending and revenues, budget surplus or deficit, and the federal debt, and, later in the session, a second resolution, which sets a binding spending ceiling and either affirms or revises the initial budget targets; conducts studies of budget matters; makes available statistics pertaining to congressional budget actions.

Democrats
Jim Sasser (Tenn.), Chairman; Ernest Hollings (S.C.), J. Bennett Johnston (La.), Donald Riegle (Mich.), James Exon (Nebr.), Frank Lautenberg (N.J.), Paul Simon (Ill.), Chris Dodd (Conn.), Paul Sarbanes (Md.), Barbara Boxer (Calif.), Patty Murray (Wash.)

Republicans
Pete Dominici (N.Mex.), Ranking Member; Chuck Grassley (Iowa), Don Nickles (Okla.), Phil Gramm (Tex.), Kit Bond (Mo.), Trent Lott (Miss.), Hank Brown (Colo.), Slade Gorton (Wash.), Judd Greg (N.H.)

No subcommittees

Committee on Commerce, Science and Transportation

254 SROB 20510. Phone 202-224-5115 (Kevin Curtin, Staff Dir.)

Jurisdiction over legislation related to U.S. Fire Administration and Fire Research Center of National Bureau of Standards; radiation hazards of consumer products and machines used in industry; all ocean-related matters, such as interoceanic canals-including Panama Canal (shared with Senate Armed Services Committee) international fishing laws and Law of the Sea, deep seabed mining (shared with Senate Energy and Natural Resources Committee), ocean charting; motor vehicle safety; the Commerce Dept. and its scientific activities, including National Oceanic and Atmospheric Administration; National Aeronautics and Space Administration, including aeronautical research and development overseas federal fire prevention, Earthquake Hazards Act, Transportation Dept. and National Transportation Safety Board, Federal Maritime Commission and Maritime Administration, maritime safety and ports, including safety security and regulation, and Interstate Commerce Commission, Regulates consumer products and services, including testing related to toxic substances.

Democrats
Ernest Hollings (S.C.), Chairman; Daniel Inouye (Hawaii), Wendell Ford (Ky.), James Exon (Nebr.), Jay Rockefeller (W.Va.), Bob Kreuger (Tex.), John Kerry (Mass.), John Breaux (La.), Richard Bryan (Nev.), Chuck Robb (Va.)

Republicans
John Danforth (Mo.), Ranking Member; Bob Packwood (Oreg.), Larry Pressler (S.Dak.), Ted Stevens (Alaska), Robert Kasten (Wis.), John McCain (Ariz.), Conrad Burns (Mont.), Slade Gorton (Wash.), Trent Lott (Miss.), Kay Bailey Hutchison (Tex.)

Subcommittees
Aviation
(D) Ford, Chm; Exon, Inouye, Kerry, Bryan
(R) Pressler, McCain, Stevens, Gorton

Communications
(D) Inouye, Chm; Hollings, Ford, Exon, Kerry, Breaux, Rockefeller, Robb
(R) Packwood, Pressler, Stevens, McCain, Burns, Gorton

Consumer
(D) Bryan, Chm.; Ford, Dorgan, Kreuger
(R) Gorton, McCain, Burns

Foreign Commerce and Tourism
(D) Kerry, Chm.; Rockefeller, Hollings, Bryan, Dorgan
(R) Gregg, Packwood, Pressler

Merchant Marine
(D) Breaux, Chm.; Inouye, Kreuger
(R) Lott, Stevens

Science, Technology, and Space
(D) Rockefeller, Chm.; Hollings, Kerry, Bryan, Robb, Kreuger
(R) Burns, Pressler, Lott, Gregg

Surface Transportation
(D) Exon, Chm.; Rockefeller, Inouye, Breaux, Robb, Dorgan, Kreuger
(R) McCain, Packwood, Burns, Lott, Gregg

National Ocean Policy Study
(D) Hollings, Chm.; Kerry, Inouye, Ford, Breaux, Robb, Kreuger
(R) Stevens, Danforth, Packwood, Pressler, Gorton, Lott, Gregg

Committee on Energy and Natural Resources
364 SDOB 20510. Phone 202-224-4971 (Benjamin S. Cooper, Staff Dir.)

Jurisdiction over legislation on energy policy, regulation and conservation, research and development, commercialization of new technologies, nonmilitary development of nuclear energy, oil and gas production and distribution (including price), liquefied natural gas projects, energy-related aspects of deepwater ports, hydro-electric power, coal production and distribution, mining and mineral conservation, leasing and the extraction of minerals from the ocean and outer continental-shelf lands, naval petroleum reserves in Alaska, coal slurry pipelines; overseas territories (Guam, American Samoa, Puerto Rico, the U.S. Virgin Islands, and the Trust Territory of the Pacific Islands).

Democrats
J. Bennett Johnston (La.), Chairman; Dale Bumpers (Ark.), Wendell Ford (Ky.), Bill Bradley (N.J.), Jeff Bingaman (N.Mex.), Daniel Akaka (Hawaii), Richard Shelby (Ala.), Paul Wellstone (Minn.), Ben Nighthorse Campbell (Colo.), Harlan Matthews (Tenn.), Robert Kreuger (Tex.)

Republicans
Malcolm Wallop (Wyo.), Ranking Member; Mark Hatfield (Oreg.), Pete Domenici (N.Mex.), Frank Murkowski (Alaska), Don Nickles (Okla.), Larry Craig (Idaho), Robert Bennett (Utah), Arlen Specter (Pa.), Trent Lott (Miss.)

Subcommittees

Renewable Energy, Energy Efficiency, and Competitiveness
(D) Bingaman, Chm.; Akaka, Bradley, Shelby, Wellstone, Matthews, Kreuger
(R) Nickles, Specter, Lott, Domenici, Murkowski, Hatfield

Mineral Resources Development and Production
(D) Akaka, Chm.; Matthews, Bumpers, Ford, Campbell
(R) Craig, Murkowski, Nickles, Bennett

Public Lands, National Parks, and Forests
(D) Bumpers, Chm.; Campbell, Bradley, Bingaman, Akaka, Shelby, Wellstone, Kreuger
(R) Murkowski, Hatfield, Lott, Domenici, Bennett, Craig, Specter

Energy Research and Development
(D) Ford, Chm.; Shelby, Bumpers, Bingaman, Wellstone, Matthews, Kreuger
(R) Domenici, Specter, Nickles, Craig, Lott

Water and Power
(D) Bradley, Chm.; Ford, Campbell
(R) Bennett, Hatfield

Committee on Environment and Public Works

458 SDOB 20510. Phone 202-224-6176 (Peter Scher, Staff Dir.)

Jurisdiction over most legislation and programs involving environmental affairs, including pollution control programs for air, water, noise, and solid waste; the National Environmental Policy Act, the Resource Conservation and Recovery Act, and the Toxic Substances Control Act, Oversight of the Environmental Protection Agency, Council on Environmental Quality, Nuclear Regulatory Commission, and U.S. Fish and Wildlife Services.

Democrats

Max Baucus (Mont.), Chairman; Daniel Patrick Moynihan (N.Y.), George Mitchell (Maine), Frank Lautenberg (N.J.), Harry Reid (Nev.), Bob Graham (Fla.), Joe Lieberman (Conn.), Howard Metzenbaum (Ohio), Harris Wofford (Pa.), Barbara Boxer (Calif.)

Republicans

John Chafee (R.I.), Ranking Member; Alan Simpson (Wyo.), Dave Durenberger (Minn.), John Warner (Va.), Bob Smith (N.H.), Launch Faircloth (N.C.), Dirk Kempthorne (Ind.)

Subcommittees

Clean Water, Fisheries, and Wildlife
(D) Graham, Chm.; Mitchell, Lautenberg, Reid, Lieberman, Wofford
(R) Chafee, Simpson, Durenberger, Warner, Jeffords, Symms

Toxic Substances, Research and Development
(D) Reid, Chm.; Lautenberg, Lieberman, Wofford, Boxer
(R) Smith, Warner, Simpson, Faircloth

Clean Air and Nuclear Regulation
(D) Lieberman, Chm.; Moynihan, Graham, Metzenbaum
(R) Simpson, Faircloth, Kempthorne

Superfund, Recycling, and Solid Waste Management
(D) Lautenberg, Chm.; Moynihan, Gramm, Metzenbaum, Wofford, Boxer
(R) Durenberger, Simpson, Smith, Warner

Water Resources, Transportation, Public Buildings, and Economic Development
(D) Moynihan, Chm.; Mitchell, Reid, Metzenbaum, Wofford, Boxer
(R) Warner, Durenberger, Smith, Kempthorne

Committee on Finance

205 SDOB 20510. Phone 202-224-4515 (Lawrence O'Donnell, Staff Dir.)

Jurisdiction over legislation relating to taxes and credits for public financing of federal elections; revenue sharing (shared with Senate Governmental Affairs Committee); international monetary matters (shared with Senate Foreign Relations and Banking, Housing and Urban Affairs Committees); tax-exempt foundations and charitable trusts; taxation of pension contributions; and sugar, including sugar imports (shared with Senate Agriculture, Nutrition and Forestry Committee). Oversees Internal Revenue Service, Treasury Dept., and Bureau of Alcohol, Tobacco and Firearms.

Democrats

Daniel Patrick Moynihan (N.Y.), Chairman; Max Baucus (Mont.), David Boren (Okla.), Bill Bradley (N.J.), George Mitchell (Maine), David Pryor (Ark.), Donald Riegle (Mich.), Jay Rockefeller (W.Va.), Tom Daschle (S.Dak.), John Breaux (La.), Kent Conrad (N.Dak.)

Republicans
Bob Packwood (Oreg.), Ranking Member; Bob Dole (Kans.), William Roth (Del.), John Danforth (Mo.), John Chafee (R.I.), David Durenberger (Minn.), Charles Grassley (Iowa), Orrin Hatch (Utah), Malcolm Wallop (Wyo.)

Subcommittees
Energy and Agricultural Taxation
(D) Daschle, Chm.; Boren, Breaux
(R) Hatch, Dole, Wallop

Health for Families and the Uninsured
(D) Riegle, Chm.; Bradley, Mitchell, Rockefeller
(R) Chafee, Roth, Durenberger, Danforth

Deficits, Debt Management, and International Debt
(D) Bradley, Chm.; Riegle
(R) Wallop

International Trade
(D) Baucus, Chm.; Moynihan, Boren, Bradley, Mitchell, Riegle, Rockefeller, Daschle, Breaux, Conrad
(R) Danforth, Packwood, Roth, Chafee, Grassley, Hatch, Wallop

Private Retirement Plans and Oversight of the Internal Revenue Service
(D) Pryor, Chm.; Moynihan
(R) Grassley

Social Security and Family Policy
(D) Breaux, Chm.; Moynihan
(R) Dole, Durenberger

Taxation
(D) Boren, Chm.; Baucus, Pryor, Conrad
(R) Roth, Packwood, Danforth

Medicare and Long Term Care
(D) Rockefeller, Chm.; Baucus, Mitchell, Pryor, Daschle, Conrad
(R) Durenberger, Packwood, Dole, Chafee, Danforth, Hatch

Committee on Foreign Relations
446 SDOB 20510. Phone 202-224-3953 (Geryld Christianson, Staff Dir.)

Jurisdiction over legislation on foreign economic assistance; foreign wars; international organizations; international economic and monetary pol-icy as it relates to U.S. foreign policy (shared with Senate Finance and Banking, Housing and Urban Affairs Committees); educational and cultural exchange programs; foreign service; human rights; international boundaries; international narcotics control; embassy security; control of international terrorism (shared with Senate Judiciary committee); exchange of prisoners between the U.S. and Canada and Mexico; protection of Americans abroad; United Nations; arms control; disarmament and nuclear nonproliferation. Oversees State Dept., Peace Corps, Intl. Dev. Cooperation Agency and U.S. Arms Control and Disarmament Agency.

Democrats
Claiborne Pell (R.I.), Chairman; Joe Biden (Del.), Paul Sarbanes (Md.), Alan Cranston (Calif.), Chris Dodd (Conn.), John Kerry (Mass.), Paul Simon (Ill.), Daniel Patrick Moynihan (N.Y.), Chuck Robb (Va.), Harris Wofford (Pa.), Russell Feingold (Wis.), Harlan Matthews Tenn.)

Republicans
Jesse Helms (N.C.), Ranking Member; Richard Lugar (Ind.), Nancy Kassebaum (Kans.), Larry Pressler (S.Dak.), Frank Murkowski (Alaska), Hank Brown (Colo.), James Jeffords (Vt.), Paul Coverdell (Ga.)

Subcommittees
African Affairs
(D) Simon, Chm.; Moynihan, Feingold
(R) Jeffords, Kassebaum

East Asian and Pacific Affairs
(D) Robb, Chm.; Biden, Kerry, Matthews
(R) Murkowski, Lugar, Pressler

European Affairs
(D) Biden, Chm.; Sarbanes, Simon, Feingold
(R) Lugar, Kassebaum, Brown

International Economic Policy, Trade, Oceans, and Environment
(D) Sarbanes, Chm.; Biden, Dodd, Kerry, Wofford, Feingold
(R) Kassebaum, Helms, Murkowski, Brown, Jeffords

Near Eastern and South Asian Affairs
(D) Moynihan, Chm.; Sarbanes, Robb, Wofford, Matthews
(R) Brown, Pressler, Jeffords, Coverdell

Terrorism, Narcotics, and International Communications
(D) Kerry, Chm.; Pell, Dodd, Simon, Moynihan
(R) Pressler, Helms, Murkowski, Coverdell

Western Hemisphere and Peace Corps Affairs
(D) Dodd, Chm.; Robb, Wofford, Matthews
(R) Coverdell, Helms, Lugar

Committee on Governmental Affairs
340 SDOB 20510. Phone 202-224-4751 (Lenord Weiss, Staff Dir.)

Jurisdiction over federal civil service; governmental information including the census; congressional organization; District of Columbia; organization and management of nuclear export policy; executive branch organization and reorganization; salary of members of Congress; relationship of U.S. to international organizations such as the United Nations, National Security Council.

Democrats
John Glenn (Ohio), Chairman; Sam Nunn (Ga.), Carl Levin (Mich.), Jim Sasser (Tenn.), David Pryor (Ark.), Joe Lieberman (Conn.), Daniel Akaka (Hawaii), Byron Dorgan (N.Dak.)

Republicans
William Roth (Del.), Ranking Member; Ted Stevens (Alaska), William Cohen (Maine), Thad Cochran (Miss.), John McCain (Ariz.)

Subcommittees
Permanent Subcommittee on Investigations
(D) Nunn, Chm.; Glenn, Levin, Sasser, Pryor, Lieberman, Dorgan
(R) Roth, Stevens, Cohen, Cochran, McCain

Federal Services, Post Office, and Civil Service
(D) Pryor, Chm.; Sasser, Akaka
(R) Stevens, Cochran

Government Information and Regulation
(D) Lieberman, Chm.; Nunn, Levin, Dorgan
(R) Cochran, Cohen, McCain

General Services, Federalism, and the District of Columbia
(D) Sasser, Chm.; Lieberman, Akaka
(R) McCain, Stevens

Oversight of Government Management
(D) Levin, Chm.; Pryor, Lieberman, Akaka, Nunn, Dorgan
(R) Cohen, Stevens, Cochran, McCain

Committee on the Judiciary
224 SDOB 20510. Phone 202-224-5225 (Catherine Russell, Staff Director)

Jurisdiction over legislation on drug abuse, including regulatory aspects of federal drug abuse programs and criminal justice system rehabilitation programs for juvenile drug abusers; international terrorism (shared with Senate Foreign Relations Committee); holidays and celebrations; judicial proceedings; constitutional amendments; civil liberties; federal judiciary; federal corrections system; protection of trade and commerce against unlawful restraints and monopolies; patents, copyrights and trademarks; bankruptcy, mutiny, espionage and counterfeiting; immigration and naturalization; revision and codification of the Statutes of the U.S.; internal security; local courts in the territories and possessions; measures relating to claims against the U.S. and State and territorial boundary lines. Oversees Justice Dept. and U.S. courts, except U.S. Tax Court; organized crime; gun control; domestic terrorism; some aspects of narcotics abuse, including control, enforcement, criminal penalties, regulation of trade, import-export control; all aspects of criminal law and procedure including rules of criminal procedure, and revision of U.S. criminal code; any claims against the U.S., Office of Justice programs; federal judicial appointments; reapportionment.

Democrats
Joe Biden (Del.), Chairman; Edward Kennedy (Mass.), Howard Metzenbaum (Ohio), Dennis DeConcini (Ariz.), Patrick Leahy (Vt.), Howell Heflin (Ala.), Paul Simon (Ill.), Herb Kohl (Wis.), Dianne Feinstein (Calif.), Carol Mosley Braun (Ill.)

Republicans
Orrin Hatch (Utah), Ranking Member; Strom Thurmond (S.C.), Alan Simpson (Wyo.), Chuck Grassley (Iowa), Arlen Specter (Pa.), Hank Brown (Colo.), William Cohen (Maine), Larry Pressler (S.Dak.)

Subcommittees
Antitrust, Monopolies, and Business Rights
(D) Metzenbaum, Chm.; DeConcini, Heflin, Simon
(R) Thurmond, Specter, Hatch

Constitution
(D) Simon, Chm.; Metzenbaum, DeConcini, Kennedy
(R) Brown, Hatch

Courts and Administrative Practice
(D) Heflin, Chm.; Metzenbaum, Kohl, Moseley-Braun
(R) Grassley, Thurmond, Cohen

Immigration and Refugee Affairs
(D) Kennedy, Chm.; Simon
(R) Simpson

Patents, Copyrights, and Trademarks
(D) DeConcini, Chm.; Kennedy, Leahy, Heflin, Feinstein
(R) Hatch, Simpson, Grassley, Brown

Technology and the Law
(D) Leahy, Chm.; Kohl, Feinstein
(R) Specter, Pressler

Juvenile Justice
(D) Kohl, Biden, Moseley-Braun
(R) Cohen, Pressler

Committee on Labor and Human Resources

428 SDOB 20510. Phone 202-224-5375 (Nick Littlefield, Staff Dir.)

Matters relating to education, labor, health, aging, and the public welfare; arts and humanities; biomedical research; drugs, vaccines, and drug labeling and packaging; occupational safety and health; health matters and national health insurance proposals; equal employment opportunities; private pension plans; labor standards; wages and hours of labor; student loan programs; railway labor and retirement. Oversees Equal Employment Opportunity Commission, National Labor Relations Board, National Mediation Board, Labor Dept., ACTION, Health and Human Services Dept., Legal Services Corp.

Democrats
Edward Kennedy (Mass.), Chairman; Claiborne Pell (R.I.), Howard Metzenbaum (Ohio), Chris Dodd (Conn.), Paul Simon (Ill.), Tom Harkin (Iowa), Barbara Mikulski (Md.), Jeff Bingaman (N.Mex.), Paul Wellstone (Minn.), Harris Wofford (Pa.)

Republicans
Nancy Kassebaum (Kans.), Ranking Member; Orrin Hatch (Utah), Strom Thurmond (S.C.),

Judd Gregg (N.H.), Dave Durenberger (Minn.), Jim Jeffords (Vt.), Dan Coats (Ind.)

Subcommittees

Aging
(D) Mikulski, Chm.; Pell, Metzenbaum, Dodd, Wofford
(R) Gregg, Durenberger, Coats

Children, Family, Drugs and Alcoholism
(D) Dodd, Chm.; Pell, Mikulski, Bingaman, Kennedy, Wellstone, Wofford
(R) Coats, Kassebaum, Jeffords, Thurmond, Durenberger, Gregg

Education, Arts, and the Humanities
(D) Pell, Chm.; Metzenbaum, Dodd, Simon, Mikulski, Bingaman, Kennedy, Wellstone, Harkin, Wofford
(R) Jeffords, Kassebaum, Hatch, Thurmond, Coats, Gregg, Durenberger

Employment and Productivity
(D) Simon, Chm.; Harkin, Mikulski, Bingaman, Wofford
(R) Thurmond, Coats, Hatch, Gregg

Disability Policy
(D) Harkin, Chm.; Metzenbaum, Simon, Bingaman
(R) Durenberger, Hatch, Jeffords

Labor
(D) Metzenbaum Chm.; Harkin, Dodd, Kennedy, Wellstone
(R) Hatch, Jeffords, Thurmond, Kassebaum

Committee on Rules and Administration

311 SROB 20510. Phone 202-224-6352 (James King, Staff Dir.)

Jurisdiction over printing, binding and distribution of Congressional publications; executive papers; depository libraries; federal elections; corrupt practices; political action committees; all matters relating to Senate office buildings and to conduct of business; banking privilege. Oversees Federal Election Commission, Library of Congress, Smithsonian Institution.

Democrats
Wendell Ford (Ky.), Chairman; Claiborne Pell (R.I.), Robert Byrd (W.Va.), Daniel Inouye (Hawaii), Dennis DeConcini (Ariz.), Daniel Patrick Moynihan (N.Y.), Chris Dodd (Conn.), Dianne Feinstein (Calif.), Harlan Matthews (Tenn.)

Republicans
Ted Stevens (Alaska), Ranking Member; Mark Hatfield (Oreg.), Jesse Helms (N.C.), John Warner (Va.), Bob Dole (Kans.), Mitch McConnell (Ky.), Thad Cochran (Miss.)

No subcommittees

Committee on Small Business
428 A SROB 20510. Phone 202-224-5175 (John Ball, Staff Dir.)

Studies and makes recommendations on problems of American small business, on programs involving minority enterprise; on environmental, energy, and pollution issues as they relate to small businesses. Oversees Small Business Administration, Occupational Safety and Health Administration as it affects small business.

Democrats
Dale Bumpers (Ark.), Chairman; Sam Nunn (Ga.), Max Baucus (Mont.), Carl Levin (Mich.), Tom Harkin (Iowa), John Kerry (Mass.), Barbara Mikulski (Md.), Joe Lieberman (Conn.), Paul Wellstone (Minn.), Harris Wofford (Pa.), Howell Heflin (Ala.), Frank Lautenberg (N.J.), Herb Kohl (Wis.), Carol Mosley-Braun (Ill.)

Republicans
Larry Pressler (S.Dak.), Ranking Member; Malcolm Wallop (Wyo.), Kit Bond (Mo.), Connie Mack (Fla.), Conrad Burns (Mont.), Ted Stevens (Alaska), Paul Coverdall (Ga.), Dirk Kempthorne (Ind.), Robert Bennett (Utah), John Chaffee (R.I.), Kay Bailey Hutchison (Tex.)

Subcommittees
Competitiveness, Capital Formation and Economic Opportunity
(D) Lieberman, Chm.; Harkin, Lautenberg
(R) Mack, Bond

Export Expansion and Agricultural Development
(D) Wofford, Chm,; Harkin, Bumpers, Lautenberg, Moseley-Braun
(R) Coverdell, Pressler, Bennett, Chaffee

Government Contracting and Paperwork Reduction
(D) Nunn, Chm.; Lieberman, Harkin, Kohl
(R) Bond, Wollop

Innovation, Manufacturing, and Technology
(D) Levin, Chm.; Kerry, Bumpers, Heflin
(R) Burns, Kempthorne, Bennett

Rural Economy and Family Farming
(D) Wellstone, Chm.; Nunn, Levin, Bumpers, Heflin, Kohl
(R) Pressler, Wallop, Burns, Coverdell, Kempthorne

Urban and Minority-Owned Business Development
(D) Kerry, Chm.; Nunn, Wellstone, Wofford, Moseley-Braun
(R) Chaffee, Mack, Pressler

Committee on Veterans Affairs
414 SROB 20510. Phone 202-224-9126 (Jim Gottlieb, Staff Dir.)

Jurisdiction over veterans' legislation, including Arlington National Cemetery. Oversees operations of Veterans' Administration.

Democrats
Jay Rockefeller (W.Va.), Chairman; Dennis DeConcini (Ariz.), George Mitchell (Maine), Bob Graham (Fla.), Daniel Akaka (Hawaii), Tom Dashle (S.Dak.), Ben Nighthorse Campbell (Colo.)

Republicans
Frank H. Murkowski (Alaska) Ranking Member; Alan Simpson (Wyo.), Strom Thurmond (S.C.), Arlen Specter (Pa.), Jim Jeffords (Vt.)

No subcommittees

SENATE SELECT COMMITTEES
Select Committee on Aging
G-31 SDOB 20510. Phone 202-224-5264 (Portia Mittelman, Staff Dir.)

Democrats
David Pryor (Ark.), Chairman; John Glenn (Ohio), Bill Bradley (N.J.), J. Bennett Johnson (La.), John Breaux (La.), Richard Shelby (Ala.), Harry Reid (Nev.), Bob Graham (Fla.), Herb Kohl (Wis.), Russell Feingold (Wis.), Bob Kreuger (Tex.)

Republicans
William Cohen (Maine), Ranking Member; Larry Pressler (S.Dak.), Charles Grassley (Iowa), Alan Simpson (Wyo.), Jim Jeffords (Vt.), John McCain (Ariz.), David Durenburger (Minn.), Larry Craig (Ind.), Conrad Burns (Mont.), Arlen Specter (Pa.)

Select Committee on Ethics

220 SHOB 20510. Phone 202-224-2981 (Victor Baird, Chief Council)

Democrats

Richard Bryan (Nev.), Chairman; Barbara Mikulski (Md.), Thomas Daschle (S.Dak.)

Republicans

Mitch McConnell (Ky.), Vice-Chairman; Robert C. Smith (N.H.), Ted Stevens (Alaska)

No Subcommittees

Select Committee on Indian Affairs

838 SHOB 20510. Phone 202-224-2251 (Patricia Zell, Staff Dir.)

Democrats

Daniel K. Inouye (Hawaii) Chairman; Dennis DeConcini (Ariz.), Thomas Daschle (S.Dak.), Kent Conrad (N.Dak.), Harry Reid (Nev.), Daniel Akaka (Hawaii), Paul Wellstone (Minn.), Paul Simon (Ill.), Byron Dorgan (N.Dak.), Ben Nighthorse Campbell (Colo.)

Republicans

John McCain (Ariz.), Ranking Member; Frank Mukowski (Alaska), Thad Cochran (Miss.), Slade Gorton (Wash.), Nancy Kassenbaum (Kans.), Pete Domenici (N.Mex.), Don Nickles (Okla.), Mark Hatfield (Oreg.)

Select Committee on Intelligence

211 SHOB 20510. Phone 202-224-1700 (Norman Bradley, Staff Dir.)

Democrats

Dennis DeConcini (Ariz.), Chairman; Howard Metzenbaum (Ohio), John Glenn (Ohio), Bob Kerry (Nebr.), Richard Bryan (Nev.), Bob Graham (Fla.), Max Baucus (Mont.), J. Bennett Johnston (La.)

Republicans

John Warner (Va.), Vice-Chairman; Alfonse D'Amato (N.Y.), John Danforth (Mo.), Slade Gorton (Wash.), John Chafee (R.I.), Ted Stevens (Ark.), Richard Lugar (Ind.), Malcolm Wallop (Wyo.)

No Subcommittees

JOINT COMMITTEES OF CONGRESS

Joint Economic Committee

G-01 SDOB; 20510-8002. Phone 202-224-5171 (Steve Quick, Ex. Dir.)

Chairman: Rep. David R. Obey (D-Wis.)
Vice-Chairman: Sen. Paul S. Sarbanes (D-Md.)

Senate Members

(D) Paul Sarbanes (Md.), Edward Kennedy (Mass.), Jeff Bingaman (N.Mex.), Richard Bryan (Nev.), Charles Robb (Va.), Byron Dorgan (N. Dak.)
(R) William Roth (Del.), Larry Craig (Idaho), Connie Mack (Fla.), Robert Bennett (Utah)

House Members

(D) David Obey (Wis.), Lee Hamilton (Ind.), Kwesi Mfume (Md.), Ron Wyden (Oreg.), Michael Andrews (Tex.)
(R) Richard Armey (Tex.), Jim Saxton (N.J.), Christopher Cox (Calif.), Jim Ramstad (Minn.)

Joint Committee on the Organization of Congress

175D Ford Bldg; 20515. Phone 202-226-0650 (Kim Wincup, Staff Dir.)

Senate Chairman: David Boren (D-Okla.)
Senate Vice-Chairman: Pete Domenici (R-N.Mex.)

House Chairman: Lee Hamilton (D-Ind.)
House Vice-Chairman: David Dreier (R-Calif.)

Senate Members

(D) Jim Sasser (Tenn.), Wendell Ford (Ky.), Harry Reid (Nev.), Paul Sarbanes (Md.), David Pryor (Ark.)
(R) Nancy Kassebaum (Kans.), Trent Lott (Miss.), Ted Stevens (Ark.), William Cohen (Maine), Richard Lugar (Ind.)

House Members

(D) David Obey (Wis.), Al Swift (Wash.), Sam Gejdenson (Conn.), John Spratt (S.C.), Eleanor Holmes Norton (D.C.)
(R) Robert Walker (Pa.), Gerald Solomon (N.Y.), Bill Emerson (Mo.), Wayne Allard (Colo.), Jennifer Dunn (Wash.)

Joint Committee on Taxation

1015 LHOB 20515. Phone 202-225-3621 (Harry L. Getmen, Chief-of-staff)

Chairman: Rep. Dan Rostenkowski (D-Ill.)
Vice-Chairman: Sen. Daniel Patrick Moynihan (D-N.Y.)

Senate Members
(D) Max Baucus (Mont.), Daniel P. Moynihan (N.Y.), David Boren (Okla.)
(R) Bob Packwood (Oreg.), Robert Dole (Kans.)

House Members
(D) Daniel Rostenkowski (Ill.), Sam Gibbons (Fla.), J.J. Pickle (Tex.)
(R) Bill Archer (Tex.), Phil Crane (Ill.)

Joint Committee on the Library

Rm. 103, Annex 1, 20515. Phone 202-226-7633 (Hilary Lieber, Staff Dir.)

Chairman: Rep. Charles Rose (D-N.C.)
Vice-Chairman: Sen. Claiborne Pell (D-R.I.)

Senate Members
(D) Claiborne Pell (R.I.), Dennis DeConcini (Ariz.), Daniel Moynihan (N.Y.)
(R) Mark Hatfield (Oreg.), Ted Stevens (Alaska)

House Members
(D) Charles Rose (N.C.), Joe Kolter (Pa.), Thomas Manton (N.Y.)
(R) Bill Barrett (Nebr.), Pat Roberts (Kans.)

Joint Committee on Printing

818 SHOB 20510. Phone 202-224-5241 (John Chambers, Staff Dir.)

Chairman: Sen. Wendall Ford (D-Ky.)
Vice Chairman: Rep. Charles Rose (D-N.C.)

Senate Members
(D) Wendell Ford (Ky.), Dennis DeConcini (Ariz.), Harlan Matthews (Tenn.)
(R) Ted Stevens (Alaska), Mark Hatfield (Oreg.)

House Members
(D) Charles Rose (N.C.), Sam Gejdenson (Conn.), Gerald Kleczka (Wis.)
(R) Pat Roberts (Kans.), Newt Gingrich (Ga.)

STANDING COMMITTEES OF THE HOUSE

Committee on Agriculture

1301 LHOB 20515. Phone 202-225-2171 (Diane Powell, Staff Dir.)

Jurisdiction over agricultural legislation, including animal and forestry industries, rural issues, nutrition, price supports. Oversees Agriculture Dept.

Democrats
E. (Kika) de la Garza (Tex.), Chairman; George Brown (Calif.), Charlie Rose (N.C.), Glenn English (Okla.), Dan Glickman (Kans.), Charles Stenholm (Tex.), Harold Volkmer (Mo.), Tim Penny (Minn.), Tim Johnson (S.Dak.), Bill Sarpalius (Tex.), Jill Long (Ind.), Gary Condit (Calif.), Cal Dooley (Calif.), Mike Kopetski (Oreg.), Collin Peterson (Minn.), Eva Clayton (N.C.), David Minge (Minn.), Earl Hilliard (Ala.), Jay Inslee (Wash.), Tom Barlow (Ky.), Earl Pomeroy (N.Dak.), Tim Holden (Pa.), Cynthia McKinney (Ga.), Scotty Baesler (Ky.), Karen Thurman (Fla.), Sanford Bishop (Ga.), Bernie Thompson (Miss.)

Republicans
Pat Roberts (Kans.), Ranking Member; Bill Emerson (Mo.), Steve Gunderson (Wis.), Tom Lewis (Fla.), Bob Smith (Oreg.), Larry Combest (Tex.), Dave Camp (Mich.), Wayne Allard (Iowa), Bill Barrett (Nebr.), Jim Nussle (Iowa), John Boehner (Ohio), Tom Ewing (Ill.), John Doolittle (Calif.), Jack Kingston (Ga.), Bob Goodlatte (Va.), Jay Dickey (Ark.), Richard Pombo (Calif.), Charles Canady (Fla.)

Subcommittees (Commodity)
General Farm Commodities
(D) Glickman, Chm.; Peterson, Volkmer, Long, Dooley, Minge, Pomeroy, Rose, English, Stenholm, Sarpalius, Condit, Barlow, Bishop, Clayton
(R) Emerson, Bob Smith, Combest, Barrett, Nussle, Boehner, Ewing, Doolittle, Dickey

Livestock
(D) Volkmer, Chm.; Baesler, Bishop, Brown, Condit, Clayton, Thurman, Minge, Inslee, Pomeroy, English, Stenholm, Peterson
(R) Tom Lewis, Emerson, Doolittle, Kingston, Goodlatte, Dickey, Pombo

Speciality Crops and Natural Resources
(D) Rose, Chm.; Baesler, Bishop, Brown, Con-

dit, Clayton, Thurman, Minge, Inslee, Pomeroy, English, Stenholm, Peterson
(R) Lewis, Emerson, Doolittle, Kingston, Goodlatte, Dickey, Pombo

Subcommittees (Operational)
Operations and Nutrition
(D) Stenholm, Chm.; Brown, Sarpalius, Dooley, Inslee, English, Glickman, Johnson, McKinney, Bishop, Volkmer, Clayton, Holden, Rose
(R) Bob Smith, Emerson, Gunderson, Allard, Barrett, Ewing, Kingston, Canady

Environment, Credit, and Rural Development
(D) English, Chm.; Johnson, Long, Clayton, Minge, Barlow, Pomeroy, Holden, McKinney, Thurman, Penney, Sarpalius, Peterson, Hilliard, Inslee, Baesler
(R) Combest, Gunderson, Camp, Allard, Barrett, Nussle, Ewing, Dickey, Pombo

Foreign Agriculture and Hunger
(D) Penny, Chm.; Rose, Barlow, McKinney, Baesler, Thurman, Pomeroy, Stenholm
(R) Allard, Lewis, Doolittle, Canady

Committee on Appropriations
H-218 The Capitol 20515-6015. Phone 202-225-2771 (Frederick Mohrman, Staff Dir.)

Jurisdiction over legislation to appropriate revenues for the government.

Democrats
Bill Natcher (Ky.), Chairman; James Whitten (Miss.), Neal Smith (Iowa), Sid Yates (Ill.), David Obey (Wis.), Louis Stokes (Ohio), Tom Bevill (Ala.), John Murtha (Pa.), Charlie Wilson (Tex.), Norman Dicks (Wash.), Martin Sabo (Minn.), Julian Dixon (Calif.), Vic Fazio (Calif.), Bill Hefner (N.C.), Steny Hoyer (Md.), Bob Carr (Mich.), Richard Durbin (Ill.), Ronald Coleman (Tex.), Alan Mollohan (W.Va.), Jim Chapman (Tex.), Marcy Kaptur (Ohio), Nancy Pelosi (Calif.), David Price (N.C.), David Skaggs (Colo.), Larry Smith (Fla.), Peter Visclosky (Ind.), Thomas Foglietta (Pa.), Esteban Edward Torres (Calif.), Buddy Darden (Ga.), Nita Lowery (N.Y.), Ray Thornton (Ark.), Jose Serranno (N.Y.), Rosa DeLauro (Conn.), James Moran (Va.), Pete Peterson (Fla.), John Olver (Mass.), Ed Pastor (Ariz.), Carrie Meek (Fla.)

Republicans
Joe McDade (Pa.), Ranking Member; John Myers (Ind.), Bill Young (Fla.), Ralph Regula (Ohio), Bob Livingston (La.), Jerry Lewis (Calif.), John Porter (Ill.), Harold Rogers (Ky.), Joe Skeen (N.Mex.), Frank Wolf (Va.), Tom DeLay (Tex.), Jim Kolbe (Ariz.), Dean Gallo (N.J.), Barbara Vucanovich (Nev.), Jim Lightfoot (Iowa), Ron Packard (Calif.), Sonny Callahan (Ala.), Helen Bentley (Md.), Jim Walsh (N.Y.), Charles Taylor (N.C.), Dave Hobson (Ohio), Earnest Istook (Okla.), Henry Bonilla (Tex.)

Subcommittees
Agriculture
(D) Durbin, Chm.; Whitten, Kaptur, Thornton, DeLauro, Peterson, Pastor, Neil Smith
(R) Skeen, Myers, Vucanovich, Walsh

Commerce, Justice, State, and Judiciary
(D) Neal Smith, Chm.; Carr, Mollohan, Moran, Skaggs, Price
(R) Rogers, Kolbe, Taylor

Defense
(D) Murtha, Chm.; Dicks, Wilson, Hefner, Sabo, Dixon, Visclosky, Darden
(R) McDade, Young, Livingston, Lewis, Skeen

District of Columbia
(D) Dixon, Chm.; Stokes, Durbin, Kaptur, Skaggs, Pelosi
(R) Walsh, Istook, Bonilla

Energy and Water Development
(D) Bevill, Chm.; Fazio, Chapman, Peterson, Pastor, Meek
(R) Myers, Gallo, Rogers

Foreign Operations, Export Financing and Related Programs
(D) Obey, Chm.; Yates, Wilson, Olver, Pelosi, Torres, Lowey, Serrano
(R) Livingston, Porter, Lightfoot, Callahan

Interior
(D) Yates, Chm.; Murtha, Dicks, Bevill, Skaggs, Coleman
(R) Regula, McDade, Kolbe, Packard

Labor, Health and Human Services, and Education
(D) Natcher, Chm.; Neal Smith, Obey, Stokes, Hoyer, Pelosi, Lowey, Serrano, DeLauro
(R) Porter, Young, Bently, Bonilla

Legislative
(D) Fazio, Chm.; Moran, Obey, Murtha, Carr, Chapman
(R) Young, Packard, Taylor

Military Construction
(D) Hefner, Chm.; Foglietta, Meek, Dicks, Dixon, Fazio, Hoyer, Coleman
(R) Vucanovich, Callahan, Bentley, Hobson

Transportation
(D) Carr, Chm.; Durbin, Sabo, Price, Coleman, Foglietta
(R) Wolf, DeLay, Regula

Treasury-Postal Service and General Government
(D) Hoyer, Chm.; Viscloskey, Darden, Olver, Bevill, Sabo
(R) Lightfoot, Wolf, Istook

VA-HUD-Ind. Agencies
(D) Stokes, Chm.; Mollohan, Chapman, Kaptur, Torres, Thornton
(R) Lewis, DeLay, Gallo

Committee on Armed Services

2120 RHOB 20515. Phone 202-225-4151 (Marilyn Elrod, Staff Dir.)

Jurisdiction over defense legislation; emergency communications and industrial planning and mobilization; military weapons procurement. Oversees arms control and disarmament matters.

Democrats
Ron Dellums (Calif.), Chairman; Sonny Montgomery (Miss.), Pat Schroeder (Colo.), Earl Hutto (Fla.), Ike Skelton (Mo.), Dave McCrudy (Okla.), Marilyn Lloyd (Tenn.), Norm Sisisky (Va.), John Spratt (S.C.), Frank McCloskey (Ind.), Solomon Otriz (Tex.), George Hochbrueckner (N.Y.), Owen Pickett (Va.), Martin Lancaster (N.C.), Lane Evans (Ill.), James Bilbray (Nev.), John Tanner (Tenn.), Glen Browder (Ala.), Gene Taylor (Miss.), Neil Abercrombie (Hawaii), Tom Andrews (Maine), Chet Edwards (Tex.), Don Johnson (Ga.), Frank Tejeda (Tex.), David Mann (Ohio), Bart Stupak (Mich.), Martin Meehan (Mass.), Jane Harman (Calif.), Paul McHale (Pa.)

Republicans
Floyd Spence (S.C.), Ranking Member; Bob Stump (Ariz.), Duncan Hunter (Calif.), John Kasich (Ohio), Herb Bateman (Va.), Jim Hansen (Utah), Curt Weldon (Pa.), John Kyl (Ariz.), Arthur Ravenel (S.C.), Bob Dornan (Calif.), Joel Hefley (Colo.), Ron Machtley (R.I.), James Sex-

ton (N.J.), Duke Cunningham (Calif.), James Inhofe (Okla.), Steve Buyer (Ind.), Peter Torkildsen (Mass.), Tillie Fowler (Fla.), John McHugh (N.Y.), James Talent (Mo.), Terry Everett (Ala.), Roscoe Bartlett (Md.)

Subcommittees
Oversight and Investigations
(D) Sisisky, Chm.; Spratt, Tanner, Browder, Edwards, Johnson, Tedjeda, Mann, Harman, Holden
(R) Hansen, Kyl, Hefley, McHugh, Everett, Dornan

Military Installations and Facilities
(D) McCrudy, Chm.; Montgomery, McCloskey, Ortiz, Hochbrueckner, Bilbray, Browder, Taylor, Abercrombie, Edwards, Johnson, Tedja, Underwood
(R) Hunter, Fowler, McHugh, Everett, Stump, Machtley, Saxton, Torkildsen

Military Forces and Personnel
(D) Skelton, Chm.; Montgomery, Pickett, Lancaster, Bilbray, Stupak, Meehan, Underwood, Harman
(R) Kyl, Ravenel, Buyer, Fowler, Talent, Bartlett

Military Acquisition
(D) Dellums, Chm.; Lloyd, Spratt, McCloskey, Pickett, Evans, Tanner, Taylor, Abercrombie, Andrews, Mann, Stupak, McHale, Holden, Geren
(R) Spence, Bateman, Weldon, Ravenal, Dornan, Hefley, Saxton, Cunningham, Inhofe

Readiness
(D) Hutto, Chm.; Ortiz, Pickett, Lancaster, Evans, Meehan, Underwood, McHale, McCurdy, Sisisky
(R) Kasich, Bateman, Weldon, Dornan, Cunningham, Inhofe

Research and Technology
(D) Schroeder, Chm.; Hochbrueckner, Lancaster, Bilbray, Browder, Edwards, Johnson, Tejeda, Meehan, Harman, Furse, Hutto, McCurdy
(R) Stump, Buyer, Torkildsen, Talent, Bartlett, Hunter, Kasich, Hansen

Committee on Banking, Finance and Urban Development

2129 RHOB 20515. Phone 202-225-7057 (Kelsay Meek, Staff Dir.)

Jurisdiction over banking including federal regulation and deposit insurance; money and credit; urban development; public and private housing; international finance; international financial and monetary organizations; financial aid to commerce and industry.

Democrats
Henry Gonzalez (Tex.), Chairman; Stephen Neal (N.C.), John LaFalce (N.Y.), Bruce Vento (Minn.), Charles Schumer (N.Y.), Barney Frank (Mass.), Paul Kanjorski (Pa.), Joe Kennedy (Mass.), Floyd Flake (N.Y.), Kweisi Mfume (Md.), Jim Bacchus (Fla.), Larry LaRocco (Idaho), Bill Orton (Utah), Maxine Waters (Calif.), Herbert Klein (N.J.), Carolyn Maloney (N.Y.), Peter Deutsch (Fla.), Luis Gutierrez (Ill.), Bobby Rush (Ill.), Lucille Roybal-Allard (Calif.), Thomas Barrett (Wis.), Elizabeth Furse (Oreg.), Nadia Velazquez (N.Y.), Albert Wynn (Md.), Cleo Fields (La.), Melvin Watt (N.C.), Maurice Hinchey (N.Y.), Eric Fingerhut (Oh.)

Republicans
Jim Leach (Iowa), Ranking Member; Bill McCollum (Fla.), Marge Roukema (N.J.), Tom Ridge (Pa.), Toby Roth (Wis.), Al McCandless (Calif.), Richard Baker (La.), Jim Nussle (Iowa), Craig Thomas (Wyo.), Sam Johnson (Tex.), Deborah Pryce (Ohio), John Linder (Ga.), Joe Knollenberg (Miss.), Rick Lazio (N.Y.), Rod Grams (Minn.), Spencer Bachus (Ala.), Mike Huffington (Calif.), Michael Castle (Del.), Peter King (N.Y.), Bernie Sanders (Soc.-Vt.)

Subcommittees
Consumer Credit and Insurance
(D) Kennedy, Chm.; Gonzalez, LaRocco, Gutierrez, Rush, Roybal-Allard, Barrett, Furse, Velazquez, Wynn, Fields, Watt, Hinchey, Kanjorski, Flake, Waters, Maloney, Deutsch, Sanders (Soc.)
(R) McCandless, Castle, King, Pryce, Linder, Knollenberg, Bereuter, Thomas, Lazio, Grams, Bachus, Baker

Economic Growth and Credit Formation
(D) Kanjorski, Chm.; Neal, LaFalce, Orton, Klein, Velazquez, Dooley, Klink, Fingerhut
(R) Ridge, McCollum, Roth, Nussle, Roukema, King

Financial Institutions Supervision, Regulation and Insurance
(D) Neal, Chm.; LaFalce, Vento, Schumer, Frank, Kanjorski, Kennedy, Flake, Mfume,

LaRocco, Orton, Bacchus, Waters, Klein, Maloney, Deutsch, Barrett, Hinchey
(R) McCollum, Leach, Baker, Nussle, Thomas, Johnson, Pryce, Linder, Lazio, Grams, Bachus, Huffington

General Oversight
(D) Flake, Chm.; Neal, Velazquez, Hinchey
(R) Roth, Ridge

Housing and Community Development
(D) Gonzalez, Chm.; Vento, Mfume, LaFalce, Waters, Klein, Maloney, Deutsch, Gutierrez, Rush, Roybal-Allard, Barrett, Furse, Velazquez, Wynn, Fields, Watt, Sanders (Soc.)
(R) Roukema, Bereuter, Ridge, Baker, Thomas, Johnson, Knollenberg, Lazio, Grams, Bachus, Castle, Pryce

International Development, Finance, Trade and Monetary Policy
(D) Frank, Chm.; Neal, LaFalce, Kennedy, Waters, LaRocco, Orton, Bacchus, Gonzalez, Kanjorski, Rush, Furse, Fields, Fingerhut, Sanders (Soc.)
(R) Bereuter, McCandless, McCollum, Roukema, Johnson, Huffington, King, Baker, Nussle, Castle

Committee on Budget

House Annex 1, 300 New Jersey Ave. SE 20515. Phone 202-226-7234 (Eileen Baumgartner, Chief-of-staff)

Jurisdiction over all concurrent budget resolutions; conducts studies of budget matters. Makes available statistics pertaining to congressional budget actions.

Democrats
Richard Gephardt (Mo.), Chairman; Dale Kildee (Mich.), Anthony Beilenson (Calif.), Martin Sabo (Minn.), Howard Berman (Calif.), Bob Wise (W.Va.), John Bryant (Tex.), John Spratt (S.C.), Charles Stenholm (Tex.), Barney Frank (Mass.), Jim Cooper (Tenn.), Louise Slaughter (N.Y.), Mike Parker (Miss.), William Coyne (Pa.), Barbara Kennelly (Conn.), Michael Andrews (Tex.), Alan Mollahan (W.Va.), Bart Gordon (Tenn.), David Price (N.C.), Jerry Costello (Ill.), Harry Johnston (Fla.), Patsy Mink (Hawaii), Bill Orton (Utah), Lucien Blackwell (Pa.), Earl Pomeroy (N.Dak.)

Republicans
John Kasich (Ohio), Alex McMillan (N.C.), Jim Kolbe (Ariz.), Chris Shays (Conn.), Olympia Snowe (Maine), Lamar Smith (Tex.), Chris Cox (Calif.), Wayne Allard (Colo.), Dan Miller (Fla.), Rick Lazio (N.Y.), Bob Franks (N.J.), Nick Smith (Mich.), Bob Inglis (S.C.), Martin Hoke (Ohio)

Committee on District of Columbia

1310 LHOB 20515. Phone 202-225-4457 (Broderick Johnson, Staff Dir.)

Oversight of all measures relating to the municipal affairs of the District of Columbia including public health and safety. Oversees National Capital Planning Commission and the Washington Metropolitan Area Transit Authority.

Democrats
Pete Starke (Calif.), Chairman; Ron Dellums (Calif.), Alan Wheat (Mo.), Jim McDermott (Wash.), Eleanor Holmes Norton (D.C.)

Republicans
Tom Bliley (Va.), Ranking Member; Dana Rohrabacher (Calif.), Jim Saxton (N.J.)

Subcommittees
Fiscal Affairs and Health
(D) McDermott, Chm.; Norton, Jefferson, Wheat, vacancy
(R) Ballenger, Saxton

Government Operations and Metropolitan Affairs
(D) Wheat, Chm.; Stark, Lewis, Jefferson
(R) Saxton, Rohrabacher

Judiciary and Education
(D) Norton, Chm.; Lewis, Stark, McDermott
(R) Rohrabacher, Ballenger

Committee on Education and Labor

2181 RHOB 20515. Phone 202-225-4527 (Patricia Rissler, Staff Dir.)

Jurisdiction over education, labor and employment matters.

Democrats
William Ford (Mich.), Chairman; Bill Clay (Mo.), George Miller (Calif.), Austin Murphy (Pa.), Dale Kildee (Mich.), Pat Williams (Mont.),

Matthew Martinez (Calif.), Major Owens (N.Y.), Tom Sawyer (Ohio), Donald Payne (N.J.), Jolene Unsoeld (Wash.), Patsey Mink (Hawaii), Robert Andrews (N.J.), Jack Reed (R.I.), Tim Roemer (Ind.), Eliot Engel (N.Y.), Xavier Becerra (Calif.), Bobby Scott (Va.), Gene Green (Tex.), Lynn Woolsey (Calif.), Carlos Romero-Barcelo (P.R.), Ron Klink (Pa.), Karan English (Ariz.), Ted Strickland (Ohio)

Republicans
William Goodling (Pa.) Ranking Member; Tom Petri (Wis.), Marge Roukema (N.J.), Steve Gunderson (Wis.), Dick Armey (Tex.), Harris Fawell (Ill.), Paul Henry (Mich.), Cass Ballenger (N.C.), Susan Molinary (N.Y.), William Barrett (Nebr.), John Boehner (Ohio), Duke Cunningham (Calif.), Peter Hoekstra (Mich.), Buck McKeon (Calif.), Dan Miller (Fla.)

Subcommittees
Elementary, Secondary, and Vocational Education
(D) Kildee, Chm.; Miller, Owens, Unsoeld, Reed, Roemer, Mink, Engel, Becerra, Green, Woolsey, English, Strickland, Payne, Romero-Barcelo
(R) Goodling, Gunderson, McKeon, Petri, Molinari, Cunningham, Miller, Roukema, Boehner

Human Resources
(D) Martinez, Chm.; Kildee, Andrews, Scott, Woolsey, Romero-Barcelo, Owens, Baesler
(R) Henry, Molinari, Barrett

Labor-Management Relations
(D) Williams, Chm.; Clay, Kildee, Miller, Owens, Martinez, Payne, Unsoeld, Mink, Klink, Murphy, Engel, Becerra, Green, Woolsey, Romero-Barcelo
(R) Roukema, Gunderson, Armey, Barrett, Boehner, Fawell, Ballenger, Hoekstra, McKeon

Labor Standards, Occupational Health and Safety
(D) Murphy, Chm.; Clay, Andrews, Miller, Strickland, Faleomavaega
(R) Fawell, Ballenger, Hoekstra

Postsecondary Education
(D) Ford, Chm.; Williams, Sawyer, Unsoeld, Mink, Andrews, Reed, Roemer, Kildee, Scott, Klink, English, Strickland, Becerra, Green
(R) Petri, Gunderson, Cunningham, Miller, Roukema, Henry, Hoekstra, McKeon, Armey

Select Education and Civil Rights
(D) Owens, Chm.; Payne, Williams, Scott, Sawyer
(R) Ballenger, Barrett, Fawell

Committee on Energy and Commerce

2125 RHOB 20515. Phone 202-225-2927 (Alan Roth, Staff Dir.)

Jurisdiction over interstate and foreign commerce generally; national energy policy; consumer affairs and consumer protection; securities and exchanges; travel and tourism; biomedical research; health and health facilities; inland waterways.

Democrats
John Dingell (Mich.), Chairman; Henry Waxman (Calif.), Phil Sharp (Ind.), Ed Markey (Mass.), Al Swift (Wash.), Cardiss Collins (Ill.), Mike Synar (Okla.), Billy Tauzin (La.), Ron Wyden (Oreg.), Ralph Hall (Tex.), Bill Richardson (N.Mex.), Jim Slattery (Kans.), John Bryant (Tex.), Rick Boucher (Va.), Jim Cooper (Tenn.), Roy Rowland (Ga.), Tom Manton (N.Y.), Edolphus Towns (N.Y.), Gerry Studds (Mass.), Richard Lehman (Calif.), Frank Pallone (N.J.), Craig Washington (Tex.), Lynn Schenk (Calif.), Sherrod Brown (Ohio), Mike Kreidler (Wash.), Marjorie Margolies Mezvinsky (Pa.), Blanche Lambert (Ark.)

Republicans
Carlos Moorhead (Calif.), Ranking Member; Tom Bliley (Va.), Jack Fields (Tex.), Mike Oxley (Ohio), Michael Bilirakis (Fla.), Dan Schaefer (Colo.), Joe Barton (Tex.), Alex McMillan (N.C.), Dennis Hastert (Ill.), Fred Upton (Mich.), Cliff Stearns (Fla.), Bill Paxton (N.Y.), Paul Gillmor (Ohio), Scott Klug (Wis.), Gary Franks (Conn.), James Greenwood (Pa.), Mike Crapo (Ind.)

Subcommittees
Commerce, Consumer Protection, and Competitiveness
(D) Collins, Chm.; Towns, Slattery, Rowland, Manton, Lehman, Pallone
(R) Stearns, McMillan, Paxon, Greenwood

Energy and Power
(D) Sharp, Chm.; Tauzin, Cooper, Lehman, Markey, Swift, Synar, Washington, Kreidler, Lambert, Hall, Boucher

(R) Bilirakis, Barton, Hastert, Stearns, Klug, Franks, Crapo

Health and the Environment
(D) Waxman, Chm; Synar, Wyden, Hall, Richardson, Bryant, Rowland, Towns, Studds, Slattery, Cooper, Pallone, Washington, Brown, Kreidler
(R) Bliley, Bilirakis, McMillan, Hastert, Upton, Paxon, Klug, Franks, Greenwood

Oversight and Investigations
(D) Dingell, Chm.; Wyden, Bryant, Brown, Margolies-Mezvinsky, Waxman, Collins
(R) Schafer, Moorhead, Upton, Gillmor

Telecommunications and Finance
(D) Markey, Chm.; Tauzin, Hall, Richardson, Slattery, Bryant, Boucher, Cooper, Manton, Lehman, Schenk, Margolies-Mezvinsky, Synar, Wyden
(R) Bliley, Fields, Oxley, Schaefer, Barton, McMillan, Hastert, Gillmor

Transportation and Hazardous Materials
(D) Swift, Chm.; Boucher, Manton, Sharp, Tauzin, Richardson, Lambert, Rowland, Studds, Pallone, Schenk, Markey
(R) Oxley, Fields, Schaefer, Upton, Paxon, Gillmor, Crapo

Committee on Foreign Affairs

2170 RHOB 20515. Phone 202-225-5021 (Michael VanDusen, Chief-of-staff)

Jurisdiction over foreign affairs legislation, including economic and military assistance programs; international boundaries, narcotics control and executive agreements; protection of Americans abroad; the U.N. and international organizations and conferences.

Democrats
Lee Hamilton (Ind.), Chairman; Sam Gejdenson (Conn.), Tom Lantos (Calif.), Robert Torricelli (N.J.), Howard Berman (Calif.), Gary Ackerman (N.Y.), Harry Johnston (Fla.), Eliot Engel (N.Y.), Eni Faleomavaega (Samoa), James Oberstar (Minn.), Charles Schumer (N.Y.), Matthew Martinez (Calif.), Robert Borski (Pa.), Donald Payne (N.J.), Robert Andrews (N.J.), Robert Menedez (N.J.), Sherrod Brown (Ohio), Cynthia McKinney (Ga.), Maria Cantwell (Wash.), Alcee

Hastings (Fla.), Eric Fingerhut (Ohio), Peter Deutsch (Fla.), Albert Wynn (Md.)

Republicans
Benjamin Gilman (N.Y.), Ranking Member; Bill Goodling (Pa.), Jim Leach (Iowa), Toby Roth (Wis.), Olympia Snowe (Maine), Henry Hyde (Ill.), Doug Bereuter (Nebr.), Chris Smith (N.J.), Dan Burton (Ind.), Jan Meyers (Kans.), Elton Gallegly (Calif.), Ileana Ros-Lehtinen (Fla.), Cass Ballenger (N.C.), Dana Rohrbacher (Calif.), David Levy (N.Y.), Donald Manzullo (Ill.), Lincoln Diaz-Balart (Fla.), Ed Royce (Calif.)

Subcommittees
Africa
(D) Johnston, Chm.; Payne, Hastings, Torricelli, Edwards
(R) Burton, Diaz-Balart, Royce

Asian and Pacific Affairs
(D) Ackerman, Chm.; Faleomavaega, Martinez, Torricelli, Brown, Fingerhut
(R) Leach, Rohrabacher, Royce, Roth

Europe and the Middle East
(D) Hamilton, Chm.; Engel, Schumer, Borski, Andrews, Brown, Hastings, Deutsch, Lantos
(R) Gilman, Goodling, Meyers, Gallegly, Levy, Leach

Economic Policy, Trade, and Environment
(D) Gejdenson, Chm.; Oberstar, McKinney, Cantwell, Fingerhut, Wynn, Johnston, Engel, Schumer
(R) Roth, Manzullo, Bereuter, Meyers, Ballenger, Rohrabacher

International Operations
(D) Berman, Chm.; Folemavaega, Martinez, Andrews, Menedez, Lantos, Johnston, Edwards
(R) Snowe, Hyde, Diaz-Balart, Levy, Manzullo

International Security, International Organizations and Human Rights
(D) Lantos, Chm.; Berman, Ackerman, Martinez, McCloskey, Sawyer
(R) Bereuter, Snowe, Smith, Burton

Western Hemisphere Affairs
(D) Torricelli, Chm.; Menedez, Oberstar, McKinney, Deutsch, Wynn
(R) Smith, Ros-Lehtinen, Ballenger, Gallegly

Committee on Government Operations
2157 RHOB 20515. Phone 202-225-5051 (Julian Epstein, Staff Dir.)

Oversees government budget and accounting issues other than appropriations; reviews regulatory process and impact of specific regulations and paperwork on the small business community and efficiency of government operations; oversees the relationship between U.S. and international organizations.

Democrats
John Conyers (Mich.), Chairman; Cardiss Collins (Ill.), Glenn English (Okla.), Henry Waxman (Calif.), Mike Synar (Okla.), Stephen Neal (N.C.), Tom Lantos (Calif.), Bob Wise (W.Va.), Major Owens (N.Y.), Edolphus Towns (N.Y.), Gary Condit (Calif.), Karen Thurman (Fla.), Lynn Woolsey (Calif.), Bobby Rush (Ill.), Carolyn Maloney (N.Y.), Thomas Barrett (Wis.)

Republicans
Bill Clinger (Pa.), Ranking Member; Al McCandless (Calif.), Dennis Hastert (Ill.), John Kyl (Ariz.), Chris Shays (Conn.), Steve Schiff (N. Mex.), Christopher Cox (Calif.), Craig Thomas (Wyo.), Ileana Ros-Lehtinen (Fla.), Ron Machtley (R.I.), Richard Zimmer (N.J.), Bill Zeliff (N.H.), John McHugh (N.Y.), Steve Horn (Calif.), Deborah Pryce (Ohio), John Mica (Fla.), Bernie Sanders (I.-Vt.), Rob Postman (Ohio)

Subcommittees
Commerce, Consumer, and Monetary Affairs
(D) Spratt, Chm.; Rush, Margolies-Mezvinsky, Collins
(R) Cox, Shays, Zeliff

Employment and Housing
(D) Peterson, Chm.; Lantos, Rush, Flake, Thurman, Collins
(R) Machtley, Shays, McHugh

Environment, Energy, and Natural Resources
(D) Synar, Chm.; Thurman, Maloney, Hayes, Washington, Towns
(R) Hasert, McHugh, Pryce, Mica

Information, Justice, Transportation, and Agriculture
(D) Condit, Chm.; Owens, Thurman, Woolsey
(R) Thomas, Ros-Lehtinen, Horn

Human Resources and Intergovernmental Relations
(D) Towns, Chm.; Waxman, Barrett, Payne, Washington
(R) Schiff, Horn, Mica

Legislation and National Security
(D) Conyers, Chm.; English, Neal, Collins, Maloney, Lantos, Brown
(R) McCandless, Clinger, Kyl, Zimmer

Committee on House Administration

H-326 The Capitol 20515. Phone 202-225-2061 (Robert Shea, Staff Dir.)

Jurisdiction over legislation and other matters relating to all federal elections; corrupt practices; oversees voter registration by mail; campaign finance; all matters related to House office buildings and House employees.

Democrats
Charlie Rose (N.C.), Chairman; Al Swift (Wash.), Bill Clay (Mo.), Sam Gejdenson (Conn.), Martin Frost (Tex.), Tom Manton (N.Y.), Steny Hoyer (Md.), Gerald Kleczka (Wis.), Dale Kildee (Mich.), Butler Derrick (S.C.), Barbara Kennelly (Conn.), Ben Cardin (Md.)

Republicans
Bill Thomas (Calif.), Ranking Member; Newt Gingrich (Ga.), Pat Roberts (Kans.), Robert Livingston (La.), Bill Barrett (Nebr.), John Boehner (Ohio), Jim Walsh (N.Y.)

Subcommittees
Accounts
(D) Gaydos, Chm.; Annunzio, Swift, Oakar, Gejdenson, Manton, Russo
(R) Gillmor, Gingrich, Dickinson, Barrett

Elections
(D) Swift, Chm.; Panetta, Frost, Gray, Hoyer
(R) Livingston, Walsh, Gillmor

Libraries and Memorials
(D) Clay, Chm.; Kolter, Frost, Gray
(R) Barrett, Roberts

Office Systems
(D) Gejdenson, Chm.; Frost, Russo, Kleczka
(R) Walsh, Dickinson

Personnel and Police
(D) Oakar, Chm.; Panetta, Kolter, Manton, Russo, Kleczka
(R) Roberts, Dickinson, Livingston

Procurement and Printing
(D) Annunzio, Chm.; Gaydos, Gray, Hoyer
(R) Edwards, Gingrich

Campaign Finance Reform Task Force
(D) Gejdenson, Chm.; Panetta, Frost, Kleczka, Gray
(R) Thomas, Edwards, Walsh

Committee on Natural Resources

1324 LHOB 20515. Phone 202-225-2761 (Daniel P. Beard, Staff Dir.)

Jurisdiction over legislation on overseas territories; natural resources; land use and planning; Department of the Interior and U.S. Forest Service; National parks and public lands; relations with Native Americans.

Democrats
George Miller (Calif.), Chairman; Phil Sharp (Ind.), Edward Markey (Mass.), Austin Murphy (Pa.), Nick Rahall (W.Va.), Bruce Vento (Minn.), Pat Williams (Mont.), Ron de Lugo (V.I.), Sam Gejdenson (Conn.), Richard Lehman (Calif.), Bill Richardson (N.Mex.), Peter DeFazio (Oreg.), Eni Faleomavaega (Samoa), Tim Johnson (S. Dak.), Larry LaRocco (Idaho), Neil Abercrombie (Hawaii), Calvin Dooley (Calif.), Carlos Romero-Barcelo (P.R.), Karan English (Ariz.), Karen Shepherd (Utah), Nathan Deal (Ga.), Maurice Hinchey (N.Y.), Robert Underwood (Guam), Patsy Mink (Hawaii), Howard Berman (Calif.), Lane Evans (Ill.), Thomas Barlow (Ky.), Thomas Barrett (Wis.)

Republicans
Don Young (Alaska), Ranking Member; James Hansen (Utah), Barbara Vucanovich (Nev.), Elton Gallegly (Calif.), Bob Smith (Oreg.), Craig Thomas (Wyo.), John Duncan (Tenn.), Joel Hefley (Colo.), John Doolittle (Calif.), Wayne Allard (Colo.), Richard Baker (La.), Ken Calvert (Calif.), Scott McInnis (Colo.), Richard Pombo (Calif.), Jay Dickey (Ark.)

Subcommittees
Native American Affairs
(D) Richardson, Chm.; Williams, Gejdenson, Falemavaega, Johnson, Abercrombie, English
(R) Thomas, Young, Baker, Calvert

Insular and International Affairs
(D) De Lugo, Chm.; Faleomavaega, Under-

wood, Romero-Barcelo, Murphy, Miller
(R) Gallegly, Vucanovich

Energy and Mineral Resources
(D) Lehman, Chm.; Sharp, Murphy, Markey, Rahall, LaRocco, Deal, DeFazio, Barlow
(R) Vucanovich, Thomas, Doolittle, Allard, McInnis, Pombo

National Parks and Public Lands
(D) Vento, Chm.; Markey, Rahall, Williams, DeFazio, Johnson, LaRocco, Abercrombie, Romero-Barcelo, English, Shepherd, Hinchey, Underwood, Murphy, Richardson, Mink
(R) Hansen, Bob Smith, Thomas, Duncan, Hefley, Doolittle, Baker, Calvert, Dickey

Oversight and Investigation
(D) Miller, Chm.; Gejdenson, Dooley, Deal, Sharp, Vento, Lehman, DeFazio, English, Shepherd, Hinchey, Abercrombie, Evans, Barrett
(R) Smith, Hansen, Vucanovich, Duncan, Doolittle, Allard, Calvert, Pombo, Dickey

Committee on the Judiciary
2138 RHOB 20515. Phone 202-225-3951 (John Yarowsky, General Counsel)

Jurisdiction over legislation on judicial proceedings; constitutional amendments; civil liberties; federal judiciary; federal corrections system; protection of trade and commerce against unlawful restraints and monopolies; patents, copyrights, and trademarks; bankruptcy, mutiny, espionage and counterfeiting; immigration and naturalization; revision and codification of the statutes of the U.S.; internal security; all legislation relating to claims against the U.S.; separation of powers and presidential succession (shared with House Government Operation Committee); internal security; reapportionment.

Democrats
Jack Brooks (Tex.), Chairman; Don Edwards (Calif.), John Conyers (Mich.), Romano Mazzoli (Ky.), Bill Hughes (N.J.), Mike Synar (Okla.), Pat Schroeder (Colo.), Dan Glickman (Kans.), Barney Frank (Mass.), Charles Schumer (N.Y.), Howard Berman (Calif.), Rick Boucher (Va.), John Bryant (Tex.), George Sangmeister (Ill.), Craig Washington (Tex.), Jack Reed (R.I.), Jerrold Nadler (N.Y.), Bobby Scott (Va.), David Mann (Ohio), Melvin Watt (N.C.)

Republicans
Hamilton Fish (N.Y.) Ranking Member; Carlos Moorhead (Calif.), Henry Hyde (Ill.), James Sensenbrenner (Wis.), Bill McCollum (Fla.), George Gekas (Pa.), Howard Coble (N.C.), Lamar Smith (Tex.), James Ramstad (Minn.), Steve Schiff (N.Mex.), Elton Gallegly (Calif.), Charles Canady (Fla.), Bob Inglis (S.C.), Bob Goodlatte (Va.)

Subcommittees
Administrative Law and Governmental Relations
(D) Bryant, Chm.; Glickman, Frank, Berman, Mann, Watt
(R) Gekas, Ramstad, Inglis, Goodlatte

Civil and Constitutional Rights
(D) Edwards, Chm.; Schroeder, Frank, Washington, Nadler
(R) Hyde, Coble, Canady

Intellectual Property and Judicial Administration
(D) Hughes, Chm.; Edwards, Conyers, Mazzoli, Synar, Frank Berman, Reed, Becerra
(R) Moorhead, Coble, Fish, Sensenbrenner, McCollum, Schiff

Crime and Criminal Justice
(D) Schumer, Chm.; Edwards, Conyers, Mazzoli, Glickman, Sangmeister, Washington, Mann
(R) Sensenbrenner, Smith, Schiff, Ramstad, Gekas

International Law, Immigration, and Refugees
(D) Mazzoli, Chm; Schumer, Bryant, Sangmeister, Nadler, Becerra
(R) McCollum, Lamar Smith, Gallegly, Canady

Economic and Commercial Law
(D) Brooks, Chm.; Conyers, Synar, Schroeder, Glickman, Berman, Boucher, Scott, Mann, Watt
(R) Fish, Gallegy, Canady, Inglis, Goodlatte, Moorhead

Committee on Merchant Marine and Fisheries
1334 LHOB 20515. Phone 202-225-4047 (Will Steele, Chief Counsel)

Jurisdiction over merchant marine generally. Oversees the Coast Guard; regulation of common carriers on water; Panama Canal; navagation and laws pertaining to navagation; international fishing treaties.

Democrats
Gerry Studds (Mass.), Chairman; Bill Hughes (N.J.), Earl Hutto (Fla.), Billy Tauzin (La.), Bill Lipinski (Ill.), Solomon Ortiz (Tex.), Tom Manton (N.Y.), Owen Pickett (Va.), George Hochbrueckner (N.Y.), Greg Laughlin (Tex.), Jolene Unsoeld (Wash.), Gene Taylor (Miss.), Jack Reed (R.I.), Lucien Blackwell (Pa.), Martin Lancaster (N.C.), Elizabeth Furse (Oreg.), Lynn Schenk (Calif.), Gene Green (Tex.), Alcee Hastings (Fla.), Dan Hamburg (Calif.), Blanche Lambert (Ark.), Anna Eshoo (Calif.), Tom Barlow (Ky.), Bart Stupak (Mich.), Bernie Thompson (Miss.)

Republicans
Jack Fields (Tex.), Ranking Member; Don Young (Alaska), Herb Bateman (Va.), Jim Saxton (N.J.), Howard Coble (N.C.), Curt Weldon (Pa.), Jim Inhofe (Okla.), Arthur Ravenel (S.C.), Wayne Gilchrest (Md.), Duke Cunningham (Calif.), Jack Kingston (Ga.), Tillie Fowler (Fla.), Michael Castle (Del.), Peter King (N.Y.), Lincoln Diaz-Balart (Fla.)

Subcommittees
Coast Guard and Navigation
(D) Tauzin, Chm.; Hughes, Hutto, Lancaster, Barlow, Stupak, Lipinski, Pickett, Hochbrueckner, Pallone, Laughlin, Schenk, Hastings, Lambert, Taylor
(R) Coble, Bateman, Gilchrest, Fowler, Castle, King, Diaz-Balart, Inhofe

Environment and Natural Resources
(D) Studds, Chm.; Hochbrueckner, Pallone, Unsoeld, Laughlin, Reed, Furse, Hamburg, Lambert, Eshoo, Hutto, Tauzin, Ortiz
(R) Saxton, Young, Weldon, Ravenel, Gilchrest, Cunningham, Castle

Merchant Marine
(D) Lipinski, Chm.; Pickett, Taylor, Andrews, Schenk, Green, Hastings, Reed, Furse, Stupak, Manton, Ackerman, Studds
(R) Bateman, Inhofe, Cunningham, Kingston, Fowler, King, Diaz-Balart

Oceanography, Gulf of Mexico and Outer Continental Shelf
(D) Ortiz, Chm.; Green, Eshoo, Laughlin, Schenk
(R) Saxton, Weldon

Fisheries Management
(D) Manton, Chm.; Hughes, Unsoeld, Taylor, Lancaster, Hamburg, Cantwell, Hutto
(R) Young, Coble, Ravenel, Kingston

Committee on Post Office and Civil Service

309 CHOB 20515. Phone 202-225-4054 (Gail Weiss, Staff Dir.)

Jurisdiction over legislation concerning postal service, franking privileges, holidays and celebrations, census, population and demography, and all officers and employers of the United States, including compensation, classification and retirement.

Democrats
William Clay (Mo.), Chairman; Pat Schroeder (Colo.), Frank McCloskey (Ind.), Gary Ackerman (N.Y.), Tom Sawyer (Ohio), Paul Kanjorski (Pa.), Eleanor Holmes Norton (D.C.), Barbara-Rose Collins (Mich.), Leslie Byrne (Va.), Mel Watt (N.C.), Al Wynn (Md.)

Republicans
John Myers (Ind.), Ranking Member; Ben Gilman (N.Y.), Donald Young (Alaska), Dan Burton (Ind.), Connie Morella (Md.), Tom Ridge (Pa.)

Subcommittees
Census, Statistics and Postal Personnel
(D) Sawyer, Chm.; McCloskey, Wynn
(R) Petri, Ridge

Civil Service
(D) McCloskey, Chm.; Schroeder, Kanjorski
(R) Burton, Morella

Compensation and Employee Benefits
(D) Norton, Chm.; Ackerman, Byrne
(R) Morella, Young

Oversight and Investigations
(D) Clay, Chm.; Hastings, Laughlin
(R) Boehlert, Saxton

Postal Operations and Services
(D) Collins, Chm.; Watt, Bishop
(R) Young, Gilman

Committee on Public Works and Transportation

2165 RHOB 20515. Phone 202-225-4472 (Paul Schoellhamer, Staff Dir.)

Jurisdiction over legislation concerning flood control and improvement of rivers and harbors; construction or maintenance of roads and post roads; public buildings and occupied or improved grounds of the United States generally; bridges and dams (other than international bridges and dams); water power; transportation, including civil aviation except railroads, railroad labor, and pensions. Oversees related transportation regulatory agencies, except the Interstate Commerce Commission as it relates to railroads, the Federal Railroad Administration, and Amtrak.

Democrats
Norman Mineta (Calif.), Chairman; James Oberstar (Minn.), Nick Rahall (W.Va.), Doug Applegate (Ohio), Ron de Lugo (V.I.), Robert Borski (Pa.), Tim Valentine (N.C.), Bill Lipinski (Ill.), James Traficant (Ohio), Peter DeFazio (Oreg.), Jimmy Hayes (La.), Bob Clement (Tenn.), Jerry Costello (Ill.), Mike Parker (Miss.), Greg Laughlin (Tex.), Pete Geren (Tex.), George Sangmeister (Ill.), Glenn Poshard (Ill.), Barbara Rose Collins (Mich.), Bud Cramer (Ala.), Eleanor Holmes Norton (D.C.), Dick Swett (N.H.), Lucien Blackwell (Pa.), Jerrold Nadler (N.Y.), Sam Coppersmith (Ariz.), Leslie Byrne (Va.), Maria Cantwell (Wash.), Patsy Danner (Mo.), Karen Shepherd (Utah), Robert Menendez (N.J.), James Clyburn (S.C.), Corrine Brown (Fla.), Nathan Deal (Fla.), James Barcia (Mich.), Dan Hamburg (Calif.), Bob Filner (Calif.), Walter Tucker (Calif.), Eddie Bernice Johnson (Tex.), Peter Barca (Wis.)

Republicans
Bud Schuster (Pa.), Ranking Member; Bill Clinger (Pa.), Tom Petri (Wis.), Sherwood Boehlert (N.Y.), James Inhofe (Okla.), Bill Emerson (Mo.), Jim Duncan (Tenn.), Bill Zeliff (N.H.), Tom Ewing (Ill.), Wayne Gilchrest (Md.), Jennifer Dunn (Wash.), Tim Hutchinson (Ark.), Bill Baker (Calif.), Mac Collins (Ga.), Jay Kim (Calif.), David Levy (N.Y.), Steve Horn (Calif.), Bob Franks (N.J.), Peter Blute (Mass.), Buck McKeon (Calif.), John Mica (Fla.), Peter Hoekstra (Mich.), Jack Quinn (N.Y.)

Subcommittees
Aviation
(D) Oberstar, Chm.; de Lugo, Lipinski, Geren, Sangmeister, Rose-Collins, Coppersmith, Borski, Valentine, DeFazio, Hayes, Clement, Costello, Parker, Laughlin, Swett, Cramer, Blackwell, Cantwell, Danner, Shepherd, Brown
(R) Clinger, Boehlert, Inhofe, Duncan, Ewing,

Gilchrest, Dunn, Collins, Kim, Levy, Horn, McKeon, Mica

Economic Development
(D) Wise, Chm.; Blackwell, Coppersmith, Clyburn, Deal, Barcia, Filner, Oberstar, Rahall, Lipinski, Traficant, Clement, Costello, Parker, Swett, Nadler, Danner, Shepherd, Menedez, Brown, Hamburg
(R) Molinari, Boehlert, Ewing, Dunn, Hutchinson, Baker, Collins, Kim, Franks, Blute, Mica, Hoekstra, Quinn

Investigations and Oversight
(D) Borski, Chm.; Rose-Collins, Wise, Laughlin, Blackwell, Byrne, Barcia, Filner, Johnson
(R) Inhofe, Duncan, Molinari, Zeliff, Gilchrest, Baker

Public Buildings and Grounds
(D) Traficant, Chm.; Norton, Johnson, Applegate, Clyburn, Tucker
(R) Duncan, Petri, Emerson

Surface Transportation
(D) Rahall, Chm.; Valentine, Clement, Costello, Laughlin, Poshard, Swett, Cramer, DeFazio, Nadler, Byrne, Cantwell, Danner, Menendez, Clyburn, Hamburg, Tucker, Johnson, Applegate, de Lugo, Lipinski, Traficant
(R) Clinger, Petri, Emerson, Zeliff, Dunn, Hutchinson, Baker, Collins, Kim, Levy, Franks, Blute, McKeon

Water Resources
(D) Applegate, Chm.; Hayes, Parker, Shepherd, Brown, Deal, Barcia, Filner, Oberstar, Rahall, Wise, Geren, Sangmeister, Poshard, Norton, Nadler, Byrne, Menendez, Hamburg, Tucker, Borski, Valentine
(R) Boehlert, Petri, Clinger, Inhofe, Emerson, Molinari, Zeliff, Ewing, Gilchrest, Hutchinson, Horn, Hoekstra, Quinn

Committee on Rules
H-312 The Capitol 20515. Phone 202-225-9486 (George Crawford, Staff Dir.)

Issues rules outlining conditions for floor debate on legislation proposed by regular standing committees, including emergency waivers under House rules; has jurisdiction over resolutions creating committees; has legislative authority to recommend changes in rules of the House.

Democrats
Joe Moakley (Mass.), Chairman; Butler Derrick (S.C.), Anthony Beilenson (Calif.), Martin Frost (Tex.), David Bonior (Mich.), Tony Hall (Ohio), Alan Wheat (Mo.), Bart Gordon (Tenn.), Louise Slaughter (N.Y.)

Republicans
Jerry Solomon (N.Y.) Ranking Member; James Quillen (Tenn.), David Dreier (Calif.), Porter Goss (Fla.)

Subcommittees
Rules of the House
(D) Beilenson, Chm.; Bonior, Hall, Slaughter
(R) Dreier, Solomon

The Legislative Process
(D) Derrick, Chm.; Frost, Wheat, Gordon
(R) Quillen, Goss

Committee on Science, Space and Technology

2321 RHOB 20515. Phone 202-225-6375 (Dr. Radford Byerly, Jr. Chief-of-staff)

Jurisdiction over legislation on all nonmilitary energy research and development, including resources, personnel, equipment, and facilities; some programs of the National Science Foundation and National Aeronautics and Space Administration.

Democrats
George Brown (Calif.), Chairman; James Scheuer (N.Y.), Marilyn Lloyd (Tenn.), Dan Glickman (Kans.), Harold Volkmer (Mo.), Ralph Hall (Tex.), David McCrudy (Okla.), Norman Mineta (Calif.), Tim Valentine (N.C.), Robert Torricelli (N.J.), Rick Boucher (Va.), James Traficant (Ohio), Jimmy Hayes (La.), John Tanner (Tenn.), Glen Browder (Ala.), Peter Geren (Tex.), Tim Roemer (Ind.), Bud Cramer (Ala.), Dick Swett (N.H.), James Barcia (Mich.), Herbert Klein (N.J.), Eric Fingerhut (Ohio), Paul McHale (Pa.), Xavier Becerra (Calif.), Jane Harman (Calif.), Don Johnson (Ga.), Sam Coppersmith (Ariz.), Anna Eshoo (Calif.), Jay Inslee (Wash.), Eddie Bernice Johnson (Tex.), David Minge (Minn.), Peter Barca (Wis.)

Republicans
Robert Walker (Pa.), Ranking Member; James Sensenbrenner (Wis.), Sherwood Boehlert (N.Y.),
Tom Lewis (Fla.), Paul Henry (Mich.), Harris Fawell (Ill.), Connie Morella (Md.), Dana Rohrabacher (Calif.), Steve Schiff (N.Mex.), Joe Barton (Tex.), Richard Zimmer (N.J.), Sam Johnson (Tex.), Ken Calvert (Calif.), Martin Hoke (Ohio), Nick Smith (Mich.), Ed Royce (Calif.), Rod Grams (Minn.), John Linder (Ga.), Peter Blute (Mass.), Jennifer Dunn (Wash.), Bill Baker (Calif.), Roscoe Bartlett (Md.)

Subcommittees
Energy
(D) Lloyd, Chm.; Scott, Cramer, Swett, Klein, McHale, Coppersmith, Inslee, Roemer, McCurdy
(R) Fawell, Schiff, Baker, Grams, Bartlett

Investigations and Oversight
(D) Hayes, Chm.; Tanner, Lloyd, Johnson, Coppersmith
(R) Henry, Morella, Barton

Science
(D) Boucher, Chm.; Hall, Valentine, Browder, Barcia, Johnson, Eshoo, Johnson, Minge
(R) Boehlert, Barton, Johnson, Nick Smith, Blute

Space
(D) Hall, Chm.; Volkmer, Toricelli, Traficant, Browder, Bacchus, Cramer, Barcia, Fingerhut, Hayes, Tanner, Geren, Roemer, Harman, Eshoo, McCurdy
(R) Sensenbrenner, Rohrabacher, Zimmer, Johnson, Hoke, Royce, Dunn, Schiff, Calvert

Technology, Environment, and Aviation
(D) Valentine, Chm.; Glickman, Geren, Roemer, Swett, Klein, McHale, Harman, Johnson, Coppersmith, Eshoo, Inslee, Johnson, Minge, Woolsey, Deal, Becerra, Torricelli, Bacchus
(R) Tom Lewis, Rohrabacher, Morella, Calvert, Nick, Smith, Grams, Linder, Blute, Bartlett, Zimmer, Hoke, Royce

Committee on Small Business

2361 RHOB 20515. Phone 202-225-5821 (Donald Terry, Staff Dir.)

Jurisdiction over legislation dealing with the Small Business Administration. Studies and makes recommendations on problems of American small businesses.

Democrats
John J. LaFalce (N.Y.), Chairman; Neal Smith

(Iowa), Ike Skelton (Mo.), Romano Mazzoli (Ky.), Ron Wyden (Oreg.), Norman Sisisky (Va.), John Conyers (Mich.), James Bilbray (Nev.), Kweisi Mfume (Md.), Floyd Flake (N.Y.), Bill Sarpalius (Tex.), Glenn Poshard (Ill.), Tom Andrews (Maine), Eva Clayton (N.C.), Martin Meehan (Mass.), Patsy Danner (Mo.), Ted Strickland (Ohio), Nadia Velazquez (N.Y.), Cleo Fields (La.), Marjorie Margolies-Mezvinsky (Pa.), Walter Tucker (Calif.), Ron Klink (Pa.), Lucille Roybal-Allard (Calif.), Earl Hilliard (Ala.)

Republicans
Jan Meyers (Kans.), Ranking Member; Larry Combest (Tex.), Richard Baker (La.), Joel Hefley (Colo.), Ron Machtley (R.I.), David Camp (Mich.), Jim Ramstad (Minn.), Sam Johnson (Tex.), Bill Zeliff (N.H.), Mac Collins (Ga.), Scott McInnis (Colo.), Mike Huffington (Calif.), James Talent (Mo.), Joe Knollenberg (Mich.), Jay Dickey (Ark.), Jay Kim (Calif.), Donald Manzullo (Ill.), Peter Torkildsen (Mass.), Rob Portman (Ohio)

Subcommittees
Rural Enterprise, Exports, and The Environment
(D) Sarpalius, Chm.; Clayton, Danner, Poshard, Strickland, Hilliard
(R) Hefley, Ramstad, Manzullo, Collins

Minority Enterprise, Finance, and Urban Development
(D) Mfume, Chm.; Conyers, Flake, Velazquez, Tucker, Fields, Roybal-Allard, Hilliard
(R) Matchley, Ramstad, Talent, Knollenberg, Dickey

Procurement, Taxation, and Tourism
(D) Bilbray, Chm.; Sisisky, Hilliard, Mfume, Clayton, Klink
(R) Baker, Knollenberg, Camp, Johnson

Regulation, Business Opportunity, and Technology
(D) Wyden, Chm.; Skelton, Strickland, Andrews, Sisisky, Bilbray, Flake, Meehan, Tucker
(R) Combest, Johnson, Dickey, Kim, Torkildsen, Huffington

SBA and The General Economy
(D) LaFalce, Chm.; Smith, Mazzoli, Poshard, Meehan, Fields, Margolies-Mezvinsky, Klink, Roybal-Allard
(R) Meyers, Camp, Zeliff, Collins, Huffington, Talent

Committee on Standards of Official Conduct (Ethics Committee)
HT-2, The Capitol 20515-6328. Phone (202) 225-7103 (Bernard Raimo, Chief Counsel)

Jurisdiction over Ethics and Government Act of 1978. House Code of Official Conduct; reviews members' financial disclosures.

Democrats
Louis Stokes (Ohio), Chairman; Benjamin Cardin (Md.), James McDermott (Wash.), Nancy Pelosi (Calif.), Buddy Darden (Ga.), Kweisi Mfume (Md.)

Republicans
Fred Grandy (Iowa), Ranking Member; Nancy Johnson (Conn.), Jim Bunning (Ky.), Porter Goss (Fla.), Jon Kyl (Ariz.), David Hobson (Ohio), Steven Schiff (N.Mex.)

No subcommittees

Committee on Veterans Affairs
335 CHOB 20515. Phone 202-225-3527 (Mack Fleming, Chief Counsel)

Jurisdiction over legislation concerning all veterans' matters, including medical care, vocational education, veterans' cemeteries, soldiers' and sailors' civil relief.

Democrats
Sonny Montgomery (Miss.), Chairman; Don Edwards (Calif.), Doug Applegate (Ohio), Lane Evans (Ill.), Tim Penny (Minn.), Roy Rowland (Ga.), Jim Slattery (Kans.), Joe Kennedy (Mass.), George Sangmeister (Ill.), Jill Long (Ind.), Chet Edwards (Tex.), Maxine Waters (Calif.), Bob Clement (Tenn.), Bob Filner (Calif.), Frank Tejeda (Tex.), Luis Gutierrez (Ill.), Scotty Baesler (Ky.), Sanford Bishop (Ga.), James Clyburn (S.C.), Michael Kreidler (Wash.), Corrine Brown (Fla.)

Republicans
Bob Stump (Ariz.), Ranking Member; Chris Smith (N.J.), Dan Burton (Ind.), Michael Bilirakis (Fla.), Tom Ridge (Pa.), Floyd Spence (S.C.), Tim Hutchinson (Ark.), Terry Everett (Ala.), Steve Buyer (Ind.), Jack Quinn (N.Y.), Spencer Bachus (Ala.), John Linder (Ga.)

Subcommittees
Hospitals and Health Care
(D) Rowland, Chm.; Kennedy, Long, Edwards,

Applegate, Clement, Filner, Tejeda, Guiterrez, Baesler, Bishop, Kreidler, Brown
(R) Stump, Christopher Smith, Burton, Bilirakis, Ridge, Hutchinson, Everett, vacancy

Compensation, Pension, and Insurance
(D) Slattery, Chm.; Applegate, Evans, Sangmeister, Edwards, Tejeda
(R) Bilirakis, Linder, Hutchinson, vacancy

Education, Training, and Employment
(D) Montgomery, Chm.; Penny, Clyburn, Rowland, Slattery, Clement
(R) Christoper Smith, Stump, Quinn, vacancy

Oversight and Investigations
(D) Evans, Chm.; Waters, Filner, Guiterrez, Clyburn, Kreidler
(R) Ridge, Everett, Bachus, Buyer

Housing and Memorial Affairs
(D) Sangmeister, Chm.; Bishop, Brown, Kreidler
(R) Burton, Spence, Buyer

Committee on Ways and Means

1102 LHOB 20515. Phone 202-225-3625 (Janice Mays, Chief Counsel)

Jurisdiction over legislation dealing with revenue measures including taxes, national debt ceiling, investment policy, trade tariffs, tax exempt foundations and charitable trusts. Oversees Internal Revenue Service, Treasury Dept.

Democrats
Dan Rostenkowski (Ill.), Chairman; Sam Gibbons (Fla.), J.J. Pickle (Tex.), Charles Rangel (N.Y.), Pete Stark (Calif.), Andy Jacobs (Ind.), Harold Ford (Tenn.), Robert Matsui (Calif.), Barbara Kennelly (Conn.), William Coyne (Pa.), Michael Andrews (Tex.), Sander Levin (Mich.), Ben Cardin (Md.), Jim McDermott (Wash.), Gerald Kleckza (Wis.), John Lewis (Ga.), L.F. Payne (Va.), Richard Neal (Mass.), Peter Hogaland (Nebr.), Michael McNulty (N.Y.), Michael Kopetski (Oreg.), William Jefferson (La.), Bill Brewster (Okla.), Mel Reynolds (Ill.)

Republicans
Bill Archer (Tex.), Ranking Member; Phil Crane (Ill.), Bill Thomas (Calif.), Clay Shaw (Fla.), Don Sundquist (Tenn.), Nancy Johnson (Conn.), Jim Bunning (Ky.), Fred Grandy (Iowa), Amo Houghton (N.Y.), Wally Herger (Calif.), Jim McCrery (La.), Mel Hancock (Mo.), Rick Santorum (Pa.)

Subcommittees
Health
(D) Stark, Chm.; Levin, Cardin, Andrews, McDermott, Kleczka, Lewis
(R) Thomas, Johnson, Grandy, McCrery

Oversight
(D) Pickle, Chm.; Ford, Rangel, Jefferson, Brewster, Kleczka, Lewis
(R) Houghton, Herger, Hancock, Santorum

Human Resources
(D) Ford, Chm.; Matsui, McDermott, Levin, Kopetski, Reynolds, Cardin
(R) Santorum, Shaw, Grandy, Camp

Select Revenue Measures
(D) Rangel, Chm.; Payne, Neal, Hogaland, McNulty, Kopetski, Jacobs
(R) Hancock, Sundquist, McCrery, Camp

Social Security
(D) Jacobs, Chm.; Pickle, Jefferson, Brewster, Reynolds
(R) Bunning, Crane, Houghton

Trade
(D) Gibbons, Chm.; Rostenkowski, Matsui, Kennelly, Coyne, Payne, Neal, Hogaland, McNulty
(R) Crane, Thomas, Shaw, Sundquist, Johnson

HOUSE SELECT COMMITTEES

Permanent Select Committee on Intelligence

H-405 The Capitol 20515. Phone 202-225-4121 (Mike Sheehey, Chief Council)

Democrats
Dan Glickman (Kans.), Chairman.; Bill Richardson (N.Mex.), Norman Dicks (Wash.), Julian Dixon (Calif.), Robert Torricelli (N.J.), Ronald Coleman (Tex.), David Skaggs (Colo.), James Bilbray (Nev.), Nancy Pelosi (Calif.), Greg Laughlin (Tex.), Bud Cramer (Ala.), Jack Reed (R.I.)

Republicans
Larry Combest (Tex.), Ranking Member; Doug Bereuter (Nebr.), Robert Dornan (Calif.), George Gekas (Pa.), Bill Young (Fla.), James Hansen (Utah), Jerry Lewis (Calif.)

Subcommittees
Legislation
(D) Coleman, Chm.; Dicks, Bilbray, Pelosi, Laughlin, Cramer
(R) Gekas, Hansen, Lewis

Oversight and Evaluation
(D) Dicks, Chm.; Pelosi, Reed, Torricelli, Coleman, Skaggs
(R) Young, Hansen, Bereuter

Program and Budget Authorization
(D) Glickman, Chm.; Richardson, Dixon, Torricelli, Skaggs, Bilbray, Laughlin, Cramer
(R) Combest, Bereuter, Dornan, Lewis

THE 103rd CONGRESS

The new Congress that was sworn in on January 5, 1993—the 103rd Congress—is one of the most unusual in the past 50 years. It is the product of numerous retirements at the end of the 102nd Congress and the wave of unrest that swept the electorate in 1992. Almost a quarter of the House and more than 10 percent of the Senate are new to those bodies. One hundred ten members of the House and a dozen new senators took the oath of office for the first time.

The Class of 1992 is much younger than the returning incumbents. As a result the greying of Congress has been reversed; for the first time in two decades, the average age of members of the new Congress is lower than it was in the previous. The new class is comprised of a record number of women and minorities, and thus have pushed almost every category of minorities to record levels.

There are record numbers of women in both the House (48) and Senate (6). There are more blacks in the House (39) than at any time in the past.

The number of Hispanics have reached record levels in the House (19), of which 13 are Mexican-Americans, three are of Cuban descent, and three are of Puerto Rican descent. A record number of Asian-American and Pacific Islanders (7) are serving in the House, among them Rep. Jay Kim, R-Calif., the first ever Korean-American to serve in Congress. In Ben Nighthorse Campbell, the Senate has its second Native American.

By a small percent, there are fewer lawyers in this Congress, but with 239 members law school graduates (181 House, 58 Senate) the law is the occupational group most represented among lawmakers. The next most prominent former professions are business and banking (155), public service (97), education (77), journalism (33), real estate (31) and farming (27). There are six physicians in the House.

Explanation of Statistics

District information. Population figures are based on the 1990 Census. Demographic breakdowns are also based on the 1990 census, including demographics for individual congressional districts which were released by the Census Bureau in March, 1993. Minority percentages are given only when a given minority represents 2 percent or more of the district's population. In some cases the racial percentages will add up to more than 100 percent because persons of Hispanic origin may be of any race. In some cases the classification of "other" is given. In the census, individual respondents list their own ethnic classification. If none is given, the person is classified as "other." Each district's politics are given as Democratic, Leans Democratic, Mixed, Leans Republican or Republican based on the results of the past half dozen presidential, senatorial and congressional elections.

Interest group ratings. At the end of every congressional session, many interest groups rate all senators and representatives according to how they voted during the past session. Typically, each interest group chooses some number of issues that came to a vote during the past session which it considers of greatest importance. It then records how each legislator voted on each of these key issues, and calculates the percentage of times each member voted the way the interest group thinks he or she should have voted. That is the number each group publishes. A *100* would indicate that the legislator voted the way the interest group would have liked every time. At the other extreme, a *00* would indicate the member never voted the way the interest would have liked. While some of the groups chose the same votes to include in their calculations, most do not. That is why ratings from groups at opposite ends of the political or special interest spectrum, are not completely inverse. For instance, a member may have voted 100 percent the way the AFL-CIO wanted, and yet still have a 25–30 rating from the Chamber of Commerce. By examining a cross section of these interest group ratings, you can develop a good view of the political leanings of each member.

THE INTEREST GROUPS

ADA—Americans for Democratic Action. The ADA describes itself as America's "oldest liberal public policy organization." It arrives at what it calls its annual "Liberal Quotient" by choosing issues such as proabortion rights, antideath penalty, anti-high-Pentagon spending and procivil rights.

ACU—American Conservative Union. This 20-year-old organization calls its annual ratings the measure of a legislator's conservatism. Military, foreign affairs and spending issues are primarily used as the test.

COPE—Committee on Political Education of the AFL-CIO. Big Labor's political lobbying arm measures legislators according to how they vote on issues the organization thinks directly effect organized labor and the working person.

COC—Chamber of Commerce of the United States. Since 1912 the voice of Big Business in Washington. Bases it ratings on issues it believes effect business and trade.

LCV—League of Conservation Voters. Organization is made up from representatives of other national proenvironmental organizations such as Friends of the Earth, Sierra Club and the Wilderness Society. It attempts to elect proenvironmental candidates to Congress. It bases its annual ratings on issues such as protecting natural resources, energy conservation and clean air-clean water.

NTLC—National Tax Limitation Committee. Organized in 1975 to seek constitutional and other limits on taxes, spending, and deficits at the federal, state and local level. In choosing which votes to analyze each member of Congress on, the NTLC studies taxing, spending, and other issues of "major fiscal consequence."

CFA—Consumer Federation of America. Lobbying organization representing the American consumer in contrast to Washington lobbies representing business and industry. It bases its annual ratings on pocketbook, product safety and health issues.

ASC—American Security Council. It says that its annual "National Security Voting Index" is a measure of a legislator's commitment to "peace through strength." Critics say it is the measure of a legislator's willingness to vote for every weapons system requested by the Pentagon. Most of its test votes involve military budgeting matters, but this year it also included the flag burning constitutional amendment.

Congressional office buildings (abbreviated)

DSOB —Dirksen Senate Office Bldg.
HSOB—Hart Senate Office Bldg.
RSOB —Russell Senate Office Bldg.
CHOB—Cannon House Office Bldg.
LHOB—Longworth House Office Bldg.
RHOB—Rayburn House Office Bldg.

CONGRESSIONAL LEADERSHIP

Senate

President Pro-Tem: Sen. Robert C. Byrd, D.-W.Va.
Majority Leader: Sen. George Mitchell, D.-Maine
Majority Whip: Sen. Wendell H. Ford, D.-Ky.
Sec. Democratic Conference: Sen. David Pryor, D.-Ark.
Chief Deputy Whip: Sen. John Braux, D.-La.
Chm. Democratic Campaign Comm.: Sen. Bob Graham, D.-Fla.
Chm. Democratic Steering Comm.: Daniel K. Inouye, D.-Hawaii
Chm. Democratic Policy Comm.: Sen. Thomas A Daschel, D.-S.Dak.
Minority Leader: Sen. Robert Dole, R.-Kans.
Minority Whip: Sen. Alan K. Simpson, R.-Wyo.
Chm. Republican Conference: Sen. Thad Cochran, R.-Miss.
Sec. Republican Conference: Sen. Trent Lott, R.-Miss.
Chm. Republican Senatorial Campaign Comm.: Sen. Phil Gramm, R-Tex.
Chm. Republican Policy Comm.: Sen. Don Nickles, R.-Okla.

House

Speaker: Rep. Thomas S. Foley, D.-Wash.
Majority Leader: Rep. Richard Gephardt, D.-Mo.
Majority Whip: Rep. David Bonior, D.-Mich.
Deputy Minority Whips
Rep. Butler Derrick, D-S.C.
Rep. Barbara Kennelly, D.-Conn.
Rep. John Lewis, D.-Ga.
Rep. William Richardson, D.-N.Mex.
Chm. Democratic Cong. Comm.: Rep. Vic Fazio, D.-Calif.
Chm. Democratic Caucus: Rep. Steny Hoyer, D.-Md.

V.-Chm. Democratic Caucus: Rep. Vic Fazio, D.-Calif.

Minority Leader: Rep. Robert Michel, R.-Ill.

Minority Whip: Rep. Newt Gingrich, R.-Ga.

Chm. Republican Conference: Rep. Richard Armey, R.-Tex.

V.-Chm. Republican Conference: Rep. Bill McCollum, R.-Fla.

Chm. Republican Congressional Comm.: Rep. Bill Paxton, R.-N.Y.

Chm. Republican Policy Comm.: Rep. Henry Hyde, R.-Ill.

ALABAMA

In 1994, with neither of Alabama's senators up for reelection, and with the congressional delegation looking solid, Alabama will look inward with all the emphasis on state politics. Governor Jim Folsom, Jr., sworn in to replace convicted former GOP Gov. Harold Guy Hunt, will try to hold the office. He could well be challenged by a trio of strong Democrats: Secretary of State Billy Joe Camp, Attorney General Jimmy Evans, and Treasurer George Wallace III. This could make the Democratic gubernatorial primary one of the more interesting contests in years.

1992 PRESIDENTIAL ELECTION: (9 Electoral votes): Clinton (D) 686,571 (41%); Bush (R) 798,439 (48%); Perot (I) 181,514 (11%); Marrou (Lib) 5,506; Fulani (NAP) 1,834; Warren (Soc Wks) 774; LaRouche (I) 680; Hagelin (NLP) 467. 1988 Bush 815,576 (60%); Dukakis 549,506 (40%); Other 13,394.

SENATORS

Howell Thomas Heflin (D)

Born June 19, 1921, Poulan, Ga; home, Tuscumbia; Birmingham-Southern College, B.A. 1941, University of Ala., J.D. 1948; United Methodist; married (Elizabeth Ann), 1 child.

Elected 1978, seat up 1996. Career: USMC, WWII; Faculty, University of Ala., 1946–48, University of N. Ala., 1948–52; Practicing atty., 1948–71, 1977–79; Chief Justice, Ala. Supreme Crt., 1971–77.

Committees: (1) Agriculture, Nutrition & Forestry; (2) Judiciary; (3) Small Business.

Election Results: 1990 Heflin 701,636 (61%); Bill Cabaniss (R) 454,906 (39%). 1984 Heflin (63%).

Interest Group Ratings:

ADA	ACU	COPE	COC
40	48	75	40

LCV	NTLC	CFA	ASC
08	33	75	90

Office: 728 HSOB 20510, 202-224-4124 (Stephen W. Raby, AA). STATE OFFICES: Fed. Crthse., 15 Lee St., Montgomery 36104, 205-832-7287 (Tim Brown, Rep.); Cardiff Hotel, Main Street, P.O. Box 228, Tuscumbia 35674, 205-381-7060 (William Gardiner, Chief-of-staff); 316 Fed. Bldg., 1800 5th Ave. N., Birmingham 35203, 205-254-1500 (Stanley Vines, Rep.); 437 Fed. Crthse., Mobile 36602, 205-690-3167 (Bob Morrissette, Rep.)

Richard Craig Shelby (D)

Born May 6, 1934, Birmingham; home, Tuscaloosa; University of Ala., B.A. 1957, LL.B. 1963; Presbyterian; married (Annette), 2 children.

Elected 1986, seat up 1998. Career: Practicing atty., 1963–78; Ala. Senate, 1970–78; U.S. House of Reps., 1978-1986.

Committees: (1) Armed Services; (2) Banking, Housing & Urban Affairs; (3) Energy & Natural Resources (4) Special Committee on Aging.

Election Results: 1992 Shelby, 1,017,332 (66%); Richard Sellers (R) (34%). 1986 Shelby 609,360 (50%), Jeremiah Denton (R) 602,537 (50%).

Interest Group Ratings:

ADA	ACU	COPE	COC
30	63	58	60

LCV	NTLC	CFA	ASC
17	33	58	100

Office: 509 HSOB 20510, 202-224-5744 (Tom Young, AA). STATE OFFICES: 1118 Greensboro Ave, P.O. Box 2570, Tuscaloosa 35403, 205-759-5047 (Connie Butler, State Dir.); 327 Fed. Bldg. Birmingham 35203, 205-731-1384 (Blair Agricola, Rep.); P.O. Box 6026, Huntsville 35806, 205-772-0460 205-772-0460 (Pam Lindley, Rep.); 113 St. Joseph St. Rm. 438, Mobile 36602 (Cathy Barter, Rep.); Fed. Crthse., 15 Lee St., Montgomery 36104, 205-832-7303 (Carol Estes, Rep.)

REPRESENTATIVES

FIRST DISTRICT

Sonny Callahan (R)

District: Six counties in southwest corner of the state including the city of Mobile. Population: 577,266—Black 28%. Politics: Republican.

Born Sept. 11, 1932, Mobile; home, Mobile; University of Ala., Mobile Extension; Roman Catholic; married (Karen), 6 children.

Elected 1984. Career: Navy, 1952–54; Finch Co. (trucking, real estate, warehousing), Pres., 1964–85; Ala. House of Reps., 1970–78; Ala. Senate, 1978–82.

Committees: (1) Appropriations.

Election Results: 1992 Callahan 125,201 (62%); William Brewer (D) 77,305 (38%). 1990 Callahan (Unopposed). 1988 Callahan 59%.

Interest Group Ratings:

ADA	ACU	COPE	COC
05	96	27	75

LCV	NTLC	CFA	ASC
00	95	20	100

Office: 2418 RHOB 20515, 202-225-4931 (Joe Bonner, AA). DISTRICT OFFICE: 2970 Cottage Hill Rd., Suite 126, Mobile 36602, 205-690-2811 (Taylor Ellis, Dist. Adm.)

SECOND DISTRICT

Terry Everett (R)

District: Southeast portion of state including entire city of Dothan, and a part of Montgomery. Population: 577,277—Black 24%. Politics: Republican.

Born Feb. 15, 1937, Dothan, Ala.; home, Enterprise; Enterprise State Junior College; Baptist; married (Barbara).

Elected 1992. Career: U.S. Air Force 1959–61; Reporter, Editor, local newspapers 1961–74. Founder & Publisher Dothan Eagle 1974–85. Owner Everett Media, Gulf Coast Media 1984–present.

Committees: (1) Armed Services; (2) Veteran Affairs.

Election Results: 1992 Everett 112,431 (51%); George Wallace, Jr. (D) 109,114 (49%).

Interest Group Ratings:
Freshman—None

Office: 208 CHOB 20515, 202-225-2901 (Clay Swanzy, AA) DISTRICT OFFICES: 3001 Zelda Rd., Montgomery 36106, 205-277-9113 (Steve Pelham, Rep. at all offices); City Hall Bldg.,

Opelika 36467, 205-493-9253; 116 S. Main St. #211, Enterprise 36330, 205-393-2996; Fed. Bldg. 100 W. Troy St., Dothan 36303 206-794-9680.

THIRD DISTRICT

Glen Browder (D)

District: East Central part of the state including cities of Anniston, Auburn and Tuskegee. Population: 577,227—Black 26%. Politics: Leans Democratic.

Born Jan. 15, 1943, Sumter, S.C.; home, Jacksonville; Presbyterian College, B.A. 1965, Emory University, M.A., Ph.D. 1965; Methodist; married (Sarah Rebecca), 1 child.

Elected April 4, 1989. Career: Sportswriter, Atlanta Journal, 1966; Investigator, U.S. Civil Service Comm., 1966; Prof., Jacksonville State University, 1971–87; Ala. House of Reps., 1982–86; Ala. Secy. of State, 1986–89.

Committees: (1) Armed Services; (2) Science, Space and Technology (on leave); (3) Budget

Election Results: 1992 Browder 118,599 (62%); Don Sledge (R) 74,101 (38%). 1990 Browder 74%. 1989 (special) Browder 65%.

Interest Group Ratings:

ADA	ACU	COPE	COC
45	48	58	50

LCV	NTLC	CFA	ASC
44	30	47	90

Office: 1221 LHOB 20515, 202-225-3261 (Bob McNeil, AA). DISTRICT OFFICES: 104 Fed. Bldg., P.O. Box 2042, Anniston 36202, 205-236-5655 (Ray Minter, Dist. AA.); Fed. Bldg., Opelika 36801, 205-745-6222 (Alice Lloyd, Mgr.)

FOURTH DISTRICT

Tom Bevill (D)

District: Entire North central part of the state including the city of Gadsden. Population: 577,227—Black 7%. Politics: Traditionally Democratic but now mixed.

Born Mar. 27, 1921, Townley; home, Jasper; University of Ala., B.S. 1943, LL.B. 1948; Baptist; married (Lou), 3 children.

Elected 1966. Career: Army, WWII; Practicing atty., 1948–67; Ala. House of Reps., 1958–66.

Committees: (1) Appropriations

Election Results: 1992 Bevill 157,937 (70%); Mickey Strickland (R) 66,907 (30%). 1990 Bevill Unopposed. 1988: Bevill 96%.

Interest Group Ratings:

ADA	ACU	COPE	COC
55	32	67	38

LCV	NTLC	CFA	ASC
19	10	60	80

Office: 2302 RHOB 20515, 202-225-4876 (Don Smith, AA). DISTRICT OFFICES: 107 Fed. Bldg., Gadsden 35901, 205-546-0201 (Mary Cochran, Mgr); 247 Fed. Bldg. Jasper 35501, 205-221-2310 (Charles Watts & Missie Hudson, Reps.); 102 Fed. Bldg., Cullman 35055, 205-734-6043 (Evelyn Stevens)

FIFTH DISTRICT

Robert "Bud" Cramer (D)

District: Far northern portion of the state including the city of Huntsville. Population: 577,227—Black 15%. Politics: Democratic.

Born Aug. 22, 1947, Huntsville, home, Huntsville; University of Ala., B.A. 1969; University of Ala. Law School J.D. 1972; Methodist; widower, 1 child.

Elected 1990. Career: Lawyer, Madison Cty. Dist. Atty. 1981–90.

Committees: (1) Public Works & Transportation; (2) Science, Space, & Technology; (3) Select Committee on Intelligence.

Election Results: 1992 Cramer 155,473 (66%); Terry Smith (R) 78,369 (34%). 1990 Cramer 67%.

Interest Group Ratings:

ADA	ACU	COPE	COC
55	44	58	50

LCV	NTLC	CFA	ASC
44	20	60	90

Office: 1318 LHOB 20515, 202-225-4801 (Mike Adcock, AA). DISTRICT OFFICES: 403 Franklin St., Huntsville 35801, 205-551-0190 (Lynn Berry, Rep.); Morgan County Courthouse, P.O. Box 668, Decatur 35602, 205-355-9400 (Lynn Berry, Rep.); 373 E. Avalon Ave., Muscle Schoals 35661, 205-381-3450 (Lynn Berry, Rep.)

SIXTH DISTRICT

Spencer Bachus (R)

District: Central part of state including parts of cities of Birimgham and Tuscaloosa. Population: 577,226—Black 9%. Politics: Leans Democratic.

Born Dec. 23, 1943, Birmingham; home, Birmingham; Auburn University, B.A. 1969; University of Ala. Law School, J.D. 1972; Baptist; (divorced), 3 children.

Elected 1992. Career: Lawyer; Ala. State Sen. 1982–83; Ala. State Rep., 1984–86; Ala. Board of Ed. 1987–91; Senior partner, Bachus, Dempsy, Carson & Steed, 1987–present.

Committees: (1) Banking, Finance & Urban Affairs; (2) Veteran Affairs.

Election Results: 1992 Bachus 146,351 (54%); Ben Erdreich (D) 125,942 (46%).

Interest Group Ratings:
None—Freshman

Office: 216 CHOB 20515, 202-225-4921 (Larry Lavender, AA) DISTRICT OFFICES: 1900 International Dr. #107, Birmingham 35243, 205-969-2296 (Donna Williams, Rep.); 3500 Mcfarland Blvd. P.O. Drawer 569, Northport 35476, 205-333-9894 (Margaret Pyle, Rep.)

SEVENTH DISTRICT

Earl F. Hilliard (D)

District: A newly created minority district in the west central part of the state, including parts of the cities of Tuscaloosa, Birmingham, and Montgomery. Population: 577,227—Black 68%. Politics: Democratic.

Born April 9, 1942, Birmingham; home, Birmingham; Moorehouse College, B.A. 1962, Howard University, J.D. 1967; Atlanta University School of Business, M.B.A. 1970; Baptist; married (Mary), 2 children.

Elected 1992. Career: State Represenative, 1974–80; State Senator, 1980–92.

Committees: (1) Agriculture; (2) Small Business.

Election Results: 1992 Hilliard 144,255 (80%); Kervin Jones (R) 36,066 (20%).

Interest Group Ratings:
None—Freshman

Office: 1007 LHOB 20515, 202-225-2665 (Tunstall Wilson, AA). DISTRICT OFFICES: 204 Fed. Bldg., Tuscaloosa 35401, 205-752-3579 (China Davidson, Dir.); 1800 5th Ave. N. #305, Birmingham 35203, 205-328-2841 (Elvira Willoughby, Rep.); 109 Fed. Bldg., Selma 36701, 205-872-2684 (Betty Callaway, Rep.)

ALASKA

The big political questions in Alaska in 1994 are whether maverick Gov. Walter Hickel, 71, will run again; and if he does, will it be as an independent as he did in 1990 when he won a surprise victory, or might he return to the Republican party (and would it welcome the former Interior Secretary back?). The state remains solidly Republican, but it's congressman-at-large, Rep. Don Young, continues to scrape by with narrow victory margins. Will he retire in 1994, or might he finally be unseated?

1992 PRESIDENTIAL ELECTION: (3 Electoral votes): Clinton (D) 63,498 (31%); Bush (R) 81,875 (40%); Perot (I) 55,085 (27%); Marrou (Lib) 1,118; Gritz (Pop) 1,095; LaRouche (I) 379; Hagelin (NLP) 355; Phillips (AmTax) 311; Fulani (NAP) 253. 1988 Bush 119,251 (62%); Dukakis 72,584 (38%).

SENATORS

Ted Stevens (R)

Born Nov. 18, 1923, Indianapolis, Ind.; home, Girdwood; University of Calif. at Los Angeles, A.B. 1947, Harvard University, LL.B. 1950; Episcopalian; married (Catherine), 6 children (5 w/ wife Anne now deceased).

Appointed Dec. 24, 1968, Elected 1970, seat up 1996. Career: Air Force, WWII; Practicing atty., 1950–53, 1961–68; U.S. Atty., 1953–56; U.S. Dept. of Interior, Legis. counsel, 1956–58, Asst. to the Secy., 1958–60, Solicitor 1960–61; Alaska House of Reps., 1964–68.

Committees: (1) Appropriations; (2) Commerce, Science & Transportation; (3) Governmental Affairs; (4) Rules & Administration (Ranking Member); (5) Select Committee on Ethics; (6) Joint Committee on the Library; (7) Joint Committee on Printing; (8) Small Business.

Election Results: 1990 Stevens 106,465 (67%); Michael Beasley (D) 51,966 (33%). 1984 Stevens 71%.

Interest Group Ratings:

ADA	ACU	COPE	COC
20	74	33	80

LCV	NTLC	CFA	ASC
08	78	17	90

Office: 522 HSOB 20510, 202-224-3004 (Lisa Sutherland, AA). STATE OFFICES: 222 W. 7th Ave., Anchorage 99513 907-271-5915 (Barbara Andrews, Manager); 206 Fed. Bldg., 101 12th Ave., Fairbanks 99701, 907-456-0261 (Janet Halverson, Asst.); 403 Fed. Bldg., Juneau 99802, 907-586-7400 (H. Gen Dickey, Asst.); 120 Trading Bay Rd., Suite 350, Kenai 99611, 907-283-5808 (Peggy Arness, Asst.); Fed. Bldg. Ketchikan 99901, 907-225-6880 (Sherri Slick, Asst.)

Frank H. Murkowski (R)

Born Mar. 28, 1933, Seattle, Wash.; home, Fairbanks; University of Santa Clara, Seattle University, B.A. 1955; Roman Catholic; married (Nancy), 6 children.

Elected 1980, seat up 1998. Career: Coast Guard, 1955–56; Alaska Commissioner of Econ. Develop., 1966–70; Pres., Alaska Natl. Bank of the North, 1971–80.

Committees: (1) Energy & Natural Resources; (2) Foreign Relations; (3) Veterans Affairs (Ranking Member); (4) Select Committee on Indian Affairs (Ranking Member).

Election Results: 1992 Murkowski 107,026 (53%); Tony Smith (D) 77,654 (39%); Mary Jordan (I) 16,498 (8%). 1986 Murkowski 97,674 (54%). 1980 Murkowski (54%).

Interest Group Ratings:

ADA	ACU	COPE	COC
25	70	30	100

LCV	NTLC	CFA	ASC
08	83	33	90

Office: 706 HSOB 20510, 202-224-6665 (Gregg Renkes, AA). STATE OFFICES: Fed. Bldg, Anchorage 99513, 907-271-3735 (Patricia Heller, Asst.); Fed. Bldg. Fairbanks 99701 (Marcia Kozie, Asst.); 965 Fed. Bldg., Juneau 99802, 907-586-7400 (H. Gen. Dickey, Asst.)

REPRESENTATIVE AT LARGE

Don Young (R)

District: Entire state. Population: 550,043—Black 4%, Native American 16%, Asian 4%. Politics: Republican.

Born June 9, 1933, Meridian, Calif.; home, Fort Yukon; Chicago State College, B.A. 1956; Episcopalian; married (Lu), 2 children.

Elected Mar. 6, 1973. Career: Construction work, 1959; Teacher, 1960–69; Riverboat captain; Fort Yukon City Cncl., 1960–64; Mayor of Fort Yukon, 1964–68; Alaska House of Reps., 1966–70; Alaska Senate, 1970-73.

Committees: (1) Natural Resources; (2) Merchant Marine & Fisheries (Ranking Member); (3) Post Office & Civil Service.

Election Results: 1992 Young 93,673 (47%); John Devens (D) 87,281 (43%); Mike Milligan (Oth) 7,694 (4%); Michael States (Oth) 12,231 (6%). 1990 Young 82,549 (51%). 1988 Young (62%).

Interest Group Ratings:

ADA	ACU	COPE	COC
25	84	67	88

LCV	NTLC	CFA	ASC
00	65	40	100

Office: 2331 RHOB 20515, 202-225-5765 (Lloyd Jones, AA). DISTRICT OFFICES: 222 W. 7th Ave. Anchorage 99513, 907-271-5978 (Roberta Norman, Asst.); 401 Fed. Bldg. Juneau 99801, 907-586-7400 (Lucy Hudson, Asst.); Fed. Bldg, Fairbanks 99701, 907-456-0210 (Royce Chapman, Asst.)

ARIZONA

After a number of confused and turbulent years, Arizona politics have settled down a bit; although it is not clear if Republican Gov. Fife Symington is going to have to stand trial on business fraud charges. The big political questions now revolve around Democratic Sen. Dennis DeConcini, one of the so-called Keating Five, five members of the Senate charged with improprieties in their dealings with S&L king Charles Keating.

DeConcini is up for reelection in 1994, and he says he fully intends to run for a third term, despite an earlier promise not to serve more than two terms. Question number one is whether Democratic Secretary of State Dick Mahony will challenge him in the Democratic primary. The probable GOP candidate, Rep. Jon Kyl, will likely give either DeConcini or Mahony a tough fight.

1992 PRESIDENTIAL ELECTION: (8 Electoral votes): Clinton (D) 526,304 (37%); Bush (R) 549,284 (38%); Perot (I) 341,638 (24%); Gritz (Pop) 7,929; Marrou (Lib) 6,579; Hagelin (NLP) 2,223; Fulani (NAP) 881. 1988 Bush 694,379 (61%); Dukakis 447,272 (39%).

SENATORS

Dennis DeConcini (D)

Born May 8, 1937, Tucson; home, Tucson; University of Ariz., B.A. 1959, LL.B. 1963; Roman Catholic; married (Susan), 3 children.

Elected 1976, seat up 1994. Career: Army, 1959–60; Practicing atty., 1963–65, 1968–73; Special Counsel, A.A. to Gov. Samuel P. Goddard, 1965–67; Pima Cnty. Atty., 1972–76.

Committees: (1) Appropriations; (2) Judiciary; (3) Rules & Administration; (4) Veterans Affairs; (5) Select Comm. on Indian Affairs; (6) Select Comm. on Intelligence (Chairman); (7) Joint Comm. on the Library; (8) Joint Comm. on Printing.

Election Results: 1988 DeConcini 660,403 (57%); DeGreen (R) 478,060 (41%). 1982 DeConcini (59%).

Interest Group Ratings:

ADA	ACU	COPE	COC
75	20	64	10

LCV	NTLC	CFA	ASC
17	33	67	40

Office: 328 HSOB 20510, 202-224-4521 (Gene Karp, AA). STATE OFFICES: Rm. C-100, 323 W. Roosevelt, Phoenix 85003, 602-261-6756 (Barry Dill, State Dir.); 2424 E. Broadway, Tucson 85719, 602-629-6831 (David Steele, Dir.); 40 N. Center Street, Suite 110, Mesa 85201, 602-261-4998 (Mary Jane Perry, Dpty. Dir.)

John Stuart McCain (R)

Born Aug. 29, 1936, Panama Canal Zone; home, Phoenix; U.S. Naval Academy, 1958, National War College, 1973–74; Episcopalian; married (Cindy), 6 children.

Elected 1986; seat up 1998. Career: Navy, 1958–80 (Captain, ret.); Dir., Navy Senate Liaison Office, 1976–80; U.S. House of Reps., 1982–1986.

Committees: (1) Armed Services; (2) Commerce, Science & Transportation; (3) Governmental Affairs; (4) Select Committee on Aging; (5) Select Committee on Indian Affairs.

Election Results: 1992 McCain 740,578 (56%); Claire Sargent (D) 421,905 (32%); Evan Mecham (I) 140,536 (11%); Kiana Delamare (I) 21,874 (2%); Ed Finkelstein (I) 6,111. 1986 McCain (60%).

Interest Group Ratings:

ADA	ACU	COPE	COC
20	85	33	90

LCV	NTLC	CFA	ASC
08	100	67	90

Office: 111 RSOB 20510, 202-224-2235 (Deb Amend, AA). STATE OFFICES: Suite 190, 5353 N. 16th Street, Phoenix 85016, 602-241-2567 (Wes Gullett, AA); 5151 Broadway, Suite 170, Tucson 85711, 602-670-6334 (Lillian Lopez Grant, Mgr.); Suite 1000, 151 N. Centennial Way, Mesa 85201, 602-835-8994 (Mary Turner, Mgr.)

REPRESENTATIVES

FIRST DISTRICT

Sam Coppersmith (D)

District: Parts of the city of Phoenix and suburbs, including Tempe and Mesa. Population: 610,872—Black 3%, Hispanic 13%, Other 6%. Politics: Leans Republican.

Born May 22, 1955, Johnstown, Pa.; home, Phoenix; Harvard University, A.B. 1976, Yale Law School, J.D. 1982; Jewish; married (Beth), 3 children.

Elected 1992. Career: Foreign Service Officer, 1977–79; Law Clerk, U.S. Court of Appeals, 1982–83; Asst. to Mayor of Phoenix, 1984–86; Practicing atty. 1986–present.

Committees: (1) Public Works & Transportation; (2) Science, Space & Technology.

Election Results: 1992 Coppersmith 125,545 (54%); John J. Rhodes III (R) 106,938 (46%).

Interest Group Ratings:
None—Freshman

Office: 1607 LHOB 20515, 202-225-2635 (Cindy Gordon, AA). DISTRICT OFFICE: 404 South Mill Ave. #C-201, Tempe 85081, 602-921-5500 (Christa Severns, Dist. Mgr.)

SECOND DISTRICT

Ed Pastor (D)

District: A newly constructed Hispanic majority district stretching from the least affluent areas of Phoenix and including most of Tucson, to the southwest corner of the state. Population: 610,871—Black 7%, Native American 5%, Hispanic 50%, Other 27%. Politics: Democratic.

Born June 28, 1943. Claypool; home, Phoenix; Ariz. State, B.S. 1966, J.D. 1974; Roman Catholic; married (Verma), 2 children.

Elected 1991. Career: Staff Member Gov. Raul Castro; Dept. Dir. Guadalupe Organization Inc.; Maricopa Co. Board of Supervisors, 1977–91.

Committees: (1) Appropriations.

Election Results: 1992 Pastor 88,010 (69%); Don Shooter (R) 40,088 (31%). 1991 (special) Pastor (56%).

Interest Group Ratings:

ADA	ACU	COPE	COC
85	12	83	13

LCV	NTLC	CFA	ASC
56	08	73	20

Office: 408 CHOB 20515, 202-225-4065 (Gene Fisher, AA). DISTRICT OFFICES: 332 E. McDowell #10, Phoenix 85004, 602-256-0551 (Ron Piceno, Rep.); 2432 E. Broadway Blvd., Tucson 85719, 602-624-9986 (Linda Leatherman, Rep.)

THIRD DISTRICT

Bob Stump (R)

District: Western part of the state including some northern and western Phoenix suburbs and the large retirement community of Sun City. Population: 610,871—Black 2%, Native American 3%, Hispanic 12%, Other 6%. Politics: Republican.

Born Apr. 4, 1927, Phoenix; home, Tolleson; Ariz. State University, B.S. 1951; Seventh Day Adventist; divorced, 3 children.

Elected 1976. Career: Navy, WWII; Cotton & grain farmer; Ariz. House of Reps., 1959–67; Ariz. Senate, 1967–76, Senate Pres., 1975–76.

Committees: (1) Armed Services; (2) Veterans Affairs (Ranking Member).

Election Results: 1992 Stump 154,242 (64%); Roger Hartstone (D) 86,894 (36%). 1990 Stump (57%). 1988 Stump (69%).

Interest Group Ratings:

ADA	ACU	COPE	COC
00	100	08	75

LCV	NTLC	CFA	ASC
00	100	00	100

Office: 211 CHOB 20515, 202-225-4576 Lisa Jackson, AA). DISTRICT OFFICE: 2001 Fed. Bldg., Phoenix 85025, 602-261-6923 (Arlene Lassila, Dist. Asst.)

FOURTH DISTRICT

Jon Llewelyn Kyl (R)

District: Includes the most affluent parts of Phoenix and Scottsdale. Population: 610,871— Hispanic 8%. Politics: Republican.

Born April 25, 1942, Oakland; home, Phoenix; University of Ariz., B.A. 1964, LL.B. 1966; Presbyterian; married (Caryll), 2 children.

Elected 1986. Career: Practicing atty., 1966–86; Chm., Metro Phoenix Chamber of Commerce, 1985–86.

Committees: (1) Armed Services; (2) Government Operations; (3) Ethics.

Election Results: 1992 Kyl 149,021 (59%); Walter Mybeck II (D) 68,355 (27%); Debbie Collings (Oth) 24,571 (10%); Tim McDermott (Oth) 11,167 (4%). 1990 Kyl (61%). 1988 Kyl (87%).

Interest Group Ratings:

ADA	ACU	COPE	COC
05	92	33	75

LCV	NTLC	CFA	ASC
00	100	13	100

Office: 2440 RHOB 20515, 202-225-3361 (Patti Alderson, AA). DISTRICT OFFICE: 4250 E. Camelback Rd., Suite 140K, Phoenix 85018, 602-840-1891 (Pamela Barbey, Rep.)

FIFTH DISTRICT

James Thomas Kolbe (R)

District: East Tucson and all of the Southeast part of the state. Population: 620,871—Black 3%, Hispanic 16%, Other 6%. Politics: Republican.

Born June 28, 1942, Evanston, Ill.; home, Patagonia; Northwestern University, B.A. 1965, Stanford University, M.B.A. 1967; United Methodist; (divorced).

Elected 1984. Career: Navy, Vietnam; Asst. to Ill. Gov. Richard Ogilvie, 1970–73; Ariz. Senate 1977–82.

Committees: (1) Appropriations; (2) Budget.

Election Results: 1992 Kolbe 166,937 (69%); Jim Toevs (D) 73,894 (31%). 1990 Kolbe (65%). 1988 Kolbe (68%).

Interest Group Ratings:

ADA	ACU	COPE	COC
25	76	25	88

LCV	NTLC	CFA	ASC
00	100	20	100

Office: 405 CHOB 20515, 202-225-2542 (Laurie Fenton, AA). DISTRICT OFFICE: Suite 112, 1661 N. Swan, Tucson 85712, 602-322-3555 (Patricia Klein, AA); Suite 160, 77 Calle Portal, Sierra Vista 85635 602-459-3115 (Billie Fabijan, Rep.)

SIXTH DISTRICT

Karan English (D)

District: A newly created, geographically large district, more than 60% rural, covering a third of the state in the northern and eastern parts. Population: 610,872—Native American 22%, Hispanic 13%, Other 6%. Politics: Democratic.

Born March 23, 1949, Berkeley, Calif.; home, Flagstaff; University of Ariz., B.A. 1975; married (Rob Elliot), 5 children.

Elected 1992. Career: Coconino Co. Board of Supervisors 1980–86; State Rep. 1987–90; State Sen. 1991–92.

Committees: (1) Education & Labor; (2) Natural Resources.

Election Results: 1992 English 120,865 (56%); Doug Wead (R) 93,653 (44%).

Interest Group Ratings:
None—Freshman

Office: 1024 LHOB 20515, 202-225-2190 (Vicki Hicks, AA). DISTRICT OFFICES: 117 E. Aspen Ave., Flagstaff 86001, 602-774-1314 (Ed Delaney, Rep.); 1818 E. Southern Ave. #3-B, Mesa 85204, 602-497-1156 (Sharon Davis, Rep.)

ARKANSAS

Arkansas is a state in which Republicans keep waiting for a breakthrough that never seems to come. Now with Bill Clinton in the White House it will be even more difficult for the GOP to make any kind of a breakthrough. Lt. Gov. Jim Guy Tucker has moved up to serve out the remainder of Clinton's term, and he will have to run for election in 1994. The Republicans would love to embarrass the President by defeating his successor, but it likely will not happen.

1992 PRESIDENTIAL ELECTION: (6 Electoral votes:) Clinton (D) 498,778 (54%); Bush (R) 333,909 (36%); Perot (I) 98,215 (11%); Fulani (NAP) 1,293; Phillips (AmTax) 1,237; Marrou (Lib) 1,194; Boren (Apath) 980; LaRouche (I) 831; Hagelin (NLP) 818; Gritz (Pop) 790; Yiamouyiannis (TkBkAm) 532; Dodge (Prob) 472; Masters (LkBack) 395. 1988 Bush 463,574 (57%); Dukakis 344,991 (43%)

SENATORS

Dale Bumpers (D)

Born Aug. 12, 1925, Charleston; home, Charleston; University of Ark., Northwestern University, LL.B. 1951; Methodist; married (Betty), 3 children.

Elected 1974, seat up 1998. Career: USMC, WWII; Practicing atty., 1951–70; Gov. of Ark., 1970–74.

Committees: (1) Appropriations; (2) Energy & Natural Resources; (3) Small Business (Chairman).

Election Results: 1992 Bumpers 545,325 (60%); Mike Huckabee (R) 362,203 (40%). 1986 Bumpers 433,092 (62%); Asa Hutchinson (R) 262,300 (38%). 1980 Bumpers (59%).

Interest Group Ratings:

ADA	ACU	COPE	COC
90	15	75	10

LCV	NTLC	CFA	ASC
50	28	92	40

Office: 229 DSOB 20510, 202-224-4843 (Mary Davis, AA). STATE OFFICE: 2527 Fed. Bldg., 700 W. Capitol, Little Rock 72201, 501-324-6286 (Martha Perry, State Rep.)

David Hampton Pryor (D)

Born Aug. 29, 1934, Camden; home, Little Rock; Henderson State University, University of Ark., B.A. 1957, LL.B. 1964; Presbyterian; married (Barbara), 3 children.

Elected 1978, seat up 1996. Career: Ed. & Publ., Ouachita Citizen, Camden, 1957–61; Ark. House of Reps., 1960–66; Practicing atty., 1964–66; U.S. House of Reps., 1967–72; Gov. of Ark., 1975–79.

Committees: (1) Agriculture, Nutrition & Forestry; (2) Finance; (3) Governmental Affairs; (4) Special Committee on Reorganization of Congress; (5) Special Committee on Aging (Chairman).

Election Results: 1990 Pryor (Unopposed). 1984 Pryor (57%).

Interest Group Ratings:

ADA	ACU	COPE	COC
90	15	75	30

LCV	NTLC	CFA	ASC
42	10	92	30

Office: 267 RSOB 20510, 202-224-2353 (Frank Thomas, AA). STATE OFFICE: 3030 Fed. Bldg., 600 W. Capitol Ave., Little Rock 72201, 501-324-6336 (Frank Thomas, St. Dir.)

REPRESENTATIVES

FIRST DISTRICT

Blanche Lambert (D)

District: The northeastern part of the state (Mississippi River Delta country) including the city of Jonesboro. Population: 588,588—Black 18%. Politics: Democratic.

Born Sept 30, 1960, Helena; home, Helena; Randolph Macon College, B.A. 1982; Episcopalian; single.

Elected 1992. Career: Lobbyist; Staff assistant, Rep. Alexander, 1982–84; Legislative affairs specialist, 1985–89; Senior Associate, The Pagnosis & Donnely Group, 1989–91.

Committees: (1) Energy & Commerce; (2) Merchant Marine & Fisheries; (3) Agriculture.

Election Results: 1992 Lambert 146,318 (70%); Terry Hayes (R) 63,876 (30%).

Interest Group Ratings:
None—Freshman

Office: 1204 LHOB 20515, 202-225-4076 (Russ Orban, AA). DISTRICT OFFICES: 615 S. Main #211, Jonesboro 72401, 501-972-4600 (Earlene Norwood, Rep.)

SECOND DISTRICT

Ray Thornton (D)

District: Central Arkansas including Little Rock. Population: 587,412—Black 18%. Politics: Leans Democratic.

Born July 26, 1928, Conway; home, Little Rock; Yale B.A. 1950, University of Ark., J.D. 1956; Church of Christ; married (Betty Jo), 3 children.

Elected 1990. Career: Lawyer priv. prac. 1956–70; Ark. Atty. Gen. 1971–73; U.S. House 1973–79; Pres. Arkansas State University 1980–84; Pres. University of Arkansas 1984–90.

Committees: (1) Appropriations.

Election Results: 1992 Thornton 149,952 (74%); Dennis Scott (R) 52,032 (26%). 1990 Thornton 101,572 (60%).

Interest Group Ratings:

ADA	ACU	COPE	COC
85	08	91	38

LCV	NTLC	CFA	ASC
25	00	60	80

Office: 1214 LHOB 20515, 202-225-2506 (Ed Fry, Staff Dir.). DISTRICT OFFICE: 1527 Fed. Bldg., 700 W. Capitol, Little Rock 72201, 501-378-5941 (vacant, Dir.)

THIRD DISTRICT

Tim Hutchinson (R)

District: The northwest part of the state including the Arkansas Ozarks with the population centering around Fort Smith and Fayetteville. Population: 589,523—Black 2%. Politics: Republican.

Born Aug 11, 1949, Gravette; home, Benntonville; Bob Jones University, B.A. 1971, University of Ark. M.A., 1971; Baptist; married (Donna), 3 children.

Elected 1992. Career: Minister; Co–owner & manager KBCV radio,1982–89; State Rep., 1984–92.

Committees: (1) Public Works & Transportation; (2) Veterans Affairs.

Election Results: 1992 Hutchinson 125,065 (50%); John VanWinkle (D) 117,486 (47%); Ralph Forbes (Oth) 6,319 (3%).

Interest Group Ratings:
None—Freshman

Office: 1541 LHOB 20515, 202-225-4301 (Ray Reid, AA). DISTRICT OFFICES: Fed. Bldg. #428, Ft. Smith 72902, 501-782-7787 (Ronnie Jones, Rep.); 35 E. Mountain #422, Fayetteville 72701, 501-442-5258 (Todd Ridge, Rep.); Fed. Bldg. #210, Harrison 72601, 501-741-6900 (Karen Hopper, Rep.)

FOURTH DISTRICT

Jay Dickey (R)

District: Southern portion of the state including city of Pine Bluff. Population: 585,202—Black 27%. Politics: Democratic.

Born Dec. 14, 1940, Pine Bluff; home, Pine Bluff; University of Ark., B.A. 1961, J.D. 1963; Methodist; divorced, 4 children.

Elected 1992. Career: Attorney 1963–92; 1972–92 businessman/owner Adventure Travel, Cindray Sign and Advertising, & Taco Bell restaurants.

Committees: (1) Small Business; (2) Agriculture; (3) Natural Resources.

Election Results: 1992 Dickey 113,580 (52%); Bill McCuen (D) 103,045 (48%).

Interest Group Ratings:
None—Freshman

Office: 1338 LHOB 20515, 202-225-3772 (Gene Bailey, AA). DISTRICT OFFICES: 100 E. 8th Ave. #2521, Pine Bluff 71601, 501-536-3376 (Rick Beardon, Rep.); P.O. Box 409, El Dorado 71731, 501-862-0236 (Rebecca Williams, Rep.); 100 Reserve St. #201, Hot Springs 71901, 501-623-5800 (Susan Carter, Rep.)

CALIFORNIA

California will be one of the nation's most politically active states in 1994. First, newly elected Sen. Dianne Feinstein will have to run for reelection as she was actually elected in 1992 to fill the last two years of the unexpired term of now Gov. Pete Wilson. She will be the GOP's number one target nationally, but given her comfortable victory margin in 1992, and her popularity she will be hard to unseat. The big question in 1994 in California is whether the Democratic sweep of 1992 was a fluke, or whether the state has moved into the Democratic column. That will be shown as GOP Gov. Pete Wilson seeks reelection. Because California's economy is down, so is his popularity. If he can win, he will become a player in the 1996 GOP presidential sweepstakes. State Treasurer Kathleen Brown (Jerry's smarter sister) is emerging from a crowded field of Democrats to be the likely challenger.

1992 PRESIDENTIAL ELECTION: (54 Electoral votes): Clinton (D) 4,815,039 (47%); Bush (R) 3,341,726 (32%); Perot (I) 2,147,409 (21%); Marrou (Lib) 44,390; Daniels (P&F) 17,149; Phillips (AmTax) 11,507. 1988: Bush 4,756,490 (52%); Dukakis 4,448,393 (48%)

SENATORS

Barbara Boxer (D)

Born Nov. 11, 1940, Brooklyn, N.Y.; home, Greenbrae; Brooklyn College, B.A. 1962; Jewish; married (Stewart), 2 children.

Elected 1992. Career: Stockbroker, researcher, 1962–65; journalist, Pacific Sun, 1972–74; District aide to U.S. Rep. John Burton, 1974–76; Marin Cnty. Bd. of Sprvsrs., 1976–82, Pres., 1980–81; U.S. House of Reps. 1982–92.

Committees: (1) Banking, Housing & Urban Affairs; (2) Environment & Public Works.

Election Results: 1992 Boxer 4,859,119 (48%); Bruce Herschensohn (R) 4,292,237 (43%); Jerome McCready 351,598 (3%); Genevieve Torres 350,460 (3%); June Genis 220,400 (2%).

Interest Group Ratings: (House)

ADA	ACU	COPE	COC
60	00	100	33

LCV	NTLC	CFA	ASC
69	00	47	20

Office: 112 HSOB 20510, 202-224-3553 (Karen Olick, AA). STATE OFFICE: 1700 Montgomery #240, San Francisco 94111, 415-403-0100; 2250 E. Imperial Hwy. #545, El Segundo 90245, 310-414-5700.

Dianne Feinstein (D)

Born June 22, 1933, San Francisco; home, San Francisco; Stanford University, B.A. 1955; Jewish; married (Richard Blum), 1 child.

Elected 1992 to fill term of Gov. Pete Wilson, seat up 1994. Career: San Francisco Board of Supervisors, 1970–78 (President 1974–78); San Francisco Mayor, 1978–88.

Committees: (1) Appropriations; (2) Judiciary.

Election Results: 1992 Feinstein 5,496,905 (55%); John Seymour (R) 3,780,880 (38%); Gerald Horne 287,167 (3%); Paul Meeuwenberg (I) 264,913 (3%); Richard Boddie 231,015 (2%).

Interest Group Ratings:
None—Freshman

Office: 331 HSOB 20510, 202-224-3841 (John Haber, AA). STATE OFFICES: 1700 Montgomery Street #305, San Francisco 94111, 415-249-4777 (Kam Kuwata, Dir. all offices); 11111 Santa Monica Blvd. #915, Los Angeles 90025, 310-914-7300; 750 B St. #1030, San Diego 92101, 619-231-9712; 1130 O St. #4015, Fresno 93721, 209-485-7430.

REPRESENTATIVES

FIRST DISTRICT

Dan Hamburg (D)

District: Far northern coast including towns of Santa Rosa and Eureka. Population: 573,082—Black 4%, Asian 4%, Hispanic 11%, Other 5%. Politics: Mixed, but still leans Democratic.

Born Oct 6, 1948, St. Louis, Mo.; home, Ukiah; Stanford, B.A. 1970, Calif. Institute for Integral Studies, M.A. 1992; No Religion Specified; married (Carrie), 4 children.

Elected 1992. Career: Founder Mariposa School, 1970–76; Chairman Ukiah Planning Commission, 1976–80; Dir. Ukiah Valley Child Development Center, 1976–80; Supervisor, Mendocino County, 1980–84; Education Project Director, 1985–86; Exec. Dir. North Coast Opportunities, 1986–89; Typesetter, 1990–92.

Committees: (1) Public Works & Transportation; (2) Merchant Marine & Fisheries.

Election Results: 1992 Hamburg 114,151 (48%); Frank Riggs (R) 106,807 (45%); Phil Baldwin (Oth) 10,278 (4%); Matthew Howard (Oth) 7,152 (3%).

Interest Group Ratings:
None—Freshman

Office: 114 CHOB 20515, 202-225-3311 (Meg Ryan O'Donnell, AA) DISTRICT OFFICES: 910-A Waugh Ln., Ukiah 95482, 707-462-1716 (Kay Spencer, Rep.); 710 E St. #140, Eureka 95501, 707-441-4949 (Clare Courtney, Rep.); 299 I St. #12, Crescent City 95531, 707-465-0112 (C. Caine-Cornell, Rep.); 817 Missouri St. #3, Fairfield 94533, 707-426-0401 (Nicki Maguire, Rep.); 1040 Main St. #103, Napa 94559, 707-254-8508 (Arlene Corsello, Rep.)

SECOND DISTRICT

Wally Herger (R)

District: Far northeast part of the state including the towns of Chico and Redding. Population: 573,322—Black 2%, Hispanic 6%, Asian 2%. Politics: Leans Republican.

Born May 20, 1945, Yuba City; home, Rio Oso; American River Community College, A.A. 1968; Calif. State University, 1968–69; Mormon; married (Pamela), 8 children.

Elected 1986. Career: Rancher, owner, Herger Gas, Inc. 1969–80; Calif. Assembly, 1981–86.

Committees: (1) Ways & Means; (2) Budget.

Election Results: 1992 Herger 161,064 (65%); Elliot Freedman (D) 69,504 (28%); Harry Pendery (Oth) 16,924 (7%). 1990 Herger (64%).

Interest Group Ratings:

ADA	ACU	COPE	COC
05	95	25	75

LCV	NTLC	CFA	ASC
06	100	13	100

Office: 2433 LHOB 20515, 202-225-3076 (John Magill, AA). DISTRICT OFFICES: 55 Independence Circle #104, Chico 95926, 916-893-8363 (Fran Peace, Dist. Mgr.); 410 Hemstead Dr. #115, Redding 96002, 916-223-5898 (Shannon Phillips, Rep.)

THIRD DISTRICT

Vic Fazio (D)

District: North central part of the state including West Sacramento and Yuka City. Population: 571,374—Black 3%, Asian 6%, Hispanic 14%, Other 8%. Politics: Democratic.

Born Oct. 11, 1942, Winchester, Mass.; home, W. Sacramento; Union College, B.A. 1965, Calif. State University; Episcopalian; married (Judy), 4 children.

Elected 1978. Career: Cong. & Legis. Consultant, 1966–75; Cofounder, The California Journal; Consultant & Asst. to Calif. Assembly Spkr., 1971; Calif. Assembly, 1975–78.

Committees: (1) Appropriations.

Election Results: 1992 Fazio 117,027 (51%); Bill Richardson (R) 91,865 (40%); Ross Crain (Oth) 19,620 (9%). 1990 Fazio (55%). 1988 Fazio (unopposed).

Interest Group Ratings:

ADA	ACU	COPE	COC
90	08	75	50

LCV	NTLC	CFA	ASC
56	00	73	60

Office: 2113 RHOB 20515, 202-225-5716 (Saundra Stuart, AA). DISTRICT OFFICES: 722-B Main St., Woodland 95695, 916-666-5521 (Richard Harris, Dist. Mgr.); 332 Pine St., Red Bluff 96080, 916-529-5629 (Richard Harris, Dist. Mgr.)

FOURTH DISTRICT

John T. Doolittle (R)

District: Northeastern California and part of the Central (San Joaquin) Valley, including the city of Auburn. Population: 571,033—Hispanic 7%. Politics: Republican.

Born Oct. 30, 1950, Glendale, Calif.; home, Rockland; University of Calif. (Santa Cruz) B.A.

1972. University of Pacific, J.D. 1978; Mormon; married (Julia), 2 children.

Elected 1990. Career: Practicing atty., 1979–81; Calif. Senate 1981–90.

Committees: (1) Agriculture; (2) Natural Resources.

Election Results: 1992 Doolittle 129,528 (50%); Patricia Malberg (D) 119,849 (46%); Patrick McHargue (Oth) 11,790 (5%). 1990 Doolittle (51%).

Interest Group Ratings:

ADA	ACU	COPE	COC
05	100	17	75

LCV	NTLC	CFA	ASC
00	89	13	100

Office: 1542 LHOB 20515, 202-225-2511 (David Lopez, AA). DISTRICT OFFICE: 2130 Professional Dr. #190, Roseville 95661, 916-786-5560 (Richard Robinson, Dist. Rep.)

FIFTH DISTRICT

Robert T. Matsui (D)

District: Most of the City of Sacramento, and its eastern suburbs. Population: 573,684—Black 13%, Asian 13%, Hispanic 15%, Other 7%. Politics: Leans Democratic.

Born Sept. 17, 1941, Sacramento; home, Sacramento; University of Calif., A.B. 1963, Hastings College of Law, University of Calif., J.D. 1966; United Methodist; married (Doris), 1 child.

Elected 1978. Career: Practicing atty., 1967–78; Sacramento City Cncl., 1971–78.

Committees: (1) Ways & Means; (2) Budget.

Election Results: 1992 Matsui 151,318 (69%); Robert Dinsmore (R) 55,381 (25%); Gordon Mors (Oth) 4,498 (2%); Tian Harter (Oth) 4,138 (2%); Chris Rufer (Oth) 4,331 (2%). 1990 Matsui (60%). 1988 Matsui (71%).

Interest Group Ratings:

ADA	ACU	COPE	COC
80	08	55	29

LCV	NTLC	CFA	ASC
69	00	80	30

Office: 2311 RHOB 20515, 202-225-7163 (Shirley Queja, AA). DISTRICT OFFICE: 8058 Fed.

Bldg., 650 Capitol Mall, Sacramento 95814, 916-551-2846 (vacant, Dist. Mgr.)

SIXTH DISTRICT

Lynn Woolsey (D)

District: Marin County, a small part of Northwest San Francisco and a part of Sonoma county. Population: 571,227—Black 2%, Asian 3%, Hispanic 9%. Politics: Democratic.

Born: Nov. 3, 1937, Seattle; home, Petaluma; University of San Francisco, B.S. 1980; married (David), 4 children.

Elected 1992. Career: Human Resources Manager, 1969–80; Petaluma City Council, 1985–92; Petaluma Vice Mayor, 1991–1992; Owner Woolsey Personnel Service, 1980–92.

Committees: (1) Education & Labor; (2) Budget.

Election Results: 1992 Woolsey 178,445 (66%); Bill Filante (R) 90,751 (34%).

Interest Group Ratings:
None—Freshman

Office: 439 CHOB 20515, 202-225-5161 (Marc Isaac, AA). DISTRICT OFFICES: 1301 Redwood Way #205, Petaluma 94954, 707-795-1462 (Elmy Burmejo, Dist. Dir.); 1050 Northgate Dr. #140, San Raphael 94903, 415-507-9554 (Elmy Burmejo, Dist. Dir.); Fed. Bldg. 777 Somona #327, Santa Rosa 95404, (Elmy Burmejo, Dist. Dir.)

SEVENTH DISTRICT

George Miller (D)

District: Parts of Contra Costa and Solana counties, including towns of Richmond and Concord. Population: 572,773—Black 17%, Asian 14%, Hispanic 13%, Other 6%. Politics: Democratic.

Born May 17, 1945, Richmond; home, Martinez; Diablo Valley Col., San Fran. State College, B.A. 1968, University of Calif. at Davis, J.D. 1972; Roman Catholic; married (Cynthia), 2 children.

Elected 1974. Career: Legislative Aide to Calif. Sen. Major. Ldr., 1969–74; Practicing atty., 1972–74.

Committees: (1) Education & Labor; (2) Natural Resources.

Election Results: 1992 Miller 147,860 (71%); Dave Scholl (R) 52,237 (25%); David Franklin (Oth) 9,491 (5%). 1990 Miller (61%); 1988 Miller (68%).

Interest Group Ratings:

ADA	ACU	COPE	COC
85	00	92	25

LCV	NTLC	CFA	ASC
75	05	87	10

Office: 2205 RHOB 20515, 202-225-2095 (John Lawrence, AA). DISTRICT OFFICES: Rm. 14, 367 Civic Dr., Pleasant Hill 94523, 415-687-3260 (Mary Lansing, Rep.); Rm. 281, 3220 Blume Dr., Richmond 94806, 415-222-4212 (Hank Royal, Asst.)

EIGHTH DISTRICT

Nancy Pelosi (D)

District: Most of San Francisco. Population: 573,247—Black 13%, Asian 28%, Hispanic 16%, Other 7%. Politics: Democratic.

Born March 26, 1940, Baltimore, Md.; home, San Francisco; Trinity College, B.A. 1962; Roman Catholic; married (Paul), 5 children.

Elected June 2, 1987. Career: San Francisco Library Comm., 1974–76; Northern Chm., State Chm., DNC, 1976–83; Chairwoman, Dem. Natl. Convention Host Comm., 1982–84; Dem. Senatorial Campaign Finance Chairwoman, 1985–86; Public relations exec., Ogilvy & Mather, 1986–87

Committees: (1) Appropriations; (2) Ethics; (3) Select Committee on Intelligence.

Election Results: 1992 Pelosi 182,564 (83%); Marc Wolin (R) 24,064 (11%); James Elwood (Oth) 7,162 (3%); Cesar Cadabes (Oth) 7,192 (3%). 1990 Pelosi (78%). 1988 Pelosi (76%).

Interest Group Ratings:

ADA	ACU	COPE	COC
90	00	92	25

LCV	NTLC	CFA	ASC
100	00	93	30

Office: 240 CHOB 20515, 202-225-4965 (Judy Lemons, AA). DISTRICT OFFICE: 13470 Fed.

Bldg., 450 Golden Gate Ave., San Francisco 94104, 415-556-4862 (Michael Yaki, Dir.)

NINTH DISTRICT

Ronald V. Dellums (D)

District: Northern Alameda County including Berkley plus a portion of Oakland. Population: 573,485—Black 32%, Asian 16%, Hispanic 12%, Other 7%. Politics: Democratic.

Born Nov. 24, 1935, Oakland; home, Berkeley; Oakland City College, A.A. 1958, San Fran. State University, B.A. 1960, University of Calif., M.S.W. 1962; Protestant; married (Roscoe), 3 children.

Elected 1970. Career: USMC, 1954–56; Psychiatric social worker, Calif. Dept. of Mental Hygiene, 1962–64; Prog. Dir., Bayview Community Ctr., 1964–65; Dir., Hunter's Pt. Bayview Youth Opp. Ctr., 1965–66; Plng. Consultant, Bay Area Social Plng. Cncl., 1966–67; Dir., San Fran. Econ. Opp. Council's Concentrated Empl. Prog., 1967–68; Berkeley City Cncl., 1967–71; Sr. Consultant, Social Dynamics, Inc. (manpower programs), 1968–70.

Committees: (1) Armed Services (Chairman).

Election Results: 1992 Dellums 154,122 (72%); Billy Hunter (R) 48,756 (23%); Dave Linn (Oth) 9,740 (5%). 1990 Dellums (62%). 1988 Dellums (67%).

Interest Group Ratings:

ADA	ACU	COPE	COC
95	00	92	25

LCV	NTLC	CFA	ASC
94	10	93	00

Office: 2108 RHOB 20515, 202-225-2661 (Carlottia Scott, Counsel). DISTRICT OFFICES: 1720 Oregon St., Rm. 6, Berkeley 94703 415-548-7767 (Ying Lee Kelley, Rep.); 201 13th St., Suite 105, Oakland 94617, 415-763-0370 (Donald Hopkins, Dist. Adm.)

TENTH DISTRICT

Bill Baker (R)

District: Parts of Alameda and Contra Costa counties, including town of Walnut Creek. Population: 572,008—Hispanic 9%, Asian 6%, Other 3%. Politics: Leans Republican.

Born Jun. 14, 1940, Oakland; home, Danville; San Jose State, B.S. 1963; Roman Catholic; married (Joanne), 4 children.

Elected 1992. Career U.S. Coast Guard Reserve, 1957–65; Financial Consultant, 1966–70; Budget Analyst, Calif. Dept. of Finance, 1971–75; Contra Costa Taxpayer Association, 1975–80; State Assemblyman, 1981–92.

Committees: (1) Public Works & Transportation; (2) Science Space & Technology.

Election Results: 1992 Baker 137,313 (52%); Wendell Williams (D) 128,942 (48%).

Interest Group Ratings:
None—Freshman

Office: 1714 LHOB 20515, 202-225-1880 (John Wallace, AA). DISTRICT OFFICES: 1801 N. California Ave. #103, Walnut Creek 94596, 510-932-8899 (Ann Jordan, Rep.)

ELEVENTH DISTRICT

Richard W. Pombo (R)

District: Parts of Sacramento and San Joaquin counties including city of Stockton. Population: 571,772—Black 6%, Asian 12%, Hispanic 21%, Other 7%. Politics: Mixed.

Born Jan. 8, 1961, Tracy; home, Tracy; Cal. State Pomona, B.S., 1983; Roman Catholic; married (Annette), 1 child.

Elected 1992. Career: Rancher. Tracy City Council, 1990–92.

Committees: (1) Agriculture; (2) Natural Resources; (3) Merchant Marine and Fisheries.

Election Results: 1992 Pombo 82,911 (47%); Patti Garamendi (D) 82,006 (46%); Christine Roberts (Oth) 12,331 (7%).

Interest Group Ratings:
None—Freshman

Office: 1519 LHOB 20515, 202-225-1947 (Matt Miller, AA). DISTRICT OFFICE: 3231 W. March Ln. #205, Stockton 95207, 209-951-3091 (Steve Ding, Rep.)

TWELFTH DISTRICT

Tom Lantos (D)

District: Peninsula south of San Francisco mostly in San Mateo County. Population: 571,535 —Black 4%, Asian 26%, Hispanic 14%, Other 5%. Politics: Democratic.

Born Feb. 1, 1928, Budapest, Hungary; home, Burlingame; University of Wash., B.A. 1949, M.A. 1950, University of Calif., Ph.D. 1953; Jewish; married (Annette), 2 children.

Elected 1980. Career: Prof., San. Fran. State University, 1950–81; Economist, Bank of America, 1952–53; TV Commentator, San Francisco, 1955–63; Dir. of Intl. Programs, Calif. State University system, 1962–71; Econ.–Foreign Policy Adviser to U.S. Sen. Joseph R. Biden, Jr., 1978–79; Member, Pres. Task Force on Defense & Foreign Policy, 1976.

Committees: (1) Foreign Affairs; (2) Government Operations.

Election Results: 1992 Lantos 149,392 (69%); Jim Tomlin (R) 50,112 (23%); George O'Brien (Oth) 7,443 (3%); Mary Weldon (Oth) 9,714 (4%). 1990 Lantos (66%). 1988 Lantos (71%).

Interest Group Ratings:

ADA	ACU	COPE	COC
95	08	92	25

LCV	NTLC	CFA	ASC
94	05	100	50

Office: 2182 RHOB 20515, 202-225-3531 (Robert King, AA). DISTRICT OFFICE: 400 El Camino Real, Suite 820, San Mateo 94402, 415-342-0300 (Evelyn Szelenyi, Rep.)

THIRTEENTH DISTRICT

Fortney H. "Pete" Stark (D)

District: Parts of Oakland and most of its Alameda County suburbs including population center of Hayward. Population: 572,441—Black 7%, Asian 19%, Hispanic 18%, Other 8%. Politics: Democratic.

Born Nov. 11, 1931, Milwaukee, Wis.; home, Oakland; MIT, B.S. 1953, University of Calif., M.B.A. 1960; Unitarian; married (Deborah), 4 children.

Elected 1972. Career: Air Force, 1955–57; Founder, Beacon Savings & Loan Assn. 1961; Founder & Pres., Security Natl. Bank, Walnut Creek, 1963–72.

Committees: (1) District of Columbia; (2) Ways & Means; (3) Joint Economic.

Election Results: 1992 Stark 117,701 (61%); Verne Teyler (R) 60,709 (31%); Roslyn Allen (Oth) 15,966 (8%). 1990 Starke (59%). 1988 Starke (73%).

Interest Group Ratings:

ADA	ACU	COPE	COC
95	04	83	13

LCV	NTLC	CFA	ASC
100	05	93	10

Office: 239 CHOB 20515, 202-225-5065 (William Vaughan, AA). DISTRICT OFFICE: 22320 Foothill Blvd., Hayward 94541, 415-635-1092 (Annie Zatlin, Rep.)

FOURTEENTH DISTRICT

Anna G. Eshoo (D)

District: Parts of San Mateo and Santa Clara counties including a portion of the city of San Jose. Population: 571,131—Black 5%, Asian 12%, Hispanic 14%. Politics: Democratic.

Born Dec. 14, 1942, New Britian, Conn.; home Atherton; Canada College, A.A. 1978; divorced, 2 children.

Elected 1992. Career: Lt. Gov. McCarthy Chief of Staff, 1981; San Mateo Co. Board of Supervisors, 1982–92.

Committees: (1) Merchant Marine & Fisheries; (2) Science, Space & Technology.

Election Results: 1992 Eshoo 136,174 (57%); Tom Huening (R) 92,091 (39%); Chuck Olson (Oth) 6,699 (3%); David Wald (Oth) 3,647 (2%).

Interest Group Ratings:
None—Freshman

Office: 1505 LHOB 20515, 202-225-8104 (John Flaherty, AA). DISTRICT OFFICE: 698 Emerson St., Palo Alto 94301, 415-323-2984 (Bruce Ives, Rep.)

FIFTEENTH DISTRICT

Norman Y. Mineta (D)

District: About half of city of San Jose, plus some suburbs and town of Santa Clara. Population: 572,485—Black 2%, Asian 11%, Hispanic 11%. Politics: Leans Democratic.

Born Nov. 12, 1931, San Jose; home, San Jose; University of Calif. at Berkeley, B.S. 1953, National University of San Diego, Ph.D. 1987; United Methodist; married (Danealia), 2 children.

Elected 1974. Career: Army, 1953-56; Owner/Agent, Mineta Insur. Agcy.; San Jose City Cncl., 1967–71, Vice Mayor, 1969–71, Mayor, 1971–75.

Committees: (1) Public Works & Transportation (Chairman); (2) Science, Space & Technology.

Election Results: 1992 Mineta 157,146 (64%); Robert Wick (R) 76,216 (31%); Duggan Dieterly (Oth) 12,469 (5%). 1990 Mineta (58%). 1988 Mineta (67%).

Interest Group Ratings:

ADA	ACU	COPE	COC
100	00	92	25

LCV	NTLC	CFA	ASC
81	00	93	30

Office: 2221 RHOB 20515, 202-225-2631 (Tim Newell, Office Dir.). DISTRICT OFFICE: Suite 310, 1245 S. Winchester Blvd., San Jose 95128, 408-984-6045 (vacant, Chief-of-staff)

SIXTEENTH DISTRICT

Don Edwards (D)

District: Santa Clara County including parts of San Jose. Population: 571,551—Black 5%, Asian 21%, Hispanic 37%, Other 18%. Politics: Democratic.

Born Jan. 6, 1915, San Jose; home, San Jose; Stanford University, B.A. 1936, Stanford University Law School, 1936–38; Unitarian; married (Edith), 5 children.

Elected 1962. Career: FBI Agent, 1940–41; Navy, WWII; Pres., Valley Title Co., 1946–62.

Committees: (1) Judiciary; (2) Veterans Affairs; (3) Foreign Affairs (Temp.).

Election Results: 1992 Edwards 89,923 (62%); Ted Bundesen (R) 45,450 (32%); Amani Kuumba (Oth) 8,756 (6%). 1990 Edwards (63%). 1988 Edwards (86%).

Interest Group Ratings:

ADA	ACU	COPE	COC
100	00	92	25

LCV	NTLC	CFA	ASC
100	00	93	20

Office: 2307 RHOB 20515, 202-225-3072 (Roberta Haeberle, AA). DISTRICT OFFICE: 1042 W. Hedding St., Suite 100, San Jose 95126, 408-247-1711 (Terry Poche, Dist. Coord.)

SEVENTEENTH DISTRICT

Sam Farr (D)

District: North Central coast including towns of Monterey and Seaside and inland agricultural area around Salinas. Population: 570,981—Black 4%, Asian 6%, Hispanic 32%, Other 19%. Politics: Democratic.

Born July 4, 1941, Carmel; home, Carmel; Willamette U., B.S. 1963, Monterey Inst. of International Studies, U. of Santa Clara; no religion specified; married (Shary), 1 child.

Elected 1993 to fill the unexpired term of Budget Director Leon Panetta. Career: Peace Corp 1967–69; Aide, Calif. St. Assembly 1969–75; Monterey County Board of Supervisors 1975–80; Member, Calif. State Assembly, 1981–93.

Committees: Not yet assigned.

Election Results: 1993 (Special) Farr 51,764 (51.9%); Bill McCampbell 42,841 (43%); 3 minor candidates (5.1%)

Interest Group Ratings:
None—Freshman

Office: 1216 LHOB 20515, 202-225-2861 (Donna Blitzer, Chief-of-Staff). DISTRICT OFFICES: Not yet established.

EIGHTEENTH DISTRICT

Gary Condit (D)

District: Mid-Central (San Joaquin) Valley including city of Modesto. Population: 571,393—Black 3%, Asian 6%, Hispanic 26%, Other 14%. Politics: Leans Democratic.

Born April 21, 1948, Salina, OK; home, Ceres;

Calif. State University, B.A. 1972; Baptist; married (Carolyn), 2 children.

Elected 1989 (special election). Career: Ceres Cty. Cncl. 1972–76; Mayor 1974–76; Cty. Bd. of Sup. 1976–82; Calif. St. Assem. 1983–89.

Committees: (1) Agriculture; (2) Government Operations.

Election Results: 1992 Condit 125,291 (84%); Kim Almstrom (Oth) 23,098 (16%). 1990 Condit (66%). 1989 (Special) Condit (52%).

Interest Group Ratings:

ADA	ACU	COPE	COC
55	48	83	75

LCV	NTLC	CFA	ASC
25	65	53	70

Office: 1123 LHOB 20515, 202-225-6131 (Mike Lynch, AA). DISTRICT OFFICES: Fed. Bldg., 415 W. 18th St., Merced 95340, 209-383-4455 (vacant, Dist. Mgr.); 920 13th Street, Modesto 95354, 209-527-1914 (Annette D'Adamo, Mgr.)

NINETEENTH DISTRICT

Richard H. Lehman (D)

District: Parts of city of Fresno and surrounding areas, including Clovis City. Population: 573,043 —Black 3%, Asian 7%, Hispanic 24%, Other 15%. Politics: Democratic.

Born July 20, 1948, Sanger; home, Fresno; Fresno City College, Calif. State University, University of Calif. at Santa Cruz; Lutheran; divorced.

Elected 1982. Career: A.A. to Calif. St. Sen. George N. Zenovich, 1970–76; Calif. Asssembly, 1976–82.

Committees: (1) Energy & Commerce; (2) Natural Resources.

Election Results: 1992 Lehman 95,147 (47%); Tal Cloud (R) 94,259 (47%); Dorothy Wells (Oth) 12,463 (6%). 1990 Lehman (Unopposed). 1988 Lehman (70%).

Interest Group Ratings:

ADA	ACU	COPE	COC
60	19	83	50

LCV	NTLC	CFA	ASC
38	15	53	40

Office: 1226 LHOB 20515, 202-225-4540 (Scott Nishioki, AA). DISTRICT OFFICE: 2377 W. Shaw #105, Fresno 93711, 209-248-0800 (David Brodie, Rep.)

TWENTIETH DISTRICT

Calvin Dooley (D)

District: South central portion of the San Joaquin Valley including parts of Bakersfield and Fresno. Population: 573,282—Black 6%, Asian 6%, Hispanic 55%, Other 38%. Politics: Mixed but leans Democratic.

Born Jan. 11, 1954 Visalia; home, Hanford; University of Calif. (Davis), B.S. 1977, Stanford (Sloan Fellow), M.A. 1987; Methodist; married (Linda), 2 children.

Elected 1990. Career: Cotton farmer, partner Dooley Farms; Adm. Asst. to Calif. St. Sen. Rose Ann Vuich.

Committees: (1) Agriculture; (2) Small Business; (3) Natural Resources.

Election Results: 1992 Dooley 66,291 (65%); Ed Hunt (R) 36,163 (35%). 1990 Dooley (55%).

Interest Group Ratings:

ADA	ACU	COPE	COC
75	20	75	50

LCV	NTLC	CFA	ASC
50	05	73	50

Office: 1227 LHOB 20515, 202-225-3341 (Lisa Quigley, AA). DISTRICT OFFICE: 711 North Court, Visalia 93291, 209-733-8348 (Susan Specht, Rep.)

TWENTY-FIRST DISTRICT

William M. Thomas (R)

District: Southeastern end of the San Joaquin Valley including parts of Bakersfield and Porterville. Population: 571,300—Black 4%, Hispanic 20%, Other 14%. Politics: Leans Republican.

Born Dec. 6, 1941, Wallace, Idaho; home, Bakersfield; Santa Ana Commun. College, A.A. 1959, San Fran. State University, B.A. 1963, M.A. 1965; Baptist; married (Sharon), 2 children.

Elected 1978. Career: Prof., Bakersfield Community College, 1965–74; Calif. Assembly, 1974–78.

Committees: (1) House Administration; (2) Ways & Means.

Election Results: 1992 Thomas 119,256 (65%);

Deborah Vollmer (D) 63,673 (35%). 1990 Thomas (59%). 1988 Thomas (71%).

Interest Group Ratings:

ADA	ACU	COPE	COC
15	90	10	88

LCV	NTLC	CFA	ASC
06	83	20	100

Office: 2209 RHOB 20515, 202-225-2915 (Catherine Abernathy, AA). DISTRICT OFFICES: 4100 Truxtun Ave., Rm. 220, Bakersfield 93309, 805-327-3611 (Robin Lake, Mgr.); 319 W. Murray St., Visalia 93291, 209-627-6549 (Bob Tapella, Rep.)

TWENTY-SECOND DISTRICT

Michael Huffington (R)

District: San Luis Obispo and Santa Barbara counties. Population: 572,891—Black 3%, Hispanic 21%, Asian 4%, Other 11%. Politics: Republican.

Born Sept. 4, 1947, Dallas, Tex.; home, Santa Barbara; Stanford, B.S., B.A. 1970, Harvard, M.B.A. 1972; Episcopalian; married (Arianna), 2 children.

Elected 1992. Career: Financial analyst, First National Bank, 1972–74; Co–Founder Simmons & Huffington, 1974–89; Dept. Asst. Secretary of Defense, 1986–88; Chairman Crest Films, 1989–92.

Committees: (1) Banking, Finance & Urban Affairs; (2) Small Business.

Election Results: 1992 Huffington 120,356 (52%); Gloria Ochoa (D) 82,137 (35%); Mindy Lorenz (Green) 22,216 (10%); Howard Dilbeck (Lib) 7,040 (3%).

Interest Group Ratings:
None—Freshman

Office: 113 CHOB 20515, 202-225-3601 (Mike Wooten, AA). DISTRICT OFFICES: 1819 State St. Suite D, Santa Barbara 93101, 805-682-6600 (Rusty Fairly, Rep.); 1060 Palm St. A, San Luis Obisbo 93401, 805-542-0426 (Brian Nestande, Rep.); 910 E. Stowell Rd., San Maria 93454, (Sharon Larrabec, Rep.)

TWENTY-THIRD DISTRICT

Elton William Gallegly (R)

District: Far northern and northwest Los Angeles suburbs including parts of Ventura County and the western San Fernando Valley. Population: 571,483—Black 3%, Hispanic 30%, Asian 5%, Other 15%. Politics: Republican.

Born Mar. 7, 1944, Huntington Park; home, Simi Valley; Calif. State University; Protestant; married (Janice), 4 children.

Elected 1986. Career: Owner & operator of real estate firm; Simi Valley City Cncl., 1979–80; Mayor, 1980–86.

Committees: (1) Foreign Affairs; (2) Natural Resources; (3) Judiciary.

Election Results: 1992 Gallegly 108,152 (54%); Anita Perez Ferguson (D) 83,543 (42%); Jay Wood (Lib) 8,584 (4%). 1990 Gallegly (58%). 1988 Gallegly (69%).

Interest Group Ratings:

ADA	ACU	COPE	COC
15	84	50	75

LCV	NTLC	CFA	ASC
06	90	27	100

Office: 2441 RHOB 20515, 202-225-5811 (Paul Bateman, AA). DISTRICT OFFICE: 300 Eaplonde Dr. #1800, Oxnard 93030, 805-483-2300 (Paula Sheil, Rep.)

TWENTY-FOURTH DISTRICT

Anthony C. Beilenson (D)

District: Northwestern Los Angeles county and parts of southern Ventura county, including Thousand Oaks and Agoura Hills. Population: 572,563—Black 2%, Hispanic 13%, Asian 6%, Other 7%. Politics: Mixed.

Born Oct. 26, 1932, New Rochelle, N.Y.; home, Los Angeles; Harvard College, A.B. 1954, LL.B. 1957; Jewish; married (Dolores), 3 children.

Elected 1976. Career: Practicing atty., 1957–59; Counsel, Calif. Assembly Comm. on Finance & Insur., 1960; Staff atty., Calif. Comp. & Insur. Fund, 1961–62; Calif. Assembly, 1963–66; Calif. Senate, 1967–77.

Committees: (1) Budget; (2) Rules.

Election Results: 1992 Beilenson 132,343 (56%); Tom McClintock (R) 91,463 (39%); John Lindblad (P&F) 12,778 (5%). 1990 Beilenson (62%). 1988 Beilenson (64%).

Interest Group Ratings:

ADA	ACU	COPE	COC
85	09	75	38

LCV	NTLC	CFA	ASC
100	30	100	40

Office: 2465 RHOB 20515, 202-225-5911 (Janet Faulstich, AA). DISTRICT OFFICES: 200 N. Westlake Blvd., Thousand Oaks 91362, 805-496-4333 (Diane Brown, Asst.); 21031 Ventura Blvd., Woodland Hills 91364, 818-999-1990 (Virginia Hatfield, Mgr.)

TWENTY-FIFTH DISTRICT

Howard P. "Buck" McKeon (R)

District: A geographically vast new district spread across northern Los Angeles County with larger population centers Palmdale and Lancaster. Population: 573,105—Black 4%, Asian 6%, Hispanic 16%, Other 8%. Politics: Leans Republican.

Born Sept. 9, 1939, Los Angeles; home, Santa Clarita; Brigham Young University, B.S. 1985; Mormon; married (Patricia), 6 children.

Elected 1992. Career: Owner Howard & Phil's Western Wear, Inc., 1960—Present; Chairman, Valencia National Bank, 1987–Present; Santa Clarita City Council, 1987–92.

Committees: (1) Education & Labor; (2) Public Works & Transportation.

Election Results: McKeon 104,552 (55%); James Gilmartin (D) 65,687 (36%); Charles Wilken (Green) 6,464 (3%); Peggy Christensen (Lib) 6,444 (3%); Nancy Lawrence (P&F) 4,782 (3%).

Interest Group Ratings:
None—Freshman

Office: 307 CHOB 20515, 202-225-1956 (Bob Cochran, AA). DISTRICT OFFICES: 23929 W. Valencia Blvd. #410, Santa Clarita 91355, 805-254-2111 (Armando Azarloze, Dist. Dir.); 1008 West Ave. M-4, Suite D, Palmdale 93551, 805-948-7833 (M. Hand, Rep.)

TWENTY-SIXTH DISTRICT

Howard Lawrence Berman (D)

District: A solidly working class district with a majority Latino population north of Los Angeles including the city of San Fernando. Population: 571,523—Black 6%, Asian 7%, Hispanic 53%. Politics: Democratic.

Born Apr. 15, 1941, Los Angeles; home, Los Angeles; University of Calif. at Los Angeles, B.A. 1962, LL.B. 1965; Jewish; married (Janis), 2 children.

Elected 1984. Career: Practicing atty., 1966–73; Calif. Assembly, 1973–82.

Committees: (1) Budget; (2) Foreign Affairs; (3) Judiciary.

Election Results: 1992 Berman 69,515 (61%); Gary Forsch (R) 33,595 (30%); Bernard Zimring (Lib) 3,280; Margery Hinds (P&F) 6,740 (6%). 1990 Berman (61%). 1988 Berman (70%).

Interest Group Ratings:

ADA	ACU	COPE	COC
85	08	73	25

LCV	NTLC	CFA	ASC
100	05	87	50

Office: 2201 RHOB 20515, 202-225-4695 (Ms. Gene Smith, AA). DISTRICT OFFICE: 14600 Roscoe Blvd., Suite 506, Panorama City 91402, 818-891-0543 (Rose Castenada, AA)

TWENTY-SEVENTH DISTRICT

Carlos J. Moorhead (R)

District: Northern and eastern Los Angeles suburbs including Glendale, part of Burbank and part of Pasadena. Population: 572,594—Black 8%, Asian 11%, Hispanic 21%, Other 10%. Politics: Republican.

Born May 6, 1922, Long Beach; home, Glendale; University of Calif. at Los Angeles, B.A. 1943, University of Southern Calif., J.D. 1949; Presbyterian; married (Valery), 5 children.

Elected 1972. Career: Army, WWII; Practicing atty.; Calif. Assembly, 1966–72.

Committees: (1) Energy & Commerce; (2) Judiciary.

Election Results: 1992 Moorhead 95,169 (49%); Doug Kahn (D) 78,559 (40%); Jesse Moorman (Oth) 10,312 (5%); Dennis Decherd (Oth) 4,427 (2%); Margaret Edwards (Oth) 6,853 (4%). 1990 Moorhead (59%). 1988 Moorhead (70%).

Interest Group Ratings:

ADA	ACU	COPE	COC
05	100	25	75

LCV	NTLC	CFA	ASC
13	100	13	100

Office: 2346 RHOB 20515, 202-225-4176 (Maxine Dean, AA). DISTRICT OFFICES: Rm. 304, 420 N. Brand Blvd., Glendale 91203, 818-247-8445 (Marilyn McKay, Rep.); Rm. 618, 301 E. Colorado Blvd., Pasadena 91101, 818-792-6168 (Peter Musurlian, Ex. Asst.)

TWENTY-EIGHTH DISTRICT

David Timothy Dreier (R)

District: Eastern Los Angeles suburbs including Pomona and West Covina. Population: 572,927—Black 6%, Asian 13%, Hispanic 24%, Other 10%. Politics: Republican.

Born July 5, 1952, Kansas City, Mo.; home, Claremont; Claremont McKenna College, B.A. 1975, M.A. 1976; Christian Scientist; single.

Elected 1980. Career: Dir. of Corp. Relations, Claremont McKenna College, 1976–78; Dir. of Pub. Affairs, Industrial Hydrocarbons, 1978–81.

Committees: (1) Rules; (2) Joint Committee on the Organization of Congress.

Election Results: 1992 Dreier 112,990 (58%); Al Wachtel (D) 72,177 (37%); Walter Sheasby (Oth) 5,869 (3%); Thomas Dominy (Oth) 4,022 (2%). 1990 Dreier (63%). 1988 Drier (69%).

Interest Group Ratings:

ADA	ACU	COPE	COC
00	100	08	75

LCV	NTLC	CFA	ASC
06	85	13	100

Office: 411 CHOB 20515, 202-225-2305 (Brad Smith, Dir.). DISTRICT OFFICE: 112 N. 2nd Ave., Covina 91723, 714-592-2857 or 818-339-9078 (Mark Harmsen, Rep.)

TWENTY-NINTH DISTRICT

Henry A. Waxman (D)

District: The Los Angeles area known as "westside," including the affluent area running from Santa Monica to Hollywood including parts of Beverly Hills. One of the wealthiest and most liberal congressional districts in the nation. Population: 571,566—Black 3%, Asian 8%, Hispanic 13%. Politics: Democratic.

Born Sept. 12, 1939, Los Angeles; home, Los Angeles; University of Calif. at Los Angeles, B.A. 1961, J.D. 1964; Jewish; married (Janet), 2 children.

Elected 1974. Career: Practicing atty., 1965–68; Calif. Assembly, 1968–74.

Committees: (1) Energy & Commerce; (2) Government Operations.

Election Results: 1992 Waxman 149,292 (66%); Mark Robbins (R) 60,995 (27%); Susan Davies (P&F) 12,996 (6%); Felix Rogin (Lib) 4,291 (2%). 1990 Waxman (69%). 1988 Waxman (72%).

Interest Group Ratings:

ADA	ACU	COPE	COC
95	00	82	25

LCV	NTLC	CFA	ASC
100	05	87	30

Office: 2408 RHOB 20515, 202-225-3976 (Phillip Schilrio, AA). DISTRICT OFFICE: 8425 W. 3rd St., Suite 400, Los Angeles 90048, 213-651-1040 (Howard Elinson, AA)

THIRTIETH DISTRICT

Xavier Becerra (D)

District: Northern Los Angeles. Population: 572,538—Black 4%, Asian 21%, Hispanic 61%, Other 31%. Politics: Democratic.

Born Jan 26, 1958, Sacramento; home Montebello; Stanford, B.A. 1980, J.D. 1984; Roman Catholic; married (Carolina), 1 child.

Elected 1992. Career: Lawyer; Calif. Dept. of Justice Deputy Atty. General, 1988–91; State Rep., 1991–92.

Committees: (1) Education & Labor; (2) Science Space & Technology; (3) Judiciary.

Election Results: 1992 Becerra (D) 45,502 (59%); Morry Waksberg (R) 18,150 (23%); Blase Bonpane (Oth) 5,852 (8%); Andrew Consalvo (Oth) 2,059 (3%); Elizabeth Nakano (Oth) 5,729 (7%).

Interest Group Ratings:
None—Freshman

Office: 1710 LHOB 20515, 202-225-6235 (Elsa Marquez, AA). DISTRICT OFFICE: 2435 Colorado Blvd. #200, Los Angeles 90041, 213-550-8962 (Henry Lozano, Rep.)

THIRTY-FIRST DISTRICT

Matthew Gilbert Martinez (D)

District: Northeastern Los Angeles county including cities of Alhambra and El Monte. Population: 572,643—Asian 23, Hispanic 59%, Other 27%. Politics: Democratic.

Born Feb. 14, 1929, Walsenburg, Colo.; home, Monterey Park; Los Angeles Trade Technical School; Roman Catholic; married (Elvira), 5 children.

Elected 1982. Career: U.S. Marine Corps, 1947–50; small business owner (furniture & upholstery), 1957–82; Monterey Park Planning Commission, 1971–74; Monterey Park City Council, 1974–76; Mayor of Monterey Park, 1976–80; Calif. State Assembly, 1980–82.

Committees: (1) Education & Labor; (2) Foreign Affairs.

Election Results: 1992 Martinez 64,430 (63%); Reuben Franco (R) 37,729 (37%). 1990 Martinez (59%). 1988 Martinez (60%).

Interest Group Ratings:

ADA	ACU	COPE	COC
95	04	91	25

LCV	NTLC	CFA	ASC
69	00	73	50

Office: 2231 RHOB 20515, 202-225-5464 (Maxine Grant, AA). DISTRICT OFFICE: 320 S. Garfield Ave. #214, Alhambria 91801, 818-458-4524 (Monte Grant, Rep.)

THIRTY-SECOND DISTRICT

Julian Carey Dixon (D)

District: Southern Los Angeles including near

suburbs and Culver City. Population: 572,595—Black 40%, Asian 8%, Hispanic 30%, other 19% Politics: Democratic.

Born Aug. 8, 1934, Washington, D.C.; home, Los Angeles; Calif. State University at L.A., B.S. 1962, Southwestern University, LL.B. 1967; Episcopalian; married (Betty), 1 child.

Elected 1979. Career: Army, 1957–60; A.A. to Calif. Sen. Merv Dymally; Calif. Assembly, 1973–79.

Committees: (1) Appropriations; (2) Select Committee on Intelligence.

Election Results: 1992 Dixon 142,271 (87%); Bob Weber (Oth) 11,470 (7%); William Williams (Oth) 9,205 (6%). 1990 Dixon (73%). 1988 Dixon (76%).

Interest Group Ratings:

ADA	ACU	COPE	COC
80	04	75	13

LCV	NTLC	CFA	ASC
94	00	93	30

Office: 2400 RHOB 20515, 202-225-7084 (Andrea Holmes, AA). DISTRICT OFFICE: 5100 W. Goldleaf Circle, Suite 208, Los Angeles 90056, 213-678-5424 (Patricia Miller, AA)

THIRTY-THIRD DISTRICT

Lucille Roybal-Allard (D)

District: Southeastern Los Angeles including South Gate City and Huntington Park. Population: 570,943—Black 4%, Asian 4%, Hispanic 84%. Politics: Democratic.

Born June 12, 1941; Los Angeles; home Bell Gardens; Temple School of Business, A.A. 1963, Calif. State at L.A., B.A. 1965; Roman Catholic; married (Edward), two children.

Elected 1992. Career: Public Relations and Fund raising Exec.; Calif. Assembly, 1987–92.

Committees: (1) Banking, Finance & Urban Affairs; (2) Small Business.

Election Results: 1992 Roybal–Allard 30,235 (63%); Robert Guzman (R) 14,383 (30%); Dale Olvera (Oth) 1,137 (2%); Tim Delia (Oth) 2,012 (4%).

Interest Group Ratings:
None—Freshman

Office: 324 CHOB 20515, 202-225-1766 (Henry Contreras, Chief-of-staff). DISTRICT OFFICE: Roybal Bldg. 255 E. Temple #1860, Los Angeles 90012, 213-628-9230 (Yolanda Chavez, Rep.)

THIRTY-FOURTH DISTRICT

Esteban Edward Torres (D)

District: Includes parts of eastern and southern Los Angeles suburbs to form a Hispanic majority district. Population: 573,047—Asian 9%, Hispanic 62%, Other 31%. Politics: Democratic.

Born Jan. 30, 1930, Miami, Ariz.; home, La Puente; E. Los Angeles Community College, A.A. 1959, Calif. State University at Los Angeles, B.A. 1963, University of Md., 1965, American University, 1966; married (Arcy), 5 children.

Elected 1982. Career: Army, Korea; Assembly–line worker, Chrysler Corp., 1953–63; Chief Steward, Local 230 UAW, 1961–63; UAW Intl. Rep., Region 6, 1963–64; Inter–Amer. Rep., 1965–68; Dir., E. Los Angeles Commun. Union, 1968–74; Asst. Dir., Intl. Affairs Dept., 1974–77; U.S. Permanent Rep. UNESCO, 1977–79; Special Asst. to the Pres., 1979–81; Pres., Intl. Enterprise & Develop. Corp., 1981–82.

Committees: (1) Appropriations.

Election Results: 1992 Torres 86,721 (62%); Jay Hernandez (R) 47,357 (34%); Carl Swinney (Oth) 6,676 (5%). 1990 Torres (61%). 1988 Torres (63%).

Interest Group Ratings:

ADA	ACU	COPE	COC
85	04	92	29

LCV	NTLC	CFA	ASC
94	00	67	30

Office: 1740 LHOB 20515, 202-225-5256 (Albert Jacques, AA). DISTRICT OFFICE: 8819 Whittier Blvd., Suite 101, Pico Rivera 90660, 213-695-0702 (James Casso, Dist. Mgr.)

THIRTY-FIFTH DISTRICT

Maxine Waters (D)

District: South–Central Los Angeles including

Gardena, Hawthorne and Inglewood. Population: 570,882—Black 43%, Asian 6%, Hispanic 43%, Other 30%. Politics: Democratic.

Born Aug. 31, 1938, St. Louis; home, Los Angeles; Calif. State University, A.B. 1970; married (Sidney), 2 children.

Elected 1990. Career: Head Start official; Calif. Assembly, 1977–90.

Committees: (1) Banking, Finance, & Urban Affairs; (2) Veterans Affairs.

Election Results: 1992 Waters 98,338 (83%); Nate Truman (R) 16,122 (14%); Carin Rogers (Oth) 1,523 (1%); Alice Miles (Oth) 2,643 (2%). 1990 Waters (80%).

Interest Group Ratings:

ADA	ACU	COPE	COC
95	00	92	13

LCV	NTLC	CFA	ASC
75	00	93	20

Office: 1207 LHOB 20515, 202-225-2201 (vacant, AA). DISTRICT OFFICE: 10124 Broadway, Los Angeles 90003, 213-757-8900 (Rod Wright, Dir.)

THIRTY-SIXTH DISTRICT

Jane Harman (D)

District: Western Los Angeles including city of Torrance. Population: 573,663—Black 3%, Asian 12%, Hispanic 15%. Politics: Mixed.

Born June 28, 1945; New York City; home, Marina del Rey; Smith College, B.A. 1966, Harvard Law School, J.D. 1969; married (Sydney), 4 children.

Elected 1992. Career: Lawyer, Businesswoman. Asst. Sen. Tunney, 1972–73; Counsel and staff dir. House Judiciary subcommittee on Constitutional rights, 1975–77; Dep. Secy. to cabinet, 1977–78; Special counsel to Defense Dept., 1979; Chair, National Lawyers Counsel, 1986–90.

Committees: (1) Armed Services; (2) Science Space & Technology.

Election Results: 1992 Harman 117,202 (49%); Joan Milke Flores (R) 100,062 (42%); Richard Greene (Oth) 12,413 (5%); Marc Denny (Oth) 5,088 (2%); Owen Staley (Oth) 5,167 (2%).

Interest Group Ratings:
None—Freshman

Office: 325 CHOB 20515, 202-225-8220 (Phil Black, AA). DISTRICT OFFICE: 5200 W. Century Blvd. #960, Los Angeles 90045, 310-348-8220 (July Sitzer, Rep.)

THIRTY-SEVENTH DISTRICT

Walter R. Tucker III (D)

District: Southern Los Angeles including cities of Compton and Carson. Population: 572,049—Black 34%, Asian 11%, Hispanic 45%. Politics: Democratic.

Born May 28, 1957; Los Angeles; home, Compton; University Southern Calif., B.A. 1978, Georgetown, J.D. 1981; Baptist; married (Robin), 2 children.

Elected 1992. Career: Attorney. Deputy Dist. Atty., L.A. Co., 1984–86; Compton City Mayor, 1991–92.

Committees: (1) Public Works & Transportation; (2) Small Business.

Election Results: 1992 Tucker 92,394 (86%); Kwaku Duren (Oth) 15,160 (14%).

Interest Group Ratings:
None—Freshman

Office: 419 CHOB 20515, 202-225-7924 (Markus Mason, AA). 145 E. Compton Blvd., Compton 90220, 310-884-9989 (Audrey Gibson, Rep.)

THIRTY-EIGHTH DISTRICT

Steve Horn (R)

District: Southeastern Los Angeles county including parts of Long Beach and Downey cities. Population: 572,657—Black 8%, Asian 9%, Hispanic 26%. Politics: Mixed.

Born May 31, 1931, San Juan Batisa; home, Long Beach; Stanford, A.B. 1953, Ph.D. 1958, Harvard, M.P.A. 1954; Protestant; married (Nini), 2 children.

Elected 1992. Career: College professor. Army Reserve Intelligence, 1954–62; Asst. to U.S. Secy. of Labor, 1959–60; Asst. to Sen. Kuchel, 1961–67; Pres. Calif. State Long Beach, 1970–88, Professor Calif. State Long Beach, 1988–92.

Committees: (1) Government Operations; (2) Public Works & Transportation.

Election Results: 1992 Horn 85,415 (48%); Evan Braude (D) 77,367 (44%); Blake Ashley (Oth) 6,374 (4%); Paul Burton (Oth) 7,934 (4%).

Interest Group Ratings:
None—Freshman

Office: 1023 LHOB 20515, 202-225-6676 (Jim Dykstra, AA). 4010 Watson Plaza Dr., Lakewood 90712, 310-425-1336 (Richard Jones, Rep.)

THIRTY-NINTH DISTRICT

Ed Royce (R)

District: Eastern Los Angeles county and parts of Orange county including Fullerton and La Habra. Population: 573,574—Black 3%, Asian 14%, Hispanic 23%. Politics: Leans Republican.

Born Oct. 12, 1951, Los Angeles; home Fullerton; Calif. State Fullerton, B.A. 1977; Roman Catholic; married (Marie), no children.

Elected 1992. Career: Tax Manager for Portland Cement, 1979–82; State Senator, 1982–92.

Committees: (1) Foreign Affairs; (2) Science Space & Technology.

Election Results: 1992 Royce 113,678 (57%); Molly McClanahan (D) 76,683 (38%); Jack Dean (Oth) 8,945 (4%).

Interest Group Ratings:
None—Freshman

Office: 1404 LHOB 20515, 202-225-4111 (Jones Bates Korich, AA). DISTRICT OFFICE: 305 N. Harbor Blvd., Fullerton 92632, 714-992-8081 (Marsha Gilchrest, Rep.)

FORTIETH DISTRICT

Jerry Lewis (R)

District: San Bernardino County west of Los Angeles including city of Redlands. Population: 573,625—Black 5%, Asian 4%, Hispanic 16%. Politics: Republican.

Born Oct. 21, 1934, Seattle, Wash; home, Redlands; University of Calif. at Los Angeles, B.A. 1956; Presbyterian; married (Arlene), 4 children, 3 stepchildren.

Elected 1978. Career: Life insur. agent, 1959–78; Field Rep. to U.S. Rep. Jerry Pettis, 1968; Calif. Assembly, 1968–78.

Committees: (1) Appropriations; (2) Select Committee on Intelligence.

Election Results: 1992 Lewis 125,874 (63%); Don Rusk (D) 62,433 (31%); Margie Akin (Oth) 11,481 (6%). 1990 Lewis (60%). 1988 Lewis (70%).

Interest Group Ratings:

ADA	ACU	COPE	COC
10	83	17	86

LCV	NTLC	CFA	ASC
00	76	13	100

Office: 2312 RHOB 20515, 202-225-5861 (Arlene Willis, AA). DISTRICT OFFICE: 1826 Orange Tree Lane, Suite 104, Redlands 92374, 714-862-6030 (Pat Cinque, Rep.)

FORTY-FIRST DISTRICT

Jay C. Kim (R)

District: Parts of Los Angeles, Orange, and San Bernadino counties including Chino and Pomona. Population: 572,663—Black 7%, Asian 10%, Hispanic 31%. Politics: Republican.

Born Mar. 27, 1939, Seoul, S. Korea; home, Diamond Bar; University Southern Calif., B.A. & M.S. 1967, Calif. State L.A., M.A. 1969; Methodist; married, (June), 3 children.

Elected 1992. Career: Engineer. Diamond Bar Mayor, 1990–92.

Committees: (1) Public Works & Transportation; (2) Small Business.

Election Results: 1992 Kim 94,867 (59%); Bob Baker (D) 56,339 (35%); Mike Noonan (Oth) 9,679 (6%).

Interest Group Ratings:
None—Freshman

Office: 502 CHOB 20515, 202-225-3201 (Sandra Garner, AA). DISTRICT OFFICES: 1131 W. 6th St. #160-A, Ontario 91762, 909-988-1055 (vacant, Rep.); 18200 Yorba Linda Blvd. #203-A, Yorba Linda 92686, 714-572-8574 (vacant, Rep.)

FORTY-SECOND DISTRICT

George E. Brown, Jr. (D)

District: Parts of San Bernardino county including towns of San Bernardino and Fontana. Population: 571,844—Black 11%, Hispanic 34%. Politics: Mixed, but now leans Republican.

Born Mar. 6, 1920, Holtville; home, Riverside; University of Calif. at Los Angeles, B.A. 1946; United Methodist; married (Marta), 7 children.

Elected 1972. Career: Army, WWII; Monterey Park City Cncl., Mayor, 1954–58; Personnel, Engineering & Management Consultant, City of Los Angeles, 1957–61; Calif. Assembly, 1959–62; U.S. House of Reps., 1962–70.

Committees: (1) Agriculture; (2) Science, Space & Technology (Chairman).

Election Results: 1992 Brown 77,996 (51%); Dick Rutan (R) 67,525 (44%); Fritz Ward (Oth) 8,212 (5%). 1990 Brown (53%). 1988 Brown (54%).

Interest Group Ratings:

ADA	ACU	COPE	COC
95	05	91	25

LCV	NTLC	CFA	ASC
81	05	100	50

Office: 2300 RHOB 20515, 202-225-6161 (Dave Contarino, AA). DISTRICT OFFICE: 657 La Cadena Dr., Colton 92324, 714-825-2472 (Wilmer Carter, Dist. Admin.)

FORTY-THIRD DISTRICT

Ken Calvert (R)

District: Western Riverside county including city of Riverside. Population: 571,231—Black 6%, Asian 4%, Hispanic 25%. Politics: Mixed.

Born Jun. 6, 1953, Corona; home, Riverside; San Diego State, B.A. 1975; no religion specified; single.

Elected 1992. Career: Real Estate Developer, 1981–92.

Committees: (1) Natural Resources; (2) Science Space & Technology.

Election Results: 1992 Calvert 82,057 (47%); Marc Takano (D) 83,291 (47%); Gary Odom (Oth) 5,740 (3%); Gene Berkman (Oth) 4,676 (3%).

Interest Group Ratings:
None—Freshman

Office: 1523 LHOB 20515, 202-225-1986 (Ed Slevin, AA). DISTRICT OFFICE: 3400 Central Ave. #200, Riverside 92506, 909-784-4300 (Sue Miller, Rep.)

FORTY-FOURTH DISTRICT

Alfred A. McCandless (R)

District: Riverside County including city of Palm Springs. Population: 571,583—Black 5%, Hispanic 28%. Politics: Republican.

Born July 23, 1927, Brawley; home, Bermuda Dunes; University of Calif. at Los Angeles, B.A. 1951; Protestant; married (Gail), 5 children.

Elected 1982. Career: USMC, 1945–46, Korea; Automobile dealer, 1959–75; Riverside Cnty. Sprvsr., 1970–82.

Committees: (1) Banking, Finance, & Urban Affairs; (2) Government Operations.

Election Results: 1992 McCandless 101,806 (54%); Georgia Smith (D) 76,910 (41%); Phil Turner (Oth) 10,785 (6%). 1990 McCandless (49%). 1988 McCandless (64%).

Interest Group Ratings:

ADA	ACU	COPE	COC
10	88	17	75

LCV	NTLC	CFA	ASC
06	95	27	100

Office: 2422 LHOB 20515, 202-225-5330 (Ms. Signy Ellerton, AA). DISTRICT OFFICES: 22690 Cactus Ave. #155, Moreno Valley 92553, 909-656-1444 (Jann Foley, Rep.); 73-700 Fred Waring Dr. #112, Palm Desert 92260, 909-656-1444 (Patricia Cross, Rep.)

FORTY-FIFTH DISTRICT

Dana Rohrabacher (R)

District: Northern Orange county including Huntington Beach and parts of Costa Mesa. Population: 570,874—Asian 11%, Hispanic 15%. Politics: Republican.

Born June 21, 1947, Coronado; home, Palos Verdes Est.; L.A. Harbor College, 1965–67,

Calif. State University, B.A. 1969, USC, M.A. 1971; Baptist; single.

Elected 1988. Career: Journalist; White House speechwriter, 1981–88.

Committees: (1) District of Columbia; (2) Science, Space & Technology; (3) Foreign Affairs.

Election Results: 1992 Rohrabacher 116,501 (54%); Patricia McCabe (D) 84,267 (39%); Gary Copeland (Oth) 14,091 (7%). 1990 Rohrabacher (59%). 1988 Rohrabacher (64%).

Interest Group Ratings:

ADA	ACU	COPE	COC
20	96	25	75

LCV	NTLC	CFA	ASC
06	100	07	90

Office: 1027 LHOB 20515, 202-225-2415 (Gary Curran, Chief-of-staff). DISTRICT OFFICE: 16162 Beach Blvd. #304, Huntington Beach 92647, 714-847-2433 (Kathleen Hollingsworth, Dist. Mgr.)

FORTY-SIXTH DISTRICT

Robert K. Dornan (R)

District: Northwestern Orange County including Santa Ana and Garden Grove. Population: 571,380—Asian 12%, Hispanic 50%. Politics: Republican.

Born April 3, 1933, New York, N.Y.; home, Garden Grove; Loyola University; Roman Catholic; married (Sallie), 5 children.

Elected 1984. Career: Air Force, 1953–58; Broadcast journalist, 1965–69; Talk show host, 1969–73; U.S. House of Representatives, 1976–82.

Committees: (1) Armed Services. (2) Permanent Select on Intelligence.

Election Results: 1992 Dornan 49,633 (50%); Robert Banuelos (D) 40,587 (41%); Richard Newhouse (Oth) 8,711 (9%). 1990 Dornan (58%). 1988 Dornan (60%).

Interest Group Ratings:

ADA	ACU	COPE	COC
05	100	17	71

LCV	NTLC	CFA	ASC
00	100	07	100

Office: 2402 RHOB 20515, 202-225-2965 (Joe Eule, AA). DISTRICT OFFICE: 300 Alicante Plaza, Suite 360, Garden Grove 92642, 714-971-9292 (Patricia Ann Fanelli, Dist. Adm.)

FORTY-SEVENTH DISTRICT

C. Christopher Cox (R)

District: Coastal and central Orange county including cities of Irvine and Laguna Beach. Population: 525,935—Black 2%, Asian 10%, Hispanic 13%. Politics: Very Mixed.

Born Oct. 16, 1952, St. Paul, Min.; home, Newport Beach; University of Southern Calif., B.A. 1973, Harvard University, M.B.A. 1977, J.D. 1977; Roman Catholic; married (Ann).

Elected 1988. Career: Clerk, U.S. Court of Appeals, 1977–78; Practicing atty., 1978–86; Sr. Assoc. Counsel, White House, 1986–88.

Committees: (1) Budget; (2) Government Operations; (3) Joint Economic Committee.

Election Results: 1992 Cox 151,143 (64%); John Anwiler (D) 71,657 (31%); Maxine Quirk (Oth) 11,538 (5%). 1990 Cox (67%). 1988 Cox (67%).

Interest Group Ratings:

ADA	ACU	COPE	COC
05	100	17	75

LCV	NTLC	CFA	ASC
00	95	13	100

Office: 206 CHOB 20515, 202-225-5611 (Jan Fujiware, AA). DISTRICT OFFICE: 400 MacArthur Blvd., Suite 430, Newport Beach 92660, 714-756-2244. (Diego Ruiz, Rep.)

FORTY-EIGHTH DISTRICT

Ronald C. Packard (R)

District: Northern San Diego county, southern Orange county and some parts of Riverside county. Population: 572,928—Black 4%, Asian 5%, Hispanic 17%. Politics: Republican.

Born Jan. 19, 1931, Meridian, Idaho; home, Oceanside; Brigham Young University, Portland State University, University of Oreg., D.M.D. 1957; Mormon; married (Jean), 7 children.

Elected 1982. Career: Navy, 1957–59; Dentist; Trustee, Carlsbad School District, 1962–70,

Chm., 1971–74; Dir., Carlsbad Chmbr. of Commerce; Carlsbad Planning Comm.; Carlsbad City Cncl., 1976–78; Mayor of Carlsbad, 1978–82.

Committees: (1) Appropriations.

Election Results: 1992 Packard 128,213 (61%); Michael Farber (D) 62,318 (30%); Ted Lowe (Oth) 8,017 (4%); Donna White (Oth) 12,336 (6%). 1990 Packard (68%). 1988 Packard (72%).

Interest Group Ratings:

ADA	ACU	COPE	COC
00	100	08	71

LCV	NTLC	CFA	ASC
00	100	13	100

Office: 2162 RHOB 20515, 202-225-3906 (David Coggin, Chief–of–staff). DISTRICT OFFICES: 221 E. Vista Way #205, Vista 92084, 619-631-1364 (Terri Tkach, Rep.); Suite 204, 629 Camino de los Mares, San Clemente 92672 714-469-2343 (Mike Eggers, Rep.)

FORTY-NINTH DISTRICT

Lynn Schenk (D)

District: Parts of San Diego and Southern suburbs. Population: 573,362—Black 5%, Asian 7%, Hispanic 13%. Politics: Mixed.

Born Jan. 5, 1945, New York City; home, San Diego; University of Calif. at Los Angeles, B.A., University of Calif. at San Diego, J.D.; Jewish; married (Hugh), 3 children.

Elected 1992. Career: Deputy Atty. General, 1971–74; Counsel San Diego Gas & Elec., 1975–76; White House Fellow, 1976–77; Deputy Calif. Secy. of Business, 1977–80; Calif. Secy. of Business, 1980–83; Comm. San Diego Port Commission, 1990–92.

Committees: (1) Energy & Commerce; (2) Merchant Marine & Fisheries.

Election Results: 1992 Schenk 118,101 (52%); Judy Jarvis (R) 96,135 (42%); John Wallner (Oth) 9,817 (4%); Milton Zaslow (Oth) 4,379 (2%).

Interest Group Ratings:
None—Freshman

Office: 315 CHOB 20515, 202-225-2040 (Tom Berry, AA). DISTRICT OFFICE: 3900 5th Ave.

#200, San Diego 92103, 619-291-1430 (Laurie Black, Rep.)

FIFTIETH DISTRICT

Bob Filner (D)

District: Parts of San Diego and eastern suburbs including Chula Vista. Population: 573,463 —Black 14%, Asian 15%, Hispanic 41%. Politics: Leans Democratic.

Born Sept. 4, 1942, Pittsburgh, Pa.; home, San Diego; Cornell University, B.A. 1963, Ph.D. 1972, University of Delaware, M.A. 1968.; Jewish; married (Jane), 2 children.

Elected 1992. Career: History Professor, San Diego State 1970–92; San Diego School Board, 1979–83; San Diego City Cncl., 1988–92.

Committees: (1) Public Works & Transportation; (2) Veteran Affairs.

Election Results: 1992 Filner 71,251 (57%); Tony Valencia (R) 35,942 (29%); Barbara Hutchinson (Oth) 14,218 (11%); Roger Batchelder (Oth) 3,927 (3%).

Interest Group Ratings:
None—Freshman

Office: 504 CHOB 20515, 202-225-8045 (Tom Sugar, AA). DISTRICT OFFICE: 333 F St. Suite A, Chula Vista 91910, 619-422-9073 (Vincent Hall, Rep.)

FIFTY-FIRST DISTRICT

Randy "Duke" Cunningham (R)

District: Central San Diego. Population: 572,982 —Black 2%, Asian 8%, Hispanic 14%. Politics: Leans Democratic.

Born Dec. 8, 1941, Los Angeles; home, Chula Vista; University of Mo., B.A. 1964, M.A. 1965, National University M.B.A. 1985; Baptist; married (Nancy), 3 children.

Elected 1990. Career: U.S. Navy, 1967–87, Vietnam POW; Dean, Nat. University School of Aviation; Businessman.

Committees: (1) Armed Services; (2) Merchant Marine & Fisheries; (3) Education & Labor.

Election Results: 1992 Cunningham 125,913 (56%); Bea Herbert (D) 77,023 (34%); Richard Roe (Oth) 4,796 (2%); Bill Holmes (Oth) 9,322 (4%); Miriam Clark (Oth) 9,502 (4%). 1990 Cunningham (46%).

Interest Group Ratings:

ADA	ACU	COPE	COC
05	96	17	75

LCV	NTLC	CFA	ASC
00	95	13	100

Office: 117 CHOB 20515, 202-225-5452 (Frank Collins, AA). DISTRICT OFFICE: 613 W. Valley Pkwy. #320, Escondido 92025, 619-737-8438 (Kathy Stafford-Taulbee, Rep.)

FIFTY-SECOND DISTRICT

Duncan Lee Hunter (R)

District: Part of San Diego City and suburbs into the Imperial Valley. Population: 573,203—Black 3%, Asian 3%, Hispanic 23%. Politics: Republican.

Born May 31, 1948, Riverside; home, Coronado; Western State University, J.D. 1976; Baptist; married (Lynne), 2 children.

Elected 1980. Career: Army, Vietnam; Practicing atty., 1976–80.

Committees: Armed Services.

Election Results: 1992 Hunter 101,936 (52%); Janet Gastil (D) 80,878 (42%); Joe Shea (Oth) 6,292 (3%); Dennis Gretsinger (Oth) 5,281 (3%). 1990 Hunter (73%). 1988 Hunter (74%).

Interest Group Ratings:

ADA	ACU	COPE	COC
15	100	27	88

LCV	NTLC	CFA	ASC
00	100	20	100

Office: 133 CHOB 20515, 202-225-5672 (Vicki Middleton, AA). DISTRICT OFFICES: 366 South Pierce St., El Cajon 92020, 619-579-3001 (Wendell Cutting, Dist. Adm.); 1101 Airport Rd., Imperial 92251, 619-353-5420 (Carole Starr, Rep.)

COLORADO

Colorado continues to be a politically confusing state. On paper it appears to be a conservative, Republican Western state, but it keeps electing Democrats. The most recent is Ben Nighthorse Campbell who won his Senate seat with surprising ease against a popular conservative. The main political question going into 1994 is whether popular Democratic Governor Roy Romer will seek reelection in a state that overwhelmingly passed term limits—12 years for all state officials (but the clock only began running with the 1990 election).

1992 PRESIDENTIAL ELECTION: (8 Electoral votes): Clinton (D) 626,528 (40%); Bush (R) 557,706 (36%); Perot (I) 362,813 (23%); Marrou (Lib) 6,827; Fulani (NAP) 1,643. 1988 Bush 727,633 (54%); Dukakis 621,093 (46%).

SENATORS

Ben Nighthorse Campbell (D)

Born April 13, 1933, Auburn, Calif.; home, Ignacio; University of Calif. at San Jose, B.A. 1957, Meisi University, Japan, 1960-64; married (Linda), 2 children.

Elected 1992. Career: Air Force, 1951–54; Colo. House of Reps., 1983–86; Horse breeder & trainer, jewelry designer, teacher. U.S. House of Reps. 1988–1992.

Committees: (1) Banking, Housing & Urban Affairs; (2) Energy & Natural Resources.

Election Results: 1992 Campbell 798,864 (55%); Terry Considine (R), 656,426 (45%).

Interest Group Ratings: (House)

ADA	ACU	COPE	COC
55	38	71	43

LCV	NTLC	CFA	ASC
44	11	53	70

Office: 380 RSOB 20510, 202-224-5852 (Ken Lane, Chief-of-staff). STATE OFFICES: 1129 Pennsylvania St., Denver 80203, 303-866-1900 (James Martin, St. Dir.); Suite 105, 830 N. Tejon St., Colorado Springs 80903 719-634-5523 (Irene Kelly, Asst.); Suite 410, 8th & Main Sts., Pueblo 81003 719-542-6987 (Christopher Wiseman, Asst.)

Hank Brown (R)

Born Feb. 12, 1940, Denver; home, Greeley; University of Colo., B.S. 1961, J.D. 1969; Congregationalist; married (Nan), 3 children.

Elected 1990. Career: Navy, Vietnam; Practicing atty., 1969; Vice Pres., Monfort of Colo., Inc., 1969–80; Colo. Senate, 1972–76, Asst. Major. Ldr., 1974–76; Greeley City Planning Comm., 1979, U.S. House 1980–90.

Committees: (1) Foreign Relations; (2) Judiciary; (3) Budget.

Election Results: 1990 Brown 568,095 (57%); Josie Heath (D) 425,543 (43%).

Interest Group Ratings.

ADA	ACU	COPE	COC
20	89	25	100

LCV	NTLC	CFA	ASC
00	94	17	80

Office: 716 HSOB 20510, 202-224-5941 (Bill Brack, Chief-of-staff). STATE OFFICES: 1200 17th St., Suite 2727, Denver 80202, 303-844-2600 (Gary Hickman, State Dir.); 228 North Cascade, Suite 106, Colorado Springs 80903, 303-634-6071; 722 Thatcher Building, 5th & Main Sts., Pueblo 81022, 303-545-9751; 215 Fed. Bldg., 400 Rood Ave., Grand Junction 81501, 303-245-9553.

REPRESENTATIVES

FIRST DISTRICT

Patricia Scott Schroeder (D)

District: Denver and parts of Aurora and Commerce City. Population: 549,068—Black 13%, Hispanic 22%. Politics: Leans Democratic.

Born July 30, 1940, Portland, Oreg.; home, Denver; University of Minn., B.A. 1961, Harvard University, J.D. 1964; United Church of Christ; married (James), 2 children.

Elected 1972. Career: Field Atty., Natl. Labor Relations Bd., 1964–66; Practicing Atty.; Lecturer, Law instructor, Commun. College of Denver, 1969–70, University of Denver, Denver Ctr., 1969, Regis College, 1970–72; Hearing officer, Colo. Dept. of Personnel, 1971–72; Legal Counsel, Colo. Planned Parenthood.

Committees: (1) Armed Services; (2) Judiciary; (3) Post Office & Civil Service.

Election Results: 1992 Schroeder 155,037 (69%); Raymond Diaz Aragon (R) 70,407 (31%). 1990 Schroeder (64%). 1988 Schroeder (70%).

Interest Group Ratings:

ADA	ACU	COPE	COC
95	04	80	50

LCV	NTLC	CFA	ASC
94	15	73	40

Office: 2208 RHOB 20515, 202-225-4431 (Daniel Buck, AA). DISTRICT OFFICE: 1600 Emerson St., Denver 80218, 303-866-1230 (Kip Cherotous, Dist. Adm.)

SECOND DISTRICT

David E. Skaggs (D)

District: Denver surburbs north including Boulder and Gilpin counties. Population: 549,072—Hispanic 9%. Politics: Leans Democratic.

Born Feb. 22, 1943, Cincinnati. Ohio; home, Boulder; Wesleyan University, B.A. 1964, M. Ed. 1964, Yale University, LL.B. 1967; Congregationalist; married (Laura), 2 stepchildren.

Elected 1986. Career: USMC, 1968–71; Colo. House of Reps., 1980–86, Dem. Minor. Ldr. 1982–85; A.A. to Rep. Timothy E. Wirth, 1975–77, Campaign Dir., 1976; Practicing atty., 1977–86.

Committees: (1) Appropriations; (2) Select Committee on Intelligence.

Election Results: 1992 Skaggs 164,790 (65%); Bryan Day (R) 88,470 (35%). 1990 Skaggs (61%). 1988 Skaggs (63%).

Interest Group Ratings:

ADA	ACU	COPE	COC
90	08	82	38

LCV	NTLC	CFA	ASC
94	05	67	30

Office: 1124 LHOB 20515, 202-225-2161 (Stephen Saunders, Chief-of-staff). DISTRICT OFFICE: 9101 Harlan, Suite 130, Westminster 80030, 303-650-7886 (Sue D'Amore, Dist. Dir.)

THIRD DISTRICT

Scott McInnis (R)

District: Western half of state, including the mountain resort communities and the population center of Pueblo. Population: 549,062—Hispanic 17%. Politics: Leans Republican.

Born May. 9, 1953, Glenwood Springs; home, Glenwood Springs; Mesa Junior College, A.A., Ft. Lewis College, B.A., St. Mary's University, J.D.; Roman Catholic; married (Lori), 3 children.

Elected 1992. Career: Attorney; Police Officer, 1976; Personnel Dir., Holy Cross Electric Assn., 1977; State Rep., 1982–92.

Committees: (1) Small Business; (2) Natural Resources.

Election Results: 1992 Mcinnis 143,050 (56%); Mike Callihan (D) 114,225 (44%).

Interest Group Ratings:
None—Freshman

Office: 512 CHOB 20515, 202-225-4761 DISTRICT OFFICES: 327 N. 7th St., Grand Junction 81501, 303-245-7107; 134 West B St., Pueblo 81003, 719-543-8200; Old Main Post Office 1060 Main Ave. Suite 107, Durango 81301, 303-259-2754; 526 Pine St., Glenwood Springs 81601, 303-928-0637.

FOURTH DISTRICT

Wayne Allard (R)

District: Northern and eastern part of the state, including Fort Collins and Greeley. Population: 549,070—Hispanic 15%. Politics: Republican.

Born Dec. 2, 1943, Fort Collins; home, Loveland; Colo. St., D.V.M., 1968; Evangelical; married (Joan), 2 children.

Elected 1990. Career: Veterinarian, 1968–1990; Colo. St. Sen. 1983–90.

Committees: (1) Agriculture; (2) Natural Resources; (3) Budget.

Election Results: 1992 Allard 139,595 (58%); Tom Redder (D) 102,004 (42%). 1990 Allard (54%).

Interest Group Ratings:

ADA	ACU	COPE	COC
05	92	10	75

LCV	NTLC	CFA	ASC
00	95	00	100

Office: 422 CHOB 20515, 202-225-4676 (Roy Palmer, AA). DISTRICT OFFICES: 307 Rocky Mt. Bldg., 315 W. Oak, Ft. Collins 80521, 303-493-9132 (Mike Bennett, Dist Dir.); 350 Greeley Nat. Plaza, 821 8th St., Greeley 80632, 303-351-7582 (Sean Conway, Rep.); 311 E. Platte, Ft. Morgan 80701, 303-867-8909 (Lewis Frank, Rep.); 243 P.O. Bldg., La Junta 81050, 303-384-7370 (Doris Morgan, Rep.); 705 S. Division Ave., Sterling 80751, 303-522-1788 (Lewis Frank, Rep.)

FIFTH DISTRICT

Joel Hefley (R)

District: Central part of state from far southern Denver suburbs and including Colorado Springs. Population: 549,066—Black 6%, Hispanic 7%. Politics: Republican.

Born April 18, 1935, Ardmore, Okla.; home, Colorado Springs; OK Baptist U., B.A. 1957, Okla. State University, M.S. 1962; Baptist; married (Lynn), 3 children.

Elected 1986. Career: Colo. House of Reps., 1977–78; Colo. Senate, 1979–86; Exec. Dir., Community Planning & Research Cncl., 1966–86.

Committees: (1) Armed Services; (2) Natural Resources; (3) Small Business.

Election Results: 1992 Hefley 167,117 (74%); Charles Oriez (D) 60,090 (26%). 1990 Hefley (69%). 1988 Hefley (75%).

Interest Group Ratings:

ADA	ACU	COPE	COC
20	92	27	88

Office: 2442 RHOB 20515, 202-225-4422 (Brian Reardon, AA). DISTRICT OFFICE: 104 S. Cascade #105, Colorado Springs 80903, 719-520-0055 (vacant, Dist. Dir.), 9605 Maroon Circle #220, Englewood 80112, 303-792-3923 (Vicki Agler, Asst.)

SIXTH DISTRICT

Dan L. Schaefer (R)

District: Denver suburbs, including parts of Aurora and Lakewood. Population: 549,056—Black 4%, Hispanic 6%. Politics: Republican.

Born Jan 25, 1936, Guttenberg, Iowa; home, Lakewood; Niagara University, B.A. 1961, Potsdam University; Roman Catholic; married (Mary), 4 children.

Elected Mar. 29, 1983. Career: USMC, 1955–57; Educator, 1961–67; Public Affairs Consultant, 1967–83; Colo. House of Reps., 1977–78; Colo. Senate, 1979–83.

Committees: (1) Energy & Commerce.

Election Results: 1992 Schaefer 140,792 (61%); Tom Kolbe (D) 90,525 (39%). 1990 Schaefer (65%). 1988 Schaefer (63%).

Interest Group Ratings:

ADA	ACU	COPE	COC
05	88	27	75

LCV	NTLC	CFA	ASC
00	95	07	100

Office: 2448 RHOB 20515, 202-225-7882 (Holly Propst, AA). DISTRICT OFFICE 3615 S. Huron St., Suite 101, Englewood 80110, 303-762-8890 (Andree Krause, Dist. Dir.)

CONNECTICUT

Republicans believe Connecticut's Democratic Senator, Joseph I. Lieberman, will be among the most vulnerable in 1994. There are a number of Republicans lining up to challenge him. In 1994 Connecticut politics will be focused on the governor's office and the question of whether maverick Republican Lowell Weicker, Jr., elected in 1990 as an independent, will run for reelection, and whether he can win. His popularity dropped because he supported the imposition of an income tax, but it has rebounded somewhat.

1992 PRESIDENTIAL ELECTION: (8 Electoral votes): Clinton (D) 682,406 (42%); Bush (R) 576,777 (36%); Perot (I) 347,407 (22%); Marrou (Lib) 5,514; Fulani (NAP 1,283). 1988 Bush 747,082 (53%); Dukakis 674,873 (47%).

SENATORS

Christopher J. Dodd (D)

Born May 27, 1944, Willimantic; home, East Haddam; Providence College, B.A. 1966, University of Louisville, J.D. 1972; Roman Catholic; divorced.

Elected 1980, seat up 1998. Career: Peace Corps, Dominican Republic, 1966–68; Army, 1969–75; Practicing atty., 1972–74; U.S. House of Reps., 1974–80.

Committees: (1) Banking, Housing & Urban Affairs; (2) Budget; (3) Foreign Relations; (4) Labor & Human Resources; (5) Rules & Administration.

Election Results: 1992 Dodd 887,734 (61%); Brook Johnson (R) 568,269 (39%). 1986 Dodd (65%). 1980 Dodd (56%).

Interest Group Ratings:

ADA	ACU	COPE	COC
75	11	92	30

LCV	NTLC	CFA	ASC
83	28	92	50

Office: 444 RSOB 20510, 202-224-2823 (Doug Susnick, AA). STATE OFFICE: Putnam Park, 100 Great Meadows Rd., Wheathersfield 06109, 203-240-3470 (Joan Hogan-Gillman, St. Dir.)

Joseph I. Lieberman (D)

Born Feb. 24, 1942, Stamford; home, New Haven; Yale, B.A. 1964, J.D. 1967; Jewish; married (Hadassah), 3 children.

Elected 1988, seat up 1994. Career: Practicing atty, 1967–present; Conn. Senate, 1970–80; Conn. Atty. Gen., 1983–88; Dir., Yale Studies in Urban Planning, 1969–88.

Committees: (1) Environment & Public Works; (2) Governmental Affairs; (3) Small Business; (4) Armed Services.

Election Results: 1988 Lieberman 688,499 (50%); Lowell Weicker (R) 678,454 (49%).

Interest Group Ratings:

ADA	ACU	COPE	COC
70	22	83	50

LCV	NTLC	CFA	ASC
100	05	92	50

Office: 316 HSOB 20510, 202-224-4041 (William Andersen, AA). STATE OFFICE: One Commercial Plaza, 21st Floor, Hartford 06106, 203-240-3566 (Sherry Brown, St. Dir.)

REPRESENTATIVES

FIRST DISTRICT

Barbara Bailey Kennelly (D)

District: Central part of the state including Hartford and suburbs. Population: 548,016—Black 14%, Asian 2%, Hispanic 10%. Politics: Democratic.

Born July 10, 1936, Hartford; home, Hartford; Trinity College (Washington, D.C.), B.A. 1958, Trinity College (Hartford, Conn.), M.A., 1971; Roman Catholic; married (James), 4 children.

Elected 1982. Career: Vice Chm., Hartford Comm. on Aging, 1971–75; Hartford Crt. of Common Cncl., 1975–79; Conn. Secy. of State, 1979–82.

Committees: (1) Ways & Means; (2) Permanent Select Committee on Intelligence; (3) Budget.

Election Results: 1992 Kennelly 164,381 (69%);

Philip Steele (R) 74,367 (31%). 1990 Kennelly (71%). 1988 Kennelly (77%).

Interest Group Ratings:

ADA	ACU	COPE	COC
100	04	92	25

LCV	NTLC	CFA	ASC
88	00	93	40

Office: 201 CHOB 20515, 202-225-2265 (Michael Prucker, AA). DISTRICT OFFICE: One Corporate Center, 11th flr., Hartford 06103, 203-240-3120 (Robert Croce, Dist. Dir.)

SECOND DISTRICT

Samuel Gejdenson (D)

District: The eastern third of the state including Windham and New London. Population: 548,041—Black 4%, Hispanic 3%. Politics: Leans Democratic.

Born May 20, 1948, Eschwege, Germany; home, Bozrah; Mitchell College, A.S. 1966, University of Conn., B.A. 1970; Jewish; separated, 2 children.

Elected 1980. Career: Conn. House of Reps., 1974–78; Legislative Liaison to the Gov. of Conn., 1979–80.

Committees: (1) Foreign Affairs; (2) House Administration; (3) Natural Resources.

Election Results: 1992 Gejdenson 123,290 (51%); Edward Munster (R) 119,415 (49%). 1990 Gejdenson (60%). 1988 Gejdenson (64%).

Interest Group Ratings:

ADA	ACU	COPE	COC
90	12	92	38

LCV	NTLC	CFA	ASC
63	05	100	30

Office: 2416 RHOB 20515, 202-225-2076 (Bob Baskin, AA). DISTRICT OFFICES: 74 W. Maine St. (P.O. Box 2000), Norwich 06360, 203-886-0139 (Naomi Otterness, Dist. Dir.); 94 Court St., Middletown 06457, 203-346-1123 (Patricia Shea, Rep.)

THIRD DISTRICT

Rosa DeLauro (D)

District: South-central part of the state including New Haven. Population: 547,765—Black 12%, Hispanic 5%, Asian 2%. Politics: Leans Democratic.

Born Mar. 2, 1943, New Haven; home, New Haven; Marymount College, B.A., 1964, Columbia University M.A., 1966; Catholic; married (Stanley Greenberg), 3 children.

Elected 1990. Career: Ex. Asst. to Mayor of New Haven, 1976–78; Develop. Adm, 1978–80; Chief-of-staff, Sen. Christopher Dodd 1980–87; ex dir., EMILY's List 1987–90.

Committees: (1) Appropriations.

Election Results: 1992 DeLauro 162,075 (66%); Tom Scott (R) 84,950 (34%). 1990 DeLauro (53%).

Interest Group Ratings:

ADA	ACU	COPE	COC
90	04	92	13

LCV	NTLC	CFA	ASC
94	00	100	20

Office: 327 CHOB 20515, 202-225-3661 (Paul Frick, AA). DISTRICT OFFICE: 265 Church St., New Haven 06510, 203-562-3718.

FOURTH DISTRICT

Christopher Shays (R)

District: Southern part of the state including the upper income New York City bedroom communities of Stamford and Greenwich, and the old industrial town of Bridgeport. Population: 547,765—Black 13%, Hispanic 11%. Politics: Republican.

Born Oct. 18, 1945, Stamford; home, Stamford; Principia College, B.A. 1968, New York University, M.B.A. 1974, M.P.A. 1978; Protestant; married (Betsi), 1 child.

Elected 1988. Career: Conn. House of Reps., 1974–87.

Committees: (1) Government Operations; (2) Budget.

Election Results: 1992 Shays 145,911 (67%); Dave Schropfer (D) 58,543 (27%); Al Smith (Oth) 11,814 (5%). 1990 Shays (76%). 1988 Shays (72%).

Interest Group Ratings:

ADA	ACU	COPE	COC
65	40	67	38

LCV	NTLC	CFA	ASC
100	85	100	70

Office: 1034 LHOB 20515, 202-225-5541 (Betsy Wright-Hawkings, AA). DISTRICT OFFICES: 10 Middle St., Bridgeport 06604, 203-579-5870 (Richard Slawsky, Mgr.); 888 Washington Blvd., Stamford 06901, 203-357-8277 (Carol Moon, Mgr.); 125 East Ave., Norwalk 06851, 203-866-6469 (Jeanne Lovejoy, Asst.)

FIFTH DISTRICT

Gary Franks (R)

District: A west-central slice of the state built around the population centers of Waterbury and Danbury. Population: 547,764—Black 5%, Hispanic 6%. Politics: Leans Republican.

Born Feb. 9, 1953, Waterbury; home, Waterbury; Yale University, B.A. 1975; Baptist; married (Donna), 2 children.

Elected 1990. Career: Real estate developer; Waterbury Bd. of Aldermen 1986–90.

Committees: (1) Energy & Commerce.

Election Results: 1992 Franks 103,998 (45%); James Lawlor (D) 74,128 (32%); Lynn Taborsak (Oth) 53,747 (23%). 1990 Franks (52%).

Interest Group Ratings:

ADA	ACU	COPE	COC
20	88	25	88

LCV	NTLC	CFA	ASC
31	80	20	100

Office: 435 CHOB 20515, 202-225-3822 (Rick Genua, AA). DISTRICT OFFICE: 135 Grand St., Waterbury 06701, 203-573-1418 (vacant, Dist. Dir.)

SIXTH DISTRICT

Nancy Lee Johnson (R)

District: Northwestern third of the state including some far western Hartford suburbs and New Britain. Population: 547,765—Black 2%, Hispanic 4%. Politics: Leans Republican.

Born Jan. 5, 1935, Chicago, Ill.; home, New Britain; University of Chicago, 1953, Radcliffe College, B.A. 1957, University of London, 1958; Unitarian; married (Theodore), 3 children.

Elected 1982. Career: Pres., Sheldon Community Guidance Clinic; Adjunct Professor, Central Conn. State College; Conn. Senate, 1977–82.

Committees: (1) Ways & Means; (2) Ethics.

Election Results: 1992 Johnson 165,002 (73%); Eugene Slason (D) 60,327 (27%). 1990 Johnson (74%). 1988 Johnson (66%).

Interest Group Ratings:

ADA	ACU	COPE	COC
40	58	42	75

LCV	NTLC	CFA	ASC
38	70	53	100

Office: 343 CHOB 20515, 202-225-4476 (Eric Thompson, AA). DISTRICT OFFICES: One Grove St., New Britain 06053, 203-223-8412 (Tom McLaughlin, Dist. Dir.); 276 Hazard Ave., Enfield 06082, 203-745-5722 (Peg Kellen, Rep.)

DELAWARE

The big story in Delaware politics in 1992 was Republican Gov. Michael N. Castle, who could not run for reelection, running for and winning the at-large Congressional seat. The question looming now is whether Republican Sen. William Roth will seek a fifth term in 1994, or whether he might step aside for Castle who clearly has Senate ambitions.

1992 PRESIDENTIAL ELECTION: (3 Electoral votes) Clinton (D) 125,997 (44%); Bush (R) 102,436 (35%); Perot (I) 59,061 (20%); Fulani (NAP) 1,112; Marrou (Lib) 965. 1988 Bush 130,581 (57%); Dukakis 99,479 (43%).

SENATORS

William Victor Roth, Jr. (R)

Born July 22, 1921, Great Falls, Mont.; home, Wilmington; University of Oreg., B.A. 1944, Harvard University, M.B.A. 1947, LL.B. 1947; Episcopalian; married (Jane), 2 children.

Elected 1970, seat up 1994. Career: Army, WWII; Practicing atty.; Chm., Del. Repub. State Committee, 1961–64; U.S. House of Reps. 1967–71.

Committees: (1) Banking, Housing & Urban Affairs; (2) Finance; (3) Governmental Affairs (Ranking Member); (4) Joint Economic.

Election Results: 1988 Roth 151,115 (62%); S. B. Woo (D) 92,378 (38%). 1982 Roth (56%).

Interest Group Ratings:

ADA	ACU	COPE	COC
25	75	27	100

LCV	NTLC	CFA	ASC
42	76	40	60

Office: 104 HSOB 20510, 202-224-2441 (John Duncan, AA). STATE OFFICES: 3021 Fed. Bldg., 844 King St., Wilmington 19801, 302-573-6291 (Jeffrey Garland, Asst.); 2215 Fed. Bldg., 300 S. New St., Dover 19901, 302-674-3308 (Marlene Elliott, Asst.); 2 S. Bedford St., Georgetown 19947, 302-856-7690 (Marlene Elliott, Asst.)

Joseph R. Biden, Jr. (D)

Born Nov. 20, 1942, Scranton, Pa.; home, Wilmington; University of Del., B.A. 1965, Syracuse University, J.D. 1968; Roman Catholic; married (Jill), 3 children.

Elected 1972; seat up 1996. Career: Practicing atty., 1968–72; New Castle Cnty. Cncl., 1970–72.

Committees: (1) Foreign Relations; (2) Judiciary (Chairman).

Election Results: 1990 Biden 112,128 (63%); Jane Brady (R) 64,682 (40%). 1984 Biden (60%).

Interest Group Ratings:

ADA	ACU	COPE	COC
83	17	81	20

LCV	NTU	CFA	ASC
86	42	80	40

Office: 221 RSOB 20510, 202-224-5042 (Edward Kaufman, Chief-of-staff). STATE OFFICES: 6021 Fed. Bldg., 844 King St., Wilmington 19801, 302-573-6345 (Bert DiClemente, Dist. Exec. Asst.); 1101 Fed. Bldg, 300 S. New St., Dover 17901, 302-678-9483 (Arleen LaPorte, Asst.); 108 Georgetown Prof. Ctr., 600 DuPont Hwy., Georgetown 19947, 302-856-9275 (Kevin Smith, Asst.)

REPRESENTATIVE

AT LARGE

Michael N. Castle (R)

District: Entire state. Population: 666,168—Black 17%, Hispanic 2%. Politics: Mixed, but leans Republican.

Born July 2, 1939, Wilmington; home, Dover; Hamilton College, B.S. 1961, Georgetown University, J.D. 1964; Roman Catholic; married (Jane), no children.

Elected 1992. Career: Lt. Gov., 1981–84; Governor, 1985–92.

Committees: (1) Banking, Finance & Urban Affairs; (2) Merchant Marine & Fisheries.

Election Results: 1992 Castle 152,761 (57%); S.B. Woo (D) 117,294 (43%).

Interest Group Ratings:
None—Freshman

Office: 1205 LHOB 20515, 202-225-4165 (Michael Ratchford, AA). DISTRICT OFFICES: 2005 Freer Fed. Off. Bldg., Dover 19901, 302-736-1666 (Carrie Shugart, Rep.); Wilmington, (Jeff Dayton, Rep.)

FLORIDA

Florida will be one of the major Senate battlegrounds in 1994. Democrats have targeted Republican Sen. Connie Mack III. They look at the 1992 election results—even if Bill Clinton did not carry the state—as showing signs that the state may be moving towards the Democrats. The popular Democratic governor, Lawton Chiles, will be running for reelection in 1994 and he should help the entire Democratic ticket.

1992 PRESIDENTIAL ELECTION: (25 Electoral votes): Clinton (D) 2,051,845 (39%); Bush (R) 2,137,752 (41%); Perot (I) 1,041,607 (20%); Marrou (Lib) 14,756. 1988 Bush 2,538,994 (61%); Dukakis 1,632,086 (39%).

SENATORS

Robert Graham (D)

Born Nov. 9, 1936, Miami; home, Miami Lakes; University of Fla., B.A. 1959, Harvard University, LL.B. 1962; United Church of Christ; married (Adele), 4 children.

Elected 1986, seat up 1998. Career: Fla. House of Reps., 1966–70; Fla. Senate, 1970–78; Gov. of Fla., 1978–1986.

Committees: (1) Environment & Public Works; (2) Veterans Affairs; (3) Special Committee on Aging; (4) Armed Services; (5) Intelligence.

Election Results: 1992 Graham 3,214,708 (66%); Bill Grant (R) 1,688,522 (34%). 1986 Graham (55%).

Interest Group Ratings:

ADA	ACU	COPE	COC
75	15	75	20

LCV	NTLC	CFA	ASC
75	22	100	100

Office: 524 HSOB 20510, 202-224-3041 (Samuel Shorstein, AA). STATE OFFICES: 325 John Knox Rd., Bldg. 600, Tallahassee 32308, 904-681-7726 (Jay Hakes, St. Dir.), 44 W. Flagler St., Suite 1715, Miami 33130, 305-536-7293 (Lula Rodriguez, Rep.), 101 E. Kennedy Blvd., Suite 3145, Tampa 33601 813-228-2476 (Michael Suarez, Rep.)

Connie Mack III (R)

Born Oct. 29, 1940, Philadelphia, Pa.; home, Cape Coral; University of Fla., B.A. 1966; Roman Catholic; married (Priscilla), 2 children.

Elected 1988; seat up 1994. Career: Banker, 1966–82; U.S. House of Reps., 1982–88.

Committees: (1) Banking, Housing & Urban Affairs; (2) Appropriations; (3) Joint Economic.

Election Results: 1988 Mack 2,049,329 (50%); Buddy MacKay (D) 2,015,717 (50%).

Interest Group Ratings:

ADA	ACU	COPE	COC
10	96	18	100

LCV	NTLC	CFA	ASC
17	89	25	100

Office: 517 HSOB 20510, 202-224-5274 (Mitchell Bainwol, AA). STATE OFFICES: 600 N. Westshore Blvd., Suite 602, Tampa 33607, 813-225-7683. (John McReynolds, Reg. Dir.), 777 Bickell Ave, Suite 704, Miami 33131 305-530-7100 (Jorge Arrizurieta, Dpty. St. Dir.), 1342 Colonial Blvd. Suite 27, Ft. Meyers 33907 813-275-6252 (Sharon Thierer, Reg. Dir.), 1211 Governor Sq. Bldg, Suite 402, Tallahassee 32301 904-681-7514 (LeeAnn Croy, Reg. Dir.), 6706 N. 9th St., Suite C8 Pensacola, 32504, 904-479-9803 (David Stafford, Rep.); 1 San Jose Pl., Suite 9, Jacksonville 32257, 904-268-7915 (Lisa Sandoser, Rep.)

REPRESENTATIVES

FIRST DISTRICT

Earl Dewitt Hutto (D)

District: Far northwest corner of the state, the "panhandle," including the city of Pensacola. Population: 562,518—Black 13%. Politics: Leans Republican.

Born May 12, 1926, Midland City, Ala.; home, Panama City; Troy St. University, B.S. 1949, Northwestern University, 1951; Baptist; married (Nancy), 2 children.

Elected 1978. Career: Navy, WWII; Pres., Earl Hutto Advertising Agency, 1974–78; Founder &

former Pres. WPEX Radio, 1960–65; TV Sports Dir., WEAR, WSFA, WJHG, 1954–72; Fla. House of Reps., 1972–78.

Committees: (1) Armed Services; (2) Merchant Marine & Fisheries.

Election Results: 1992 Hutto 110,044 (55%); Terry Ketchel (R) 90,098 (45%). 1990 Hutto (52%). 1988 Hutto (67%).

Interest Group Ratings:

ADA	ACU	COPE	COC
15	83	36	88

LCV	NTLC	CFA	ASC
6	80	33	100

Office: 2435 RHOB 20515, 202-225-4136 (Gary Pulliam, AA). DISTRICT OFFICES: 4300 Bayou Blvd., Suite 25A, (P.O. Box 17689), Pensacola 32522, 904-478-1123 (Ben Collins, Dist. Adm.); P.O. Box 459, Panama City 32402, 904-763-0709 (Earl Hadaway, Dist. Adm.); Courthouse Annex, Shalamar 32579, 904-651-3111 (Larry Williamson, Rep.)

SECOND DISTRICT

Pete Peterson (D)

District: The northern counties including the city of Tallahassee. Population: 562,519—Black 23%. Politics: Conservative Democratic.

Born June 26, 1935, Omaha, Neb.; home, Marianna; University of Tampa, B.S., 1976; University of Central Mich., M.A. public administration, 1977; Catholic; married (Carlotta Ann), 3 children.

Elected 1990. Career: U.S. Air Force 1958–85 (POW Vietnam six years); faculty, Fla. State Univ., 1985–87; headmaster Dozier School (Fla.), 1987–90.

Committees: (1) Appropriations.

Election Results: 1992 Peterson 155,284 (74%); Ray Wagner (R) 53,519 (26%). 1990 Peterson (57%).

Interest Group Ratings:

ADA	ACU	COPE	COC
75	19	64	38

LCV	NTLC	CFA	ASC
38	10	67	70

Office: 426 CHOB 20515, 202-225-5235 (Suzanne Farmer, AA). DISTRICT OFFICES: 930 Thomasville Rd. #101, Tallahassee 32303, 904-561-3979 (Tom Pitcock, Rep.); 30 W. Govt. St. #203, Panama City, 904-785-0812 (Alexa Peas, Rep.)

THIRD DISTRICT

Corrine Brown (D)

District: Black majority district that winds through the north central and eastern coastal regions, including parts of city of Jacksonville. Population: 562,519—Black 55%, Hispanic 3%. Politics: Democratic.

Born Nov. 11, 1946, Jacksonville; home, Jacksonville; Fla. A.& M., B.A. 1969, University of Fla., M.S. 1974; Baptist; divorced, 1 child.

Elected 1992. Career: State Rep. 1982–92; Professor Fla. Comm. College Jacksonville, 1977–92.

Committees: (1) Public Works & Transportation; (2) Veterans Affairs.

Election Results: 1992 Brown 89,625 (60%); Don Weidner (R) 60,586 (40%).

Interest Group Ratings:
None—Freshman

Office: 1037 LHOB 20515, 202-225-0123 (Ronnie Simmons, Rep.) DISTRICT OFFICE: 815 S. Main St. Suite 275, Jacksonville 32207, 904-398-8567 (Shelda Shaw, Rep.); 75 Ivanhoe Blvd., Orlando 32802, 407-425-1234 (Reginald McGill, Rep.); 401 SE 1st Ave. #316, Gainesville 32601, 904-375-6003 (Jean Haley, Rep.); 250 N. Beach St. #80-1, Daytona Beach 32114, 904-254-4622 (Naomi Cooper, Rep.)

FOURTH DISTRICT

Tillie Fowler (R)

District: Northern Atlantic coastal counties, including parts of Daytona Beach and Jacksonville. Population: 562,518—Black 6%, Hispanic 3%. Politics: Leans Republican.

Born Dec. 23, 1942, Medgeville, Ga.; home, Jacksonville; Emory University, A.B. 1964, J.D. 1967; Episcopalian; married (Buck), 2 children.

Elected 1992. Career: Asst. to Rep. Stephens, 1967–69; White House Office of Consumer Affairs, 1970–71; Jacksonville City Counsel, 1985–92.

Committees: (1) Armed Services; (2) Merchant Marine & Fisheries.

Election Results: 1992 Fowler 127,758 (56%); Mattox Hair (D) 99,554 (44%).

Interest Group Ratings:
None—Freshman

Office: 413 CHOB 20515, 202-225-2501 (David Gillialand, AA). DISTRICT OFFICES: 4452 Hendricks Ave., Jacksonville 32207, 904-739-6600 (Susie Wiles, Rep.); 533 N. Nova Rd., Ormond Beach 32174, 904-672-0754 (Georgia Flynn, Rep.)

FIFTH DISTRICT

Karen L. Thurman (D)

District: Northwestern coast including parts of Gainsville and Port Richie. Population: 562,518 —Black 6%, Hispanic 3%. Politics: Mixed.

Born Jan. 12, 1951, Rapid City, S.Dak.; home, Dunnellon; Santa Fe Community College, A.A. 1971, University of Fla., B.A. 1973; Episcopalian; married (John), 2 children.

Elected 1992. Career: Teacher. Dunnellon City Counsel, 1976–82; Mayor of Dunellon, 1981–82; State Sen., 1982–92.

Committees: (1) Agriculture; (2) Government Operations.

Election Results: 1992 Thurman 129,677 (53%); Tom Hogan (R) 114,331 (47%).

Interest Group Ratings:
None—Freshman

Office: 130 CHOB 20515, 202-225-1002 (Nora Matus, AA). DISTRICT OFFICES: One Courthouse Sq. #102, Iverness 34450, 904-637-9945 (Anne Morgan, Dist. Dir.); 5700 SW 34th St. #425, Gainsville 32608, 904-336-6614; 5623 U.S. 19 South #206, Newport Richie 34652, 813-849-4496.

SIXTH DISTRICT

Cliff Stearns (R)

District: North central part of the state including town of Ocala and parts of Jacksonville. Population: 562,518—Black 7%, Hispanic 3%. Politics: Leans Republican.

Born Apr. 16, 1941, Washington, D.C.; home, Ocala; George Washington University, B.S. 1963; Presbyterian; married (Joan), 3 children.

Elected 1988. Career: Owner & pres., Stearns House Inc., 1972–present.

Committees: (1) Energy & Commerce.

Election Results: 1992 Stearns 142,499 (65%); Phil Denton 75,806 (35%). 1990 Stearns (59%). 1988 Stearns (54%).

Interest Group Ratings:

ADA	ACU	COPE	COC
05	92	11	75

LCV	NTLC	CFA	ASC
25	90	08	100

Office: 332 CHOB 20515, 202-225-5744 (Jack Seum, Chief-of-staff). DISTRICT OFFICE: 115 SE 25th Ave., Ocala 32671, 904-351-8777 (Sharon Brooks, Dist. Exec. Asst.)

SEVENTH DISTRICT

John L. Mica (R)

District: North central eastern coast including parts of Daytona Beach and Orlando. Population: 562,518—Black 4%, Hispanic 6%. Politics: Leans Republican.

Born Jan. 27, 1943, Binghamton, N.Y.; home, Winter Park; Miami Dade Community College, A.A. 1965, University of Fla., B.A. 1967; Episcopalian; married (Pat), 2 children.

Elected 1992. Career: State Rep., 1976–80; Chief of Staff for Sen. Hawkins, 1986–92.

Committees: (1) Government Operations; (2) Public Works & Transportation.

Election Results: 1992 Mica 125,755 (56%); Dan Webster (D) 96,889 (44%).

Interest Group Ratings:
None—Freshman

Office: 427 CHOB 20515, 202-225-4035 (Russell Roberts, AA). DISTRICT OFFICES: 237 Fernwood #105, Fern Park 32720, 904-339-8080 (Dick Harkey, Rep.); 840 Deltona #G, Deltona 32725, 407-860-1499 (C.J. Drake, Rep.); 1395 Delbauton #2B, Ft. Orange 32127, 904-756-9798 (John Booker, Rep.)

EIGHTH DISTRICT

Bill McCollum (R)

District: Most of Orange county including parts of Orlando and Winter Park. Population: 562,518 —Black 5%, Hispanic 11%. Politics: Republican.

Born July 12, 1944, Brooksville; home, Altamonte Springs; University of Fla., B.A. 1965, J.D. 1968; Episcopalian; married (Ingrid), 3 children.

Elected 1980. Career: Navy, 1969–72; Practicing atty., 1973–81; Chm., Seminole Cnty. Repub. Exec. Comm., 1976.

Committees: (1) Banking, Finance & Urban Affairs; (2) Judiciary.

Election Results: 1992 McCollum 141,011 (69%); Chuck Kovaleski (D) 64,763 (31%). 1990 McCollum (60%). 1988 McCollum (Unopposed).

Interest Group Ratings:

ADA	ACU	COPE	COC
15	92	25	86

LCV	NTLC	CFA	ASC
19	90	13	100

Office: 2266 RHOB 20515, 202-225-2176 (Vaughn Forrest, Chief-of-staff). DISTRICT OFFICE: 605 E. Robinson St. #605, Orlando 32801, 407-872-1962 (John Ariale, Rep.)

NINTH DISTRICT

Michael Bilirakis (R)

District: Gulf coastal counties of Pasco, Pinellas and Hillsborough, north of Tampa, including population center of Clearwater. Population: 562,518—Black 3%, Hispanic 4%. Politics: Republican.

Born July 16, 1930, Tarpon Springs; home, Palm Harbor; University of Pittsburgh, B.S. 1959, University of Fla., J.D. 1963; Greek Orthodox; married (Evelyn), 2 children.

Elected 1982. Career: Air Force, Korea; Steelworker, 1955–59; Govt. contract negotiator, 1959–60; Petroleum engineer, 1960–63; Practicing atty., 1969–83.

Committees: (1) Energy & Commerce; (2) Veterans Affairs.

Election Results: 1992 Bilirakis 157,786 (59%); Cheryl Knapp (D) 110,002 (41%). 1990 Bilirakis (58%). 1988 Bilirakis (Unopposed).

Interest Group Ratings:

ADA	ACU	COPE	COC
20	80	42	75

LCV	NTLC	CFA	ASC
19	85	27	100

Office: 2240 RHOB 20515, 202-225-5755 (Robert Meyers, AA). DISTRICT OFFICES: 1100 Cleveland St., Suite 1600, Clearwater 33515, 813-441-3721 (Pat Faber, Dist. Dir.); 4111 Land-O-Lakes Blvd. #306, Land-O-Lakes 34639, 813-996-7441 (Shirley Miaoulis, Rep.)

TENTH DISTRICT

C.W. Bill Young (R)

District: St. Petersburg and environs. Population: 562,518—Black 9%,. Politics: Leans Republican.

Born Dec. 16, 1930, Harmarville, Pa.; home, Largo; United Methodist; married (Beverly), 6 children.

Elected 1970. Career: Aide to U.S. Rep. William C. Cramer, 1957–60; Fla. Senate, 1960–70, Minor. Ldr., 1966–70.

Committees: (1) Appropriations; (2) Select Committee on Intelligence.

Election Results: 1992 Young 149,657 (57%); Karen Moffitt (D) 114,890 (43%). 1990 Young (Unopposed). 1988 Young (73%).

Interest Group Ratings:

ADA	ACU	COPE	COC
15	76	42	63

LCV	NTLC	CFA	ASC
25	70	33	100

Office: 2407 RHOB 20515, 202-225-5961 (Douglas Gregory, AA). DISTRICT OFFICES: 801 W. Bay Drive, Rm. 606, Largo 33540 813-581-0980 (George Cretekos, AA); 627 Fed. Bldg., 144 First Ave. S, St. Petersburg 33701, 813-893-3191 Pauline Arnold, Asst.)

ELEVENTH DISTRICT

Sam M. Gibbons (D)

District: Parts of Hillsborough county including city of Tampa. Population: 562,519—Black 17%, Hispanic 14%. Politics: Leans Democratic.

Born Jan. 20, 1920, Tampa; home, Tampa; University of Fla., J.D. 1947; Presbyterian; married (Martha), 3 children.

Elected 1962. Career: U.S. Army, WWII; Practicing attorney, 1947–62; Fla. House of Representatives, 1952–58; Fla. State Senate, 1958–62.

Committees: (1) Ways & Means; (2) Joint Committee on Taxation.

Election Results: 1992 Gibbons 100,816 (57%); Mark Sharpe (R) 77,451 (43%). 1990 Gibbons (68%). 1988 Gibbons (Unopposed).

Interest Group Ratings:

ADA	ACU	COPE	COC
65	22	50	25

LCV	NTLC	CFA	ASC
50	00	87	60

Office: 2204 RHOB 20515, 202-225-3376 (Janice Stoorza, AA). DISTRICT OFFICES: 2002 N. Lois Ave. #260, Tampa 33607, 813-870-2101 (Gregg Wonders, Mgr.); 201 S. Kings Ave., Rm. 6, Brandon 33511, 813-689-2847.

TWELFTH DISTRICT

Charles T. Canady (R)

District: Central part of state taking in six counties including city of Lakeland. Population 562,519—Black 13%, Hispanic 6%. Politics: Republican.

Born Jun. 22, 1954, Lakeland; home Lakeland; Haverford College, B.A. 1976, Yale, J.D. 1979; Presbyterian; single.

Elected 1992. Career: Attorney. State Rep. 1984–90.

Committees: (1) Agriculture; (2) Judiciary.

Election Results: 1992 Canady 100,298 (52%); Tom Mims (D) 92,228 (48%).

Interest Group Ratings:
None—Freshman

Office: 1107 LHOB 20515, 202-225-1252 (Clark Reid, AA). DISTRICT OFFICES: Fed. Bldg. 124 S. Tennessee Ave., Lakeland 33801, 813-688-2651 Sue Loftin, Rep.)

THIRTEENTH DISTRICT

Dan Miller (R)

District: Central western coast, including city of Sarasota. Population: 562,518—Black 5%, Hispanic 4%. Politics: Republican.

Born May 30, 1942, Highland Park, Mich.; home, Bradenton; University of Fla., B.S. 1964, Emory University, M.B.A. 1965, Louisiana State University, Ph.D. 1970; Episcopalian; married (Glenda), 2 children.

Elected 1992. Career: Businessman. College Professor, 1969–83.

Committees: (1) Budget; (2) Education & Labor.

Election Results: 1992 Miller 158,826 (58%); Rand Snell (D) 115,725 (42%).

Interest Group Ratings:
None—Freshman

Office: 510 CHOB 20515, 202-225-5015 (Katherine Calhoun Wood, AA). DISTRICT OFFICES: 1751 Mound St. #A2, Sarasota 34236, 813-951-6643 (Ralph Davitto, Rep.); 2424 Manatee #104, Bradenton 34205, 813-951-2972 (Sandra Groseclose, Rep.); 4000 S. Tamiami Trail A-124, Venice 34293, 813-493-2044 (Mike Demming, Rep.)

FOURTEENTH DISTRICT

Porter Goss (R)

District: Southwest Gulf coast, including cities of Naples, and Fort Myers. Population: 562,518 —Black 6%, Hispanic 7%. Politics: Leans Republican.

Born Nov. 26, 1938, Waterbury, Conn.; home, Sanibel; Yale, B.A. 1960; Presbyterian; married (Mariel), 4 children.

Elected, 1988. Career: Central Intelligence Agency 1960–71; Newspaper publisher, 1973–88; Mayor of Sanibel, Fla.; Lee Cnty. Commissioner.

Committees: (1) Rules; (2) Ethics.

Election Results: 1992 Goss 223,410 (82%); James King (Oth) 48,874 (18%). 1990 Goss (Unopposed). 1988 Goss (71%).

Interest Group Ratings:

ADA	ACU	COPE	COC
05	88	17	75

LCV	NTLC	CFA	ASC
31	95	33	100

Office: 330 CHOB 20515, 202-225-2536 (Sheryl Wooley, Chief-of-staff). DISTRICT OFFICES: 2000 Main St., Suite 407, Ft. Myers 33901, 813-332-4677 ; 3301 Tamiami Trail East #F212, Naples 33962, 818-774-8060.

FIFTEENTH DISTRICT

Jim Bacchus (D)

District: Central Atlantic coastal counties including city of Melbourne. Population: 562,519 —Black 8%, Hispanic 3%. Politics: Leans Republican.

Born June 21, 1949, Nashville, Tenn; home, Belle Isle; Vanderbilt University, B.A., 1971, Yale University, M.A. 1973, Fla. State University, J.D. 1978; Presbyterian; married (Rebecca), 2 children.

Elected 1990. Career: Lawyer; Govt. advis; Reporter, Orlando Sentinel; Aide, Fla. Gov. Ruebin Askew, 1978; Special Asst. U.S. Trade Negot.; atty. priv. prac.

Committees: (1) Banking, Finance & Urban Affairs; (2) Science, Space & Technology.

Election Results: 1992 Bacchus 132,284 (51%); Bill Tolley (R) 128,749 (49%). 1990 Bacchus (52%).

Interest Group Ratings:

ADA	ACU	COPE	COC
70	29	55	13

LCV	NTLC	CFA	ASC
88	10	87	90

Office: 432 CHOB 20515, 202-225-3671 (Linda Hennesse, AA). DISTRICT OFFICES: 874 Dickson Blvd., Cocoa 32922, 407-632-1776 (Dale Ketcham, Dist. Dir.)

SIXTEENTH DISTRICT

Tom Lewis (R)

District: South central Atlantic coast including parts of West Palm Beach and Port St. Lucie.

Population: 562,519—Black 4%, Hispanic 6%. Politics: Republican.

Born Oct. 26, 1924, Philadelphia, Pa.; home, North Palm Beach; Palm Beach Junior College, 1956–57, University of Fla. 1958–59; United Methodist; married (Marian), 3 children.

Elected 1982. Career: Air Force, WWII & Korea; Corp. Exec., Pratt & Whitney Aircraft, 1957–73; Mayor/Councilman, North Palm Beach, 1964–71; Fla. House of Reps., 1972–80; Fla. Senate 1980–82.

Committees: (1) Agriculture; (2) Science, Space & Technology.

Election Results: 1992 Lewis 157,190 (61%); John Comerford (D) 101,179 (39%). 1990 Lewis (Unopposed). 1988 Lewis (Unopposed).

Interest Group Ratings:

ADA	ACU	COPE	COC
10	96	27	83

LCV	NTLC	CFA	ASC
19	80	20	100

Office: 2351 RHOB 20515, 202-225-5792 (Karen Hogan, AA). DISTRICT OFFICES: 4440 PGA Blvd., Suite 406, Palm Beach Gardens 33410 407-627-6192 (Ed Chase, Dist. Dir.); 7601 S. Hwy. One, Suite 200, Port St. Lucie, 34952, 407-283-7989 (Ann Decker, Dist. Mgr.)

SEVENTEENTH DISTRICT

Carrie Meek (D)

District: North Miami and suburbs including town of Coral City. Population: 562,519—Black 58%, Hispanic 23%. Politics: Democratic.

Born Apr. 29, 1926, Tallahassee; home, Miami; Florida A.& M., B.A. 1946, University of Michigan, M.A. 1949; Baptist; divorced, 3 children.

Elected 1992. Career: College professor, 1961–92; State Rep., 1979–82; State Sen., 1982–92.

Committees: Appropriations.

Election Results: 1992 Meek (Unopposed).

Interest Group Ratings:
None—Freshman

Office: 404 CHOB 20515, 202-225-4506 (Peggy Demon, AA). DISTRICT OFFICE: 25 W. Flager

St. #1015, Miami 33130, 305-381-9541 (Gary Forchion, Rep.)

EIGHTEENTH DISTRICT

Ileana Ros-Lehtinen (R)

District: Parts of Miami and Miami Beach. Population: 562,519—Black 4%, Hispanic 67%. Politics: Leans Republican.

Born July 15, 1952, Havana, Cuba; home, Miami; Fla. International University, B.A. 1975, M.S. 1987; Roman Catholic; married (Dexter Lehtinen), 2 children.

Elected 1989 (Special Election). Career: Teacher, private school administrator, Fla. House of Reps., 1982–86; Fla. Sen. 1986–89.

Committees: (1) Foreign Affairs; (2) Government Operations.

Election Results: 1992 Ros-Lehtinen 104,715 (67%); Magda Davis (D) 52,095 (33%). 1990 Ros-Lehtinen (62%). 1989 (special) Ros-Lehtinen (58%).

Interest Group Ratings:

ADA	ACU	COPE	COC
25	78	50	57

LCV	NTLC	CFA	ASC
56	70	53	100

Office: 127 CHOB 20515, 202-225-3931 (Maurico Tamargo, AA). DISTRICT OFFICE: 5757 Blue Lagoon, Suite 240, Miami 33126, 305-262-1800 (Debra Musgrove, Dist. Dir.)

NINETEENTH DISTRICT

Harry A. Johnston II (D)

District: Southeast Atlantic coast including Coral Springs and parts of Boca Raton. Population: 562,519—Black 3%, Hispanic 6%. Politics: Leans Democratic.

Born December 2, 1931, West Palm Beach; home, West Palm Beach; Va. Military Institute, B.S. 1953, University of Fla., J.D. 1958; Presbyterian; married (Mary), 2 children.

Elected 1988. Career: U.S. Army, 1953–55; Practicing attorney, 1958–88; Florida State Senate.

Committees: (1) Foreign Affairs; (2) Budget.

Election Results: 1992 Johnston 177,376 (63%); Larry Metz (R) 103,819 (37%). 1990 Johnston (66%). 1988 Johnston (55%).

Interest Group Ratings:

ADA	ACU	COPE	COC
90	12	67	38

LCV	NTLC	CFA	ASC
94	11	60	30

Office: 204 CHOB 20515, 202-225-3001 (Suzanne Stoll, AA). DISTRICT OFFICE: 1501 Corporate Dr., Suite 250 Boynton Beach 33426, 407-732-4000 (Diane Birnbaum, Dist. Adm.); Margate City Hall 5790 Margate Blvd., Margate 33063, 305-972-6454.

TWENTIETH DISTRICT

Peter Deustch (D)

District: Southern most part of the state including Hollywood and the Keys. Population: 562,518—Black 4%, Hispanic 12%. Politics: Leans Democratic.

Born Apr. 1, 1957, Bronx, N.Y.; home, Lauderhill; Swarthmore, B.A. 1979, Yale, J.D. 1982; Jewish; married (Lori), 2 children.

Elected 1992. Career: Lawyer; State Rep., 1982–92.

Committees: (1) Banking, Finance & Urban Affairs; (2) Foreign Affairs.

Election Results: 1992 Deutsch 130,895 (59%); Beverly Kennedy (R) 91,289 (41%).

Interest Group Ratings:
None—Freshman

Office: 425 CHOB 20515, 202-225-7931 (Henry Ellenbogen, AA). DISTRICT OFFICES: 10100 Pines Blvd., Pembrook Pines 33025, 305-437-3936 (Juliana Walsh, Dist. Dir.)

TWENTY-FIRST DISTRICT

Lincoln Diaz-Balart (R)

District: Western Dade county including Hialeah. Population 562,519—Black 4%, Hispanic 70%. Politics: Leans Republican.

Born Aug. 13, 1954, Havana, Cuba; home, Miami; University of S. Fla., B.A. 1976, Cambridge (England), Diploma, Case Western Reserve, J.D. 1979; Roman Catholic; married (Christina), 2 children.

Elected 1992. Career: Lawyer; State Rep., 1978–88; State Sen., 1989–92; Dade Co. Chairman, 1991–92.

Committees: (1) Foreign Affairs; (2) Merchant Marine & Fisheries.

Election Results: 1992 Diaz-Balart (Unpoppossed).

Interest Group Ratings:
None—Freshman

Office: 509 CHOB 20515, 202-225-4211 (Jeff Bartel, AA). DISTRICT OFFICES: 8525 N.W. 53rd Terr. #102, Miami 33166, 305-470-8555 (Ana Carbonell, Dist. Dir.)

TWENTY-SECOND DISTRICT

E. Clay Shaw, Jr. (R)

District: Parts of Broward, Dade, and Palm Beach counties including parts of Fort Lauderdale and North Miami. Population: 562,519—Black 3%, Hispanic 13%. Politics: Leans Republican.

Born Apr. 19, 1939, Miami; home, Fort Lauderdale; Stetson University, B.A. 1961, University of Alabama, M.B.A. 1963, Stetson University, J.D. 1966; Roman Catholic, married (Emilie), 4 children.

Elected 1980. Career: Practicing atty., 1966–68; Fort Lauderdale Asst. City Atty., 1968, Chief City Prosecutor, 1968–69, Assoc. Municipal Judge, 1969–71, City Commissioner, 1971–73, Vice Mayor, 1973–75, Mayor 1975–80.

Committees: (1) Ways & Means.

Election Results: 1992 Shaw 128,254 (58%);

Gwen Margolis (D) 91,540 (42%). 1990 Shaw (Unopposed). 1988 Shaw (66%).

Interest Group Ratings:

ADA	ACU	COPE	COC
15	84	25	75

LCV	NTLC	CFA	ASC
19	90	33	100

Office: 2267 RHOB 20515, 202-225-3026 (Lee Johnson, AA). DISTRICT OFFICE: 1512 E. Broward Blvd. #101, Ft. Lauderdale 33301, 305-522-1800 (Dorothy Stewart, Dist. Mgr.)

TWENTY-THIRD DISTRICT

Alcee L. Hastings (D)

District: Southern Atlantic coast including parts of Ft. Lauderdale, Pompano Beach, and West Palm Beach. Population: 562,519—Black 52%, Hispanic 9%. Politics: Democratic.

Born Sept. 5, 1936, Altamonte Springs; home, Miami; Fisk University, B.A. 1957, Fla. A.& M., J.D. 1963; African Methodist Episcopal; divorced, 3 children.

Elected 1992. Career: Attorney, 1964–77; Judge, Broward Co., 1977–79; Federal Judge, 1979–89.

Committees: (1) Foreign Affairs; (2) Merchant Marine & Fisheries.

Election Results: 1992 Hastings 84,207 (65%); Ed Fielding (R) 44,758 (35%).

Interest Group Ratings:
None—Freshman

Office: 1039 LHOB 20515, 202-225-1313 (Trey Coleman, AA). DISTRICT OFFICE: 270 W. Oakland Pk. Blvd., Ft. Lauderdale 33311, 305-733-2800 (Cert Kennedy, Rep.)

GEORGIA

Georgia has become a confusing state, politically. Bill Clinton carried the state in 1992, but at the same time Democratic Sen. Wyche Fowler was narrowly defeated for reelection in a runoff running by former state senator Paul Coverdell. The question for 1994 is whether Democratic Gov. Zell Miller will run for reelection, and whether he will win.

1992 PRESIDENTIAL ELECTION: (13 Electoral votes) Clinton (D) 1,005,889 (44%); Bush (R) 989,804 (43%); Perot (I) 307,857 (13%); Marrou (Lib) 7,455. 1988 Bush 1,070,089 (60%); Dukakis 715,635 (40%).

SENATORS

Samuel Augustus Nunn (D)

Born Sept. 8, 1938, Perry; home, Perry; Ga. Institute of Technology, 1959, Emory University, A.B. 1962; United Methodist; married (Colleen), 2 children.

Elected 1972, seat up 1996. Career: Coast Guard, 1959–60; Farmer, Practicing atty., 1963–72; Ga. House of Reps., 1968–72.

Committees: (1) Armed Services (Chairman); (2) Governmental Affairs; (3) Small Business.

Election Results: 1990 Nunn (Unopposed). 1984 Nunn (80%).

Interest Group Ratings:

ADA	ACU	COPE	COC
65	30	91	50

LCV	NTLC	CFA	ASC
67	39	75	60

Office: 303 DSOB 20510, 202-224-3521 (Bob Hurt, AA). STATE OFFICES: 75 Spring St., Suite 1700, Atlanta 30303, 404-331-4811 (Tommy Dortch, St. Dir.); 915 Main St., Perry 31069, 912-987-1458 (Jim Peterson, Asst.); 130 Fed. Bldg., Gainesville 30501, 404-532-9976 (Charles Wurst, Asst.); 101 U.S. P.O. Bldg., Columbus 31902, 404-327-3270 (Olan Faulk, Asst.); Suite A-307, 120 Barnard St., Savannah 31402, 912-944-4300 (Elizabeth Way, Asst.)

Paul Coverdell (R)

Born Jan. 20, 1939, Des Moines, Ia.; home, Atlanta; University of Missouri, B.A. 1961; Presbyterian; married (Donna), 1 child.

Elected 1992, seat up 1998. Career: Army, 1962–64; President and Chairman, Coverdell & Co., 1965–92; Ga. State Senate, 1970–89; Director U.S. Peace Corps, 1989–92.

Committees: (1) Agriculture, Nutrition & Forestry; (2) Foreign Relations.

Election Results: 1992 (Runoff) Coverdell 630,023 (51%); Wyche Fowler, Jr. (Incumbent D), 613,846 (49%). (General Election—majority required to win): Fowler 1,098,658 (49%); Coverdell 1,067,294 (48%); Jim Hudson (Lib) 69,779 (3%).

Interest Group Ratings:
None—Freshman

Office: 200 RSOB 20510, 202-224-3643 STATE OFFICE: 100 Colony Square 410, 1175 Peach St., Atlanta 30361, 404-347-2202 (Eric Tannenblatt, Rep.)

REPRESENTATIVES

FIRST DISTRICT

Jack Kingston (R)

District: Atlantic Coast counties including cities of Waycross and Brunswick, and parts of Savannah. Population: 589,546—Black 23%. Politics: Leans Republican.

Born Apr. 24, 1955, Bryan, Tex.; home, Savannah; University of Ga., B.S. 1977; Episcopalian; married (Elizabeth), 4 children.

Elected 1992. Career: Insurance Broker, 1979–92; State Rep., 1985–92.

Committees: (1) Agriculture; (2) Merchant Marine & Fisheries.

Election Results: 1992 Kingston 99,204 (57%); Barbara Christmas (D) 75,044 (43%).

Interest Group Ratings:
None—Freshman

Office: 1229 LHOB 20515, 202-225-5831 (Paul Powell, AA). DISTRICT OFFICES: 6605 Abercorn St. Suite 102, Savannah 31405, 912-352-

0101 (Peggy Lee Mowers, Dist. Dir.); Statesboro Fed. Bldg. #220, Statesboro 30458, 912-489-8797 (Floyd Thackson, Mgr.); Brunswick Fed. Bldg. 805 Gloucester St. #304, Brunswick 31520, 912-265-9010 (Becki Bernier, Mgr.), 208 Tebeau St., Waycross 31501, 912-287-1180 (Malcolm Vass, Mgr.)

SECOND DISTRICT

Sanford Bishop (D)

District: Southwest part of the state including towns of Albany, Valdosta and parts of Macon. Population: 591,699—Black 57%. Politics: Democratic.

Born Feb. 4, 1947, Mobile, Ala.; home, Columbus; Morehouse College, B.A. 1968, Emory University, J.D. 1971; Baptist; divorced.

Elected 1992. Career: Lawyer; Ga. House of Reps., 1976-90; State Sen., 1990–92.

Committees: (1) Agriculture; (2) Veterans Affairs.

Election Results: 1992 Bishop 94,943 (64%); Jim Dudley (R) 54,036 (36%).

Interest Group Ratings:
None—Freshman

Office: 1632 LHOB 20515, 202-225-3631 (Sylvia McCoy, AA). DISTRICT OFFICES: 225 Pine Ave., Albany 31702, 912-439-8067 (Sandra Pointer, Asst.); 401 N. Patterson, Valdosta 31601, (Bridget Singleton, Rep); 682 Cherry St. #1113, Macon 31201, Steve Balk, Rep.)

THIRD DISTRICT

Mac Collins (R)

District: West central part of the state including Columbus and Griffin. Population: 591,328—Black 18%. Politics: Leans Republican.

Born Oct. 15, 1944, Jackson; home, Jackson; United Methodist; married (Julie), 4 children.

Elected 1992. Career: Ga. National Guard, 1964–70; Trucking Co. Owner; State Sen., 1988–92.

Committees: (1) Public Works & Transportation; (2) Small Business.

Election Results: 1992 Collins (R) 112,640 (55%); Richard B. Ray (D) (incumbent) 90,969 (45%).

Interest Group Ratings:
None—Freshman

Office: 1118 LHOB 20515, 202-225-5901 (Jay Morgan, AA) DISTRICT OFFICES: 5074 Beall-Wood #200, Columbus 31904, 706-327-7228 (Shirley Gillespie, Rep.); 173 N. Main St., Jonesboro 30236, 404-603-3395 (Ronnie Chance, Rep.)

FOURTH DISTRICT

John Linder (R)

District: Part of the City of Atlanta, and its western suburbs. Population: 588,293—Black 12%, Asian 4%, Hispanic 3%. Politics: Leans Democratic.

Born Sept. 9, 1942, Deer River, Minn.; home, Dunwoody; University of Minn., B.A. 1964, D.D.S. 1967; Presbyterian; married (Lynne), 2 children.

Elected 1992. Career: U.S. Air Force, 1967–69; Dentist 1969–82; Pres., Linder Financial Corp., 1977–92; State Rep., 1977–90.

Committees: (1) Banking, Finance & Urban Affairs; (2) Science, Space & Technology; (3) Veterans Affairs.

Election Results: 1992 Linder 126,502 (51%); Cathey Steinberg (D) 123,819 (49%).

Interest Group Ratings:
None—Freshman

Office: 1605 LHOB 20515, 202-225-4272 (Rick Halcomb, AA). DISTRICT OFFICE: 3003 Chamblee-Tucker Rd. #140, Atlanta 30341, 404-936-9400 (Bob Varga, Exec. Dir.)

FIFTH DISTRICT

John R. Lewis (D)

District: Parts of Fulton, Cobb, Clayton, and DeKalb counties, including part of Atlanta. Population: 586,485—Black 62%. Politics: Democratic.

Born Feb. 21, 1940, Troy, Ala.; home, Atlanta; American Baptist Theological Seminary, B.A. 1961, Fisk University, B.A. 1963; Baptist; married (Lillian), 1 child.

Elected 1986. Career: Chairman, Student Non-violent Coordinating Committee, 1963–66; Associate Director, Field Foundation, 1966–67; Director of Community Organizations, Southern Regional Council, 1967–70; Executive Director, Voter Education Project, 1970–77; Associate Director, ACTION, 1977–80; Director of Consumer Affairs, Consumer Cooperative Bank, 1980–81; Member, Atlanta City Council, 1982–86.

Committees: (1) Ways & Means.

Election Results: 1992 Lewis 147,443 (72%); Paul Stabler (R) 56,898 (28%). 1990 Lewis (76%). 1988 Lewis (78%).

Interest Group Ratings:

ADA	ACU	COPE	COC
95	00	92	13

LCV	NTLC	CFA	ASC
88	05	100	10

Office: 329 CHOB 20515, 202-225-3801 (Linda Chastang, AA). DISTRICT OFFICE: Equitable Bldg., Suite 750, 100 Peachtree St. NW, Atlanta 30303, 404-659-0116 (Michael German, Dist. Mgr.)

SIXTH DISTRICT

Newton Leroy Gingrich (R)

District: North central part of the state including parts of Marietta and Roswell. Population: 587,118—Black 6%. Politics: Leans Republican.

Born June 17, 1943, Harrisburg, Pa.; home, Jonesboro; Emory University, B.A. 1965, Tulane University, M.A. 1968, Ph.D. 1971; Baptist; married (Marianne), 2 children.

Elected 1978. Career: Asst. Prof., West Ga. College, 1970–78.

Committees: (1) House Administration (Ranking Member); (2) Joint Committee on the Library.

Election Results: 1992 Gingrich 158,670 (58%); Tony Center (D) 116,147 (42%). 1990 Gingrich (50%). 1988 Gingrich (59%).

Interest Group Ratings:

ADA	ACU	COPE	COC
10	100	22	88

LCV	NTLC	CFA	ASC
06	100	20	100

Office: 2428 RHOB 20515, 202-225-4501 (Annette Thompson, AA). DISTRICT OFFICE: 3823 Roswell Rd. #200, Marietta 30062, 404-565-6398 (Jeff Wansley, Rep.)

SEVENTH DISTRICT

George "Buddy" Darden (D)

District: Northwest corner of the state including 11 counties and towns of Rome and Marietta. Population: 588,071—Black 13%. Politics: Democratic.

Born Nov. 22, 1943, Sparta; home, Marietta; North Ga. College, George Washington University, University of Ga., B.A. 1965, J.D. 1967; United Methodist; married (Lillian), 2 children.

Elected 1983. Career: Assistant District Attorney, Cobb County, 1968–73; District Attorney, 1973–77; Practicing attorney, 1977–83; Georgia House of Representatives, 1981–83.

Committees: (1) Appropriations; (2) Ethics.

Election Results: 1992 Darden 111,259 (57%); Al Beverly (R) 82,820 (43%). 1990 Darden (60%). 1988 Darden (65%).

Interest Group Ratings:

ADA	ACU	COPE	COC
70	32	58	50

LCV	NTLC	CFA	ASC
38	15	60	100

Office: 2303 RHOB 20515, 202-225-2931 (Bob Gaylor, AA). DISTRICT OFFICES: 376 Powder Springs St., Suite 100, Marietta 30064, 404-422-4480 (Paul Ervin, Chief-of-staff); 301 Fed. Bldg., Rome 30161, 404-291-7777 (Sharon Helton, Mgr.); 315 Bradley St., Carrollton 30117, 404-832-0553 (Bill Hemrick, Mgr.); City Hall 200 Ridley Ave., Lagrange 30240, 706-882-4578 (Hilda Raley, Mgr.)

EIGHTH DISTRICT

James Roy Rowland (D)

District: South central part of the state including part of the city of Macon. Population: 591,615—Black 21%. Politics: Democratic.

Born Feb. 3, 1926, Johnson Cnty; home, Dublin; Emory University, South Ga. College, University of Ga., Medical College of Ga., M.D. 1952; United Methodist; married (Luella), 3 children.

Elected 1982. Career: Army, WWII; Practicing physician 1954–82; Ga. House of Reps. 1976–82.

Committees: (1) Energy & Commerce; (2) Veterans Affairs.

Election Results: 1992 Rowland 107,601 (56%); Robert Cunningham (R) 85,774 (44%). 1990 Rowland (69%). 1988 Rowland (Unopposed).

Interest Group Ratings:

ADA	ACU	COPE	COC
50	48	58	63

LCV	NTLC	CFA	ASC
19	33	60	100

Office: 2134 RHOB 20515, 202-225-6531 (Selby McCash, AA). DISTRICT OFFICES: P.O. Box 6258, Macon 31208, 912-474-0150 (Bill Stembridge, Dist. Mgr.); 1810 N. Ashley St. #5, Valdosta 31602, 912-333-0118; 2410 Westgate Blvd. #109, Albany 31707, 912-889-9040; 200 Carl Venson Pkwy., Warner Robbins 31088, 912-328-6404.

NINTH DISTRICT

Nathan Deal (D)

District: Northern part of the state including cities of Gainesville and Dalton. Population: 586,222—Black 4%. Politics: Democratic.

Born Aug. 25, 1942, Millen; home, Gainesville; Mercer University, B.A. 1964, J.D. 1966; Baptist; married (Sandra), 4 children.

Elected 1992. Career: Army, 1966–68; Asst. Dist. Atty., 1970–71; Judge, Hall Co., 1971–72; Practicing atty., 1972–92; State Sen. 1980–92.

Committees: (1) Natural Resources; (2) Public Works & Transportation.

Election Results: 1992 Deal 114,020 (59%); Daniel Becker (R) 77,877 (41%).

Interest Group Ratings:
None—Freshman

Office: 1406 LHOB 20515, 202-225-5211 (Andy Maddox, AA). DISTRICT OFFICES: 311 Green St. #302, Gainesville 30501, 404-535-2592 (Don Parks, Dist. Mgr.); 307 Selridge St., Dalton 30720, 706-226-5320 (Don Parks, Dist. Mgr.); 109

N. Main St., Lafayette 30728, 706-638-7042 (Don Parks, Dist. Mgr.)

TENTH DISTRICT

Don Johnson (D)

District: Northeastern part of the state including population centers of Athens and parts of Augusta. Population: 591,644—Black 18%. Politics: Democratic.

Born Jan. 30, 1948, Royston; home, Royston; University of Ga., B.A. 1970, J.D. 1973, London School of Economics, M.A. 1978; Baptist; married (Suzanne), 3 children.

Elected 1992. Career: U.S. Air Force, 1978–81; Staff Atty. House Ways & Means Committee, 1973–76; Practicing Atty. 1976–92; State Sen., 1987–92.

Committees: (1) Armed Services; (2) Science, Space & Technology.

Election Results: 1992 Johnson 108,494 (54%); Ralph Hudgens (R) 92,776 (46%).

Interest Group Ratings:
None—Freshman

Office: 226 CHOB 20515, 202-225-4101 (Beverly Bell, AA). DISTRICT OFFICES: 220 College Ave. #200, Athens 30601, 706-353-6444 (Jane Kidd, Rep.); 2050 Walton Way #212, Augusta 30904, 706-736-3373 (Roberta Bush, Rep.); 1108 Hunter St., Covington 30209, 706-787-8667 (Cathy Dobbs, Rep.)

ELEVENTH DISTRICT

Cynthia McKinney (D)

District: Black majority district covering central part of the state, including parts of Augusta and Savannah. Population: 586,195—Black 64%. Politics: Democratic.

Born Mar. 17, 1955, Atlanta; home, Lithonia; University of Southern Calif., B.A., Fletcher School of Law & Diplomacy, Ph.D. candidate; Roman Catholic; divorced, 1 child.

Elected 1992. Career: State Rep., 1988–92.

Committees: (1) Agriculture; (2) Foreign Affairs.

Election Results: 1992 McKinney 120,187 (73%); Woodrow Lovett (R) 44,359 (27%).

Interest Group Ratings:
None—Freshman

Office: 124 CHOB 20515, 202-225-1605 (Andrea Young, AA). DISTRICT OFFICE: 1 S. DeKalb Center 2853 Candler Rd. #9, Decatur 30034, 404-244-9902 (Ouida Lamar, Rep.)

HAWAII

Sen. Daniel Akaka, 70, has announced he will seek reelection in 1996. Popular two time Gov. John Waihee, who cannot seek a third term in 1994, says he will not challenge Akaka. There has been some talk that Rep. Patsy Mink, now in her second incarnation in Congress, might decide to retire again. If so she would open the way for Waihee. The interesting contest in 1994 is for governor with two strong Republicans, former Rep. Pat Saiki and Honolulu Mayor Frank Fasi fighting it out to see who will challenge the likely Democratic candidate, Lt. Gov. Ben Cayetano.

1992 PRESIDENTIAL ELECTION: (4 Electoral votes): Clinton (D) 179,310 (48%); Bush (R) 136,822 (37%); Perot (I) 53,003 (14%); Gritz (Pop) 1,452; Marrou (Lib) 1,119; Fulani (NAP) 720; Hagelin (NLP) 416. 1988 Dukakis 192,364 (55%); Bush 158,625 (45%).

SENATORS

Daniel K. Inouye (D)

Born Sept. 7, 1924, Honolulu; home, Honolulu; University of Hawaii, B.A. 1950, George Washington University, J.D. 1952; United Methodist; married (Margaret), 1 child.

Elected 1962, seat up 1998. Career: Army, WWII; Honolulu Asst. Pros. Atty., 1953–54; Practicing atty., 1954–59; Hawaii Territorial Senate, 1958–59; U.S. House of Reps. 1959–62.

Committees: (1) Appropriations; (2) Commerce, Science & Transportation; (3) Rules & Administration; (4) Select Committee on Indian Affairs (Chairman).

Election Results: 1992 Inouye, 207,794 (58%); Rick Reed (R) 97,653 (27%); Linda Martin (I) 49,789 (14%). 1986 Inouye (74%). 1980 Inouye (78%).

Interest Group Ratings:

ADA	ACU	COPE	COC
65	04	92	10

LCV	NTLC	CFA	ASC
42	11	92	50

Office: 722 HSOB 20510, 202-224-3934 (Patrick Deleon, AA). STATE OFFICES: 7325 Fed. Bldg., 300 Ala Moana Blvd., Honolulu 96850, 808-541-2542 (Jennifer Goto, Rep.); 101 Aupuni St., Suite 205, Hilo 96720 808-935-1114 (Bill Kikuchi, Asst.)

Daniel Kahikina Akaka (D)

Born Sept. 11, 1924, Honolulu; home, Honolulu; University of Hawaii, B.A.Ed. 1952, M.A.Ed. 1966; Congregrationalist; married (Mary Mildred), 5 children.

Elected 1990, seat up 1996. Career: Pub. sch. teacher, principal, program specialist, 1953–71; Dir., Hawaii Ofc. of Econ. Opp., 1971–74; Spec. Asst. in Human Resources, Ofc. of the Gov. of Hawaii, 1975–76; Dir., Progressive Neighborhoods Program, 1975–76; U.S. House of Reps. 1976–90.

Committees: (1) Energy & Natural Resources; (2) Veterans Affairs; (3) Governmental Affairs; (4) Select Committee on Indian Affairs.

Election Results: 1990 Akaka 188,900 (54%); Patricia F. Saiki (R) 155,978 (45%).

Interest Group Ratings:

ADA	ACU	COPE	COC
90	00	92	20

LCV	NTLC	CFA	ASC
92	05	92	20

Office: 720 HSOB 20510, 202-224-6361 (James Sakai, AA). STATE OFFICE: 3104 Prince Kuhio Bldg., Honolulu 96850, 808-541-2534 (Mike Kitamura, Dist. Adm.)

REPRESENTATIVES

FIRST DISTRICT

Neil Abercrombie (D)

District: Eastern half of Oahu including Honolulu. Population: 554,119—Asian and Pacific Islander 67%, Black 2%, Hispanic 6%. Politics: Democratic.

Born June 26, 1938, Buffalo, N.Y.; home, Honolulu; Union College, B.A. 1959, University of Hawaii, M.A. 1964, Ph.D. 1974; married (Nancy).

Elected 1990. Career: Hawaii House of Reps., 1974–78; Hawaii Senate, 1978–86; U.S. House of Reps., 1986–87; Honolulu Cty. Cnsl. 1988–90.

Committees: (1) Armed Services; (2) Natural Resources.

Election Results: 1992 Abercrombie 128,942 (76%); Warner Sutton (R) 41,415 (24%). 1990 Abercrombie (61%).

Interest Group Ratings:

ADA	ACU	COPE	COC
95	00	91	13

LCV	NTLC	CFA	ASC
88	00	100	20

Office: 1440 LHOB 20515, 202-225-2726 (Patrick McCain, AA). DISTRICT OFFICE: 4104 Fed. Bldg, 300 Ala Moana Blvd., Honolulu 96850, 808-546-8997 (Steve Beaudry, Mgr.)

SECOND DISTRICT

Patsy T. Mink (D)

District: Western half of Oahu and all Outer Islands. Population: 554,110—Asian and Pacific Islander 57%, Black 2%, Hispanic 9%. Politics: Democratic.

Born Dec. 26, 1927, Paia (Maui), Hawaii; home, Honolulu; University of Hawaii, B.A., 1948, University of Chicago, J.D., 1951; Protestant; married (John F. Mink), 1 child.

Elected, September 1990 (Special Election). Career: Hawaii Terr. House, 1956–58; Hawaii Terr. Sen., 1958–59; Hawaii State Sen. 1962–64; U.S. House of Reps. 1965–77; Asst. Secy. of State, 1978–81; Pres. Amer. For Dem. Action, 1981–83; Mbr. Honolulu Cty. Cncl. 1983–87, Chm., 1984–87.

Committees: (1) Education and Labor; (2) Budget; (3) Natural Resources; (4) Government Operations.

Election Results: 1992 Mink 131,256 (77%); Kamuela Price (R) 39,963 (23%). 1990 Mink (68%). 1990 (special) Mink (62%).

Interest Group Ratings:

ADA	ACU	COPE	COC
100	00	100	25

LCV	NTLC	CFA	ASC
100	00	100	30

Office: 2135 RHOB 20515, 202-225-4906 (vacant, AA). DISTRICT OFFICE: 5104 Fed. Bldg., 300 Ala Moana Blvd., Honolulu 96850, 808-541-1986 (Earl Arruda, Dist. AA)

IDAHO

Idaho, one of the most Republican of states, has elected a Democrat governor every year since 1970. In 1994 Cecil Andrus, arguably the popular politician in the state, will be precluded from running for a third consecutive term. This is a race that the GOP would love to win. It is not yet clear who will be either party's standard bearer, but Democratic Attorney General Larry EchoHawk is an early favorite.

1992 PRESIDENTIAL ELECTION: (4 Electoral votes): Clinton (D) 136,734 (28%); Bush (R) 202,421 (42%); Perot (I) 130,282 (27%); Gritz (Pop) 10,259 (2%); Marrou (Lib) 1,161; Fulani (NAP) 610. 1988 Bush 253,467 (63%); Dukakis (D) 147,420 (37%).

SENATORS

Dirk Kempthorne (R)

Born Oct. 29, 1951, San Diego; home, Boise; University of Idaho, B.A. 1975; Methodist; married (Patricia), 2 children.

Elected 1992, seat up 1998. Career: FMC Corp. Public Affairs Mgr., 1980–86; Boise Mayor, 1986–92.

Committees: (1) Armed Services; (2) Environment & Public Works.

Election Results: 1992 Kempthorne 269,209 (57%); Richard Stallings (D) 207,124 (43%).

Interest Group Ratings:
None—Freshman

Office: 367 DSOB 20510, 202-224-6142 STATE OFFICES: 304 N. 8th St. #338, Boise 83702, 208-334-1776 (Phil Reberger, Rep.); 118 N. 2nd St. #1, Coeur d'Alene 83814, 208-664-5490 (Steve Judy, Asst.); 2539 Channing Way, Suite 240, Idaho Falls 83404, 208-522-9779 (Dixie Richardson, Rep.); 250 S. 4th St. #207, Pocatello 83201, 208-236-6775 (Sally Greenslade, Rep.); 401 2nd St. North #106, Twin Falls, 83301, 208-734-2515 (Orrie Sinclair, Rep.); 633 Main St. #103, Lewiston 83501, 208-743-1492 (Carolyn Durant, Rep.)

Larry Craig (R)

Born July 20, 1945, Midvale; home, Midvale; University of Idaho, B.S. 1969, George Washington University, M.A. 1971; United Methodist; married (Suzanne), 3 children.

Elected 1990. Seat up 1996. Career: Rancher, 1971–74; Idaho Senate, 1974–80; U.S. House of Reps., 1980–90.

Committees: (1) Energy & Natural Resources; (2) Agriculture.

Election Results: 1990 Craig 178,653 (61%); Ron Twilegar (D) 112,752 (39%).

Interest Group Ratings:

ADA	ACU	COPE	COC
00	100	17	90

LCV	NTLC	CFA	ASC
00	89	00	70

Office: 313 HSOB 20510, 202-224-2752 (Greg Casey, AA). STATE OFFICES: 304 N. 8th St. #149, Boise 83702, 208-342-7985 (Jeff Malman, Rep.); 103 N. 4th St., Coeur d'Alene 83814, 208-667-6130 (Sandy Potano, Rep.); 2539 Channing Way, Idaho Falls 83404, 208-523-5541 (Jeff Schrode, Rep.); 633 Main St., Lewiston 83501, 208-743-0792 (Norm Semenko, Rep.); 250 S. 4th St., Pocatello 83201, 208-236-6817 (Valarie Watkins, Rep.); 1292 Addison Ave. E., Twin Falls 83301, 208-734-6780 (Lewie Eilers, Rep.)

REPRESENTATIVES

FIRST DISTRICT

Larry La Rocco (D)

District: North and west portions of the state including Lewiston and Boise. Population: 503,357—Hispanic 5%, Other 3%. Politics: Leans Republican.

Born Aug. 26, 1946, Van Nuys, Calif.; home, Boise; University of Portland (Oreg.) B.A., 1967, Boston University, M.A., 1969, Johns Hopkins School of International Studies; Roman Catholic; married (Chris), 2 children.

Elected 1990. Career: Stockbroker; Asst. to U.S. Sen. Frank Church, 1975–81.

Committees: (1) Banking, Housing and Urban Affairs; (2) Natural Resources.

Election Results: 1992 LaRocco 139,899 (61%); Rachel Gilbert (R) 90,487 (39%). 1990 La Rocco (53%).

Interest Group Ratings:

ADA	ACU	COPE	COC
80	24	75	50

LCV	NTLC	CFA	ASC
50	15	73	60

Office: 1117 LHOB 20515, 202-225-6611 (Gary Wenske, Chief-of-staff). DISTRICT OFFICES: 304 N. 8th St., Rm. 136, Boise 83702, 208-343-4211 (Tom Knappenberger, Press Sec.); 408 Sherman Ave., Suite 206, Coeur d'Alene 83814, 208-667-2111 (Jeff Bell, Rep.); 621 Main St., Suite G, Lewiston 83501, 208-746-6694 (Debbi Fitzgerald, Rep.)

SECOND DISTRICT

Michael D. Crapo (R)

District: Eastern half of the state including Pocatello and Idaho Falls. Population: 503,392— Hispanic 6%. Politics: Republican.

Born May 20, 1951, Idaho Falls; home, Idaho Falls; Brigham Young University, B.A. 1973, Harvard University, J.D. 1977; Mormon; married (Susan), 5 children.

Elected 1992. Career: Attorney; State Sen., 1984–92.

Committees: (1) Energy & Commerce.

Election Results: 1992 Crapo 139,612 (63%); J.D. Williams (D) 81,354 (37%).

Interest Group Ratings:
None—Freshman

Office: 437 CHOB 20515, 202-225-5531 (Jane Wittmeyer, AA). DISTRICT OFFICES: 304 N. 8th St. #444, Boise 83702, 208-334-1953 (Janet Jeffries, Dist. Dir.); 488 Blue Lakes Blvd. #105, Twin Falls 83301, 208-734-7219 (Linda Norris, Rep.); 2539 Channing Suite 330, Idaho Falls 83404, 208-523-6701 (Laurel Hall, Rep.); Fed. Bldg. 250 S. 4th St. #220, Pocatello 83201, 208-236-6734 (Dawn Hatch, Rep.)

ILLINOIS

Illinois represented one of the biggest victories in 1992 for the Democrats. The Chicago machine showed that it could still turn out voters, and more significantly, the blue collar suburbs returned to the Democratic column. The big question for 1994 is whether the Democrats can keep the momentum and can recapture the governor's mansion. First term incumbent GOP Gov. Jim Edgar will be trying for a second term, and several Democrats are lining up to challenge him. The Democrats are ready to spend whatever it takes to try to regain control of state politics, and this will be one of the hot races in 1994.

1992 PRESIDENTIAL ELECTION: (22 Electoral votes): Clinton (D) 2,449,663 (49%); Bush (R) 1,732,879 (34%); Perot (I) 839,950 (17%); Marrou (Lib) 9,106; Fulani (NAP) 5,174; Gritz (Pop) 3,512; Hagelin (NLP) 2,715; Warren (SocWks) 1,341. 1988 Bush 2,298,648 (51%); Dukakis 2,180,657 (49%).

SENATORS

Carol Moseley-Braun (D)

Born Aug. 16, 1947, Chicago; home, Chicago; University of Ill., B.A. 1967, University of Chicago, J.D. 1972; Roman Catholic; divorced (now engaged), 1 child.

Elected 1992, seat up 1998. Career: Asst. U.S. Attorney, 1973–77; Ill. House of Reps., 1978–88; Cook County Recorder of Deeds, 1989–92.

Committees: (1) Judiciary; (2) Banking, Housing & Urban Affairs.

Election Results: 1992 Moseley-Braun 2,555,304 (55%); Richard Williamson (R) 2,107,955 (45%)

Interest Group Ratings:
None—Freshman

Office: 320 HSOB 20510, 202-224-2854 (Paul Stilp, Mgr.). STATE OFFICES: 117 Fed. Bldg. 600 E. Monroe St., Springfield 62701, 217-492-4162 (Craig Lovitt, Mgr.); Fed. Bldg. 230 S. Dearborn Suite 3996, Chicago 60604, 312-353-5420 (Joann Pierce, Mgr.); Fed. Bldg. 105 S. 6th St., Mt. Vernon 62864, (Clark Gyure, Mgr.)

Paul Simon (D)

Born Nov. 29, 1928, Eugene, Oreg.: home, Macanda; University of Oreg., Dana College; Lutheran; married (Jeanne), 2 children.

Elected 1990, seat up 1996. Career: Ed.–Pub., Troy Tribune & Weekly newspaper chain owner 1948–66; Army, 1951–53; Ill. House of Reps., 1955–63; Ill. Senate, 1963–69; Lt. Gov. of Ill., 1969–73; Instr., Harvard University, Sangamon State University, 1972–74; U.S. House of Reps., 1974–84.

Committees: (1) Budget; (2) Foreign Relations; (3) Judiciary; (4) Labor & Human Services; (5) Select Committee on Indian Affairs.

Election Results: 1990 Simon 2,075,493 (65%); Lynn Martin (R) 1,120,179 (35%). 1984 Simon (50%).

Interest Group Ratings:

ADA	ACU	COPE	COC
95	07	92	10

LCV	NTLC	CFA	ASC
92	05	100	50

Office: 462 DSOB 20510, 202-224-2152 (Jeremy Karpatkin, Chief-of-staff). STATE OFFICES: 3892 Fed. Bldg., 230 S. Dearborn, Chicago 60604, 312-353-4952 (Nancy Chen, Dir.); 3 W. Old Capital Plaza, Suite 1, Springfield 62701, 217-492-4960 (Joe Dunn, Ex. Asst.); 250 W. Cherry, Rm. 115B, Carbondale 62901, 618-457-3653 (Donna Eastman, Asst.)

REPRESENTATIVES

FIRST DISTRICT

Bobby L. Rush (D)

District: South side of Chicago. Population: 571,530—Black 70%, Hispanic 4%. Politics: Democratic.

Born Nov 23, 1946, Albany, Ga.; home, Chicago; Roosevelt University, B.A.; Protestant; married (Carolyn), 5 children.

Elected 1992. Career: Alderman, 1983–92.

Committees: (1) Banking, Finance & Urban Affairs; (2) Government Operations.

Election Results: 1992 Rush 187,926 (82%); Jay Walker (R) 41,363 (18%).

Interest Group Ratings:
None—Freshman

Office: 1725 LHOB 20515, 202-225-4372 (Maurice Daniel, AA).DISTRICT OFFICE: 9730 S. Western Ave. #237, Evergreen Park 60642, 708-422-4055 (Chuck Krezwick, Rep.); 655 E. 79th St., Chicago 60619, 312-224-6500 (vacant, Rep.)

SECOND DISTRICT

Melvin J. Reynolds (D)

District: South Side of Chicago and near suburbs including Harvey. Population: 571,530—Black 68%, Hispanic 7%, Other 4%. Politics: Democratic.

Born Jan. 8, 1952, Mound Bayou, Miss.; home, Chicago; Chicago City College, A.A. 1972; University of Ill., B.A. 1974; Oxford, Masters in Law (Rhodes Scholar), Harvard, M.P.A.; Baptist; married (Marisol), 1 child.

Elected 1992. Career: College Professor.

Committees: (1) Ways & Means.

Election Results: 1992 Reynolds 172,191 (85%); Ron Blackstone (R) 31,118 (15%).

Interest Group Ratings:
None—Freshman

Office: 514 CHOB 20515, 202-225-0773 (Charles Kelly, AA). DISTRICT OFFICE: 525 E. 103rd St. Chicago 60628, 312-568-7900 (Damon Rockett, Dist. Dir.); 17926 S. Halsted, Homewood 60430, 708-957-9955 (Kay Cronin, Rep.)

THIRD DISTRICT

William O. Lipinski (D)

District: South central Chicago and near suburbs. Population: 571,531—Black 2%, Hispanic 7%. Politics: Leans Democratic.

Born Dec. 22, 1937, Chicago; home, Chicago; Loras College, 1957–58; Roman Catholic; married (Rosemarie), 2 children.

Elected 1982. Career: Chicago Parks & Recreation Dept., 1958–75; Chicago City Alderman, 1975–83.

Committees: (1) Merchant Marine & Fisheries; (2) Public Works & Transportation.

Election Results: 1992 Lipinski 156,900 (63%); Harry Lepinske (R) 91,447 (37%). 1990 Lipinski (68%). 1988 Lipinski (61%).

Interest Group Ratings:

ADA	ACU	COPE	COC
50	48	67	29

LCV	NTLC	CFA	ASC
38	11	67	40

Office: 1501 LHOB 20515, 202-225-5701 (George Edwards, AA). DISTRICT OFFICE: 5832 S. Archer Ave., Chicago 60638, 312-886-0481 (vacant, Rep.); 12717 S. Richland Ave., Palos Heights 60463, 708-371-7460.

FOURTH DISTRICT

Luis V. Gutierrez (D)

District: A newly created Hispanic majority district snaking through the northwest and southwest of Chicago and parts of Northlake and Cicero. Population 571,530—Hispanic 65%, Black 6%, Asian 3%, Other 42%. Politics: Democratic.

Born Dec. 10, 1953, Chicago; home, Chicago; North East Ill. University, B.A. 1974; Roman Catholic; married (Zoraida), 2 children.

Elected 1992. Career: Social Worker; Staff Asst. to Mayor Washington; Alderman, 1987–92.

Committees: (1) Banking, Finance & Urban Affairs; (2) Veterans Affairs.

Election Results: 1992 Gutierrez 83,340 (77%); Hildegarde Rodriguez-Schieman (R) 24,426 (23%).

Interest Group Ratings:
None—Freshman

Office: 1208 LHOB 20515, 202-225-8203 (Doug Scofield, AA). DISTRICT OFFICES: 3181 N. Elston Ave., Chicago 60618, 312-509-0999 (Steve Shavers, Rep.)

FIFTH DISTRICT

Dan Rostenkowski (D)

District: North and northwest sides of Chicago. Population: 571,530—Asian 6%, Hispanic 13%. Politics: Democratic.

Born Jan. 2, 1928, Chicago; home, Chicago; Loyola University, 1948–51; Roman Catholic; married (LaVerne), 4 children.

Elected 1958. Career: Army, Korea; Ill. House of Reps., 1953–55; Ill. Senate, 1955–59.

Committees: (1) Ways & Means (Chairman); (2) Joint Committee on Taxation (Chairman).

Election Results: 1992 Rostenkowski 128,818 (59%); Elias Zenkich (R) 88,360 (41%). 1990 Rostenkowski (79%). 1988 Rostenkowski (75%).

Interest Group Ratings:

ADA	ACU	COPE	COC
95	00	82	38

LCV	NTLC	CFA	ASC
25	05	93	80

Office: 2111 RHOB 20515, 202-225-4061 (Virginia Fletcher, AA). DISTRICT OFFICE: 4849 N. Milwaukee #101, Chicago 60630, 312-481-0111 (Nancy Panzke, Rep.)

SIXTH DISTRICT

Henry John Hyde (R)

District: Far western Chicago suburbs including city of Wheaton. Population: 571,530—Asian 5%, Hispanic 5%. Politics: Republican.

Born Apr. 18, 1924, Chicago; home, Bensenville; Georgetown University, B.S. 1947, Loyola University, J.D. 1949; Roman Catholic; widowed, 4 children.

Elected 1974. Career: Navy, WWII; Practicing atty., 1950–75; Ill. House of Representatives, 1967–74, Majority Leader, 1971–72.

Committees: (1) Foreign Affairs; (2) Judiciary.

Election Results: 1992 Hyde 164,739 (66%); Barry Watkins (D) 86,737 (34%). 1990 Hyde (67%). 1988 Hyde (74%)

Interest Group Ratings:

ADA	ACU	COPE	COC
15	94	44	75

LCV	NTLC	CFA	ASC
13	84	33	100

Office: 2110 RHOB 20515, 202-225-4561 (Judy Wolverton, AA). DISTRICT OFFICE: Suite 200, 50 East Oak St., Addison 60101, 312-832-5950 (Patrick Durante, Exec. Asst.)

SEVENTH DISTRICT

Cardiss Collins (D)

District: Downtown and westside Chicago, and near west suburbs. Population: 571,530—Black 66%, Hispanic 4%, Asian 3%. Politics: Democratic.

Born Sept. 24, 1931, St. Louis, Mo.; home, Chicago; Northwestern University; Baptist; widowed, 1 child.

Elected June 5, 1973. Career: Stenographer, Ill. Dept. of Labor; Secy., Accountant & Revenue Auditor, Ill. Dept. of Revenue.

Committees: (1) Energy & Commerce; (2) Government Operations.

Election Results: 1992 Collins 166,236 (83%); Norman Boccio (R) 33,141 (17%). 1990 Collins (80%). 1988 Collins (89%).

Interest Group Ratings:

ADA	ACU	COPE	COC
85	94	92	14

LCV	NTLC	CFA	ASC
56	00	93	10

Office: 2308 RHOB 20515, 202-225-5006 (Rufus Myers, AA). DISTRICT OFFICES: 3880 Fed. Bldg., 230 S. Dearborn St., Chicago 60604, 312-353-5754 (James Garrett, Dist. Adm.); 328 West Lake, Oak Park 60302, 312-383-1400 (Robert Kettlewell, Dist. Adm.)

EIGHTH DISTRICT

Philip Miller Crane (R)

District: Far northwest Chicago suburbs including town of Palatine. Population: 571,530—Black 2%, Asian 4%, Hispanic 6%. Politics: Republican.

Born Nov. 3, 1930, Chicago; home, Chicago; DePauw University, Hillsdale College, B.A. 1952, Ind. University, M.A. 1961, Ph.D. 1963,

University of Mich., 1954, University of Vienna, Austria, 1953–56; Protestant; married (Arlene), 8 children.

Elected 1969. Career: Advertising Manager, 1956–58; Instructor, Indiana University, 1959–62; Assistant Professor, Bradley University, 1963–67; Director of Schools, Westminster Academy, 1967–68.

Committee: Ways & Means.

Election Results: 1992 Crane 132,855 (58%); Sheila Smith (D) 96,397 (42%). 1990 Crane (Unopposed). 1988 Crane (75%).

Interest Group Ratings:

ADA	ACU	COPE	COC
00	100	08	71

LCV	NTLC	CFA	ASC
00	100	07	90

Office: 233 CHOB 20515, 202-225-3711 (Robert Coleman, AA). DISTRICT OFFICES: Suite 101, 1450 S. New Wilke Rd., Arlington Heights 60005, 708-394-0790 (Jack McKenney, Dist. Rep.); 300 N. Milwaukee Suite C, Lake Villa 60046, 708-265-9000 (Carol Toft, Asst.)

NINTH DISTRICT

Sidney R. Yates (D)

District: North side Chicago, Park Ridge, and Skokie. Population: 571,530—Black 12%, Asian 10%, Hispanic 10%. Politics: Democratic.

Born Aug. 27, 1909, Chicago; home, Chicago; University of Chicago, Ph.D. 1931, J.D. 1933; Jewish; married (Adeline), 1 child.

Elected 1964. Career: Practicing atty.; Asst. Atty. for Ill. State Bank Receiver, 1935–37; Asst. Atty. Gen. attached to Ill. Commerce Comm., 1937–40; Navy, WWII; U.S. House of Reps., 1949–63; U.N. Rep. Trusteeship Council, 1963–64.

Committee: Appropriations.

Election Results: 1992 Yates 156,949 (72%); Herb Sohn (R) 62,327 (28%). 1990 Yates (71%). 1988 Yates (66%).

Interest Group Ratings:

ADA	ACU	COPE	COC
95	00	100	29

LCV	NTLC	CFA	ASC
88	06	73	20

Office: 2109 RHOB 20515, 202-225-2111 (Mary Bain, AA). DISTRICT OFFICES: 3920 Fed. Bldg, 230 S. Dearborn St., Chicago 60604, 312-353-4596 (Mary Bain, Mgr.); 2100 Ridge Ave., Rm. 2700, Evanston, 60204, 312-328-2610 (George Van Dusen, Dir.)

TENTH DISTRICT

John Edward Porter (R)

District: North Shore and northwest Chicago suburbs, including town of Waukegan. Population: 571,530—Black 6%, Hispanic 7%, Asian 4%. Politics: Republican.

Born June 1, 1935, Evanston; home, Winnetka; MIT, Northwestern University, B.A., B.S. 1957, University of Mich., J.D. 1961; Presbyterian; married (Kathryn), 5 children.

Elected 1980. Career: Atty., U.S. Dept. of Justice, 1961–63; Practicing atty., 1963–80; Ill. House of Reps., 1973–79.

Committee: Appropriations.

Election Results: 1992 Porter 153,801 (65%); Michael Kennedy (D) 84,650 (35%). 1990 Porter (69%). 1988 Porter (73%).

Interest Group Ratings:

ADA	ACU	COPE	COC
30	74	33	88

LCV	NTLC	CFA	ASC
56	90	40	90

Office: 1026 LHOB 20515, 202-225-4835 (Rob Bradner, AA). DISTRICT OFFICES: 104 Wilmot Rd., Suite 410, Deerfield 60015, 708-940-0202 (Ginny Hotaling, Ex. Asst.); 1650 Arlington Hgts. Rd., Suite 204, Arlington Heights. 60004, 708-392-0303 (Bonnie Nelson, Asst.); 601A County Bldg., 18 N. County St., Waukegan 60085, 708-662-0101 (Dee Jay Davis, Asst.)

ELEVENTH DISTRICT

George E. Sangmeister (D)

District: South and southwestern Chicago suburbs including Joliet and Calumet City. Population: 571,528—Black 9%, Hispanic 6%. Politics: Leans Republican.

Born Feb. 16, 1931, Frankfort; home, Mokena;

Joliet Junior College, 1949–51, Elmhurst College, B.A. 1957, LL.D. 1960, J.D. 1970; Lutheran; married (Doris), 2 children.

Elected 1988. Career: Army, 1951–53; Practicing atty. 1960–88; Justice of the Peace, Will Cty., 1961–63; Magistrate of the Circuit Crt., 1963–64; State's Atty., 1964–68; Ill. House of Reps., 1973–76; Ill. Senate, 1977–88.

Committees: (1) Judiciary; (2) Veterans Affairs; (3) Public Works and Transportation.

Election Results: 1992 Sangmeister 133,400 (56%); Robert Herbolsheimer (R) 106,480 (44%). 1990 Sangmeister (59%). 1988 Sangmeister (50%).

Interest Group Ratings:

ADA	ACU	COPE	COC
70	24	83	25

LCV	NTLC	CFA	ASC
63	05	80	20

Office: 1032 LHOB 20515, 202-225-3635 (Emma Beckler, AA). DISTRICT OFFICES: 101 N. Joliet St., Joliet 60431, 815-740-2028 (Emma Beckler, AA); 213 Gold Coast Lane, Calumet City 60409, 708-862-2590 (Marge Freidman, Rep.); 102 W. Madison, Ottawa 61350, 815-433-0085 (Tom Walsh, Rep.)

TWELFTH DISTRICT

Jerry F. Costello (D)

District: Southwest part of state including cities of East St. Louis and Carbondale. Population: 571,530—Black 17%. Politics: Democratic.

Born Sept. 25, 1949, East St. Louis; home, Belleville; Belleville Area College, 1972, Maryville College of the Sacred Heart, B.A. 1972; Roman Catholic; married (Georgia), 3 children.

Elected 1988 (Special election). Career: Sheriff, St. Clair Cty.; Chief Investigator, Ill. Attorney's Off., 1970–75; Dir. of Court Srvcs., 20th Judicial Circuit, 1975–80; Chm., St. Clair Cty. Board.

Committees: (1) Public Works & Transportation; (2) Budget.

Election Results: 1992 Costello 168,761 (71%); Mike Starr (R) 68,123 (29%). 1990 Costello (66%). 1988 Costello (53%).

Interest Group Ratings:

ADA	ACU	COPE	COC
60	44	83	14

LCV	NTLC	CFA	ASC
56	16	73	60

Office: 119 CHOB 20515, 202-225-5661 (Brian Lott, AA). DISTRICT OFFICES: 1363 Niedringhaus Ave., Granite City 62040 618-451-7065 (Debbie Saltage, Dist. Mgr.); 8787 State St., Suite 207, East St. Louis 62201 618-397-8833 (Mel Frierson, Asst.); 327 W. Main St., Belleville 62220, 618-233-8026 (Brian Lott, Rep.); 250 W. Cherry, Carbondale 62091, 618-529-3791 (Jenny Gehrig, Rep.)

THIRTEENTH DISTRICT

Harris W. Fawell (R)

District: Southwest Chicago suburbs including Downers Grove. Population: 571,531—Black 3%, Asian 4%, Hispanic 3%. Politics: Republican.

Born Mar. 25, 1929, West Chicago; home, Naperville; North Central College, 1947–49, Chicago Kent College of Law, J.D. 1953; United Methodist; married (Ruth), 3 children.

Elected 1984. Career: Practicing atty., 1953–84; Ill. Senate, 1963–77.

Committees: (1) Education & Labor; (2) Science, Space & Technology.

Election Results: 1992 Fawell 179,245 (68%); Dennis Temple (D) 82,974 (32%). 1990 Fawell (66%). 1988 Fawell (70%).

Interest Group Ratings:

ADA	ACU	COPE	COC
25	84	17	88

LCV	NTLC	CFA	ASC
44	90	27	100

Office: 2342 RHOB 20515, 202-225-3515 (Alan Mertz, Chief-of-staff). DISTRICT OFFICE: 115 West 55th St., Suite 100. Clarendon Hills 60514, 708-655-2052 (Barbara Graham, Rep.)

FOURTEENTH DISTRICT

John Dennis Hastert (R)

District: North central part of the state including cities of De Kalb and Elgin. Population: 571,530—Black 4%, Hispanic 10%, Other 5%. Politics: Republican.

Born Jan. 2, 1942, Aurora, Ill.; home, Yorkville; Wheaton College, B.A. 1964, Northern Ill. University, M.S. 1967; Protestant; married (Jean), 2 children.

Elected 1986. Career: Family restaurant, 1965–75; Teacher & coach, Yorkville H.S., 1965–81; Ill. House of Reps., 1981–86.

Committees: (1) Government Operations; (2) Energy & Commerce.

Election Results: 1992 Hastert 155,271 (67%); Jonathan Reich (D) 75,286 (33%). 1990 Hastert (67%). 1988 Hastert (74%).

Interest Group Ratings:

ADA	ACU	COPE	COC
05	92	25	75

LCV	NTLC	CFA	ASC
13	95	20	90

Office: 2453 RHOB 20515, 202-225-2976 (Scott Palmer, Chief-of-staff). DISTRICT OFFICES: 27 N. River, Batavia 60510, 708-406-1114 (Lisa Post, Off. Mgr.)

FIFTEENTH DISTRICT

Vacant pending special election.

District: Central part of the state including towns of Bloomington and Champaign. Population: 571,532—Black 7%. Politics: Republican.

SIXTEENTH DISTRICT

Donald Manzullo (R)

District: Northwest corner of the state including city of Rockford. Population: 571,530—Black 5%, Hispanic 3%. Politics: Leans Republican.

Born Mar. 24, 1944, Rockford; home, Egan; American University, B.A. 1967, Marquette University, J.D., 1970; Baptist; married (Freda), 3 children.

Elected 1992. Career: Lawyer, 1970-92.

Committees: (1) Foreign Affairs; (2) Small Business.

Election Results: 1992 Manzullo 142,388 (56%); John W. Cox Jr. (D) (Incumbent) 113,555 (44%).

Interest Group Ratings:
None—Freshman

Office: 506 CHOB 20515, 202-225-5676 (Jim Thacker, AA). DISTRICT OFFICES: 3929 Broadway #1, Rockford 61108, 815-394-1213 (Pam Bunting, Rep.); 181 N. Virginia, Crystal Lake 60014, 815-356-9800 (Kathryn McNally, Rep.)

SEVENTEENTH DISTRICT

Lane Evans (D)

District: Western part of the state including cities of Rock Island, Moline and Galesburg. Population: 571,530—Black 3%, Hispanic 3%. Politics: Leans Democratic.

Born Aug. 4, 1951, Rock Island; home, Rock Island; Augustana College, B.A. 1974, Georgetown University, J.D. 1978; Roman Catholic; single.

Elected 1982. Career: USMC, 1969–71; Practicing atty., 1978–82.

Committees: (1) Armed Services; (2) Veterans Affairs.

Election Results: 1992 Evans 156,233 (60%); Ken Schloemer (R) 103,719 (40%). 1990 Evans (67%). 1988 Evans (65%).

Interest Group Ratings:

ADA	ACU	COPE	COC
95	04	100	13

LCV	NTLC	CFA	ASC
100	00	100	20

Office: 2335 RHOB 20515, 202-225-5905 (Dennis King, AA). DISTRICT OFFICES: Rm. 5, 1535 47th Ave., Moline 61265, 309-793-5760 (Phillip Hare, Dist. Asst.); 125 E. Main St., Galesburg 61401, 309-342-4411 (Joyce Bean, Mgr.)

EIGHTEENTH DISTRICT

Robert H. Michel (R)

District: City of Peoria and parts of Springfield. Population: 571,580—Black 5%. Politics: Republican.

Born Mar. 2, 1923, Peoria; home, Peoria; Bradley

University, B.S. 1948; Apostolic Christian; married (Corinne), 4 children.

Elected 1956. Career: Army, WWII; A.A. to U.S. Rep. Harold Velde, 1949–56.

Committees: Minority Leader.

Election Results: 1992 Michel 156,533 (58%); Ronald Hawkins (D) 114,413 (42%). 1990 Michel (Unopposed). 1988 Michel (55%).

Interest Group Ratings:

ADA	ACU	COPE	COC
10	87	25	88

LCV	NTLC	CFA	ASC
06	95	33	100

Office: 2112 RHOB 20515, 202-225-6201 (Sue Bell, Ex. Asst.). DISTRICT OFFICES: 100 N.E. Monroe, Rm. 107, Peoria 61602, 309-671-7027 (Ray LaHood, Chief-of-staff); 236 W. State St., Jacksonville 62650, 217-245-1431 (Craig Findley, Spec. Asst.)

NINETEENTH DISTRICT

Glenn Poshard (D)

District: Southeastern Illinois including city of Decatur. Population: 571,530—Black 4%. Politics: Democratic.

Born Oct. 30, 1945, White County; home, Carterville; University of Southern Ill., B.S. 1970, M.S. 1974, Ph.D. 1984; Baptist; married (Betty Jo), 2 children.

Elected 1988. Career: Teacher, School administrator; Ill. Senate 1983–88.

Committees: (1) Public Works & Transportation; (2) Small Business.

Election Results: 1992 Poshard 187,137 (69%); Douglas Lee (R) 83,515 (31%). 1990 Poshard (84%). 1988 Poshard (65%).

Interest Group Ratings:

ADA	ACU	COPE	COC
65	36	83	25

LCV	NTLC	CFA	ASC
56	20	80	30

Office: 107 CHOB 20515, 202-225-5201 (David Stricklin, AA). DISTRICT OFFICES: New Route 13 West, Marion 62959, 618-993-8532 (Judy Hampton, Mgr.) 201 E. Nolan, W. Frankfort 62896, 618-937-6402 (Tim Martin, Asst.); 363 S. Main St., Decatur 62521, 217-362-9011 (Louise Nolan, Asst.); 600 Airport Rd., Matoon 61938, 217-234-7032 (Paul Black, Asst.); 444 S. Willow St., Effingham 62401, 217-342-7220 (Sam Medernach, Asst.); 801 W. 9th St., P.O. Box 818, Mt. Carmel 62863, 618-262-7723 (Shirley Stevenson, Asst.)

TWENTIETH DISTRICT

Richard J. Durbin (D)

District: South central part of the state including city of Edwardsville, and parts of Springfield. Population: 571,480—Black 4%. Politics: Leans Democratic.

Born Nov. 21, 1944; East St. Louis; home, Springfield; Georgetown University, B.S. 1966, J.D. 1969; Roman Catholic; married (Loretta), 3 children.

Elected 1982. Career: Staff of Sen. Paul H. Douglas, 1966–69; Staff of Lt. Gov. Paul Simon, 1969–72; Legal Counsel to Ill. Sen. Judiciary Comm., 1972–82; Prof., Southern Ill. School of Medicine, 1978–82.

Committees: (1) Appropriations; (2) Budget.

Election Results: 1992 Durbin 154,869 (57%); John Shimkus (R) 119,219 (43%). 1990 Durbin (66%). 1988 Durbin (69%).

Interest Group Ratings:

ADA	ACU	COPE	COC
90	04	83	13

LCV	NTLC	CFA	ASC
69	00	87	10

Office: 2463 RHOB 20515, 202-225-5271 (Ed Greenlegs, Chief-of-staff). DISTRICT OFFICES: 525 S. 8th St., Springfield 62703, 217-492-4062 (Michael Daly, Dist. Dir.); 221 E. Broadway, Centralia 62801, 618-532-4265 (Patti Henry, Rep.); 400 St. Louis St. #2, Edwardsville 62025, (Jerry Soehlka, Rep.)

INDIANA

Indiana remains one of the most conservative states outside the West or Deep South. On paper it would appear to be overwhelmingly Republican. In fact it has given very solid majorities to all GOP presidential candidates save two, since the end of World War II. But Indiana voters can also be contrary. They will elect, and reelect a Democratic governor, such as the present incumbent Evan Bayh. They will occasionally elect a Democratic senator, and they have been known to elect a majority of Democrats to the state legislature. Favorite son Dan Quayle has returned home, and disavows any interest in any statewide office. That's probably because none are really open. GOP Sen. Richard Lugar is up for reelection, and will be a sure winner unless he surprises voters by deciding to retire. If this happens, Quayle could make a try to return to the Senate. Otherwise, the former vice president should be taken at his word: that he will sit the next one out and will run for the White House in the year 2000.

1992 PRESIDENTIAL ELECTION: (12 Electoral votes): Clinton (D) 837,792 (37%); Bush (R) 969,697 (43%); Perot (I) 450,112 (20%); Fulani (NAP) 8,181; Marrou (Lib) 7,285. 1988 Bush 1,280,292 (60%); Dukakis 850,851 (40%).

SENATORS

Richard Green Lugar (R)

Born Apr. 4, 1932, Indianapolis; home, Indianapolis; Denison University, B.A. 1954; Rhodes Scholar, Oxford University, M.A. 1956; United Methodist; married (Charlene), 4 children.

Elected 1976, seat up 1994. Career: Navy, 1957–60; Vice Pres. & Treasurer, Thomas L. Green & Co., 1960–67; Indianapolis Board of School Commissioners, 1964–67; Mayor of Indianapolis, 1968–75; Repub. Nominee for U.S. Senate, 1974; Visiting Prof., University of Indianapolis, 1975.

Committees: (1) Agriculture, Nutrition & Forestry (Ranking Member); (2) Foreign Relations; (3) Select Committee on Intelligence; (4) Joint Committee on the Organization of Congress.

Election Results: 1988 Lugar 1,430,525 (68%);

Jack Wickes (D) 668,778 (32%). 1982 Lugar (54%).

Interest Group Ratings:

ADA	ACU	COPE	COC
10	85	17	100

LCV	NTLC	CFA	ASC
33	82	17	100

Office: 306 HSOB 20510, 202-224-4814 (Marty Morris, AA). STATE OFFICES: 1180 Market Tower, 10 W. Market St., Indianapolis 46204, 317-226-5555 (Sue Ann Gilroy, St. Dir.); 3158 Fed. Bldg., 1300 S. Harrison St., Fort Wayne 46802, 219-422-1505 (Matt Kelty, Dir.); Rm. 103, 5530 Sohl Ave., Hammond 47320, 219-937-5380 (Tim Sanders, Dir.); 103 Fed. Ctr., 1201 E. 10th St., Jeffersonville 47132, 812-288-3377 (Harold Gutzwiller, Dir.); 122 Fed. Bldg., 101 N.W. 7th St., Evansville 47708, 812-465-6313 (Frank Gulledge, Dir.)

Daniel R. Coats (R)

Born May 16, 1943, Jackson, Mich.; home, Fort Wayne; Wheaton College, B.A. 1965, Ind. University, J.D. 1971; Baptist; married (Marcia), 3 children.

Appointed, 1989 (to fill unexpired term of Vice President Dan Quayle. Elected to 2-year term 1990. Elected to full term 1992. Seat up 1998. Career: Army, 1966–68; Asst. Vice Pres. & Legal Counsel, Mutual Security Life Insur. Co., 1972–76; Dist. Rep. for U.S. Rep. Dan Quayle, 1976–80; U.S.House of Reps., 1980–88.

Committees: (1) Armed Services; (2) Labor & Human Resources.

Election Results: 1992 Coats 1,243,172 (58%); Joseph Hogsett (D) 882,737 (42%). 1990 Coats (54%).

Interest Group Ratings:

ADA	ACU	COPE	COC
10	93	33	90

LCV	NTLC	CFA	ASC
17	100	50	90

Office: 404 RSOB 20510, 202-224-5623. (David Gribbons, AA). STATE OFFICES: 1180 Market

Tower, 10 W. Market St., Indianapolis 46204, 317-226-5555 (Curt Smith, St. Dir.); 340 Fed. Bldg., 1300 S. Harrison St., Ft. Wayne 46802, 219-422-1505 (Matt Kelty, Reg. Dir.); 5530 Sohl Ave., Hammond 47320, 219-937-5380 (Tim Sanders, Dir.); 103 Fed. Ctr., 1201 E. 10th St., Jeffersonville 47132, 812-288-3377 (Harold Gutzwiller, Dir.); 122 Fed. Bldg., 101 NW 7th St., Evansville 47708, 812-465-6313 Frank Gulledge, Dir.)

REPRESENTATIVES

FIRST DISTRICT

Peter J. Visclosky (D)

District: Far northwest corner of the state including far southern Chicago suburbs and the old industrial belt of Gary and Hammond. Population: 554,416—Black 21%, Hispanic 9%. Politics: Democratic.

Born Aug. 13, 1949, Gary; home, Merrillville; Ind. University, B.S. 1970, University of Notre Dame, J.D. 1973, Georgetown University, LL.M. 1982; Roman Catholic; married (Anne Marie O'Keefe), 2 children.

Elected 1984. Career: Legal Asst., Off. of the Manhattan Dist. Atty., 1972; Practicing atty., 1973–76, 1983–84; Aide to U.S. Rep. Adam Benjamin, Jr. 1977–82.

Committees: (1) Appropriations.

Election Results: 1992 Viscloski 146,816 (69%); David Vucich (R) 64,767 (31%). 1990 Visclosky (66%). 1988 Visclosky (77%).

Interest Group Ratings:

ADA	ACU	COPE	COC
85	16	100	50

LCV	NTLC	CFA	ASC
38	25	87	50

Office: 2464 RHOB 20515, 202-225-2461. (Charles Brimmer, AA). DISTRICT OFFICE: 215 W. 35th Ave., Gary 46408, 219-884-1177 (Adam Adams, Dist. Dir.); 6070 Central Ave., Portage 46368, 219-763-2904 (vacant, Rep.); 166 Lincoln Way, Valparaiso 46383, 219-464-0315 (vacant, Rep.)

SECOND DISTRICT

Philip Riley Sharp (D)

District: East central part of the state including cities of Muncie and Richmond. Population: 554,416—Black 4%. Politics: Conservative Democratic.

Born July 15, 1942, Elwood, Ind.; home, Muncie; DePauw University, Georgetown University, B.S. 1964, Oxford University, 1966, Georgetown University, Ph.D. 1974; United Methodist; married (Marilyn), 2 children.

Elected 1974. Career: Legis. Aide to U.S. Sen. Vance Hartke, 1964–69; Asst. & Assoc. Prof., Ball State University, 1969–74.

Committees: (1) Energy & Commerce; (2) Natural Resources.

Election Results: 1992 Sharp 130,881 (59%); William Frazier (R) 90,593 (41%). 1990 Sharp (59%). 1988 Sharp (53%).

Interest Group Ratings:

ADA	ACU	COPE	COC
85	25	75	38

LCV	NTLC	CFA	ASC
38	20	80	50

Office: 2217 RHOB 20515, 202-225-3021 (Ron Gyure, AA). DISTRICT OFFICES: 2900 W. Jackson, Suite 101, Muncie 47304, 317-747-5566 (Rick Gann, Asst.); 331 Franklin Suite A, Columbus 47201, 812-372-3637 (Carol Ann Sewell, Asst.); 17 Main Post Off. Bldg., 400 N. A St., Richmond 47374 317-966-6125 (Sally Cook, Asst.)

THIRD DISTRICT

Tim Roemer (D)

District: North central counties including city of South Bend. Population: 554,416—Black 7%. Politics: Leans Republican.

Born Oct. 30, 1956, South Bend; home, South Bend; University of Calif. (San Diego), B.A. 1979, Notre Dame, M.A. 1982, Ph.D. 1986; Roman Catholic; married (Sally), 1 child.

Elected 1990. Career: Instructor, American University; Legs. aide to U.S. Sen. Dennis DeConcini, 1983–88.

Committees: (1) Education and Labor; (2) Science, Space & Technology.

Election Results: 1992 Roemer 121,269 (57%); Carl Baxmeyer (R) 89,709 (43%). 1990 Roemer (51%).

Interest Group Ratings:

ADA	ACU	COPE	COC
55	40	58	63

LCV	NTLC	CFA	ASC
44	40	67	60

Office: 415 CHOB 20515, 202-225-3915 (Bernard Toon, AA). DISTRICT OFFICE: 217 N. Main St., South Bend 46601, 219-288-3301 (Patricia Odyga, Dist. Dir.)

FOURTH DISTRICT

Jill Long (D)

District: Northeast corner of the state including city of Fort Wayne. Population: 554,416—Black 6%. Politics: Leans Republican.

Born July 15, 1952, Warsaw; home, Larwill; Valparaiso University, B.S. 1974, Indiana University, M.B.A. 1978, Ph.D. 1984; Methodist; single.

Elected March 1989 (Special Election). Career: Farmer; Asst. professor, Indiana University–Purdue University at Ft. Wayne; Valparaiso City Council, 1983.

Committees: (1) Agriculture; (2) Veterans Affairs.

Election Results: 1992 Long 129,980 (62%); Charles Pierson (R) 78,716 (38%). 1990 Long (61%). 1989 (special) Long (51%).

Interest Group Ratings:

ADA	ACU	COPE	COC
80	24	75	63

LCV	NTLC	CFA	ASC
44	30	80	50

Office: 1513 LHOB 20515, 202-225-4436 (Inga Smulkstys, AA). DISTRICT OFFICE: 3105 Fed. Bldg., 1300 S. Harrison St., Ft. Wayne 46802, 219-424-3041 (Mary Schmidt, Dist. Dir.); 105 E. Mitchell, Kendallville 46755, 219-347-5471; 1190 U.S. 27 North, Berne 46711, 219-589-8699.

FIFTH DISTRICT

Steve Buyer (R)

District: North central part of the state including cities of Kokomo and Marion. Population: 554,415—Black 2%. Politics: Conservative Democratic.

Born Nov. 26, 1958, Rensselar; home, Monticello; The Citadel, B.S. 1980, Valparaiso University, J.D. 1984; United Methodist; married (Joni), 2 children.

Elected 1992. Career: Special Asst. U.S. Atty., 1984–87, Deputy Atty. Gen., 1986–87; Practicing Atty. 1987–92.

Committees: (1) Armed Services; (2) Veteran Affairs.

Election Results: 1992 Buyer 112,492 (51%); James Jontz (D-Incumbent) 107,973 (49%).

Interest Group Ratings:
None—Freshman

Office: 1419 LHOB 20515, 202-225-5037 (Kelly Craven, AA). DISTRICT OFFICES: 120 E. Mulberry #106, Kokomo 46902, 317-454-7551 (Linda Worsham-Ameen, Rep.)

SIXTH DISTRICT

Dan Burton (R)

District: Central counties including parts of Indianapolis and its suburbs, and city of Carmel. Population: 554,416 Politics: Republican.

Born June 21, 1938, Indianapolis; home, Indianapolis, Ind. University, 1956–57, Cincinnati Bible Seminary, 1958–60; Protestant; married (Barbara), 3 children.

Elected 1982. Career: Army, 1956–57; Founder, Dan Burton Insur. Agency; Ind. House of Reps., 1967–68, 1977–80; Ind. Senate, 1969–70, 1981–82.

Committees: (1) Foreign Affairs; (2) Post Office & Civil Service; (3) Veterans Affairs.

Election Results: 1992 Burton 181,786 (73%); Natalie Bruner (D) 68,304 (27%). 1990 Burton (63%). 1988 Burton (73%).

Interest Group Ratings:

ADA	ACU	COPE	COC
10	100	25	86

LCV	NTLC	CFA	ASC
13	100	00	100

Office: 2411 RHOB 20515, 202-225-2276 (Kevin Binger, AA). DISTRICT OFFICES: 8900 Keystone at the Crossing, Suite 1050, Indianapolis 46240, 317-848-0201 (James Atterholt, AA); 435 E. Main St. Suite J-3, Greenwood 46142, 317-882-3640 (Mary Fredricks, Rep.)

SEVENTH DISTRICT

John T. Myers (R)

District: West central counties including cities of Terre Haute and Lafayette. Population: 554,416—Black 2%. Politics: Republican.

Born Feb 8,1927, Covington; home, Covington; Ind. State University B.S. 1951; Episcopalian; married (Carol), 2 children.

Elected 1966. Career: Army, WWII; Cashier & Trust Officer, Foundation Trust Co., 1954–66.

Committees: (1) Appropriations; (2) Post Office & Civil Service (Ranking Member).

Election Results: 1992 Myers 129,189 (59%); Ellen Wedum (D) 88,005 (41%). 1990 Myers (58%). 1988 Myers (62%).

Interest Group Ratings:

ADA	ACU	COPE	COC
00	84	17	75

LCV	NTLC	CFA	ASC
06	75	20	100

Office: 2372 RHOB 20515, 202-225-5805 (Ronald Hardman, AA). DISTRICT OFFICES: 107 Fed. Bldg., Terre Haute 47808, 812-238-1619 (Lynn Nicoson, Dist. Rep.); 107 Fed. Bldg., Lafayette 27901, 317-423-1661 (Jane Long, Asst.)

EIGHTH DISTRICT

Frank McCloskey (D)

District: Southwest counties, including city of Evansville. Population: 544,416—Black 3%. Politics: Leans Democratic.

Born June 12, 1939, Philadelphia, Pa.; home, Bloomington; Ind. University, A.B. 1968, J.D. 1971; Roman Catholic; married (Roberta), 2 children.

Elected 1982. Career: Air Force, 1957–61; Mayor of Bloomington, 1971–82.

Committees: (1) Armed Services; (2) Post Office & Civil Service; (3) Foreign Affairs (temp.).

Election Results: 1992 McCloskey 113,018 (53%); Richard Mourdock (R) 98,241 (47%). 1990 McCloskey (55%). 1988 McCloskey (62%).

Interest Group Ratings:

ADA	ACU	COPE	COC
95	12	83	25

LCV	NTLC	CFA	ASC
56	00	93	50

Office: 306 CHOB 20515, 202-225-4636 (Melinda Plaisier, AA). DISTRICT OFFICES: 208 City Center, Bloomington 47404, 812-334-1111 (vacant, Dist. Dir.); 10 NE 4th St., Washington 47501, 812-254-6646 (Ronald Critchlow, Mgr.); 124 Fed. Bldg., 101 NW 7th St., Evansville 47708, 812-465-6484 (Patti Turpin, Mgr.)

NINTH DISTRICT

Lee H. Hamilton (D)

District: Southeast Ohio River counties including city of Jeffersonville and town of New Albany. Population: 544,416—Black 2%. Politics: Leans Democratic.

Born Apr. 20, 1931, Daytona Beach, Fla.; home, Nashville; DePauw University, B.A. 1952, Goethe University, Frankfurt, Germany, 1952–53, Ind. University, J.D. 1956; United Methodist; married (Nancy), 3 children.

Elected 1964. Career: Practicing atty., 1956–64.

Committees: (1) Foreign Affairs; (2) Joint Economic Committee; (3) Joint Committee on the Organization of Congress (Co–Chairman).

Election Results: 1992 Hamilton 160,823 (70%); Michael Bailey (R) 70,030 (30%). 1990 Hamilton (69%). 1988 Hamilton (71%).

Interest Group Ratings:

ADA	ACU	COPE	COC
80	32	75	63

LCV	NTLC	CFA	ASC
44	30	60	70

Office: 2187 RHOB 20515, 202-225-5315 (Jonathon Friedman, Ex. Asst.). DISTRICT OFFICES

107 Fed. Ctr. Bldg, 1201 E. 10th St., Jefferson-ville 47130, 812-288-3999 (Wayne Vance, AA)

TENTH DISTRICT

Andrew Jacobs, Jr. (D)

District: Majority of city of Indianapolis, and some surrounding suburbs. Population: 544,416 —Black 30%. Politics: Democratic.

Born Feb. 24, 1932; Indianapolis; home, Indianapolis; Ind. University, B.S. 1955, LL.B. 1958; Roman Catholic; married (Kim), 2 children.

Elected 1974. Career: USMC, Korea; Practicing atty., 1958–65, 1973–74; Ind. House of Reps., 1959–60; U.S. House of Reps. 1965–73.

Committee: Ways & Means.

Election Results: 1992 Jacobs 111,339 (64%); Janos Horvath (R) 61,641 (36%). 1990 Jacobs (66%). 1988 Jacobs (61%).

Interest Group Ratings:

ADA	ACU	COPE	COC
85	20	83	25

LCV	NTLC	CFA	ASC
75	40	100	30

Office: 2313 RHOB 20515, 202-225-4011 (David Wildes, AA). DISTRICT OFFICES: 441-A Fed. Bldg., 46 E. Ohio St. Indianapolis 46204, 317-269-7331 (Loretta Raikes, Mgr.)

IOWA

Iowa continues to be a state that is Democratic in its cities and heavily Republican in its rural areas. This combination often gives mixed results, as seen in the state's mixed congressional delegation. The question in 1994 is whether Iowans will reelect Republican Gov. Terry Branstead to a fourth term. He has had easy campaigns and hard campaigns in the past, mostly tied to the quality of his Democratic opponent. A strict opponent of abortion, there is some thought this issue will work against Branstead in a close campaign. If he wins reelection, it is believed he will take on incumbent Democratic Sen. Tom Harkin in 1996. That would make for a very interesting Senate contest.

1992 PRESIDENTIAL ELECTION: (7 Electoral votes): Clinton (D) 583,669 (44%); Bush (R) 503,077 (38%); Perot (I) 251,795 (19%); Hagelin (NLP) 2,568; Gritz (Pop) 898; Ehlers (Ind) 876; Marrou (Lib) 649; Yiamouyiannis (TkBkAm) 485; Herer (GrassRts) 441; Phillips (AmTax) 287; Warren (SocWks) 209; LaRouche (I) 138; Fulani (NAP) 133; Daniels (P&F) 132. 1988 Dukakis 667,085 (55%); Bush (R) 541,540 (45%)

SENATORS

Charles Ernest Grassley (R)

Born Sept. 17, 1933, New Hartford; home, New Hartford; University of Northern Iowa, B.A. 1955, M.A. 1956, University of Iowa, 1957-58; Baptist; married (Barbara), 5 children.

Elected 1980, seat up 1998. Career: Farmer; Iowa House of Reps., 1959–74; U.S. House of Reps., 1974–80.

Committees: (1) Finance; (2) Budget; (3) Judiciary; (4) Small Business; (5) Agriculture, Nutrition, & Forestry.

Election Results: 1992 Grassley 894,235 (72%); Jean Lloyd-Jones (D) 349,461 (28%). 1986 Grassley (66%). 1980 Grassley (53%).

Interest Group Ratings:

ADA	ACU	COPE	COC
30	74	17	90

LCV	NTLC	CFA	ASC
25	83	50	50

Office: 135 HSOB 20510, 202-224-3744 (Robert Ludwiczak, AA). STATE OFFICES: 721 Fed. Bldg., 210 Walnut St., Des Moines 50309, 515-284-4890 (Henry Wulff, Iowa Admin.); 210 Waterloo Bldg., 531 Commercial St., Waterloo 50701, 319-232-6657 (Fred Schuster, Rep.); 116 Fed. Bldg., 131 E. 4th St., Davenport 52801, 319-322-4331 (Vada Reed, Rep.); 103 Fed. Bldg., 320 6th St., Sioux City 51101, 712-233-1860 (Michele Wing, Rep.); 206 Fed. Bldg., 101 1st St. S.E., Cedar Rapids 52401, 319-363-6832 (Janice Swanson, Rep.).

Thomas R. Harkin (D)

Born Nov. 19, 1939, Cumming; home, Cumming; Iowa State University, B.S. 1962, Catholic University, J.D. 1972; Roman Catholic; married (Ruth), 2 children.

Elected 1990, seat up 1996. Career: Navy, 1962–67; Staff of U.S. Rep. Neal Smith, 1969–70; Staff of U.S. House Select Comm. on U.S. Involvement in SE Asia, 1970–73; Practicing atty., 1973–74; U.S. House of Reps., 1974–84.

Committees: (1) Agriculture, Nutrition & Forestry; (2) Appropriations; (3) Labor & Human Resources; (4) Small Business.

Election Results: 1990 Harkin 525,074 (54%); Tom Tauke (R) 446,851 (46%). 1984 Harkin (55%).

Interest Group Ratings:

ADA	ACU	COPE	COC
85	00	91	17

LCV	NTLC	CFA	ASC
33	00	75	40

Office: 531 HSOB 20510, 202-224-3254 (Dan Smith, AA). STATE OFFICES: 733 Fed. Bldg., 733 Fed. Bldg. 210 Walnut St., Des Moines 50309, 515-284-4574 (Ellen Huntoon, St. Adm.); 317 Fed. Bldg., Council Bluffs 51502, 712-325-5533 (E. Huntoon, Reg. Dir.); Lindale Mall, Box 74884 Lindale Mall, Cedar Rapids 52407, 319-393-6374 (Ellen Huntoon, Reg. Dir.); 314B Fed. Bldg., 131 E. 4th St., Davenport, 52801, 319-322-1338 (Ellen Huntoon, Reg. Dir.); 315 Fed. Bldg. 350 W. 6th St., Dubuque 52001, 319-582-2130 (Ellen Huntoon, Reg. Dir.); 110 Fed. Bldg. 320

6th St., Sioux City 51101, 712-252-1550 (Ellen Huntoon, Reg. Dir.)

REPRESENTATIVES

FIRST DISTRICT

James A. S. Leach (R)

District: Southeast portion of the state including cities of Davenport and Cedar Rapids. Population: 555,229.—Black 3% Politics: Leans Republican.

Born Oct. 15, 1942, Davenport; home, Davenport; Princeton University, B.A. 1964, Johns Hopkins University, M.A. 1966, London School of Economics, 1966–68; Episcopalian; married (Elisabeth), 2 children.

Elected 1976. Career: Staff Asst., U.S. Rep. Donald Rumsfeld, 1965–66; U.S. Foreign Svc., 1968–69; 1971–72; A.A. to Dir. of U.S. Office of Equal Opp., 1969–70; Pres., Flamegas Co., Inc., propane gas marketers, 1973–76; Dir., Fed. Home Loan Bank Bd., Midwest Region, 1975–76.

Committees: (1) Banking, Finance & Urban Affairs; (2) Foreign Affairs.

Election Results: 1992 Leach 177,335 (69%); Jan Zonneveld (D) 81,225 (31%). 1990 Leach (Unopposed). 1988 Leach (61%).

Interest Group Ratings:

ADA	ACU	COPE	COC
60	40	33	63

LCV	NTLC	CFA	ASC
31	70	67	70

Office: 2186 LHOB 20515, 202-225-6576 (Bill Tate, AA). DISTRICT OFFICES: 209 W. 4th St., Davenport 52801, 319-326-1841 (Linda Weeks, AA); 102 S. Clinton #505, Iowa City 52240, 319-351-0789 (Ginny Burrus, Asst.); 308 10th St. SE, Cedar Rapids 52403, 319-363-4773 (Tom Cope, Rep.)

SECOND DISTRICT

Jim Nussle (R)

District: Northeast counties including cities of Dubuque and Waterloo. Population: 555,494. Politics: Mixed, but overall leans Republican.

Born June 27, 1960, Des Moines; home, Manchester; Luther College, B.A. 1983, Drake University, J.D. 1985; Lutheran; married (Leslie), 2 children.

Elected 1990. Career: Lawyer, Delaware Cty. Att. 1987–90.

Committees: (1) Agriculture; (2) Banking, Finance & Urban Affairs.

Election Results: 1992 Nussle 134,033 (51%); David Nagle (Incumbent) 130,833 (49%). 1990 Nussle (50%).

Interest Group Ratings:

ADA	ACU	COPE	COC
25	76	25	88

LCV	NTLC	CFA	ASC
06	80	33	90

Office: 308 CHOB 20515, 202-225-2911 (Steve Greiner, AA). DISTRICT OFFICES: 501 W. Lowell, Shenandoah 51601, 712-246-1984 (Corrinne Gilbert, Dist. Cord.); 220 W. Salem, Indianola 50125, 515-961-0591; 413 Kellogg, Ames 50010, 515-232-1288; 347 E. 2nd St., Ottumwa 52505, 515-683-3551; 311 N. 3rd, Burlington 52601, 319-753-6415.

THIRD DISTRICT

James Ross Lightfoot (R)

District: Southern counties, including the city of Ottumwa. Population: 555,299. Politics: Leans Republican.

Born Sept. 27, 1939, Sioux City; home, Shenandoah; Roman Catholic; married (Nancy), 4 children.

Elected 1984. Career: Army, 1955–56; Mgr., farm equip. manufacturing facility, 1970–76; Corsican City Comm., 1974–76; businessman, radio broadcaster & farm editor, 1976–84.

Committees: (1) Appropriations.

Election Results: 1992 Lightfoot 125,835 (51%); Elaine Baxter (D) 120,728 (49%). 1990 Lightfoot (67%). 1988 Lightfoot (64%).

Interest Group Ratings:

ADA	ACU	COPE	COC
15	87	25	88

LCV	NTLC	CFA	ASC
00	90	33	100

Office: 2444 RHOB 20515, 202-225-3806 (Barbara Millunci, AA). DISTRICT OFFICES: 501 W. Lowell, Shenandoah 51601, 712-246-1984 (Eleanor Sligar, Dist. Rep.); 105 Pearl, Council Bluffs 51501, 712-235-5572 (Dorothy Smith, Rep.); 220 W. Salem, Indianola 50125, 515-961-0591 (Janice Goode, Rep.); 908 1st Ave. S., Warden Plaza, Suite 7, Ft. Dodge 50501, 515-955-5319 (Sue Duvall, Rep.)

FOURTH DISTRICT

Neal Edward Smith (D)

District: Southwestern counties including cities of Des Moines and Council Bluffs. Population: 555,276—Black 3%. Politics: Democratic.

Born March 23, 1920, Hedrick; home, Altoona; University of Mo., Syracuse University, Drake University, B.A. 1950; United Methodist; married (Beatrix), 2 children.

Elected 1958. Career: Farmer; Army Air Corps, WWII; Asst. Polk Cty. Atty., 1950–52; Practicing atty., 1952–58; Chm., Polk Cty. Bd. of Social Welfare, 1956.

Committees: (1) Appropriations; (2) Small Business.

Election Results: 1992 Smith 156,617 (63%); Paul Lunde (R) 93,084 (37%). 1990 Smith (Unopposed). 1988 Smith (72%).

Interest Group Ratings:

ADA	ACU	COPE	COC
75	17	75	57

LCV	NTLC	CFA	ASC
25	10	60	60

Office: 2373 RHOB 20515, 202-225-4426 (Tom Dawson, AA). DISTRICT OFFICES: 544 Insurance Exchange Bldg., Des Moines 50309, 515-284-4634 (Kay Bolton, Asst.); 40 Pearl St., Council Bluffs 51503, 712-323-5976 (Jane Bell, Rep.)

FIFTH DISTRICT

Frederick Lawrence Grandy (R)

District: Northwest counties including city of Sioux City. Population: 555,457. Politics: Leans Republican.

Born June 29, 1948, Sioux City; home, Sioux City; Harvard College, B.A. 1970; Episcopalian; married (Catherine), 3 children.

Elected 1986. Career: Asst. to U.S. Rep. Wiley Mayne, 1970–71; Professional actor, 1971–85.

Committees: (1) Ways & Means; (2) Standards of Official Conduct.

Election Results: 1992 Grandy (Unopposed). 1990 Grandy (72%). 1988 Grandy (64%).

Interest Group Ratings:

ADA	ACU	COPE	COC
15	88	25	88

LCV	NTLC	CFA	ASC
00	75	27	90

Office: 418 CHOB 20515, 202-225-5476 (Craig Tufty, AA). DISTRICT OFFICES: 4501 Southern Hills Dr. #21, Sioux City 51106, 712-276-5800 (Lori Grosbeck, Dist. Dir.); 822 Central Ave. #102, Ft. Dodge 50501, 515-573-2738 (Sue Duvall, Rep.); 14 W. 5th Street, Spencer 51301 712-262-6480 (George Moriarity, Farm Rep.)

KANSAS

Kansas is a heavily Republican state, and the GOP is embarrassed that a Democrat, Joan Finney, occupies the governor's mansion. They will have a chance to do something about that in 1994, and will be going all out to defeat her. Neither of the state's senators is up for reelection, and the entire House delegation looks solid.

1992 PRESIDENTIAL ELECTION: (6 Electoral votes): Clinton (D) 387,488 (34%); Bush (R) 445,790 (39%); Perot (I) 310,458 (27%); Marrou (Lib) 4,386. 1988 Bush 549,049 (56%); Dukakis 422,636 (43%)

SENATORS

Robert Dole (R)

Born July 22, 1923, Russell; home, Russell; University of Kans., Washburn Municipal University, A.B., LL.B. 1952; United Methodist; married (Elizabeth), 1 child.

Elected 1968, seat up 1998. Career: Army, WWII; Kans. House of Reps., 1951–53; Russell Cty. Atty., 1953–61; U.S. House of Reps., 1961–69; Chm., Repub. Natl. Comm., 1971–73.

Committees: Minority Leader. (1) Agriculture, Nutrition & Forestry; (2) Finance; (3) Rules & Administration; (4) Joint Committee on Taxation.

Election Results: 1992 Dole 700,534 (64%); Gloria O'Dell (D) 349,379 (32%); Christina Campbell-Cline (I) 45,709 (4%). 1986 Dole (70%). 1980 Dole (64%).

Interest Group Ratings:

ADA	ACU	COPE	COC
05	93	17	90

LCV	NTLC	CFA	ASC
00	72	25	100

Office: 141 HSOB 20510, 202-224-6521 (Dan Stanley, AA). STATE OFFICES: 636 Minnesota Ave., Kansas City, Kans. 66101, 913-371-6108 (Gayle Grosch, Rep.); 392 Fed. Bldg., 444 SE Quincy, Topeka 66603, 913-295-2745 (Judy Brown, Reg. Adm.); 100 N. Broadway, Wichita 67202, 316-263-4956 (David Spears, St. Dir.); 310 N. Pine, Pittsburg 66762, 316-232-2030 (Jill Maycomber, Reg. Rep.)

Nancy Landon Kassebaum (R)

Born July 29, 1932, Topeka; home, Wichita; University of Kans., B.A. 1954, University of Mich., M.A. 1956; Episcopalian; divorced, 4 children.

Elected 1984, seat up 1996. Career: Member, Maize School Board, 1972–75; Staff of U.S. Sen. James B. Pearson, 1975.

Committees: (1) Foreign Relations; (2) Labor & Human Resources (Ranking Member); (3) Joint Committee on the Organization of Congress.

Election Results: 1990 Kassebaum 574,584 (74%); Dick Williams (D) 206,250 (26%). 1984 Kassebaum (76%).

Interest Group Ratings:

ADA	ACU	COPE	COC
25	67	25	100

LCV	NTLC	CFA	ASC
33	56	33	90

Office: 302 RSOB 20510, 202-224-4774 (Dave Bartel, AA). STATE OFFICES: Fed. Bldg., 444 SE Quincy St., Topeka 66683, 913-295-2888 (Jacque Kimbrough, Reg. Dir.); 911 N. Main, Garden City 67846, 316-276-3423 (Betty Jo Roberts, Dir.); 4200 Somerset, Suite 152, Prairie Village 66208, 913-648-3103 (Michael Harper, St. Dir.); 111 N. Market, Wichita 67202, 316-269-6251 (Georgia Ptacek, Reg. Dir.)

REPRESENTATIVES

FIRST DISTRICT

Charles Patrick Roberts (R)

District: One of the nation's largest districts covering the entire western two-thirds of the state—several thousand square miles spread over 58 counties. Main population centers: West Salina and Dodge City. Population: 619,370—Hispanic 5%. Politics: Republican.

Born Apr. 20, 1936, Topeka; home, Dodge City; Kans. State University, B.A. 1958; United Methodist; married (Franki), 3 children.

Elected 1980. Career: USMC, 1958–62; Coowner, editor, *The Westsider* (Ariz. Newspaper) 1962–

67; A.A. to U.S. Sen. Frank Carlson, 1966–
68; A.A. to U.S. Rep. Keith G. Sebelius, 1968–
80.

Committees: (1) Agriculture; (2) House Administration; (3) Joint Committee on the Library; (4)
Joint Committee on Printing.

Election Results: 1992 Roberts 193,541 (70%);
Duane West (D) 83,672 (30%). 1990 Roberts
(62%). 1988 Roberts (Unopposed).

Interest Group Ratings:

ADA	ACU	COPE	COC
10	88	17	88

LCV	NTLC	CFA	ASC
00	80	33	100

Office: 1125 LHOB 20515, 202-225-2715 (D.
Leroy Towns, AA). DISTRICT OFFICES: 100
Military Plaza (P.O. Box 550), Dodge City 67801,
316-227-2244 (Phyllis Ross, Dist. AA); P.O. Box
128, Norton 67654, 913-877-2454 (Karen Reedy,
Rep.); P.O. Box 1334, Salina 67402, 913-825-5409
(Betty Duwe, Rep.); P.O. Box 1128, Hutchinson
67504, (Jamie Fall, Rep.)

SECOND DISTRICT

Jim Slattery (D)

District: Eastern counties including city of
Topeka. Population: 619,391—Black 6%, Hispanic 3%. Politics: Leans Republican.

Born Aug. 4, 1948, Atchison; home, Topeka;
Washburn University, B.S. 1970, J.D. 1974,
Netherlands School of International Economics,
1969–70; Roman Catholic; married (Linda), 2
children.

Elected 1982. Career: Kans. House of Reps.,
1972–78, Chm. of Dem. Policy Group, 1975–79,
Speaker Pro Tem. 1977–79; Kans. Acting Secy.
of Revenue, 1979; Real estate & develop.,
Brosius, Slattery & Meyer, Inc., 1977–82.

Committees: (1) Veterans Affairs; (2) Energy &
Commerce.

Election Results: 1992 Slattery 150,849 (58%);
Jim Van Slyke (R) 109,674 (42%). 1990 Slattery
(63%). 1988 Slattery (73%).

Interest Group Ratings:

ADA	ACU	COPE	COC
75	28	83	50

LCV	NTLC	CFA	ASC
63	50	67	90

Office: 2243 LHOB 20515, 202-225-6601 (Howard
Bauleke, Staff Dir.). DISTRICT OFFICE: 803
Jayhawk Tower 700 SW Jackson, Topeka 66603,
913-233-2503 (Carol McDowell, AA); 1001 N.
Broadway Suite C, Pittsburg 66762, 316-231-6040
(Tom Beall, Rep.)

THIRD DISTRICT

Jan Meyers (R)

District: Kansas suburbs of greater Kansas City,
including Kansas City (Kans.) and Overland
Park. Population: 619,439—Black 9%, Hispanic
3%. Politics: Republican.

Born July 20, 1928, Lincoln; home, Superior;
Williams Wood College, A.A. 1948, University
of Nebr., B.A. 1951; United Methodist; married
(Louis), 2 children.

Elected 1984. Career: Member, Overland Park
City Cncl., 1967–72; Kans. Senate, 1972–84.

Committees: (1) Foreign Affairs; (2) Small Business.

Election Results: 1992 Meyers 169,668 (61%);
Tom Love (D) 109,548 (39%). 1990 Meyers
(60%). 1988 Meyers (74%).

Interest Group Ratings:

ADA	ACU	COPE	COC
30	72	36	88

LCV	NTLC	CFA	ASC
50	63	40	100

Office: 2338 RHOB 20515, 202-225-2865 (Brian
Gaston, AA). DISTRICT OFFICE: 204 Fed.
Bldg., 812 N. 7th, Kansas City Kans. 66101,
913-621-0832 (Mike Murray, Dist. AA), Rm.
217, 7133 W. 95th St., Overland Park 66212
913-383-2013 (Lori Phillips, Rep.); 708 W. 9th
St., Lawrence 66044, 913-842-9313 (Ann Wik-
lund, Rep.)

FOURTH DISTRICT

Daniel Robert Glickman (D)

District: South central portion of the state including Wichita. Population: 619,374—Black
7%, Hispanic 4%. Politics: Leans Republican.

Born Nov. 24, 1944, Wichita; home, Wichita; University of Mich., B.A. 1966; George Washington University, J.D. 1969; Jewish; married (Rhoda), 2 children.

Elected 1976. Career: Atty., Securities & Exch. Comm., 1971–73; Practicing atty., 1973–76; Pres., Wichita Bd. of Ed., 1975–76.

Committees: (1) Agriculture; (2) Judiciary; (3) Science, Space & Technology; (4) Permanent Select Committee on Intelligence (Chairman).

Election Results: 1992 Glickman 139,854 (55%); Eric Yost (R) 114,269 (45%). 1990 Glickman (71%). 1988 Glickman (64%).

Interest Group Ratings:

ADA	ACU	COPE	COC
75	32	64	63

LCV	NTLC	CFA	ASC
50	17	73	100

Office: 2371 RHOB 20515, 202-225-6216 (Mark Pearl, AA). DISTRICT OFFICES: 134 U.S. Courthouse, Wichita 67201, 316-262-8396 (Melissa Greg, AA); 325 N. Pennsylvania #9, Independence 67301, 316-331-8056 (John Lechlighter, Rep.)

KENTUCKY

It will be a quiet two years in Kentucky politics as no statewide offices are being contested until 1995. Actually, most of the political interest in the state is focusing on the expected 1996 reelection bid of Republican Sen. Mitch McConnell. Democrats consider him vulnerable, if they can find a candidate of stature to oppose him.

1992 PRESIDENTIAL ELECTION: (8 Electoral votes): Clinton (D) 664,246 (45%); Bush (R) 616,517 (42%); Perot (I) 203,628 (14%); Hagelin (NLP) 4,578; Marrou (Lib) 977; Gritz (Pop) 686; Fulani (NAP) 420; Phillips (AmTax) 149. 1988 Bush 731,446 (56%); Dukakis 579,077 (44%)

SENATORS

Wendell Hampton Ford (D)

Born Sept. 8, 1924, Daviess Cty; home, Owensboro; University of Ky., Md. School of Insurance; Baptist; married (Jean), 2 children.

Elected 1974, seat up 1998. Career: Army, WWII; Family insur. bus.; Chf. A.A. to Gov. Bert Combs; Ky. Senate, 1965–67; Lt. Gov., 1967–71; Gov., 1971–74.

Committees: (1) Commerce, Science & Transportation; (2) Energy & Natural Resources; (3) Rules & Administration (Chairman); (4) Joint Committee on Printing (Chairman).

Election Results: 1992 Ford 835,883 (64%); David Williams (R) 477,040 (36%). 1986 Ford (75%). 1980 Ford (65%).

Interest Group Ratings:

ADA	ACU	COPE	COC
75	15	92	10

LCV	NTLC	CFA	ASC
17	33	75	30

Office: 173A RSOB 20510, 202-224-4343 (James Fleming, AA). STATE OFFICES: 172-C New Fed. Bldg., 600 Fed. Pl., Louisville 40202, 502-582-6251 (Doris Walsh, Mgr.); 305 Fed. Bldg., Frederica St., Owensboro 42301, 502-685-5158 (Gloria Murphy, Dir.); 343 Waller Ave., Suite 204, Lexington 40504, 606-233-2484 (Rusty Cheuvront, Rep.); 19 U.S. Courthouse, Covington 41011, 606-491-7929 (Janet Gerding, Rep.)

Mitch McConnell (R)

Born Feb. 20, 1942, Sheffield, Ala.; home, Louisville; University of Louisville, B.A. 1964, University of Ky., J.D. 1967; Baptist; married (Elaine), 3 children.

Elected 1984, seat up 1996. Career: Chief Legis. Asst. to U.S. Sen. Marlow Cook, 1967–69; Dpty. Asst. Atty. Gen., 1974–76; Judge/Exec., Jefferson Cty., Ky., 1977–1985.

Committees: (1) Agriculture, Nutrition & Forestry; (2) Appropriations; (3) Ethics; (4) Rules.

Election Results: 1990 McConnell 476,810 (52%); Harvey Sloan (D) 436,470 (48%). 1984 McConnell (50%).

Interest Group Ratings:

ADA	ACU	COPE	COC
15	89	18	100

LCV	NTLC	CFA	ASC
17	83	42	90

Office: 120 RSOB 20510, 202-224-2541 (Steven Law, AA). STATE OFFICES: 136C Fed. Bldg., 600 Martin Luther King Pl., Louisville 40202, 502-582-6304 (Larry Cox, St. Dir.); 307 Fed. Bldg., Covington 41011, 606-261-6304 (Kathy Mueller, Rep.); Irvin Cobb Bldg., 602 Broadway, Paducah 42001, 502-442-4554 (Susan Tharp); 1501 S. Main St., Suite N, London 40741, 606-864-2026 (Janie Catron, Dir.); 305 Fed. Bldg., 241 Main St., Bowling Green 42101 502-781-1673 (Robbin Morrison, Rep.); 155 E. Main St., Suite 210, Lexington 40508, 606-252-1781 (Pat Allen, Rep.)

REPRESENTATIVES

FIRST DISTRICT

Tom Barlow (D)

District: Western third of the state including city of Paducah. Population: 614,226—Black 8%. Politics: Democratic.

Born Aug. 7, 1940, Washington, D.C.; home, Paducah; Haverford College, B.A. 1962; Methodist; married (Shirley), 2 children.

Elected 1992. Career: Asst. V.P. of Fidelity Bank, 1963–68; Natural Resource Defense Council, 1971–82; Business Consultant, 1982–86; Dir. of Sales for Central Services, 1986–92.

Committees: (1) Agriculture; (2) Merchant Marine & Fisheries.

Election Results: 1992 Barlow 128,233 (60%); Steve Hamrick (R) 82,991 (39%); Marvin Seat (Reform) 1,012 (0%).

Interest Group Ratings:
None—Freshman

Office: 1533 LHOB 20515, 202-225-3115 (Bobby Miller, AA). DISTRICT OFFICES: 1 Executive Blvd., Paducah 42001, 502-444-7216 (Bob Buchanan, Dist. Dir.); 222 1st St., Henderson 42420, 502-831-1834; 1315 S. Virginia St., Hopkinsville 42240, 502-886-5821.

SECOND DISTRICT

William Huston Natcher (D)

District: West central portion of the state including city of Owensboro. Population: 564,883 —Black 5%. Politics: Leans Democratic.

Born Sept 11, 1909, Bowling Green; home, Bowling Green; Western Ky. State College, A.B. 1930, Ohio State University, LL.B. 1933; Baptist; widower, 2 children.

Elected Aug. 1, 1953. Career: Practicing atty., 1934–53; Fed. Conciliation Commissioner, W. Dist. of Ky., 1936–37; Warren Cty. Atty., 1937–49; Navy, WWII; Commonwealth Atty., 8th Judicial Dist. of Ky., 1951–53.

Committee: (1) Appropriations.

Election Results: 1992 Natcher 126,808 (61%); Bruce Bartley (R) 79,619 (39%). 1990 Natcher (66%). 1988 Natcher (61%).

Interest Group Ratings:

ADA	ACU	COPE	COC
85	16	83	50

LCV	NTLC	CFA	ASC
31	00	80	70

Office: 2333 RHOB 20515, 202-225-3501 (Diane Rihely, AA). DISTRICT OFFICES: 414 E. 10th St., Bowling Green 42101, 502-842-7376 (Sharon Martin, Asst.); 312 N. Mulberry St. Suite

4, Elizabethtown 42701, 502-765-4630 (Kathy Poyner, Asst.)

THIRD DISTRICT

Romano Louis Mazzoli (D)

District: Louisville and suburbs. Population: 613,603—Black 18%. Politics: Leans Democratic.

Born Nov. 2, 1932, Louisville; home, Louisville; College of Notre Dame, B.S. 1954, University of Louisville, J.D. 1960; Roman Catholic; married (Helen), 2 children.

Elected 1970. Career: Army, 1954–56; Law Department, L & N Railroad Co., 1960–62; Practicing atty., 1962–70; Lecturer, Bellarmine College, 1964–68; Ky. State Senate, 1968–70.

Committees: (1) Judiciary; (2) Small Business.

Election Results: 1992 Mazzoli 148,066 (53%); Susan Stokes (R) 132,689 (47%). 1990 Mazzoli (61%). 1988 Mazzoli (70%).

Interest Group Ratings:

ADA	ACU	COPE	COC
70	28	75	38

LCV	NTLC	CFA	ASC
56	10	100	60

Office: 2246 RHOB 20515, 202-225-5401 (Jane Kirby, AA). DISTRICT OFFICE: 551 Fed. Bldg., 600 Fed. Pl., Louisville 40202, 502-582-5129 (Charles Mattingly, AA)

FOURTH DISTRICT

Jim Bunning (R)

District: Northern counties including towns of Covington and Ashland. Population: 614,425— Black 2%. Politics: Republican.

Born Oct. 23, 1931, Campbell County; home, Ft. Thomas; Xavier University, B.S. 1953; Roman Catholic; married (Mary), 9 children.

Elected 1986. Career: Professional baseball player, 1950–71; Investment broker & agent, 1960–86; Ft. Thomas City Cncl., 1977–79; Ky. Senate, 1979–83.

Committees: (1) Ways and Means; (2) Budget; (3) Ethics.

Election Results: 1992 Bunning 139,466 (62%);

Floyd Poore (D) 86,713 (38%). 1990 Bunning (69%). 1988 Bunning (74%).

Interest Group Ratings:

ADA	ACU	COPE	COC
10	90	27	71

LCV	NTLC	CFA	ASC
00	95	89	90

Office: 2437 RHOB 20515, 202-225-3465 (Dave York, AA). DISTRICT OFFICES: 1717 Dixie Hwy., Suite 160, Fort Wright 41011, 606-341-2602 (Debbie McKinney, Dist. Adm.); 704 W. Jefferson St. #219, LaGrange 40031, 502-222-2188 (Oteka Brab, Rep.); 1405 Greenup Ave. #236, Ashland 41101, 606-325-9898 (Darlynn Barber, Rep.)

FIFTH DISTRICT

Harold Dallas Rogers (R)

District: Southeastern counties including towns of Middlesboro and Pikesville. Population: 614,119. Politics: Republican.

Born Dec. 31, 1937, Barrier; home, Somerset; University of Ky., B.A. 1962, J.D. 1964; Baptist; married (Shirley), 3 children.

Elected 1980. Career: Practicing atty., 1964–69; Pulaski–Rockcastle Commonwealth Atty., 1969–81.

Committees: (1) Appropriations.

Election Results: 1992 Rogers 113,809 (54%); John Hays (D) 97,768 (46%). 1990 Rogers (Unopposed). 1988 Rogers (Unopposed).

Interest Group Ratings:

ADA	ACU	COPE	COC
25	80	50	88

LCV	NTLC	CFA	ASC
06	65	33	90

Office: 2468 CHOB 20515, 202-225-4601 (Kevin Fromer, AA). DISTRICT OFFICE: 203 E. Mt. Vernon, Somerset 42501, 606-679-8346 (Robert Mitchell, Dist. Adm.); 601 Main St., Hazard 41701, 606-439-0794 (Dudley Crouch, Rep.); 806 Hambley Blvd., Pikesville 41501, 606-432-4388 (Jeff Speaks, Rep.)

SIXTH DISTRICT

Scotty Baesler (D)

District: Central counties including cities of Lexington and Frankfort. Population: 614,270— Black 8%. Politics: Mixed, leans Republican.

Born July 9, 1941, Lexington; home, Lexington; University of Ky., B.S. 1963, J.D. 1966; Christian; married (Alice), 2 children.

Elected 1992. Career: Attorney, 1966–92; Lexington Vice Mayor, 1981–92.

Committees: (1) Agriculture; (2) Veteran Affairs.

Election Results: 1992 Baesler 135,021 (61%); Charles Ellinger (R) 87,636 (39%).

Interest Group Ratings:
None—Freshman

Office: 508 CHOB 20515, 202-225-4706 (Chuck Atkins, AA).DISTRICT OFFICE: 444 E. Main St. #103, Lexington 40507, 606-253-1124 (Bob Wiseman, Rep.)

LOUISIANA

Politically, Louisiana remains the most offbeat state in the union. With its nonpartisan election system, Democrats are elected in what appears to be Republican districts, life long Democrats suddenly call themselves Republicans and are elected, and Republicans are elected from districts that are otherwise solidly Democratic. With no statewide contests until 1995, currently the state's biggest political question concerns the approval of a huge gambling casino in New Orleans and who will run it.

1992 PRESIDENTIAL ELECTION: (9 Electoral votes): Clinton (D) 815,530 (46%); Bush (R) GOP 731,619 (41%); Perot (I) 210,604 (12%); Gritz (Pop) 19,289; Marrou (Lib) 3,477; Daniels (P&F) 2,001; Phillips (AmTax) 1,535; Fulani (NAP) 1,415; LaRouche (I) 1,124; Hagelin (NLP) 1,090; Yiamouyiannis (TkBkAm) 1,070. 1988 Bush 880,830 (55%); Dukakis 715,612 (45%)

SENATORS

J. Bennett Johnston, Jr. (D)

Born June 10, 1932, Shreveport; home, Shreveport; Washington and Lee University, 1950–51, 1952–53, U.S. Military Academy, 1951–52, La. State University, LL.B. 1956; Baptist; married (Mary), 4 children.

Elected 1972, seat up 1996. Career: Army, 1956–59; Practicing atty., 1959–72; La. House of Reps., 1964–68; La. Senate, 1968–72.

Committees: (1) Appropriations; (2) Budget; (3) Energy & Natural Resources; (4) Select Committee on Intelligence.

Election Results: (nonpartisan election) 1990 Johnston 749,552 (53%), David Duke (R) 605,681 (43%); 1984 Johnston (86%).

Interest Group Ratings:

ADA	ACU	COPE	COC
70	23	75	20

LCV	NTLC	CFA	ASC
25	05	75	60

Office: 136 HSOB 20510, 202-224-5824 (John Lynn, AA). STATE OFFICES: 1010 Fed. Bldg., 500 Camp St., New Orleans 70130, 504-589-2427 (Charamine Caccioppi, Ex. Asst.); 7A12 Fed.

Bldg., 500 Fannin St., Shreveport 71101, 318-676-3085 (Julie Rogers, Ex. Asst.); 1 American Pl., Suite 1510, Baton Rouge 70825, 504-389-0395 James Oakes, State Dir.)

John B. Breaux (D)

Born Mar. 1, 1944, Crowley; home, Lafayette; University of Southwestern La., B.A. 1964, La. State University, J.D. 1967; Roman Catholic; married (Lois), 4 children.

Elected 1986, seat up 1998. Career: Practicing atty., 1967–68; Legis. Asst. Dist. Mgr. to U.S. Rep. Edwin W. Edwards, 1968–72; U.S. House of Reps., 1972–87.

Committees: (1) Commerce, Science & Transportation; (2) Finance; (3) Special Committee on Aging.

Election Results: (nonpartisan election) 1992 Breaux (Unopposed). 1986 Breaux 723,586 (53%), W. Henson Moore (R) 646,311 (47%).

Interest Group Ratings:

ADA	ACU	COPE	COC
60	30	67	10

LCV	NTLC	CFA	ASC
25	17	83	60

Office: 516 HSOB 20510, 202-224-4623 (David Strauss, Chief-of-staff). STATE OFFICES: 301 Fed. Bldg, 705 Jefferson, Lafayette 70501, 318-264-6871 (Raymond Cordova, Ex. Asst.); 1005 Fed. Bldg, 501 Magazine St., New Orleans 70130, 504-589-2531 (J. Martin Walke, Ex. Asst.); 102A Wash. Sq. Annex Bldg., 211 N. 3rd St., Monroe 71202, 318-325-3320 (Jean Bates, Asst.); 1 American Place #2020, Baton Rouge 70825, (Bob Mann, Rep.)

REPRESENTATIVES

FIRST DISTRICT

Robert L. Livingston, Jr. (R)

District: Parts of five parishes north of New Orleans including suburban areas. Population: 602,859—Black 10%, Hispanic 4%. Politics: Leans Republican.

180

Born Apr. 30, 1943, Colorado Springs, Colo.; home, New Orleans; Tulane University, B.A. 1967, J.D. 1968; Episcopalian; married (Bonnie), 4 children.

Elected Aug. 27, 1977. Career: Navy, 1961–63; Asst. U.S. Atty., 1970–73; Chf. Spec. Prosecutor, Orleans Parish Dist. Atty.'s Off., 1974–75; Chf. Prosecutor, La. Atty. Gen.'s Off., Organized Crime Unit, 1975–76.

Committees: (1) Appropriations.

Election Results: 1992 Livingston (Unopposed); 1990 Livingston (83%); 1988 Livingston (79%).

Interest Group Ratings:

ADA	ACU	COPE	COC
10	95	30	83

LCV	NTLC	CFA	ASC
00	84	20	100

Office: 2368 LHOB 20515, 202-225-3015 (J. Allan Martin, AA). DISTRICT OFFICES: 111 Veterans Blvd., Suite 700, Metairie 70005, 504-589-2753 (Rick Legendre, Dist Mgr.); 300 E. Thomas St., Hammond 70401, 504-542-9616 (Rick Legendre, Dist Mgr.)

SECOND DISTRICT

William J. Jefferson (D)

District: City of New Orleans and parts of Jefferson Parish and Orleans Parish. Population: 602,689—Black 61%, Hispanic 4%. Politics: Democratic.

Born Mar. 14, 1947, Lake Providence, La.; home, New Orleans; Southern University, B.A., 1969, Harvard University, J.D., 1972; Baptist; married (Andrea), 5 children.

Elected 1990. Career: Lawyer; U.S. Army; Clerk U.S. Court of Appeals; Leg. Asst. U.S. Sen. J. Bennett Johnston; La. St. Senate 1981–90.

Committees: (1) Ways & Means.

Election Results: 1992 Jefferson (Unopposed). 1990 Jefferson (52%).

Interest Group Ratings:

ADA	ACU	COPE	COC
85	00	92	29

LCV	NTLC	CFA	ASC
63	00	87	20

Office: 428 CHOB 20515, 202-225-6636 (Weldon Rougeau, AA). DISTRICT OFFICE: 501 Magazine St., New Orleans 70130, 504-589-2274 (Stephanie Edwards, Rep.)

THIRD DISTRICT

W.J. "Billy" Tauzin (D)

District: Cajun Louisiana—Southeastern parishes including town of Thiboudax. Population: 602,950—Black 22%, Hispanic 2%. Politics: Democratic.

Born June 14, 1943, Chackbay; home, Thibodaux; Nicholls State University, B.A. 1964, La. State University, J.D. 1967; Roman Catholic; divorced, 5 children.

Elected May 22, 1980. Career: Legis. Aide, La. Senate, 1964–68; Practicing atty., 1968–80; La. House of Reps., 1971–79.

Committees: (1) Energy & Commerce; (2) Merchant Marine & Fisheries.

Election Results: 1992 Tauzin (Unopposed). 1990 Tauzin (87%). 1988 Tauzin (89%).

Interest Group Ratings:

ADA	ACU	COPE	COC
40	71	55	75

LCV	NTLC	CFA	ASC
13	60	47	100

Office: 2330 RHOB 20515, 202-225-4031 (Dan Tate, AA). DISTRICT OFFICES: 1041 Fed. Bldg., 500 Camp St., New Orleans 70130, 504-589-6366 (Wayne Fernandez, Dist. Mgr.); 107 Fed. Bldg., Houma 70360, 504-876-3033 (Tom Lyons, Rep.); 210 E. Main St., New Iberia 70560, 318-367-8231 (Bonnie Landry, Rep.)

FOURTH DISTRICT

Cleo Fields (D)

District: A newly created black majority district that runs through and around 28 northern and eastern parishes. Population: 602,884—Black 66%. Politics: Democratic.

Born Nov. 22, 1962, Baton Rouge; home, Baton Rouge; Southern University, B.A. 1984, J.D. 1987; Baptist; married (Debra).

Elected 1992. Career: State Sen., 1987–92.

Committees: (1) Banking, Finance & Urban Affairs; (2) Small Business.

Election Results: 1992 Cleo Fields 142,822 (74%); Charles Jones (D) 50,796 (26%).

Interest Group Ratings:
None—Freshman

Office: 513 CHOB 20515, 202-225-8490 (Johnny Anderson, AA). DISTRICT OFFICES: 700 N. 10th St., Baton Rouge 70802, 504-343-9773; 610 Texas Ave. #201, Shreveport 71101, 318-221-9924; 301 N. Main St., Opelousas 70570, 318-942-9691.

FIFTH DISTRICT

James Otis McCrery III (R)

District: State's northern parishes including city of Shreveport. Population: 602,816—Black 22%. Politics: Leans Republican.

Born Sep. 18, 1949, Shreveport; home, Leesville; La. Technical University, B.A. 1971; La. State University, J.D. 1975; United Methodist; married (Johnette).

Elected 1988. Career: Practicing atty., 1975–78; Staff of U.S. Rep. Claude Leach, 1979; Asst. City Atty., Shreveport, La., 1979–81; Staff of U.S. Rep. Buddy Roemer, 1981–84; Regional Mgr. of Govt. Affairs, Georgia–Pacific Corp., 1984–88.

Committees: (1) Ways & Means.

Election Results: 1992 McCrery 153,232 (63%); Jerry Huckaby (D) 89,923 (37%). 1990 McCrery (54%); 1988 McCrery (68%).

Interest Group Ratings:

ADA	ACU	COPE	COC
05	91	10	83

LCV	NTLC	CFA	ASC
13	74	20	100

Office: 225 CHOB 20515, 202-225-2777 (Grace Wiegers, AA). DISTRICT OFFICES: 6425 Youree Dr. #260, Shreveport 71105, 318-676-3080 (Richard Hunt, Rep.); 2400 Forsythe St., Monroe 71201, 318-388-6105 (Lee Fletcher, Rep.)

SIXTH DISTRICT

Richard Hugh Baker (R)

District: East central part of the state including

parts of Baton Rouge. Population: 602,854—Black 15%, Hispanic 2%. Politics: Leans Republican.

Born May 22, 1948, New Orleans; home, Baton Rouge; La. State University, B.A. 1971; United Methodist; married (Karen), 2 children.

Elected 1986. Career: Real estate broker, 1971–86; La. House of Reps., 1972–86.

Committees: (1) Banking, Finance & Urban Affairs; (2) Small Business; (3) Natural Resources.

Election Results: (nonpartisan election) 1992 Baker 123,869 (51%); Clyde Holloway 120,900 (49%). 1990 Baker (Unopposed); 1988 Baker (Unopposed).

Interest Group Ratings:

ADA	ACU	COPE	COC
00	100	20	86

LCV	NTLC	CFA	ASC
00	89	20	100

Office: 434 CHOB 20515, 202-225-3901 (Tim Carpenter, AA). DISTRICT OFFICES: 5757 Corporate Blvd., Suite 104, Baton Rouge 70806, 504-929-7711; 3406 Rosalino St., Alexandria 71301, 318-445-5504; 100 E. Texas St., Leesville 71446, 318-238-5443.

SEVENTH DISTRICT

James A. Hayes (D)

District: Southwest parishes including cities of Lake Charles and Lafayette. Population: 602,921—Black 20%. Politics: Democratic.

Born Dec. 21, 1946, Lafayette; home, Lafayette; University of South West La., B.A. 1967, Tulane University, J.D. 1970; United Methodist; married (Leslie), 3 children.

Elected 1986. Career: Asst. City Atty., Lafayette, 1971–72; Asst. Dist. Atty., Lafayette Parish, 1974–83; La. Commissioner of Financial Institutions, 1983–85.

Committees: (1) Public Works & Transportation; (2) Science, Space & Technology; (3) Government Operations.

Election Results: 1992 Hayes (Unopposed). 1990 Hayes (57%). 1988 Hayes (Unopposed).

Interest Group Ratings:

ADA	ACU	COPE	COC
30	65	55	100

LCV	NTLC	CFA	ASC
06	53	47	80

Office: 2432 RHOB 20515, 202-225-2031 (John Doyle, AA). DISTRICT OFFICES: 109 E. Vermillion, Lafayette 70501, 318-233-4773 (Louis Perret, Asst.); 901 Lake Shore Dr., Suite 402, Lake Charles 70601, 318-433-1613 (Sheryl Sinegal, Asst.)

MAINE

The GOP considers Maine to be a Republican state and Maine Republicans are still in shock after President George Bush ran third behind Bill Clinton and Ross Perot. They will not have much of a chance for a comeback in 1994. Senate Majority Leader George J. Mitchell is up for reelection, and should have little trouble winning a third term.

1992 PRESIDENTIAL ELECTION: (4 Electoral votes): Clinton (D) 263,420 (39%); Bush (R) 206,504 (30.3%); Perot (I) 206,820 (30.4%); Marrou (Lib) 2,060; Phillips (AmTax) 595; Fulani (NAP) 471. 1988 Bush 304,087 (56%); Dukakis 240,509 (44%)

SENATORS

William S. Cohen (R)

Born Aug. 28, 1940, Bangor; home, Bangor; Bowdoin College, B.A. 1962, Boston University, LL.B. 1965; Unitarian Universalist; divorced, 2 children.

Elected 1978, seat up 1996. Career: Practicing atty., 1965–68; Asst. Penobscot Cty. Atty., 1968–69; Bangor City Cncl., 1969–72, Mayor of Bangor, 1971–72; U.S. House of Reps., 1972–78.

Committees: (1) Armed Services; (2) Governmental Affairs; (3) Special Committee on Aging; (4) Judiciary.

Election Results: 1990 Cohen 306,980 (61%); Neil Rolde (D) 193,925 (39%). 1984 Cohen (73%).

Interest Group Ratings:

ADA	ACU	COPE	COC
40	48	33	70

LCV	NTLC	CFA	ASC
67	50	67	80

Office: 322 HSOB 20510, 202-224-2523 (Robert Tyrer, AA). STATE OFFICES: 150 Capitol St., Augusta 04330, 207-622-8414 (Jan Anderson, Rep.); 204 Fed. Bldg., 202 Harlow St., Bangor 04401, 207-945-0417 (Don Carrigan, Rep.); 109 Alfred St., Biddeford 04005, 207-283-1101 (Linda Leeman, Rep.); 11 Lisbon St., Lewiston 04240,

207-784-6969 (Eric Howes, Rep.); 10 Moulton St., Portland 04101, 207-780-3575 (Bill Johnson, Rep.); 169 Academy, Presque Isle 04769, 207-764-3266 (Dayle Ashby, Rep.)

George J. Mitchell (D)

Born Aug. 20, 1933, Waterville; home, South Portland; Bowdoin College, B.A. 1954, Georgetown University, J.D. 1960; Roman Catholic; divorced, 1 child.

Appointed May 17, 1980, elected 1982, seat up 1994. Career: Army counter–intelligence, 1954–56; U.S. Dept. of Justice, 1960–62; Executive Asst. to U.S. Senator Edmund S. Muskie, 1962–65; Practicing atty., 1965–77; Asst. Attorney, Cumberland Cty., 1971; U.S. Attorney for Maine, 1977–79; U.S. District Judge for Maine, 1979–80.

Committees: Majority leader. (1) Environment & Public Works; (2) Finance; (3) Veterans Affairs.

Election Results: 1988 Mitchell 452,590 (81%); Jasper Wyman (R) 104,758 (19%). 1982 Mitchell (61%).

Interest Group Ratings:

ADA	ACU	COPE	COC
95	00	83	20

LCV	NTLC	CFA	ASC
83	11	100	40

Office: 176 RSOB 20510, 202-224-5344 (Mary McAleney, AA). STATE OFFICES: 537 Congress St, Portland 01401, 207-874-0883 (Larry Benoit, Senior Rep.); 101C Fed. Bldg., 40 Western Ave., Augusta 04330, 207-622-8292 (Tom Bertocci, Rep.); 231 Main St., Biddeford 04005, 207-282-4144 (Judith Cadorette, Rep.); 387 Main St., Rockland 04841, 207-596-0311 (Tom Bertocci, Rep.); 235 Fed. Bldg., 202 Harlow St., Bangor 04401, 207-945-0451 (Clyde MacDonald, Rep.); 157 Main St., Lewiston 04240, 207-784-0163 (Janet Welsh, Rep.); 33 College Ave., Waterville 04901, 207-873-3361 (Janet Dennis, Rep.); 6 Church St., Presque Isle 04769, 207-764-5601 (Mary Leblanc, Rep.)

REPRESENTATIVES

FIRST DISTRICT

Thomas H. Andrews (D)

District: South part of the state including cities of Portland and Augusta. Population: 636,484. Politics: Leans Democratic.

Born March 27, 1953, N. Easton, Mass.; home, Portland; Bowdoin College, B.A., 1976; Protestant; married (Debra).

Elected 1990. Career: Dir., Maine Assoc. of Handicapped; Maine State House, 1983–85; Maine State Sen. 1985–90; founder, Maine Studies Center, 1987.

Committees: (1) Armed Services; (2) Small Business; (3) Merchant Marine and Fisheries.

Election Results: 1992 Andrews 231,363 (65%); Linda Bean (R) 126,079 (35%). 1990 Andrews (61%).

Interest Group Ratings:

ADA	ACU	COPE	COC
100	04	92	25

LCV	NTLC	CFA	ASC
100	00	93	30

Office: 1530 LHOB 20515, 202-225-6116 (Craig Brown, AA). DISTRICT OFFICE: 136 Commercial St., Portland 04101, 207-772-8240 (Joe Cowie, Dist. Dir.)

SECOND DISTRICT

Olympia J. Snowe (R)

District: Northern two–thirds of the state including cities of Lewiston and Bangor. Population: 591,442. Politics: Leans Republican.

Born Feb. 21, 1947, Augusta; home, Auburn; University of Maine, B.A. 1969; Greek Orthodox; married (Gov. John McKernan).

Elected 1978. Career: Dir., Superior Concrete Co.; Member, Bd. of Voter Regis., Auburn, Maine, 1971–73; Maine House of Reps., 1973–76; Maine Senate, 1976–78.

Committees: (1) Foreign Affairs; (2) Budget.

Election Results: 1992 Snowe 152,285 (49%); Patrick McGowan (D) 130,958 (42%); Jonathan Carter (I) 29,953 (10%). 1990 Snowe (51%). 1988 Snowe (66%).

Interest Group Ratings:

ADA	ACU	COPE	COC
50	60	58	50

LCV	NTLC	CFA	ASC
63	35	67	80

Office: 2268 RHOB 20515, 202-225-6306 (Judy Butler, AA). DISTRICT OFFICES: 1 Cumberland Pl., Suite 306, Bangor 04401, 207-945-0432 (Kevin Raye, Rep.); 169 Academy St., Presque Isle 04769, 207-764-5124 (Marion Higgins, Asst.); 2 Great Falls Plaza, Suite 7B, Auburn 04210, 207-786-2451 (John Richter, Asst.)

MARYLAND

Two major questions loom on the horizon for Maryland. The first is whether incumbent Democratic Sen. Paul Sarbanes will seek reelection in 1994. If he does not, a free-for-all will ensue among Democrats who might seek to succeed him. On the state level, Gov. William Donald Shaffer cannot run again, and the wide open Democratic primary will feature a showdown between metropolitan Baltimore and the Washington, D.C. suburbs, a political battle that has been brewing for years.

1992 PRESIDENTIAL ELECTION: (10 Electoral votes): Clinton (D) 941,979 (50%); Bush (R) 671,609 (35%); Perot (I) 271,198 (14%); Marrou (Lib) 4,603; Fulani (NAP) 2,726. 1988 Bush 834,202 (51%); Dukakis 793,939 (49%).

SENATORS

Paul Spyros Sarbanes (D)

Born Feb. 3, 1933, Salisbury; home, Baltimore; Princeton University, A.B. 1954, Rhodes Scholar, Oxford University, B.A. 1957, Harvard University, LL.B. 1960; Greek Orthodox; married (Christine), 3 children.

Elected 1976, seat up 1994. Career: Law Clerk to Judge Morris A. Soper, U.S. 4th Circuit Crt. of Appeals, 1960–61; Practicing atty., 1961–62, 1965–70; A.A. to Chm. Walter W. Heller of the Pres. Cncl. of Econ. Advisers, 1962–63; Exec. Dir., Baltimore Charter Revision Comm., 1963–64; Md. House of Delegates, 1966–70; U.S. House of Reps., 1971–77.

Committees: (1) Banking, Housing & Urban Affairs; (2) Foreign Relations; (3) Joint Economic Committee (Vice Chairman).

Election Results: 1988 Sarbanes 999,166 (62%); Alan Keyes (R) 617,537 (38%). 1982 Sarbanes (63%).

Interest Group Ratings:

ADA	ACU	COPE	COC
100	00	92	10

LCV	NTLC	CFA	ASC
92	05	100	40

Office: 309 HSOB 20510, 202-224-4524 (Marvin Moss, AA). STATE OFFICES: 1518 Fed. Bldg.,

31 Hopkins Plaza, Baltimore 21201, 301-962-4436 (Emily Gibbs, St. Dir.); Suite 206, 141 Baltimore St., Cumberland 21502, 301-724-0695 (Nina Conway, Rep.); Suite 115, 111 Baptist St., Salisbury 21801, 301-860-2131 (Ellen Murdock, Rep.)

Barbara A. Mikulski (D)

Born July 20, 1936, Baltimore; home, Baltimore; Mount Saint Agnes College, B.A. 1958, University of Md., M.S.W. 1965; Roman Catholic; single.

Elected 1986, seat up 1998. Career: Caseworker, Baltimore Dept. of Soc. Svcs.; Adjunct prof., Loyola College, 1958–71; Baltimore City Cncl., 1971–76; U.S. House of Reps., 1976–86.

Committees: (1) Appropriations; (2) Labor & Human Resources; (3) Ethics.

Election Results: 1992 Mikulski 1,247,386 (71%); Alan Keyes (R) 503,956 (29%). 1986 Mikulski 675,225 (61%); Linda Chavez (R) 437,411 (39%).

Interest Group Ratings:

ADA	ACU	COPE	COC
100	00	92	00

LCV	NTLC	CFA	ASC
67	17	92	40

Office: 709 HSOB 20510, 202-224-4654 (Lynn Battaglia, Chief-of-staff). STATE OFFICES: 253 World Trade Center, Baltimore 21202-3041, 301-962-4510 (Terry Curtis, St. Adm.); 60 West St., Annapolis 21401, 301-263-1805 (Denise Nooe, Dir.); Suite 103, 9658 Baltimore Ave., College Park 20740, 301-345-5517 (Patrice Little-Murray, Dir.); Suite 402, 82 W. Washington St., Hagerstown 21740, 301-797-2826 (Brian Poffenberger, Rep.); 213 W. Main St., Salisbury 21801, 301-546-7711 (Cindy Birge, Rep.)

REPRESENTATIVES

FIRST DISTRICT

Wayne T. Gilchrest (R)

District: Eastern Shore and southern Maryland counties including cities of Annapolis and

Salisbury. Population: 597,684—Black 15%. Politics: Very mixed, but leans Democratic.

Born Apr. 15, 1946, Rahway, N.J.; home, Kennedyville; Del. State University, 1973, Loyola College (Baltimore); Methodist; married (Barbara), 3 children.

Elected 1990. Career: High school teacher.

Committees: (1) Merchant Marine & Fisheries; (2) Public Works & Transportation.

Election Results: 1992 Gilchrest (R) 114,017 (52%); Tom McMillen (D-Incumbent) 106,914 (48%). 1990 Gilchrest (57%).

Interest Group Ratings:

ADA	ACU	COPE	COC
30	64	36	75

LCV	NTLC	CFA	ASC
88	80	47	100

Office: 412 CHOB 20515, 202-225-5311 (Tony Caligiuri, AA). DISTRICT OFFICES: 1 Plaza E., Salisbury 21801, 410-749-3184 (Sue Sullivan, Rep.); 335 High St., Chestertown 21620, 410-778-9407 (Karen Kendall, Rep.); 101 Crain Hwy. #509, Glen Burnie 21061, 410-760-3372 (Kathy Hicks, Rep.)

SECOND DISTRICT

Helen Delich Bentley (R)

District: Northern Baltimore suburbs including parts of Harford and Baltimore counties. Population: 597,683—Black 6%, Asian 2%. Politics: Leans Republican.

Born Nov. 28, 1923, Ely, Nev.; home, Lutherville; University of Mo., B.A. 1944, University of Nev., George Washington University; Greek Orthodox; married (William).

Elected 1984. Career: Reporter & Maritime Ed., *The Sun*, Baltimore, 1945–69; Chmn., Fed. Maritime Comm., 1969–75; Businesswoman, 1975–85; Columnist & Ed., *World Ports Magazine*, 1981–85.

Committees: (1) Appropriations.

Election Results: 1992 Bentley 157,194 (65%); Michael Hickey (D) 85,931 (35%). 1990 Bentley (74%). 1988 Bentley (71%).

Interest Group Ratings:

ADA	ACU	COPE	COC
25	80	50	100

LCV	NTLC	CFA	ASC
06	60	53	100

Office: 1610 LHOB 20515, 202-225-3061 (Pat Wait, AA). DISTRICT OFFICES: 400 Shell Bldg., 200 E. Joppa Rd., Towson 21204, 301-337-7222 (Sandra Dawson, Mgr.); 45 N. Main, Bel Air 21014, 410-838-2517; 115 W. Bel Air Ave., Aberdeen 21001, 410-272-7099; 4513-R Mountain Rd., Pasadena 21122, (Chuck Cresswell, Dist. Dir.)

THIRD DISTRICT

Benjamin Louis Cardin (D)

District: Eastern parts of Baltimore, and northern and southern suburbs. Population: 597,680 —Black 17%, Asian 2%, Hispanic 2%. Politics: Democratic.

Born Oct. 5, 1943, Baltimore; home, Baltimore; University of Pittsburgh, B.A. 1964, University of Md., LL.B., J.D. 1967; Jewish; married (Myrna), 2 children.

Elected 1986. Career: Md. House of Delegates, 1966–86, Speaker, 1979–86; Practicing atty., 1967–86.

Committees: (1) Ways and Means.

Election Results: 1992 Cardin (D) 156,085 (74%); William Bricker (R) 56,125 (26%). 1990 Cardin (70%). 1988 Cardin (73%).

Interest Group Ratings:

ADA	ACU	COPE	COC
95	04	83	38

LCV	NTLC	CFA	ASC
81	10	100	40

Office: 227 CHOB 20515, 202-225-4016 (David Koshgarian, AA). DISTRICT OFFICE: 540 E. Belvedere Ave., Suite 201, Baltimore 21212, 301-443-8886 (Bailey Fine, Dist. Mgr.)

FOURTH DISTRICT

Albert R. Wynn (D)

District: Newly created Black majority district including parts of Prince George's and Montgomery counties. Population: 597,690—Black 58%, Asian 5%, Hispanic 6%. Politics: Democratic.

Born Sept. 10, 1951, Philadelphia; home, Largo; University of Pittsburgh, B.A. 1973; Georgetown, J.D., 1977; Baptist; married (Alice).

Elected 1992. Career: Dir. Prince George's Co. Consumer Protection Comission, 1977–81; Lawyer, 1981–92; State Delegate, 1982–86; State Sen., 1986–92.

Committees: (1) Banking, Finance & Urban Affairs; (2) Foreign Affairs; (3) Post Office and Civil Service.

Election Results: 1992 Wynn (D) 132,776 (76%); Michele Dyson (R) 42,743 (24%).

Interest Group Ratings:
None—Freshman

Office: 423 CHOB 20515, 202-225-8699 (Luis Navarro, AA).DISTRICT OFFICES: 8700 Central Ave. #307, Landover 20785, 301-350-5055 (Don Juan Williams, Rep.); 8601 Georgia Ave. #201, Silver Spring 20910, 301-588-7328 (Lou D'Ovidio, Rep.)

FIFTH DISTRICT

Steny Hamilton Hoyer (D)

District: Prince George's County (Washington, D.C. suburbs) and southern counties. Population: 597,681—Black 19%, Asian 3%, Hispanic 2%. Politics: Democratic.

Born June 14, 1939, New York City; home, District Heights; University of Md., B.S. 1963, Georgetown University, J.D. 1966; Baptist; married (Judith), 3 children.

Elected May 19, 1981. Career: Md. Senate, 1966–78, Pres., 1974–78; Mbr., Md. Bd. for Higher Education, 1978–81.

Committee: (1) Appropriations; (2) House Administration.

Election Results: 1992 Hoyer 113,280 (55%); Larry Hogan (R) 92,636 (45%). 1990 Hoyer (81%). 1988 Hoyer (79%).

Interest Group Ratings:

ADA	ACU	COPE	COC
90	17	75	38

LCV	NTLC	CFA	ASC
44	00	87	70

Office: 1705 LHOB 20515, 202-225-4131 (Samuel Wynkoop, Chief-of-staff). DISTRICT OFFICES: 4201 Northview Dr. #403, Bowie 20716, 301-464-6440 (Betty Richardson, Rep.); 21 Industrial Park Dr. #101, Waldorf 20602, 301-705-9633.

SIXTH DISTRICT

Roscoe Bartlett (R)

District: Western portion of the state including far suburbs of both Washington and Baltimore. Population: 597,688—Black 4%. Politics: Mixed, but leans Democratic.

Born June 3, 1926, Moreland, Ky.; home, Frederick; University of Md., B.S. 1948, M.S. 1950, Ph.D. 1952; Seventh Day Adventist; married (Ellen), 10 children.

Elected 1992. Career: College Professor, 1952–56; Engineer, Researcher, 1956–74; Founder, Roscoe Bartlett & Assoc., 1974–92.

Committees: (1) Armed Services; (2) Science, Space & Technology.

Election Results: 1992 Bartlett (R) 119,684 (54%); Thomas Hattery (D) 100,753 (46%).

Interest Group Ratings:
None—Freshman

Office: 312 CHOB 20515, 202-225-2721 (Tim Wooford, AA).DISTRICT OFFICES: 100 W. Franklin, Hagerstown 21740, 301-797-6043 (Rita Downs, Rep.); 15 E. Main St. #110, Westminster 20157, 410-857-1115 Nancy Stockdale, Rep.); 5831 Buckeystown Pike E., Frederick 21701, 301-694-3030 (Sally Bloomfield, Rep.)

SEVENTH DISTRICT

Kweisi Mfume (D)

District: Central and western Baltimore. Population: 597,680—Black 71%. Politics: Democratic.

Born Oct. 24, 1948, Baltimore; home, Baltimore; Morgan State University, B.S. 1976, Johns Hopkins University, M.A. 1984; Baptist; divorced, 5 children.

Elected 1986. Career: Baltimore City Cncl., 1979–87.

Committees: (1) Banking, Finance & Urban Affairs; (2) Small Business; (3) Ethics.

Election Results: 1992 Mfume 147,133 (85%); Kenneth Kondner (R) 25,013 (15%). 1990 Mfume (85%). 1988 Mfume (87%).

Interest Group Ratings:

ADA	ACU	COPE	COC
95	00	92	13

LCV	NTLC	CFA	ASC
75	05	93	10

Office: 2419 RHOB 20515, 202-225-4741 (Tammy Hawley, AA). DISTRICT OFFICES: 3000 Druid Park Drive, Baltimore 21205, 301-367-1900 (Ruth Simms, Dist. Dir.); 2203 N. Charles St., Baltimore 21218, 301-235-2700 (Carol Swann, Sen. Rep.); 1825 Woodlawn, Baltimore 21207, 410-298-5997 (Ruth Simmer, Rep.)

EIGHTH DISTRICT

Constance Albanese Morella (R)

District: Montgomery County (suburban Washington, D.C.). Population: 587,682—Black 8%, Asian 8%, Hispanic 6%. Politics: Leans Democratic.

Born Feb. 12, 1931, Somerville, Mass.; home, Bethesda; Boston University, A.B. 1954; American University, M.A. 1967; Roman Catholic; married (Anthony), 3 children.

Elected 1986. Career: Teacher, 1956–70; Md. House of Delegates, 1979–86.

Committees: (1) Science, Space & Technology; (2) Post Office & Civil Service.

Election Results: 1992 Morella 189,420 (72%); Ed Heffernan (D) 72,190 (28%). 1990 Morella (77%). 1988 Morella (63%).

Interest Group Ratings:

ADA	ACU	COPE	COC
70	35	50	38

LCV	NTLC	CFA	ASC
81	45	80	70

Office: 223 CHOB 20515, 202-225-5341 (David Nathan, AA). DISTRICT OFFICE: 51 Monroe 507, Rockville 20850, 301-424-3501 (Mary Brown, Dist. Dir.)

MASSACHUSETTS

As it is every six years, the big political question in the Bay State for 1994 is: what will Teddy do? Sen. Edward Kennedy is up for reelection once again, and he gives every indication that he will run again for a sixth term. If he does, as usual, the GOP will throw everything at him they can. As in the past, he should win easily. In 1992, the "throw–the–bums out" atmosphere permeated Massachusetts politics, two Republicans, Peter G. Torkildsen and Peter I. Blute, defeated Democratic incumbents in Democratic districts. The Democrats will be going all out to win those districts back. Finally, GOP Gov. William Weld must run for reelection in 1994. If he can win, and he may face a tough race, he will become a player in the 1996 GOP presidential primary.

1992 PRESIDENTIAL ELECTION: (12 Electoral votes) Clinton (D) 1,315,016 (48%); Bush (R) 804,534 (29%); Perot (I) 630,440 (23%); Marrou (Lib) 7,084; Fulani (NAP) 3,219; Phillips (AmTax) 2,744; Hagelin (NLP) 1,710; LaRouche (I) 1,099. 1988 Dukakis 1,387,398 (54%); Bush 1,184,323 (46%).

SENATORS
Edward M. Kennedy (D)

Born Feb. 22, 1932, Boston; home, Boston; Harvard University, B.A. 1956, Academy of International Law, The Hague, The Netherlands, 1958, University of Virginia, LL.B. 1959; Roman Catholic; married (Victoria), 3 children.

Elected 1962, seat up 1994. Career: Army, 1951–53; Asst. Dist. Atty., Suffolk Cty., 1961–62.

Committees: (1) Armed Services; (2) Judiciary; (3) Labor & Human Resources (Chairman); (4) Joint Economic Committee.

Election Results: 1988 Kennedy 1,693,344 (65%); Joseph Malone (R) 884,267 (34%). 1982 Kennedy (61%).

Interest Group Ratings:

ADA	ACU	COPE	COC
100	00	92	20

LCV	NTLC	CFA	ASC
100	05	100	40

Office: 315 RSOB 20510, 202-224-4543 (Paul Donovan, AA). STATE OFFICE: 2400 JKF Fed. Bldg., Govt. Ctr., 10 Causeway St., Boston 02203, 617-565-3170 (Barbara Souliotis, Staff Dir.)

John Kerry (D)

Born Dec. 11, 1943, Denver, Colo.; home, Boston; Yale University, A.B. 1966, Boston College of Law, LL.B. 1976; Roman Catholic; divorced, 2 children.

Elected 1984, seat up 1996. Career: Navy, Vietnam; Organizer, Vietnam Veterans Against the War; Asst. Dist. Atty., Middlesex Cty., 1976–81; Practicing atty., 1981–82; Lt. Gov. of Mass., 1982–84.

Committees: (1) Banking, Housing & Urban Affairs; (2) Commerce, Science & Transportation; (3) Foreign Relations; (4) Small Business; (5) Select Committee on Intelligence.

Election Results: 1990 Kerry 1,180,209 (57%); Jim Rappaport (R) 892,624 (43%). 1984 Kerry (55%).

Interest Group Ratings:

ADA	ACU	COPE	COC
100	00	83	10

LCV	NTLC	CFA	ASC
92	11	92	40

Office: 421 RSOB 20510, 202-224-2742 (David Leiter, AA). STATE OFFICES: 1 Bowdoin St. 10th Fl., Boston 02214, 617-565-8519 (Chris Greeley, Dir.), 145 State St., Springfield 01103, 413-785-4610 (Bill Bradley, Rep.)

REPRESENTATIVES

FIRST DISTRICT
John W. Olver (D)

District: The Berkshires country of western Massachusetts including city of Amherst. Population: 601,643—Black 2%, Hispanic 5%. Politics: Traditional Republicanism.

Born Sept. 3, 1936, Honesdale, Pa.; home, Amherst; Rensselar Polytechnic Institute, B.S. 1955, Tufts, M.S. 1956, Massachusetts Institute of Technology, Ph.D. 1961; no religion specified; married (Rose), 1 child.

Elected 1991 (special). Career: Mass. House of Reps., 1969–73; Mass. Senate, 1973–91.

Committees: (1) Appropriations.

Election Results: 1992 Olver 134,954 (54%); Patrick Larkin (R) 113,796 (46%). 1991 (special) Olver (50%).

Interest Group Ratings:

ADA	ACU	COPE	COC
100	00	92	25

LCV	NTLC	CFA	ASC
100	00	100	40

Office: 1323 LHOB 20515, 202-225-5335 (Jonathan Klein, AA). DISTRICT OFFICES: 187 High St., Holyoke 01040, 413-532-7010 (Pat Sackery, Dist. Dir.); 78 Center St., Pittsfield 01201, 413-442-0946 (Pat Sackery, Dist. Dir.); 881 Main St., Fitchburg 01420, 508-342-8722 (Pat Sackery, Dist. Dir.)

SECOND DISTRICT

Richard E. Neal (D)

District: West central part of the state including the city of Springfield. Population: 601,642—Black 6%, Hispanic 6%. Politics: Democratic.

Born Feb. 14, 1949, Worcester; home, Springfield; American International College, B.A. 1972, University of Hartford, M.B.A. 1976; Roman Catholic; married (Maureen), 4 children.

Elected 1988. Career: College teacher, 1973–82; Asst. to the Mayor of Springfield, 1973–78; high school teacher, 1978–80; Springfield City Councilmember 1978–83; Mayor of Springfield, 1984–88.

Committees: (1) Ways & Means.

Election Results: 1992 Neal 131,147 (63%); Anthony Ravosa, Jr. (R) 76,780 (37%). 1990 Neal (Unopposed). 1988 Neal (80%).

Interest Group Ratings:

ADA	ACU	COPE	COC
90	00	92	13

LCV	NTLC	CFA	ASC
88	00	100	10

Office: 131 CHOB 20515, 202-225-5601 (Morgan

Broman, AA). DISTRICT OFFICES: 309 Fed. Office Bldg., 1550 Main St., Springfield 01103, 413-785-0325 (James Leydon, AA); 4 Congress St., Milford 01757, 508-634-8198 (Virginia Purcell, Rep.)

THIRD DISTRICT

Peter I. Blute (R)

District: Central part of the state including the city of Worcester. Population: 601,642—Black 2%, Hispanic 4%. Politics: Democratic.

Born Jan. 28, 1956, Worcester; home, Shrewsbury; Boston College, B.A. 1978; Roman Catholic; married (Roberta).

Elected 1992. Career: Mass. House of Reps., 1987–92.

Committees: (1) Public Works & Transportation; (2) Science, Space & Technology.

Election Results: 1992 Blute 131,406 (53%); Joseph D. Early (D) (Incumbent) 115,493 (47%).

Interest Group Ratings:
None—Freshman

Office: 1029 LHOB 20515, 202-225-6101 (Bob March, AA). DISTRICT OFFICES: 1079 Mechanics Tower, 100 Front St., Worcester 01608, 508-752-6789 (Mary Jane McKenna, Rep.); 1039 S. Main St., Fall River 02724, 508-675-3400 (Lou Cabral, Rep.); 7 Main St. #200, Attleboro 02703, 508-223-3100 (Gary Moran, Rep.)

FOURTH DISTRICT

Barney Frank (D)

District: A strange shaped district growing out of politically charged 1980 redistricting. It encompasses wide swath of south and southwestern Boston suburbs and town of Fall River. Population: 601,642—Black 2%, Asian 2%, Hispanic 2%. Politics: Leans Democratic.

Born Mar. 31, 1940, Bayonne, N.J.; home, Newton; Harvard University, B.A. 1962, J.D. 1977; Jewish; single.

Elected 1980. Career: Chf. of Staff to Boston Mayor Kevin White, 1968–71; A.A. to U.S. Rep. Michael Harrington, 1971–72; Mass. House of Reps., 1973–80; Lecturer on Pub. Policy, Harvard JFK School of Government, 1979–80.

Committees: (1) Banking, Finance & Urban Affairs; (2) Budget; (3) Judiciary.

Election Results: 1992 Frank 182,207 (72%); Edward McCormick III (R) 70,628 (28%). 1990 Frank (66%). 1988 Frank (70%).

Interest Group Ratings:

ADA	ACU	COPE	COC
100	00	83	25

LCV	NTLC	CFA	ASC
100	10	100	10

Office: 2404 RHOB 20515, 202-225-5931 (Peter Kovar, AA). DISTRICT OFFICES: 29 Crasts., Newton 02158, 617-332-3920 (Dorothy Reichard, Dist. Dir.); 10 Purchase St., Fall River 02722), 508-674-3551 (Amelia Wright, Mgr.; 558 Pleasant St., New Bedford 02740, 508-999-6462 (Elise Sousa, Rep.); 89 Main St., Bridgewater 02324, 508-697-9403 (Garth Patterson, Rep.)

FIFTH DISTRICT

Martin T. Meehan (D)

District: Far northern Boston suburbs including cities of Lowell and Lawrence. Population: 601,643—Black 2%, Hispanic 8%. Politics: Democratic.

Born Dec. 30, 1956, Lowell; home, Lowell; University of Mass., B.S. 1978, M.S. 1981, Suffolk, J.D., 1986; Roman Catholic; single.

Elected 1992. Career: Dept. Secy. for Securities and Corporations, 1986–90; Asst. Dist. Atty. for Middlesex Co., 1991–92.

Committees: (1) Armed Services; (2) Small Business.

Election Results: 1992 Meehan (D) 134,417 (58%); Paul Cronin (R) 96,827 (42%).

Interest Group Ratings:
None—Freshman

Office: 1223 LHOB 20515, 202-225-3411 (Steve Joncas, AA). DISTRICT OFFICE: 11 Kearney St., Lowell 01852, 508-459-0101 (vacant, Rep.); Bay State Bldg. 11 Lawrence St., Lawrence 01840, 508-681-6200 (Bob LaRochell, Rep.); Walker Bldg. #102 255 Main St., Marlboro 01752, 508-460-9292 (Maryanne Presco–Ricca, Rep.)

SIXTH DISTRICT

Peter G. Torkildsen (R)

District: North Shore Boston suburbs including towns of Lynn and Peabody. Population: 601,643 —Hispanic 3%. Politics: Democratic.

Born Jan. 28, 1956, Milwaukee, Wis.; home, Danvers; University of Mass., B.A. 1982, Harvard University, M.P.A. 1990; Roman Catholic; single.

Elected 1992. Career: Service Coordinator Visiting Nurse Assn. of Boston, 1982–84; State Rep. 1985–90; Commissioner Mass. Dept. of Labor and Industries, 1991–92.

Committees: (1) Armed Services; (2) Small Business.

Election Results: 1992 Torkildsen 158,577 (55%); Nicholas Mavroules (D) (Incumbent) 130,597 (45%).

Interest Group Ratings:
None—Freshman

Office: 120 CHOB 20515, 202-225-8020 (Steven Sutton, AA). DISTRICT OFFICES: 70 Washington St., Salem 01970, 508-741-1600 (Judy Cypret, Rep.); 156 Broad St. #106, Lynn 01901, 617-599-2424 (vacant, Rep.)

SEVENTH DISTRICT

Edward J. Markey (D)

District: Nearer northern Boston suburbs including Medford and Malden. Population: 601,642. Politics: Democratic.

Born July 11, 1946, Malden; home, Malden; Boston College, B.A. 1968, J.D. 1972; Roman Catholic; married, (Susan).

Elected 1976. Career: Practicing atty.; Mass. House of Reps., 1973–76.

Committees: (1) Energy & Commerce; (2) Natural Resources.

Election Results: 1992 Markey 182,850 (70%); Stephen Sohn (R) 78,194 (30%). 1990 Markey (unopposed). 1988 Markey (Unopposed).

Interest Group Ratings:

ADA	ACU	COPE	COC
100	00	83	25

LCV	NTLC	CFA	ASC
88	00	93	30

Office: 2133 RHOB 20515, 202-225-2836 (Dan Rabinovite, AA). DISTRICT OFFICE: 5 High St. #101, Medford 02155, 617-396-2900 (Carol Lederman, Rep.)

EIGHTH DISTRICT

Joseph Patrick Kennedy II (D)

District: Portions of Boston and suburbs including city of Cambridge. Population: 601,643— Black 23%, Asian 6%, Hispanic 11%. Politics: Democratic.

Born Sept. 24, 1952, Boston; home, Brighton; University of Mass., B.A. 1976; Roman Catholic; divorced, 2 children.

Elected 1986. Career: Peace Corps, 1974; Community Services Administration, 1977–79; Founder & President, Citizens Energy Corp., 1979–86.

Committees: (1) Banking, Finance & Urban Affairs; (2) Veterans Affairs.

Election Results: 1992 Kennedy 114,125 (83%); Alice Nakash (I) 23,795 (17%). 1990 Kennedy (75%). 1988 Kennedy (80%).

Interest Group Ratings:

ADA	ACU	COPE	COC
95	08	83	25

LCV	NTLC	CFA	ASC
100	00	100	50

Office: 1210 LHOB 20515, 202-225-5111 (Michael Powell, AA). DISTRICT OFFICE: 605 The Schrafft Ctr., 529 Main St., Charlestown 02129, 617-242-0200 (Frank Castello, Dist. Dir.)

NINTH DISTRICT

John Joseph Moakley (D)

District: Boston and near southern suburbs. Population: 601,643—Black 7%, Hispanic 5%. Politics: Democratic.

Born Apr. 27, 1927, Boston; home, Boston; University of Miami, Suffolk University, LL.B. 1956; Roman Catholic; married (Evelyn).

Elected 1972. Career: Navy, WWII; Mass. House of Reps., 1953–65, Major., Whip, 1957; Practicing atty., 1957–72; Mass. Senate, 1965–69; Boston City Cncl. 1971.

Committee: (1) Rules (Chairman).

Election Results: 1992 Moakley 175,187 (76%); Martin Conboy (R) 54,061 (24%). 1990 Moakley (71%). 1988 Moakley (Unopposed).

Interest Group Ratings:

ADA	ACU	COPE	COC
85	04	92	25

LCV	NTLC	CFA	ASC
50	05	93	30

Office: 235 CHOB 20515, 202-225-8273 (John Weinfurter, AA). DISTRICT OFFICES: 220 World Trade Ctr., Boston 02210, 617-565-2920 (Roger Kineavy, Dist. Mgr.); 4 Court St., Taunton 02780, 508-824-6676 (Karen Pacheco, Asst.); Fed Bldg. 166 Main St., Brockton 02401, 508-587-6053 (Joe Moynihan, Rep.)

TENTH DISTRICT

Gerry Eastman Studds (D)

District: South Shore Boston suburbs, southeast corner of the state including Cape Cod. Population: 601,642—Black 2%. Politics: Leans Democratic.

Born May 12, 1937, Mineola, N.Y.; home, Cohasset; Yale University, B.A. 1959, M.A.T. 1961; Episcopalian; single.

Elected 1972. Career: U.S. Foreign Service, 1961–62; Assistant, Domestic Peace Corps consultant, 1962–63; Legislative Assistant to U.S. Sen. Harrison J. Williams, 1964; Prep. school teacher, 1965–69

Committees: (1) Energy & Commerce; (2) Merchant Marine & Fisheries.

Election Results: 1992 Studds 188,720 (62%); Daniel Daly (R) 75,686 (25%); Jon Bryan (I) 39,111 (13%). 1990 Studds (52%). 1988 Studds (67%).

Interest Group Ratings:

ADA	ACU	COPE	COC
100	00	83	25

LCV	NTLC	CFA	ASC
88	00	100	20

Office: 237 CHOB 20515, 202-225-3111 (Steven Schwadron, AA). DISTRICT OFFICES: 225 Water St. #201, Plymouth 02360, 508-747-5500 (vacant, Rep.); 1212 Hancock St., Quincy 02169, 617-770-3700 (Mary Lou Butler, Rep.,); 146 Main St., Hyannis 02601, 508-771-0666 (Mark Forest, Rep.)

MICHIGAN

Michigan politics in 1993–94 is entering an interesting cycle. Democratic Sen. Donald W. Riegle, one of the Keating Five—so named for their dealings with the deposed S&L kingpin, is up for reelection and Republicans think he is very vulnerable. But their ability to defeat him will depend on the quality of opponent they will put up. In the past, the Michigan GOP has had problems getting first class candidates willing to take on a Senate incumbent. Democrats, meantime, believe that they will be able to defeat first term Republican Gov. John Engler, who won in an upset four years ago. Here again, the problem is finding a first class opponent. If the Democrats can, it will be a tight race.

1992 PRESIDENTIAL ELECTION: (18 Electoral votes): Clinton (D) 1,868,709 (44%); Bush (R) 1,559,713 (36%); Perot (I) 822,461 (19%); Marrou (Lib) 10,115; Phillips (AmTax) 8,348; Hagelin (NLP) 3,593; Halyard (WksLg) 1,466. 1988 Bush 1,969,435 (54%); Dukakis 1,673,496 (46%).

SENATORS
Donald W. Riegle, Jr. (D)

Born Feb. 4, 1938, Flint; home, Flint; Flint Jr. College, Western Mich. University, University of Mich., B.A. 1960, Mich. St. University, M.B.A. 1961, Harvard University, 1964–66; United Methodist; married (Lori), 5 children.

Elected 1976, seat up 1994. Career: Sr. Financial Analyst, IBM Corp., 1961–64; Faculty Mbr., Mich. St. University, Boston University, Harvard University, University of Southern Calif.; U.S. House of Reps., 1966–76.

Committees: (1) Banking, Housing & Urban Affairs (Chairman); (2) Budget; (3) Finance.

Election Results: 1988 Riegle 2,116,865 (60%); Jim Dunn (R) 1,348,216 (39%). 1982 Riegle (58%).

Interest Group Ratings:

ADA	ACU	COPE	COC
95	04	92	38

LCV	NTLC	CFA	ASC
75	11	83	40

Office: 105 DSOB 20510, 202-224-4822 (David

Krawitz, AA). STATE OFFICES: 1155 Brewery Park Blvd. Suite 343, Detroit 48207, 313-226-3188 (Cecilia Walker, Dir.); 30800 Van Dyke, 3rd floor, Warren 48093, 313-573-9017 (Bill Wenzell, Dir.); Suite 910, 352 Saginaw St., Flint 48502, 313-766-5115 (Jill Weide, Rep.); Suite 705, 109 W. Michigan Ave., Lansing 48933, 517-377-1713 (Ginny Haas, Rep.); 716 Fed. Bldg., Grand Rapids 49503, 616-456-2592 (Brad Miller, Rep.); 309 E. Front St., Traverse City 49685, 616-946-1300 (Christopher Wright, Rep.); 323 Post Off. Bldg., 200 W. Washington, Marquette 49855, 906-228-7457 (John Nelson, Rep.)

Carl M. Levin (D)

Born June 28, 1934, Detroit; home, Detroit; Swarthmore College, B.A. 1956, Harvard University, LL.B. 1959; Jewish; married (Barbara), 3 children.

Elected 1978, seat up 1996. Career: Practicing atty; Asst. Atty. Gen. of Mich. & Gen. Counsel for the Mich. Civil Rights Comm., 1964–67; Spec. Asst. Atty. Gen. of Mich. & Chief Appellate Defender for the City of Detroit, 1967–69; Detroit City Cncl., 1969–78, Pres., 1973–78.

Committees: (1) Armed Services; (2) Governmental Affairs; (3) Small Business.

Election Results: 1990 Levin 1,450,331 (58%); Bill Schuette (R) 1,036,140 (42%). 1984 Levin (52%).

Interest Group Ratings:

ADA	ACU	COPE	COC
100	00	92	20

LCV	NTLC	CFA	ASC
75	11	100	40

Office: 459 RSOB 20510, 202-224-6221 (Gordon Kerr, AA). STATE OFFICES: 1860 Fed. Bldg., 477 Michigan Ave., Detroit 48226, 313-226-6020 (Kelvin Smyth, Mich. Dir.); 102 Fed. Bldg., 145 Water St., Alpena 49707, 517-354-5520 (Thad McCollum, Asst.); 623 Ludington, Suite 200, Escanaba 49829, 906-789-0052 (Vacant, Rep.); 134 Fed. Bldg., 110 Michigan Ave. NW, Grand Rapids 49503, 616-456-2531 (Richard Tormala, Rep.); 116 W. Ottawa St., Suite 402, Lansing 48933, 517-377-1508 (James Turner, Rep.,); 301

E. Genessee St., Suite 101, Saginaw 48607, 517-754-4562 (James Turner, Rep.); 24580 Cunningham, Rm. 110, Warren 48091, 313-759-0477 (David Loosing, Rep.)

REPRESENTATIVES

FIRST DISTRICT

Bart Stupak, (D)

District: The Northern quarter of the state including the entire Upper Peninsula. Population: 580,956. Politics: Mixed.

Born Feb. 29, 1952, Milwaukee, Wis.; home Menominee; Northwest Mich. Community College, A.A. 1972, Saginaw Valley State, B.S. 1977, Thomas Cooley Law School, J.D. 1981; Roman Catholic; married (Laurie), 2 children.

Elected 1992. Career: State Police Officer, 1973–84; Attorney, 1984–92; State Rep., 1989–90.

Committees: (1) Armed Services; (2) Merchant Marine & Fisheries.

Election Results: 1992 Stupak 144,930 (55%); Phil Ruppe (R) 116,948 (45%).

Interest Group Ratings:
None—Freshman

Office: 317 CHOB 20515, 202-225-4735 (Ann Beser, AA). DISTRICT OFFICES: 160 E. State St., Traverse City 49684, 616-929-4711 (Scott Schloegel, Rep.); 1229 W. Washington, Marquette 49855, 906-228-3700 (Glenda Gray, Rep.); 2501 14th Ave. S., Escanaba 49829, 906-786-4504 (Cindy Frazer, Rep.)

SECOND DISTRICT

Peter Hoekstra (R)

District: Western part of the state including cities of Muskegon and Holland. Population: 580,956—Black 4%. Politics: Republican.

Born Oct. 30, 1930, Groningen, The Netherlands; home, Holland; Hope College, B.A. 1975, University of Mich., M.B.A. 1977; Christian Reformed; married (Diane), 3 children.

Elected 1992. Career: businessman, V.P., Herman Miller Inc., 1977–92.

Committees: (1) Education & Labor; (2) Public Works & Transportation.

Election Results: 1992 Hoekstra 152,282 (63%); John Miltner (D) 84,179 (35%); Dick Jacobs (Libert) 4,731 (2%).

Interest Group Ratings:
None—Freshman

Office: 1319 LHOB 20515, 202-225-4401 (Doug Coopman, AA). DISTRICT OFFICES: 42 W. 10th St., Holland 49423, 616-395-0030; 900 3rd St. #203, Muskegon 49440, 616-722-8386; 120 W. Harris St., Cadillac 49601, 616-775-0050.

THIRD DISTRICT

Paul Brentwood Henry (R)

District: South central part of the state including all of Kent and Ionia counties and city of Grand Rapids as well as parts of Barry county. Population: 580,956—Black 7%, Hispanic 3%. Politics: Republican.

Born July 9, 1942, Chicago, Ill.; home, Grand Rapids; Wheaton College, B.A. 1963, Duke University, M.A. 1968, Ph.D. 1970; Christian Reformed; married (Karen), 3 children.

Elected 1984. Career: Peace Corps, 1963–65; Acting Dir., Republican Conf., 1969; Instructor, Duke University, 1969–70; Prof., Calvin College, 1970–78; Mbr., Mich. Bd. of Ed., 1975–78; Mich. House of Reps., 1979–82; Mich. Senate, 1983–84.

Committees: (1) Education & Labor; (2) Science, Space & Technology.

Election Results: 1992 Henry (R) 164,518 (63%); Carol Kooistra (D) 96,666 (37%). 1990 Henry (75%). 1988 Henry (73%).

Interest Group Ratings:

ADA	ACU	COPE	COC
35	80	58	88

LCV	NTLC	CFA	ASC
44	65	33	90

Office: 1526 LHOB 20515, 202-225-3831 (Mary Lobisco, AA). DISTRICT OFFICE: 166 Fed. Bldg., 110 Michigan Ave., Grand Rapids 49503, 616-451-8383 (Anne Knox, Dist. Adm.)

FOURTH DISTRICT

David Camp (R)

District: Wide portion of north central Michigan including city of Midland. Population: 580,956. Politics: Republican.

Born July 9, 1953, Midland; home, Midland; Albion College, B.A. 1975, University of Calif. (San Diego), J.D., 1978; Roman Catholic; single.

Elected 1990. Career: Atty. priv. prac. 1978–90; A.A. to U.S. Rep. Bill Schuette 1984–87.

Committees: (1) Ways and Means.

Election Results: 1992 Camp 157,032 (64%); Lisa Donaldson (D) 87,662 (36%). 1990 Camp (66%).

Interest Group Ratings:

ADA	ACU	COPE	COC
05	84	25	75

LCV	NTLC	CFA	ASC
13	75	27	100

Office: 137 CHOB 20515, 202-225-3561 (John Guzik, AA). DISTRICT OFFICES: 135 Ashman, Midland 48640, 517-631-2552 (Scott Haines, Dist. Dir.); Matthews Building, 308 West Main Street, Owosso 48867, 517-723-6759; 3508 W. Houghton Lake Dr. #1, Houghton Lake 48629, 517-366-4922 (Karin Boven, Rep.)

FIFTH DISTRICT

James A. Barcia (D)

District: Eastern part of the state including cities of Saginaw and Bay City. Population: 580,956 —Black 8%, Hispanic 3%. Politics: Leans Democratic.

Born Feb. 25, 1952, Bay City; home Bay City; Saginaw Valley State, B.A. 1974; Roman Catholic; married (Vicki).

Elected 1992. Career: Service Coordinator, Mich. Community Blood Ctr., 1974–75; State Rep., 1977–82; State Sen., 1983–92.

Committees: (1) Public Works & Transportation; (2) Science, Space & Technology.

Election Results: 1992 Barcia 147,657 (61%); Keith Muxlow (R) 92,791 (39%).

Interest Group Ratings:
None—Freshman

Office: 1717 LHOB 20515, 202-225-8171 (Roger Szemarj, AA). DISTRICT OFFICES: 301 E. Genesee #502, Saginaw 48607, 517-754-6075 (Jim Lewis, Rep.); 3741 E. Wilder Rd., Bay City 48706, 517-667-0003 (Deborah Zarazua, Rep.); 5409 Pierson Rd., Flushing 48433, 313-732-7501 (Mark Salogar, Rep.)

SIXTH DISTRICT

Frederick S. Upton (R)

District: Southwest corner of the state including cities of Kalamazoo, Benton Harbor and St. Joseph. Population: 580,956—Black 10%. Politics: Republican.

Born Apr. 23, 1953, St. Joseph; home, St. Joseph; University of Mich., B.A. 1975; Protestant; married (Amey), 2 children.

Elected 1986. Career: Staff of U.S. Rep. David Stockman, 1976–80; Dir., Leg. Affairs, Office of Mgt. & Budget, 1981–85.

Committees: (1) Energy and Commerce.

Election Results: 1992 Upton 143,943 (62%); Andy Davis (D) 89,020 (38%). 1990 Upton (58%). 1988 Upton (71%).

Interest Group Ratings:

ADA	ACU	COPE	COC
30	72	50	88

LCV	NTLC	CFA	ASC
25	70	40	100

Office: 2439 LHOB 20515, 202-225-3761 (Joan Hillebrands, AA). DISTRICT OFFICES: 421 Main St., St. Joseph 49085, 616-982-1986 (Jack Baker, Dist. Adm.); 535 S. Burdick #225, Kalamazoo 49007, 616-385-0039 (Jeff Breneman, Rep.)

SEVENTH DISTRICT

Nick Smith (R)

District: Southern part of the state including cities of Jackson and Battle Creek. Population: 580,957—Black 6%. Politics: Republican.

Born Nov. 5, 1934, Addison; home, Addison; Mich. State, B.A. 1957, University of Del., M.S.

1959; Congregationalist; married (Bonnalyn), 4 children.

Elected 1992. Career U.S. Air Force, 1959–61; Dir. of Energy, U.S. Dept. of Agriculture, 1972–74; State Rep., 1978–82; State Sen. 1982–92.

Committees: (1) Budget; (2) Science, Space & Technology.

Election Results: 1992 Smith 133,323 (87%); Kenneth Proctor (Libert) 20,071 (13%).

Interest Group Ratings:
None—Freshman

Office: 1708 LHOB 20515, 202-225-6276 (Rob Hartwell, AA). DISTRICT OFFICES: 209 E. Washington #200 D, Jackson 49201, 517-783-4486 (Brian Phiede, Rep.); 121 S. Cochran Ave., Charlotte 48813, 517-543-0055 (Mary Douglas, Dist. Adm.)

EIGHTH DISTRICT

Robert Carr (D)

District: South central part of the state including city of Lansing. Population: 580,956—Black 6%, Hispanic 3%. Politics: Leans Democratic.

Born Mar. 27, 1943, Janesville, Wis.; home, Okemos; University of Wis., B.S. 1965, J.D. 1968, Mich. State University, 1968–69; Baptist; married (Kate), 2 children.

Elected 1982. Career: Staff Mbr., Mich. Senate Minor. Ldr.'s Ofc., 1968–69; A.A. to Atty. Gen. of Mich., 1969–70; Asst. Atty. Gen. of Mich., 1970–72; U.S. House of Reps., 1975–81.

Committees: Appropriations.

Election Results: 1992 Carr (D) 135,491 (51%); Dick Chrysler (R) 131,804 (49%). 1990 Carr (Unopposed). 1988 Carr (59%).

Interest Group Ratings:

ADA	ACU	COPE	COC
70	22	75	57

LCV	NTLC	CFA	ASC
25	20	60	50

Office: 2347 RHOB 20515, 202-225-4872 (Howard Edelson, Chief-of-staff). DISTRICT OFFICES: 2848 E. Grand River, Suite 1, East Lansing 48823, 517-351-7203 (Carol Conn, Dist. AA);

3487 Linden Rd. Suite D, Flint 48507, 313-230-0873 (Eddie McDonald, Rep.)

NINTH DISTRICT

Dale E. Kildee (D)

District: Eastern central part of the state including cities of Flint and Pontiac. Population: 580,956—Black 32%, Hispanic 3%. Politics: Democratic.

Born Sept. 16, 1929, Flint; home, Flint; Sacred Heart Seminary, Detroit, B.A. 1952, University of Mich., M.A. 1961, Rotary Fellow, University of Peshawar, Pakistan; Roman Catholic; married (Gayle), 3 children.

Elected 1976. Career: High school teacher, 1954–64; Mich. House of Reps., 1965–75; Mich. Senate, 1975–77.

Committees: (1) Budget; (2) Education & Labor.

Election Results: 1992 Kildee 133,980 (54%); Megan O'Neill (R) 112,322 (46%). 1990 Kildee (68%). 1988 Kildee (76%).

Interest Group Ratings:

ADA	ACU	COPE	COC
90	04	92	25

LCV	NTLC	CFA	ASC
75	00	93	30

Office: 2239 RHOB 20515, 202-225-3611 (Christopher Mansour, Chief-of-staff). DISTRICT OFFICES: 316 W. Water St. Flint 48503, 313-239-1437 (Gary Sullenger, Dist. Dir.); 1829 N. Perry St., Pontiac 48340, 313-373-9337.

TENTH DISTRICT

David E. Bonior (D)

District: Counties just northeast of Detroit including city of Port Huron. Population: 580,956—Black 2%. Politics: Leans Republican.

Born June 6, 1945, Hamtramck; home, Mt. Clemens; University of Iowa, B.A. 1967, Chapman College, M.A. 1972; Roman Catholic; married (Judy), 2 children.

Elected 1976. Career: Probation officer & adoption caseworker, 1967–68; Air Force, 1968–72; Mich. House of Reps., 1973–77.

Committee: (1) Rules.

Election Results: 1992 Bonior 134,946 (55%); Douglas Carl (R) 111,776 (45%). 1990 Bonior (66%). 1988 Bonior (54%).

Interest Group Ratings:

ADA	ACU	COPE	COC
80	00	91	29

LCV	NTLC	CFA	ASC
69	00	73	30

Office: 2207 RHOB 20515, 202-225-2106 (Sarah Dufendach, AA). DISTRICT OFFICES: 59 N. Walnut, Suite 305, Mt. Clemens 48043, 313-469-3232 (Christine Koch, AA); 526 Water St., Port Huron 48060, 313-987-8889 (Tim Morse, Asst.)

ELEVENTH DISTRICT

Joe Knollenberg (R)

District: Parts of Oakland and Wayne counties northwest of Detroit, including portions of Livonia and Southfield. Population: 580,956—Black 4%. Politics: Republican.

Born Nov. 28, 1933, Mattoon, Ill.; home, Bloomfield Hills; E. Ill. University, B.S. 1955; Roman Catholic; married (Sandra), 2 children.

Elected 1992. Career: Army, 1955–57; Owner Troy Allstate Insurance, 1962–92.

Committees: (1) Banking, Finance & Urban Affairs; (2) Small Business.

Election Results: 1992 Knollenberg 166,982 (59%); Walter Briggs (D) 117,030 (41%).

Interest Group Ratings:
None—Freshman

Office: 1218 LHOB 20515, 202-225-5802 (Paul Welday, AA). DISTRICT OFFICES: 30833 Northwestern Hwy. #214, Farmington Hills 48334, 313-851-1366 (Pat Wierzeick, Rep.); 15439 Meddlebelt Rd., Livonia 48154, 313-425-7557 (Denise Radpke, Rep.)

TWELFTH DISTRICT

Sander Martin Levin (D)

District: Northern Detroit suburbs including cities of Warren and Sterling Heights. Population: 580,956—Black 4%. Politics: Leans Democratic.

Born Sept. 6, 1931, Detroit; home, Southfield; University of Chicago, B.A. 1952, Columbia University, M.A. 1954, Harvard University, LL.B. 1957; Jewish; married (Victoria), 4 children.

Elected 1982. Career: Practicing atty.; Oakland Bd. of Sprvrs., 1961–64; Mich. Senate, 1964–70; Adj. Prof., Wayne St. University, 1971–74; Asst. Admin., Agency for Intl. Develop., 1977–81.

Committees: Ways & Means.

Election Results: 1992 Levin 137,615 (54%); John Pappageorge (R) 119,448 (46%). 1990 Levin (68%). 1988 Levin (70%).

Interest Group Ratings:

ADA	ACU	COPE	COC
95	04	83	38

LCV	NTLC	CFA	ASC
75	00	93	20

Office: 106 CHOB 20515, 202-225-4961 (vacant, AA). DISTRICT OFFICE: 2107 E. 14 Mile Rd. #130, Sterling Heights 48310, 313-268-4444 (Dan Mulhern, Rep.)

THIRTEENTH DISTRICT

William David Ford (D)

District: Western Detroit suburbs including city of Ann Arbor. Population: 580,956—Black 11%, Hispanic 2%. Politics: Leans Democratic.

Born Aug. 6, 1927, Detroit; home, Taylor; Wayne State University, 1947–48, NE St. Teachers College, University of Denver, B.S. 1949, J.D. 1951; United Church of Christ; married (Mary), 2 children.

Elected 1964. Career: Navy, 1944–46; Practicing atty., 1951–60; Taylor Township Justice of the Peace, 1955–57; Melvindale City Atty., 1957–59; Mich. Senate, 1962–64.

Committees: (1) Education & Labor (Chairman).

Election Results: 1992 Ford 119,072 (53%); Robert Geake (R) 103,497 (47%). 1990 Ford (63%). 1988 Ford (64%).

Interest Group Ratings:

ADA	ACU	COPE	COC
95	00	100	25

LCV	NTLC	CFA	ASC
50	00	73	20

Office: 2107 RHOB 20515, 202-225-6261 (David Geiss, AA). DISTRICT OFFICES: Fed. Bldg., 3716 Newberry St., Wayne 48184, 313-722-1411 (Patricia Tallmadge, Dist. Mgr.); 31 S. Huron St., Ypsilanti 48197. 313-482-6636 (Dee Dogan, Asst.)

FOURTEENTH DISTRICT

John Conyers, Jr. (D)

District: North Central Detroit including some suburbs including Highland Park. Population: 580,956—Black 69%. Politics: Democratic.

Born May 16, 1929, Detroit; home, Detroit; Wayne St. University, B.A. 1957, LL.B. 1958; Baptist; married (Monica), 1 child.

Elected 1964. Career: Army, Korea; Legis. Asst. to U.S. Rep. John D. Dingell, 1958–61; Practicing atty., 1959–61; Referee, Mich. Workmen's Compensation Dept., 1961–63.

Committees: (1) Government Operations (Chairman); (2) Judiciary. (3) Small Business.

Election Results: 1992 Conyers 165,172 (84%); John Gordon (R) 32,054 (16%). 1990 Conyers (91%). 1988 Conyers (91%).

Interest Group Ratings:

ADA	ACU	COPE	COC
90	00	89	13

LCV	NTLC	CFA	ASC
81	05	73	10

Office: 2426 RHOB 20515, 202-225-5126 (Joan Gorman, AA). DISTRICT OFFICE: 669 Fed. Bldg., 231 W. Lafayette St., Detroit 48226, 313-961-5670 (Roy Plowden, Chief-of-staff)

FIFTEENTH DISTRICT

Barbara-Rose Collins (D)

District: Central Detroit and some suburbs including Grosse Pointe. Population: 580,956—Black 70%, Hispanic 4%. Politics: Democratic.

Born Apr. 13, 1939, Detroit; home, Detroit; Wayne St. Univ.; Pan African Orthodox Church; widow, 2 children.

Elected 1990. Career: Detroit Sch. Bd., 1970–73; Mich. House 1975–81; Det. City Cncl., 1982–90.

Committees: (1) Public Works and Transportation; (2) Post Office and Civil Service; (3) Government Operations.

Election Results: 1992 Collins 148,755 (82%); Charles Vincent (R) 31,564 (18%). 1990 Collins (88%).

Interest Group Ratings:

ADA	ACU	COPE	COC
95	00	90	13

LCV	NTLC	CFA	ASC
63	00	87	10

Office: 1108 LHOB 20515, 202-225-2261 (Miniard Culpepper, AA). DISTRICT OFFICE: 1155 Brewery Park Blvd. #353, Detroit 48207, 313-567-2233 (vacant, Rep.)

SIXTEENTH DISTRICT

John D. Dingell (D)

District: Detroit suburbs of southeast Wayne County and Monroe County. Population: 580,956. Politics: Mixed, but leans Democratic.

Born July 8, 1926, Colorado Springs, Colo.; home, Trenton; Georgetown University, B.S. 1949, LL.D. 1952; Roman Catholic; married (Deborah), 4 children.

Elected Dec. 13, 1955. Career: Army, WWII; Park ranger; Practicing atty., 1952–55; Wayne Cnty. Asst. Prosecuting Atty., 1953–55.

Committees: Energy & Commerce (Chairman).

Election Results: 1992 Dingell 156,964 (67%); Frank Beaumont (R) 75,694 (33%). 1990 Dingell (67%). 1988 Dingell (97%).

Interest Group Ratings:

ADA	ACU	COPE	COC
90	00	83	25

LCV	NTLC	CFA	ASC
38	00	87	50

Office: 2328 RHOB 20515, 202-225-4071 (Marda Robilliard, AA). DISTRICT OFFICES: 5461 Schaefer Rd., Dearborn 48126, 313-846-1276 (Connie Shorter, Rep.); 241 E. Elm, Suite 105, Monroe 48161, 313-243-1849 (Donna Hoffer, Asst.)

MINNESOTA

Incumbent GOP Sen. David F. Durenberger has been indicted on fraud charges, and even if he is found not guilty, it will certainly hinder his ability to run for reelection in 1994. If he runs, he will likely be challenged in the GOP primary, and Democrats are lining up to take him on. Likewise, Republican Gov. Arne Carlson, a narrow winner in 1990, is also up for reelection. The Democrats' biggest problem may be to figure out who to put in which race.

1992 PRESIDENTIAL ELECTION: (10 Electoral votes): Clinton (D) 1,019,901 (44%); Bush (R) 746,622 (32%); Perot (I) 561,589 (24%); Marrou (Lib) 3,287; Gritz (Pop) 3,237; Herer (GrassRts) 2,587; Hagelin (NLP) 1,395; Warren (Soc.Wks) 984; Fulani (NAP) 950; Phillips (AmTax) 703; LaRouche (Ind) 597. 1988 Dukakis 1,106,975 (54%); Bush 958,199 (46%).

SENATORS

David F. Durenberger (R)

Born Aug. 19, 1934, Collegeville; home Minneapolis; St. John's University, B.A. 1955, University of Minn., J.D. 1959; Roman Catholic; 4 children.

Elected 1978, seat up 1994. Career: Army, 1955–57; Practicing atty., 1959–66; Exec. Secy. to Gov. Harold LeVander, 1967–71; Mgr., Intl. Licensing Div., H.B. Fuller Co., 1971–78.

Committees: (1) Environment & Public Works; (2) Finance; (3) Labor & Human Resources.

Election Results: 1988 Durenberger 1,176,210 (56%); Hubert H. Humphrey III (DFL) 856,694 (41%). 1982 Durenberger (53%).

Interest Group Ratings:

ADA	ACU	COPE	COC
25	42	50	60

LCV	NTLC	CFA	ASC
50	56	75	80

Office: 154 RSOB 20510, 202-224-3244 (Rick Evans, Chief-of-staff). STATE OFFICE: 1020 Plymouth Bldg., 12 S. 6th St., Minneapolis 55402, 612-370-3382 (Bill Fritts, Mgr.)

Paul Wellstone (DFL)

Born July 21, 1944, Washington, D.C.; home, Northfield; University of North Carolina, B.A., 1965, Ph.D. 1969; Jewish; married (Sheila), 3 children.

Elected 1990; seat up 1996. Career: professor, Carleton College.

Committees: (1) Energy & Natural Resources; (2) Labor and Human Resources; (3) Small Business; (4) Select Committee on Indian Affairs.

Election Results: 1990 Wellstone 833,252 (52%), Rudy Boschwitz (Incumbent R) 784,658 (48%).

Interest Group Ratings:

ADA	ACU	COPE	COC
100	00	92	10

LCV	NTLC	CFA	ASC
100	11	100	40

Office: 717 HSOB 20510, 202-224-5641 (Kari Moe, Chief-of-staff). STATE OFFICES: 2550 University Ave., St. Paul 55101, 612-645-0323 (Jeff Blodgett, St. Dir.); 105 2nd Ave. S., VA 55792, 218-741-1075 (Kim Stokes, Rep.); 417 Litchfield Ave. SW, Williams 56201, 612-231-0001 (Tom Meium, Rep.)

REPRESENTATIVES

FIRST DISTRICT

Timothy J. Penny (DFL)

District: Southeastern counties including cities of Rochester and Austin. Population: 546,887. Politics: Mixed, but leans Democrat Farm Labor.

Born Nov. 19, 1951, Albert Lea; home New Richland; Winona State University, B.A. 1974; University of Minnesota; Lutheran; married (Barbara), 4 children.

Elected 1982. Career: Minn. Senate, 1976–82.

Committees: (1) Agriculture; (2) Veterans Affairs.

Election Results: 1992 Penny 205,704 (74%); Timothy Droogsma (R) 72,600 (26%). 1990 Penny (78%). 1988 Penny (70%).

Interest Group Ratings:

ADA	ACU	COPE	COC
45	53	50	50

LCV	NTLC	CFA	ASC
69	40	53	60

Office: 436 CHOB 20515, 202-225-2472 (Steven Bosacker, AA). DISTRICT OFFICES: 108 W. Park Square, Owatonna 55060, 507-455-9151 (Jim Hagerty, Dist. Mgr.)

SECOND DISTRICT

David Minge (D)

District: Southwestern quarter of the state. Population: 546,887. Politics: Republican.

Born Mar. 19, 1942, Clarkfield; home Montevideo; St. Olaf College, B.A. 1964, University of Chicago, J.D. 1967; Lutheran; married (Karen), 2 children.

Elected 1992. Career: Practicing atty., 1967–70, 1977–92; Law professor, 1970–77.

Committees: (1) Agriculture; (2) Science, Space & Technology.

Election Results: 1992 Minge 131,888 (50%); Cal Ludeman (R) 131,302 (50%).

Interest Group Ratings:
None—Freshman

Office: 1508 LHOB 20515, 202-225-2331 (Rick Jauert, AA). DISTRICT OFFICES: 542 1st St. S., Montevideo 56265, 612-269-9311 (Norma Brick-Samuelson, Rep.); 938 4th Ave. Box 367, Windom 56101, 507-831-0115 (Cheryl Thomas, Rep.); 108 E. 3rd St., Chaska 55318, 612-448-6567 (Kim Isenberg, Rep.)

THIRD DISTRICT

James Ramstad (R)

District: Southern and western Twin Cities suburbs, including city of Bloomington. Population: 546,888. Politics: Republican.

Born May 6, 1946, Jamestown, N.Dak.; home, Minnetonka; University of Minn., B.A. 1968, George Washington University, J.D., 1973; Protestant; single.

Elected 1990. Career: Lawyer; U.S. Army 1973–75; Aide Minn. St. House; Spec. Asst. U.S. Reps.

Tom Kleppe, Bill Frenzel; Adjunct prof. American University; priv. prac.; Minn. St. Senate, 1981–90.

Committees: (1) Judiciary; (2) Small Business.

Election Results: 1992 Ramstad 199,872 (66%); Paul Mandell (D) 104,431 (34%). 1990 Ramstad (66%).

Interest Group Ratings:

ADA	ACU	COPE	COC
30	68	42	75

LCV	NTLC	CFA	ASC
50	75	53	80

Office: 322 CHOB 20515, 202-225-2871 (Maybeth Christensen, AA). DISTRICT OFFICE: 8120 Pennsylvania Ave. S., Bloomington 55431, 612-881-4600 (Erik Paulsen, Rep.)

FOURTH DISTRICT

Bruce F. Vento (DFL)

District: St. Paul and suburbs. Population: 546,887—Black 4%, Hispanic 3%, Asian 5%. Politics: Leans Democratic.

Born Oct. 7, 1940, St. Paul; home St. Paul; University of Minnesota, A.A. 1961; Wis. State University, B.S. 1965; Roman Catholic; married (Mary Jean), 3 children.

Elected 1976. Career: Teacher, 1965–76; Minn. House of Reps., 1971–77, Asst. Major. Ldr., 1974–76.

Committees: (1) Banking, Finance & Urban Affairs; (2) Natural Resources.

Election Results: 1992 Vento 159,326 (61%); Ian Maitland (R) 101,313 (39%). 1990 Vento (65%). 1988 Vento (72%).

Interest Group Ratings:

ADA	ACU	COPE	COC
100	00	92	25

LCV	NTLC	CFA	ASC
94	00	87	30

Office: 2304 RHOB 20515, 202-225-6631 (Lawrence Romans, AA). DISTRICT OFFICE: Galtier Plaza, 175 5th St. East, St. Paul 55101, 612-290-3724 (Cathy Hope, Dist. Dir.)

FIFTH DISTRICT

Martin Olav Sabo (DFL)

District: Minneapolis and suburbs. Population: 546,887—Black 10%, Asian 4%. Politics: Leans Democrat Farm Labor.

Born Feb. 28, 1938, Crosby, N.Dak.; home Minneapolis; Augsburg College, B.A. 1959, University of Minn.; Lutheran; married (Sylvia), 2 children.

Elected 1978. Career: Minn. House of Reps., 1961–79, Minor. Ldr., 1969–73, Spkr., 1973–79.

Committee: (1) Appropriations; (2) Budget (Chairman); (3) Select Committee on Intelligence.

Election Results: 1992 Sabo 174,027 (69%); Stephen Moriarty (R) 77,059 (31%). 1990 Sabo (73%). 1988 Sabo (72%).

Interest Group Ratings:

ADA	ACU	COPE	COC
100	00	92	25

LCV	NTLC	CFA	ASC
81	05	100	30

Office: 2336 RHOB 20515, 202-225-4755 (Michael Erlandson, AA). DISTRICT OFFICE: 462 Fed. Courts Bldg., 110 S. 4th St., Minneapolis 55401, 612-348-1649 (Kathleen Anderson, Mgr.)

SIXTH DISTRICT

Rod Grams (R)

District: Northern Twin Cities suburbs. Population: 546,888. Politics: Leans Democrat Farm Labor.

Born Feb. 4, 1948, Princeton; home, Anoka; Carroll College, 1975; Lutheran; married (Laurel), 4 children.

Elected 1992. Career: Engineering Consultant, 1968–74; News Anchor and Producer, 1974–91; President Sun Ridge Builders, 1991–92.

Committees: (1) Banking, Finance & Urban Affairs; (2) Science, Space & Technology.

Election Results: 1992 Grams 133,349 (47%); Gerry Sikorski (D) (Incumbent) 99,769 (35%); Dean Barkley (I) 48,213 (17%).

Interest Group Ratings:
None—Freshman

Office: 1713 LHOB 20515, 202-225-2271 (Chris Erikstrump, AA). DISTRICT OFFICE: 2013 2nd Ave. N., Anoka 55303, 612-427-5921 (Barb Sykora, Dist. Dir.)

SEVENTH DISTRICT

Collin C. Peterson (DFL)

District: Northwestern quarter of the state including towns of St. Cloud and Moorhead. Population: 546,888. Politics: Leans Democrat Farm Labor.

Born June 29, 1944, Fargo, N.Dak.; home, Detroit Lakes; Lutheran; divorced, 3 children.

Elected 1990. Career: Accountant; Minn. Senate, 1977–86.

Committees: (1) Agriculture; (2) Government Operations.

Election Results: 1992 Peterson 133,737 (51%); Bernie Omann (R) 129,973 (49%). 1990 Peterson (54%).

Interest Group Ratings:

ADA	ACU	COPE	COC
65	24	75	63

LCV	NTLC	CFA	ASC
63	25	80	60

Office: 1133 LHOB 20515, 202-225-2165 (Rebecca Donovan, Asst.). DISTRICT OFFICES: 714 Lake Ave., Suite 107, Detroit Lakes 56501, 218-847-3133 (Sharon Jasperson, Dir.); Fed. Bldg., 720 W. Germain, St. Cloud 56301, 612-259-0559; Minn. Wheat Growers Bldg., Red Lake Falls 56750, (Willis Eken, Rep.); 3333 W. Division #210, St. Cloud 56301, 612-259-0599 (Mike Sullivan, Rep.)

EIGHTH DISTRICT

James L. Oberstar (DFL)

District: Northeast quarter of the state including city of Duluth. Population: 546,887. Politics: Leans Democrat Farm Labor.

Born Sept. 10, 1934, Chisholm; home Chisholm; College of St. Thomas, B.A. 1956, College of Europe, Bruges, Belgium, M.A. 1957; Roman Catholic; widower, 4 children.

Elected 1974. Career: Teacher, U.S. Navy, Haiti,

1959–63; Admin. Asst. to U.S. Rep. John A. Blatnik, 1963–74; Administrator, U.S. House of Reps. Committee on Public Works, 1971–74.

Committees: (1) Foreign Affairs; (2) Public Works & Transportation.

Election Results: 1992 Oberstar 144,958 (66%); Phil Herwig (R) 73,705 (34%). 1990 Oberstar (71%). 1988 Oberstar (75%).

Interest Group Ratings:

ADA	ACU	COPE	COC
90	04	92	25

LCV	NTLC	CFA	ASC
88	05	87	20

Office: 2366 RHOB 20515, 202-225-6211 (Tom Reagan, AA). DISTRICT OFFICES: 231 Fed. Bldg., 515 W. First St., Duluth 55802, 218-727-7474 (Jackie Morris, Asst.); City Hall, 316 W. Lake St., Chisholm 55719, 218-254-5761 (Deann Stish, Asst.); Brainerd City Hall, 501 Laurel St., Brainerd 56401, 218-828-4400 (Ken Hasskamp, Asst.)

MISSISSIPPI

Mississippi remains something of a political contradiction. All five of its congressmen are Democrats who won by wide margins. The current governor is a popular Democrat, as are most of its local office holders. But it votes Republican in presidential contests, and both its senators are Republicans. One, Sen. Trent Lott, should easily win reelection in 1994.

1992 PRESIDENTIAL ELECTION: (7 Electoral votes) Clinton (D) 392,929 (41%); Bush (R) 481,583 (50%); Perot (I) 84,496 (9%); Marrou (Lib) 2,788; Fulani (NAP) 2,591; Phillips (AmTax) 1,592; Hagelin (NLP) 1,140; Gritz (Pop) 504. 1988 Bush 551,745 (60%); Dukakis 360,892 (40%).

SENATORS

Thad Cochran (R)

Born Dec. 7, 1937, Pontotoc; home, Jackson; University of Miss., B.A. 1959, J.D. 1965, Rotary Fellow, Trinity College, Dublin, Ireland, 1963–64; Baptist; married (Rose), 2 children.

Elected 1978; seat up 1996. Career: Navy, 1959–61; Practicing atty., 1965–72; U.S. House of Reps., 1973–78.

Committees: (1) Agriculture, Nutrition & Forestry; (2) Appropriations; (3) Governmental Affairs; (4) Rules; (5) Select Committee on Indian Affairs.

Election Results: 1990 Cochran (Unopposed). 1984 Cochran (58%).

Interest Group Ratings:

ADA	ACU	COPE	COC
10	85	17	100

LCV	NTLC	CFA	ASC
00	65	25	90

Office: 326 RSOB 20510, 202-224-5054 (Margo Carlisle, Chief-of-staff). STATE OFFICE: 188 E. Capitol, Suite 614, Jackson 39201, 601-965-4459 (Wiley Carter, AA)

Trent Lott (R)

Born Oct. 9, 1941, Grenada; home, Pascagoula; University of Miss., B.A. 1963, J.D. 1967; Baptist; married (Patricia), 2 children.

Elected 1988; seat up 1994. Career: Practicing atty., 1967–68; A.A. to U.S. Rep. William M. Colmer, 1968–72; U.S. House of Reps., 1972–88.

Committees: (1) Armed Services; (2) Commerce, Science & Transportation; (3) Budget; (4) Special Committee on Organization of Congress; (5) Energy & Natural Resources.

Election Results: 1988 Lott 510,380 (54%); Wayne Dowdy (D) 436,339 (46%).

Interest Group Ratings:

ADA	ACU	COPE	COC
10	100	17	90

LCV	NTLC	CFA	ASC
00	78	25	100

Office: 487 RSOB 20510, 202-224-6253 (John Lundy, Chief-of-staff). STATE OFFICES: 245 E. Capitol St., Suite 226, Jackson 39201, 601-965-4644 (Guy Hovis, Rep.); 3100 S. Pascagoula St., Pascagoula 39567, 601-762-5400 (Bill Pope, Rep.); #1 Government Plaza, Suite 428, Gulfport 39503, 601-832-6126 (Bobby Thomas, Rep.); P.O. Box 1474, Oxford 38655, 601-234-3774 (Bill Canty, Rep.); 200 E. Washington St., Greenwood 38930, 601-453-5681 (Carolyn Overstreet, Rep.); 101 S. Lafayette, Starkville 39756, 601-323-1414 (Jack Miller, Rep.)

REPRESENTATIVES

FIRST DISTRICT

Jamie L. Whitten (D)

District: Northeastern part of the state including city of Tupelo. Population: 514,584—Black 23%. Politics: Democratic.

Born Apr. 18, 1910, Cascilla; home, Charleston; University of Miss.; Presbyterian; married (Rebecca), 2 children.

Elected 1941. Career: Practicing atty.; School principal; Miss. House of Reps., 1932–33; Dist. Prosecuting Atty., 17th Judicial Dist., 1933–41.

Committees: (1) Appropriations (Chairman).

Election Results: 1992 Whitten 120,987 (60%); Clyde Whitaker (R) 82,275 (40%). 1990 Whitten (65%). 1988 Whitten (78%).

Interest Group Ratings:

ADA	ACU	COPE	COC
50	29	78	50

LCV	NTLC	CFA	ASC
13	07	67	80

Office: 2314 RHOB 20515, 202-225-4306 (Hal DeCell, AA). DISTRICT OFFICES: P.O. Bldg., 3 N. Square, Charleston 38921, 601-647-2413 (Buddie Bishop, Dir.); Fed. Bldg, Oxford 38655, 601-234-9064 (Debbie Little, Rep.); Fed. Bldg., Tupelo 38801 (Billy Ballard, Rep.)

SECOND DISTRICT

Bernie Thompson (D)

District: Mississippi Delta country: the west-central part of the state including cities of Vicksburg and Greenville. Population: 514,845 —Black 63%. Politics: Democratic.

Born Jan. 28, 1948, Bolton; home, Bolton; Tougaloo College, B.A. 1968, Jackson State University, M.A. 1972; Methodist; married (London Johnson), 1 child.

Elected 1993. Career: Bolton Board of Aldermen, 1969–73; Mayor of Bolton, 1973–79; Hinds Cty. Supervisor, 1980-93.

Committees: (1) Agriculture; (2) Merchant Marine & Fisheries.

Election Results: 1993 (Special to replace Mike Espy, appointed Secretary of Agriculture) Thompson 71,432 (55%); Hayes Dent (R) 58,508 (45%).

Interest Group Ratings:
None—Freshman

Office: 1408 LHOB 20515, 202-225-5876 (Dave Craxton, AA). DISTRICT OFFICES: Not Yet Established.

THIRD DISTRICT

G.V. "Sonny" Montgomery (D)

District: East-central counties including Meridian. Population: 515,314—Black 31%. Politics: Democratic.

Born Aug. 5, 1920, Meridian; home, Meridian; Miss. St. University, B.S. 1943; Episcopalian; single.

Elected 1966. Career: Army, WWII & Korea; Owner, Montgomery Insur. Agcy.; Miss. Senate, 1956-66.

Committees: (1) Armed Services; (2) Veterans Affairs (Chairman).

Election Results: 1992 Montgomery 160,576 (81%); Michael Williams (R) 37,447 (19%). 1990 Montgomery (Unopposed). 1988 Montgomery (89%).

Interest Group Ratings:

ADA	ACU	COPE	COC
30	64	25	88

LCV	NTLC	CFA	ASC
06	55	40	100

Office: 2184 RHOB 20515, 202-225-5031 (Andre Clemandot, AA). DISTRICT OFFICES: Fed. Bldg., Meridian 39301, 601-693-6681 (Jeanette Noe, Dist. Rep.); Golden Triangle Airport, Columbus 39701, 601-327-2766 (Clara Peterson, Asst.); 110-D Airport Rd., Pearl 39208, 601-932-2410 (Daniel Kimbrough, Spec. Rep.)

FOURTH DISTRICT

Mike Parker (D)

District: Southwestern part of the state including city of Jackson. Population: 513,853—Black 41%. Politics: Democratic.

Born Oct. 31, 1949, Laurel; home, Brookhaven; William Carey College, B.A. 1970; Presbyterian; married (Rosemary), 3 children.

Elected 1988. Career: Owner, Brookhaven Funeral Home, Franklin-Parker Funeral Home, Consolidated Life Insurance Co.

Committees: (1) Budget; (2) Public Works & Transportation.

Election Results: 1992 Parker 131,660 (72%); Jack McMillan (R) 42,585 (23%); James Meredith (I) 9,013 (5%). 1990 Parker (81%). 1988 Parker (55%).

Interest Group Ratings:

ADA	ACU	COPE	COC
30	68	25	88

LCV	NTLC	CFA	ASC
13	60	33	100

Office: 1410 LHOB 20515, 202-225-5865 (Arthur Rhodes, AA). DISTRICT OFFICES: 245 E. Capitol St., Suite 222, Jackson 39201, 601-965-4085 (Ed Cole, Ex. AA); Chancery Ct. Annex, Columbia 39429, 601-731-1622 (Rick Hux, Rep.); 230 S. Whitworth St., Brookhaven 39601, 601-835-0706 (Sharon London, Asst.); 521 Main St., Natchez 39120, 601-446-7250 (Connie Merick, Rep.); 728 ½ Sawmill Rd., Laurel 39440, 601-425-4999 (Donna Gibbs, Rep.)

FIFTH DISTRICT

Gene Taylor (D)

District: Southeast corner of the state including Gulf Coast countries and cities of Hattiesburg and Biloxi. Population: 514,656—Black 20%. Politics: Democratic.

Born Sept. 17, 1953, New Orleans La.; home, Bay St. Louis; Tulane University, B.A., 1976; Roman Catholic; married (Margaret), 3 children.

Elected 1989 (Special Election). Career: Sales

Rep., Bay St. Louis Cty. Council 1981–83; Miss. St. Senate 1984–89.

Committees: (1) Armed Services; (2) Merchant Marine & Fisheries.

Election Results: 1992 Taylor 118,750 (63%); Paul Harvey (R) 66,809 (36%); Shawn O'Hara (I) 2,621 (1%). 1990 Taylor (81%). 1989 (special) Taylor (65%).

Interest Group Ratings:

ADA	ACU	COPE	COC
30	76	50	50

LCV	NTLC	CFA	ASC
31	75	47	70

Office: 214 CHOB 20515, 202-225-5772 (Wayne Weidie, AA). DISTRICT OFFICES: 2424 14th Street, Gulfport 39501, 601-864-7670 (Beau Gex, Dir.); 215 Fed. Bldg. 701 Main St., Hattiesburg 39401, 601-582-3246 (Jerry Martin, Rep.); 706 Watts Ave., Pascagoula 39567, 601-762-1770 (Brian Martin, Rep.)

MISSOURI

Missouri represents a typical midwestern state of the 90s—the cities are solidly Democratic while the suburbs and rural areas heavily Republican. This means with the growth of the suburbs, the state as a whole now leans Republican, with the governor and both senators from the GOP. A wide open Senate race is in the offing for Missouri in 1994. Incumbent Republican John Danforth has announced he will not run again. It is assumed that popular former GOP Gov. John Ashcroft, who was unable to succeed himself in 1992, will be the GOP frontrunner. The Democrats will have a large field of potential candidates.

1992 PRESIDENTIAL ELECTION: (11 Electoral votes): Clinton (D) 1,053,040 (44%); Bush (R) 811,057 (34%); Perot (I) 518,250 (22%); Marrou (Lib) 7,924. 1988 Bush 1,081,163 (52%); Dukakis 1,004,040 (48%).

SENATORS

John Claggett Danforth (R)

Born Sept. 5, 1936, St. Louis; home Newburg; Princeton University, B.A. 1958, Yale University, B.D., LL.B. 1963; Episcopalian; married (Sally), 5 children.

Elected 1976, seat up 1994. Career: Practicing atty., 1963–68; Ordained clergyman; Atty. Gen. of Mo., 1968–76.

Committees: (1) Commerce, Science & Transportation (Ranking Member); (2) Finance; (3) Select Committee on Intelligence.

Election Results: 1988 Danforth 1,407,416 (68%); Jeremiah Nixon (D) 660,045 (32%). 1982 Danforth (51%).

Interest Group Ratings:

ADA	ACU	COPE	COC
25	74	25	90

LCV	NTLC	CFA	ASC
08	67	58	80

Office: 249 RSOB 20510, 202-224-6154 (Robert McDonald, AA). STATE OFFICES: 705 Plaza Towers, 1736 E. Sunshine, Springfield 65804, 417-881-7068 (Brad Bodenhausen, Asst.); Old P.O. Bldg., Rm. 228, 815 Olive St., St. Louis 63101, 314-539-6381 (Carla Roeber, Asst.); 1233

Jefferson St., Jefferson City 65101, 314-635-7292 (Clair Elsberry, Asst.); 943 U.S. Courthouse, 811 Grand Ave., Kansas City 64106, 816-426-6101 (Rachel Steele, Asst.); 214 Fed. Bldg., 339 Broadway, Cape Girardeau 63701, 314-334-7044 (Tom Schulte, Asst.)

Christopher Samuel "Kit" Bond (R)

Born Mar. 6, 1939, St. Louis; home Mexico, Mo.; Princeton University, B.A. 1960, University of Va., LL.B. 1963; Presbyterian; married (Carolyn), 1 child.

Elected 1986, seat up 1998. Career: Practicing atty., 1964–69; Mo. Asst. Atty. Gen., 1969–70; Mo. Auditor, 1970–72; Gov. of Mo., 1972–84.

Committees: (1) Appropriations; (2) Banking, Housing & Urban Affairs; (3) Budget; (4) Small Business.

Election Results: 1992 Bond 1,221,453 (54%); Geri Rothman-Serot (D) 1,057,357 (46%). 1986 Bond (53%).

Interest Group Ratings:

ADA	ACU	COPE	COC
25	76	33	100

LCV	NTLC	CFA	ASC
08	76	50	100

Office: 293 RSOB 20510, 202-224-5721 (Warren Erdman, AA). STATE OFFICES: 8000 Maryland Ave. #1050, St. Louis 63105, 314-727-7773 (Jo-Ann Digman, Dir.); 510 NE 291 Hwy., Lee's Summit 64063, 816-524-6141 (Brad Scott, Dpty. AA); 312 Monroe St., Jefferson City 65101, 314-634-2488 (Mary Beth Dobbs, Spec. Asst.); 214 Fed. Bldg., 339 Broadway, Cape Girardeau 63701, 314-334-7044 (Tom Schulte, Asst.); 1736 Sunshine Ave., Rm. 705, Springfield 65804, 417-881-7086 (Sally Dinka, Asst.)

REPRESENTATIVES

FIRST DISTRICT

William L. Clay (D)

District: St. Louis City and northeast St. Louis County. Population: 568,285—Black 52%. Politics: Democratic.

Born Apr. 30, 1931, St. Louis; home St. Louis; St. Louis University, B.S. 1953; Roman Catholic; married (Carol), 3 children.

Elected 1968. Career: Real estate broker; Life insur. business, 1959–61; St. Louis City Alderman, 1959–64.

Committees: (1) Education & Labor; (2) House Administration; (3) Post Office & Civil Service (Chairman).

Election Results: 1992 Clay 158,418 (68%); Arthur Montgomery (R) 74,308 (32%). 1990 Clay (61%). 1988 Clay (72%).

Interest Group Ratings:

ADA	ACU	COPE	COC
95	00	91	13

LCV	NTLC	CFA	ASC
75	00	87	10

Office: 2306 RHOB 20515, 202-225-2406 (Harriet Pritchett, AA). DISTRICT OFFICES: 6197 Delmar Blvd., St. Louis 63112, 314-725-5770 (Pearlie Evans, Asst.); 12263 Bellefontaine Rd., St. Louis 63138, 314-355-6811 (Virginia Cook, Asst.)

SECOND DISTRICT

James M. Talent (R)

District: Western St. Louis County. Population: 568,306—Black 4%, Asian 2%. Politics: Leans Republican.

Born Oct. 18, 1956, St. Louis; home Chesterfield; Washington University, B.A. 1978, University of Chicago, J.D. 1981; Presbyterian; married (Brenda), 1 child.

Elected 1992. Career: Law clerk, 1981–82; College Professor, 1981–83; Practicing atty., 1983–92; State Rep., 1985–92.

Committees: (1) Armed Services; (2) Small Business.

Election Results: 1992 Talent 157,556 (51%); Joan Kelly Horn (D) (Incumbent) 148,658 (49%).

Interest Group Ratings:
None—Freshman

Office: 1022 LHOB 20515, 202-225-2561 (Mark Strand, AA). DISTRICT OFFICES: 555 N. New Ballas #315, St. Louis 63141, 314-872-9561 (Barbara Cooper, Dist. Dir.); 820 S. Main St. #206, St.

Charles 63301, 314-949-6826 (Barbara Cooper, Dist. Dir.)

THIRD DISTRICT

Richard A. Gephardt (D)

District: South St. Louis City, plus southeast St. Louis County and Jefferson County. Population: 568,326. Black 2%. Politics: Democratic.

Born Jan. 31, 1941, St. Louis; home St. Louis; Northwestern University, B.S. 1962, University of Mich., J.D. 1965; Baptist; married (Jane), 3 children.

Elected 1976. Career: Practicing atty., 1965–76; St. Louis City Alderman, 1971–76.

Committees: Majority Leader.

Election Results: 1992 Gephardt 173,906 (66%); Mack Holekamp (R) 89,978 (34%). 1990 Gephardt (57%). 1988 Gephardt (63%).

Interest Group Ratings:

ADA	ACU	COPE	COC
85	00	78	25

LCV	NTLC	CFA	ASC
44	00	87	40

Office: 1432 LHOB 20515, 202-225-2671 (Dr. Andrea King, AA). DISTRICT OFFICE: 9959 Gravois, St. Louis 63123, 314-631-9959 (Mary Resnick, Asst.)

FOURTH DISTRICT

Isaac Newton "Ike" Skelton IV (D)

District: Central and west-central part of the state up to western Kansas City suburbs including city of Jefferson City. Population: 569,146—Black 3%. Politics: Leans Democratic.

Born Dec. 20, 1931, Lexington; home Lexington; Wentworth Military Acad., University of Mo., A.B. 1953, LL.B. 1956; Disciples of Christ; married (Susan), 3 children.

Elected 1976. Career: Lafayette Cty. Prosecuting Atty., 1957–60; Spec. Asst. Atty. Gen. of Mo., 1961–63; Practicing atty., 1957–76; Mo. Senate, 1971–76.

Committees: (1) Armed Services; (2) Small Business.

Election Results: 1992 Skelton 176,884 (70%); John Carley (R) 74,575 (30%). 1990 Skelton (62%). 1988 Skelton (72%).

Interest Group Ratings:

ADA	ACU	COPE	COC
45	65	67	86

LCV	NTLC	CFA	ASC
06	16	53	100

Office: 2227 RHOB 20515, 202-225-2876 (John Pollard, AA). DISTRICT OFFICES: 514-B N. 7 Hwy., Blue Springs 64014, 816-228-4242 (Robert Hagedorn, Dir.); 1616 Industrial Dr., Jefferson City 65101, 314-635-3499 (Carol Scott, Asst.); Fed. Bldg., 319 South Lamine, Sedalia 65301, 816-826-2675 (Arletta Garrett, Asst.); 219 N. Adams, Lebanon 65536, 417-532-7964 (Shirley Clark, Rep.)

FIFTH DISTRICT

Alan Wheat (D)

District: Kansas City and eastern suburbs. Population: 569,130—Black 24%, Hispanic 3%. Politics: Democratic.

Born Oct. 16, 1951, San Antonio, Tex.; home Kansas City; Grinnell College, B.A. 1972; Church of Christ; married (Yolanda).

Elected 1982. Career: Economist, Dept. of HUD, Kansas City & Mid–America Regional Cncl., 1972–74; Aide to Jackson Cty. Exec., Mike White 1974–75; Mo. House of Reps., 1976–82.

Committees: (1) District of Columbia; (2) Rules.

Election Results: 1992 Wheat 150,693 (62%); Edward Moody (R) 93,421 (38%). 1990 Wheat (62%). 1988 Wheat (70%).

Interest Group Ratings:

ADA	ACU	COPE	COC
95	00	91	13

LCV	NTLC	CFA	ASC
88	00	100	20

Office: 2334 RHOB 20515, 202-225-4535 (Margaret Broadaway, AA). DISTRICT OFFICES: 935 U.S. Courthouse, 811 Grand Ave., Kansas City 64106, 816-842-4545 (Gerald Grimaldi, Dist. Dir.); 301 W. Lexington, Suite 221, Independence 64050, 816-833-4545 (Sheila Thompson, Asst.)

SIXTH DISTRICT

Pat Danner (D)

District: Northwestern part of the state including city of St. Joseph. Population: 569,131—Black 2%. Politics: Leans Republican.

Born Jan. 13, 1934, Louisville, Ky.; home Smithfield; Northeast Missouri State, B.A. 1972,; Roman Catholic; married (Mark Meyer), 4 children.

Elected 1992. Career: Dist. Asst. Rep. Litton, 1973–76; Co–Chairman Ozark Regional Council, 1977–81; State Sen. 1983–92.

Committees: (1) Public Works & Transportation; (2) Small Business.

Election Results: 1992 Danner 148,889 (55%); Tom Coleman (R) (Incumbent) 119,638 (45%).

Interest Group Ratings:
None—Freshman

Office: 1217 LHOB 20515, 202-225-7041 (Doug Gray, AA). DISTRICT OFFICES: P.O. Box 201, S. 8th St. #333, St. Joseph 64501, 816-233-9818 (Rosie Haertling, Rep.); 5754 Bldg. #3 Suite 2, Kansas City 64118 (Lou Carson, Rep.)

SEVENTH DISTRICT

Melton D. Hancock (R)

District: Southwestern part of the state including cities of Springfield and Joplin. Population: 568,017. Politics: Leans Republican.

Born Sept. 14, 1929, Cape Fair. Home, Springfield; Southwest Mo. St. College, B.S. 1951; Protestant; married (Sug), 3 children.

Elected 1988. Career: International Harvester; Insur. exec., 1959–69; Owner, security co., 1969–88.

Committees: (1) Ways & Means.

Election Results: 1992 Hancock 160,251 (62%); Pat Deaton (D) 99,642 (38%). 1990 Hancock (52%). 1988 Hancock (53%).

Interest Group Ratings:

ADA	ACU	COPE	COC
10	96	25	75

LCV	NTLC	CFA	ASC
00	100	07	100

Office: 129 CHOB 20515, 202-225-6536 (Duncan Haggart, AA). DISTRICT OFFICES: 302 Fed. Bldg., Joplin 64801, 417-781-1041 (Bea White, Asst.); 2840 A. E. Chestnut Expwy., Springfield 65806, 417-862-4317 (Barbara Dixon, Asst.)

EIGHTH DISTRICT

Bill Emerson (R)

District: Southeastern part of the state including city of Cape Girardeau. Population: 568,385 —Black 4%. Politics: Leans Republican.

Born Jan. 1, 1938, St. Louis; home Cape Girardeau; Westminster College, B.A. 1959, University of Baltimore, LL.B. 1964; Presbyterian; married (Jo Ann), 4 children.

Elected 1980. Career: Spec. Asst. to U.S. Rep. Bob Ellsworth, 1961–65; A.A. to U.S. Rep. Charles Mathias, 1965–70; Dir. of Govt. Relations, Fairchild Indus., 1970–73; Dir. of Public Affairs, Interstate Natural Gas Assn., 1974–75; Exec. Asst. to Chm, Fed. Election Comm., 1975; Dir., Fed. Relations, TRW, Inc., 1975–79; Govt. relations consultant, 1979–80.

Committees: (1) Agriculture; (2) Public Works & Transportation.

Election Results: 1992 Emerson 147,398 (63%); Thad Bullock (D) 86,695 (37%). 1990 Emerson (57%). 1988 Emerson (58%).

Interest Group Ratings:

ADA	ACU	COPE	COC
20	92	42	88

LCV	NTLC	CFA	ASC
06	65	33	100

Office: 2454 CHOB 20515, 202-225-4404 (Keith Kirk, Ex. Asst.). DISTRICT OFFICES: Fed. Bldg., 339 Broadway, Cape Girardeau 63701, 314-335-0101 (Lloyd Smith, Chief-of-staff); 612 Pine St., Rolla 65401, 314-364-2455 (Iris Bernhardt, Mgr.)

NINTH DISTRICT

Harold L. Volkmer (D)

District: Northeastern part of the state including city of Columbia. Population: 568,347—Black 4%. Politics: Leans Democratic.

Born Apr. 4, 1931, Jefferson City; home Hannibal; Jefferson City Jr. College, St. Louis University, University of Mo., LL.B. 1955; Roman Catholic; married (Shirley), 3 children.

Elected 1976. Career: Army, 1955–57; Mo. Asst. Atty. Gen.; Marion Cty. Prosecuting atty., 1960–66; Mo. House of Reps., 1967–76.

Committees: (1) Agriculture; (2) Science, Space & Technology.

Election Results: 1992 Volkmer 124,696 (50%); Rick Hardy (R) 118,806 (47%); Duane Burghard (I) 7,108 (3%). 1990 Volkmer (58%). 1988 Volkmer (68%).

Interest Group Ratings:

ADA	ACU	COPE	COC
50	40	91	50

LCV	NTLC	CFA	ASC
19	21	73	80

Office: 2409 RHOB 20515, 202-225-2956 (James Spurling, AA). DISTRICT OFFICES: 370 Fed. Bldg., 801 Broadway, Hannibal 63401, 314-221-1200 (Lee Viorel, Oprs. Sup.); 912 E. Walnut, Columbia, MO 65201 (Ewell Lawson, Asst.); 122 Bourke, Macon 63552, 816-385-5615 (Carol Phillips, Asst.)

MONTANA

Montana may face a bruising Senate battle in 1994. Republican incumbent Conrad Burns is up for reelection, and Democrats believe he can be beaten. The logical choice to oppose Burns would seem to be at-large Rep. Pat Williams who is coming off a bruising battle which saw him defeat Montana former GOP Rep. Ron Marlenee when the two were thrown against each other when the state lost one of its two congressional districts. Some believe it might be just as easy to face Burns, as run statewide again against Marlenee, who will likely make a try to return to Washington.

1992 PRESIDENTIAL ELECTION: (3 Electoral votes): Clinton (D) 153,899 (38%); Bush (R) 143,702 (35%); Perot (I) 106,869 (26%); Gritz (Pop) 3,630; Marrou (Lib) 976. 1988 Bush 189,598 (53%); Dukakis 168,120 (47%).

SENATORS

Max Baucus (D)

Born Dec. 11, 1941, Helena; home Missoula; Stanford University, B.A. 1964, LL.B. 1967; Protestant; married (Wanda), 1 child.

Elected 1978, seat up 1996. Career: Staff Atty., Civil Aeronautics Bd., 1967–69; Legal Staff, Securities & Exchange Comm., 1969–71, Legal Asst. to the Chm., 1970–71; Practicing atty., 1971–74; Mont. House of Reps., 1973–74; U.S. House of Reps., 1974–78.

Committees: (1) Agriculture, Nutrition & Forestry; (2) Environment & Public Works (Chairman); (3) Finance; (4) Small Business; (5) Select Committee on Intelligence; (6) Joint Committee on Taxation.

Election Results: 1990 Baucus 217,451 (70%); Allen Kolstad (R) 93,984 (30%). 1984 Baucus (57%).

Interest Group Ratings:

ADA	ACU	COPE	COC
95	04	75	20

LCV	NTLC	CFA	ASC
58	05	100	50

Office: 511 HSOB 20510, 202-224-2651 (Greg Mastel, Chief-of-staff). STATE OFFICES: 32 N. Last Chance Gulch, Helena 59601, 406-449-5480 (Holly Luck, Asst.); 202 Fratt Bldg., 2817 2nd Ave. N., Billings 59101, 406-657-6970 (Sharon Peterson, Asst.); 114 Fed. Bldg., 32 E. Babcock, Bozeman 59715, 406-586-6104 (Dave McAlpen, Asst.); Silver Bow Center, 125 W. Granite, Butte 59701, 406-782-8700 (Kim Krueger, Asst.); 107 5th St. N., Great Falls 59401, 406-761-1574 (Bernice Olsen, Asst.); 211 N. Higgins, Rm. 102, Missoula 59802, 406-329-3123 (Carlene Nimlos, Rep.); 1715 S. Main St., Kalisville 59901, 406-756-1150 (Tracy Crabtree, Rep.)

Conrad Burns (R)

Born Jan. 25, 1935, Gallatin, Mo.; home, Billings; University of Md., 1952–54; Lutheran; married (Phyllis), 2 children.

Elected 1988, seat up 1994. Career: USMC, 1955–57; Radio & TV broadcaster; Yellowstone Cty. Commissioner, 1987–88.

Committees: (1) Commerce, Science & Transportation; (2) Appropriations; (3) Small Business.

Election Results: 1988 Burns 189,445 (52%); John Melcher (Incumbent D) 175,809 (48%).

Interest Group Ratings:

ADA	ACU	COPE	COC
05	89	25	100

LCV	NTLC	CFA	ASC
00	83	08	90

Office: 183 DSOB 20510, 202-224-2644 (Jack Ramirez, AA). STATE OFFICES: 208 N. Montana Ave., Suite 202A, Helena 59601, 406-449-5401 (Betti Hill, Rep.); 2708 1st Ave., Billings 59101, 406-252-0550 (Dwight McKay, St. Dir.); 415 N. Higgins, Missoula 59802, 406-329-3528 (Julie Altemus, Rep.); 104 4th St., N., Great Falls 59401, 406-452-9585 (Kathy Sparr, Rep.)

REPRESENTATIVES

AT LARGE

Pat Williams (D)

District: Entire state. Population: 779,065—Native American 6%. Politics: Leans Democratic.

Born Oct. 30, 1937, Helena; home Helena; University of Mont., University of Denver, B.A. 1961; Roman Catholic; married (Carol), 3 children.

Elected 1978. Career: Pub. school teacher; Mont. House of Reps., 1967, 1969; Humphrey Presidential Campaign, 1968; Exec. Asst. to U.S. Rep. John Melcher, 1969–71; Mont. State Coord., Family Ed. Prog., 1971–78.

Committees: (1) Education & Labor; (2) Natural Resources; (3) Agriculture.

Election Results: 1992 Williams 202,929 (50%); Ron Marlenee (R) (Incumbent) 189,165 (47%); Jerome Wilverding (Lib) 10,398 (3%). 1990 Williams (61%). 1988 Williams (61%).

Interest Group Ratings:

ADA	ACU	COPE	COC
85	08	92	50

LCV	NTLC	CFA	ASC
38	00	67	20

Office: 2457 RHOB 20515, 202-225-3211 (Jim Foley, AA). DISTRICT OFFICES: 316 N. Park Ave. #443, Helena 59624, 406-443-7878 (Joe Lamson, Rep.); 305 W. Mercury #306, Butte 59701, 406-723-4404 (Marsha Brown, Rep.); 214 N. 29th St., Billings 59101, 406-256-1019 (Mike Barton, Rep.); Courthouse Annex, 325 2nd Ave. N., Great Falls 59401, 406-771-1242 (Lorian Donohoe, Rep.)

NEBRASKA

Another state of political contradictions. Looking at its three congressional districts, the state seems solidly Republican outside Omaha (although Lincoln is starting to vote almost Democratic). Yet both its senators are Democrats, and in 1990 Democrat Ben Nelson ousted Republican Gov. Kay Orr in a major surprise. In 1994 Nelson must run for reelection, and the GOP wants to office back. Also in 1994, Sen. Bob Kerrey also must run for a new 6-year term. There was some disappointment with his rather inept presidential run in 1992, but he should win reelection easily.

1992 PRESIDENTIAL ELECTION: (5 Electoral votes): Clinton (D) 214,064 (29%); Bush (R) 339,109 (47%); Perot (I) 172,043 (24%); Marrou (Lib) 1,277; Fulani (NAP) 815; Hagelin (NLP) 688. 1988 Bush 389,394 (60%); Dukakis 254,426 (40%).

SENATORS

J. James Exon (D)

Born Aug. 9, 1921, Geddes, S.Dak.; home Lincoln; University of Omaha; Episcopalian; married (Patricia), 3 children.

Elected 1978, seat up 1996. Career: Army, WWII; Branch Mgr., Universal Finance Co., 1946–54; Pres., Exon's Inc., office equip. business, 1954–70; Gov. of Nebr. 1970–78.

Committees: (1) Armed Services; (2) Budget; (3) Commerce, Science & Transportation.

Election Results: 1990 Exon 342,638 (59%); Hal Daub (R) 237,193 (41%). 1984 Exon (52%).

Interest Group Ratings:

ADA	ACU	COPE	COC
75	26	83	30

LCV	NTLC	CFA	ASC
42	17	75	60

Office: 528 HSOB 20510, 202-224-4224 (Gregory Pallas, Chief-of-staff). STATE OFFICES: 1624 Farnham St. #700, Omaha 68102, 402-341-1776 (Catherine Dahquist, Rep.); 287 Fed. Bldg., 100 Centennial Mall N., Lincoln 68508, 402-437-5591 (Frances White, Rep.); 275 Fed. Bldg., North Platte 69101, 308-534-2006 (Clair Nicholas, Rep.); 2106 1st Ave., Scottsbluff 69361, 308-632-3595 (Pat Redel, Rep.)

Joseph Robert Kerrey (D)

Born Aug. 27, 1943, Lincoln; home, Lincoln; University of Nebr., B.S. 1965; Congregationalist; divorced, 2 children.

Elected 1988, seat up 1994. Career: Navy 1967–69; Entrepreneur, 1969–83; Gov. of Nebr. 1983–87.

Committees: (1) Agriculture, Nutrition & Forestry; (2) Appropriations; (3) Select Committee on Intelligence.

Election Results: 1988 Kerrey 378,717 (57%); David Karnes (R) 278,250 (42%).

Interest Group Ratings:

ADA	ACU	COPE	COC
90	00	91	25

LCV	NTLC	CFA	ASC
50	17	75	30

Office: 303 HSOB 20510, 202-224-6551 (Paul Johnson, AA). STATE OFFICES: 294 Fed. Bldg., 100 Centennial Mall N., Lincoln 68508, 402-437-5246 (Eugene Glock, Ag. Rep.); 7602 Pacific St., Rm. 205, Omaha 68114, 402-391-3411 (Lonnie Michael, St. Dir.); 2106 First Ave., Scottsbluff 69361, 308-632-3595 (Patricia Redel, Rep.)

REPRESENTATIVES

FIRST DISTRICT

Douglas Kent Bereuter (R)

District: Eastern part of the state, except Omaha area, but including the city of Lincoln. Population: 526,297. Politics: Republican.

Born Oct. 6, 1939, York; home Utica; University of Nebr., B.A. 1961, Harvard University, M.C.P. 1963, M.P.A. 1973; Lutheran; married (Louise), 2 children.

Elected 1978. Career: Army, 1963–65; Urban Planner, U.S. Dept. of HUD, 1965–66; Div. Dir., Dept. of Econ. Dev., 1967–68; Dir., Nebr. St. Plng. Office, 1968–70; Chm., Urban Dev. Cmte., 1973–74; Nebr. Senate, 1974–78.

Committees: (1) Banking, Finance & Urban Affairs; (2) Foreign Affairs; (3) Permanent Select Committee on Intelligence.

Election Results: 1992 Bereuter 141,000 (60%); Gerry Finnegan (D) 95,397 (40%). 1990 Bereuter (65%). 1988 Bereuter (67%).

Interest Group Ratings:

ADA	ACU	COPE	COC
20	79	33	88

LCV	NTLC	CFA	ASC
25	70	47	90

Office: 2348 RHOB 20515, 202-225-4806 (Susan Olsen, AA). DISTRICT OFFICES: 1045 K St., Lincoln 68508, 402-437-5400 (Jim Barr, Mgr.); 502 N. Broad St., Fremont 68025, 402-727-0888 (Dave Heineman, Rep.)

SECOND DISTRICT

Peter D. Hoagland (D)

District: Omaha and immediate environs. Population: 526,567—Black 10%, Hispanic 3%. Politics: Leans Republican.

Born Nov. 17, 1941, Omaha; home, Omaha; Stanford University, B.A. 1963, Yale University, LL.B. 1968; Episcopalian; married (Barbara), 5 children.

Elected 1988. Career: Army, 1963–65; Clerk, U.S. District Court, Washington, D.C., 1969–70; Public defender, 1970–73; Practicing atty., 1974–78; Nebr. Senate, 1979–88.

Committees: (1) Ways & Means.

Election Results: 1992 Hoagland 118,486 (51%); Ronald Staskiewicz (R) 112,779 (49%). 1990 Hoagland (58%). 1988 Hoagland (51%).

Interest Group Ratings:

ADA	ACU	COPE	COC
85	24	75	50

LCV	NTLC	CFA	ASC
63	10	87	100

Office: 1113 LHOB 20515, 202-225-4155 (Kathleen Ambrose, AA). DISTRICT OFFICE: 8424 Fed. Bldg., 215 N. 17th St., Omaha 68102, 402-221-4216 (Paul Landow, Mgr.)

THIRD DISTRICT

William Barrett (R)

District: Central and western parts of the state including city of Grand Island. Population: 525,521—Hispanic 3%. Politics: Leans Republican.

Born Feb. 9, 1929, Lexington, Nebr.; home, Lexington; Hastings College, B.A., 1952; Presbyterian; married (Elsie), 4 children.

Elected 1990. Career: Insurance & Real Estate Co. owner, Nebr. Legs., 1979–90, speaker 1987–90.

Committees: (1) Agriculture; (2) Education & Labor; (3) House Administration.

Election Results: 1992 Barrett 168,177 (72%); Lowell Fisher (D) 66,202 (28%). 1990 Barrett (51%).

Interest Group Ratings:

ADA	ACU	COPE	COC
10	84	25	88

LCV	NTLC	CFA	ASC
00	65	27	100

Office: 1213 LHOB 20515, 202-225-6435 (Jeri Finke, AA). DISTRICT OFFICES: 312 W. 3rd St., P.O. Box 308, Grand Island 68802, 308-381-5555 (Bruce Rieker, Dir.); 1502 2nd Ave., Suite 2, Scottsbluff 69361, 307-622-3333 (Greg Stull, Rep.)

NEVADA

The GOP considers Nevada a Republican state and is reeling from Clinton's 1992 victory. The GOP also failed in its attempt to unseat first term Democratic Sen. Harry Reid. Now, in 1994, it will try to defeat the state's other Democratic Sen. Richard Bryan, as well as Democratic Gov. Bob Miller. It may well be that the strongest GOP candidate for either office is incumbent Rep. Barbara Vuncanovich. But she passed up making the Senate race in 1992, and she showed weakness in her narrow House reelection. Things are not looking up for the GOP in Nevada.

1992 PRESIDENTIAL ELECTION: (4 Electoral votes): Clinton (D) 188,169 (37%); Bush (R) 174,775 (35%); Perot (I) 131,856 (26%); Gritz (Pop) 2,876; "None of These" 2,525; Marrou (Lib) 1,819; Phillips (AmTax) 673; Fulani (NAP) 480; Hagelin (NLP) 337. 1988 Bush 205,942 (60%); Dukakis 132,716 (38%).

SENATORS

Harry M. Reid (D)

Born Dec. 2, 1922, Searchlight. Home, Searchlight; Utah St. University, B.S. 1961, George Washington University, J.D. 1964; Mormon; married (Landra), 5 children.

Elected 1986, seat up 1998. Career: Practicing atty.; City Atty., Henderson, 1964–66; Nev. Assembly, 1968–70; Lt. Gov. of Nev., 1970–74; Chm., Nev. Gaming Comm., 1977–81; U.S. House of Reps., 1982–86.

Committees: (1) Appropriations; (2) Environment & Public Works; (3) Select Committee on Aging.

Election Results: 1992 Reid 247,732 (52%); Demar Dahl (R) 194,527 (41%); "None of These" 12,815; H. Kent Cromwell 7,091; Joe Garcia, Jr. 11,045. 1986 Reid (50%).

Interest Group Ratings:

ADA	ACU	COPE	COC
80	23	73	10

LCV	NTLC	CFA	ASC
67	22	75	70

Office: 324 HSOB 20510, 202-224-3542 (Reynaldo Martinez, Chief-of-staff). STATE OFFICES: 300

Booth St., Suite 4024, Reno 89509, 702-784-5568 (Wendell Newman, Reg. Mgr.); 500 E. Charleston, Las Vegas 89104, 702-474-0041 (Marge Van Hoove, Rep.); 600 E. Williams, Suite 302, Carson City 89701, 702-882-7343 (Wendall Newman, Reg. Mgr.)

Richard H. Bryan (D)

Born July 16, 1937, Washington, D.C.; home, Carson City; University of Nev., B.A. 1959; University of Calif., LL.B. 1963; Episcopalian; married (Bonnie), 3 children.

Elected 1988, seat up 1994. Career: Dpty. Dist. Atty., Clark Cty., 1964–66; Clark Cty. Public Defender 1966–68; Counsel, Clark Cty. Juvenile Court, 1968–69; Nev. Assembly 1969–73; Nev. Senate 1973–79; Atty. Gen. of Nev. 1978–83; Gov. of Nev. 1982–88.

Committees: (1) Banking, Housing & Urban Affairs; (2) Commerce, Science & Transportation; (3) Joint Economic Committee; (4) Ethics; (5) Select Committee on Intelligence.

Election Results: 1988 Bryan 175,548 (50%); Chic Hecht (Incumbent R) 161,336 (46%); Others (4%).

Interest Group Ratings:

ADA	ACU	COPE	COC
80	19	67	10

LCV	NTLC	CFA	ASC
67	28	83	70

Office: 364 RSOB 20510, 202-224-6244 (Jean Neal, AA). STATE OFFICES: 300 Las Vegas Blvd. S., Suite 140, Las Vegas 89101, 702-388-6605 (Lou Gamage, Rep.); 300 Booth St., Suite 2014, Reno 89509, 702-784-5007 (Marlene Joiner, St. Dir.); 600 E. William, Suite 304, Carson City 89701, 702-885-9111 (Tom Baker, Rep.)

REPRESENTATIVES

FIRST DISTRICT

James H. Bilbray (D)

District: City of Las Vegas and Surrounding suburbs. Population: 600,957—Black 10%, Asian 4%, Hispanic 12%. Politics: Leans Democratic.

Born May 19, 1938, Las Vegas. Home, Las Vegas; University of Nev., American University, B.A. 1962, J.D. 1964; Roman Catholic; married (Michaelene), 3 children.

Elected 1986. Career: Staff Asst. to U.S. Sen. Howard Cannon, 1960–62; Dpty Dist. Atty., Clark Cty., Nev., 1964–68; University Regent, University of Nev., 1968–72; Alt. Municipal Judge, Las Vegas 1978–80; Nev. Senate, 1980–86.

Committees: (1) Armed Services; (2) Small Business; (3) Select Committee on Intelligence.

Election Results: 1992 Bilbray 127,292 (58%); J. Coy Pettyjohn (R) 83,527 (38%); Scott Kjar (Lib) 8,914 (4%). 1990 Bilbray (64%). 1988 Bilbray (64%).

Interest Group Ratings:

ADA	ACU	COPE	COC
70	33	75	63

LCV	NTLC	CFA	ASC
56	05	67	100

Office: 2431 RHOB 20515, 202-225-5965 (John Fadgen, AA). DISTRICT OFFICE: 1785 E. Sahara Ave., Suite 445, Las Vegas 89104, 702-792-2424 (Rene Diamond, Dist. Dir.)

SECOND DISTRICT

Barbara F. Vucanovich (R)

District: Entire state north, south and west of Las Vegas including the part of city of North Las Vegas. Population: 600,867—Black 3%, Native American 2%, Asian 3%, Hispanic 9%. Politics: Leans Republican.

Born June 22, 1921, Camp Dix, N.J. Home, Reno; Manhattanville College; Roman Catholic; married (George), 5 children.

Elected 1982. Career: Owner, Nev. franchise of Evelyn Wood Speed Reading Co., 1964–68; Owner, travel agcy., 1968–74; Campaign staff for U.S. Sen. Paul Laxalt, 1974, 1980; Dist. Rep. for U.S. Sen. Paul Laxalt, 1974–81.

Committees: (1) Appropriations.

Election Results: 1992 Vucanovich 125,118 (48%); Pete Sferrazza (D) 113,364 (44%); Dan Becan (Lib) 7,312 (3%); Daniel Hansen (I) 12,831 (5%). 1990 Vucanovich (63%). 1988 Vucanovich (57%).

Interest Group Ratings:

ADA	ACU	COPE	COC
05	96	17	75

LCV	NTLC	CFA	ASC
19	90	20	100

Office: 2202 RHOB 20515, 202-225-6155 (Michael Pieper, AA). DISTRICT OFFICES: 3038 Fed. Bldg, 300 Boothe St., Reno 89509, 702-784-5003 (Olive Hill, Rep.); 19 W. Brooke Ave., Suite B, N. Las Vegas 89030, 702-399-3555 (Joan Dimmitt, Rep.); 401 Railroad St., Rm. 307, Elko 89801, 702-738-4064 (Pete Ludwig, Rep.)

NEW HAMPSHIRE

New Hampshire requires its governors to run for reelection every two years, so newly elected Republican Steve Merrill will have to run for a second term in 1994. It will be the only state-wide contest, and he should win a second term. Despite the surprise Clinton victory in 1992, New Hampshire remains one of the most Republican of states.

1992 PRESIDENTIAL ELECTION: (4 Electoral votes): Clinton (D) 207,264 (39%); Bush (R) 199,623 (38%); Perot (I) 120,029 (23%); Marrou (Lib) 4,576; Fulani (NAP) 461; Hagelin (NLP) 262. 1988 Bush 279,770 (63%); Dukakis 162,335 (37%).

SENATORS

Judd Gregg (R)

Born Feb. 14, 1947, Nashua; home, Nashua; Columbia University, A.B. 1969, Boston University, J.D. 1972, L.L.M. 1975; Protestant; married (Kathy), 3 children.

Elected 1992, seat up 1998. Career: Partner, Sullivan, Greg & Horton, 1975–80; N.H. Exec. Council, 1978–80; U.S. House of Representatives, 1981–88; Governor of N.H., 1989–92.

Committees: (1) Commerce, Science & Transportation; (2) Labor & Human Resources.

Election Results: 1992 Gregg 247,215 (50%); John Rauh (D) 232,846 (48%); Larry Brady 9,577 (2%).

Interest Group Ratings:
None—Freshman

Office: 393 RSOB 20510, 202-224-3324 (Martha Austin, AA) STATE OFFICES: 125 Main St., Concord 03301, 603-225-7115 (Joel Maiola, State Dir.); 28 Webster St., Manchester 03104, 603-622-7979; 136 Pleasant St., Berlin 03570, 603-752-2604; 99 Pease Blvd., Portsmouth 03801, 603-431-2171.

Robert C. Smith (R)

Born Mar. 20, 1941, Trenton, N.J.; home, Tuftonboro; Lafayette College, B.A., 1965; Roman Catholic; married (Mary Jo), 3 children.

Elected 1990, seat up 1996. Career: Air Force, 1965–67; Teacher, 1975–85; Real Estate Broker;

Chm., Wentworth Sch. Bd., 1978–83; U.S. House 1985–90.

Committees: (1) Armed Services; (2) Environment & Public Works.

Election Results: 1990 Smith 118,854 (67%); John Durkin (D) 91,786 (33%).

Interest Group Ratings:

ADA	ACU	COPE	COC
05	96	25	90

LCV	NTLC	CFA	ASC
25	94	17	70

Office: 332 DSOB 20510, 202-224-2841 (Pat Pettey, AA). STATE OFFICES: 46 S. Main St., Concord 03301, 603-228-0453 (Jim Courtovich, Rep.); Gateway Bldg. 50 Phillipe Cote St., Manchester 03101, 603-634-5000 (Mark Aldrich, Rep.)

REPRESENTATIVES

FIRST DISTRICT

William Zeliff (R)

District: Southeastern part of the state including city of Manchester. Population: 554,360. Politics: Republican.

Born June 12, 1936, East Orange, N.J.; home, Jackson; University of Conn., B.S. 1959, Protestant; married (Sydna), 3 children.

Elected 1990. Career: DuPont Co., 1961–76; Innkeeper, Christmas Farm Inn 1976–90. No previous political office.

Committees: (1) Government Operations; (2) Public Works & Transportation; (3) Small Business.

Election Results: 1992 Zeliff 134,575 (56%); Bob Preston (D) 107,189 (44%). 1990 Zeliff (55%).

Interest Group Ratings:

ADA	ACU	COPE	COC
20	92	25	88

LCV	NTLC	CFA	ASC
06	85	13	100

Office: 224 CHOB 20515, 202-225-5456 (Marshall Cobleith, Chief-of-staff). DISTRICT OFFICES: Technology Center, 340 Commercial St., 2nd

Fl., Manchester 03101, 603-699-6330 (Kathy Schneiderat, Rep.); 601 Spaulding Turnpike #28, Portsmouth 03801, 603-433-1601 (Pam Kocher, Dist Mgr.)

SECOND DISTRICT

Richard Nelson Swett (D)

District: Western and northern parts of the state including towns of Concord and Nashua. Population: 554,892. Politics: Republican.

Born May 1, 1957, Bryn Mawr, Pa.; home, Bow; Yale University, B.A., 1979; Mormon; married (Katrina), 6 children.

Elected 1990. Career: Architect.

Committees: (1) Public Works & Transportation; (2) Science, Space & Technology.

Election Results: 1992 Swett 157,199 (63%); Bill Hatch (R) 91,090 (37%). 1990 Swett (53%).

Interest Group Ratings:

ADA	ACU	COPE	COC
85	32	83	38

LCV	NTLC	CFA	ASC
94	50	80	60

Office: 230 CHOB 20515, 202-225-5206 (Dr. Kay King, AA). DISTRICT OFFICES: 18 N. Main Street, Concord 03301, 603-224-6621 (Shireen Tilley, Rep.); 5 Coliseum Ave., Nashua 03063, 603-880-6142 (Paul Bagley, Rep.); 127 Main St., Littleton 03561, 603-444-1321 (Richard Polansky, Rep.)

NEW JERSEY

Can New Jersey's Democratic Gov. James Florio make one of the most remarkable comebacks in recent political history? Voters were so angry at him in 1991 for pushing through the state's largest tax hike ever, after making a no new taxes pledge, that it looked like he might face a recall effort. The thought that he would even run for reelection seemed out of the question. But now he is not only running for a second term in the 1993 election, but he has a solid chance of winning. Republicans are hopeful they can unseat Democratic Sen. Frank Lautenberg in 1994. But he solidly beat a very attractive GOP candidate in 1988, and would look to do so again.

1992 PRESIDENTIAL ELECTION: (15 Electoral votes): Clinton (D) 1,377,414 (43%); Bush (R) 1,316,028 (41%); Perot (I) 507,952 (16%); Marrou (Lib) 6,173; Bradford (I) 4,605; Fulani (NAP) 3,308; LaRouche (I) 2,394; Phillips (AmTax) 2,035; Daniels (P&F) 1,938; Gritz (Pop) 1,611; Halyard (WksLg) 1,601; Warren (SocWks) 1,408; Hagelin (NLP) 1,314. 1988 Bush 1,699,634 (57%); Dukakis 1,275,063 (43%).

SENATORS

Bill Bradley (D)

Born July 28, 1943, Crystal City, Mo.; home, Denville; Princeton University, B.A. 1965, Rhodes Scholar, Oxford University, M.A. 1968; Protestant; married (Ernestine), 2 children.

Elected 1978, seat up 1996. Career: U.S. Olympic Team, 1964; Pro basketball player, New York Knicks, 1967–77.

Committees: (1) Energy & Natural Resources; (2) Finance; (3) Special Committee on Aging.

Election Results: 1990 Bradley 972,056 (51%); Christine Todd Whitman (R) 916,359 (49%). 1984 Bradley (64%).

Interest Group Ratings:

ADA	ACU	COPE	COC
85	04	91	22

LCV	NTLC	CFA	ASC
83	19	75	40

Office: 731 HSOB 20510, 202-224-3224 (vacant,

AA). STATE OFFICES: 1609 Vauxhall Rd., Union 07083, 201-688-0960 (Kevin Rigby, St. Dir.); 1 Greentree Ctr., Rte. 73, Marlton 08053, 609-983-4143 (James Pennestri, Rep.)

Frank R. Lautenberg (D)

Born Jan. 23, 1924, Paterson; home, Montclair; Columbia University, B.S. 1949; Jewish; separated, 4 children.

Elected 1982, seat up 1994. Career: Army, WWII; Cofounder, Automatic Data Processing, 1952–82; Commissioner, Port Authority of N.Y. & N.J., 1978–82.

Committees: (1) Appropriations; (2) Budget; (3) Environment & Public Works; (4) Small Business.

Election Results: 1990 Lautenberg 1,599,905 (54%); Peter Dawkins (R) 1,349,937 (46%). 1982 Lautenberg (51%).

Interest Group Ratings:

ADA	ACU	COPE	COC
100	04	92	30

LCV	NTLC	CFA	ASC
92	17	83	40

Office: 506 HSOB 20510, 202-224-4744 (Eve Lubalin, AA). STATE OFFICES: 1 Gateway Ctr., Suite 1510, Newark 07102, 201-645-3030 (Tim O'Donovan, St. Dir.); 208 Whitehorse Pike, Suite 18, Barrington 08007, 609-757-5353 (Karen Elkins, Dpty. St. Dir.)

REPRESENTATIVES

FIRST DISTRICT

Robert E. Andrews (D)

District: The New Jersey suburbs of Philadelphia including the city of Camden. Population: 594,630—Black 16%, Hispanic 6%. Politics: Democratic.

Born Aug. 4, 1957, Camden, N.J.; home, Bellmawr; Buchnell University, B.A., 1979, Cornell, J.D., 1982; Episcopalian; single.

Elected 1990. Career: Lawyer, Law prof., Rutgers University, Camden Cty. Bd. of Freeholders, 1986–90, Director, 1990.

Committees: (1) Education & Labor; (2) Foreign Affairs.

Election Results: 1992 Andrews 150,560 (70%); Lee Solomon (R) 63,607 (30%). 1990 Andrews (56%).

Interest Group Ratings:

ADA	ACU	COPE	COC
70	32	83	N/A

LCV	NTLC	CFA	ASC
69	15	73	70

Office: 1005 LHOB 20515, 202-225-6501 (Ken Holdsman, Leg. Dir.). DISTRICT OFFICE: 16 Summerdale Sq., Barrington 08083, 609-627-9000 (Lynn Kmiec, Rep.)

SECOND DISTRICT
William John Hughes (D)

District: Southern part of the state including Atlantic City. Population: 594,630—Black 14%, Hispanic 7%, Other 4%. Politics: Democratic.

Born Oct. 17, 1932, Salem; home, Ocean City; Rutgers University, A.B. 1955, J.D. 1958; Episcopalian; married (Nancy), 4 children.

Elected 1974. Career: Practicing atty., 1959–74; Cape May Cty. Asst. Prosecutor, 1960–70.

Committees: (1) Judiciary; (2) Merchant Marine & Fisheries.

Election Results: 1992 Hughes 127,987 (57%); Frank LoBiondo (R) 95,231 (43%). 1990 Hughes (88%). 1988 Hughes (66%).

Interest Group Ratings:

ADA	ACU	COPE	COC
80	20	83	25

LCV	NTLC	CFA	ASC
88	38	93	60

Office: 241 CHOB 20515, 202-225-6572 (Mark Brown, AA). DISTRICT OFFICES: 222 New Road, Suite 405, Linwood 08221, 609-927-9063 (John Mruz, Dist. Dir.); 151 N. Broadway, P.O. Box 248, Pennsville 08070, 609-678-3333 (Bernice Willadsen, Asst.)

THIRD DISTRICT
H. James Saxton (R)

District: South Jersey's Philadelphia suburbs, including Cherry Hill, and extending east to include southern Ocean County. Population: 594,630—Black 8%, Hispanic 3%. Politics: Leans Republican.

Born Jan. 22, 1943, Scranton, Pa.; home, Vincentown; East Stroudsburg State College, B.A. 1965, Temple University, 1967–68; United Methodist; separated, 2 children.

Elected 1984. Career: Teacher, 1965–68; Real estate broker, 1968–84, N.J. House of Reps., 1975–81; N.J. Senate, 1981–84.

Committees: (1) Armed Services; (2) Merchant Marine & Fisheries; (3) District of Columbia.

Election Results: 1992 Saxton 142,850 (62%); Timothy Ryan (D) 89,347 (38%). 1990 Saxton (60%). 1988 Saxton (69%).

Interest Group Ratings:

ADA	ACU	COPE	COC
15	80	50	75

LCV	NTLC	CFA	ASC
38	68	33	100

Office: 438 CHOB 20515, 202-225-4765 (Bill Jarrell, Chief-of-staff). DISTRICT OFFICES: 115 High St., Mt. Holly 08060, 609-261-5800 (Sandra Condit, Rep.); 1 Maine Ave., Cherry Hill 08002, 609-428-0520 (Dee Denton, Rep.); 7 Hadley Ave., Toms River 08753, 908-914-2020 (Patricia Brogan, Asst.)

FOURTH DISTRICT
Christopher H. Smith (R)

District: Central part of the state including city of Trenton. Population: 594,630—Black 12%, Hispanic 5%. Politics: Leans Democratic.

Born Mar. 4, 1953, Rahway; home, Hamilton Township; Worcester College, England, 1974, Trenton St. College, B.S. 1975; Roman Catholic; married (Marie), 4 children.

Elected 1980. Career: Sales exec., family–owned sporting goods business, 1975–78; Exec. Dir., N.J. Right to Life, 1976–78; Legis. Agent, N.J. Senate & Assembly, 1979.

Committees: (1) Foreign Affairs; (2) Veterans Affairs.

Election Results: 1992 Smith 139,304 (63%); Brian Hughes (D) 80,550 (37%). 1990 Smith (65%). 1988 Smith (66%).

Interest Group Ratings:

ADA	ACU	COPE	COC
40	68	67	75

LCV	NTLC	CFA	ASC
44	55	60	100

Office: 2353 RHOB 20515, 202-225-3765 (Martin Dannenfelser, AA). DISTRICT OFFICES: 1720 Greenwood, Trenton 08609, 609-890-2800 (Joyce Golden, Dir.); 427 High St., Rm. 1, Burlington 08016, 609-386-5534 (Pidge Carroll, Asst.); 100 Lacy Rd. #38-A, Whiting 08759, 908-350-2300 (Lorretta Charbonneau, Reg. Dir.)

FIFTH DISTRICT

Marge Scafati Roukema (R)

District: Far north and western part of the state including town of Ridgewood. Population: 594,630—Asian 4%, Hispanic 3%. Politics: Leans Republican.

Born Sept. 19, 1929, Newark; home, West Orange; Montclair State College, B.A. 1951, Rutgers University; Protestant; married (Richard), 2 children.

Elected 1980. Career: High school teacher, 1951–55; Ridgewood Bd. of Educ., 1970–73; Cofounder, Ridgewood Sr. Citizens Housing Corp., 1973.

Committees: (1) Banking, Finance & Urban Affairs; (2) Education & Labor.

Election Results: 1992 Roukema 193,468 (74%); Frank Lucas (D) 66,746 (26%). 1990 Roukema (77%). 1988 Roukema (76%).

Interest Group Ratings:

ADA	ACU	COPE	COC
50	68	42	N/A

LCV	NTLC	CFA	ASC
38	53	47	90

Office: 2244 RHOB 20515, 202-225-4465 (Steve Wilson, AA). DISTRICT OFFICES: 1200 E. Ridgewood Ave., Ridgewood 07450, 201-447-3900 (Frank Covelli, Chief-of-staff); 1500 Rte. 517 Suite 105, Hackettstown 07840, 908-850-4747.

SIXTH DISTRICT

Frank J. Pallone, Jr. (D)

District: Central Jersey Shore including towns of Asbury Park and Long Branch. Population: 594,630—Black 11%, Hispanic 6%, Asian 5%. Politics: Leans Democratic.

Born Oct. 30, 1951, Long Branch; home, Long Branch; Middlebury College, B.A. 1973, The Fletcher School, M.A. 1974; Rutgers University, J.D. 1978; Roman Catholic; married (Sarah).

Elected 1988. Career: Law clerk, 1978–79; Practicing atty., 1980–88; Counsel, Protective Svcs. for the Elderly, 1982–83; N.J. Senate, 1983–88; City Councilor, Long Branch, N.J., 1982–88.

Committees: (1) Energy & Commerce; (2) Merchant Marine & Fisheries.

Election Results: 1992 Pallone 111,653 (54%); Joseph Kyrillos (R) 95,585 (46%). 1990 Pallone (51%). 1988 Pallone (52%).

Interest Group Ratings:

ADA	ACU	COPE	COC
90	28	83	38

LCV	NTLC	CFA	ASC
88	40	87	80

Office: 420 CHOB 20515, 202-225-4671 (Russ McGuik, AA). DISTRICT OFFICES: 540 Broadway, Suite 119, Long Branch 07740, 908-571-1140 (Patrick Gillespie, Dist. Rep.); IEI Bldg. Suite 33, Hwy. 36, Hazlet 07730, 908-264-9104 (Mike Beson, Rep.); 67-69 Church St. Kilmer Sq., New Brunswick 08901, 908-249-8892

SEVENTH DISTRICT

Bob Franks (R)

District: North–central part of the state including city of Woodbridge. Population: 594,629—Black 10%, Hispanic 5%, Asian 5%. Politics: Mixed, but leans Republican.

Born Sept. 21, 1951, Hackensack; home, New Providence; DePauw, B.A. 1973, Southern Methodist, J.D. 1976; Christian; single.

Elected 1992. Career: N.J. General Assembly, 1979-82.

Committees: (1) Budget; (2) Public Works & Transportation.

Election Results: 1992 Franks 127,726 (56%); Leonard Sendelsky (D) 101,548 (44%).

Interest Group Ratings:
None—Freshman

Office: 429 CHOB 20515, 202-225-5361 (Gregg Edwards, AA). DISTRICT OFFICES: 2333 Morris Ave. B-17, Union 07083, 908-686-5576 (Betty Bauer, Rep.)

EIGHTH DISTRICT

Herbert C. Klein (D)

District: Northeastern part of the state including parts of the cities of Paterson and Passaic. Population: 594,629—Black 13%, Hispanic 18%, Asian 4%, Other 9%. Politics: Democratic.

Born June 24, 1930, Newark; home, Clifton; Rutgers, B.A. 1950, Harvard University, J.D. 1953; Jewish; married (Jacqueline), 2 children (one deceased).

Elected 1992. Career: Attorney, 1953–92; N.J. General Assembly, 1973–76.

Committees: (1) Banking, Finance & Urban Affairs; (2) Science, Space & Technology.

Election Results: 1992 Klein 91,262 (49%); Joseph Bubba (R) 80,734 (43%); Gloria Kolodziej (Oth) 15,618 (8%).

Interest Group Ratings:
None—Freshman

Office: 1728 LHOB 20515, 202-225-5751 (Joe Hansen, AA). DISTRICT OFFICES: 200 Fed. Plaza 500, Patterson 07505, 201-523-5152 (Nellie Pou, Rep.); Post Office Bldg. 13 Municipal Plaza, Bloomfield 07003, 201-645-6299 (Jane Meyers, Rep.)

NINTH DISTRICT

Robert G. Torricelli (D)

District: Northern New York City bedroom communities including communities of Fort Lee and Hackensack. Population: 594,630—Black 6%, Hispanic 11%, Asian 7%. Politics: Democratic.

Born Aug. 26, 1951, Paterson; home, Englewood; Rutgers University, B.A. 1974, J.D. 1977, Kennedy Sch. of Govt., Harvard University, M.P.A. 1980; United Methodist; divorced.

Elected 1982. Career: Asst. to N.J. Gov. Brendan Byrne, 1975–77; Counsel to Vice Pres. Walter Mondale, 1978–81; Practicing atty., 1981–82.

Committees: (1) Foreign Affairs; (2) Science, Space & Technology; (3) Select Committee on Intelligence.

Election Results: 1992 Torricelli 132,201 (61%); Patrick Roma (R) 83,867 (39%). 1990 Torricelli (58%). 1988 Torricelli (68%).

Interest Group Ratings:

ADA	ACU	COPE	COC
85	16	83	33

LCV	NTLC	CFA	ASC
63	05	87	90

Office: 2159 RHOB 20515, 202-225-5061 (Rob Henken, AA). DISTRICT OFFICE: 25 Main St., Court Plaza, Hackensack 07601, 201-646-1111 (Lynn Horwitz, Rep.)

TENTH DISTRICT

Donald M. Payne (D)

District: Northeastern part of the state including city of East Orange, as well as parts of Newark and Jersey City. Population: 594,630— Black 60%, Hispanic 12%. Politics: Democratic.

Born July 16, 1934, Newark; home, Newark; Seton Hall University, B.A. 1957; Baptist; widower, 2 children.

Elected 1988. Career: Exec. Prudential Ins. Co.; V.P. Urban Data Systems; Pres. YMCAs of USA; Essex Cty. Bd. of Freeholders 1972–78; Newark City Council, 1982–89.

Committees: (1) Education & Labor; (2) Foreign Affairs; (3) Government Operations.

Election Results: 1992 Payne 104,817 (79%); Alfred Palermo (R) 28,061 (21%). 1990 Payne (83%). 1988 Payne (86%).

Interest Group Ratings:

ADA	ACU	COPE	COC
95	00	91	13

LCV	NTLC	CFA	ASC
81	00	93	10

Office: 417 CHOB 20515, 202-225-3436 (Maxine James, AA). DISTRICT OFFICE: 1435B Fed. Bldg., 970 Broad St., Newark 07102, 201-645-3213 (Richard Thigpen, Dist. Adm.)

ELEVENTH DISTRICT

Dean A. Gallo (R)

District: North-central part of the state including all of Morris county as well as parts of Essex, Sussex, Passaic, and Somerset counties. Population: 594,630—Black 3%, Asian 4%, Hispanic 4%. Politics: Leans Republican.

Born Nov. 23, 1935, Boonton; home, Parsippany; United Methodist; divorced, 2 children.

Elected 1984. Career: Parsippany–Troy Hills Cncl., 1968–71, Pres., 1970–71; Morris Cty. Bd. of Freeholders, 1971–75, Dir., 1973–75; N.J. House of Reps., 1975–84.

Committees: (1) Appropriations.

Election Results: 1992 Gallo 179,803 (73%); Ona Spiridellis (D) 65,024 (27%). 1990 Gallo (66%). 1988 Gallo (70%).

Interest Group Ratings:

ADA	ACU	COPE	COC
25	76	33	75

LCV	NTLC	CFA	ASC
81	60	27	100

Office: 2447 RHOB 20515, 202-225-5034 (Donna Mullin, Chief-of-staff). DISTRICT OFFICES: 1 Morris St., Morristown 07960, 201-984-0711 (Carol Ricker, Dist. Mgr.); 22 N. Sussex St., Dover 07801, 201-328-7413 (Joan Bramhall, Rep.); 3 Fairfield Ave., W. Caldwell 07006, 201-228-9262 (Joan Hamilton, Rep.)

TWELFTH DISTRICT

Richard Zimmer (R)

District: Central part of the state including towns of Princeton and Ewing. Population: 594,063—Black 5%, Asian 4%, Hispanic 3%. Politics: Leans Republican.

Born Aug. 16, 1944, Newark; home, Flemington; Yale University, B.A., 1966, LL.B. 1969; Jewish; married (Marfy), 2 children.

Elected 1990. Career: Lawyer; N.J, Assembly, 1982–87; N.J. Senate 1987–90.

Committees: (1) Government Operations; (2) Science, Space & Technology.

Election Results: 1992 Zimmer 167,127 (67%); Frank Abate (D) 80,731 (33%). 1990 Zimmer (67%).

Interest Group Ratings:

ADA	ACU	COPE	COC
40	76	42	63

LCV	NTLC	CFA	ASC
50	80	40	90

Office: 228 CHOB 20515, 202-225-5801 (Dave Karvelas, AA). DISTRICT OFFICES: P.O. Bldg., 133 Franklin Corner Rd., Lawrenceville 08648, 609-895-1559 (Tom Blakley, Dist. Mgr.); 36 W. Main St., Freehold 07728, 908-309-9020; 119 Main St., Flemington 08822, 908-788-1952.

THIRTEENTH DISTRICT

Robert Menendez (D)

District: Northeastern part of the state including parts of Newark and Jersey City. Population: 594,630—Black 14%, Hispanic 41%, Asian 5%, Other 14%. Politics: Democratic.

Born Jan. 1, 1954, New York City; home, Union City; St. Peters College, B.A. 1976, Rutgers, J.D. 1979; Roman Catholic; married (Jane), 2 children.

Elected 1992. Career: Union City Board of Education, 1974–82; Mayor of Union City, 1986–92; N.J. General Assembly, 1987–91; N.J. State Senate, 1991–92.

Committees: (1) Foreign Affairs; (2) Public Works & Transportation.

Election Results: 1992 Menendez 88,358 (68%); Fred Theemling, Jr. (R) 42,524 (32%).

Interest Group Ratings:
None—Freshman

Office: 1531 LHOB 20515, 202-225-7919 (Michael Hutton, AA). DISTRICT OFFICES: 911 Bergan Ave., Jersey City 07302, 201-222-2828 (Patti McGuire, Rep.); 654 Ave. C, Bayonne 07002, 201-823-2900 (Dennis Collins, Rep.); 275 Hobart St., Perth Amboy 08861, 908-324-6212 (Jose Alvarez, Rep.)

NEW MEXICO

This traditionally Republican state is becoming more Democratic in part because of the heavy influx of new Hispanic voters. Republicans would like to think they can defeat incumbent Democratic Sen. Jeff Bingaman in 1994. But that would seem possible only if the GOP can convince Rep. Steven Schiff to give up a safe House seat to make the race. That does not seem likely. Also in 1994, New Mexico's governor will be allowed to run for a third consecutive term for the first time. That means the probable reelection of popular Democrat Bruce King.

1992 PRESIDENTIAL ELECTION: (5 Electoral votes): Clinton (D) 259,500 (46%); Bush (R) 212,393 (38%); Perot (I) 91,539 (16%); Marrou (Lib) 1,466; Hagelin (NLP) 646; Phillips (AmTax) 608; Fulani (NAP) 364; Warren (SocWks) 189; LaRiva (Wks-Wld) 178; Dodge (Prob) 127. 1988 Bush 260,792 (52%); Dukakis 236,528 (48%).

SENATORS

Pete V. Domenici (R)

Born May 7, 1932, Albuquerque; home, Albuquerque; St.Joseph's College, 1950–52, University of N.Mex., B.S. 1954, Denver University, LL.B. 1958; Roman Catholic; married (Nancy), 8 children.

Elected 1972, seat up 1996. Career: Practicing atty., 1958–72; Albuquerque City Comm., 1966–70, Mayor Ex–Officio, 1967–70.

Committees: (1) Appropriations; (2) Budget (Ranking Member); (3) Energy & Natural Resources; (4) Banking, Housing & Urban Affairs.

Election Results: 1990 Domenici 294,226 (73%); Tom Benavides (D) 109,375 (27%). 1984 Domenici (72%).

Interest Group Ratings:

ADA	ACU	COPE	COC
15	78	17	78

LCV	NTLC	CFA	ASC
00	72	33	100

Office: 427 DSOB 20510, 202-224-6621 (Chas Gentry, AA). STATE OFFICES: 625 Silver Ave., SW, Suite 120, Albuquerque 87102, 505-766-3481 (Fran Langholf, Dir.); New P.O. Bldg, 5 Fed. Place, Santa Fe 87501, 505-988-6511 (Maggie

Murray, Dir.); Sunbelt Plaza 1065 S. Main St. Bldg D, Las Cruces 88005, 505-526-5475 (Darlene Garcia, Dir.); 140 Fed. Bldg. Roswell 88201, 505-623-6170 (Poe Corn, Dir.)

Jeff Bingaman (D)

Born Oct. 1943, El Paso, Tex.; home, Santa Fe; Harvard College, B.A. 1965, Stanford Law School, LL.B. 1968; United Methodist; married (Anne), 1 child.

Elected 1982, seat up 1994. Career: N.Mex. Asst. Atty. Gen., 1969; Practicing atty., 1970–78; N.Mex. Atty. Gen., 1979–82.

Committees: (1) Armed Services; (2) Energy & Natural Resources; (3) Labor & Human Resources; (4) Joint Economic Committee

Election Results: 1988 Bingaman 321,983 (63%); Bill Valentine (R) 186,579 (37%). 1982 Bingaman (54%).

Interest Group Ratings:

ADA	ACU	COPE	COC
75	04	92	20

LCV	NTLC	CFA	ASC
58	17	75	40

Office: 524 HSOB 20510, 202-224-5521 (Patrick VonBargen, Chief of Staff.). STATE OFFICES: 625 Silver Ave. SW, Suite 130, Albuquerque 87102, 505-766-3636 (Ricardo Zuniga, St. Cord.); 119 E. Marcy, Suite 101, Santa Fe 87501, 505-988-6647 (Dolores Garcia, Ex. Asst.); 148 Loredo Town Ctr., 505 Main St., Las Cruces 88001, 505-523-6561 (Alice Salcido, Dist. Dir.); 114 E. 4th St. Suite 103, Roswell 88201, 505-622-7113 (Lynn Ditto, Asst.)

REPRESENTATIVES

FIRST DISTRICT

Steven H. Schiff (R)

District: City of Albuquerque and Torrance county. Population: 505,491—Black 3%, Native American 3%, Hispanic 38%, Other 16%. Politics: Very mixed, but leaning Republican.

Born Mar. 18, 1947, Chicago, Ill.; home, Albuquerque; University of Ill. at Chicago, B.A. 1968,

University of N.Mex., J.D. 1972; Jewish; married (Marcia), 2 children.

Elected 1988. Career: Asst. Dist. Atty., Bernalillo Cty., 1972–77; Practicing atty., 1977–79; Asst. Cty. Atty. & Counsel, Albuquerque Police Dept., 1979–81; Dist. Atty., Bernalillo Cty., 1981–88.

Committees: (1) Government Operations; (2) Science, Space & Technology; (3) Judiciary; (4) Ethics.

Election Results: 1992 Schiff 127,560 (63%); Robert Aragon (D) 76,188 (37%). 1990 Schiff (70%). 1988 Schiff (51%).

Interest Group Ratings:

ADA	ACU	COPE	COC
25	72	58	88

LCV	NTLC	CFA	ASC
13	70	20	90

Office: 1009 LHOB 20515, 202-225-6316 (Pete Rintye, AA). DISTRICT OFFICE: 625 Silver Ave, S.W., Suite 140, Albuquerque 87102, 505-766-2538 (Martha Morgan, Dist. Dir.)

SECOND DISTRICT

Joseph Richard Skeen (R)

District: Southern and half of the state including cities of Las Cruces and Roswell. Population: 504,659—Black 2%, Native American 4%, Hispanic 42%, Other 10%. Politics: Republican.

Born June 30, 1927, Roswell: home, Picacho; Tex. A&M University, B.S. 1950; Roman Catholic; married (Mary), 2 children.

Elected 1980. Career: Navy, WWII; Engineer, Navajo Reservation, 1950–51; Sheep rancher, 1951–80; N.Mex. Senate, 1960–70, Minor. Ldr., 1965–70; Repub. Nominee for Gov. of N.Mex., 1974, 1978.

Committees: Appropriations.

Election Results: 1992 Skeen 94,826 (56%); Dan Sosa Jr. (D) 73,118 (44%). 1990 Skeen (Unopposed). 1988 Skeen (Unopposed).

Interest Group Ratings:

ADA	ACU	COPE	COC
20	76	42	88

LCV	NTLC	CFA	ASC
06	60	27	100

Office: 2367 RHOB 20515, 202-225-2365 (Suzanne Eisold, AA). DISTRICT OFFICES: 1065 S. Main St. Suite A, Las Cruces 88005, 505-527-1771 (Dorothy Conway, Dist. Rep.); 127 Fed Bldg., 500 N. Richardson Ave., Roswell 88201, 505-622-0055 (Alice Eppers, Dist. Rep.)

THIRD DISTRICT

Bill Richardson (D)

District: Northern half of the state including cities of Farmington and Santa Fe. Population: 504,919—Native American 20%, Hispanic 35%, Other 13%. Politics: Democratic.

Born Nov. 15, 1947, Pasadena, Calif.: home, Santa Fe; Tufts University, B.A. 1970, Fletcher School of Law & Diplomacy, M.A. 1971; Roman Catholic; married (Barbara).

Elected 1982. Career: Staff, N.Mex. House of Reps., 1981–72; State Dept. Off. of Congressional Relations, 1973–75; Staff, Sen. Subcomm. on Foreign Relations Assistance, 1975–78; Business, 1978–82.

Committees: Majority Whip. (1) Energy & Commerce; (2) Natural Resources; (3) Permanent Select Committee on Intelligence.

Election Results: 1992 Richardson 121,026 (67%); F. Gregg Bemis Jr. (R) 53,949 (30%); Ed Nagel (Libert) 4,700 (3%). 1990 Richardson (74%). 1988 Richardson (73%).

Interest Group Ratings:

ADA	ACU	COPE	COC
75	33	73	57

LCV	NTLC	CFA	ASC
63	00	67	80

Office: 2349 RHOB 20515, 202-225-6190 (Isabelle Watkins, AA). DISTRICT OFFICES: 548 Agua Fria, Santa Fe 87501, 505-988-7230 (Sam Taylor, Dist. Dir.); Gallup City Hall, 2nd & Aztec, Gallup 87301, 505-722-6522 (Rose Custer, Asst.); San Miguel Cty. Cthse., Las Vegas 87701, 505-425-7270 (Rebecca Montoya, Asst.); 602 Mitchell, Clovis 88101, 505-769-3380 (Becky Geer, Rep.)

NEW YORK

New York Democrats are still badly split as a result of the bloody Senate primary in 1992 in which state Attorney General Bob Abrams narrowly won the right to oppose GOP Sen. Al D'Amato, and then lost to D'Amato in the general election. Thus, it is a good thing for the Democrats that Governor Mario Cuomo has taken himself out of contention for a Supreme Court seat and says that he will run for a fourth term. This will keep New York politics stable. Had he left for Washington, it would have opened a major office and a dozen top Democrats would have been after the job. As it stands now, it is likely that as controversial as he is in some areas, Cuomo will win an easy reelection victory. Democratic Sen. Daniel Patrick Moynihan must run in 1994 for a new 6-year term. He has given every indication that he will do so, and he should win easily.

1992 PRESIDENTIAL ELECTION: (33 Electoral votes): Clinton (D) 3,246,787 (50%); Bush (R) 2,250,676 (34%); Perot (I) 1,029,038 (16%); Warren (SocWks) 18,388; Marrou (Lib) 16,386; Fulani (NAP) 12,557; Hagelin (NLP) 6,122. 1988 Bush 3,081,871 (48%); Dukakis 3,347,882 (52%).

SENATORS

Daniel Patrick Moynihan (D)

Born Mar. 16, 1927, Tulsa, Okla.; home, W. Davenport; Community College of New York, 1943, Tufts University, B.A. 1948, M.A. 1949, Ph.D. 1961, LL.D. 1968; Roman Catholic; married (Elizabeth), 3 children.

Elected 1976, seat up 1994. Career: Navy, 1944–47; University prof.; Aide to Gov. Averell Harriman, 1955–58; U.S. Asst. Secy. of Labor, 1963–65; Dir., Joint Ctr. for Urban Studies, MIT & Harvard, 1966–69; Asst. to the Pres. for Urban Affairs, 1969–70; Ambassador to India, 1973–75; Ambassador to the U.N., 1975–76.

Committees: (1) Environment & Public Works; (2) Finance (Chairman); (3) Foreign Relations; (4) Rules & Administration; (5) Joint Committee on the Library; (6) Joint Committee on Taxation.

Election Results: 1988 Moynihan 4,048,649 (67%); Robert McMillan (R) 1,875,784 (31%). 1982 Moynihan (65%).

Interest Group Ratings:

ADA	ACU	COPE	COC
100	00	83	10

LCV	NTLC	CFA	ASC
67	11	92	40

Office: 464 RSOB 20510, 202-224-4451 (Richard Eaton, AA). STATE OFFICES: 405 Lexington Ave., Suite 4101, New York 10074, 212-661-5150 (David Warner, Reg. Dir.); Guaranty Bldg., 28 Church St., Buffalo 14202, 716-846-4097 (Jim B. Kane, Reg. Dir.); 214 Main St., Oneonta 13820, 607-433-2310 (Barbara Rainville, Reg. Dir.)

Alfonse M. D'Amato (R)

Born Aug. 1, 1937, Brooklyn; home, Island Park; Syracuse University, B.S. 1959, J.D. 1961; Roman Catholic; separated, 4 children.

Elected 1980, seat up 1998. Career: Nassau Cty. Public Admin., 1965–68; Hempstead Town Receiver of Taxes, 1969, Sprvsr., 1971–77, Presiding Sprvsr., Vice Chmn. Nassau Cty. Bd. of Sprvsrs., 1977–80.

Committees: (1) Appropriations; (2) Banking, Housing & Urban Affairs (Ranking Member); (3) Select Committee on Intelligence.

Election Results: 1992 D'Amato 3,007,882 (51%); Robert Abrams (D) 2,899,888 (49%). 1986 D'Amato (57%). 1980 D'Amato (45%).

Interest Group Ratings:

ADA	ACU	COPE	COC
30	52	70	60

LCV	NTLC	CFA	ASC
58	78	67	100

Office: 520 HSOB 20510, 202-224-6542 (Michael Kinsella, AA). STATE OFFICES: 420 Fed. Bldg. One Clinton Ave., Albany 12207, 518-472-4343 (Dave Pulito, Dir.); 620 Fed. Bldg., 111 West Huron, Buffalo 14202, 716-846-4111 (Jane O'Bannon, Ex. Asst.); 7 Penn Plaza, Suite 600, New York 10001, 212-947-7390 (Margaret Dillon, Ex. Asst.); 1259 Fed. Bldg., 100 South Clinton Street, Syracuse 13260, 315-423-5471 (Gretchen Ralph, Ex. Asst.); 304 Fed. Bldg., 100 State Street, Rochester 14614, 716-263-5866 (Joan Mueller, Ex. Asst.)

REPRESENTATIVES

FIRST DISTRICT

George J. Hochbrueckner (D)

District: Eastern half of Long Island in Suffolk County. Population: 580,388—Black 4%, Hispanic 5%. Politics: Mixed, but leans Democratic.

Born Sept. 20, 1938, Jamaica, Queens; home, Coram; State University of N.Y., Stonybrook, Hofstra University; Roman Catholic; married (Carol Ann), 4 children.

Elected 1986. Career: Navy, 1956–59; Engineer, 1961–75; N.Y. Assembly, 1975–84.

Committees: (1) Armed Services; (2) Merchant Marine & Fisheries.

Election Results: 1992 Hochbrueckner 111,418 (51%); Edward Romaine (R) 105,069 (49%). 1990 Hochbrueckner (56%). 1988 Hochbrueckner (51%).

Interest Group Ratings:

ADA	ACU	COPE	COC
95	04	92	25

LCV	NTLC	CFA	ASC
75	00	93	50

Office: 229 CHOB 20515, 202-225-3826 (Tom Downs, AA). DISTRICT OFFICES: 3771 Nesconset Hwy., Suite 213, Centereach 11720, 516-689-6767 (Ellen Joyce, Mgr.); 437 E. Main, Riverhead 11901, 516-727-2152 (Marge Acevedo, Mgr.)

SECOND DISTRICT

Rick Lazio (R)

District: Western half of Long Island, western Suffolk County. Population: 580,337—Black 10%, Hispanic 10%. Politics: Leans Democratic.

Born Mar. 13, 1958, W. Islip; home, Brightwaters; Vassar, B.A. 1980, American University, J.D. 1983; Roman Catholic; married (Patricia), 1 child.

Elected 1992. Career: Suffolk County Asst. Dist. Attorney, 1983–88; Practicing Attorney, 1989–Present; Suffolk Cty. Legislature, 1989–92.

Committees: (1) Banking, Finance & Urban Affairs; (2) Budget.

Election Results: 1992 Lazio 104,264 (53%); Thomas J. Downey (Incumbent D) 91,465 (47%).

Interest Group Ratings:
None—Freshman

Office: 314 CHOB 20515, 202-225-3335 (Phil Boyle, AA). DISTRICT OFFICE: 126 W. Main St., Babylon 11702, 516-893-9010 (Christopher Williams, Rep.)

THIRD DISTRICT

Peter King (R)

District: North Shore of Long Island in Nassau County including Long Beach City and Hicksville. Population: 580,337—Black 2%, Hispanic 4%, Asian 3%. Politics: Leans Republican.

Born Apr. 5, 1944, New York City; home, Seaford; Saint Frances College, B.A. 1965, Notre Dame, J.D. 1968; Roman Catholic; married (Rosemary), 2 children.

Elected 1992. Career: Campaign Manager, Norm Lent for Congress, 1972; Nassau Cty. Comptroller, 1981–92.

Committees: (1) Banking, Finance & Urban Affairs; (2) Merchant Marine & Fisheries.

Election Results: 1992 King 118,345 (49%); Steve Orlins (D) 112,063 (47%); Louis Roccanova 6,889; Ben-Zion Heyman 2,949.

Interest Group Ratings:
None—Freshman

Office: 118 CHOB 20515, 202-225-7896 (John Hymes, AA). DISTRICT OFFICES: 1003 Hark Blvd., Massapequa Park 11762, 516-541-4225

FOURTH DISTRICT

David Levy (R)

District: Western portion of Long Island's Nassau County including communities of Mineola, Hempstead and Rockville Centre. Population: 580,388—Black 16%, Hispanic 8%, Asian 3%. Politics: Republican.

Born Dec. 18, 1953, Johnson Cty., Ind.; home, Baldwin; Hofstra University, B.A. 1974, J.D. 1979; Jewish; married (Tracy), 2 children.

Elected, 1992. Career: Practicing atty.; Hempstead Town Council, 1988–92.

Committees: (1) Foreign Affairs; (2) Public Works & Transportation.

Election Results: 1992 Levy 107,285 (50%); Philip Schiliro (D) 97,583 (46%); Vincent Garbitelli 9,168 (4%).

Interest Group Ratings:
None—Freshman

Office: 116 CHOB 20515, 202-225-5516 (Arthur DeCello, AA).DISTRICT OFFICE: 203 Rockaway Ave., Valley Stream 11580, 516-872-9550 (Donald Fonte, Rep.)

FIFTH DISTRICT

Gary L. Ackerman (D)

District: Central Queens including the Kew Gardens section. Population: 580,337—Black 3%, Asian 11%, Hispanic 7%. Politics: Democratic.

Born Nov. 19, 1942, Brooklyn; home, Flushing; Queens College, B.A. 1965; Jewish; married (Rita), 3 children.

Elected Mar. 1, 1983. Career: Pub. sch. teacher, 1966–72; Newspaper ed. & pub.; Adv. agcy. owner; N.Y. Senate, 1979–83.

Committees: (1) Foreign Affairs; (2) Post Office & Civil Service; (3) Banking, Finance & Urban Affairs (temp.).

Election Results: 1992 Ackerman 97,425 (52%); Allan Binder (R) 86,316 (46%); Andrew Duff (C) 5,180 (3%). 1990 Unopposed. 1988 Unopposed.

Interest Group Ratings:

ADA	ACU	COPE	COC
70	00	91	33

LCV	NTLC	CFA	ASC
75	00	67	40

Office: 2445 RHOB 20515, 202-225-2601 (Jedd Moskowitz, AA). DISTRICT OFFICES: 218-14 Northern Blvd., Bayside 11361, 718-423-2154 (Arthur Flug, Dist. Adm.); 229 Main St., Huntington 11743, 516-423-2154 (Anne McShane, Rep.)

SIXTH DISTRICT

Floyd H. Flake (D)

District: Western Queens including neighborhoods of Ozone Park and Jamaica. Population:

580,337—Black 56%, Hispanic 17%, Asian 6%. Politics: Democratic.

Born Jan. 30, 1945, Los Angeles, Calif.; home, Jamaica, Queens; Wilberforce University, B.A., 1967; Payne Theological Seminary, 1967–69, Northeastern University, 1974–75; Saint John's University, 1982–85; African Methodist Episcopal; married (Elaine), 4 children.

Elected 1986. Career: Mktg. Analyst, XeroxCorp. 1969–70; Assoc. Dean & Dir. of Student Activities, 1970–73; Dean of Students & Chaplin, Boston University, 1973–76; Pastor, Allen A.M.E. Church.

Committees: (1) Banking, Finance & Urban Affairs; (2) Small Business; (3) Government Operations.

Election Results: 1992 Flake 92,654 (81%); Dianand Bhagwandin (R) 21,276 (19%). 1990 Flake (72%); 1988 Flake (86%).

Interest Group Ratings:

ADA	ACU	COPE	COC
90	00	92	13

LCV	NTLC	CFA	ASC
75	00	93	20

Office: 1035 LHOB 20515, 202-225-3461 (Edwin Reed, AA). DISTRICT OFFICE: 196-06 Linden Blvd., St. Alban 11412, 718-949-5600 (Sam Moon, Rep.)

SEVENTH DISTRICT

Thomas J. Manton (D)

District: Portions of both the Bronx and Queens including the Astoria and Jackson Heights areas. Population: 580,337—Black 10%, Asian 11%, Hispanic 17%. Politics: Democratic.

Born Nov. 3, 1932, New York City; home, Sunnyside; Saint John's University, B.B.A. 1958, LL.B. 1962; Roman Catholic; married (Diane), 4 children.

Elected 1984. Career: USMC, 1951–53; New York City Police Dept., 1955–60; IBM salesman, 1960–64; Practicing atty., 1964–84; New York City Council, 1970–84.

Committees: (1) Energy & Commerce; (2) Merchant Marine & Fisheries; (3) House Administration.

Election Results: 1992 Manton 67,843 (56%); Dennis Shea (R) 52,734 (44%). 1990 Manton 65%. 1988 Manton (Unopposed).

Interest Group Ratings:

ADA	ACU	COPE	COC
85	08	83	29

LCV	NTLC	CFA	ASC
38	05	80	60

Office: 203 CHOB 20515, 202-225-3965 (David Springer, AA). DISTRICT OFFICES: 46-12 Queens Blvd., Sunnyside 11104, 718-706-1400 (Fran Craft, Dir.); 2114 Williamsbridge Rd., Bronx 10461, 718-931-1400 (Fran Mahoney, Rep.)

EIGHTH DISTRICT

Jerrold Nadler (D)

District: Northern Queens centered around the Flushing area along with small sections of the eastern Bronx and suburban western Nassau County. Population: 580,337—Black 9%, Asian 6%, Hispanic 13%. Politics: Democratic.

Born Jun. 13 1947, Brooklyn; home, Manhattan; Columbia University, B.A. 1970, Fordham University, J.D. 1978 ; Jewish; married (Joyce Miller), 1 child.

Elected 1992. Career: Asst. to State Sen. Jack Bronston, 1966–68; Asst. to Assemblyman Richard Gottfried, 1972; Lobbyist, 1972–76; N.Y. General Assembly, 1976–92.

Committees: (1) Judiciary; (2) Public Works & Transportation.

Election Results: 1992 Nadler 126,832 (81%); David Askren (R) 24,227 (16%); Margaret Byrnes (I) 4,873 (3%).

Interest Group Ratings:
None—Freshman

Office: 424 CHOB 20515, 202-225-5635 (Amy Green, AA). DISTRICT OFFICE: 1841 Broadway #800, New York 10023, 212-489-3530 (Neil Goldstein, Rep.)

NINTH DISTRICT

Charles E. Schumer (D)

District: Central and southern Brooklyn. Population: 580,338—Black 3%, Asian 6%, Hispanic 8%. Politics: Democratic.

Born Nov. 23, 1950, Brooklyn; home, Brooklyn; Harvard College, B.A. 1971, Harvard Law School, J.D. 1974; Jewish; married (Iris), 2 children.

Elected 1980. Career: Practicing atty.; N.Y. Assembly, 1974–80.

Committees: (1) Banking, Finance & Urban Affairs; (2) Foreign Affairs; (3) Judiciary.

Election Results: 1992 Schumer 111,399 (89%); Alice Gaffney (I) 14,273 (11%). 1990 Schumer 80%. 1988 Schumer 78%.

Interest Group Ratings:

ADA	ACU	COPE	COC
95	00	82	25

LCV	NTLC	CFA	ASC
88	05	100	30

Office: 2412 LHOB 20515, 202-225-6616 (Marcus Kunian, AA). DISTRICT OFFICES: 1628 Kings Hwy., Brooklyn 11229, 718-965-5400 (Florence Stachel, Ex. Asst.); 7315 Yellowstone Blvd., Forest Hills 11375, 718-268-8200 (Verona Sullivan, Rep.); 90-16 Rockaway Beach Blvd., Rockaway 11693, 718-945-9200

TENTH DISTRICT

Edolphus Towns (D)

District: Northern Brooklyn centered on the Bedford-Stuyvesant area. Population: 580,335—Black 61%, Hispanic 20%, Other 10%. Politics: Democratic.

Born July 21, 1934, Chadbourn, N.C.; home, Brooklyn; N.C. A&T State University, B.S. 1956, Adelphi University, M.S.W. 1973; Presbyterian; married (Gwendolyn), 2 children.

Elected 1982. Career: Army, 1956–58; Prof., Medgar Evers College; Asst. Admin., Beth Israel Hospital, 1965–75; Dpty. Borough Pres. of Brooklyn, 1976–82.

Committees: (1) Government Operations; (2) Public Works & Transportation.

Election Results: 1992 Towns 93,271 (96%); Owen Augustin (I) 4,320 (4%). 1990 Towns 93%. 1988 Towns 87%.

Interest Group Ratings:

ADA	ACU	COPE	COC
80	00	82	14

LCV	NTLC	CFA	ASC
69	00	80	10

Office: 2232 RHOB 20515, 202-225-5936 (Brenda Pillon, Chief-of- staff). DISTRICT OFFICE: 545 Broadway 2nd Floor., Brooklyn 11236, 718-387-8696 (vacant, Dir.)

ELEVENTH DISTRICT

Major R. Owens (D)

District: Central Brooklyn centered on the Crown Heights section. Population: 580,337—Black 74%, Hispanic 12%, Asian 3%, Other 4%. Politics: Democratic.

Born June 28, 1936, Memphis, Tenn.; home, Brooklyn; Morehouse College, B.A. 1956, Atlanta University, M.S. 1957; Baptist; married (Maria), 5 children.

Elected 1982. Career: Vice Pres., Metropolitan Council of Housing, 1964; Community Coord., Brooklyn Pub. Library, 1964–65; Exec. Dir., Brownsville Community Council, 1966–68; Commissioner, N.Y.C. Community Development Agency, 1968–73; Dir., Community Media Library Program, Columbia University, 1974; N.Y. Senate 1974–82.

Committees: (1) Education & Labor; (2) Government Operations.

Election Results: 1992 Owens 75,574 (95%); Michael Gaffney (I) 4,122 (5%). 1990 Owens 95%. 1988 Owens 93%.

Interest Group Ratings:

ADA	ACU	COPE	COC
85	00	92	13

LCV	NTLC	CFA	ASC
94	05	93	10

Office: 2305 RHOB 20515, 202-225-6231 (Jacqueline Ellis, AA). DISTRICT OFFICE: 289 Utica Ave., Brooklyn 11213, 718-773-3100 (Evette Garner, Dir.)

TWELFTH DISTRICT

Nydia Velazquez (D)

District: Parts of Brooklyn, Manhattan and Queens. Population: 580,340—Black 14%, Asian 20%, Hispanic 58%, Other 32%. Politics: Democratic.

Born Mar. 28, 1953, Yabucoa, P.R.; home, Brooklyn; University of Puerto Rico, B.A. 1974, New York University, M.S. 1976; no religion specified; divorced.

Elected 1992. Career: College Professor, 1976–83; Asst. to Rep. Ed Towns, 1983; N.Y. City Council, 1984–92.

Committees: (1) Banking, Finance & Urban Affairs; (2) Small Business.

Election Results: 1992 Velazquez 51,608 (77%); Angel Diaz (R) 13,945 (21%); Ruben Franco (I) 1,420 (2%).

Interest Group Ratings:
None—Freshman

Office: 132 CHOB 20515, 202-225-2361 (Karen Ackerman, AA).DISTRICT OFFICE: 815 Broadway, Brooklyn 11206, 718-599-3658 (Manny Rosa, Rep.)

THIRTEENTH DISTRICT

Susan Molinari (R)

District: Staten Island and the western section of Brooklyn including Bensonhurst and Brooklyn Heights. Population: 580,337—Black 6%, Asian 5%, Hispanic 7%. Politics: Leans Republican.

Born March 27, 1958, Staten Island; home, Staten Island; State University of N.Y. (Albany), B.A. 1980, M.A., 1982; Roman Catholic; divorced.

Elected Mar., 1990 (Special Election). Career: New York Cty. Council 1985–90.

Committees: (1) Education and Labor; (2) Public Works.

Election Results: 1992 Molinari 102,715 (56%); Sal Albanese (D) 70,447 (38%); Kathleen Murphy (I) 10,428 (6%). 1990 Molinari 60%. 1990 (special) Molinari 59%.

Interest Group Ratings:

ADA	ACU	COPE	COC
35	64	58	88

LCV	NTLC	CFA	ASC
44	65	47	100

Office: 123 CHOB 20515, 202-225-3371 (Dan Leonard, AA). DISTRICT OFFICES: 14 New Dorp Lane, Staten Island 10306, 718-987-8400 (Barbara Palumb, Rep.); 9818 4th Ave., Brooklyn 11209, 718-630-5277 (Ellen Long, Rep.)

FOURTEENTH DISTRICT

Carolyn Maloney (D)

District: America's "Silk Stocking" district — the affluent East Side of Manhattan now expanded to include more blue collar areas of Greenpoint in Brooklyn and Astoria in Queens. Population: 580,337—Black 5%, Asian 6%, Hispanic 11%. Politics: Leans Republican.

Born Feb. 18, 1948, Greensboro, N.C.; home, New York City; Greensboro College, A.B. 1968; Presbyterian; married (Clifton), 2 children.

Elected 1992. Career: Teacher, 1972–74; N.Y.C. Board of Education Industry Education Coordinator, 1974–77; Aide, N.Y. Assembly Committee on Housing, 1978; State Sen. Minority Leader Director of Special Projects, 1979–81; N.Y. City Council, 1982–92.

Committees: (1) Banking, Finance & Urban Affairs; (2) Government Operations.

Election Results: 1992 Maloney 94,613 (51%); Bill Green (R.-Incumbent) 89,423 (49%).

Interest Group Ratings:
None—Freshman

Office: 1504 LHOB 20515, 202-225-7944 (Jeremy Rabinowitz, AA). DISTRICT OFFICE: 950 3rd Ave. 19th Floor, New York 10022, 212-832-6531 (Victor Montesinos, Rep.)

FIFTEENTH DISTRICT

Charles Bernard Rangel (D)

District: Harlem. Population: 580,337—Black 47%, Hispanic 46%, Other 22%. Politics: Democratic.

Born June 11, 1930, New York City; home, New York City; New York University, B.S. 1957, Saint John's University, J.D. 1960; Roman Catholic; married (Alma), 2 children.

Elected 1970. Career: Army, Korea; Asst. U.S. Atty., South Dist. of N.Y., 1961; Legal Counsel to Manhattan Borough Pres. Percy Suttibm 1964–66; N.Y. Assembly, 1966–70.

Committees: (1) Ways & Means.

Election Results: 1992 Rangel 97,398 (95%); Jose Suero (I) 4,817 (5%). 1990 Rangel 97%; 1988 Rangel 97%.

Interest Group Ratings:

ADA	ACU	COPE	COC
95	00	100	25

LCV	NTLC	CFA	ASC
69	00	93	20

Office: 2252 RHOB 20515, 202-225-4365 (Patricia Bradley, Ex. Asst.). DISTRICT OFFICES: 163 W. 125 St., Rm. 730, New York 10027, 212-663-3900 (Vivian Jones, Dist. Adm.); 601 W. 181st St., New York 10033, 212-927-5333 (Rita Kardeman, Rep.); 2110 First Ave., New York 10029, 212-348-9630 (Juanita Laugier, Rep.)

SIXTEENTH DISTRICT

Jose E. Serrano (D)

District: South Bronx. Population: 580,338—Black 42%, Hispanic 60%, Other 35%. Politics: Democratic.

Born Oct. 24, 1943, Mayaguez, P.R.; home, Bronx; Roman Catholic; married (Mary), 3 children, 2 step children.

Elected Mar., 1990 (Special Election). Career: Army 1964–66; N.Y. Cty. Comm. Sch. Bd., 1969–75; N.Y. Assembly, 1975–90.

Committees: (1) Appropriations.

Election Results: 1992 Serrano 81,632 (91%); Michael Walters (R) 7,868 (9%). 1990 Serrano 93%. 1990 (special) Serrano 92%.

Interest Group Ratings:

ADA	ACU	COPE	COC
95	00	91	13

LCV	NTLC	CFA	ASC
88	00	93	10

Office: 336 CHOB 20515, 202-225-4361 (Ellyn Toscano, Chief-of-staff). DISTRICT OFFICE: 890 Grand Concourse, Bronx 10451, 212-860-6200 (Caridad Pena, AA)

SEVENTEENTH DISTRICT

Eliot L. Engel (D)

District: West Side of Manhattan and Riverdale

section of the Bronx. Population: 580,337—Black 42%, Asian 4%, Hispanic 29%, Other 14%. Politics: Democratic.

Born Feb. 18, 1947, the Bronx, New York; home, the Bronx; Hunter-Lehman College, B.A. 1969, Lehman College, M.A. 1973; Jewish; married (Pat), 2 children.

Elected 1988. Career: Teacher & guidance counselor, 1969–77; N.Y. State Assemblyman, 1977–78.

Committees: (1) Foreign Affairs; (2) Education & Labor.

Election Results: 1992 Engel 92,802 (81%); Martin Richman (R) 15,898 (14%); Kevin Brawley (C,RTL) 2,977; Martin O'Grady 2,861. 1990 Engel 61%. 1988 Engel 56%.

Interest Group Ratings:

ADA	ACU	COPE	COC
95	04	91	25

LCV	NTLC	CFA	ASC
94	00	93	50

Office: 1434 LHOB 20515, 202-225-2464 (John Mills, Legs. Asst.). DISTRICT OFFICES: 3655 Johnson, Bronx 10463, 718-796-9700 (Arnold Linhardt, AA); Rm. 3, Dreiser Community Ctr., 177 Dreiser Loop, Bronx 10475, 212-320-2314 (Ester Keller, Dir.)

EIGHTEENTH DISTRICT

Nita M. Lowey (D)

District: Central and southern Westchester County. Population: 580,337—Black 7%, Hispanic 10%, Asian 8%. Politics: Leans Democratic.

Born July 5, 1937, the Bronx; home, Harrison; Mount Holyoke College, B.A. 1959; Jewish; married (Stephen), 3 children.

Elected 1988. Career: Anti-Poverty Citizen Participation Officer, N.Y. Dept. of State; Dpty. Dir., Div. of Econ. Oppty.; Asst. to Secy. of State for Econ. Dev. & Neighborhood Preservation; Advisor, N.Y. State Childcare Comm.; N.Y. Asst. Secy. of State, 1985–87.

Committees: (1) Appropriations.

Election Results: 1992 Lowey 102,269 (55%); Joseph DioGuardi (R) 83,282 (45%). 1990 Lowey 62%. 1988 Lowey 50%.

Interest Group Ratings:

ADA	ACU	COPE	COC
100	00	92	25

LCV	NTLC	CFA	ASC
88	00	93	30

Office: 1424 LHOB 20515, 202-225-6506 (Scott Fleming, AA). DISTRICT OFFICES: 235 Mamaroneck Ave., White Plains, 10605, 914-428-1707 (Deborah Bohren, Dist. Dir.); 97-45 Queens Blvd. #505, Rego Park 11374, 718-897-3602

NINETEENTH DISTRICT

Hamilton Fish, Jr. (R)

District: The lower Hudson Valley including Westchester and Putnam counties. Population: 580,337—Black 7%, Hispanic 5%. Politics: Republican.

Born June 3, 1926, Washington, D.C.; home, Millbrook; Harvard College, A.B. 1949, New York University, LL.B. 1957; Episcopalian; married (Mary Ann), 4 children.

Elected 1968. Career: Navy, WWII; Vice Consul, U.S. Foreign Svc., Ireland, 1951–53; Practicing atty., 1957–68; Counsel, N.Y. Assembly Judiciary Comm., 1961; Dutchess Cty. Civil Defense Dir., 1967–68.

Committees: (1) Judiciary (Ranking Member); (2) Joint Economic Committee.

Election Results: 1992 Fish 125,417 (60%); Neil McCarthy (D) 81,941 (40%). 1990 Fish 71%. 1988 Fish 75%.

Interest Group Ratings:

ADA	ACU	COPE	COC
40	48	58	43

LCV	NTLC	CFA	ASC
81	55	60	100

Office: 2354 RHOB 20515, 202-225-5441 (Nicholas Hayes, AA). DISTRICT OFFICES: 2 Church St., Ossining 10562, 914-762-7561 (Janice Traber, Dist. Adm.); 70 Gleneida Ave., Carmel 10512, 914-225-5200 (Dolly Pederson, Mgr); 235 Rt. 9, Suite 209, Wappingers Falls 12590, 914-297-5711 (Helen Fuimarello, Mgr.)

TWENTIETH DISTRICT

Benjamin A. Gilman (R)

District: New York City suburbs in Rockland and Orange counties, including the Catskills. Population: 580,338—Black 8%, Hispanic 6%, Asian 3%. Politics: Leans Republican.

Born Dec. 6, 1922, Poughkeepsie; home, Middletown; University of Pa., B.S. 1946, N.Y. Law School, LL.B.1950; Jewish; married (Gail), 3 children, 2 stepchildren.

Elected 1972. Career: Army Air Corps, WWII; Asst. Atty. Gen. of N.Y. State, 1953–55; Practicing atty., 1955–72; Atty., N.Y. Temp. Comm. on the Courts; N.Y. Assembly, 1967–72.

Committees: (1) Foreign Affairs; (2) Post Office and Civil Service (Ranking Member).

Election Results: 1992 Gilman 139,712 (67%); Jonathan Levine (D) 61,630 (29%); Robert Garrison 8,045 (4%). 1990 Gilman 68%. 1988 Gilman 71%.

Interest Group Ratings:

ADA	ACU	COPE	COC
75	32	92	50

LCV	NTLC	CFA	ASC
81	50	100	90

Office: 2185 RHOB 20515, 202-225-3776 (Nancy Colandrea, AA). DISTRICT OFFICES: 407 E. Main St., Middletown 10940, 914-343-6666 (Molly Aumick, Mgr.); 377 Rte. 59, Monsey 10952, 914-357-9000 (Ann Cortese, Asst.); 32 Main St., Hastings-on-Hudson 10706, 914-478-5550 (Valerie Jennings, Rep.)

TWENTY-FIRST DISTRICT

Michael R. McNulty (D)

District: Hudson and Mohawk Valleys including cities of Albany and Schenectady. Population: 516,943—Black 5%. Politics: Democratic.

Born Sept. 16, 1947, Troy; home, Green Island; Holy Cross, B.A. 1969; Roman Catholic; married (Nancy), 4 children.

Elected 1958. Career: Exec. Asst. to the Mayor of Green Island, 1969–70; Supervisor, Green Island, 1970–78; Mayor of Green Island, 1977–82; N.Y. Assembly, 1982–88.

Committees: (1) Ways & Means.

Election Results: 1992 McNulty 147,173 (62%); Nancy Norman (R) 82,668 (35%); William Donnelly 7,108 (3%). 1990 McNulty 64%. 1988 McNulty (62%).

Interest Group Ratings:

ADA	ACU	COPE	COC
90	12	91	38

LCV	NTLC	CFA	ASC
25	15	80	70

Office: 217 CHOB 20515, 202-225-5076 (Lana Helfrich, Chief of Staff.). DISTRICT OFFICE: Fed. Bldg., Albany 12207, 518-465-0700 (Charles Diamond, Dist. AA); 29 Jay St., Schenectady 12305, 518-374-4547 (Bob Carr, Mgr.); 33 2nd St., Troy 12180, 518-271-0822 (Domenica Millington, Mgr.); 9 Market St., Amsterdam 12010, 518-3400 (Elaine DeVito, Rep.)

TWENTY-SECOND DISTRICT

Gerald B.H. Solomon (R)

District: Upper Hudson Valley south to Dutchess County, including the city of Poughkeepsie. Population: 580,337—Black 2%, Hispanic 2%. Politics: Republican.

Born Aug. 14, 1930, Okeechobee, Fla.; home, Glens Falls; Siena College, Saint Lawrence University; Presbyterian; married (Freda), 5 children.

Elected 1978. Career: USMC, Korea; Queensbury Town Sprvsr., 1967–72; N.Y. Assembly, 1972–78.

Committees: (1) Rules (Ranking Member).

Election Results: 1992 Solomon 154,416 (66%); David Roberts (D) 80,713 (34%). 1990 Solomon (68%). 1988 Solomon (72%).

Interest Group Ratings:

ADA	ACU	COPE	COC
15	96	58	63

LCV	NTLC	CFA	ASC
19	90	20	100

Office: 2265 RHOB 20515, 202-225-5614 (Herb Koster, AA). DISTRICT OFFICES: Gaslight Square, 285 Broadway, Saratoga Springs 12866, 518-587-9800 (Jeff Turner, Rep.); 337 Fairview Ave., Hudson 12534; 518-828-0181 (Pat Hart, Asst.); 21 Bay St., Glens Falls 12801, 518-792-3013 (Dan Orsini, Asst.)

TWENTY-THIRD DISTRICT

Sherwood Louis Boehlert (R)

District: Central portion of the state including cities of Rome and Utica. Population: 580,337—Black 3%. Politics: Republican.

Born Sept. 28, 1936, Utica; home, New Hartford; Utica College, Syracuse University, B.S. 1961; Roman Catholic; married (Marianne), 4 children.

Elected 1982. Career: Army, 1956–58; Mgr., pub. relations, Wyandotte Chemicals Corp., 1961–64; Chf. of Staff to Rep. Alexander Pirnie, 1964–73; Chf. of Staff to Rep. Donald Mitchell, 1973–79; Cty. Exec., Oneida Cty., 1979–82.

Committees: (1) Public Works & Transportation; (2) Science, Space & Technology.

Election Results: 1992 Boehlert 126,879 (64%); Paula DiPerna (D) 56,841 (29%); Geoffrey Grace 7,496 (4%); Randall Terry (RTL) 8,045 (4%). 1990 Boehlert (84%). 1988 Boehlert (Unopposed).

Interest Group Ratings:

ADA	ACU	COPE	COC
75	40	75	50

LCV	NTLC	CFA	ASC
88	45	80	100

Office: 1127 LHOB 20515, 202-225-3665 (Margaret Moore, Ex. Asst.). DISTRICT OFFICE: 200 Fed. Bldg., 10 Broad St., Rm. 200, Utica 13501, 315-793-8146, 800-235-2525 (Randy Wilcox, Ex. Asst.)

TWENTY-FOURTH DISTRICT

John McHugh (R)

District: Far northern counties including cities of Plattsburgh and Watertown. Population: 580,338—Black 3%. Politics: Republican.

Born Sept. 29, 1948, Watertown; home, Pierrepont Manor; Utica College, B.A. 1970, State University of New York Albany, M.A.; Roman Catholic; married (Katherine).

Elected 1992. Career: Asst. to Mayor of Watertown, 1970–75; Asst. to Sen. Douglas Barclay, 1976–84; State Sen., 1984–92.

Committees: (1) Armed Services; (2) Government Operations.

Election Results: 1992 McHugh 116,254 (61%); Margaret Ravenscroft (D) 44,798 (23%); Morrison Hosley 25,848 (14%); Stephen Burke 4,330 (2%).

Interest Group Ratings:
None—Freshman

Office: 416 CHOB 20515, 202-225-4611 (Cary Brick, AA). DISTRICT OFFICES: 404 A Key Bank Bldg. 200 Washington, Watertown 13601, 315-782-3150; 104 Fed. Bldg., Plattsburgh 12921, 518-563-1406; 104 W. Utica St., Oswego 13126, 315-342-5664

TWENTY-FIFTH DISTRICT

James T. Walsh (R)

District: Syracuse and environs. Population: 580,337—Black 7%. Politics: Mixed, but leaning Republican.

Born June 19, 1947, Syracuse; home: Syracuse; Saint Bonaventure, B.A. 1970; Roman Catholic; married (Dede), 3 children.

Elected 1988. Career: Peace Corps, 1970–72; Dept. of Social Services caseworker, 1972–74; Telephone co. mktg. exec., 1974–78; Syracuse Common Council, 1977–88; Pres., Syracuse Common Council, 1985–88.

Committees: (1) Appropriations.

Election Results: 1992 Walsh 132,279 (56%); Rhea Jezer (D) 105,364 (44%). 1990 Walsh 63%. 1988 Walsh 57%.

Interest Group Ratings:

ADA	ACU	COPE	COC
25	72	75	75

LCV	NTLC	CFA	ASC
50	80	53	100

Office: 1330 LHOB 20515, 202-225-3701 (Arthur Jutton, AA). DISTRICT OFFICES: 1269 Fed Bldg., Clinton Sq., Syracuse 13260, 315-423-5657 (James O'Conner, Rep.); 1 Lincoln, Auburn 13021, 315-255-0649 (Vivian Norman, Rep.)

TWENTY-SIXTH DISTRICT

Maurice Hinchey (D)

District: Ulster and Sullivan counties and the southern counties running along Pennsylvania border, including cities of Binghamton and Ithaca.

Population: 580,338—Black 6%, Hispanic 4%, Asian 2%. Politics: Democratic.

Born Oct. 27, 1938, New York City; home, Saugerties; State University of New York New Paltz, M.A. 1970 ; Roman Catholic; married (Ilene), 3 children.

Elected 1992. Career: N.Y. General Assembly, 1975–92.

Committees: (1) Banking, Finance & Urban Affairs; (2) Natural Resources.

Election Results: 1992 Hinchey 114,133 (51%); Bob Moppert (R) 105,037 (47%); Mary Dixon 6,556 (3%).

Interest Group Ratings:
None—Freshman

Office: 1313 LHOB 20515, 202-225-6335 (Elanor Nash-Brown, AA). DISTRICT OFFICES: 291 Wall St., Kingston 12401, 914-331-4466; 100-A Fed. Bldg., Binghamton 13901, 607-773-2768; Carriage House—Terrace Hill, Ithaca 14850, 607-273-1388

TWENTY-SEVENTH DISTRICT

L. William Paxon (R)

District: West central counties including Buffalo suburbs. Population: 580,337—Black 3%. Politics: Republican.

Born April 29, 1954, Buffalo; home, Newstead; Canisius College, B.A. 1977; Roman Catholic; single.

Elected 1988. Career: Member, Erie County Legislature, 1978–82; N.Y. State Assembly, 1983–88.

Committees: (1) Energy & Commerce.

Election Results: 1992 Paxon 150,451 (63%); W. Douglas Call (D) 86,631 (37%). 1990 Paxon 56%. 1988 Paxon 53%.

Interest Group Ratings:

ADA	ACU	COPE	COC
10	92	33	75

LCV	NTLC	CFA	ASC
06	75	20	100

Office: 1314 LHOB 20515, 202-225-5265 (Michael Hook, AA). DISTRICT OFFICES: 5500 Main St., Williamsville 14221, 716-634-2324 (Matt Koch, Dist. Mgr.); 10 E. Main, Victor 14564, 716-742-1600

TWENTY-EIGHTH DISTRICT

Louise M. Slaughter (D)

District: Rochester and environs including town of Batavia. Population: 580,337—Black 14%, Hispanic 4%. Politics: Leans Democratic.

Born Aug. 14, 1929, Harlan Cty., Ky.; home, Fairport; University of Ky., B.A. 1951, M.S. 1953; Episcopalian; married (Robert), 3 children.

Elected 1986. Career: Monroe Cty. Leg., 1976–79; Regional Coord., Lt. Gov. Mario Cuomo, 1976–79; N.Y. Assembly, 1983–86.

Committees: (1) Budget; (2) Rules.

Election Results: 1992 Slaughter 138,318 (55%); William Polito (R) 111,233 (45%). 1990 Slaughter 59%. 1988 Slaughter 57%.

Interest Group Ratings:

ADA	ACU	COPE	COC
95	04	92	25

LCV	NTLC	CFA	ASC
100	15	93	30

Office: 2421 RHOB 20515, 202-225-3615 (Monica Mills, Chief of Staff.). DISTRICT OFFICE: 311 Fed. Bldg., 100 State St., Rochester 14614, 716-232-4850 (Chris Rumfola, Dist. Dir.)

TWENTY-NINTH DISTRICT

John J. LaFalce (D)

District: Niagara Falls, Buffalo suburbs of Tonawanda and Amherst and part of Rochester and suburbs. Population: 580,337—Black 5%, Hispanic 3%. Politics: Mixed, but leans Democratic.

Born Oct. 6, 1939, Buffalo; home, Tonawanda; Canisius College, B.S. 1961, Villanova University, J.D. 1964; Roman Catholic; married (Patricia), 1 child.

Elected 1974. Career: Army, 1965–67; Practicing atty.; N.Y. Senate, 1971–72; N.Y. Assembly, 1973–74.

Committees: (1) Banking, Finance & Urban Affairs; (2) Small Business (Chairman).

Election Results: 1992 LaFalce 124,276 (55%); William Miller Jr. (R) 95,328 (42%); Kenneth Kowalski (RTL) 7,118 (3%). 1990 LaFalce 54%. 1988 LaFalce 73%.

Interest Group Ratings:

ADA	ACU	COPE	COC
85	12	100	25

LCV	NTLC	CFA	ASC
44	05	87	20

Office: 2310 RHOB 20515, 202-225-3231 (Ronald Moselka, AA). DISTRICT OFFICES: Fed. Bldg., 111 W. Huron St., Buffalo 14202, 716-846-4056 (Peter Hadrovic, Dist. Rep.); Main P.O. Bldg., Niagara Falls 14302, 716-284-9976 (Rebekah Muscoreil, Asst.); 302 Fed. Bldg., 100 State Street, Rochester 14614, 716-263-6424 (Hanny Heyen, Asst.)

THIRTIETH DISTRICT

Jack Quinn (R)

District: Buffalo. Population: 580,337—Black 17%, Hispanic 2%. Politics: Leans Democratic.

Born Apr. 13, 1951, Buffalo; home, Hamburg; Sienna College, B.A. 1973, State University of New York Buffalo, M.A. 1975; Roman Catholic; married (Mary Beth), 2 children.

Elected 1992. Career: English Teacher, 1975–82; Hamburg Town Council, 1982–83; Hamburg Town Supervisor, 1984–92.

Committees: (1) Public Works & Transportation; (2) Veteran Affairs.

Election Results: 1992 Quinn 119,102 (52%); Dennis Gorski (D) 105,391 (46%); Mary Refermat 5,857 (3%).

Interest Group Ratings:
None—Freshman

Office: 331 CHOB 20515, 202-225-3306 (Mary Lou Palmer, AA). DISTRICT OFFICE: 403 Main St. 510, Buffalo 14202, 716-845-5257

THIRTY-FIRST DISTRICT

Amory "Amo" Houghton, Jr. (R)

District: Western half of the Southern tier counties including towns of Jamestown and Elmira. Population: 580,337. Politics: Leans Republican.

Born Aug. 7, 1926, Corning; home, Corning; Harvard, B.A. 1950, M.B.A. 1952; Episcopalian; married (Priscilla), 4 children.

Moderate; elected 1986. Career: USMC, WWII; Corning Glass Works, 1951–86, Chm. of the Bd., C.E.O., 1964–83.

Committees: (1) Ways & Means.

Election Results: 1992 Houghton 143,463 (71%); Joseph Leahey (D) 49,379 (24%); Gretchen McManus 10,190 (5%). 1990 Houghton 69%. 1988 Houghton 96%.

Interest Group Ratings:

ADA	ACU	COPE	COC
30	68	50	88

LCV	NTLC	CFA	ASC
13	90	27	100

Office: 1110 LHOB 20515, 202-225-3161 (Brian Fitzpatrick, AA). DISTRICT OFFICES: 700 Westgate Plaza, W. State St., Olean 14760, 716-372-2127 (Nancy Clark, Dist. Dir.); 32 Denison Pkwy. W., Corning 14830, 607-937-3333 (John Fox, Dir.); 122 Fed. Bldg., Prendergast & 3rd Sts., Jamestown 14701, 716-484-0252 (Mickey Brown, Mgr.)

NORTH CAROLINA

After several highly charged political years, North Carolina gets a rest in 1993–94. No statewide offices will be contested until 1996. The state is still recovering from a redistricting battle that saw both the creation of the state's first minority district and the creation of a new congressional district that went to the Republicans. While they are resting, North Carolina voters can ponder the question: will Sen. Jesse Helms retire in 1996? If he does, he will set off a major political free-for-all in both parties.

1992 PRESIDENTIAL ELECTION: (14 Electoral votes): Clinton (D) 1,107,857 (43%); Bush (R) 1,128,446 (43%); Perot (I) 354,554 (14%); Marrou (Lib) 5,393. 1988 Bush 1,237,258 (58%); Dukakis 890,167 (42%).

SENATORS

Jesse Alexander Helms (R)

Born Oct. 18, 1921, Monroe; home, Raleigh; Wingate Junior College, Wake Forest University, 1941; Baptist; married (Dorothy), 3 children.

Elected 1972, seat up 1996. Career: Navy, WWII; City Ed., Raleigh Times; Dir., News & Programs, Tobacco Radio Network, WRAL; A.A. to U.S. Sen. Willis Smith, 1951–53 & Alton Lennon, 1953; Exec. Dir., N. C. Bankers Assn., 1953–60; Raleigh City Cncl., 1957–61; Exec. V.P., WRAL–TV & Tobacco Radio Network, 1960–72.

Committees: (1) Agriculture, Nutrition & Forestry; (2) Foreign Relations (Ranking Member); (3) Rules & Administration; (4) Select Committee on Ethics.

Election Results: 1990 Helms 1,070,343 (52%); Harvey Gantt (D) 968,998 (48%). 1984 Helms (52%).

Interest Group Ratings:

ADA	ACU	COPE	COC
05	100	13	100

LCV	NTLC	CFA	ASC
00	100	00	80

Office: 403 DSOB 20510-3301, 202-224-6342 (Darrell Neurenberg, AA). STATE OFFICES: 314 P.O. Bldg., (P.O. Box 2888), Raleigh 27602, 919-856-4630 (Frances Jones, Dir.); Fed. Bldg.,

(P.O. Box 2944), Hickory 28603, 704-322-5170 (Jo Murray, Dir.)

Lauch Faircloth (R)

Born Jan. 14, 1928, Sampson Co.; home, Clinton; Presbyterian; divorced, 1 child.

Elected 1992, seat up 1998. Career: Farmer/Businessman, 1947–present; Chairman N.C. Highway Commission, 1968–73; N.C. Secy. of Commerce, 1977–83.

Committees: (1) Armed Services; (2) Environment & Public Works; (3) Banking, Housing & Urban Affairs.

Election Results: 1992 Faircloth 1,276,831 (52%); Terry Sanford (Incumbent D) 1,176,939 (48%).

Interest Group Ratings:
None—Freshman

Office: 702 HSOB 20510-3304, 202-224-3154 (Vic Barfield, AA).STATE OFFICES: 310 New Bern Ave. Suite 306, Raleigh 27601, 919-856-4791 (Mary Bear, Rep.); 401 W. Trade St. Suite 219, Charlotte 28202, (Susan Hays, Rep.); Fed. Bldg. Suite 16, 37 Battery Park, Asheville 28801, 704-251-0165 (Scotty Morgan, Rep.); Fed. Bldg. 251 Main St. Suite 422, Winston Salem 27101, 919-631-5313 (Mary Bagnal, Rep.)

REPRESENTATIVES

FIRST DISTRICT

Eva Clayton (D)

District: A Newly created black majority district in the northeastern part of the state running through 28 counties and parts of 12 cities. Population: 552,394—Black 57%. Politics: Democratic.

Born Sept. 16, 1934, Savannah, Ga.; home, Littleton; Johnson C. Smith University, B.S. 1955, N.C. Central University, M.S. 1962; Presbyterian; married (Theaoseus), 4 children.

Elected 1992. Career: N.C. Dept. of Natural Resources & Community Development, 1977–81; Founder, Technical Resources International,

1981–92; Warren Cty. Board of Commissioners; 1982–92.

Committees: (1) Agriculture; (2) Small Business.

Election Results: 1992 Clayton 115,508 (68%); Ted Tyler (R) 54,133 (32%).

Interest Group Ratings:
None—Freshman

Office: 222 CHOB 20515, 202-225-3101 (Lan Woog Long, AA). DISTRICT OFFICES: P.O. Box 676, Warrenton 27589, 919-257-4800 (Chas Worth, Dist. Dir.); 400 W. 5th, Greenville 27834, 919-758-8800

SECOND DISTRICT

Itimous Thaddeus "Tim" Valentine, Jr. (D)

District: North central counties including parts of cities of Durham and Rocky Mount. Population: 552,378—Black 22%. Politics: Democratic.

Born Mar. 15, 1926, Nash County; home, Nashville; The Citadel, A.B. 1948, University of N. C., LL.B., 1952; Baptist; married (Barbara), 4 children.

Elected 1982. Career: Air Force, WWII; N.C. House of Reps., 1955–60; Legal Advisor to the Gov., 1965, Counsel, 1967.

Committees: (1) Public Works & Transportation; (2) Science, Space & Technology.

Election Results: 1992 Valentine 112,367 (55%); Don Davis (R) 92,164 (45%). 1990 Valentine (75%). 1988 Valentine (Unopposed).

Interest Group Ratings:

ADA	ACU	COPE	COC
45	48	42	29

LCV	NTLC	CFA	ASC
38	37	40	80

Office: 2229 RHOB 20515, 202-225-4531 (Ed Nagy, AA). DISTRICT OFFICES: 3310 Croasville Dr. #302, Durham 27705, 919-383-9405 (A.B. Swindell, Dist. AA); 101 Triangle Court, Nashville 27856, 919-459-8881

THIRD DISTRICT

H. Martin Lancaster (D)

District: Eastern and central counties including

town of Goldsboro. Population: 552,387—Black 21%. Politics: Democratic.

Born Mar. 24, 1943, Wayne Cty.; home, Goldsboro; University of N.C., Chapel Hill, A.B. 1965, J.D. 1967; Presbyterian; married (Alice), 2 children.

Elected 1986. Career: Navy, 1967–70; N.C. House of Reps., 1978–86; Practicing atty.

Committees: (1) Armed Services; (2) Merchant Marine & Fisheries; (3) Small Business (Temp.).

Election Results: 1992 Lancaster 100,602 (56%); Tommy Pollard (R) 80,062 (44%). 1990 Lancaster (60%). 1988 Lancaster (Unopposed).

Interest Group Ratings:

ADA	ACU	COPE	COC
25	10	60	90

LCV	NTLC	CFA	ASC
45	58	50	75

Office: 2436 RHOB 20515, 202-225-3415 (Charles Rawls, AA). DISTRICT OFFICE: 103 Fed. Bldg., 134 N. John St., Goldsboro 27530, 919-736-1844 (David Hepler, AA)

FOURTH DISTRICT

David Eugene Price (D)

District: Central counties including cities of Raleigh and parts of Chapel Hill. Population: 552,387—Black 20%. Politics: Leans Democratic.

Born Aug. 17, 1940, Johnson City, Tenn.; home, Chapel Hill; Mars Hill College, University of N.C., Chapel Hill, B.A. 1961, Yale University, B.D. 1964, Ph.D. 1969; Baptist; married (Lisa), 2 children.

Elected 1986. Career: Leg. Aide, Sen. E.L. Barlett, 1963–67; Pol. Sci. Prof., Duke University, 1973–85.

Committees: (1) Appropriations; (2) Budget.

Election Results: 1992 Price 170,753 (66%); Vicky Goudie (R) 89,147 (34%). 1990 Price (58%). 1988 Price (58%).

Interest Group Ratings:

ADA	ACU	COPE	COC
85	12	67	25

LCV	NTLC	CFA	ASC
56	00	80	60

Office: 2458 RHOB 20515, 202-225-1784 (Eugene Conti, AA). DISTRICT OFFICES: 225 Hillsborough St., Suite 330, Raleigh 27603, 919-856-4611 (Joan Ewing, Mgr.); 1777 Chapel Hill-Durham Blvd., Suite 202, Chapel Hill 27514, 919-967-8500 (Gay Eddy, Asst.)

FIFTH DISTRICT

Stephen Lybrook Neal (D)

District: Northwestern Piedmont counties including parts of city of Winston-Salem. Population: 552,386—Black 15%. Politics: Leans Republican.

Born Nov. 7, 1934, Winston-Salem; home, Winston-Salem; University of Calif. at Santa Barbara, University of Hawaii, A.B. 1959; Presbyterian; married (Landis), 2 children.

Elected 1974. Career: Bank executive, 1959–66; Newspaper publisher, 1966–75; Pres., Community Press, Inc., Suburban Newspapers, Inc., King Publishing Co. & Yadkin Printing Co., Inc.

Committees: (1) Banking, Finance & Urban Affairs; (2) Government Operations.

Election Results: 1992 Neal 117,256 (54%); Richard Burr (R) 101,605 (46%). 1990 Neal (60%). 1988 Neal (53%).

Interest Group Ratings:

ADA	ACU	COPE	COC
65	27	50	29

LCV	NTLC	CFA	ASC
81	10	73	70

Office: 2469 RHOB 20515, 202-225-2071 (Robert Wrigley, AA). DISTRICT OFFICE: Piedmont Plaza 2, 2000 W. 1st St. #508, Winston-Salem 27104, 919-631-5125 (Jim Phillips, Dist. AA)

SIXTH DISTRICT

John Howard Coble (R)

District: Central part of the state including parts of Greensboro and High Point. Population: 552,385—Black 7%. Politics: Republican.

Born Mar. 18, 1931, Greensboro; home, Greensboro; Guilford College, A.B. 1958, University of N.C., Chapel Hill, J.D. 1962; Presbyterian; single.

Elected 1984. Career: State Farm Insurance agent, 1961–67; Asst. Dist. Atty., Guilfone County, 1967–69; N.C. House of Reps., 1969, 1979–84; Asst. U.S. Atty., Middle District of N.C., 1969–73;

Commissioner, N.C. Dept. of Revenue, 1973–77; Practicing atty., 1979–84.

Committees: (1) Judiciary; (2) Merchant Marine & Fisheries.

Election Results: 1992 Coble 161,880 (71%); Robin Hood (D) 66,810 (29%). 1990 Coble (67%). 1988 Coble (62%).

Interest Group Ratings:

ADA	ACU	COPE	COC
10	92	25	75

LCV	NTLC	CFA	ASC
06	90	27	90

Office: 403 CHOB 20515, 202-225-3065 (Edward McDonald, AA). DISTRICT OFFICES: 324 W. Market St., Greensboro 27402, 919-333-5005 (Jan Scott, Rep.); 1404 Piedmont Dr. Suite A, Lexington 27293, 704-246-8230 (Connie Leonard, Rep.); 124 W. Elm St., Graham 27253, 919-229-0159 (Janine Osborne, Rep.); 510 Ferndale Blvd., High Point 27260, 919-886-5106 (Carolyn McGahey, Rep.); 241 Sunset Ave. Suite 101, Asheboro 27203, 919-626-3060 (Sally Corrigan, Rep.)

SEVENTH DISTRICT

Charles Grandison Rose III (D)

District: Southeast coastal plain counties including parts of cities of Wilmington and Fayetteville. Population: 552,386—Black 19%, Native American 7%, Hispanic 3%. Politics: Leans Democratic.

Born Aug. 10, 1939. Fayetteville; home, Fayetteville; Davidson College, A.B. 1961, University of N.C., LL.B. 1964; Presbyterian; married (Joan), 3 children.

Elected 1972. Career: Practicing atty., 1964–72; Chf. Dist. Crt. Prosecutor, 12th Judicial Dist., 1967–70.

Committees: (1) Agriculture; (2) House Administration (Chairman).

Election Results: 1992 Rose 85,684 (58%); Robert Anderson (R) 61,267 (42%). 1990 Rose (65%). 1988 Rose (67%).

Interest Group Ratings:

ADA	ACU	COPE	COC
95	04	83	38

LCV	NTLC	CFA	ASC
50	00	67	40

Office: 2230 RHOB 20515, 202-225-2731 (Andrea Turner-Scott, AA). DISTRICT OFFICES: 208 P.O. Bldg. Wilmington 28401, 919-343-4959 (Judy Bentley, Asst.); 218 Fed. Bldg., Fayetteville 28301, 919-323-0260 (Judith Laws-Kirchman, Dist. Cord.)

EIGHTH DISTRICT

W.G. "Bill" Hefner (D)

District: South central counties including town of Kannapolis and parts of Salisbury. Population: 552,387—Black 23%. Politics: Leans Democratic.

Born Apr. 11, 1930, Elora, Tenn.; home, Concord; Baptist; married (Nancy), 2 children.

Elected 1974. Career: entertainment & radio business, 1954–74; Mbr., Harvesters Quartet.

Committees: (1) Appropriations.

Election Results: 1992 Hefner 109,779 (61%); Coy Privette (R) 70,177 (39%). 1990 Hefner (55%). 1988 Hefner (52%).

Interest Group Ratings:

ADA	ACU	COPE	COC
40	06	88	17

LCV	NTLC	CFA	ASC
13	00	83	50

Office: 2470 RHOB 20515, 202-225-3715 (William McEwen, AA). DISTRICT OFFICES: 101 Union St., S., Concord 28025, 704-786-1612 (Virginia Jochems, Dist. Adm.); 507 W. Innes St., Suite 225, Salisbury 28144, 704-636-0635 (Sharon Sheelor, Mgr.); 230 E. Franklin St., Rockingham 28379, 919-997-2070 (David Perry, Mgr.)

NINTH DISTRICT

J. Alex McMillan III (R)

District: Parts of cities of Charlotte and Gastonia. Population: 552,387—Black 9%. Politics: Republican.

Born May 9, 1932, Charlotte; home, Charlotte; University of N.C., B.A. 1954, University of Va., M.B.A. 1958; Presbyterian; married (Caroline), 2 children.

Elected 1984. Career: Army Intelligence, 1954–56; Businessman, Harris–Teeter Super Markets,

Ruddick Corp., R.S. Dickson & Co., Carolina Paper Board Co., 1958–83; Mecklenburg Cty. Bd. of Commissioners, 1973.

Committees: (1) Energy & Commerce; (2) Budget.

Election Results: 1992 McMillan 145,455 (67%); Rory Blake (D) 71,415 (33%). 1990 McMillan (62%). 1988 McMillan (66%).

Interest Group Ratings:

ADA	ACU	COPE	COC
15	84	33	88

LCV	NTLC	CFA	ASC
19	90	27	100

Office: 401 CHOB 20515, 202-225-1976 (Frank Hill, AA). DISTRICT OFFICES: 401 W. Trade St., Rm. 222, Charlotte 28202, 704-372-1976 (Bob Morgan, Rep.); 224 S. New Hope Rd. Suite H, Gastonia 28052-54 704-861-1976 (vacant, Rep.)

TENTH DISTRICT

Thomas Cass Ballenger (R)

District: Western counties including town of Hickory and parts of Statesville. Population: 552,386—Black 5%. Politics: Republican.

Born Dec. 6, 1926, Hickory; home, Hickory; University of N.C., Chapel Hill 1944–45, Amherst College, B.A. 1948; Episcopalian; married (Donna), 3 children.

Elected 1986. Career: Army, WWII; Founder & Chm., Plastic Packaging Inc.; Catawba Cty. Bd. of Commissioners, 1966–74, Chm. 1970–74; N.C. House of Reps., 1974–76; N.C. Senate, 1976–86.

Committees: (1) Education & Labor; (2) District of Columbia.

Election Results: 1992 Ballenger 148,900 (65%); Ben Neill (D) 78,979 (35%). 1990 Ballenger (62%). 1988 Ballenger (61%).

Interest Group Ratings:

ADA	ACU	COPE	COC
10	92	25	75

LCV	NTLC	CFA	ASC
06	95	27	100

Office: 2238 RHOB 20515, 202-225-2576 (Patrick Murphy, AA). DISTRICT OFFICES: P.O. Box 1830, Hickory 28603, 704-327-6100 (Thomas Luckadoo, Dist. Dir.); P.O. Box 1881, Clemmons 27012, 919-766-9455 (Tom Luckadoo, Rep.)

ELEVENTH DISTRICT

Charles H. Taylor (R)

District: Western counties including city of Asheville. Population: 552,387—Black 7%. Politics: Republican.

Born Jan. 23, 1941, Brevard, N.C.; home, Brevard; Wake Forest University, B.A. 1963, J.D., 1967; Baptist; married (Elizabeth), 3 children.

Elected 1990. Career: Tree farmer; N.C. State House, 1967–71, N.C. Senate 1973–75.

Committees: (1) Appropriations.

Election Results: 1992 Taylor 130,103 (55%); John Stevens (D) 107,894 (45%). 1990 Taylor (51%).

Interest Group Ratings:

ADA	ACU	COPE	COC
15	87	25	86

LCV	NTLC	CFA	ASC
06	95	27	100

Office: 516 CHOB 20515, 202-225-6401 (Roger France, AA). DISTRICT OFFICE: 22 S. Pack Sq., Suite 330, Asheville 28801, 704-251-1988 (Bruce Briggs, Dist. Rep.)

TWELFTH DISTRICT

Melvin Watt (D)

District: The newly created Black majority "I–85" district winds through the entire central part of the state including 10 counties and parts of 12 cities. Population 552,387—Black 57%. Politics: Democratic.

Born Aug. 26, 1945, Steele Creek; home, Charlotte; University of N.C., B.S. 1967, Yale, J.D. 1970; Presbyterian; married (Eulada), 2 children.

Elected 1992. Career: Lawyer, 1971–92; State Sen., 1985–86.

Committees: (1) Banking, Finance & Urban Affairs; (2) Judiciary.

Election Results: 1992 Watt 126,836 (72%); Barbara Washington (R) 49,191 (28%).

Interest Group Ratings: None—Freshman

Office: 1232 LHOB 20515, 202-225-1510 (Joan Kennedy, AA). DISTRICT OFFICES: 214 N. Church St. #130, Charlotte 28202, 704-344-9950 (Don Baker, Dist. Dir.); 301 S. Green St. #212, Greensboro 27402, 919-379-9403 (Pamela Stubbs, Rep.); 315 E. Chapel St. #202, 919-688-3004 (Tracy Lovett, Rep.)

NORTH DAKOTA

North Dakota continues among the strangest of states, politically. Again in 1992, it remained solidly Republican in presidential voting, while electing two Democratic senators and an at-large Congressman to go along with a new Republican governor. Sen. Kent Conrad, who did not run for reelection for his own seat but then ran for and won the unexpired term of the late Quentin Burdick, will have to run for reelection once again in 1994. He should win a new 6-year term easily.

1992 PRESIDENTIAL ELECTION: (3 Electoral votes): Clinton (D) 98,928 (32%); Bush (R) 135,498 (44%); Perot (I) 70,703 (23%); LaRouche (I) 662; Marrou (Lib) 405; Warren (SocWks) 242; Hagelin (NLP) 231; Fulani (NAP) 181. 1988 Bush 165,517 (57%); Dukakis 127,081 (43%).

SENATORS

Byron Leslie Dorgan (D)

Born May 14, 1942, Dickinson; home, Regent; University of N.Dak., B.S. 1965, University of Denver, M.B.A. 1966; Lutheran; married (Kimberly), 3 children.

Elected 1992, seat up 1998. Career: Martin–Marietta Exec. Develop. Prog., 1966–67; N.Dak. Dpty. Tax Commissioner, 1967–68, Tax Commissioner, 1969–80. U.S. House 1980–92.

Committees: (1) Commerce, Science & Transportation; (2) Government Affairs; (3) Joint Committee on Economics; (4) Select Committee on Indian Affairs.

Election Results: 1992 Dorgan 178,443 (60%); Steve Sydness (R) 117,832 (40%).

Interest Group Ratings: House Record

ADA	ACU	COPE	COC
70	28	83	38

LCV	NTLC	CFA	ASC
56	30	87	40

Offices: 713 HSOB 20510, 202-224-2551 (Lucy Calautti, AA). STATE OFFICES: 312 Fed. Bldg., Bismarck 58502, 701-250-4618 (Mark Fredricks, Rep.); 112 Roberts, P.O. Box 2250, Fargo 58107, 701-239-5389 (Kevin Carvell, Rep.)

Kent Conrad (D)

Born May 12, 1948, Bismarck; home, Bismarck; University of Mo., Stanford University, B.A. 1972, George Washington University, M.B.A. 1975; Unitarian; married (Lucy), 2 children.

Elected 1986, resigned own seat in 1992. Then ran to fill the unexpired term of the late Quentin Burdick in a special election in 1992. Seat up 1994. Career: Asst. to N.Dak. Tax Commissioner, 1974–80; Dir., Mgt. Planning & Personnel, N.Dak. Tax Dept., 1980; N.Dak. Tax Commissioner, 1981–86.

Committees: (1) Agriculture, Nutrition & Forestry; (2) Budget; (3) Finance; (4) Select Committee on Indian Affairs.

Election Results: 1992 Special Election: 1986 (old seat) Conrad 143,932 (50%); Mark Andrews (Incumbent R) 141,797 (49%).

Interest Group Ratings:

ADA	ACU	COPE	COC
90	12	75	20

LCV	NTLC	CFA	ASC
17	39	75	60

Offices: 724 HSOB 20510, 202-224-2043 (Mary Wakefield, Chief-of-staff). STATE OFFICES: 232 Fed. Bldg., 3rd & Rosser Ave., Bismarck 58501, 701-258-4648 (Mr. Lynn Clancy, St. Dir.); 306 Fed. Bldg., 657 2nd Ave. N., Fargo 58102, 701-232-8030 (Lois Schneider, Rep.); 100 1st St., S.W., Suite 105, Minot 58701, 701-852-0703 (Mavis Williamson, Rep.); 104 Fed. Bldg., 102 N. 4th St., Grand Forks 58201, 701-775-9601 (James Hand, Rep.)

REPRESENTATIVE AT LARGE

Earl Pomeroy (D)

District: Entire State. Population: 638,800—Native American 4%, Hispanic 1%. Politics: Mixed.

Born Sept. 2, 1952, Valley City; home, Bismarck; University of N.Dak., B.A. 1974, J.D. 1979; Presbyterian; married (Kirby).

Elected 1992. Career: Attorney, 1979–84; State Rep., 1980–84; State Insurance Commissioner, 1984–92.

Committees: (1) Agriculture; (2) Budget.

Election Results: 1992 Pomeroy 168,415 (59%); John Korsmo (R) 117,041 (41%).

Interest Group Ratings: None—Freshman

Offices: 318 CHOB 20515, 202-225-2611 (Karen Fredrickson, AA). DISTRICT OFFICES: 337 Fed. Bldg. 304 E. Broadway, Bismarck 58501, 701-224-0355 (Gail Skaley, Dist. Dir.); 226 Fed. Bldg. 657 2nd Ave., Fargo 58102, 701-235-9760

OHIO

The Democrats have targeted Ohio in 1994. Their first priority is the reelection of Sen. Howard Metzenbaum. Given his popularity, this should not be difficult to accomplish, although if Republican Secretary of State Robert Taft II, decides to make the race, it could be close. The Democrats' second priority is to try to win back two traditional Democratic congressional districts, the 10th and 15th, that were taken from troubled incumbents by Republicans in 1992. Finally, the Democrats would like to unseat GOP Gov. George Voinovich. That will not be likely unless they can find a strong candidate. That may be a tall order.

1992 PRESIDENTIAL ELECTION: (21 Electoral votes): Clinton (D) 1,965,155 (40%); Bush (R) 1,875,664 (38%); Perot (I) 1,024,479 (21%); Marrou (Lib) 7,443; Fulani (NAP) 6,349; Gritz (Pop) 4,620; Hagelin (NLP) 3,737; LaRouche (I) 2,743. 1988 Bush 2,411,719 (55%); Dukakis 1,934,922 (45%).

SENATORS

John Herschel Glenn, Jr. (D)

Born July 18, 1921, Cambridge; home, Columbus; Muskingum College, B.S. 1943; Presbyterian; married (Anna), 2 children.

Elected 1974, seat up 1998. Career: USMC, 1942–65; NASA Astronaut, 1959–65, First American to orbit the Earth, 1962; Vice Pres., Royal Crown Cola Co., 1966–68, Pres., Royal Crown Intl., 1967–69.

Committees: (1) Armed Services; (2) Governmental Affairs (Chairman); (3) Select Committee on Aging; (4) Select Committee on Intelligence.

Election Results: 1992 Glenn 2,418,464 (55%); Michael DeWine (R) 1,992,793 (45%). 1986 Glenn 1,949,208 (62%). 1980 Glenn (69%).

Interest Group Ratings:

ADA	ACU	COPE	COC
80	11	75	10

LCV	NTLC	CFA	ASC
75	22	92	50

Office: 503 HSOB 20510, 202-224-3353 (Mary Jane Veno, AA). STATE OFFICES: 600 Fed Bldg, 200 N. High St., Columbus 43215, 614-469-6697

(Dale Butland, St. Dir.); Fed. Cthse., 201 Superior Ave., Cleveland 44114, 216-522-7095 (Caroline Arnold, Asst.); 10407 Fed. Bldg, 550 Main St., Cincinnati 45202, 513-684-3265 (Rosemary Mathews, Asst.); 234 N. Summit #726, Toledo 43604, 419-259-7592 (Marion Schenkenberger, Rep.)

Howard M. Metzenbaum (D)

Born June 4, 1917, Cleveland; home, Lyndhurst; Ohio State University, B.A. 1939; LL.D. 1941; Jewish; married (Shirley), 4 children.

Elected 1976, seat up 1994. Career: Practicing atty; Co–founder, Airport Parking Co. of America, ComCorp Communications Corp.; Chm. of the Bd., ITT Consumer Services Corp., 1966–68; Ohio House of Reps., 1943–46; Ohio Senate, 1947–50; Campaign Mgr. for Sen. Stephen M. Young, 1958, 1964.

Committees: (1) Environment & Public Works; (2) Judiciary; (3) Labor & Human Resources; (4) Select Committee on Intelligence.

Election Results: 1988 Metzenbaum 2,480,038 (57%); George Voinovich (R) 1,872,716 (43%). 1982 Metzenbaum (57%).

Interest Group Ratings:

ADA	ACU	COPE	COC
90	00	100	11

LCV	NTLC	CFA	ASC
100	22	92	40

Office: 140 RSOB 20510, 202-224-2315 (Joel Johnson, AA). STATE OFFICES: 405 Fed. Bldg., 200 N. High St., Columbus 43215, 614-469-6774 (John Maynard, Mgr.); 2915 Fed. Bldg., 1240 E. 9th St., Cleveland 44199, 216-522-7272 (Candy Korn, Mgr.); 100 Fed. Plaza E., Ste 510, Youngstown 44503, 216-746-1132; 10411 Fed. Bldg., 550 Main St., Cincinnati 45202, 513-684-3894 (Pat Phelan, Mgr.); 234 Summit St., Rm. 722, Toledo 43603, 419-259-7536 (Jerry Brown, Mgr.)

REPRESENTATIVES

FIRST DISTRICT

David Mann (D)

District: Western portions of Cincinnati and

Hamilton County suburbs. Population: 570,900
—Black 30%. Politics: Mixed. City is heavily
Democratic, while suburbs are heavily Republican.

Born Sept. 25, 1939, Cincinnati; home, Cincinnati; Harvard, A.B. 1961, LL.B. 1968; Methodist; married (Elizabeth), 3 children.

Elected 1992. Career: Navy, 1961–65; Practicing atty., Cincinnati City Cncl., 1974–92; mayor 1980–82, 1991.

Committees: (1) Armed Services; (2) Judiciary.

Election Results: 1992 Mann 117,689 (51%); Jim Berns (I) 12,444 (5%); Steve Grote (I) 99,741 (43%).

Interest Group Ratings:
None—Freshman

Office: 503 CHOB 20515, 202-225-2216 (Hannah Marget, Rep.). DISTRICT OFFICE: 2210 Kroger Bldg. 114 Vine St., Cincinnati 45202, 513-684-2723 (Tim Reiker, Rep.)

SECOND DISTRICT

Rob Portman (R)

District: Eastern Cincinnati and suburbs and southwestern counties. Population: 570,902—Black 2%. Politics: Republican.

Born Dec. 19, 1955, Cincinnati; home, Hyde Park; Dartmouth College, B.A., 1979, University of Mich., J.D., 1984; Methodist, married (Jane), 2 children.

Elected 1993, special election to fill term of Rep. Bill Gradison. Career: Lawyer; Assoc. Patton, Boggs & Blow, 1984–86; priv. prac., Graydon, Head, Ritchey, 1987–88; 1992–93; Spec. Asst. to Pres. George Bush, 1988–92.

Committees: (1) Government Operations; (2) Small Business

Election Results: 1993 (special) Portman 53,177 (70%); Lee Hornberger (D) 22,685 (30%).

Interest Group Ratings:
None—Freshman

Office: 238 CHOB, 20515, 202-225-3164 (TBA, AA). DISTRICT OFFICE: 8010 Fed. Bldg, 550 Main Street, Cincinnati 45202, 513-684-2456 (Annette Wishard, Rep.)

THIRD DISTRICT

Tony P. Hall (D)

District: Montgomery county including city of Dayton. Population: 570,901—Black 18%. Politics: Leans Democratic.

Born Jan. 16, 1942, Dayton; home, Dayton; Denison University, A.B. 1964; Presbyterian; married (Janet), 2 children.

Elected 1978. Career: Peace Corps, Thailand, 1966–67; Real estate broker, 1968–78; Ohio House of Reps. 1969–72; Ohio Senate, 1973–78.

Committees: (1) Rules.

Election Results: 1992 Hall 144,854 (60%); Peter Davis (R) 98,049 (40%). 1990 Hall (Unopposed). 1988 Hall (77%).

Interest Group Ratings:

ADA	ACU	COPE	COC
60	25	67	25

LCV	NTLC	CFA	ASC
44	05	67	40

Office: 2264 RHOB 20515, 202-225-6465 (Murray Rapp, AA). DISTRICT OFFICE: 501 Fed. Bldg., 200 W. 2nd St., Dayton 45402, 513-225-2843 (William Monita, Dir.)

FOURTH DISTRICT

Michael G. Oxley (R)

District: A group of mostly rural west–central counties that include the cities of Lima and Findley. Population: 570,901—Black 5%. Politics: Republican.

Born Feb. 11, 1944, Findlay; home, Findlay; Miami University of Ohio, B.A. 1966, Ohio State University, J.D. 1969; Lutheran; married (Patricia), 1 child.

Elected June 25, 1981. Career: FBI Spec. Agent, 1969–72; Ohio House of Reps. 1972–81; Practicing atty., 1972–81.

Committees: (1) Energy & Commerce.

Election Results: 1992 Oxley 145,484 (61%); Raymond Ball (D) 91,718 (39%). 1990 Oxley (62%). 1988 Oxley (Unopposed).

Interest Group Ratings:

ADA	ACU	COPE	COC
05	96	17	86

LCV	NTLC	CFA	ASC
44	95	20	100

Office: 2233 RHOB 20515, 202-225-2676 (James Conzelman, AA). DISTRICT OFFICES: 3121 W. Elm Plaza, Lima 45805, 419-999-6455 (Kelly Kirk, Rep.); 24 W. 3rd St., Rm. 314, Mansfield 44902, 419-522-5757 (Philip Holloway, Rep.); 100 E. Main Cross St., Findlay 45840, 419-423-3210 (Bonnie Dunbar, Rep.)

FIFTH DISTRICT

Paul E. Gillmor (R)

District: North central portion of the state including cities of Bowling Green and Sandusky. Population: 570,901—Black 2%, Hispanic 3%. Politics: Republican.

Born Feb. 1, 1939, Tiffin; home, Clinton; Ohio Wesleyan, B.A. 1961, University of Mich., J.D. 1964; married (Karen), 2 children.

Elected 1988. Career: Air Force, 1964–66; Ohio Senate 1967–88.

Committees: (1) Energy & Commerce.

Election Results: 1992 Gillmor (Unopposed). 1990 Gillmor (73%). 1988 Gillmor (61%).

Interest Group Ratings:

ADA	ACU	COPE	COC
20	80	50	75

LCV	NTLC	CFA	ASC
19	60	33	100

Office: 1203 LHOB 20515, 202-225-6405 (Marl Wellman, AA). DISTRICT OFFICES: 148 E. Southboundry, Perrysburg 43551, 419-872-2500 (Tim Brown, Rep.); 120 Jefferson St., 2nd Fl., Port Clinton 43452 419-734-1999 (Tom Brown, Rep.)

SIXTH DISTRICT

Ted Strickland (D)

District: A wide ranging district in the south–central part of the state running from the outskirts of Cincinnati to the eastern border. Includes cities of Portsmouth and Marietta. Population: 570,901. Politics: Republican.

Born Aug. 4, 1941, Portsmouth; home, Lucasville; Asbury College, B.A., M.A., University of Ky., Ph.D.; Methodist; married (Frances).

Elected 1992. Career: College Professor.

Committees: (1) Education & Labor; (2) Small Business.

Election Results: 1992 Strickland 121,223 (51%); Bob McEwen (R) (Incumbent) 117,681 (49%).

Interest Group Ratings:
None—Freshman

Office: 1429 LHOB 20515, 202-225-5705 (Riley Grimes, AA). DISTRICT OFFICES: 1236 Gallia St., Portsmouth 45662, 614-353-5171

SEVENTH DISTRICT

David L. Hobson (R)

District: A semi–circular district in the western central part of the state including city of Springfield. Population: 570,902—Black 5%. Politics: Republican.

Born Oct. 17, 1936, Cincinnati; home, Springfield; Ohio Wesleyan University, B.A. 1958, Ohio State, J.D., 1963; Methodist; married (Carolyn), 3 children.

Elected 1990. Career: Chm. Bd., Financial Land Corp.; Ohio St. Senate 1983–90.

Committees: (1) Appropriations; (2) Budget; (3) Standards of Ethical Conduct.

Election Results: 1992 Hobson 162,764 (71%); Clifford Heskett (D) 65,525 (29%). 1990 Hobson (62%).

Interest Group Ratings:

ADA	ACU	COPE	COC
15	80	33	88

LCV	NTLC	CFA	ASC
13	80	33	100

Office: 1507 LHOB 20515, 202-225-4324 (Mary Beth Carozza, AA). DISTRICT OFFICES: 150 N. Limestone St., Rm. 220, Springfield 45501, 513-325-0474 (Eileen Austria, Rep.); 212 S. Broad St. #55, Lancaster 43130, 614-654-5149

EIGHTH DISTRICT

John A. Boehner (R)

District: West end of the state including towns of Middletown and Hamilton. Population: 570,901 —Black 3%. Politics: Republican.

Born Nov. 17, 1949, Cincinnati; home, West Chester; Xavier, B.S., 1977; Roman Catholic; married (Deborah), 2 children.

Elected 1990. Career: Businessman, pres. Nucite Sales Co.; Ohio House of Reps., 1985–90.

Committees: (1) Agriculture; (2) Education & Labor; (3) House Administration.

Election Results: 1992 Boehner 167,485 (71%); Fred Sennet (D) 68,159 (29%). 1990 Boehner (61%).

Interest Group Ratings:

ADA	ACU	COPE	COC
05	96	17	88

LCV	NTLC	CFA	ASC
00	95	13	100

Office: 1020 LHOB 20515, 202-225-6205 (Barry Jackson, AA). DISTRICT OFFICES: 5617 Liberty Fairfield Rd., Hamilton 45011, 513-894-6003 (Sue Clark, Dir.); 12 S. Plum St., Troy 45373, 513-339-1524 (Chuck Mohler, Rep.)

NINTH DISTRICT

Marcy Kaptur (D)

District: Toledo and suburbs. Population: 570,901 —Black 12%, Hispanic 3%. Politics: Democratic.

Born June 17, 1946, Toledo; home, Toledo; University of Wis., B.A. 1968, University of Mich., M.A.U.P. 1974; Roman Catholic; single.

Elected 1982. Career: Urban planner, Toledo–Lucas Cty. Planning Comm., 1969–75; Development & Urban Planning Consultant, 1975–77; Asst. Dir. for Urban Affairs, Domestic Policy Staff, White House, 1977–80; Dpty. Secy., National Consumer Coop. Bank, 1980–81.

Committees: (1) Appropriations.

Election Results: 1992 Kaptur 176,877 (77%); Ken Brown (R) 52,431 (23%). 1990 Kaptur (78%). 1988 Kaptur (81%).

Interest Group Ratings:

ADA	ACU	COPE	COC
75	08	100	14

LCV	NTLC	CFA	ASC
56	00	87	40

Office: 2104 RHOB 20515, 202-225-4146 (Fairborz Fatemi, AA). DISTRICT OFFICE: 719 Fed. Bldg., 234 Summit St., Toledo 43604, 419-259-7500 (Steve Katich, Mgr.)

TENTH DISTRICT

Martin R. Hoke (R)

District: Parts of Cleveland and western suburbs. Population: 570,903—Hispanic 4%. Politics: Republican.

Born May 18, 1952, Lakewood; home, Shaker Heights; Amherst College, B.A. 1973, Case Western Reserve, J.D. 1980; Presbyterian; divorced, 3 children.

Elected 1992. Career: Attorney, Businessman, 1980–92.

Committees: (1) Budget; (2) Science Space and Technology.

Election Results: 1992 Hoke 134,711 (57%); Mary Rose Oakar (D) (Incumbent) 102,573 (43%).

Interest Group Ratings:
None—Freshman

Office: 212 CHOB 20515-3510, 202-225-5871 (Ed Cassidy, AA). DISTRICT OFFICES: 21270 Lorain Rd., Fairview Park 44126, 216-356-2010 (vacant, Rep.)

ELEVENTH DISTRICT

Louis Stokes (D)

District: Central and eastern Cleveland plus some suburbs and Cleveland Heights. Population: 570,901—Black 59%. Politics: Democratic.

Born Feb. 23, 1925, Cleveland; home, Cleveland; Western Reserve University, 1946–48, Cleveland State University, J.D. 1953; United Methodist; married (Jeanette), 4 children.

Elected 1968. Career: Army 1943–46; Practicing atty., 1954–68.

Committees: (1) Appropriations.

Election Results: 1992 Stokes 152,328 (78%); Beryl Rothschild (R) 43,152 (22%). 1990 Stokes (80%); 1988 Stokes (86%).

Interest Group Ratings:

ADA	ACU	COPE	COC
95	00	92	14

LCV	NTLC	CFA	ASC
81	00	100	10

Office: 2365 RHOB 20515, 202-225-7032 (Reginald Gilliam, AA). DISTRICT OFFICES: 2947 New Fed. Bldg., 1240 E. 9th St., Cleveland 44199, 216-522-4900 (Jewell Gilbert, Dist. Mgr.); 2140 Lee Rd., Suite 211, Cleveland Hgts. 44118, 216-522-4907 (Juanita Connor-Phillips, Rep.)

TWELFTH DISTRICT

John R. Kasich (R)

District: Central part of the state including parts of Columbus and suburbs. Population: 570,902 —Black 23%. Politics: Republican.

Born May 13, 1952, McKees Rocks, Pa.; home, Westerville; Ohio State University, B.S. 1974; Roman Catholic; divorced.

Elected 1982. Career: A.A. to State Sen. Donald Lukens, 1975–77; Ohio Senate, 1979–82.

Committees: (1) Armed Services; (2) Budget.

Election Results: 1992 Kasich 169,548 (71%); Bob Fitrakis (D) 68,250 (29%). 1990 Kasich (72%). 1988 Kasich (80%).

Interest Group Ratings:

ADA	ACU	COPE	COC
15	84	42	86

LCV	NTLC	CFA	ASC
25	75	33	100

Office: 1131 LHOB 20515, 202-225-5355 (Don Thibaut, Chief-of-staff). DISTRICT OFFICE: 400 Fed. Bldg., 200 N. High St., Columbus 43215, 614-469-7318 (Tod Bowen, Rep.)

THIRTEENTH DISTRICT

Sherrod Brown (D)

District: Three northern counties including some far Cleveland suburbs but mainly Lorain County with cities of Lorain and Elyria. Population: 570,894—Black 5%, Hispanic 3%. Politics: Leans Democratic.

Born Nov. 9, 1952, Mansfield; home, Chippewa Lake; Yale, B.A. 1974, Ohio State, M.A. 1979, M.P.A. 1981; Presbyterian; divorced, 2 children.

Elected 1992. Career: State Rep., 1975–83; Ohio Secy. of State, 1983–91; College Prof., 1991–92.

Committees: (1) Energy & Commerce; (2) Foreign Affairs; (3) Post Office and Civil Service.

Election Results: 1992 Brown 133,489 (60%); Margaret Mueller (R) 88,202 (40%).

Interest Group Ratings:
None—Freshman

Office: 1407 LHOB 20515, 202-225-3401 (Rhod Shawe, AA). DISTRICT OFFICE: Not yet established.

FOURTEENTH DISTRICT

Thomas C. Sawyer (D)

District: Akron and environs. Population: 570,900 —Black 11%. Politics: Leans Democratic.

Born Aug. 15, 1945, Akron; home, Akron; University of Akron, B.A. 1968, M.A. 1970; Presbyterian; married (Joyce), 1 child.

Elected 1986. Career: Ohio House of Reps., 1977–83; Mayor of Akron, 1983–86.

Committees: (1) Education & Labor; (2) Post Office & Civil Service; (3) Foreign Affairs (temp.); (4) Ethics.

Election Results: 1992 Sawyer 163,454 (68%); Robert Morgan (R) 77,953 (32%). 1990 Sawyer (60%). 1988 Sawyer (75%).

Interest Group Ratings:

ADA	ACU	COPE	COC
95	04	83	38

LCV	NTLC	CFA	ASC
63	00	100	30

Office: 1414 LHOB 20515, 202-225-5231 (Rochelle Dornatt, Ex. AA). DISTRICT OFFICE: 405 Fed. Bldg., 2 S. Main St., Akron 44308, 216-375-5710 (Judi Shapiro, Dist. Adm.)

FIFTEENTH DISTRICT

Deborah Pryce (R)

District: Western Columbus and suburbs. Population: 570,902—Black 5%. Politics: Republican.

Born July 29, 1951, Warren; home, Dublin; Ohio State, B.A. 1973, Capital University, J.D. 1976; Presbyterian; married (Randy Walker), 2 children.

Elected 1992. Career: Judge, Ohio Dept. of Insurance, 1976–77; Asst. Columbus City Atty., 1978–85, Franklin Cty. Judge, 1986–92; Practicing atty., 1977–92.

Committees: (1) Banking, Finance & Urban Affairs; (2) Government Operations.

Election Results: 1992 Pryce 115,710 (44%); Richard Cordray (D) 97,599 (37%); Linda Reidelbach (I) 47,178 (18%).

Interest Group Ratings:
None—Freshman

Office: 128 CHOB 20515, 202-225-2015 (Tom Wolfe, AA). DISTRICT OFFICE: 200 N. High St., Columbus 43215, 614-469-5614 (Marcee McCreary, Rep.)

SIXTEENTH DISTRICT

Ralph S. Regula (R)

District: Several northeast counties including city of Canton and Wooster. Population: 570,902 —Black 5%. Politics: Leans Republican.

Born Dec. 3, 1924, Beach City; home, Navarre; Mount Union College, B.A. 1948, Wm. McKinley Sch. of Law, LL.B 1952; Episcopalian; married (Mary), 3 children.

Elected 1972. Career: Navy, WWII; Teacher & school principal, 1948–55; Practicing atty., 1952–73; Ohio Bd. of Educ., 1961–64; Ohio House of Reps., 1965–66; Ohio Senate, 1967–72.

Committees: (1) Appropriations.

Election Results: 1992 Regula 156,963 (64%); Warner Mendenhall (D) 89,509 (36%). 1990 Regula (59%). 1988 Regula (79%).

Interest Group Ratings:

ADA	ACU	COPE	COC
35	72	67	100

LCV	NTLC	CFA	ASC
25	60	33	100

Office: 2309 RHOB 20515, 202-225-3876 (Barbara Wainman, AA). DISTRICT OFFICE: 4150 Belden Village Ave., N.W., Canton 44718, 216-489-4414 (Jeannette Griffin, Mgr.)

SEVENTEENTH DISTRICT

James A. Traficant, Jr. (D)

District: Youngstown and environs including towns of Warren and Salem. Population: 514,172 —Black 10%. Politics: Democratic.

Born May 8, 1941, Youngstown; home, Poland; University of Pittsburgh, B.S. 1963; Youngstown State University, M.S. 1973, M.S. 1976; Roman Catholic; married (Patricia), 2 children.

Elected 1984. Career: Dir., Mahoning Cty. Drug Program, 1971–81; Sheriff, 1981–85.

Committees: (1) Public Works & Transportation; (2) Science, Space & Technology.

Election Results: 1992 Traficant 214,433 (84%); Salvador Pansino (R) 40,381 (16%). 1990 Traficant (78%). 1988 Traficant (77%).

Interest Group Ratings:

ADA	ACU	COPE	COC
85	08	90	50

LCV	NTLC	CFA	ASC
50	15	80	20

Office: 2446 RHOB 20515, 202-225-5261 (H. West Richards, Chief-of-staff). DISTRICT OFFICES: 11 Overhill Rd., Youngstown 44514, 216-788-2414 (Henry DiBlasio, Dist. AA); 5555 Youngstown-Warren Rd. #2685, Niles 44446, 216-652-5649 (vacant, Rep.); 109 W. 3rd St., E. Liverpool 43920, 216-385-5921 (Carrie Davis, Rep.)

EIGHTEENTH DISTRICT

E. Douglas Applegate (D)

District: Group of Hill Country eastern counties including cities of Steubenville and Zanesville. Population: 570,900. Politics: Democratic.

Born Mar. 27, 1928, Steubenville; home, Steubenville; Presbyterian; married (Betty), 2 children.

Elected 1976. Career: Ohio House of Reps., 1961–68; Ohio Senate, 1968–76.

Committees: (1) Public Works & Transportation; (2) Veterans Affairs.

Election Results: 1992 Applegate 164,390 (68%); Bill Ress (R) 76,868 (32%). 1990 Applegate (74%). 1988 Applegate (78%).

Interest Group Ratings:

ADA	ACU	COPE	COC
70	12	92	38

LCV	NTLC	CFA	ASC
44	15	80	30

Office: 2183 RHOB 20515, 202-225-6265 (James Hart, AA). DISTRICT OFFICES: 46060 National Rd. W., Clairsville 43950, 614-695-4600 (Susan Witten, Rep.); 610 Ohio Valley Tower, 500 Market St., Steubenville 43952, 614-283-3716 (Julie Ellen, Rep.); 225 Underwood, Zanesville 43701, 614-452-7203 (Mary Funk, Rep.); 1330 4th St., N.W., New Philadelphia 44663, 216-343-9112 (Nancy Leggett, Rep.)

NINETEENTH DISTRICT

Eric D. Fingerhut (D)

District: South Cleveland suburbs to northeastern corner of the state, including Ashtabula. Population: 570,901—Black 2%. Politics: Leans Democratic.

Born May 6, 1959, University Heights; home, Cleveland; Northwestern, B.A. 1951, Stanford, J.D. 1984; Jewish; single.

Elected 1992. Career: Staff Atty. Older Persons Law Office of Cleveland, 1984–85; Cleveland Works, 1987–89; Practicing atty., 1989–92.

Committees: (1) Foreign Affairs; (2) Space Science & Technology; (3) Banking, Finance and Urban Affairs.

Election Results: 1992 Fingerhut 137,140 (53%); Robert Gardner (R) 123,308 (47%).

Interest Group Ratings:
None—Freshman

Office: 431 CHOB 20515, 202-225-5731 (David Fleshler, AA). DISTRICT OFFICE: 2550 Sum Center Rd. #385, Willoughby Hills 44094, 216-943-1919 (Bob Triozzi, Rep.)

OKLAHOMA

The politics of this state remain narrowly balanced between Democrat and Republican. The unexpected retirement of popular Republican Gov. Henry Bellmon in 1990 set off a mad scramble among both Democratic and Republican hopefuls, and ended up with Democrat David Walters winning by a surprisingly comfortable margin. He must now run for reelection in 1994, and the GOP thinks he can be beaten.

1992 PRESIDENTIAL ELECTION: (8 Electoral votes): Clinton (D) 473,066 (34%); Bush (R) 592,929 (43%); Perot (I) 319,978 (23%); Marrou (Lib) 4,486. 1988 Bush 678,244 (58%); Dukakis 483,373 (42%).

SENATORS

David Lyle Boren (D)

Born Apr. 21, 1941, Washington, D.C.; home, Seminole; Yale University, B.A. 1963, Rhodes Scholar, Oxford University, 1965, University of Okla., J.D. 1968; United Methodist; married (Molly), 2 children.

Elected 1978, seat up 1996. Career: Okla. House of Reps., 1968–74; Prof. & Chm., Dept. of Govt., Okla. Baptist University, 1968–74; Practicing atty.; Gov. of Okla., 1975–79.

Committees: (1) Agriculture, Nutrition & Forestry; (2) Finance; (3) Small Business; (4) Joint Committee on the Organization of Congress.

Election Results: 1990 Boren 733,715 (83%); Stephen Jones (R) 148,438 (17%). 1984 Boren (76%).

Interest Group Ratings:

ADA	ACU	COPE	COC
60	35	50	50

LCV	NTLC	CFA	ASC
42	29	67	80

Office: 453 RSOB 20510, 202-224-4721 (David Cox, AA). STATE OFFICES: 621 N. Robinson, Rm. 370, Oklahoma City 73102, 405-231-4381 (Patty Mellow, Dir.); Fed. Bldg., 440 S. Houston, Tulsa 74127, 918-581-7785 (Shreese Wilson, Mgr.); City Hall, Seminole 74868, 405-382-6480 (Ann Dubler, Mgr.)

Donald Lee Nickles (R)

Born Dec. 6, 1948, Ponca City; home, Ponca City; Okla. State University, B.B.A. 1971; Roman Catholic; married (Linda), 4 children.

Elected 1980, seat up 1998. Career: Natl. Guard, 1970–76; Vice Pres. & Gen. Mgr., Nickles Machine Corp., 1976–80; Okla. Senate, 1979–80.

Committees: (1) Appropriations; (2) Budget; (3) Energy & Natural Resources.

Election Results: 1992 Nickles 757,876 (59%); Steve Lewis (D) 494,350 (38%); Thomas Ledgerwood 20,972; Roy Edwards 21,225. 1986 Nickles (55%). 1980 Nickles (53%).

Interest Group Ratings:

ADA	ACU	COPE	COC
00	96	08	89

LCV	NTLC	CFA	ASC
00	100	08	80

Office: 133 HSOB 20510, 202-224-5754 (Les Brorsen, AA). STATE OFFICES: 1820 Liberty Tower, 100 N. Broadway, Oklahoma City 73102, 405-231-4941 (Grant Todd, Rep.); 3310 Mid-Continent Tower, 409 South Boston, Tulsa 74103, 918-581-7651 (Karl Ahlgren, Rep.); 1916 Lake Rd., Ponca City 74604, 405-767-1270 (Cheryl Fletcher, St. Dir.); 115 Federal Building, 5th & E Aves., 201 Lawton Nat. Bk. Bldg., 601 D Ave., Lawton 73501, 405-357-9878 (Billie Jo Penn, Rep.)

REPRESENTATIVES

FIRST DISTRICT

James M. Inhofe (R)

District: Tulsa and Tulsa County. Population: 524,564—Black 10%, Native American 5%, Hispanic 2%. Politics: Republican.

Born Nov. 17, 1934, Des Moines, Iowa; home, Tulsa; University of Tulsa, B.A. 1959; Presbyterian; married (Kay), 4 children.

Elected 1986. Career: Okla. House of Reps., 1966–68; Okla. Senate, 1968–76; Mayor of Tulsa, 1978–84.

Committees: (1) Merchant Marine & Fisheries; (2) Public Works & Transportation; (3) Armed Services.

Election Results: 1992 Inhofe 119,211 (53%); John Selph (D) 106,619 (47%). 1990 Inhofe (56%). 1988 Inhofe (52%).

Interest Group Ratings:

ADA	ACU	COPE	COC
10	96	36	75

LCV	NTLC	CFA	ASC
00	100	27	100

Office: 442 CHOB 20515, 202-225-2211 (V. Bruce Thompson, AA). DISTRICT OFFICE: 1924 S. Utica #530, Tulsa 74104, 918-581-7111 (Marcia Perry, Dir.)

SECOND DISTRICT

Michael L. Synar (D)

District: Northeastern part of the state except Tulsa. Population: 524,264—Black 5%, Native American 17%. Politics: Democratic.

Born Oct. 17, 1950, Vinita; home, Muskogee; University of Okla., B.A. 1972, J.D. 1977, Northwestern University, M.S. 1973, University of Edinburgh, Rotary International Scholar, 1974; Episcopalian; single.

Elected 1978. Career: Rancher, practicing atty., real estate broker.

Committees: (1) Energy & Commerce; (2) Government Operations; (3) Judiciary.

Election Results: 1992 Synar 118,542 (56%); Jerry Hill (R) 87,657 (41%); William Vardeman (I) 7,314 (3%). 1990 Synar (61%). 1988 Synar (65%).

Interest Group Ratings:

ADA	ACU	COPE	COC
95	00	83	25

LCV	NTLC	CFA	ASC
81	00	87	30

Office: 2329 RHOB 20515, 202-225-2701 (Deborah Wesslund, AA). DISTRICT OFFICE: 2B22 Fed. Bldg., 125 S. Main, Muskogee 74401, 918-687-2533 (Gene Wallace, AA)

THIRD DISTRICT

William Brewster (D)

District: Southeast and central part of the state including Stillwater and Ardmore. Population 524,264—Black 4%, Native American, 11%. Politics: Conservative Democratic.

Born Nov. 8, 1941, Ardmore; home, Marietta; Southwest Oklahoma State, B.S. (pharmacology), 1968; Baptist; married (Suzie), 1 child.

Elected 1990. Career: Pharmacist, rancher, real estate co. owner; Okla. State House 1983–90.

Committees: (1) Ways & Means.

Election Results: 1992 Brewster 155,934 (75%); Robert Stokes (R) 51,725 (25%). 1990 Brewster (80%).

Interest Group Ratings:

ADA	ACU	COPE	COC
60	48	50	75

LCV	NTLC	CFA	ASC
25	00	47	100

Office: 1727 LHOB 20515, 202-225-4565 (Phyllis Kreis, AA). DISTRICT OFFICES: P.O. Box 1607., Ada 74801, 405-436-1980 (James Ross, Dir.); 118 Fed. Bldg., McAlester 74501, 918-423-5951; 123 W. 7th Ave, Suite 206, Stillwater 74074, 405-743-1400 (Robert Felts, Rep.); 101 W. Main St., Ardmore 73401, 405-226-6300 (Sissy Kiser, Rep.)

FOURTH DISTRICT

Dave McCurdy (D)

District: Southwestern part of the state and a small part of Oklahoma City. Population: 524,265 —Black 7%, Native American 5%, Hispanic 4%. Politics: Leans Democratic.

Born Mar. 30, 1950, Canadian, Tex.; home, Norman; University of Okla., B.A. 1972, J.D. 1975, University of Edinburgh, 1977–78; Lutheran; married (Pamela), 3 children.

Elected 1980. Career: Okla. Asst. Atty. Gen., 1975–77; Practicing atty., 1977–80.

Committees: (1) Armed Services; (2) Science, Space & Technology.

Election Results: 1992 McCurdy 140,841 (71%); Howard Bell (R) 58,235 (29%). 1990 McCurdy (74%). 1988 McCurdy (83%).

Interest Group Ratings:

ADA	ACU	COPE	COC
70	32	64	75

LCV	NTLC	CFA	ASC
38	25	60	90

Office: 2344 RHOB 20515, 202-225-6165 (Stephen Patterson, AA). DISTRICT OFFICES: 330 W. Gray, Suite 110, Norman 73070, 405-329-6500 (Vaughn Clark, Dist. AA); 103 Fed. Bldg., Lawton 73501, 405-357-2131 (Joe Hall, Rep.)

FIFTH DISTRICT

Earnest J. Istook (R)

District: Winding district covering parts of Oklahoma City and suburbs extending through the north central counties. Population: 524,264—Black 6%, Native American 5%, Hispanic 3%. Politics: Republican.

Born Feb. 11, 1950, Ft. Worth, Tex.; home, Oklahoma City; Baylor University, B.A. 1971, Oklahoma City University, J.D. 1977; Mormon; married (Judy), 5 children.

Elected 1992. Career: Reporter, 1972–77; Practicing attorney, 1978–92; State Rep. 1986–92; Warr Acres City Council, 1988–92.

Committees: (1) Appropriations.

Election Results: 1992 Istook 123,237 (53%); Laurie Williams (D) 107,579 (47%).

Interest Group Ratings:
None—Freshman

Office: 1116 LHOB 20515, 202-225-2132 (Brian Lopina, AA). DISTRICT OFFICES: 5400 N.W.

Grand Blvd. #505, Oklahoma City 73112, 405-942-3636 (Dwight Dissler, Rep.)

SIXTH DISTRICT

Glenn English (D)

District: Western (panhandle) part of the state including some parts of Oklahoma City. Population: 524,264—Black 13%, Hispanic 4%, Native American 5%. Politics: Democratic.

Born Nov. 30, 1940, Cordell; home, Cordell; Southwestern State College, B.A. 1964; United Methodist; married (Jan), 2 children.

Elected 1974. Career: Chf. Asst., Major Caucus, Calif. Assembly; Exec. Dir., Okla. Dem. Party, 1969–73; Petroleum leasing business.

Committees: (1) Agriculture; (2) Government Operations.

Election Results: 1992 English 134,734 (68%); Bob Anthony (R) 64,068 (32%). 1990 English (80%). 1988 English (73%).

Interest Group Ratings:

ADA	ACU	COPE	COC
55	56	67	75

LCV	NTLC	CFA	ASC
38	45	47	60

Office: 2206 RHOB 20515, 202-225-5565 (Scott Ingham, Spec. Asst.). DISTRICT OFFICES: 252 Old P.O. Bldg., 215 Dean A. McGee Ave., Oklahoma City 73102, 405-231-5511 (Gary Dage, AA); Fed. Bldg., P.O. Box 3612, Enid 73702, 405-233-9224 (Amie Schenandoah, Rep.); 1007 Main St., Woodward 73801, 405-256-5752 (Dana Franks, Rep.)

OREGON

The political question of the moment in Oregon is whether GOP Sen. Bob Packwood will face a recall election, if he is not unseated by the Senate Ethics Committee over charges of sexual harassment of his employees. Almost an afterthought will be the reelection campaign of Gov. Barbara Roberts. She won only a very narrow victory in 1990, but is popular and will be difficult to dislodge.

1992 PRESIDENTIAL ELECTION: (7 Electoral votes): Clinton (D) 538,793 (43%); Bush (R) 404,301 (32%); Perot (I) 316,334 (25%); Marrou (Lib) 3,722; Fulani (NAP) 2,661. 1988 Dukakis 575,071 (53%); Bush 517,731 (47%).

SENATORS

Mark O. Hatfield (R)

Born July 12, 1922, Dallas; home, Tigard; Willamette University, B.A. 1943, Stanford University, M.A. 1948; Baptist; married (Antoinette), 4 children.

Elected 1966, seat up 1996. Career: Navy, WWII; Assoc. Prof. of Pol. Sci., Dean of Students, Willamette University, 1949–57; Oreg. House of Reps., 1951–55; Oreg. Senate, 1955–57; Secy. of State of Oreg., 1957–59; Gov. of Oreg., 1959–67.

Committees: (1) Appropriations (Ranking Member); (2) Energy & Natural Resources; (3) Rules & Administration; (4) Joint Committee on the Library; (5) Joint Committee on Printing.

Election Results: 1990 Hatfield 541,035 (54%); Harry Lonsdale (D) 463,438 (46%). 1984 Hatfield (67%).

Interest Group Ratings:

ADA	ACU	COPE	COC
70	23	75	56

LCV	NTLC	CFA	ASC
42	44	67	40

Office: 711 HSOB 20510, 202-224-3753 (Steve Nelson, AA). STATE OFFICES: 727 Center St. S.E. #305, Salem 97301, 503-588-9510 (Ray Naff, Dir.); 121 S.W. Salmon #1420, Portland 97204, 503-326-3386 (Mike Salsgiver, Chief Rep.)

Robert William Packwood (R)

Born Sept. 11, 1932, Portland; home, Aloha; Willamette University, B.A. 1954, New York University, LL.B. 1957; Unitarian; divorced.

Elected 1968, seat up 1998. Career: Law clerk, Oreg. Supreme Crt., 1957–58; Practicing atty., 1958–68; Oreg. House of Reps., 1963–69.

Committees: (1) Commerce, Science & Transportation; (2) Finance (Ranking Member); (3) Joint Committee on Taxation.

Election Results: 1992 Packwood 612,238 (52%); Les AuCoin (D) 558,015 (48%). 1990 Packwood (63%). 1980 Packwood (52%).

Interest Group Ratings:

ADA	ACU	COPE	COC
60	33	50	30

LCV	NTLC	CFA	ASC
25	56	50	90

Office: 259 RSOB 20510, 202-224-5244 (Elaine Franklin, Chief-of-staff). STATE OFFICE: 101 S.W. Main St., Suite 240, Portland 97204-3210, 503-326-3370 (Emily Barlow, Rep.)

REPRESENTATIVES

FIRST DISTRICT

Elizabeth Furse (D)

District: Northwest corner of the state including part of Portland and western suburbs. Population: 568,461—Asian 3%, Hispanic 4%. Politics: Leans Democratic.

Born Oct. 13, 1936, Nairobi, Kenya; home, Hillsboro; Evergreen State College, B.A. 1974; Protestant; married (John Platt), 2 children.

Elected 1992. Career: Dir. Restoration Program for Native American Tribes, 1980–86.

Committees: (1) Banking & Finance; (2) Merchant Marine & Fisheries; (3) Armed Services.

Election Results: 1992 Furse 118,133 (54%); Tony Meeker (R) 100,955 (46%).

Interest Group Ratings:
None—Freshman

Office: 316 CHOB 20515, 202-225-0855 (Jenorie Kluel, AA). DISTRICT OFFICE: 2701 N.W. Vaughn #860, Portland 97201, 503-326-2901 (Phillis Oster, Rep.)

SECOND DISTRICT

Robert F. Smith (R)

District: Eastern two–thirds of the state including cities of Bend and Medford. Population: 568,464—Native American 2%, Hispanic 5%. Politics: Republican.

Born June 16, 1931, Portland; home, Burns; Willamette University, B.A. 1953; Presbyterian; married (Kaye), 3 children.

Elected 1982. Career: Cattle rancher; Oreg. House of Reps., 1960–72, Spkr. 1968–72; Oreg. Senate, 1972–82.

Committees: (1) Agriculture; (2) Natural Resources.

Election Results: 1992 Smith 166,394 (67%); Denzel Ferguson (D) 82,823 (33%). 1990 Smith (68%). 1988 Smith (63%).

Interest Group Ratings:

ADA	ACU	COPE	COC
05	92	25	75

LCV	NTLC	CFA	ASC
00	75	13	100

Office: 118 CHOB 20515, 202-225-6730 (Paul Unger, Chief-of-staff). DISTRICT OFFICES: 259 Barnett Rd. Suite E, Medford 97501, 503-776-4646 (Leigh Johnson, Dist. AA); 771 Ponderosa Village, Burns 97720, 503-573-6112 (Ruby Filler, Rep.)

THIRD DISTRICT

Ron Wyden (D)

District: Eastern Portland and suburbs. Population: 568,465—Black 6%, Asian 4%, Hispanic 3%. Politics: Leans Democratic.

Born May 3, 1949, Wichita, Kans.; home, Portland; Stanford University, B.A. 1971, University of Oreg., J.D. 1974; Jewish; married (Laurie), 2 children.

Elected 1980. Career: Campaign aide to Sen. Wayne Morse, 1972, 1974; Practicing atty., 1974–80; Co–dir. & Co–founder, Oreg. Gray Panthers, 1974–80; Dir., Oreg. Legal Svcs. for the Elderly,

1977–79; Prof., University of Oreg., 1976, Portland State University, 1979, University of Portland, 1980.

Committees: (1) Energy & Commerce; (2) Small Business; (3) Joint Economic Committee.

Election Results: 1992 Wyden 177,745 (81%); Al Ritter (R) 40,752 (19%). 1990 Wyden (81%). 1988 Wyden (99%).

Interest Group Ratings:

ADA	ACU	COPE	COC
95	00	73	25

LCV	NTLC	CFA	ASC
81	00	100	30

Office: 1111 LHOB 20515, 202-225-4811 (Windy Horwitz, AA). DISTRICT OFFICE: 500 N.E. Multnomah, Suite 250, Portland 97232, 503-231-2300 (Lou Savage, Dist. AA)

FOURTH DISTRICT

Peter A. DeFazio (D)

District: Southwest part of the state including city of Eugene. Population: 568,465. Politics: Leans Democratic.

Born May 27, 1947, Needham, Mass.; home, Springfield; Tufts University, B.A. 1969, University of Oreg., M.S. 1977; Roman Catholic; married (Myrnie).

Elected 1986. Career: Air Force, 1967–71; District Office Dir., Rep. James Weaver, 1977–82; Lane Cty. Bd. of Commissioners, 1982–86, Chm., 1984–86.

Committees: (1) Natural Resources; (2) Public Works & Transportation.

Election Results: 1992 DeFazio 183,358 (72%); Richard Schulz (R) 71,446 (28%). 1990 DeFazio (86%). 1988 DeFazio (72%).

Interest Group Ratings:

ADA	ACU	COPE	COC
90	09	82	25

LCV	NTLC	CFA	ASC
75	00	87	30

Office: 1233 LHOB 20515, 202-225-6416 (Jeff Stier, Legs. Dir.). DISTRICT OFFICES: 215 S. 2nd, Coos Bay 97420, 503-269-2609 (Jana Doerr, Rep.); Fed. Bldg., 211 E. 7th Ave. Eugene 97401, 503-965-6732 (Deborah Farrington, Mgr.); 612 S.E. Jackson #9, P.O. Box 2460, Roseburg 97470, 503-440-3523 (Chris Conroy, Rep.)

PENNSYLVANIA

Republicans would like to think they will be able to mount a strong challenge to the reelection of Democratic Sen. Harris Wofford, who is running again only three years after winning a special election. But in that time he has established a solid base, and is very popular. It will take a major upset to unseat him. In even less trouble is Democratic Gov. Robert Casey who also faces reelection in 1994. He is controversial for his solid pro–life stance in the abortion debate, but that seems to sit well with a majority of Pennsylvania voters.

1992 PRESIDENTIAL ELECTION: (23 Electoral votes): Clinton (D) 2,229,759 (45%); Bush (R) 1,778,769 (36%); Perot (I) 896,423 (18%); Marrou (Lib) 21,315; Fulani (NAP) 6,895. 1988 Bush 2,291,297 (51%); Dukakis 2,183,928 (49%).

SENATORS

Harris Wofford (D)

Born Apr. 9, 1926, New York City; home, Bryn Mawr; University of Chicago, B.A. 1948, Yale University, LL.B. 1954, Howard University, J.D. 1954; Roman Catholic; married (Clare), 3 children.

Elected 1991, seat up 1994. Career: U.S. Army, 1944–45; Campaign Advisor to John F. Kennedy, 1960; President Bryn Mawr College, 1966–70; Professor Notre Dame Law, 1970–77; Practicing attorney, 1978–90.

Committees: (1) Foreign Relations; (2) Environment & Public Works; (3) Labor & Human Resources.

Election Results: 1991 Wofford 1,828,188 (55%); Dick Thornburgh (R) 1,505,640 (46%).

Interest Group Ratings:

ADA	ACU	COPE	COC
100	00	92	20

LCV	NTLC	CFA	ASC
67	25	83	60

Office: 521 DSOB 20510, 202-224-6324 (Steve Schutt, AA). STATE OFFICES: 9456 Fed. Bldg., 6th & Arch Sts., Philadelphia 19106, 215-597-9914 (Todd Bernstein, Ex. Asst.); 2031 Fed. Bldg., 100 Liberty Ave., Pittsburgh 15222, 412-562-0533 (Mary Van Shura, AA); U.S. Cthse., 3rd & Chestnut Sts., Harrisburg 17108, 717-233-5849 (LaVerna Fountain, Dir.); 130 Fed. Bldg., Perry Sq., Erie 16501, 814-454-7114 (Mary Fiolek, Rep.); 814 Scranton Electric Bldg., 507 Linden St., Scranton 18503, 717-347-2341 (Tim McGrath, Asst.)

Arlen Specter (R)

Born Feb. 12, 1930, Wichita, Kans.; home, Philadelphia; University of Pa., B.A. 1951, Yale University, LL.B. 1956; Jewish; married (Joan), 2 children.

Elected 1980, seat up 1998. Career: Air Force, 1951–53; Practicing atty.; Asst. Counsel, Warren Comm., 1964; Pa. Asst. Atty. Gen., 1964–65; Philadelphia Dist. Atty., 1966–74, City Cncl., 1979.

Committees: (1) Appropriations; (2) Judiciary; (3) Veterans Affairs; (4) Energy & Natural Resources.

Election Results: 1992 Specter 2,344,397 (51%); Lynn Yeakel (D) 2,215,472 (49%). 1986 Specter (56%). 1990 Specter (50%).

Interest Group Ratings:

ADA	ACU	COPE	COC
65	30	83	60

LCV	NTLC	CFA	ASC
50	50	75	90

Office: 530 HSOB 20510, 202-224-4254 (Berry Caldwell, AA). STATE OFFICES: 9400 Fed. Bldg., 600 Arch Street, Suite 9400, Philadelphia 19106, 215-597-7200 (Patrick Meehan, Ex. Dir.); 2031 Fed. Bldg., Liberty & Grant Sts., Pittsburgh 15222, 412-644-3400 (Yvonne O'Connor, Ex. Dir.); 1159 Fed. Bldg., 228 Walnut St., Harrisburg 17101, 717-782-3951 (Steve Dunkle, Ex. Dir.); 118 Fed. Bldg., 617 State St., Erie 16501, 814-453-3010 (Patricia Root, Dir.); 225 N. Washington Ave, Suite 503, Scranton 18503, 717-346-2006 (Andrew Wallace, Dir.)

REPRESENTATIVES

FIRST DISTRICT

Thomas M. Foglietta (D)

District: Central Philadelphia and Chester. Population: 565,842—Black 52%, Hispanic 10%. Politics: Democratic.

Born Dec. 3, 1928, Philadelphia; home, Philadelphia; St. Joseph's College, B.A. 1949, Temple University, J.D. 1952; Catholic; single.

Elected 1980. Career: Practicing atty., 1952–80; Philadelphia City Cncl., 1955–75; Regional Dir., U.S. Dept. of Labor, 1976.

Committees: (1) Appropriations.

Election Results: 1992 Foglietta 150,183 (81%); Craig Snyder (R) 35,345 (19%). 1990 Foglietta (79%). 1988 Foglietta (76%).

Interest Group Ratings:

ADA	ACU	COPE	COC
80	00	91	33

LCV	NTLC	CFA	ASC
56	00	100	20

Office: 341 CHOB 20515, 202-225-4731 (Anthony Green, AA). DISTRICT OFFICE: 10-402 Fed. Bldg., 600 Arch St., Philadelphia 19106, 215-925-6840 (Stanley White, Rep.)

SECOND DISTRICT

Lucien Blackwell (D)

District: West Philadelphia and suburbs. Population: 565,650—Black 62%. Politics: Democratic.

Born Aug. 1, 1931, Philadelphia; home, Philadelphia; Baptist; married (Jannie), 3 children.

Elected 1991 (special). Career: U.S. Army, Korea; Union President Intl. Longshoreman Assn.; Philadelphia City Council; Chairman Philadelphia Gas Commission; Commissioner, Delaware Port Authority; Pa. State Rep.

Committees: (1) Budget; (2) Public Works & Transportation.

Election Results: 1992 Blackwell 160,786 (77%); Larry Hollin (R) 47,393 (23%). 1991 (special) Blackwell (76%).

Interest Group Ratings:

ADA	ACU	COPE	COC
90	00	100	29

LCV	NTLC	CFA	ASC
69	00	100	20

Office: 410 CHOB 20515, 202-225-4001 (Corliss

Clemonts-James, Chief of Staff). DISTRICT OFFICE: 3901 Market St., Philadelphia 19104, 215-387-2543 (Maurice Floyd, Rep.)

THIRD DISTRICT

Robert A. Borski (D)

District: Northeast Philadelphia. Population: 565,866—Black 5%, Hispanic 5%, Asian 3%. Politics: Democratic.

Born Oct. 20, 1948, Philadelphia; home, Philadelphia; University of Baltimore, B.A. 1971; Catholic; married (Karen), 5 children.

Elected 1982. Career: Stockbroker, Philadelphia Stock Exchange, 1972–76; Pa. House of Reps., 1976–82.

Committees: (1) Foreign Affairs; (2) Public Works & Transportation.

Election Results: 1992 Borski 125,596 (60%); Charles Dougherty (R) 89,909 (40%). 1990 Borski (59%). 1988 Borski (63%).

Interest Group Ratings:

ADA	ACU	COPE	COC
80	16	83	29

LCV	NTLC	CFA	ASC
56	05	87	70

Office: 2161 RHOB 20515, 202-225-8251 (Alan Slomowitz, AA). DISTRICT OFFICE: 7141 Frankford Ave., Philadelphia 19135, 215-335-3355 (John Dempsey, Dist. Dir.); 2630 Memphis St., Philadelphia 19124, 215-426-4616

FOURTH DISTRICT

Ron Klink (D)

District: Far western part of the state north of Pittsburgh including Beaver County and the town of New Castle. Population: 565,792—Black 3%. Politics: Democratic.

Born Sept. 23, 1951, Canton, Ohio; home, Jeannette; United Church of Christ; married (Linda), 2 children.

Elected 1992. Career: Reporter, 1978–92; Restaurant owner, 1981–92.

Committees: (1) Education & Labor; (2) Small Business; (3) Banking Finance and Urban Affairs.

Election Results: 1992 Klink 186,346 (79%); Gordon Johnston (R) 48,332 (21%).

Interest Group Ratings:
None—Freshman

Office: 1130 LHOB 20515, 202-225-2565 (Brent Ayer, AA). DISTRICT OFFICES: 11279 Center Hwy., N. Huntingdon 15642, 412-864-8681 (Joe Brimmeier, Rep.); 250 Insurance St. Suite 305, Beaver 15009, 412-728-3005 (Tony Campbell, Rep.); Municipal Bldg. 2700 D Rochester Rd., Mars 16046, 412-772-6080 (Dick Picio, Rep.); 304 E. North St., New Castle 16101, 312-654-9036 (Rita Foley, Rep.)

FIFTH DISTRICT

William F. Clinger, Jr. (R)

District: A wide swatch of rural central and north-central counties including city of State College. Population: 565,813. Politics: Republican.

Born Apr. 4, 1929, Warren; home, Warren; Johns Hopkins University, B.A. 1951, University of Va., LL.B. 1965; Presbyterian; married (Julia), 4 children.

Elected 1978. Career: Navy, 1951–55; Adv. Dept., New Process Co., 1955–62; Practicing atty., 1965–75, 1977–78; Chf. Counsel, U.S. Dept. of Commerce, Econ. Develop. Admin., 1975–77.

Committees: (1) Government Operations; (2) Public Works & Transportation.

Election Results: 1992 Clinger (Unopposed). 1990 Clinger (59%). 1988 Clinger (62%).

Interest Group Ratings:

ADA	ACU	COPE	COC
10	90	08	88

LCV	NTLC	CFA	ASC
13	60	27	100

Office: 2160 RHOB 20515, 202-225-5121 (James Clarke, AA). DISTRICT OFFICES: 315 South Allen Street, Suite 219, State College 16801, 814-238-1776 (Patrick Conway, Rep.); 605 Pennbank Building, 315 2nd Ave., Warren 16365, 814-726-3910 (Richard Peltz, Adm.)

SIXTH DISTRICT

Tim Holden (D)

District: Eastern part of the state outside the Philadelphia area including the city of Reading. Population: 565,760—Hispanic 3%. Politics: Leans Democratic.

Born Mar. 5, 1957, St. Clair; home, St. Clair; Bloomsburg State, B.S., 1979; Roman Catholic; Separated.

Elected 1992. Career: Schuylkill Co. Sheriff, 1985–92.

Committees: (1) Agriculture (2) Armed Services.

Election Results: 1992 Holden 106,939 (52%); John Jones (R) 97,156 (48%).

Interest Group Ratings:
None—Freshman

Office: 1421 LHOB 20515, 202-225-5546 (Tom Gajewski, AA). DISTRICT OFFICE: 633 Court St., Reading 19601, 215-371-9931 (Tim Smith, Rep.); 303 Meridian Bank Bldg., Pottsville 17901, 717-624-2122 (Connie Conavola, Rep.)

SEVENTH DISTRICT

Wayne Curtis Weldon (R)

District: Southwest Philadelphia Suburbs. Population: 565,746—Black 4%. Politics: Leans Republican.

Born July 22, 1947, Marcus Hook; home, Aston; West Chester State College, B.A. 1969; Protestant; married (Mary), 5 children.

Elected 1986. Career: Teacher, Vice Principal, 1969–76; Dir. Training & Manpower Dev., INC Corp., 1976–81; Mayor, Marcus Hook, 1977–82; Delaware Cty. Cncl., 1981–86, Chm. 1985–86.

Committees: (1) Armed Services; (2) Merchant Marine & Fisheries.

Election Results: 1992 Weldon 179,541 (66%); Frank Daly (D) 93,453 (34%). 1990 Weldon (65%). 1988 Weldon (68%).

Interest Group Ratings:

ADA	ACU	COPE	COC
25	80	83	88

LCV	NTLC	CFA	ASC
38	75	33	100

Office: 2452 CHOB 20515, 202-225-2011 (Douglas Ritter, AA). DISTRICT OFFICES: 1554 Garett Rd., Upper Darby 19082, 215-259-0700 (Dennis

Lynch, Dist. Mgr.); 300 S. Valley Rd. #212, Paoli 19301, 215-940-9064 (vacant, Rep.)

EIGHTH DISTRICT

Jim Greenwood (R)

District: Northern Philadelphia suburbs; Bucks County. Population: 565,787—Black 3%. Politics: Leans Democratic.

Born May 4, 1951, Philadelphia; home, Erwinna; Dickinson College, B.A. 1973; Presbyterian; married (Christina), 4 children.

Elected 1992. Career: Asst. to State Rep. Renniger, 1972–76; Bucks Cty. Children and Youth Social Service, 1977–80; State Rep., 1981–86; State Sen., 1978–92.

Committees: (1) Energy & Commerce.

Election Results: 1992 Greenwood 129,737 (53%); Peter Kostmayer (D–Incumbent) 114,039 (47%).

Interest Group Ratings:
None—Freshman

Office: 515 CHOB 20515, 202-225-4276 (Judy Borger, Rep.) DISTRICT OFFICES: Not Yet Established.

NINTH DISTRICT

E. G. "Bud" Shuster (R)

District: Wide area of semi–rural south central part of the state including city of Altoona. Population: 565,803. Politics: Republican.

Born Jan. 23, 1932, Glassport; home, Everett; University of Pittsburgh, B.S. 1954, Duquesne University, M.B.A. 1960, American University, Ph.D. 1967; United Church of Christ; married (Patricia), 5 children.

Elected 1972. Career: Army, 1954–56; V.P., Radio Corp. of Am.; Operator, Shuster Farms.

Committees: (1) Public Works & Transportation.

Election Results: 1992 Shuster (Unopposed). 1990 Shuster (Unopposed). 1988 Shuster (Unopposed).

Interest Group Ratings:

ADA	ACU	COPE	COC
05	100	58	88

LCV	NTLC	CFA	ASC
00	95	13	90

Office: 2188 RHOB 20515, 202-225-2431 (Ann Eppard, AA). DISTRICT OFFICES: RD 2, Box 711, Altoona 16601, 814-946-1653 (Judy Giansante, Asst.); 179 E. Queen St., Chambersburg 17201, 717-264-8308 (Steven Minnich, Rep.)

TENTH DISTRICT

Joseph M. McDade (R)

District: Eastern half of northern counties bordering on New York State and including the city of Scranton. Population: 565,681. Politics: Republican.

Born Sept. 29, 1931, Scranton; home, Clarks Summit; University of Notre Dame, B.A. 1953, University of Pa., LL.B. 1956; Roman Catholic; married (Sarah), 5 children.

Elected 1962. Career: Clerk to Chf. Fed. Judge John W. Murphy, 1956–57; Practicing atty., 1957–62; Scranton City Solicitor, 1962.

Committees: (1) Appropriations.

Election Results: 1992 McDade 1,187,318 (90%); Albert Smith (Lib) 19,800 (10%). 1990 McDade (Unopposed). 1988 McDade (73%).

Interest Group Ratings:

ADA	ACU	COPE	COC
15	76	75	86

LCV	NTLC	CFA	ASC
13	75	47	100

Office: 2370 RHOB 20515, 202-225-3731 (Deborah Weatherly, AA). DISTRICT OFFICES: 538 Spruce St., Suite 514, Scranton 18503, 717-346-3834 (Michael Russen, Dist. Rep.); 240 W. 3rd #230, Williamsport 17701, 717-327-8161

ELEVENTH DISTRICT

Paul Edmund Kanjorski (D)

District: Northeast coal country including city of Wilkes–Barre. Population: 565,913. Politics: Very mixed, but leans Democratic.

Born April 2, 1937, Nanticoke; home, Nanticoke; Temple University, 1961, Dickinson University, J.D. 1965; Roman Catholic; married (Nancy), 1 child.

Elected 1984. Career: Practicing atty., 1966–84; Nanticoke City Solicitor, 1969–81; Admin. Law Judge, 1972–80.

Committees: (1) Banking, Finance & Urban Affairs; (2) Post Office & Civil Service.

Election Results: 1992 Kanjorski 138,557 (67%); Michael Fescina (R) 66,743 (33%). 1990 Kanjorski (Unopposed). 1988 Kanjorski (Unopposed).

Interest Group Ratings:

ADA	ACU	COPE	COC
80	16	83	25

LCV	NTLC	CFA	ASC
50	05	67	40

Office: 2429 CHOB 20515, 202-225-6511 (Karen Feather, AA). DISTRICT OFFICES: 10 E. South St., Wilkes-Barre 18701, 717-825-2200 (Joe Terrana, Dist. Dir.); 860 Spruce St., Kulpmont 17834, 717-373-1541 (Henry Sgrow, Rep.)

TWELFTH DISTRICT

John P. Murtha (D)

District: Southwest part of the state including city of Johnstown. Population: 565,794. Politics: Democratic.

Born June 17, 1932, New Martinsville, W.Va.; home, Johnstown; University of Pitt., B.A. 1962, Indiana University of Pa.; Roman Catholic; married (Joyce), 3 children.

Elected Feb. 5, 1974. Career: USMC, Korea, Vietnam; Owner, Johnstown Minute Car Wash; Pa. House of Reps., 1969–74.

Committees: (1) Appropriations.

Election Results: 1992 Murtha (Unopposed). 1990 Murtha (62%). 1988 Murtha (Unopposed).

Interest Group Ratings:

ADA	ACU	COPE	COC
65	24	92	63

LCV	NTLC	CFA	ASC
25	10	73	90

Office: 2423 RHOB 20515, 202-225-2065 (William Allen, Ex. Asst.). DISTRICT OFFICES: Vine & Walnut Sts., 2nd Floor, Centre Town Mall, Johnstown 15907, 814-535-2642 (John Hugya, Dist. AA); 15 P.O. Bldg., 201 N. Center St., Somerset 15501, 814-445-6041 (Virginia Tressler, Mgr.)

THIRTEENTH DISTRICT

Marjorie Margolies Mezvinsky (D)

District: Northwest Philadelphia suburbs including most of the Montgomery County. Population: 565,793—Black 6%, Asian 3%. Politics: Republican.

Born June 21, 1942, Philadelphia; home, Narberth; University of Pa., 1962; Jewish; married (Edward), 11 children (9 adopted).

Elected 1992. Career: Television Reporter, 1967–92.

Committees: (1) Energy & Commerce; (2) Small Business.

Election Results: 1992 Margolies Mezvinsky 127,534 (50%); John Fox (R) 126,445 (50%).

Interest Group Ratings:
None—Freshman

Office: 1516 RHOB 20515, 202-225-6111 (Jim Pearthree, AA). DISTRICT OFFICES: 1 Presidential Blvd. #200, Bala Cynwyd 19004, 215-667-3666 (Linda August, Rep.)

FOURTEENTH DISTRICT

William J. Coyne (D)

District: All of Pittsburgh plus a few suburbs. Population: 565,787—Black 18%. Politics: Democratic.

Born Aug. 24, 1936, Pittsburgh; home, Pittsburgh; Robert Morris College, B.S. 1965; Roman Catholic; single.

Elected 1980. Career: Army, Korea; Corporate accountant; Pa. House of Reps., 1970–72; Pittsburgh City Cncl., 1974–80.

Committees: (1) Ways & Means; (2) Budget.

Election Results: 1992 Coyne 164,827 (73%); Byron King (R) 60,932 (27%). 1990 Coyne (72%). 1988 Coyne (79%).

Interest Group Ratings:

ADA	ACU	COPE	COC
95	04	92	50

LCV	NTLC	CFA	ASC
63	05	93	30

Office: 2455 RHOB 20515, 202-225-2301 (Coleman Conroy, AA). DISTRICT OFFICE: 2009 Fed. Bldg., 1000 Liberty Ave., Pittsburgh 15222, 412-644-2870 (James Rooney, Ex. Asst.)

FIFTEENTH DISTRICT

Paul McHale (D)

District: East part of the state north of Philadelphia including cities of Allentown and Bethlehem. Population: 565,810. Politics: Leans Republican.

Born Jul. 26, 1950, Bethlehem; home, Bethlehem; Lehigh University, B.A. 1972, Georgetown University, J.D. 1977; Roman Catholic; married (Katherine), 3 children.

Elected 1992. Career: USMC, 1972–74, Saudi Arabia 1991; Practicing atty., 1977–92; State Rep., 1983–91.

Committees: (1) Armed Services; (2) Science, Space & Technology.

Election Results: 1992 McHale 110,865 (53%); Don Ritter (R–Incumbent) 99,482 (47%).

Interest Group Ratings:
None—Freshman

Office: 511 RHOB 20515, 202-225-6411 (Herbert Giobbi, AA). DISTRICT OFFICES: 26 E. 3rd St., Bethlehem 18015, 215-866-0916; One Center Square Suite 203, Allentown 18101, 215-439-8861; 633 Ferry St., Easton 18042, 215-258-8383; 168 Main St., Pennsburgh 18073, 215-541-0614

SIXTEENTH DISTRICT

Robert Smith Walker (R)

District: Southeast part of the state including large parts of Lancaster and Chester counties. Population: 565,835—Black 5%, Hispanic 4%. Politics: Republican.

Born Dec. 23, 1942, Bradford; home, East Petersburg; Millersville University, B.S. 1964, University of Del., M.A. 1968; Presbyterian; married (Sue).

Elected 1976. Career: Teacher, 1964–67; A. A. to U.S. Rep. Edwin D. Eshleman, 1967–76.

Committees: (1) Science, Space & Technology (Ranking Member).

Election Results: 1992 Walker 137,818 (65%); Robert Peters (D) 74,648 (35%). 1990 Walker (66%). 1988 Walker (74%).

Interest Group Ratings:

ADA	ACU	COPE	COC
10	96	25	88

LCV	NTLC	CFA	ASC
06	100	07	100

Office: 2369 RHOB 20515, 202-225-2411 (Connie Thumma, AA). DISTRICT OFFICES: Cty. Cthse., 50 N. Duke St., 5th Flr., Lancaster 17603, 717-393-0666 (Marc Phillips, AA); Exton Commons #595, Exton 19341, 215-363-8409

SEVENTEENTH DISTRICT

George W. Gekas (R)

District: Central part of the state including cities of Harrisburg and Williamsport. Population: 565,742—Black 7%. Politics: Republican.

Born April 14, 1930, Harrisburg; home, Harrisburg; Dickinson College, B.A. 1952, Dickinson Law School, J.D. 1958; Greek Orthodox; married (Evangeline).

Elected 1982. Career: Asst. Dist. Atty., Dauphin Cty., 1960–66; Pa. House of Reps., 1967–75; Pa. Senate, 1977–83.

Committees: (1) Judiciary; (2) Select Committee on Intelligence.

Election Results: 1992 Gekas 150,074 (70%); Bill Sturges (D) 65,826 (30%). 1990 Gekas (Unopposed). 1988 Gekas (Unopposed).

Interest Group Ratings:

ADA	ACU	COPE	COC
15	88	18	88

LCV	NTLC	CFA	ASC
19	85	20	100

Office: 2410 LHOB 20515, 202-225-4315 (Allan Cagnoli, AA). DISTRICT OFFICES: 302 Govs. Plaza North Bldg., 2101 N. Front St., Harrisburg 17110, 717-232-5123 (Arlene Eckels, Asst.); 222 S. Market #102A, Elizabethtown 17022, 717-367-6669 (Michele Spane, Rep.); 108-B Mun. Bldg. 400 S. 8th St., Lebanon 17402, 717-273-1451 (Reg Nynan, Rep.)

EIGHTEENTH DISTRICT

Richard Santorum (R)

District: Eastern and southern Pittsburgh suburbs in Allegheny County. Population: 565,781 —Black 8%. Politics: Leans Republican.

Born May 10, 1958, Winchester, Va.; home, Pittsburgh; Penn. State University, B.A., 1980, University of Pitt., M.B.A., 1981, Dickinson School of Law, J.D., 1986; Roman Catholic; married (Karen), 2 children.

Elected 1990. Career: Adm. Asst. Pa. St. Senate 1982–86; Atty. priv. prac. (Pittsburgh) 1986-90.

Committees: (1) Ways & Means.

Election Results: 1992 Santorum 153,154 (61%); Frank Pecora (D) 96,736 (39%). 1990 Santorum (51%).

Interest Group Ratings:

ADA	ACU	COPE	COC
20	83	58	88

LCV	NTLC	CFA	ASC
19	90	33	90

Office: 1222 LHOB 20515, 202-225-2135 (Mark Rogers, AA). DISTRICT OFFICES: 606 Weyman Rd., Pittsburgh 15236, 412-882-3205 (Mark Rodgers, Rep.); 541 5th Ave., McKeesport 15132, 412-664-4049 (John Verbanac, Rep.)

NINETEENTH DISTRICT

William Franklin Goodling (R)

District: South central portion of the state including city of York. Population: 565,831—Black 3%. Politics: Republican.

Born Dec. 5, 1927, Loganville; home, Jacobus; University of Md., B.S. 1945, Western Md. University, M.A.Ed. 1956; United Methodist; married (Hilda), 2 children.

Elected 1974. Career: Army, 1946–48; Pub. sch. teacher & admin., 1952–74.

Committees: (1) Foreign Affairs; (2) Education & Labor (Ranking Member).

Election Results: 1992 Goodling 96,883 (45%); Paul Kilker (D) 73,849 (34%); Thomas Humbert (I) 43,939 (20%). 1990 Goodling (Unopposed). 1988 Goodling (77%).

Interest Group Ratings:

ADA	ACU	COPE	COC
10	83	33	75

LCV	NTLC	CFA	ASC
19	74	27	100

Office: 2263 RHOB 20515, 202-225-5836 (Rob Green, AA). DISTRICT OFFICES: 2020 Yale Ave., Camp Hill 17011, 717-763-1988 (Nancy Newcomer, Dist. Cord.); Fed. Bldg., 200 S. George St., York 17405, 717-843-8887 (Betty Lou Tarasovic, Asst.); 212 N. Hanover St., Carlisle 17013, 717-243-5432 (Dr. Charles Walters, Staff); 140 Baltimore St., Rm. 210, Gettysburg 17325, 717-334-3430 (Muriel Brendle, Asst.)

TWENTIETH DISTRICT

Austin J. Murphy (D)

District: Southwest corner of the state including cities of Uniontown and Washington. Population: 565,815—Black 3%. Politics: Democratic.

Born June 17, 1927, North Charleroi; home, Monongahela; Duquesne University, B.A. 1949, University of Pittsburgh, LL.B. 1952; Roman Catholic; married (Mona), 6 children.

Elected 1976. Career: USMC, WWII; Practicing atty., Washington Cty. Asst. Dist. Atty., 1956–57; Pa. House of Reps., 1959–71; Pa. Senate, 1971–77.

Committees: (1) Education & Labor; (2) Natural Resources; (3) Foreign Affairs (temp.).

Election Results: 1992 Murphy 114,408 (51%); Bill Townsend (R) 108,261 (49%). 1990 Murphy (63%). 1988 Murphy (72%).

Interest Group Ratings:

ADA	ACU	COPE	COC
65	33	83	38

LCV	NTLC	CFA	ASC
50	10	53	30

Office: 2210 RHOB 20515, 202-225-4665 (Frederick McLuckie, AA). DISTRICT OFFICES: 306 Fallowfield Ave., Charleroi 15022, 412-489-4217 (vacant, Dist. Adm.); 96 N. Main, Washington 15301, 412-228-2777 (Paulette Bienek, Rep.); 4551 East Penn St., Uniontown 15401, 412-438-1490 (Jacqueline Joseph, Asst.); 8 S. 4th St., Youngwood 15697, 412-925-1370.

TWENTY-FIRST DISTRICT

Tom Ridge (R)

District: Northwest corner of the state including city of Erie. Population: 565,645—Black 4%. Politics: Very mixed.

Born Aug. 26, 1945, Munhall; home, Erie; Harvard College, B.A. 1967, Dickinson School of Law, J.D. 1972; Roman Catholic; married (Michele), 2 children.

Elected 1982. Career: Army, 1968–70; Practicing atty., 1972–82.

Committees: (1) Banking, Finance & Urban Affairs; (2) Veterans Affairs; (3) Post Office and Civil Service.

Election Results: 1992 Ridge 149,857 (67%); John Harkins (D) 74,049 (33%). 1990 Ridge (Unopposed). 1988 Ridge (79%).

Interest Group Ratings:

ADA	ACU	COPE	COC
30	68	50	63

LCV	NTLC	CFA	ASC
19	65	40	80

Office: 1714 LHOB 20515, 202-225-5406 (Mark Campbell, AA). DISTRICT OFFICES: 108 Fed. Bldg., 617 State St., Erie 16501, 814-456-2038 (Anne DiTuillio, Mgr.); 305 Chestnut St., Meadville 16335, 814-724-8414 (Jody Bruckner, Mgr.); 91 E. State St., Sharon 16146, 412-981-8440 (Carol Weber, Mgr.); 327 N. Main St., Butler 16001, 412-285-7005 (Joan Janaszek, Rep.)

RHODE ISLAND

Republican Sen. John H. Chafee is up for ree-lection in 1994. If he runs he will win easily. If he should decide to retire after three terms, the political landscape of the state will be changed tremendously, and there will be a free-for-all in both parties to choose candidates to be his successor.

1992 PRESIDENTIAL ELECTION: (4 Electoral votes): Clinton (D) 198,877 (47%); Bush (R) 121,864 (29%); Perot (I) 94,717 (23%); Fulani (NAP) 1,771; Marrou (Lib) 650; LaRouche (I) 470; Phillips (AmTax) 287; Hagelin (NLP) 227. 1988 Dukakis 216,668 (56%); Bush 169,730 (44%).

SENATORS

Claiborne Pell (D)

Born Nov. 22, 1918, New York, N.Y.; home, Newport; Princeton University, A.B. 1940, Columbia University, A.M. 1946; Episcopalian; married (Nuala), 4 children.

Elected 1960, seat up 1996. Career: Coast Guard, WWII; U.S. Foreign Svc. & State Dept., Czechoslovakia & Italy, 1945–52; Exec. Asst. to R.I. Dem. St. Chm., 1952, 1954; Consultant, Dem. Natl. Comm., 1953–60.

Committees: (1) Foreign Relations (Chairman); (2) Labor & Human Resources; (3) Rules & Administration; (4) Joint Committee on the Library (Vice Chairman).

Election Results: 1990 Pell 216,253 (62%); Claudine Schneider (R) 133,552 (38%). 1984 Pell (73%).

Interest Group Ratings:

ADA	ACU	COPE	COC
80	08	82	30

LCV	NTLC	CFA	ASC
83	17	92	50

Office: 335 RSOB 20510, 202-224-4642 (Thomas Hughes, Chief-of-staff). STATE OFFICE: 418 Fed. Bldg., Providence 02903, 401-528-5456 (John Cummings, Ex. Asst.)

John H. Chafee (R)

Born Oct. 22, 1922, Providence; home, Warwick; Yale University, B.A. 1947, Harvard University, LL.B. 1950; Episcopalian; married (Virginia), 5 children.

Elected 1976, seat up 1994. Career: USMC, WWII, Korea; Practicing atty., 1952–63; R.I. House of Reps., 1957–63, Minor. Ldr., 1959–63; Gov. of R.I., 1963–69; Sec. of the Navy 1969–72.

Committees: (1) Environment & Public Works (Ranking Member); (2) Finance; (3) Small Business.

Election Results: 1990 Chafee 217,273 (55%); Richard Licht (D) 180,717 (45%). 1982 Chafee (51%).

Interest Group Ratings:

ADA	ACU	COPE	COC
40	44	17	80

LCV	NTLC	CFA	ASC
67	33	33	90

Office: 567 DSOB 20510, 202-224-2921 (David Griswold, Chief-of-staff). STATE OFFICE: 301 Fed. Bldg., Kennedy Plaza, Providence 02903, 401-528-5294 (Michael Ryan, Dir.)

REPRESENTATIVES

FIRST DISTRICT

Ronald K. Machtley (R)

District: Eastern portion of the state including eastern portion of Providence and towns of Pawtucket and Newport. Population: 501,677— Black 3%, Hispanic 4%. Politics: Leans Democratic.

Born July 13, 1948, Johnstown, Pa.; home, Portsmouth; U.S. Naval Acad., B.S. 1970, Suffolk University Law School, J.D. 1978; Presbyterian; married (Katie), 2 children.

Elected 1988. Career: Navy, 1970–75; Practicing atty., 1976–88.

Committees: (1) Armed Services; (2) Government Operations; (3) Small Business.

Election Results: 1992 Machtley 130,282 (74%); David Carlin (D) 45,460 (26%). 1990 Machtley (55%). 1988 Machtley (56%).

Interest Group Ratings:

ADA	ACU	COPE	COC
55	44	50	38

LCV	NTLC	CFA	ASC
88	60	80	100

Office: 326 CHOB 20515, 202-225-4911 (Rowdy Yates, Chief-of-staff). DISTRICT OFFICE: 200 Main St., Pawtucket 02860, 401-725-9400 (Marc Palazzo, Dist. Dir.)

SECOND DISTRICT

John F. Reed (R)

District: West two–thirds of the state including western half of Providence and town of Warwick. Population: 501,787—Black 4%, Hispanic 5%. Politics: Leans Democratic.

Born Nov. 12, 1949, Providence; home, Cranston; U.S. Military Acad., B.S., 1971, Harvard University, M.P.P. 1972, J.D., 1982; Roman Catholic; single.

Elected 1990. Career: U.S. Army, 1972–80, private law practice, 1981–90; R.I. St. Senate 1984–90.

Committees: (1) Judiciary; (2) Education and Labor; (3) Merchant Marine and Fisheries; (4) Select Committee on Intelligence.

Election Results: 1992 Reed 138,780 (75%); James Bell (R) 47,456 (25%). 1990 Reed (59%).

Interest Group Ratings:

ADA	ACU	COPE	COC
90	04	92	13

LCV	NTLC	CFA	ASC
94	00	100	20

Office: 1510 LOHB 20515, 202-225-2735 (J.B. Poersch, AA). DISTRICT OFFICE: Garden City Center 100 Midway Place #5, Cranston 02920, 401-943-3100 (Ray Simone, Dist. Dir.)

SOUTH CAROLINA

The dominant political question in South Carolina is whether GOP Sen. Strom Thurmond will retire at the end of this term, and not run for reelection in 1996. Most assume he will retire, given that he will be 94 in 1996. But with Strom Thurmond, you can never tell. The most popular politician in the state is GOP Gov. Carroll Campbell who cannot run for reelection in 1994. If Thurmond retires, Campbell will undoubtedly run for the seat, and will go into the contest as the odds-on-favorite. If Thurmond decides to run again, then Campbell is faced with sitting on the sidelines until 1998 when Democratic Sen. Fritz Hollings comes up for reelection. If this happens, look for Campbell to position himself to be the vice presidential choice on the 1996 GOP ticket.

1992 PRESIDENTIAL ELECTION: (8 Electoral votes): Clinton (D) 476,665 (40%); Bush (R) 574,061 (48%); Perot (I) 138,141 (12%); Marrou (Lib) 2,710; Phillips (AmTax) 2,485; Fulani (NAP) 1,223. 1988 Bush 599,871 (62%); Dukakis 367,511 (38%).

SENATORS

James Strom Thurmond (R)

Born Dec. 5, 1902, Edgefield; home, Aiken; Clemson College, B.S. 1923; Baptist; married (Nancy), 4 children.

Elected 1954, seat up 1996. Career: Teacher & coach, 1923–29; Edgefield County Superintendant of Education, 1929–33; Practicing atty., 1930–38, 1951–55; S.C. State Senate, 1933–38; Circuit Judge, 1938–46; Army, WWII; Gov. of S.C., 1947–51; U.S. Senate, 1954–56.

Committees: (1) Armed Services (Ranking Member); (2) Judiciary; (3) Labor & Human Resources; (4) Veterans Affairs.

Election Results: 1990 Thurmond 475,399 (66%); Bob Cunningham (D) 241,826 (34%); 1984 Thurmond (67%).

Interest Group Ratings:

ADA	ACU	COPE	COC
10	89	25	100

LCV	NTLC	CFA	ASC
00	83	33	90

Office: 217 RSOB 20510-4001, 202-224-5972 (Robert "Duke" Short, AA). STATE OFFICES: 1558 Fed., Bldg., 1835 Assembly St., Columbia 29201, 803-765-5494 (Warren Abernathy, Rep.); 600 Fed. Bldg., 334 Meeting St., Charleston 29403, 803-724-4516 (Phillip Fairchild, Rep.); 211 York St., N.E., Suite 29, Aiken 29801, 803-649-2591 (Eliz. McFarland, Rep.); Fed. Bldg., 401 W. Evans St., Florence 29501, 803-662-8873 (Raleigh Ward, Rep.)

Ernest F. Hollings (D)

Born Jan. 1, 1922, Charleston; home, Charleston; The Citadel, B.A. 1942, University of S.C., LL.B. 1947; Lutheran; married (Peatsy), 4 children.

Elected 1966, seat up 1998. Career: Army, WWII; Practicing atty.; S.C. House of Reps., 1949–54, Speaker Pro Temp., 1951–54; Lt. Gov. of S.C., 1955–59; Gov. of S.C., 1959-63.

Committees: (1) Appropriations; (2) Budget; (3) Commerce, Science & Transportation (Chairman).

Election Results: 1992 Hollings 578,749 (51%); Thomas Hartnett (R) 550,900 (49%). 1986 Hollings (63%). 1980 Hollings (70%).

Interest Group Ratings:

ADA	ACU	COPE	COC
35	63	50	60

LCV	NTLC	CFA	ASC
42	39	58	60

Office: 125 RSOB 20510, 202-224-6121 (David Rudd, AA). STATE OFFICES: 1551 Fed. Bldg., 1835 Assembly St., Columbia 29201, 803-765-5731 (Samuel B. King, Rep.); 112 Custom House, 200 E. Bay St., Charleston 29401; 803-724-4525 (Joe Maupin, Rep.); 126 Fed. Bldg., 300 E. Washington St., Greenville 29304, 803-233-5366 (Ben Alexander, Rep.,); 103 Fed. Bldg, 201 Magnolia St., Spartanburg 29301, 803-585-3702 (Lynn Berry, Rep.)

REPRESENTATIVES

FIRST DISTRICT

Arthur Ravenel, Jr. (R)

District: Southeastern part of the state including city of Charleston. Population: 520,338—Black 32%. Politics: Leans Republican.

Born Mar. 29, 1927, St. Andrews Parish; home, Mount Pleasant; College of Charleston, B.A. 1950; French Huguenot; married (Jean), 6 children, 4 stepchildren.

Elected 1986. Career: USMC, 1945–46; Realtor, general contractor, cattleman; S.C. House of Reps., 1952–58; S.C. Senate, 1980–86.

Committees: (1) Armed Services; (2) Merchant Marine & Fisheries.

Election Results: 1992 Ravenel 117,599 (66%); Bill Oberst Jr. (D) 59,538 (34%). 1990 Ravenel (65%). 1988 Ravenel (64%).

Interest Group Ratings:

ADA	ACU	COPE	COC
40	80	42	75

LCV	NTLC	CFA	ASC
69	100	47	100

Office: 231 CHOB 20515, 202-225-3176 (Delores DeCosta, Mgr.). DISTRICT OFFICES: 640 Fed. Bldg., 334 Meeting St., Charleston 29403, 803-724-4175 (Sharon Chellis, AA); 206 Laurel St., Conway 29526, 803-248-2660 (Barbara Browning, Rep.); 829-E Front St., Georgetown 29440, 803-527-6868 (Elma Harrelson, Rep.)

SECOND DISTRICT

Floyd D. Spence (R)

District: Central part of the state including city of Columbia. Population: 522,688—Black 35%. Politics: Leans Republican.

Born Apr. 9, 1928, Columbia; home, Lexington; University of S.C., A.B. 1952, LL.B. 1956; Lutheran; married (Debbie), 4 children.

Elected 1970. Career: Navy, 1952–54; Practicing atty.; S.C. House of Reps., 1956–62; S.C. Senate, 1966–70, Minor. Ldr., 1966–70.

Committees: (1) Armed Services; (2) Veterans Affairs.

Election Results: 1992 Spence 148,032 (88%); Geb Sommer (Libert) 20,714 (12%). 1990 Spence (89%). 1988 Spence (53%).

Interest Group Ratings:

ADA	ACU	COPE	COC
15	92	42	75

LCV	NTLC	CFA	ASC
06	95	27	100

Office: 2405 RHOB 20515, 202-225-2452 (Kenneth Black, AA). DISTRICT OFFICES: 916 Bay St., Columbia 29902, 803-521-2530 (Mary Howard, Rep.); 1681 Chestnut St., N.E., Orangeburg 29116-1609, 803-536-4641 (Chessye Powell, Asst.); 40 Town Center Palmetto Pkwy., Hilton Head 29928, 803-842-7212 (Sarah Brielove, Rep.); 66 E. RR Ave. P.O. Box 550, Estill 29918, 803-625-3177 (Mary Eleanor Bowers, Rep.)

THIRD DISTRICT

Butler Derrick (D)

District: Western part of the state including towns of Anderson and Aiken. Population: 519,280—Black 23%. Politics: Leans Democratic.

Born Sept. 30, 1936, Springfield, Mass.; home, Edgefield; Erskine College, Lander College, University of S.C., University of Ga., LL.B. 1965; Episcopalian; divorced, 2 children.

Elected 1974. Career: Practicing atty., 1965–74; S.C. House of Reps., 1969–74.

Committees: Chief Deputy Majority Whip. (1) Rules; (2) House Administration.

Election Results: 1992 Derrick 118,927 (61%); Jim Bland (R) 75,558 (39%). 1990 Derrick (58%). 1988 Derrick (54%).

Interest Group Ratings:

ADA	ACU	COPE	COC
80	28	58	63

LCV	NTLC	CFA	ASC
44	05	80	80

Office: 221 CHOB 20515, 202-225-5301 (Lynn Richardson, AA). DISTRICT OFFICES: McDuffie St., Anderson 29622, 803-224-7401 (Barbara Gaines, Mgr.); 211 York St., N.E., Rm. 5, Aiken 29801, 803-649-5571 (Susan Griffin, Asst.); 101 Fed. Bldg., 120 Main St., Greenwood 29622, 803-223-8251 (Elestine Norman, Asst.)

FOURTH DISTRICT

Bob Inglis (R)

District: Northwestern textile counties including city of Greenville and Spartanburg. Population: 520,525—Black 19%. Politics: Democratic.

Born Oct. 11, 1959, Savannah, Ga.; home, Greenville; Duke, B.A. 1981, University of Va., J.D. 1984; Presbyterian; married (Mary Anne), 3 children.

Elected 1992. Career: Practicing Attorney, 1984–92.

Committees: (1) Budget.

Election Results: 1992 Inglis 99,878 (51%); Liz Patterson (D) (Incumbent) 94,179 (49%).

Interest Group Ratings:
None—Freshman

Office: 1237 LHOB 20515, 202-225-6030 (Jeff Fedorchak, Chief of Staff). DISTRICT OFFICES: 300 E. Washington #101, Greenville 29601, 803-232-1141 (Maxon Metcalf, Dist. Adm.); 201 Magnolia #108, Spartanburg 29301, 803-582-6422; 405 W. Main, Union 29379, 803-427-2205.

FIFTH DISTRICT

John M. Spratt, Jr. (D)

District: Eleven north central counties. Population: 519,716—Black 32%. Politics: Democratic.

Born Nov. 1, 1942, Charlotte, N.C.; home, York; Davidson College, A.B. 1964, Oxford University, M.A., 1966, Yale University, LL.B. 1969; Presbyterian; married (Jane), 3 children.

Elected 1982. Career: Operations Off. of Asst. Secy. of Defense, 1969–71; Practicing atty., 1971–82; Pres., Bank of Ft. Mill, 1973–82; Pres., Spratt Insur. Agcy., 1973–82.

Committees: (1) Armed Services; (2) Government Operations.

Election Results: 1992 Spratt 111,439 (61%); Bill Horne (R) 71,604 (39%). 1990 Spratt (Unopposed). 1988 Spratt (70%).

Interest Group Ratings:

ADA	ACU	COPE	COC
75	28	67	50

LCV	NTLC	CFA	ASC
56	00	100	100

Office: 1536 LHOB 20515, 202-225-5501 (Ellen Buchanan, AA). DISTRICT OFFICES: Fed. Bldg., P.O. Box 350, Rock Hill 29731, 803-327-1114 (Robert Hopkins, Dist. Adm.); 39 E. Calhoun St., Sumter 29150, 803-773-3362 (Linda Mixon, Rep.); P.O. Box 25, Darlington 29532, 803-393-3998 (Joanne Langley, Rep.)

SIXTH DISTRICT

James E. Clyburn (D)

District: Eastern part of the state including city of Florence. Population: 519,273—Black 41%. Politics: Democratic.

Born July 21, 1940, Sumter; home, Columbia; S.C. State, B.A. 1962; African Methodist Episcopal; married (Emily), 3 children.

Elected 1992. Career: High School Teacher, 1962–65; Exec. Dir. Commission for S.C. Farm Workers, 1968–72; S.C. Human Affairs Commissioner, 1974–92.

Committees: (1) Public Works & Transportation; (2) Veteran Affairs.

Election Results: 1992 Clyburn 119,282 (65%); John Chase (R) 64,372 (35%).

Interest Group Ratings:
None—Freshman

Office: 319 CHOB 20515, 202-225-3315 (Bill DeLoach,AA). DISTRICT OFFICES: 1703 Gervais St., Columbia 29211, 803-799-1100; 181 E. Evans St. Suite 314, Florence 29502, 803-662-1212; City Hall 4900 Lacrosse Rd. 1st Floor, N. Charleston 29418, 803-747-9660.

SOUTH DAKOTA

On paper South Dakota would seem a Republican state, but based on results politics here remain quite mixed with the governor and one senator Republican, the other senator and the at-large congressman Democrats. In 1992 the GOP failed in an attempt to unseat first term Democratic Sen. Tom Daschle. Now it is the Democrats turn. In 1994 they will try to defeat GOP Gov. Walter D. Miller, who succeeded the late George Mickelson after his death in a plane crash in 1993. Then in 1996 the Democrats will try to unseat GOP Sen. Larry Pressler. Both look like tough assignments.

Governor: Walter Dale Miller (R) (605-773-3212); succeeded the late Gov. George S. Mickelson (R), killed in a plane crash, April, 1993. Next election Nov. 1994. Lt. Governor: Vacant

1992 PRESIDENTIAL ELECTION: (3 Electoral votes): Clinton (D) 124,861 (37%); Bush (R) 136,671 (41%); Perot (I) 73,296 (22%); Marrou (Lib) 862; Hagelin (NLP) 424; Fulani (NAP) 112. 1988 Bush 165,516 (53%); Dukakis 145,632 (47%).

SENATORS

Larry Pressler (R)

Born Mar. 29, 1942, Humboldt; home, Humboldt; University of S.Dak., B.A. 1964, Rhodes Scholar, Oxford University, 1966, Harvard University, M.A., J.D. 1971; Roman Catholic; married (Harriet), 1 stepchild.

Elected 1978, seat up 1996. Career: Army, Vietnam; U.S. House of Reps., 1975–79.

Committees: (1) Commerce, Science & Transportation; (2) Foreign Relations; (3) Small Business; (4) Judiciary.

Election Results: 1990 Pressler 135,443 (52%); Ted Muenster (D) 116,431 (45%); Dean Sinclair (I) 6,548 (3%). 1984 Pressler (74%).

Interest Group Ratings:

ADA	ACU	COPE	COC
20	85	17	90

LCV	NTLC	CFA	ASC
08	83	33	100

Office: 283 RHOB 20510, 202-224-5842 (Doug

Miller, Chief-of-staff). STATE OFFICES: Empire Mall, 4001 W. 41st St., Sioux Falls 57106, 605-361-3052 (Jill Schieffer, St. Dir.); 520 S. Main, Aberdeen 57401, 605-226-7471 (Shanon Garey, Rep.); 112 Rushmore Mall, Rapid City 57701, 605-341-1185 (Darrell Draper, Rep.)

Thomas Andrew Daschle (D)

Born Dec. 9, 1947, Aberdeen; home, Aberdeen; S.Dak. State University, B.A. 1969; Roman Catholic; married (Linda), 3 children.

Elected 1986, seat up 1998. Career: Air Force, 1969–72; Legis. Asst. to U.S. Sen. James Abourezk, 1972–77; U.S. House of Reps., 1978–86.

Committees: (1) Agriculture, Nutrition & Forestry; (2) Finance; (3) Select Committee on Indian Affairs; (4) Veterans' Affairs; (5) Ethics.

Election Results: 1992 Daschle 216,869 (66%); Charlene Haar (R) 108,573 (33%); Gus Hercules 4,347. 1986: Daschle (52%).

Interest Group Ratings:

ADA	ACU	COPE	COC
95	22	75	20

LCV	NTLC	CFA	ASC
58	22	92	60

Office: 317 HSOB 20510, 202-224-2321 (Peter Rouse, AA). STATE OFFICES: 810 S. Minnesota, Sioux Falls 57184, 605-334-9596 (Rick Weiland, St. Dir.); 615 S. Main St., Aberdeen 57401, 605-225-8823 (Beth Smith, Rep.); 816 S. 6th St., Rapid City 57709, 605-348-7551 (Arnold Snortland, Rep.)

REPRESENTATIVE AT LARGE

Timothy Peter Johnson (D)

District: Entire state. Population: 696,004—Native American 7%, Hispanic 3%. Politics: Mixed.

Born Dec. 28, 1946, Canton; home, Vermillion; University of S.Dak., B.A. 1969, M.A. 1970, J.D. 1975; Lutheran; married (Barbara), 3 children.

Elected 1986. Career: Budget advisor, Mich. Senate, 1971–72; Practicing atty., S.Dak. House of Reps., 1978–82; S.Dak. Senate, 1982–86.

Committees: (1) Agriculture; (2) Natural Resources.

Election Results: 1992 Johnson 229,648 (71%); John Timmer (R) 89,123 (28%); Robert Newland (Libert) 3,932 (1%). 1990 Johnson (67%). 1988 Johnson (72%).

Interest Group Ratings:

ADA	ACU	COPE	COC
70	32	67	50

LCV	NTLC	CFA	ASC
69	05	80	50

Office: 2438 RHOB 20515, 202-225-2801 (Drey Samuelson, AA). DISTRICT OFFICES: 515 S. Dakota St., Sioux Falls, 57102, 605-332-8896 (Sharon Bertram, St. Dir.); 809 South St, Suite 104, Rapid City, 57709, 605-341-3990 (Darrell Shoemaker, Rep.); 615 S. Main, Aberdeen 57401, 605-226-3440 (Luci Weigel, Asst.)

TENNESSEE

Both of Tennessee's Democratic senators will have to run for reelection in 1994 and this will be the key state the GOP targets. Sen. James Sasser looks safe, so the GOP will be aiming at the seat held by Vice President Al Gore, and now held by appointee Harlan Mathews. It is not clear if Mathews will run for the seat. If he doesn't, there will be a long line of Democrats waiting for their shot. The GOP's best chance would seem to be to convince Rep. John Duncan to leave a safe House seat to make the run. It is not at all clear if he is willing.

1992 PRESIDENTIAL ELECTION: (11 Electoral votes): Clinton (D) 933,620 (47%); Bush (R) 840,899 (42%); Perot (I) 199,787 (10%); Marrou (Lib) 1,691; Brisben (Soc) 1,266; Fulani (NAP) 708; Gritz (Pop) 696; Hagelin (NLP) 587; Phillips (AmTax) 541; Daniels (P&F) 480; LaRouche (I) 453; Dodge (Prob) 354; Warren (SocWks) 265; Yiamouyiannis (TkBkAm) 229. 1988 Bush 939,434 (58%); Dukakis 677,715 (42%).

SENATORS

James Ralph Sasser (D)

Born Sept. 30, 1936, Memphis; home, Nashville; University of Tenn., Vanderbilt University, B.A. 1958, J.D. 1961; United Methodist; married (Mary), 2 children.

Elected 1976, seat up 1994. Career: Practicing atty., 1961–76; Chm., Tenn. State Dem. Comm., 1973–76.

Committees: (1) Budget (Chairman); (2) Appropriations; (3) Banking, Housing & Urban Affairs; (4) Governmental Affairs.

Election Results: 1988 Sasser 1,020,061 (65%); Bill Anderson (R) 541,033 (35%). 1982 Sasser (62%).

Interest Group Ratings:

ADA	ACU	COPE	COC
95	07	83	10

LCV	NTLC	CFA	ASC
50	11	92	40

Office: 363 RSOB 20510, 202-224-3344 (Craven Crowell, Chief-of-staff). STATE OFFICES: 569 U.S. Crthse., Nashville 37203, 615-736-7353 (Bill Hauks, St. Cord.); 239 Fed. Bldg., 900 Georgia Ave., Chattanooga 37402, 615-756-8836 (Gloria Daniels, Rep.); 320 P.O. Bldg., 501 Main St., Knoxville 37902, 615-673-4204 (Vicki Nance, Cord.); 390 Fed. Bldg., 167 N. Main, Memphis 38103, 901-521-4187 (Calvin Anderson, Spec. Asst.); B-8 Fed. Bldg., Jackson 38301, 901-424-6600 (Neal Smith, Cord.); Tri-City Airport, Blountville 37617, 615-323-6207 (Paul Bivens, Asst.)

Harlan Mathews (D)

Born Jan. 17, 1927; home, Nashville; Jacksonville State College, A.B., 1949, Vanderbilt University, M.A., 1952, Nashville College of Law, LL.B., 1962; Baptist, married (Patsey), 2 children.

Appointed, 1992 to fill portion of unexpired term of Vice President Albert Gore. Seat up in 1996, but special election will be held in 1994. Career: U.S. Navy, WWII; Commissioner, Tenn. Dept. of Finance, 1961–71; Sr. V.P., Amcon Corp., 1971–73; Asst. to Tenn. Comptroller, 1973–74; Tenn. State Treas., 1974–87; Asst. to the Gov., 1987–92.

Committees: (1) Energy & Natural Resources; (2) Foreign Relations.

Election Results: Appointed

Interest Group Ratings:
None—Freshman

Office: 506 DSOB 20510, 202-224-1036 (Estie Harris, AA). STATE OFFICES: 3322 Westland #120, Nashville 37203, 615-736-5129 (Sandy Stapleton, State Dir.); 403 Fed. Bldg. 167 N. Main St., Memphis 38103, 901-544-4224; 315 P.O. Bldg., 501 Main St., Knoxville 37902, 615-545-4253.

REPRESENTATIVES

FIRST DISTRICT

James Henry Quillen (R)

District: Far northeastern corner of the state including the tri–cities of Johnson City, Kingsport and Bristol. Population: 541,875. Politics: Republican.

Born Jan. 11, 1916, Wayland, Va.; home, Kingsport; United Methodist; married (Cecile).

Elected 1962. Career: Founder & Pub., Kingsport Press, 1934–35, Kingsport Times, 1935–36, Johnson City Times, 1939–44; Navy, WWII; Pres. & Bd. Chm., real estate & insur. business; Dir., 1st Tenn. Bank, Kingsport; Tenn. House of Reps., 1955–62.

Committees: (1) Rules.

Election Results: 1992 Quillen 115,095 (71%); J. Carr Christian (D) 48,122 (29%). 1990 Quillen (Unopposed). 1988 Quillen (80%).

Interest Group Ratings:

ADA	ACU	COPE	COC
05	92	33	75

LCV	NTLC	CFA	ASC
06	84	27	90

Office: 102 CHOB 20515, 202-225-6356 (Frances Currie, AA). DISTRICT OFFICE: 157 P.O. Bldg., Kingsport 37662, 615-247-8161 (Betty Vaughn, Ex. Sec.)

SECOND DISTRICT

John J. Duncan, Jr. (R)

District: Eastern part of the state including city of Knoxville. Population: 541,864—Black 7%. Politics: Leans Republican.

Born July 21, 1947, Lebanon; home, Knoxville; University of Tenn., B.S. 1969, George Washington University, J.D. 1973; Presbyterian, married (Lynn), 4 children.

Elected 1988. Career: Judge, Knox Cty., 1980–88.

Committees: (1) Public Works & Transportation; (2) Banking, Finance & Urban Affairs; (3) Natural Resources.

Election Results: 1992 Duncan 148,203 (74%); Troy Goodale (D) 52,766 (26%). 1990 Duncan (81%). 1988 Duncan (56%).

Interest Group Ratings:

ADA	ACU	COPE	COC
25	84	42	63

LCV	NTLC	CFA	ASC
06	100	33	70

Office: 115 CHOB 20515, 202-225-5435 (Judy Whitbred, AA). DISTRICT OFFICE: 318 P.O.

Bldg., Knoxville 37902, 615-523-3772 (Mildred MacRae, Ex. Sec.); Courthouse, Athens 37303, 615-745-4671 (Linda Higdon, Rep.); 200 E. Broadway #419, Maryville 37801, 615-984-5464 (Shirley Lambert, Rep.)

THIRD DISTRICT

Marilyn Lloyd (D)

District: Southeast portion of the state including cities of Chattanooga and Oak Ridge. Population: 541,866—Black 12%. Politics: Leans Democratic.

Born Jan. 3, 1929, Ft. Smith, Ark.; home, Chattanooga; Shorter College, 1967–70; Church of Christ; married (Robert Fowler), 4 children.

Elected 1974. Career: Co–owner & Mgr., WTTI Radio, Dalton, Ga.

Committees: (1) Armed Services; (2) Science, Space & Technology.

Election Results: 1992 Lloyd 106,900 (51%); Zach Wamp (R) 103,409 (49%). 1990 Lloyd (57%). 1988 Lloyd (57%).

Interest Group Ratings:

ADA	ACU	COPE	COC
45	50	64	63

LCV	NTLC	CFA	ASC
25	63	67	80

Office: 2406 RHOB 20515, 202-225-3271 (Sue Carlton, AA). DISTRICT OFFICES: 253 Fed. Bldg., 900 Georgia Ave., Chattanooga 37401, 615-267-9108 (Anita Ebersole, Dist. AA); 1211 Fed. Bldg., Oak Ridge 37830, 615-576-1977 (Martha Wallus, Dist. AA)

FOURTH DISTRICT

Jim Cooper (D)

District: Covers a wide rural area running from northeast corner to southwestern border. Population: 541,868—Black 4%. Politics: Leans Democratic.

Born June 19, 1954, Nashville; home, Shelbyville; University of N.C., B.A. 1975, Rhodes Scholar, Oxford University, B.A., M.A. 1977, Harvard Law School, J.D. 1980; Episcopalian; married (Martha), 2 children.

Elected 1982. Career: Practicing atty., 1980–81.

Committees: (1) Energy & Commerce; (2) Small Business; (3) Budget.

Election Results: 1992 Cooper 99,113 (66%); Dale Johnson (R) 50,097 (34%). 1990 Cooper (69%). 1988 Cooper (Unopposed).

Interest Group Ratings:

ADA	ACU	COPE	COC
70	32	67	63

LCV	NTLC	CFA	ASC
63	50	80	100

Office: 125 CHOB 20515, 202-225-6831 (David Withrow, AA). DISTRICT OFFICES: 116 Depot St., Shelbyville 37160, 615-684-1114 (Walter Wood, Dist. Dir.); City Hall, 7 S. High St., Winchester 37398, 615-967-4150 (Judy Wofford, Rep.); 208 E. First North St., Morristown 37814, 615-587-9000 (Joyce Hopson, Rep.) 311 S. Main St., Crossville 38555, 615-484-1864 (Mickey Eldridge, Rep.)

FIFTH DISTRICT

Bob Clement (D)

District: Nashville and Davidson County and some northern suburbs. Population: 541,910—Black 23%. Politics: Leans Democratic.

Born Sept. 23, 1943, Nashville; home, Nashville; University of Tenn., B.S. 1967, Memphis State University, M.B.A. 1968; Methodist; married (Mary), 4 children.

Elected January 19, 1988. Career: Army 1969–71; Tenn. Public Service comm., 1972–79; Bob Clement & Assoc., 1979; Bd. of Dir., Tenn. Valley Authority, 1979–81; owner, Charter Equities, 1981–83; Pres., Cumberland University, 1983–87.

Committees: (1) Veteran Affairs; (2) Public Works & Transportation.

Election Results: 1992 Clement 125,181 (72%); Thomas Stone (R) 49,385 (28%). 1990 Clement (72%). 1988 Clement (Unopposed).

Interest Group Ratings:

ADA	ACU	COPE	COC
65	39	75	63

LCV	NTLC	CFA	ASC
38	15	53	90

Office: 1230 CHOB 20515, 202-225-4311 (David

Flander, AA). DISTRICT OFFICES: 552 U.S. Crthse., Nashville 37203, 615-736-5295 (Dottie Moore, Dist. Adm.); 2701 Jefferson St., Suite 103, Nashville 37208, 615-320-1363 (Gail Stafford, Rep.); 510 Main St., Springfield 37172, 615-384-6600 (Nancy Hall, Rep.)

SIXTH DISTRICT

Barton Jennings Gordon (D)

District: North central counties including city of Murfreesboro. Population: 541,977—Black 6%. Politics: Democratic.

Born Jan. 24, 1949, Rutherford Cty.; home, Murfreesboro; Middle Tenn. University, B.S. 1971, University of Tenn., J.D. 1973; United Methodist; single.

Elected 1984. Career: Practicing atty., 1974–84; Chm., Tenn. Dem. Party, 1981–83.

Committees: (1) Rules; (2) Budget.

Election Results: 1992 Gordon 119,599 (58%); Marsha Blackburn (R) 85,959 (42%). 1990 Gordon (70%). 1988 Gordon (76%).

Interest Group Ratings:

ADA	ACU	COPE	COC
70	25	67	50

LCV	NTLC	CFA	ASC
56	05	67	70

Office: 103 CHOB 20515, 202-225-4231 (Jeff Whorley, AA). DISTRICT OFFICES: Courthouse Sq., 106 S. Maple, Murfreesboro 37130, 615-896-1986 (Kent Syler, Dist. AA)

SEVENTH DISTRICT

Donald Kenneth Sundquist (R)

District: stretching north-south from western Nashville suburbs into Memphis also including city of Clarksville. Population: 541,937—Black 12%. Politics: Mixed, but leans Republican.

Born Mar. 15, 1936, Moline, Ill.; home, Memphis; Augustana College, B.A. 1957; Lutheran; married (Martha), 3 children.

Elected 1982. Career: Navy, 1957–59; Josten's Inc., 1961–72; Partner, Graphic Sales of America, 1972, President, 1973–82.

Committees: (1) Ways & Means.

Election Results: 1992 Sundquist 126,768 (63%); David Davis (D) 75,010 (37%). 1990 Sundquist (62%). 1988 Sundquist (80%).

Interest Group Ratings:

ADA	ACU	COPE	COC
05	96	18	75

LCV	NTLC	CFA	ASC
06	100	27	90

Office: 339 CHOB 20515, 202-225-2811 (Thomas McNamara, AA). DISTRICT OFFICES: 5909 Shelby Oaks Dr., Suite 213, Memphis 38134, 901-382-5811 (Gwen Hurd, Rep.); 117 S. 2nd St., Clarksville 37040, 615-552-4406 (Kathy Higinbotham, Asst.)

EIGHTH DISTRICT

John S. Tanner (D)

District: Western counties including city of Jackson and part of Shelby County. Population: 541,907—Black 20%. Politics: Democratic.

Born Sept. 22, 1942, Halls; home, Union City; University of Tenn., B.S. 1967, J.D. 1968; married (Betty Ann), 2 children.

Elected 1988. Career: Practicing atty., 1968–77; Tenn. House of Reps., 1976–88.

Committees: (1) Armed Services; (2) Science, Space & Technology.

Election Results: 1992 Tanner 134,444 (84%); Lawrence Barnes (I) 9,598 (6%); Millard McKissack (I) 4,628 (3%); John Vinson (I) 5,412 (3%); David Ward (I) 6,922 (4%). 1990 Tanner (Unopposed). 1988 Tanner (62%).

Interest Group Ratings:

ADA	ACU	COPE	COC
65	50	58	38

LCV	NTLC	CFA	ASC
25	35	53	90

Office: 1427 LHOB 20515, 202-225-4714 (Kelly Sharbel, AA). DISTRICT OFFICES: 203 W. Church St., Union City 38261, 901-885-7070 (Joe Hill, Dist. Dir.); 2836 Coleman Rd., Memphis 38128, 901-382-3220 (Margaret Black, Mgr.); B-7 Fed. Bldg., Jackson 38301, 901-423-4848 (Martha Truell, Mgr.)

NINTH DISTRICT

Harold Eugene Ford (D)

District: Memphis. Population: 541,981—Black 59%. Politics: Democratic.

Born May 20, 1945, Memphis; home, Memphis; Tenn. State University, B.S. 1967, John Gupten College, A.A. 1969; Howard University, M.B.A. 1982; Baptist; married (Dorothy), 3 children.

Elected 1974. Career: Tenn. House of Reps., 1971–75.

Committees: (1) Ways & Means.

Election Results: 1992 Ford 123,269 (67%); Charles Black (R) 60,603 (33%). 1990 Ford (65%). 1988 Ford (82%).

Interest Group Ratings:

ADA	ACU	COPE	COC
85	05	86	29

LCV	NTLC	CFA	ASC
63	00	73	10

Office: 2211 RHOB 20515, 202-225-3265 (Gerald Delk, AA). DISTRICT OFFICE: 369 Fed. Bldg., 167 Main St., Memphis 38103, 901-544-4131 (John Lowery, Adm.)

TEXAS

A lot of Texas politics today revolves around whether or not Sen. Phil Gramm is going to challenge for the GOP presidential nomination in 1996. His seat is up that year, and while under Texas law it is possible for him to contest for both seats, that will be very difficult, especially if he wins the nomination. So lines are already starting to form for candidates eager to succeed him. Democratic Gov. Ann Richards is expected to easily win reelection in 1994. She would be the early front runner if she was willing to make the race. There are a half dozen top Republicans who would love to have the opportunity, and are hoping that Gramm will make the run for the Oval Office.

1992 PRESIDENTIAL ELECTION: (32 Electoral votes): Clinton (D) 2,279,269 (37%); Bush (R) 2,460,334 (40%); Perot (I) 1,349,947 (22%); Marrou (Lib) 19,582. 1988 Bush 3,014,007 (56%); Dukakis 2,331,286 (44%).

SENATORS

Phil Gramm (R)

Born July 8, 1942, Ft. Benning, Ga.; home, College Station; University of Ga., B.A. 1964, Ph.D. 1967; Episcopalian; married (Wendy), 2 children.

Elected 1984, seat up 1996. Career: Prof., Tex. A&M University, 1967–78; U.S. House of Reps., 1978–84.

Committees: (1) Appropriations; (2) Banking, Housing & Urban Affairs; (3) Budget.

Election Results: 1990 Gramm 2,292,519 (62%); Hugh Palmer (D) 1,425,137 (38%). 1984 Gramm (59%).

Interest Group Ratings:

ADA	ACU	COPE	COC
00	93	08	100

LCV	NTLC	CFA	ASC
00	94	17	80

Office: 370 RSOB 20510, 202-224-2934 (Ruth Cymber, AA). STATE OFFICES: 2323 Bryan St., Dallas 75202, 214-767-3000 (Joan Moore, St. Dir.); 222 E. Van Buren., Suite 404, Harlingen 78550, 512-423-6118 (Delfina Medina, Mgr.); 712 Main St., Suite 2400, Houston 77002, 713-229-2766 (Dale Laine, Reg. Dir.); 113 Fed. Bldg., 1205 Texas Ave., Lubbock 79401, 806-743-7533 (Jennifer Crabtree, Reg. Dir.); 123 Pioneer Plaza, Rm 665, El Paso 79901, 915-534-6896 (Margie Velez, Mgr.); 201 InterFirst Plaza Bldg., 102 N. College St., Tyler 75701, 214-593-0902 (Steve Moss, Dir.)

Kathyrn "Kay" Bailey Hutchison (R)

Born July 22, 1943, Galveston; home, Dallas; University of Tex., B.A. 1992, University of Tex. Law School, J.D. 1967; Episcopalian; married (Ray Hutchison), 2 children.

Elected, May, 1993 to fill the unexpired term of Treasury Secretary Lloyd Bentsen; seat up 1994. Career: Television reporter, Houston, 1967–72; member Texas State Legis., 1972–76; member, National Transportation Safety Board, 1976–79; banking executive and owner McGraw Candy Company, 1980–90; Texas state treasurer, 1990–93.

Committees: (1) Armed Services; (2) Small Business; (3) Commerce, Science & Transportation

Election Results: 1993 Hutchison 1,183,766 (67%); Bob Kruger (D) 574,089 (33%).

Interest Group Ratings:
None—Freshman

Office: 703 HSOB 20510, 202-224-5922 (John Savercool, Acting AA). STATE OFFICES: 961 Fed. Bldg., 300 E. 8th St., Austin 78701, 512-482-5834; 1919 Smith St., Suite 800, Houston 77002, 713-653-3456; 7C14 Fed. Bldg., 1111 Commerce St., Dallas 75242, 214-767-0577.

REPRESENTATIVES

FIRST DISTRICT

Jim Chapman (D)

District: Northeast corner of the state including city of Texarkana. Population: 566,217—Black 18%, Hispanic 3%. Politics: Democratic.

Born Mar. 8, 1945, Washington, D.C.; home, Sulphur Springs; University of Tex., B.A. 1968, Southern Methodist University, J.D. 1970; United Methodist; married (Betty), 2 children.

Elected Aug. 3, 1985. Career: Practicing atty.; D.A., 8th Judicial Dist. of Tex., 1976–84.

Committees: (1) Appropriations.

Election Results: 1992 Chapman (Unopposed). 1990 Chapman (61%). 1988 Chapman (62%).

Interest Group Ratings:

ADA	ACU	COPE	COC
75	24	75	25

LCV	NTLC	CFA	ASC
13	05	80	70

Office: 2417 RHOB 20515, 202-225-3035 (William Moore, AA). DISTRICT OFFICES: P.O. Box 538, Sulphur Springs 75483, 214-885-8682 (Bill Brannen, Dist. Adm.); G-15 Fed. Bldg., 100 E. Houston, Marshall 75670, 214-938-8386 (vacant, Dir.); 1000 James Bowie St., New Boston 75570, 214-628-5594 (Marie Martin, Asst.)

SECOND DISTRICT

Charles Nesbitt Wilson (D)

District: Sixteen counties of East Texas including the towns of Lufkin and Orange. Population: 566,217—Black 17%, Hispanic 6%, Native American 3%. Politics: Democratic.

Born June 1, 1933, Trinity; home, Lufkin; U.S. Naval Academy, B.S. 1956; United Methodist; divorced.

Elected 1972. Career: Navy, 1956–60; Mgr., Retail Lumber Store, 1961–72; Tex. House of Reps., 1960–66; Tex. Senate, 1966–72.

Committees: (1) Appropriations.

Election Results: 1992 Wilson 116,948 (56%); Donna Peterson (R) 91,100 (44%). 1990 Wilson (55%). 1988 Wilson (88%).

Interest Group Ratings:

ADA	ACU	COPE	COC
65	45	82	71

LCV	NTLC	CFA	ASC
31	10	53	100

Office: 2256 RHOB 20515, 202-225-2401 (Peyton Walters, AA). DISTRICT OFFICE: 701 N. 1st St., Rm. 201, Lufkin 75901, 409-637-1770 (Shaun Davis, Dist. Dir.)

THIRD DISTRICT

Sam Johnson (R)

District: North Dallas and northern suburbs. Population: 566,217—Black 4%, Asian 3%, Hispanic 6%. Politics: Republican.

Born Sept. 19, 1947, Dallas; home, Dallas; Southern Methodist University, B.A., George Washington, M.A.; United Methodist; married (Shirley), 3 children.

Elected 1991. Career: U.S. Air Force, 1950–79; Owner Homebuilding Company, 1979–present; Tex. House of Reps., 1984–92.

Committees: (1) Banking, Finance & Urban Affairs; (2) Education & Labor.

Election Results: 1992 Johnson 201,670 (86%); Noel Kopala (Libert) 32,542 (14%).

Interest Group Ratings:

ADA	ACU	COPE	COC
10	100	25	88

LCV	NTLC	CFA	ASC
00	100	13	100

Office: 1030 LHOB 20515, 202-225-4201 (Mary Jane Maddox, AA). DISTRICT OFFICES: 9400 N. Central Expressway #610, Dallas 75231, 214-739-0182 (Maty Lynn Murrell, Rep.); 1912 Ave K #204, Plano 75074, 214-423-2017 (Jerry Durham, Rep.)

FOURTH DISTRICT

Ralph M. Hall (D)

District: Rural northeast part of the state including cities of Tyler and Longview. Population: 566,217—Black 8%, Hispanic 4%. Politics: Democratic.

Born May 3, 1923, Fate; home, Rockwall; University of Tex., Tex. Christian University, Southern Methodist University, LL.B. 1951; United Methodist; married (Mary Ellen), 3 children.

Elected 1980. Career: Navy, WWII; Rockwall Cty. Judge, 1950–62; Tex. Senate, 1962–72; Pres. & CEO, Texas Aluminum Corp.; Gen. Counsel, Texas Extrusion Co., Inc.; Practicing atty.

Committees: (1) Energy & Commerce; (2) Science, Space & Technology.

Election Results: 1992 Hall 127,987 (60%); David Bridges (R) 83,867 (40%). 1990 Hall (Unopposed). 1988 Hall (66%).

Interest Group Ratings:

ADA	ACU	COPE	COC
40	76	50	63

LCV	NTLC	CFA	ASC
00	63	47	100

Office: 2236 RHOB 20515, 202-225-6673 (James Cole, AA). DISTRICT OFFICES: 104 N. San Jacinto St., Rockwall 75087, 214-771-9118 (Diane Milliken, Dist. Dir.); 119 Fed. Bldg., Sherman 75090, 214-892-1112 (Mike Allen, Asst.); 211 Fed. Bldg., Tyler 75702, 214-597-3729 (Martha Glover, Asst.)

FIFTH DISTRICT

John Wiley Bryant (D)

District: Central Dallas, plus its eastern and southern suburbs. Population: 566,217—Black 16%, Hispanic 18%, Other 10%. Politics: Leans Democratic.

Born Feb. 22, 1947, Lake Jackson; home, Dallas; Southern Methodist University, B.A. 1969, J.D. 1972; United Methodist; married (Janet), 3 children.

Elected 1982. Career: Practicing atty., 1972–82; Chief counsel, Tex. Senate Subcommittee on Consumer Affairs, 1973; Tex. House of Reps., 1974–83.

Committees: (1) Budget; (2) Energy & Commerce; (3) Judiciary.

Election Results: 1992 Bryant 98,160 (61%); Richard Stokley (R) 62,181 (39%). 1990 Bryant (61%). 1988 Bryant (61%).

Interest Group Ratings:

ADA	ACU	COPE	COC
80	14	82	38

LCV	NTLC	CFA	ASC
75	13	73	40

Office: 205 CHOB 20515, 202-225-2231 (Randy White, AA). DISTRICT OFFICE: 8035 East R. L. Thornton Freeway, Suite 518, Dallas 75228, 214-767-6554 (Norma Minnis, AA)

SIXTH DISTRICT

Joe Linus Barton (R)

District: Long narrow district designed to join far suburbs of both Dallas–Fort Worth and Houston, and includes parts of Arlington and Ft. Worth. Population: 566,217—Black 4%, Hispanic 5%. Politics: Leans Republican.

Born Sept. 15, 1949, Waco; home, Ennis; Texas A&M University, B.S. 1972, Purdue University, M.S. 1973; United Methodist; married (Janet), 3 children.

Elected 1984. Career: Asst. to Vice Pres., Ennis Business Forms, 1973–81; White House Fellow, 1981–82; Consultant, Atlantic Richfield Co., 1982–84.

Committees: (1) Energy & Commerce; (2) Science, Space & Technology.

Election Results: 1992 Barton 188,762 (72%); John Dietrich (D) 73,787 (28%). 1990 Barton (67%). 1988 Barton (68%).

Interest Group Ratings:

ADA	ACU	COPE	COC
05	100	27	75

LCV	NTLC	CFA	ASC
00	90	13	100

Office: 1514 LHOB 20515, 202-225-2002 (Catherine Gillespie, AA). DISTRICT OFFICES: 101 First Republic Bank Bldg., 303 West Knox, Ennis 75119, 214-875-8488; 3509 Hulen, Suite 110, Ft. Worth 76107, 817-737-7737; 2019 E. Lamar Blvd., #100, Arlington 76006, 817-543-1000 (Harold Samuels, Dist. Dir.)

SEVENTH DISTRICT

Bill Archer (R)

District: Western Houston and suburbs. Population: 566,217—Black 6%, Asian 6%, Hispanic 12%. Politics: Republican.

Born Mar. 22, 1928, Houston; home, Houston; Rice University, 1945–46, University of Tex., B.B.A. 1949, LL.B 1951; Roman Catholic; married (Sharon), 5 children, 2 stepchildren.

Elected 1971. Career: Air Force, 1951–53; Pres., Uncle Johnny Mills, Inc., 1953–61; Hunters Creek Village Cncl. & Mayor Pro Temp., 1955–

62; Tex. House of Reps., 1966–70; Dir., Heights State Bank, Houston, 1967–70; Practicing atty., 1968–71.

Committees: (1) Ways & Means (Ranking Member); (2) Joint Committee on Taxation.

Election Results: 1992 Archer (Unopposed). 1990 Archer (Unopposed). 1988 Archer (79%).

Interest Group Ratings:

ADA	ACU	COPE	COC
00	100	17	75

LCV	NTLC	CFA	ASC
13	89	13	100

Office: 1236 LHOB 20515, 202-225-2571 (Donald Carlson, AA). DISTRICT OFFICE: 1003 Wirt Rd., Suite 311, Houston 77055, 713-467-7493 (Anne Clutterbuck, Dist. Dir.)

EIGHTH DISTRICT

Jack Fields (R)

District: Houston suburbs and eastern Harris County. Population: 566,217—Black 5%, Hispanic 7%. Politics: Leans Republican.

Born Feb. 3, 1952, Humble; home, Humble; Baylor University, B.A. 1974, J.D. 1977; Baptist; married (Lynn), 2 children.

Elected 1980. Career: Practicing atty.; Vice Pres., Rosewood Memorial Funeral Home & Cemetery. 1977–80.

Committees: (1) Energy & Commerce; (2) Merchant Marine & Fisheries.

Election Results: 1992 Fields 172,881 (76%); Charles Robinson (D) 53,164 (24%). 1990 Fields (Unopposed). 1988 Fields (68%).

Interest Group Ratings:

ADA	ACU	COPE	COC
05	96	25	75

LCV	NTLC	CFA	ASC
00	100	13	90

Office: 2228 RHOB 20515, 202-225-4901 (Robert Ferguson, AA). DISTRICT OFFICES: 320 First Rep. Bank Bldg., 12605 E. Freeway, Houston 77015, 713-451-6334 (Jim Finley, Dist. AA); 9810 FM1960-Bypass West Suite 165, Dearbrook Plaza, Humble 77338, 713-540-8000; 300 W. Davis #507, Corroe 77301, 409-756-8044; 111 E. University #216, College Station 77840, 409-846-6068.

NINTH DISTRICT

Jack B. Brooks (D)

District: Stretches from southern Houston suburbs to Beaumont and Galveston. Population: 566,217—Black 22%, Hispanic 9%. Politics: Leans Democratic.

Born Dec. 18, 1922, Crowley, La.; home, Beaumont; Lamar Junior College, 1939–41, University of Tex., B.J. 1943, J.D. 1949; United Methodist; married (Charlotte), 3 children.

Elected 1952. Career: USMC, WWII; Tex. House of Reps., 1946–50; Practicing atty., 1949–52.

Committees: (1) Judiciary (Chairman).

Election Results: 1992 Brooks 118,607 (56%); Steve Stockman (R) 94,980 (44%). 1990 Brooks (58%). 1988 Brooks (Unopposed).

Interest Group Ratings:

ADA	ACU	COPE	COC
75	23	83	33

LCV	NTLC	CFA	ASC
31	17	80	70

Office: 2449 RHOB 20515, 202-225-6565 (Sharon Matts, AA). DISTRICT OFFICES: 230 Fed. Bldg., 300 Willow St., Beaumont 77701, 409-839-2508 (Diana Coffey, Asst.); 216 U.S. P.O. & Crthse., 601 25th St., Galveston 77550, 409-766-3608 (Dorthea Lewis, Asst.)

TENTH DISTRICT

James Jarrell "Jake" Pickle (D)

District: City of Austin and environs. Population: 566,217—Black 11%, Hispanic 21%. Politics: Democratic.

Born Oct. 11, 1913, Roscoe; home, Austin; University of Tex., B.A. 1938; United Methodist; married (Beryl), 3 children.

Elected Dec. 17, 1963. Career: Area Dir., Natl. Youth Admin., 1938–41; Navy, WWII; Coorganizer, KVET Radio, Austin; Adv. & P.R., 1945–63; Dir., Tex. Dem. Exec. Comm., 1957–60; Mbr., Tex. Employment Comm., 1961–63.

Committees: (1) Ways & Means; (2) Joint Committee on Taxation.

Election Results: 1992 Pickle 177,233 (72%);

Herbert Spiro (R) 68,646 (28%). 1990 Pickle (67%). 1988 Pickle (93%).

Interest Group Ratings:

ADA	ACU	COPE	COC
65	33	64	63

LCV	NTLC	CFA	ASC
38	26	73	80

Office: 242 CHOB 20515, 202-225-4865 (Barbara Pate, AA). DISTRICT OFFICE: 763 Fed. Bldg., 303 8th St. E., Austin 78701, 512-482-5921 (Paul Hilgers, Dist. Adm.)

ELEVENTH DISTRICT

Chet Edwards (D)

District: Mainly rural, central part of the state including city of Waco. Population: 566,217—Black 16%, Hispanic 12%. Politics: Democratic.

Born Nov. 24, 1951, Corpus Christi; home, Waco; Texas A&M University, B.A., 1974, Harvard University, M.B.A., 1976; Methodist; married (Lea Ann).

Elected 1990. Career: Radio station owner; aide U.S. Rep. Marvin Teague, 1974–77; Tex. St. Senate 1983–90.

Committees: (1) Armed Services; (2) Veterans Affairs.

Election Results: 1992 Edwards 119,206 (67%); James Broyles (R) 57,813 (33%). 1990 Edwards (54%).

Interest Group Ratings:

ADA	ACU	COPE	COC
55	40	75	63

LCV	NTLC	CFA	ASC
25	16	60	100

Office: 328 CHOB 20515, 202-225-6105 (Jay Neel, AA). DISTRICT OFFICE: 710 Univ. Tower, 700 S. Univ. Parks Dr., Waco 76706, 817-752-9600 (Jim Haddox, Mgr.)

TWELFTH DISTRICT

Preston M. "Pete" Geren (D)

District: Parts of Fort Worth and suburbs including northwest Tarrant County. Population: 566,217—Black 8%, Hispanic 15%. Politics: Democratic.

Born Jan. 29, 1952, Fort Worth; home, Fort Worth; Georgia Tech, University of Tex., B.A., 1974, J.D. 1978; Baptist; married (Rebecca), 2 children.

Elected 1989 (special election). Career: Lawyer, private practice 1979–82, 1984–89; Asst. Sen. Lloyd Bensten 1982–84.

Committees: (1) Public Works and Transportation; (2) Science, Space & Technology; (3) Armed Services.

Election Results: 1992 Geren 125,343 (63%); David Hobbs (R) 74,334 (37%). 1990 Geren (71%). 1989 (Special) Geren (51%).

Interest Group Ratings:

ADA	ACU	COPE	COC
45	60	55	88

LCV	NTLC	CFA	ASC
13	55	33	90

Office: 1730 LHOB 20515, 202-225-5071 (Lionell Collins, AA). DISTRICT OFFICE: 100 E. 15th St., Suite 500, Ft. Worth 76102, 817-338-0909 (Bill Souder, Dist. Dir.)

THIRTEENTH DISTRICT

Bill Sarpalius (D)

District: Eastern panhandle counties including cities of Amarillo and Wichita Falls. Population: 566,217—Black 8%, Hispanic 19%. Politics: Democratic.

Born June 10, 1948, Los Angeles, Calif.; home, Austin; Clarendon Junior College, A.S. 1970; Tex. Tech., B.S. 1972, W. Tex. State University, M.A. 1978; Methodist; divorced, 1 child.

Elected 1988. Career: Teacher 1972–77; Speaker, Tex. House of Rep., 1977–79; Tex. Senate, 1981–88.

Committees: (1) Small Business; (2) Agriculture.

Election Results: 1992 Sarpalius 118,370 (60%); Beau Boulter (R) 77,783 (40%). 1990 Sarpalius (56%). 1988 Sarpalius (52%).

Interest Group Ratings:

ADA	ACU	COPE	COC
40	64	50	75

LCV	NTLC	CFA	ASC
06	55	47	90

Office: 126 CHOB 20515, 202-225-3706 (Phil

Duncan, AA). DISTRICT OFFICES: 817 South Polk St., Amarillo 79114, 806-371-8844 (vacant, Dist. AA); 1000 La Mar St., Rm. 208, Wichita Falls 76301, 817-767-0541 (Aaron Alejandro, Dist. Mgr.)

FOURTEENTH DISTRICT

Greg Laughlin (D)

District: Gulf Coast counties. Population: 566,217—Black 11%, Hispanic 24%. Politics: Leans Democratic.

Born Jan. 21, 1942, Bay City; home, West Columbia; Texas A&M, B.A. 1964; University of Tex., J.D. 1967; Methodist; married (Ginger), 2 children.

Elected 1988. Career: Army 1967–69; Asst. District Atty., Harrison Cty., 1970–74; Practicing atty., 1974–88.

Committees: (1) Merchant Marine & Fisheries; (2) Public Works & Transportation; (3) Select Committee on Intelligence; (4) Post Office and Civil Service.

Election Results: 1992 Laughlin 137,184 (72%); Humberto Garza (R) 54,567 (28%). 1990 Laughlin (55%). 1988 Laughlin (53%).

Interest Group Ratings:

ADA	ACU	COPE	COC
45	52	50	63

LCV	NTLC	CFA	ASC
19	40	53	100

Office: 236 CHOB 20515, 202-225-2831 (Bob Grasso, AA). DISTRICT OFFICES: 312 S. Main St., Victoria 77901, 512-578-7955 (Howdy Leal, Dist. Dir.); 102 N. L.B.J., Hays Co. Courthouse Annex 3, San Marcos 78666, 512-396-1400 (Linda Collinsworth, Rep.); 111 N. 10th, W. Columbia 77486, 409-345-1414 (Bruce Creary, Rep.)

FIFTEENTH DISTRICT

E. "Kika" de la Garza (D)

District: Southern part of the state including border city of McAllen. Population: 566,217—Hispanic 75%, Other 23%. Politics: Democratic.

Born Sept. 22, 1927, Mercedes; home, Mission; Edinburg Junior College, St. Mary's University,

San Antonio, LL.B 1952; Roman Catholic; married (Lucille), 3 children.

Elected 1964. Career: Navy, WWII, Army, Korea; Practicing atty., 1952–64; Tex. House of Reps., 1952–64.

Committees: (1) Agriculture (Chairman).

Election Results: 1992 de la Garza 86,197 (60%); Tom Haughey (R) 56,811 (40%). 1990 de la Garza (Unopposed). 1988 de la Garza (94%).

Interest Group Ratings:

ADA	ACU	COPE	COC
70	19	75	43

LCV	NTLC	CFA	ASC
31	11	80	70

Office: 1401 LHOB 20515, 202-225-2531 (Bernice McGuire, AA). DISTRICT OFFICE: 1418 Beech St., McAllen 78501, 512-682-5545 (Norma Brewster, Asst.)

SIXTEENTH DISTRICT

Ronald D'Emory Coleman (D)

District: Far western corner of the state including border city of El Paso. Population: 566,217—Black 4%, Hispanic 70%. Politics: Democratic.

Born Nov. 19, 1941, El Paso; home, El Paso; University of Tex., B.A. 1963, J.D. 1967; University of Kent, England, 1981; Presbyterian; married (Tammy), 2 children.

Elected 1982. Career: Practicing atty.; Teacher, El Paso public schools, Tex. School for the Deaf; Army, 1967–69; Asst. El Paso Cty. Atty., 1969, First Asst., 1971; Tex. House of Reps., 1973–82.

Committees: (1) Appropriations.

Election Results: 1992 Coleman 66,731 (52%); Chip Taberski (R) 61,870 (48%). 1990 Coleman (Unopposed). 1988 Coleman (Unopposed).

Interest Group Ratings:

ADA	ACU	COPE	COC
85	12	83	29

LCV	NTLC	CFA	ASC
69	00	80	50

Office: 440 CHOB 20515, 202-225-4831 (Paul Rogers, AA). DISTRICT OFFICE: 723 Fed. Bldg., 700 E. San Antonio Ave., El Paso 79901, 915-534-6200 (Luis Mata, Dist. Dir.)

SEVENTEENTH DISTRICT

Charles W. Stenholm (D)

District: West Texas plains counties including city of Abilene. Population: 566,217—Black 4%, Hispanic 17%. Politics: Democratic.

Born Oct. 26, 1938, Stamford; home, Avoca; Tarleton State Junior College, 1959, Tex. Technologic University, B.S. 1961; M.S. 1962; Lutheran; married (Cynthia), 3 children.

Elected 1978. Career: Teacher, 1962–65; Exec. Vice Pres., Rolling Plains Cotton Growers, 1965–68; Mgr., Stamford Electric Coop., 1968–76; Farmer, 1976–78.

Committees: (1) Agriculture; (2) Budget.

Election Results: 1992 Stenholm 136,107 (66%); Jeannie Sadowski (R) 69,834 (34%). 1990 Stenholm (Unopposed). 1988 Stenholm (Unopposed).

Interest Group Ratings:

ADA	ACU	COPE	COC
30	72	25	57

LCV	NTLC	CFA	ASC
00	60	40	100

Office: 1211 LHOB 20515, 202-225-6605 (Lois Auer, AA). DISTRICT OFFICES: 903 E. Hamilton, Stamford 79553, 915-773-3623 (Bill Longley, Dist. Mgr.); 2101 Fed. Bldg., 300 Pine St., Abilene 79604, 915-673-7221 (Elaine Talley, Rep.)

EIGHTEENTH DISTRICT

Craig Washington (D)

District: Central Houston. Population: 566,217 —Black 51%, Hispanic 15%. Politics: Democratic.

Born Oct. 21, 1941, Longview; home, Houston; Prairie View A&M, B.S. 1966, Texas Southern, J.D., 1969; divorced, 5 children.

Elected 1989 (Special election). Career: Lawyer, Tex. House of Reps., 1973–83; Tex. St. Senate, 1983–89.

Committees: (1) Energy & Commerce; (2) Judiciary.

Election Results: 1992 Washington 110,794 (68%); Edward Blum (R) 52,984 (32%). 1990

Washington (Unopposed). 1989 (special) Washington (56%).

Interest Group Ratings:

ADA	ACU	COPE	COC
90	00	83	13

LCV	NTLC	CFA	ASC
88	00	80	10

Office: 1711 LHOB 20515, 202-225-3816 (Licia Green, AA). DISTRICT OFFICE: 1919 Smith, Suite 820, Houston 77002, 713-739-7339 (Sidney Braquett, Counsel)

NINETEENTH DISTRICT

Larry Ed Combest (R)

District: High plains country in the Northwest part of the state, including the cities of Lubbock and Odessa. Population: 527,805—Black 5%, Hispanic 25%. Politics: Republican.

Born Mar. 20, 1945, Memphis; home, Lubbock; West Tex. State University, B.B.A. 1969; United Methodist; married (Sharon), 2 children.

Elected 1984. Career: Farmer; teacher, 1970–71; Dir., U.S. Agric. Stabilization & Conserv. Svc., Graham, Tex., 1971; Aide to U.S. Sen. John Tower, 1971–78; Founder & Pres., Combest Distributing Co., 1978–1985.

Committees: (1) Agriculture; (2) Small Business; (3) Permanent Select Committee on Intelligence.

Election Results: 1992 Combest 161,896 (77%); Terry Moser (D) 47,326 (23%). 1990 Combest (Unopposed). 1988 Combest (68%).

Interest Group Ratings:

ADA	ACU	COPE	COC
10	100	33	88

LCV	NTLC	CFA	ASC
00	80	20	100

Office: 1511 LHOB 20515, 202-225-4005 (Robert Lehman, AA). DISTRICT OFFICES: 613 Fed. Bldg., 1205 Texas Ave., Lubbock 79401, 806-763-1611 (Mary Whistler, Rep.); 3800 E. 42nd St., Odessa 79762, 915-362-2631 (Jenny Welch, Rep.); 5809 S. Western #205, Amarillo 79110, 806-353-9945 (Margo Colquitt, Rep.); 511 W. Ohio, Midland 79701, 915-687-0926 (Susan Webb, Rep.)

TWENTIETH DISTRICT

Henry B. Gonzalez (D)

District: Central San Antonio. Population: 566,217—Black 3%, Hispanic 20%. Politics: Democratic.

Born May 3, 1916, San Antonio; home, San Antonio College; San Antonio Junior College, A.A., University of Tex., St. Mary's University, LL.B., J.D. 1943; Roman Catholic; married (Bertha), 8 children.

Elected 1961. Career: Bexar County Chief Probation Officer, 1946; Deputy Director, San Antonio Housing Authority, 1950–51; San Antonio City Council, 1953–56, Mayor Pro Temp., 1955–56; Tex. State Senate, 1956–61.

Committees: (1) Banking, Finance & Urban Affairs (Chairman).

Election Results: 1992 Gonzalez (Unopposed). 1990 Gonzalez (Unopposed). 1988 Gonzalez (71%).

Interest Group Ratings:

ADA	ACU	COPE	COC
80	04	92	38

LCV	NTLC	CFA	ASC
63	00	87	30

Office: 2413 RHOB 20515, 202-225-3236 (Jennifer Sada, Leg. Dir.). DISTRICT OFFICE: B-124 Fed. Bldg., 727 E. Durango St., San Antonio 78206, 512-229-6195 (vacant, Dir.)

TWENTY-FIRST DISTRICT

Lamar S. Smith (R)

District: San Antonio suburbs and environs including parts of San Angelo and Austin. Population: 566,217—Black 2%, Hispanic 14%, Other 21%. Politics: Republican.

Born Nov. 19, 1947, San Antonio; home, San Antonio; Yale University, B.A., 1968, S. Methodist University, J.D., 1975; Christian Scientist; married (Beth), 2 children.

Elected 1986. Career: Mgt. Intern, Small Bus. Admin., 1969–70; Bus. & Fin. Reporter, Christian Science Monitor, 1970–72; Practicing atty., 1975–76; Tex. House of Reps., 1981–82; Bexar Cty. Commissioner, 1982–85.

Committees: (1) Judiciary; (2) Budget.

Election Results: 1992 Smith 190,712 (75%); James Gaddy (D) 62,791 (25%). 1990 Smith (75%). 1988 Smith (93%).

Interest Group Ratings:

ADA	ACU	COPE	COC
20	88	36	88

LCV	NTLC	CFA	ASC
13	75	33	100

Office: 2443 RHOB 20515, 202-225-4236 (John Lampmann, AA). DISTRICT OFFICES: 1100 N.E. Rt. 410 Suite 460, San Antonio 78209, 210-821-5024 (Earlene Stone, Dist. Dir.); 201 W. Wall St., Suite 104, Midland 79701, 915-687-5232 (Lori Johns, Mgr.); 1006 Junction Hwy., Kerrville 78028, 512-895-1414 (Kathy Loeffler, Mgr.); 33 E. Twohig, Suite 302, San Angelo 76903, 915-653-3971 (Jo Powell-Brooks, Dir.); 211 E. Main St. #318, Roundrock 78664, 512-218-4221.

TWENTY-SECOND DISTRICT

Tom DeLay (R)

District: Southwest Houston and suburbs including Fort Bend, Harris and Brazoria Counties. Population: 566,217—Black 8%, Asian 7%, Hispanic 16%. Politics: Leans Republican.

Born Apr. 8, 1947, Laredo; home, Sugar Land; University of Houston, B.S. 1970; Baptist; married (Christine), 1 child.

Elected 1984. Career: Owner, Albo Pest Control; Tex. House of Reps., 1978–84.

Committees: (1) Appropriations.

Election Results: 1992 DeLay 146,639 (68%); Richard Konrad (D) 67,520 (32%). 1990 DeLay (71%). 1988 DeLay (67%).

Interest Group Ratings:

ADA	ACU	COPE	COC
05	100	08	71

LCV	NTLC	CFA	ASC
00	100	13	100

Office: 407 CHOB 20515, 202-225-5951 (Kenneth Carroll, AA). DISTRICT OFFICE: 12603 S.W. Freeway, Suite 285, Stafford 77477, 713-240-3700 (Janice Reynolds, Dist. Dir.)

TWENTY-THIRD DISTRICT

Henry Bonilla (R)

District: Southwest San Antonio suburbs to the border including city of Laredo. Population: 566,217—Black 3%, Hispanic 63%, Other 22%. Politics: Democratic.

Born Jan. 2, 1954, San Antonio; home, San Antonio; University of Texas, B.A. 1976; Roman Catholic; married (Deborah), 2 children.

Elected 1992. Career: Television Reporter, 1976–80; Asst. Press Sec. Gov. Thornburgh (Pa.); News Producer WABC (New York), 1982–85; News Dir. WTAF (Philadelphia), 1985–86; Producer KENS (San Antonio), 1986–92.

Committees: (1) Appropriations.

Election Results: 1992 Bonilla 98,012 (61%); Albert Bustamante (D- Incumbent) 63,496 (39%).

Interest Group Ratings:
None—Freshman

Office: 1529 LHOB 20515, 202-225-4511 (Steve Ruhlen, AA). DISTRICT OFFICES: 11120 Wurzbach Suite 300, San Antonio 78230, 210-697-9055 (Phil Ricks, Dist. Dir.); 1300 Matamoros St. Suite 113B, Loredo 78040, 210-726-4682 (Patricia Zuniga, Rep.); Fed. Courthouse Bldg. 111 E. Broadway Suite 101, Del Rio 78840, 210-774-6547 (Ida Nino, Rep.); 4400 N. Big Spring Suite 211, Midland 79705, 915-686-8833 (Melissa Columbus, Rep.)

TWENTY-FOURTH DISTRICT

Martin Frost (D)

District: South Dallas and some western suburbs. Population: 566,217—Black 19%, Hispanic 22%. Politics: Democratic.

Born Jan. 1, 1942, Glendale, Calif.; home, Dallas; University of Mo., B.A., B.J. 1964, Georgetown University, J.D. 1970; Jewish; married (Valerie), 3 children.

Elected 1978. Career: Reporter, 1964–65; Staffwriter, *CQ Weekly Report*, 1965–67; Clerk, U.S. Dist. Judge Sarah T. Hughes, 1970–71; Practicing atty., 1972–78.

Committees: (1) House Administration; (2) Rules.

Election Results: 1992 Frost 104,167 (60%); Steve Masterson (R) 70,036 (40%). 1990 Frost (Unopposed). 1988 Frost (93%).

Interest Group Ratings:

ADA	ACU	COPE	COC
75	25	73	57

LCV	NTLC	CFA	ASC
56	00	60	90

Office: 2459 RHOB 20515, 202-225-3605 (Matt Angle, AA). DISTRICT OFFICES: 1319 NCNB Tower, 400 S. Zang Blvd., Dallas 75208, 214-767-2816 (Cinda Crawford, Dist. Dir.); 3020 S.E. Loop #820, Ft. Worth 76140, 817-293-9231; 318 W. Main St. #102, Arlington 76076, 817-795-3291 (Mike Spears, Rep.)

TWENTY-FIFTH DISTRICT

Michael A. Andrews (D)

District: South Houston and southeast suburbs. Population: 566,217—Black 27%, Hispanic 17%. Politics: Leans Democratic.

Born Feb. 7, 1944, Houston; home, Houston; University of Tex., B.A. 1967, Southern Methodist University, J.D. 1970; United Methodist; married (Ann), 2 children.

Elected 1982. Career: Law clerk, U.S. Dist. Judge for Southern Dist. of Texas, 1970–72; Asst. D.A., Harris Cty., Tex., 1972–76; Practicing atty., 1976–82.

Committees: (1) Ways & Means; (2) Budget; (3) Joint Economic Committee.

Election Results: 1992 Andrews 97,656 (59%); Dolly McKenna (R) 68,407 (41%). 1990 Andrews (Unopposed). 1988 Andrews (71%).

Interest Group Ratings:

ADA	ACU	COPE	COC
70	38	55	63

LCV	NTLC	CFA	ASC
38	20	80	100

Office: 303 CHOB 20515, 202-225-7508 (Ann Rowan, Chief-of-staff.). DISTRICT OFFICES: 12102 Fed. Bldg., 515 Rusk, Houston 77002, 713-229-2244 (vacant, Rep.); 1001 E. Southmore, Suite 810, Pasadena 77503, 713-473-4334 (Joseph Jiamfortone, Dist. Dir.)

TWENTY-SIXTH DISTRICT

Richard Keith Armey (R)

District: Dallas–Fort Worth suburbs including Carrollton. Population: 566,217—Black 4%, Asian 4%, Hispanic 9%. Politics: Leans Republican.

Born July 7, 1940, Cando, N.Dak.; home, Copper Canyon; Jamestown College, B.A. 1963, University of N.Dak., M.A. 1964, University of Okla., Ph.D. 1969; Presbyterian; married (Susan), 5 children.

Elected 1984. Career: Instr., University of Mont., 1964, University of Okla., 1965–66, Prof., West Tex. State University, 1967, Austin College, 1968–71, North Tex. State University, 1972–74, Chm., Econ. Dept., 1977–84.

Committees: (1) Budget; (2) Education & Labor.

Election Results: 1992 Armey 150,209 (73%); John Wayne Caton (D) 55,237 (27%). 1990 Armey (70%). 1988 Armey (69%).

Interest Group Ratings:

ADA	ACU	COPE	COC
00	100	08	Tk

LCV	NTLC	CFA	ASC
00	100	07	100

Office: 301 CHOB 20515, 202-225-7772 (Kerry Knott, AA). DISTRICT OFFICE: 9901 Valley Ranch Parkway E., Irving 75063, 214-556-2500 (Jean Campbell, Dist. Dir.)

TWENTY-SEVENTH DISTRICT

Solomon P. Ortiz (D)

District: Southern Gulf Coast counties including cities of Corpus Christi and Brownsville. Population: 566,217—Black 2%, Hispanic 66%, Other 18%. Politics: Democratic.

Born June 3, 1937, Robstown; home, Corpus Christi; Del Mar College, Institute of Applied Science, 1962, National Sherriffs' Training Institute, 1977; United Methodist; divorced, 2 children.

Elected 1982. Career: Army, 1960–62; Nueces Cty. Constable, 1965–68, Commissioner, 1969–76, Sheriff, 1977–82.

Committees: (1) Armed Services; (2) Merchant Marine & Fisheries.

Election Results: 1992 Ortiz 87,223 (57%); Jay Kimbrough (R) 66,449 (43%). 1990 Ortiz (Unopposed). 1988 Ortiz (Unopposed).

Interest Group Ratings:

ADA	ACU	COPE	COC
60	40	83	75

LCV	NTLC	CFA	ASC
19	10	87	80

Office: 2136 RHOB 20515, 202-225-7742 (Florencio Rendon, AA). DISTRICT OFFICES: 3649 Leopard, Suite 510, Corpus Christi 78408, 512-883-5868 (Mary Clary, Dist. Mgr.); 3505 Boca Chica Blvd., Suite 438, Brownsville 78521, 512-541-1242 (vacant, Mgr.)

TWENTY-EIGHTH DISTRICT

Frank Tejeda (D)

District: Parts of San Antonio and southern counties. Population: 566,217—Black 9%, Hispanic 60%, Other 22%. Politics: Democratic.

Born Oct. 2, 1945, San Antonio; home, San Antonio; Saint Mary's University, B.A. 1970, University of Calif., J.D. 1974, Harvard, M.P.A. 1980, Yale, LL.M. 1989; Roman Catholic; divorced, 3 children.

Elected 1992. Career: State Rep. 1977–86; State Sen., 1987–92.

Committees: (1) Armed Services; (2) Veteran Affairs.

Election Results: 1992 Tejeda 122,068 (87%); David Slatter (Lib) 18,158 (13%).

Interest Group Ratings:
None—Freshman

Office: 323 CHOB 20515, 202-225-1640 (Jeffery Mindelsohn, AA). DISTRICT OFFICE: 1313 S.E. Military Dr. #115, San Antonio 78214, 210-924-7383 (Frances Ruiz, Rep.)

TWENTY-NINTH DISTRICT

Gene Green (D)

District: Parts of Houston and suburbs including Pasadena and Baytown. Population: 566,217—Black 10%, Hispanic 61%, Other 34%. Politics: Democratic.

Born Oct. 17, 1947, Houston; home, Houston; University of Houston, B.S. 1971; Methodist; married (Helen), 2 children.

Elected 1992. Career: State Rep., 1974–85; State Sen., 1986–92.

Committees: (1) Education & Labor; (2) Merchant Marine & Fisheries.

Election Results: 1992 Green 63,192 (66%); Clark Ervin 32,754 (34%).

Interest Group Ratings:
None—Freshman

Office: 1004 LHOB 20515, 202-225-1688 (Moses Mercado, AA). DISTRICT OFFICE: 5502 Lawndale, Houston 77023, 713-923-9961 (Rhonda Jackson, Rep.)

THIRTIETH DISTRICT

Eddie Bernice Johnson (D)

District: Parts of Dallas and suburbs including parts of Irvine and Arlington. Population: 566,217—Black 50%, Hispanic 17%. Politics: Democratic.

Born Dec. 1935, Waco; home, Dallas; Notre Dame University, Prof. Nursing 1955, Texas Christian, B.S. 1967, Southern Methodist, M.P.A. 1976; Baptist; divorced, 1 child.

Elected 1992. Career: Nurse 1957–72; Exec. Asst. Neiman–Marcus, 1972–75; Consultant Zales Corp., 1976–77; State Rep., 1972–77; Dept. of HEW., 1977–81; Visiting Nurse Assn. of Tex., 1981–87; State Sen., 1986–92.

Committees: (1) Public Works & Transportation; (2) Science, Space & Technology.

Election Results: 1992 Johnson 107,830 (74%); Lucy Cain (R) 37,853 (26%).

Interest Group Ratings:
None—Freshman

Office: 1721 LHOB 20515, 202-225-8885 (Lee Nobles, AA). DISTRICT OFFICE: 2515 McKinney Ave. #1565, Dallas 75201, 214-922-8885 (Lisa Hembry, Dist. Mgr.)

UTAH

The big political news of 1992 in this most Republican of states was the election of two Democrats to Congress. This has breathed new life in the Utah Democratic Party. But this new confidence extends only so far, and not as far as believing that GOP Sen. Orrin Hatch can be upset in 1994.

1992 PRESIDENTIAL ELECTION: (5 Electoral votes): Clinton (D) 182,850 (25%); Bush (I) 320,950 (43%); Perot (I) 202,823 (27%); Gritz (Pop) 28,392 (4%); Marrou (Lib) 1,913; Hagelin (NLP) 1,324; LaRouche (I) 1,099; Fulani (NAP) 419; Phillips (AmTax) 392; Smith (Amer) 290; Warren (SocWks) 277; Daniels (P&F) 187; Brisben (Soc) 160. 1988 Bush 426,858 (67%); Dukakis 206,853 (33%).

SENATORS

Robert Bennett (R)

Born Sept. 18, 1933, Salt Lake City; home, Salt Lake City; University of Utah, B.A. 1957; Mormon; married (Joyce McKay), 6 children.

Elected 1992, seat up 1998. Career: CEO The Franklin Institute, 1984–92.

Committees: (1) Banking, Housing & Urban Affairs; (2) Energy & Natural Resources.

Election Results: 1992 Bennett 418,309 (58%); Wayne Owens (D) 300,404 (42%).

Interest Group Ratings:
None—Freshman

Office: 241 DSOB 20510, 202-224-5444 (Greg Hopkins, AA). STATE OFFICES: 4225 Fed. Bldg. 125 S. State Salt Lake City 84138, 801-524-5933; 1410 Fed. Bldg. 324 25th St. Ogden 84401, 801-625-5676; 51 S. University #310, Provo 84601, 801-379-2525; 196 E. Tabernacle, St. George 84770, 801-628-5514.

Orrin Grant Hatch (R)

Born Mar. 22, 1934, Pittsburgh, Pa.; home, Midvale; Brigham Young University, B.S. 1959, University of Pittsburgh, LL.B. 1962; Mormon; married (Elaine), 6 children.

Elected 1976, seat up 1994. Career: Practicing atty., 1963–76.

Committees: (1) Judiciary (Ranking Member); (2) Labor & Human Resources; (3) Finance; (4) Select Committee on Intelligence.

Election Results: 1988 Hatch 430,089 (67%); Brian Moss (D) 203,364 (32%). 1982 Hatch (58%).

Interest Group Ratings:

ADA	ACU	COPE	COC
05	96	17	100

LCV	NTLC	CFA	ASC
00	94	33	100

Office: 135 RSOB 20510, 202-224-5251 (Wendy Higginbotham, AA). STATE OFFICES: 3438 Fed. Bldg., 125 S. State St., Salt Lake City 84138, 801-524-4380 (Ronald Madsen St. AA); 109 Fed. Bldg., 88 W. 100 N., Provo 84601, 801-375-7881 (Catherine Johnson, Dir.); 1410 Fed. Bldg., 325 25th St., Ogden 84401, 801-625-5672 (Norma Holmgren, Dir.); 10 N. Main St., Cedar City 84720, 801-586-8435 (Jeannine Holt, Rep.)

REPRESENTATIVES

FIRST DISTRICT

James V. Hansen (R)

District: Western half of the state including Ogden. Population: 547,286—Hispanic 5%. Politics: Republican.

Born Aug. 14, 1932, Salt Lake City; home, Farmington; University of Utah, B.S. 1961; Mormon; married (Ann), 5 children.

Elected 1980. Career: Navy, Korea; Insurance co. exec.; Farmington City Cncl., 1966–72; Utah House of Reps., 1972–80, Speaker, 1978–80.

Committees: (1) Armed Services; (2) Natural Resources;(3) Select Committee on Intelligence.

Election Results: 1992 Hansen 159,601 (65%); Ron Holt (D) 68,549 (28%); William Lawrence (I) 16,463 (7%). 1990 Hansen (54%). 1988 Hansen (60%).

Interest Group Ratings:

ADA	ACU	COPE	COC
05	100	18	100

LCV	NTLC	CFA	ASC
06	100	13	100

Office: 2466 RHOB 20515, 202-225-0453 (Nancee Blockinger, Chief of Staff). DISTRICT OFFICES: 1017 Fed. Bldg., 324 25th St., Ogden 84401, 801-393-8362 (Peter Jenks, St. AA); 435 E. Tabernacle, Suite 305, St. George 84770, 801-628-1071 (Rick Arial, Rep.)

SECOND DISTRICT

Karen Shepherd (D)

District: Salt Lake City and county. Population: 574,241—Hispanic 5%. Politics: Mixed.

Born July 5, 1940, Silver City, N.Mex.; home, Salt Lake City; University of Utah, B.A. 1962, Brigham Young University, M.A. 1963; Protestant; married (Vincent), 2 children.

Elected 1992. Career: High School Teacher, 1964–74; Dir. Salt Lake Co. Social Services, 1975–78; Editor Network Magazine, 1978–84; President Webster Publishing, 1984–88; Dir. of Development University of Utah, 1988–90; State Sen., 1988–92.

Committees: (1) Public Works & Transportation; (2) Natural Resources.

Election Results: 1992 Shepherd 127,543 (52%); Enid Greene (R) 118,013 (48%).

Interest Group Ratings:
None—Freshman

Office: 414 CHOB 20515, 202-225-3011 (Michael Burke, AA). DISTRICT OFFICE: 2311 Bennett Fed. Bldg. 125 S. State St., Salt Lake City 84138, 801-524-4394 (Robyn Matheson, Rep.)

THIRD DISTRICT

William Orton (D)

District: Eastern half of the state including city of Provo. Population: 574,323—Native American 3%, Hispanic 5%. Politics: Republican.

Born Sept. 22, 1949, North Ogden; home, Provo; Brigham Young University, B.S., 1973, J.D., 1979; Mormon; single.

Elected 1990. Career: aide, U.S. House Ways & Means Comm., U.S. Sen. Finance Comm.

Committees: (1) Budget; (2) Banking, Finance & Urban Affairs.

Election Results: 1992 Orton 134,190 (62%); Richard Harrington (R) 83,104 (38%). 1990 Orton (62%).

Interest Group Ratings:

ADA	ACU	COPE	COC
55	56	42	63

LCV	NTLC	CFA	ASC
25	67	40	80

Office: 1122 LHOB 20515, 202-225-7751 (Sheldon Kinsel, AA). DISTRICT OFFICES: 55 S. Union, #317, Provo 84601, 801-379-2500; 3540 South 40th West #410, W. Valley City 84120, 801-964-5828 (Missy Larsen, Rep.)

VERMONT

Vermont continues to be a state that elects its officials without much regard to party label. In 1992, it reelected a Republican senator, elected a Democratic governor and reelected a Socialist congressman. In 1994 Republican Sen. James Jeffords is up for reelection. He does not expect much difficulty. One of the more interesting political stories here is the rise of Lt. Gov. Barbara Snelling, widow of former Gov. Dick Snelling. She is coming into her own and likely will be a political force in the future.

1992 PRESIDENTIAL ELECTION: (3 Electoral votes): Clinton (D) 130,607 (46%); Bush (R) 86,030 (30%); Perot (I) 64,452 (23%); Marrou (Lib) 390; Phillips (AmTax) 209; Hagelin (NLP) 181; Fulani (NAP) 171; Warren (SocWks) 43; LaRouche (I) 39. 1988 Bush 123,166 (51%); Dukakis 116,419 (49%).

SENATORS

Patrick Leahy (D)

Born Mar. 31, 1940, Montpelier; home, Burlington; St. Michael's College, B.A. 1961, Georgetown University, J.D. 1964; Roman Catholic; married (Marcelle), 3 children.

Elected 1974, seat up 1998. Career: Practicing atty., 1964–74; Chittenden Cty. States Atty., 1966–74.

Committees: (1) Agriculture, Nutrition & Forestry (Chairman); (2) Appropriations; (3) Judiciary.

Election Results: 1992 Leahy 145,653 (55%); James Douglas (R) 116,847 (45%). 1986 Leahy (63%). 1980 Leahy (50%)

Interest Group Ratings:

ADA	ACU	COPE	COC
100	00	100	10

LCV	NTLC	CFA	ASC
100	11	100	40

Office: 433 RSOB 20510, 202-224-4242 (Ellen Lovell, AA). STATE OFFICES: Cthse. Plaza, 199 Main St., Burlington 05401, 802-863-2525 (Thomas Davis, Dir.); 340 Fed. Bldg., Montpelier 05602, 802-229-0569 (Robert Paquin, Asst.)

James M. Jeffords (R)

Born May 11, 1934, Rutland; home, Rutland; Yale University, B.S.I.A. 1956, Harvard Univer-

sity, LL.B. 1962; Congregationalist; married (Elizabeth), 2 children.

Elected 1988, seat up 1994. Career: Navy, 1956–59; Practicing atty., Vt. Senate, 1967–68; Atty. Gen. of Vt., 1969–73; U.S. House of Reps., 1974–88.

Committees: (1) Labor & Human Resources; (2) Foreign Relations.

Election Results: 1988 Jeffords 163,183 (70%); Bill Gray (D) 71,460 (30%).

Interest Group Ratings:

ADA	ACU	COPE	COC
65	27	56	60

LCV	NTLC	CFA	ASC
75	18	75	60

Office: 513 HSOB 20510, 202-224-5141 (Susan Boardman-Russ, AA). STATE OFFICES: 138 Main St., Montpelier 05602, 802-223-5273 (Susan Butler, Dist. Mgr.); 30 Airport Rd. S., Rm. 7, Burlington 05403, 802-951-6732 (Diana Harrington, Mgr.); 2 S. Main St., Rutland 05701, 802-773-3879 (Mary Sheldon, Mgr.)

REPRESENTATIVE AT LARGE

Bernard Sanders (Soc)

District: Entire state. Population: 562,758. Politics: Leans Republican.

Born Sept. 8, 1941, Brooklyn, N.Y.; home, Burlington; University of Chicago, B.A., 1964; Jewish; married (Jane), 4 children.

Elected 1990. Career: College teacher, free lance writer; mayor, Burlington, 1981–88.

Committees: (1) Banking, Finance & Urban Affairs; (2) Government Operations.

Election Results: 1992 Sanders 152,551 (60%); Lewis Young (D) 20,989 (8%); Tim Philbin (R) 82,443 (32%). 1990 Sanders (56%).

Interest Group Ratings:

ADA	ACU	COPE	COC
95	00	100	13

LCV	NTLC	CFA	ASC
100	15	100	10

Office: 213 CHOB 20515, 202-225-4115 (Doug Boucher, AA). DISTRICT OFFICE: 1 Church St. 2nd Floor, Burlington 05401, 802-862-0697 (Anthony Pollina, Rep.)

VIRGINIA

Few states have changed more politically than Virginia in the 1980's. It went from a solidly conservative Republican state, to one which today is very mixed thanks to the influx of Democrats into its northern counties which are suburbs of Washington, D.C. The state's congressional delegation has gone from 9-1 Republican to 7-4 Democratic. Over the past several years, Democratic Sen. Charles Robb has been beset with problems. He says he will run for reelection in 1994, and the biggest question is whether he will be challenged by his number one rival, Democratic Gov. Doug Wilder. Wilder himself faces a stiff reelection challenge in November, 1993.

1992 PRESIDENTIAL ELECTION: (13 Electoral votes): Clinton (D) 1,036,288 (41%); Bush (R) 1,148,332 (45%); Perot (I) 347,059 (14%); LaRouche (I) 11,691; Marrou (Lib) 5,619; Fulani (NAP) 3,119. 1988 Bush 1,305,131 (60%); Dukakis 860,767 (40%).

SENATORS

John W. Warner (R)

Born Feb. 18, 1927, Washington, D.C.; home, Atoka; Washington & Lee University, B.S. 1949, University of Va., LL.B. 1953; Episcopalian; divorced.

Elected 1978, seat up 1996. Career: Navy, WWII, USMC, Korea; Law Clerk to U.S. Crt. of Appeals Chf. Judge E. Barrett Prettyman, 1953–54; Practicing atty., 1954–56, 1960–69; Asst. U.S. Atty., 1956–60; Under Secy. of the U.S. Navy, 1969–72, Secy., 1972–74; Dir., Amer. Rev. Bicentennial Comm., 1974–76.

Committees: (1) Armed Services; (2) Environment & Public Works; (3) Select Committee on Intelligence.

Election Results: 1990 Warner 872,764 (82%); Nancy Spannaus (I) 196,257 (18%). 1984 Warner (70%).

Interest Group Ratings:

ADA	ACU	COPE	COC
20	74	17	100

LCV	NTLC	CFA	ASC
08	83	25	90

Office: 225 RSOB 20510, 202-224-2023 (Susan Magill, AA). STATE OFFICES: 1100 E. Main St., 2nd Fl., Richmond 23219, 804-771-2579 (Paul Powell, St. Dir.); 490 World Trade Ctr, Norfolk 23510, 804-441-3079 (Loretta Tate, Mgr.); 235 Fed. Bldg., 180 E. Main St., Abingdon 24210, 703-628-8158 (Cathie Gollehon, Mgr.); 1003 Dominion Bk. Bldg., 213 S. Jefferson, Roanoke 24011, 703-982-4676 (Camellia Crowder, Rep.)

Charles S. Robb (D)

Born June 26, 1939, Phoenix, Ariz.; home, McLean; University of Wis., B.B.A. 1961, University of Va., J.D. 1973; Episcopalian; married (Lynda Bird), 3 children.

Elected 1988, seat up 1994. Career: U.S. Marine Corps 1961–70; Clerk, U.S. Court of Appeals, 1973; Practicing atty., 1974–77; Lt. Governor of Va., 1978–82; Governor of Va., 1972–86.

Committees: (1) Joint Economic Committee; (2) Commerce, Science & Transportation; (3) Foreign Relations; (4) Armed Services.

Election Results: 1988 Robb 1,474,086 (71%); Maurice Dawkins (R) 593,652 (29%).

Interest Group Ratings:

ADA	ACU	COPE	COC
60	30	75	30

LCV	NTLC	CFA	ASC
67	17	92	100

Office: 493 RSOB 20510, 202-224-4024 (Roland McKelroy, AA). STATE OFFICES: 1001 E. Broad St., Richmond 23219, 804-771-2221 (Christine Bridge, St. Dir.); 999 Waterside Dr., Suite 107, Norfolk 23510, 804-441-3124 (Tyrone Hicks, Dpty. St. Dir.); Dominion Bk. Bldg., Main St., Clintwood 24288, 703-926-4104 (Jimmy O'Quinn, Rep.)

REPRESENTATIVES

FIRST DISTRICT

Herbert H. Bateman (R)

District: Wide ranging district in the southeast part of the state including parts of cities of

Newport News and Hampton. Population: 562,677—Black 18%. Politics: Mixed, but leans Republican.

Born Aug. 7, 1928, Elizabeth City, N.C.; home, Newport News; College of William & Mary, B.A. 1949, Georgetown University School of Law, J.D. 1956; Presbyterian; married (Laura), 2 children.

Elected 1982. Career: Teacher, Hampton School, 1949–51; Air Force, 1951–53; Law Clerk, U.S. Court of Appeals, 1956–57; Practicing atty., 1957–82; Va. State Senate, 1968–82.

Committees: (1) Armed Services; (2) Merchant Marine & Fisheries.

Election Results: 1992 Bateman 132,685 (60%); Andrew Fox (D) 89,353 (40%). 1990 Bateman (51%). 1988 Bateman (73%).

Interest Group Ratings:

ADA	ACU	COPE	COC
10	84	17	88

LCV	NTLC	CFA	ASC
06	95	33	100

Office: 2350 RHOB 20515, 202-225-4261 (Dan Scandling, AA). DISTRICT OFFICES: 739 Thimble Shoals Boulevard, Newport News 23606, 804-873-1132 (Dee Benton, Dist. Dir.); 4712 Southpoint Pkwy., Fredericksburg 22407, (Ruth Jessie, Rep.); P.O. Box 447, Accomac, 23301, 804-787-7836 (Suzanne Beasley, Asst.)

SECOND DISTRICT

Owen B. Pickett (D)

District: Southeast corner of the state, including parts of Norfolk and Virginia Beach. Population: 562,276—Black 17%, Asian 4%, Hispanic 3%. Politics: Leans Democratic.

Born Aug. 31, 1930, Richmond; home, Virginia Beach; Va. Polytechnic Institute and State University, B.S. 1952, University of Richmond, LL.B. 1955; Baptist; married (Sybil), 3 children.

Elected 1986. Career: Practicing atty; Va. House of Delegates, 1972–86.

Committees: (1) Armed Services; (2) Merchant Marine & Fisheries.

Election Results: 1992 Pickett 99,127 (56%); Jim

Chapman (R) 77,789 (44%). 1990 Pickett (78%). 1988 Pickett (61%).

Interest Group Ratings:

ADA	ACU	COPE	COC
35	52	25	88

LCV	NTLC	CFA	ASC
19	55	33	100

Office: 2430 RHOB 20515, 202-225-4215 (Jeanne Evans, AA). DISTRICT OFFICES: 112 E. Little Creek Rd. #216, Norfolk 23505, 804-583-5892 (Jeanne Evans, Dist. Dir.); 2710 Virginia Blvd., Virginia Beach 23452, 804-486-3710

THIRD DISTRICT

Robert C. Scott (D)

District: Eastern central part of the state including parts of Norfolk and Richmond. Population: 562,431—Black 64%. Politics: Democratic.

Born Apr. 30, 1947, Washington, D.C., home, Newport News; Harvard, B.A. 1969, Boston College, J.D. 1973; Episcopalian; divorced.

Elected 1992. Career: Attorney, 1973–92; State Rep., 1978–81; State Sen., 1982-92.

Committees: (1) Education & Labor; (2) Judiciary; (3) Science, Space & Technology.

Election Results: 1992 Scott 130,998 (79%); Daniel Jenkins (R) 35,348 (21%).

Interest Group Ratings:
None—Freshman

Office: 501 CHOB 20515, 202-225-8351 (Tamara Copeland, Leg. Asst.) DISTRICT OFFICE: P.O. Box 56, Newport News 23607, 804-380-1000

FOURTH DISTRICT

Norman Sisisky (D)

District: Southeast part of the state including cities of Chesapeake and Portsmouth. Population: 562,466—Black 32%. Politics: Leans Democratic.

Born June 9, 1927, Baltimore, Md.; home, Petersburg; Va. Commonwealth University, B.S. 1949; Jewish; married (Rhoda), 4 children.

Elected 1982. Career: Navy, 1945–46; Pres.,

Petersburg Pepsi–Cola Bottling Co.; Va. House of Delegates, 1974–82.

Committees: (1) Armed Services; (2) Small Business.

Election Results: 1992 Sisisky 144,965 (69%); Tony Zevgolis (R) 66,405 (31%). 1990 Sisisky (78%). 1988 Sisisky (Unopposed).

Interest Group Ratings:

ADA	ACU	COPE	COC
55	48	55	88

LCV	NTLC	CFA	ASC
13	44	47	100

Office: 2352 CHOB 20515, 202-225-6365 (Jan Faircloth, AA). DISTRICT OFFICES: 309 County St., Suite 204, Portsmouth 23704, 804-393-2068 (vacant, Dist. Rep.); 425-H S. Main St., Emporia 23847, 804-634-5575 (Rick Franklin, Rep.); 43 River Rd., Petersburg 23805, 804-732-2544 (Rick Franklin, Rep.)

FIFTH DISTRICT

Lewis Franklin Payne, Jr. (D)

District: Southern tobacco counties including population center of Danville. Population: 562,268—Black 25%. Politics: Leans Democratic.

Born Jul. 9, 1945, Amherst; home, Nellysford; Va. Military Institute, B.S. 1967, University of Va., Colgate, M.B.A. 1973; Presbyterian, married (Susan), 4 children.

Elected 1988. Career: Engineering Assoc., C&P Telephone Co., 1970–71; Planning & Dev. Mgr., Wintergreen, Va., 1973–75; Pres., Wintergreen Devlopment, Inc., Chm. of Board, 1985–88.

Committees: (1) Ways & Means.

Election Results: 1992 Payne 132,867 (69%); Bill Hurlburt (R) 59,756 (31%). 1990 Payne (Unopposed). 1988 Payne (54%).

Interest Group Ratings:

ADA	ACU	COPE	COC
65	32	50	63

LCV	NTLC	CFA	ASC
38	30	60	100

Office: 1119 LHOB 20515, 202-225-4711 (Jim Johnson, AA). DISTRICT OFFICES: 301 P.O. Bldg, Danville 24541, 804-792-1280 (Jennifer Moorefield, Mgr.); Fed. Bldg., 103 S. Main St., Farmville 23901, 804-392-8331 (Margaret Watkins, Mgr.); 103 E. Water St. #302, Charlottesville 22902, 804-295-6372 (Greg Kelly, Mgr.)

SIXTH DISTRICT

Robert W. Goodlatte (R)

District: Blue Ridge portion of the western part of the state including city of Roanoke. Population: 562,572—Black 11%. Politics: Leans Democratic.

Born Sep. 22, 1952, Holyoke, Mass.; home, Roanoke; Bates College, B.A. 1974, Washington & Lee, J.D. 1977; Christian Scientist; married (Maryellen), 2 children.

Elected 1992. Career: Office Manager Rep. Butler, 1977-79; Attorney, 1979–92.

Committees: (1) Agriculture; (2) Judiciary.

Election Results: 1992 Goodlatte 126,590 (60%); Stephen Musselwhite (D) 83,967 (40%).

Interest Group Ratings:
None—Freshman

Office: 214 CHOB 20515, 202-225-5431 (Tim Phillips, AA). DISTRICT OFFICES: 540 Crestar Plaza, 10 Franklin St. S.E., Roanoke 24011, 703-982-4672 (Steve Landes, Dist. Dir.); 114 N. Central Ave., Staunton 24401, 703-885-3861 (Pete Larkin, Rep.); 2 S. Main St. Suite A, Harrisonburg 22801, 703-432-2391 (Phoebe Orebaugh, Rep.); 916 Main St. Suite 300, Lynchburg 24504, (Clarkie Jester, Rep.)

SEVENTH DISTRICT

Thomas Jerome Bliley, Jr. (R)

District: Parts of Richmond and counties to the North. Population: 562,643—Black 10%. Politics: Leans Republican.

Born Jan. 28, 1932, Chesterfield; home, Richmond; Georgetown University, B.A. 1952; Roman Catholic; married (Mary Virginia), 2 children.

Elected 1980. Career: Navy, 1952–55; Owner, funeral home, 1955–80; Richmond City Cncl., 1968, Vice Mayor, Richmond, 1968–70, Mayor, 1970–77; Pres., Joseph W. Bliley Co., 1972–80.

Committees: (1) District of Columbia; (2) Energy & Commerce.

Election Results: 1992 Bliley 209,919 (83%); Gerald Berg (I) 42,971 (17%). 1990 Bliley (66%). 1988 Bliley (Unopposed).

Interest Group Ratings:

ADA	ACU	COPE	COC
15	96	25	86

LCV	NTLC	CFA	ASC
00	89	13	100

Office: 2241 RHOB 20515, 202-225-2815 (Linda Pedigo, AA). DISTRICT OFFICES: 4914 Fitzhugh Ave., Suite 101, Richmond 23230, 804-771-2809 (Karen Marcus, Dist. Cord.); 763 Madison Rd. #207, Culpepper 22701, 703-825-8960 (Anita Essalih, Rep.)

EIGHTH DISTRICT

James P. Moran, Jr. (D)

District: Washington, D.C. suburbs in southern Fairfax County including city of Alexandria. Population: 562,484—Black 13%, Asian 7%, Hispanic 9%. Politics: Leans Democratic.

Born May 14, 1945, Buffalo, N.Y.; home, Alexandria; Holy Cross, B.A., 1967, University of Pittsburgh, M.A., 1970; Roman Catholic; married (Mary), 4 children.

Elected 1990. Career: Investment Banker; Alexandria City Cncl., 1979–84; vice–mayor 1982–84; mayor 1985–1990.

Committees: (1) Appropriations.

Election Results: 1992 Moran 135,698 (57%); Kyle McSlarrow (R) 101,447 (43%). 1990 Moran (52%).

Interest Group Ratings:

ADA	ACU	COPE	COC
80	12	73	50

LCV	NTLC	CFA	ASC
63	05	73	60

Office: 430 CHOB 20515, 202-225-4376 (Mame Reiley, Chief-of-staff). DISTRICT OFFICE: 5115 Franconia Red., Alexandria 22310, 703-971-4700, (Susie Warner, Dist. Dir.)

NINTH DISTRICT

Rick Boucher (D)

District: Far southwest corner of the state including towns of Blacksburg and Bristol. Population: 562,380. Politics: Mixed, but currently leans Democratic.

Born Aug. 1, 1946, Abingdon; home, Abingdon; Roanoke College, B.A. 1968, University of Va., J.D. 1971; United Methodist; single.

Elected 1982. Career: Practicing atty., 1971–82; Va. Senate, 1975–1982.

Committees: (1) Energy & Commerce; (2) Judiciary; (3) Science, Space & Technology.

Election Results: 1992 Boucher 132,915 (63%); L. Garrett Weddle (R) 78,014 (37%). 1990 Boucher (Unopposed). 1988 Boucher (63%).

Interest Group Ratings:

ADA	ACU	COPE	COC
90	08	82	38

LCV	NTLC	CFA	ASC
44	00	87	30

Office: 2245 RHOB 20515, 202-225-3861 (Ridge Schuyler, AA). DISTRICT OFFICES: 188 E. Main St., Abingdon 24210, 703-628-1145 (Donna Stanley, Dist. Adm.); 311 Shawnee Ave. E., Big Stone Gap 24319, 703-523-5450 (Janet Cantrell, Asst.); 112 N. Washington Ave., Pulaski 24301, 703-980-4310 (Becki Gunn, Asst.)

TENTH DISTRICT

Frank R. Wolf (R)

District: Far north of the state including Washington, D.C. suburbs in Fairfax and Loudon counties. Population: 562,664—Black 6%, Asian 3%, Hispanic 2%. Politics: Leans Republican.

Born Jan. 30, 1939, Philadelphia, Pa.; home, Vienna; Pa. State University, B.A. 1961; Georgetown University, J.D. 1965; Presbyterian; married (Carolyn), 5 children.

Elected 1980. Career: Army (Reserves), 1962–67; Legis. Asst. to U.S. Rep. Edward Biester, 1968–71; Asst. to Sec. of Interior Rogers Morton, 1971–74; Dpty. Asst. Secy., U.S. Dept. of Interior, 1974–75; Practicing atty.; 1975–80.

Committees: (1) Appropriations.

Election Results: 1992 Wolf 143,778 (65%); Raymond Vickery (D) 75,744 (35%). 1990 Wolf (62%). 1988 Wolf (68%).

Interest Group Ratings:

ADA	ACU	COPE	COC
20	84	42	88

LCV	NTLC	CFA	ASC
13	95	33	100

Office: 104 CHOB 20515, 202-225-5136 (Charles White, AA). DISTRICT OFFICES: 13873 Park Center Rd., Herndon 22071, 703-709-5800 (Judith McCary, Dir.); 110 N. Cameron St., Winchester 22601, 703-667-0990 (Donna Crowley, Asst.)

ELEVENTH DISTRICT

Leslie L. Byrne (D)

District: Washington, D.C. suburbs in Fairfax and Prince William counties. Population: 562,497 —Black 8%, Asian 8%, Hispanic 7%. Politics: Mixed.

Born Oct. 27, 1946, Salt Lake City, Utah; home, Annandale; Roman Catholic; married (Larry), 2 children.

Elected 1992. Career: Founder Quintech Assoc., 1984–92; State Rep., 1985–92.

Committees: (1) Public Works & Transportation; (2) Post Office and Civil Service.

Election Results: 1992 Byrne 113,461 (52%); Henry Butler (R) 103,091 (48%).

Interest Group Ratings:
None—Freshman

Office: 1609 LHOB 20515, 202-225-1492 (Maggie Luca, AA). DISTRICT OFFICE: 7620 Little River Turnpike, Annandale 22003, 703-750-1992 (Janet Reaves, Rep.)

WASHINGTON

The surprise senate victory of Democrat Patty Murray was the State of Washington's big political story of 1992. That coupled with Bill Clinton's victory, the gubernatorial victory of Democrat Mike Lowry, and close wins in some marginal congressional districts is said by Washington Democrats to show the state is moving into the Democratic column. That theory will be quickly tested as GOP Sen. Slade Gorton runs for reelection in 1994. Gorton has never had a deep base of support, and could well be vulnerable. A lot will depend on the strength of the challenger the Democrats can find.

1992 PRESIDENTIAL ELECTION: (11 Electoral votes): Clinton (D) 856,056 (44%); Bush (R) 610,166 (31%); Perot (I) 470,491 (24%); Marrou (Lib) 6,422; Gritz (Pop) 4,037; Hagelin (NLP) 2,088; Phillips (AmTax) 1,882; Fulani (NAP) 1,538; Daniels (P&F) 995; LaRouche (I) 692; Warren (SocWks) 443. 1988 Dukakis 844,554 (51%); Bush 800,182 (49%).

SENATORS

Patty Murray (D)

Born Oct. 11, 1950, Bothell; home, Seattle; Washington State University, B.A. 1972; Roman Catholic; married (Rob), 2 children.

Elected 1992. Seat up 1998. Career: Lobbyist 1981–88; Wash. State Sen., 1988–92.

Committees: (1) Appropriations; (2) Banking & Urban Affairs; (3) Rules & Administration.

Election Results: 1992 Murray 1,036,845 (55%); Rod Chandler (R) 857,610 (45%).

Interest Group Ratings:
None—Freshman

Office: 302 HSOB 20510, 202-224-2621 (Michael Timmeny, AA). STATE OFFICE: 2988 Jackson Fed. Bldg. 915 2nd Ave., Seattle 98174, 206-553-5545 (Michael Temple, Rep.)

Slade Gorton (R)

Born Jan. 8, 1928, Chicago, Ill.; home, Olympia; Dartmouth, A.B. 1950; Columbia University, LL.B. 1953; Episcopalian; married (Sally), 3 children.

Elected 1988, seat up 1994. Career: Army 1946–47; Air Force 1953–56; U.S. House of Representatives, 1956–69; Atty. Gen. of Wash., 1969–80; U.S. Senate, 1981–85.

Committees: (1) Appropriations; (2) Commerce, Science & Transportation; (3) Select Committee on Intelligence; (4) Budget; (5) Select Committee on Indian Affairs.

Election Results: 1988 Gorton 944,359 (51%); Michael Lowry (D) 904,183 (49%).

Interest Group Ratings:

ADA	ACU	COPE	COC
25	72	36	90

LCV	NTLC	CFA	ASC
17	72	33	90

Office: 730 HSOB 20510, 202-224-3441 (Jack McRae, AA). STATE OFFICES: 3206 Fed. Bldg. 915 Second Ave., Seattle 98174, 206-442-0350 (Veda Jellan, Dir.); 697 U.S. Crthse, W. 920 Riverside Dr., Spokane 99201, 509-456-2507 (Dan Kirschner, Dir.); Fed. Bldg., 500 W. 12th St, Vancouver 98660, 206-696-7838 (Cathy Treadwell, Dir.); 119 Morris Bldg., 23 S. Wenatchee Ave., Wenatchee 98670 509-663-2118 (Don Moos, Dir.); 402 E. Yakima Ave., Yakima 98901, 509-353-2507 (Sandra Linde, Rep.); 1530 Grand Ridge Blvd. #212, Kennewick 99336, 509-783-0640 (Susanne Heaston, Rep.)

REPRESENTATIVES

FIRST DISTRICT

Maria Cantwell (D)

District: Northern Seattle and suburbs. Population: 540,745—Asian 5%. Politics: Mixed.

Born Oct. 13, 1958, Indianapolis, Ind.; home, Mountlake Terrace; Miami of Ohio, B.A. 1980; Roman Catholic; single.

Elected 1992. Career: State Rep., 1987–92; Public Relations Consultant, 1980–92.

Committees: (1) Foreign Affairs; (2) Public Works & Transportation.

Election Results: 1992 Cantwell 128,885 (57%); Gary Nelson (R) 96,540 (43%).

Interest Group Ratings:
None—Freshman

Office: 1520 LHOB 20515, 202-225-6311 (Lisa Piccione, Rep.). DISTRICT OFFICE: 21905 64th Ave. W., Mountlake Terrace 98043, 206-640-0233 (Michael Daller, Rep.)

SECOND DISTRICT

Al Swift (D)

District: Northwest portion of the state including part of Olympic peninsula and the city of Everett. Population: 540,739—Native American 2%, Hispanic 3%. Politics: Leans Democratic.

Born Sept. 12, 1935, Tacoma; home, Bellingham; Whitman College, 1953–55, Central Wash. University, B.A. 1957; Unitarian; married (Paula), 2 children.

Elected 1978. Career: Broadcaster & Director of Public Affairs, KVOS–TV, Bellingham, Wash., 1957–62, 1969–77; Administrative Assistant to U.S. Representative Lloyd Meeds, 1965–69 & 1977.

Committees: (1) Energy & Commerce; (2) House Administration.

Election Results: 1992 Swift 116,118 (56%); Jack Metcalf (R) 89,923 (44%). 1990 Swift (55%). 1988 Swift (Unopposed).

Interest Group Ratings:

ADA	ACU	COPE	COC
90	04	75	25

LCV	NTLC	CFA	ASC
71	00	87	40

Office: 1502 LHOB 20515, 202-225-2605 (Janet Thiessen, AA). DISTRICT OFFICES: 302 Fed. Bldg., 3002 Colby, Everett 98201, 206-252-3188 (Jill McKinnie, Dir.); 308 Fed. Bldg., 104 West Magnolia, Bellingham 98225, 206-733-4500 (Andy Anderson, Dir.)

THIRD DISTRICT

Jolene Unsoeld (D)

District: Southwest corner of the state including cities of Olympia and Vancouver. Population: 540,745—Asian 2%, Hispanic 2%. Politics: Democratic.

Born Dec. 3, 1931, Corvallis, Oreg.; home, Olympia; Oreg. State University, 1949–51; widowed, 4 children.

Elected 1988. Career: Dir., English Language Institute, 1965–67; Wash. State legislature, 1984–88.

Committees: (1) Education & Labor; (2) Merchant Marine & Fisheries.

Election Results: 1992 Unsoeld 124,393 (56%); Pat Fiske (R) 96,773 (44%). 1990 Unsoeld (54%). 1988 Unsoeld (50%).

Interest Group Ratings:

ADA	ACU	COPE	COC
90	00	100	38

LCV	NTLC	CFA	ASC
81	10	87	30

Office: 1527 LHOB 20515, 202-225-3536 (Dan Evans, AA). DISTRICT OFFICES: 207 Fed. Bldg., Olympia 98501, 206-753-9528 (Clover Lockland, Dist. Dir.); 601 Main St, Rm. 505, Vancouver 98661, 206-696-7942 (Donna Levin, Rep.)

FOURTH DISTRICT

Jay Inslee (D)

District: Central part of the state east of the Cascades including city of Yakima. Population: 540,744—Hispanic 16%. Politics: Leans Republican.

Born Feb. 9, 1951, Seattle; home, Selah; University of Wash., B.A. 1973, Willamette University, J.D. 1976; Protestant; married (Trudi), 3 children.

Elected 1992. Career: Practicing atty., 1976–92; City Prosecutor Selah, 1976–82; State Rep., 1988–92.

Committees: (1) Agriculture; (2) Science, Space & Technology.

Election Results: 1992 Inslee 91,118 (51%); Richard Hastings (R) 86,127 (49%).

Interest Group Ratings:
None—Freshman

Office: 1431 LHOB 20515, 202-225-5816 (Lisa Garza, Chief of Staff). DISTRICT OFFICES: 701 N. 1st St. Suite B, Yakima 98901, 800-759-1871 (Brian Legate, Rep.); 3311 N. Clearwater #105,

Kennewick 99336, 509-783-0310 (Tom Bennett, Rep.); 112 N. Mission St., Wenatchee 98801, 509-662-4294 (Stephanie Gillioand, Rep.)

FIFTH DISTRICT

Thomas S. Foley (D)

District: Eastern part of the state including city of Spokane. Population: 540,744—Hispanic 3%. Politics: Leans Democratic.

Born Mar. 6, 1929, Spokane; home, Spokane; University of Wash., B.A. 1951, LL.B. 1957; Roman Catholic; married (Heather).

Elected 1964. Career: Practicing atty., 1957; Spokane Cty. Asst. Prosecuting Atty., 1958–60; Inst., Gonzaga University School of Law, 1958–60; Asst. Atty. Gen. of Wash., 1960–61; Asst. Chf. Clerk & Spec. Counsel, U.S. Senate Comm. on Interior & Insular Affairs, 1961–63.

Committees: (1) Speaker.

Election Results: 1992 Foley 123,110 (55%); John Sonneland (R) 99,692 (45%). 1990 Foley (69%). 1988 Foley (76%).

Interest Group Ratings:
Speaker Does Not Vote

Office: 1201 LHOB 20515, 202-225-2006 (Susan Moos, AA). DISTRICT OFFICES: W. 601 1st Ave., 2nd flr. W., Spokane 99204, 509-353-2155 (Janet Gilpatrick, Dist. Asst.); 12929 E. Sprague, Spokane 99216, 509-926-4434 (Jeanne Zappone, Rep.); 28 W. Main, Walla Walla 99362, 509-529-3789 (Patricia Gregg, Dist. Asst.)

SIXTH DISTRICT

Norman D. Dicks (D)

District: Puget Sound area including city of Tacoma and environs. Population: 540,742—Black 5%, Asian 4%, Hispanic 3%. Politics: Leans Democratic.

Born Dec. 16, 1940, Bremerton; home, Bremerton; University of Wash., B.A. 1963, J.D. 1968; Lutheran; married (Suzanne), 2 children.

Elected 1976. Career: Off. of U.S. Sen. Warren G. Magnuson, Legis. Asst., 1968–73, A.A., 1973–76.

Committees: (1) Appropriations; (2) Select Committee on Intelligence.

Election Results: 1992 Dicks 121,162 (70%); Lauri Phillips (R) 51,297 (30%). 1990 Dicks (62%). 1988 Dicks (68%).

Interest Group Ratings:

ADA	ACU	COPE	COC
80	08	73	25

LCV	NTLC	CFA	ASC
44	10	93	60

Office: 2467 RHOB 20515, 202-225-5916 (Donna Taylor, Mgr.). DISTRICT OFFICES: 1019 Pacific Ave., Suite 916, Tacoma 98402, 206-593-6536 (Tim Thompson, Dist. Cord.); 301 Great Northwest Bldg., Bremerton 98310, 206-479-4011 (Mary Bowen, Rep.)

SEVENTH DISTRICT

James A. McDermott (D)

District: Seattle and suburbs. Population: 547,747—Black 10%, Asian 12%, Hispanic 4%. Politics: Leans Democratic.

Born Dec. 28, 1936, Chicago, Ill.; home, Seattle; Wheaton College, B.S. 1958, University of Ill., M.D. 1963; Episcopalian; divorced, 2 children.

Elected 1988. Career: Navy, 1968–70; Private psychiatric practice, 1970–83; Regional Medical Officer, U.S. Foreign Svc., 1987–88; Wash. House of Reps., 1970–73; Wash. Senate, 1974–87.

Committees: (1) Ways & Means; (2) District of Columbia; (3) Standards of Official Conduct (Chairman).

Election Results: 1992 McDermott 198,657 (81%); Glenn Hampson (R) 45,351 (19%). 1990 McDermott (76%). 1988 McDermott (76%).

Interest Group Ratings:

ADA	ACU	COPE	COC
95	00	83	25

LCV	NTLC	CFA	ASC
81	05	93	30

Office: 1707 LHOB 20515, 202-225-3106 (Charles Williams, AA). DISTRICT OFFICE: 1809 7th Ave., Suite 1212, Seattle 98104, 206-442-7170 (Nancy James, Mgr.)

EIGHTH DISTRICT

Jennifer Dunn (R)

District: Seattle suburbs and adjoining counties including city of Bellevue. Population: 540,742 —Asian 5%. Politics: Leans Republican.

Born July 29, 1949, Seattle; home, Bellevue; Stanford, B.A., 1963; Episcopalian; divorced, 2 children.

Elected 1992. Career: Chairman Washington State Republican Party, 1981–92.

Committees: (1) Public Works & Transportation; (2) Science, Space & Technology.

Election Results: 1992 Dunn 129,475 (60%); George Tamblyn (D) 73,654 (34%); Bob Adams (I) 12,354 (6%).

Interest Group Ratings:
None—Freshman

Office: 1641 LHOB 20515, 202-225-7761 (Phil Bond, AA). DISTRICT OFFICE: 50 116th Ave. S.E. #201, Bellevue 98004, 206-450-0161 (Dick Larsen, Rep.)

NINTH DISTRICT

Mike Kreidler (D)

District: Parts of King, Pierce, and Thurston counties and Tacoma city. Population: 540,744— Black 5%, Asian 6%, Hispanic 4%. Politics: Leans Democratic.

Born Sept. 28, 1943, Tacoma; home, Olympia; Pacific University, B.S. 1967, Dr. of Optometry 1969, University of Calif. at Los Angeles, M.A. 1972; Church of Christ; married (Lela), 3 children.

Elected 1992. Career: Optometrist Olympia Group Health, 1972–92; State Rep., 1977–84; State Sen., 1985–92.

Committees: (1) Energy & Commerce; (2) Veteran Affairs.

Election Results: 1992 Kreidler 94,656 (53%); Pete von Reichbauer (R) 73,763 (42%); Timothy Brill (I) 2,886 (2%); Brian Wilson (I) 5,787 (3%).

Interest Group Ratings:
None—Freshman

Office: 1535 LHOB 20515, 202-225-8901 (Bob Crane, AA). DISTRICT OFFICES: P.O. Box 907, Puyallup 98371, 206-840-5688 (Evan Simpson, Rep.); 31919 1st Ave. #140, Federal Way 98003, 206-946-0553

WEST VIRGINIA

This is the nation's most Democratic state, with the Republican Party all but invisible. Democratic Sen. Robert Byrd, now with 35 years service in the Senate, says he will seek a seventh term. If he does, and it now appears he will run again, he will win easily. If, however, Byrd decides to retire, a major contest will develop among Democrats over who will replace him.

1992 PRESIDENTIAL ELECTION: (5 Electoral votes): Clinton (D) 327,784 (49%); Bush (R) 239,252 (35%); Perot (I) 106,488 (16%); Marrou (Lib) 1,808. 1988 Dukakis 339,112 (52%); Bush 307,824 (48%).

SENATORS

Robert Carlyle Byrd (D)

Born Nov. 20, 1917, N. Wilkesboro, N.C.; home, Sophia; American University, LL.B., J.D. 1963; Baptist; married (Erma), 2 children.

Elected 1958, seat up 1994. Career: W.V. House of Reps. 1946–50; W.V. Senate, 1950–52; U.S. House of Reps., 1953–58.

Committees: (1) Appropriations (Chairman); (2) Armed Services; (3) Rules & Administration.

Election Results: 1988 Byrd 410,983 (65%); Jay Wolfe (R) 223,564 (35%). 1988 Byrd (69%).

Interest Group Ratings:

ADA	ACU	COPE	COC
100	19	92	20

LCV	NTLC	CFA	ASC
42	17	75	30

Office: 311 HSOB 20510, 202-224-3954 (Joan Drummond, AA). STATE OFFICE: 1019 Fed Bldg., 500 Quarrier St., Charleston 25301, 304-342-5855 (Ann Barth, Dir.)

John D. Rockefeller IV (D)

Born June 18, 1937, New York, N.Y.; home, Charleston; Harvard University, A.B. 1961, Inter'l Christian University, Tokyo, 1957–60; Presbyterian; married (Sharon), 4 children.

Elected 1984, seat up 1996. Career: Natl. Adv. Cncl. of Peace Corps, 1961; Asst. to Peace Corps

Dir. Sargent Shriver, 1962–63; VISTA worker, 1964–66; W.V. House of Delegates, 1966–68; W.V. Secy. of State, 1968–72; Pres., W.V. Wesleyan College, 1973–75; Gov. of W.V., 1976–84.

Committees: (1) Commerce, Science & Transportation; (2) Finance; (3) Veterans Affairs.

Election Results: 1990 Rockefeller 274,614 (69%); John Yoder (R) 126,035 (31%). 1984 Rockefeller (52%).

Interest Group Ratings:

ADA	ACU	COPE	COC
100	07	91	20

LCV	NTLC	CFA	ASC
75	00	75	40

Office: 109 HSOB 20510, 202-224-6472 (R. Lane Bailey, AA). STATE OFFICES: 200 L&S Bldg., 812 Quarrier St., Charleston 25301, 304-347-5372 (Lou Ann Martin, St. Dir.); 115 S. Kanawha St., Suite 1, Beckley 25801, 304-253-9704 (Dennis Altizer, Rep.); 200 Adams St., Suite A, Fairmont 26554, 304-367-0122 (Larry Lemon, Cord.)

REPRESENTATIVES

FIRST DISTRICT

Alan B. Mollohan (D)

District: Northern panhandle that is actually close to Pittsburgh, and includes city of Wheeling. Population: 598,056—Black 2%. Politics: Democratic.

Born May 14, 1943; Fairmont; home, Fairmont; College of William & Mary, B.A. 1966, W.V. University, College of Law, J.D. 1970; Baptist; married (Barbara), 5 children.

Elected 1982. Career: Practicing atty., 1970–82.

Committees: (1) Appropriations; (2) Budget.

Election Results: 1992 Mollohan (Unopposed). 1990 Mollohan (67%). 1988 Mollohan (75%).

Interest Group Ratings:

ADA	ACU	COPE	COC
70	21	100	43

LCV	NTLC	CFA	ASC
38	00	73	90

Office: 2242 RHOB 20515, 202-225-4172 (Mary McGovern, AA). DISTRICT OFFICES: 213 Fed. Bldg. P.O. Box 720, Morgantown 26507, 304-292-3019 (Lotta Near, Rep.); 1117 Fed. Bldg., 425 Juliana St., Parkersburg 26101, 304-428-0493 (Allenetta Kaufman, Rep.); 316 Fed. Bldg., Wheeling 26003, 304-232-5390 (Cathy Abraham, Rep.); 209 P.O. Bldg., 500 W. Pike St., Clarksburg 26301, 304-623-4422 (Ann Merandi, Rep.)

SECOND DISTRICT

Robert E. Wise (D)

District: Central part of the state including city of Charleston and environs. Population: 597,921 —Black 3%. Politics: Democratic.

Born Jan. 6, 1948, Washington, D.C.; home, Clendenin; Duke University, B.A. 1970, Tulane University, J.D. 1975; Episcopalian; married (Sandy), 2 children.

Elected 1982. Career: Practicing atty., 1975–80; Dir. W.V. for Fair & Equitable Assessment of Taxes, Inc., 1977–80; W.V. Senate, 1980–82.

Committees: (1) Budget; (2) Public Works & Transportation.

Election Results: 1992 Wise 143,923 (71%); Samuel Cravotta (R) 58,666 (29%). 1990 Wise (Unopposed). 1988 Wise (74%).

Interest Group Ratings:

ADA	ACU	COPE	COC
80	17	92	38

LCV	NTLC	CFA	ASC
44	00	93	40

Office: 2434 RHOB 20515, 202-225-2711 (Lowell Johnson, AA). DISTRICT OFFICES: 107 Pennsylvania Ave., Charleston 25302, 304-342-7170 (Joyce Edwards, Mgr.); 102 E. Martins St., Martinsburg 25401, 304-264-8810 (Chip Slaven, Rep.)

THIRD DISTRICT

Nick Joe Rahall II (D)

District: Southern coal counties including cities of Huntington and Beckley. Population: 597,500 —Black 4%. Politics: Democratic.

Born May 20, 1949, Beckley; home, Beckley; Duke University, A.B. 1971, George Washington University; Presbyterian; divorced, 3 children.

Elected 1976. Career: Aide to Sen. Robert C. Byrd, 1971–74; Pres., Mountaineer Tour & Travel Agency, 1974; Pres., W.V. Broadcasting Corp.

Committees: (1) Natural Resources; (2) Public Works & Transportation.

Election Results: 1992 Rahall 119,500 (66%); Ben Waldman (R) 61,887 (34%). 1990 Rahall (52%). 1988 Rahall (61%).

Interest Group Ratings:

ADA	ACU	COPE	COC
70	20	100	38

LCV	NTLC	CFA	ASC
63	10	73	30

Office: 2269 RHOB 20515, 202-225-3452 (Kent Keyser, AA). DISTRICT OFFICES: 110-½ Main St., Beckley 25801, 304-252-5000 (vacant, Rep.); 815 5th Ave., Huntington 25701, 304-522-6425 (Pat Cannon, Rep.); 1005 Fed. Bldg., Bluefield 24701, 304-325-6222 (Vicki Goins, Rep.); 220 Stratton, Logan 25601, 304-752-4934 (Anna Marcum, Rep.)

WISCONSIN

Wisconsin is one of a number of midwestern states that splits almost evenly between Democratic urban dwellers and Republicans in the suburbs and rural areas. Democrats were much buoyed here in 1992 with the victory of Senate candidate Russ Feingold, and Bill Clinton's big victory. In 1994 they hope to reelect Sen. Herb Kohl and to defeat GOP Gov. Tommy Thompson. Their chances of the former are significantly higher than of unseating the popular Thompson.

1992 PRESIDENTIAL ELECTION: (11 Electoral votes): Clinton (D) 1,036,316 (41%); Bush (R) 926,646 (37%); Perot (I) 542,470 (22%); Marrou (Lib) 3,122; Gritz (Pop) 2,208; Daniels (P&F) 1,796; Phillips (AmTax) 1,720; Brisben (Soc) 1,178; Hagelin (NLP) 1,045; Fulani (NAP) 629; LaRouche (I) 615; Herer (GrassRts) 395; Warren (SocWks) 388. 1988 Dukakis 1,122,090 (52%); Bush 1,043,584 (48%).

SENATORS

Russell Feingold (D)

Born Mar. 2, 1953, Janesville; home, Milwaukee; Oxford (Rhodes Scholar), 1977, Harvard, J.D. 1979; Jewish; married (Mary), 2 children, 2 stepchildren.

Elected 1992. Seat up 1998. Career: Practicing Attorney, Foley & Lardner, 1979–84; Wis. Senate, 1983–92.

Committees: (1) Agriculture, Nutrition & Forestry; (2) Foreign Relations.

Election Results: 1992 Feingold 1,284,285 (53%); Robert W. Kasten Jr. (R-Incumbent) 1,123,715 (47%).

Interest Group Ratings:
None—Freshman

Office: 502 HSOB 20510, 202-224-5323 (Ruth LaRocque, Adm. Dir.). STATE OFFICES: 8383 Greenway, Middleton 53562, 608-828-1200 (Jim Rudolph, Rep.); 517 E. Wisconsin Ave. #408, Milwaukee 53202, 414-276-7282 (Cecilia Peterson, Rep.)

Herb Kohl (D)

Born Feb. 7, 1935, Milwaukee; home, Milwaukee; University of Wis., B.A. 1956, Harvard University, M.B.A. 1958; Jewish; single.

Elected 1988, seat up 1994. Career: Kohl Corp., grocery & dept. stores, 1959–70, Pres., 1970–79; Herbert Kohl Investments, 1979–88; owner, Milwaukee Bucks basketball team.

Committees: (1) Judiciary; (2) Appropriations; (3) Small Business.

Election Results: 1988 Kohl 1,128,625 (52%); Susan Engeleiter (R) 1,030,440 (48%).

Interest Group Ratings:

ADA	ACU	COPE	COC
95	11	83	30

LCV	NTLC	CFA	ASC
83	33	83	50

Office: 330 HSOB 20510, 202-224-5653 (Chris Coffin, Chief-of-staff). STATE OFFICES: 205 E. Wisconsin Ave., Milwaukee 53202, 414-297-4451 (Teri Houfek, Mgr.); 14 W. Mifflin St., Suite 312, Madison 53703, 608-264-5338 (Eve Galanter, Rep.); 3409 Golf Rd., Eau Claire 54071, 715-832-8424 (Marge Bunce, Rep.); 625 52nd St., Suite 303, Kenosha 53140, 414-657-7719 (Lois O'Keefe, Rep.); 4321 W. College Ave. #235, Appleton 54914, 414-738-1640 (Marlene Mielke, Rep.)

REPRESENTATIVES

FIRST DISTRICT

Peter W. Barca (D)

District: Far southeastern counties of the state including cities of Racine, Kenosha and Janesville. Population: 543,530—Black 5%, Hispanic 3%. Politics: Democratic.

Born August 7, 1955, Kenosha; home, Kenosha; University of Wis. (Milwaukee), B.S., 1977, University of Wis. (Madison), M.S., 1982; Roman Catholic; married (Kathy), 2 children.

Elected 1993, special election to fill the term of Defense Secretary Les Aspin. Career: Teacher, camp director, job training specialist; member, State Assembly, 1985–93.

Committees: (1) Public Works and Transportation; (2) Science, Space, and Technology

Election Results: 1993 (special) Barca 55,578 (49.9%); Mark W. Neumann (R) 54,838 (49.3%).

Interest Group Ratings:
None—Freshman

Office: 1719 LHOB 20515, 202-225-3031 (AA TBA). DISTRICT OFFICE: (TBA)

SECOND DISTRICT

Scott L. Klug (R)

District: South–central part of the state including town of Madison. Population: 543,532. Politics: Mixed between liberal Democratic Madison and conservative Republican farm country surrounding it.

Born Jan. 16, 1953, Milwaukee; home, Madison; Lawrence University, B.S., 1975, Northwestern University, M.S.J., 1976, University of Wis., M.B.A., 1990; Roman Catholic; married (Teresa), 3 children.

Elected 1990. Career: Broadcast journalist, news anchor, businessman.

Committees: (1) Energy & Commerce.

Election Results: 1992 Klug 181,845 (63%); Ada Deer (D) 107,480 (37%). 1990 Klug (53%).

Interest Group Ratings:

ADA	ACU	COPE	COC
40	56	33	63

LCV	NTLC	CFA	ASC
50	80	47	80

Office: 1224 LHOB 20515, 202-225-2906 (Brandon Schotz, AA). DISTRICT OFFICE: 16 N. Carroll St., Suite 600, Madison 53703, 608-657-9200 (Judy Lowell, Dist. Dir.)

THIRD DISTRICT

Steven Craig Gunderson (R)

District: Western counties along the Mississippi including cities of Eau Claire and La Crosse. Population: 543,533. Politics: Mixed, but overall leans Democratic.

Born May 10, 1951, Eau Claire; home, Pleasantville; University of Wis., B.A. 1973, Brown School of Broadcasting, 1974; Lutheran; single.

Elected 1980. Career: Wis. Assembly, 1974–79; Leg. Dir. for U.S. Rep. Toby Roth, 1979.

Committees: (1) Agriculture; (2) Education & Labor.

Election Results: 1992 Gunderson 145,200 (57%); Paul Sacia (D) 107,458 (43%). 1990 Gunderson (61%). 1988 Gunderson (68%).

Interest Group Ratings:

ADA	ACU	COPE	COC
40	64	50	88

LCV	NTLC	CFA	ASC
25	55	40	100

Office: 2235 RHOB 20515, 202-225-5506 (Kris Deininger, AA). DISTRICT OFFICE: P. O. Box 247, Black River Falls 54615, 715-284-7431 (Marlene Hanson, Chief-of-staff)

FOURTH DISTRICT

Gerald D. Kleczka (D)

District: Southern Milwaukee and suburbs including Waukesha. Population: 543,527—Hispanic 6%. Politics: Democratic.

Born Nov. 26, 1943, Milwaukee; home, Milwaukee; University of Wis.; Roman Catholic; married (Bonnie).

Elected 1984. Career: Accountant; Wis. Assembly, 1968–72; Wis. Senate, 1974–84, Asst. Major. Ldr., 1977–82.

Committees: (1) Ways & Means.

Election Results: 1992 Kleczka 172,903 (67%); Joseph Cook (R) 84,463 (33%). 1990 Kleczka (69%). 1988 Kleczka (Unopposed).

Interest Group Ratings:

ADA	ACU	COPE	COC
80	04	82	25

LCV	NTLC	CFA	ASC
38	00	93	10

Office: 2301 RHOB 20515, 202-225-4572 (vacant, AA). DISTRICT OFFICES: 5032 W. Forest Home Ave., Milwaukee 53219, 414-297-1140 (Kathryn Hein, Dir.); 414 Westmoreland Blvd #105., Waukesha 53186, 414-549-6360 (Lorie Grabow, Rep.)

FIFTH DISTRICT

Thomas M. Barrett (D)

District: Northern Milwaukee and suburbs including Wauwatosa. Population: 543,530—Black 35%. Politics: Democratic.

Born Dec. 8, 1953, Milwaukee; home, Milwaukee; University of Wis., B.A. 1976, J.D. 1980; Roman Catholic; married (Christie).

Elected 1992. Career: Attorney, 1980–84; State Assembly, 1984–89; State Sen., 1989–92.

Committees: (1) Banking Finance & Urban Affairs; (2) Government Operations.

Election Results: 1992 Barrett 159,446 (70%); Donalda Ann Hammersmith (R) 68,676 (30%).

Interest Group Ratings:
None—Freshman

Office: 313 CHOB 20515, 202-225-3571 (Janet Pirano, AA). DISTRICT OFFICE: 135 W. Wells St. #618, Milwaukee 53203, 414-297-1331 (Ann DeLeo, Rep.)

SIXTH DISTRICT

Thomas E. Petri (R)

District: Central part of the state including towns of Oshkosh, Fond du Lac, and Manitowoc. Population: 543,652. Politics: Republican.

Born May 28, 1940, Marinette; home, Fond du Lac; Harvard University, A.B. 1962, J.D. 1965; Lutheran; married (Anne), 1 child.

Elected Apr. 3, 1979. Career: Law Clerk to Federal Judge James Doyle, 1965; Peace Corps, 1966–67; White House Aide, 1969; Practicing atty., 1970–79; Wis. Senate, 1973–79.

Committees: (1) Education & Labor; (2) Public Works & Transportation; (3) Standards of Official Conduct; (4) Post Office and Civil Service (Temp.).

Election Results: 1992 Petri 143,843 (53%); Peggy Lautenschlager (D) 128,353 (47%). 1990 Petri (Unopposed). 1988 Petri (74%).

Interest Group Ratings:

ADA	ACU	COPE	COC
25	76	25	63

LCV	NTLC	CFA	ASC
44	95	53	80

Office: 2262 RHOB 20515, 202-225-2476 (Joseph Flader, AA). DISTRICT OFFICES: 14 Western

Ave., Fond du Lac 54935, 414-922-1180 (Sue Kerkman, Dist. Dir.); 105 Washington Ave., Rm. 112, Oshkosh 54901, 414-231-6333 (Frank Frassetto, Asst.)

SEVENTH DISTRICT

David R. Obey (D)

District: Northwest third of the state including towns of Wausau and Superior. Population: 543,529. Politics: Democratic.

Born Oct. 3, 1938, Okmulgee, Okla.; home, Wausau; University of Wis., M.A. 1960; Roman Catholic; married (Joan), 2 children.

Elected Apr. 1, 1969. Career: Real estate broker; Wis. Assembly, 1963–69.

Committees: (1) Appropriations; (2) Joint Economic Committee.

Election Results: 1992 Obey 165,975 (64%); Dale Vannes (R) 91,775 (36%). 1990 Obey (62%). 1988 Obey (62%).

Interest Group Ratings:

ADA	ACU	COPE	COC
100	00	92	38

LCV	NTLC	CFA	ASC
73	00	87	30

Office: 2462 RHOB 20515, 202-225-3365 (Joseph Crapa, Staff Dir.). DISTRICT OFFICE: Fed. Bldg., 317 First St., Wausau 54401, 715-842-5606 (Jerry Madison, Dist. Dir.)

EIGHTH DISTRICT

Toby Roth (R)

District: Northeast portion of the state including cities of Green Bay and Appleton. Population: 543,404—Native American 3%. Politics: Republican.

Born Oct. 10, 1938, Strasburg, N.Dak.; home, Appleton; Marquette University, B.A. 1961; Roman Catholic; married (Barbara), 3 children.

Elected 1978. Career: Realtor; Wis. House of Reps., 1973–79.

Committees: (1) Banking, Finance & Urban Affairs; (2) Foreign Affairs.

Election Results: 1992 Roth 191,649 (70%); Catherine Helms (D) 82,032 (30%). 1990 Roth (54%). 1988 Roth (70%).

Interest Group Ratings:

ADA	ACU	COPE	COC
15	83	08	75

LCV	NTLC	CFA	ASC
13	80	27	70

Office: 2234 RHOB 20515, 202-225-5665 (Joe Western, AA). DISTRICT OFFICES: 2301 S. Oneida St., Green Bay 54307, 414-494-2800 (Ann Boltz, Rep.); 126 N. Oneida St., Appleton 54911, 414-739-4167 (John Fink, Rep.); P.O. Box 254 Marinette 54143, 715-735-5845 (Howie Witt, Rep.)

NINTH DISTRICT

F. James Sensenbrenner, Jr. (R)

District: Milwaukee suburbs including Sheboygan and Beaver Dam. Population: 543,532. Politics: Republican.

Born June 14, 1943, Chicago, Ill.; home, Menomonee Falls; Stanford University, A.B. 1965, University of Wis., J.D. 1968; Episcopalian; married (Cheryl), 2 children.

Elected 1978. Career: Practicing atty.; Staff of U.S. Rep. Arthur Younger, 1965; Wis. Assembly, 1969–75; Wis. Senate, 1975–78.

Committees: (1) Judiciary; (2) Science, Space & Technology.

Election Results: 1992 Sensenbrenner 192,915 (71%); Ingrid Buxton (D) 77,358 (29%). 1990 Sensenbrenner (Unopposed). 1988 Sensenbrenner (75%).

Interest Group Ratings:

ADA	ACU	COPE	COC
15	92	17	88

LCV	NTLC	CFA	ASC
25	95	13	90

Office: 2332 RHOB 20515, 202-225-5101 (Todd Schultz, AA). DISTRICT OFFICE: 120 Bishops Way, Rm. 154, Brookfield 53005, 414-784-1111 (Tom Schreivel, Dir.)

WYOMING

Wyoming remains typical of many western states that are uniformly Republican when it comes to voting for president or senator or members of the U.S. House, but who then turn around and elect a Democratic governor. The major question on the political horizon is whether Sen. Malcolm Wallop will seek another term in 1994 or whether he might retire in favor of former Defense Secretary (and former Wyoming congressman) Dick Cheney. Cheney is too young and too political to retire, and Wallop's seat is the only one in view for him. Democratic Gov. Michael Sullivan is up for reelection in 1994, and should win a third term easily.

1992 PRESIDENTIAL ELECTION: (3 Electoral votes): Clinton (D) 67,858 (34%); Bush (R) 79,515 (40%); Perot (I) 51,182 (26%); Marrou (Lib) 819; Fulani (NAP) 264. 1988 Bush 106,814 (61%); Dukakis 67,077 (39%).

SENATORS

Malcolm Wallop (R)

Born Feb. 27, 1933, New York, N.Y.; home, Big Horn; Yale University, B.A. 1954; Episcopalian; married (French), 4 children.

Elected 1976, seat up 1994. Career: Rancher; Army, 1955–57; Wyo. House of Reps., 1969–72; Wyo. Senate, 1973–76.

Committees: (1) Energy & Natural Resources (Ranking Member); (2) Finance; (3) Small Business; (4) Select Committee on Intelligence.

Election Results: 1988 Wallop 91,143 (50%); John Vinich (D) 89,821 (50%). 1982 Wallop (57%).

Interest Group Ratings:

ADA	ACU	COPE	COC
10	100	25	100

LCV	NTLC	CFA	ASC
00	88	08	70

Office: 237 RSOB 20510, 202-224-6441 (Patti McDonald, AA). STATE OFFICES: 2201 Fed. Bldg., Casper 82601, 307-261-5415 (Mona White, Dir.); 2009 Fed. Ctr., Cheyenne 82001, 307-634-0626 (Byra Kite, Dir.); P.O. Bldg., Lander 82520, 307-332-2293 (Pam Redfield, Dir.); 2515 Foothill Blvd., Rock Springs 82901, 307-382-5127 (Billie

Jelouchan, Dir.); 40 S. Main, Sheridan 82801, 307-672-6456 (Evelyn Ebzbry, Dir.)

Alan K. Simpson (R)

Born Sept. 2, 1931, Denver, Colo.; home, Cody; University of Wyo., B.S. 1954, J.D. 1958; Episcopalian; married (Ann), 3 children.

Elected 1978, seat up 1996. Career: Practicing atty., 1959–78; Wyo. Asst. Atty. Gen., 1959; Cody City Atty., 1959–69; Wyo. House of Reps., 1964–77, Major. Floor Ldr. 1975–76, Speaker Pro-Temp., 1977.

Committees: (1) Environment & Public Works; (2) Judiciary; (3) Veterans Affairs.

Election Results: 1990 Simpson 100,800 (64%); Kathy Helling (D) 56,692 (36%). 1984: Simpson (78%).

Interest Group Ratings:

ADA	ACU	COPE	COC
15	89	17	90

LCV	NTLC	CFA	ASC
00	72	42	100

Office: 261 DSOB 20510, 202-224-3424 (Donald Hardy, AA). STATE OFFICES: 2007 Fed. Bldg., 2120 Capitol Ave., Cheyenne 82001, 307-772-2477 (Dee Rodekohr, St. Off. Mgr.); 1731 Sheridan Ave., Cody 82414, 307-527-7121 (Karen McCreary, Rep.); 3201 Fed. Ctr., 100 E. B St., Casper 82601, 307-261-5172 (Cherie Burd, Chief-of-staff); 300 S. Gillette Ave., Gillette 82716, 307-682-7091 (Robin Bailey, Rep.); 2020 Grand Ave., Rm. 411, Laramie 82070, 307-745-5303 (Angela Dougherty, Rep.); 2515 Foothill Blvd., Suite 220, Rock Springs 82901, 307-382-5079 (Lynette Shanaghty, Rep.)

REPRESENTATIVE AT LARGE

Craig Thomas (R)

District: Entire state. Population: 453,588— Native American 2%, Hispanic 6%. Politics: Republican.

Born Feb. 13, 1933, Cody; home, Casper; University of Wyo. B.A. 1955; LaSalle University,

LL.B. 1959; Methodist; married (Susan), 4 children.

Elected 1989 (Special Election). Career: V.P., Wyo. Farm Bureau, 1959–66; Am. Farm Bureau, 1966–75; Mgr. Wyo. Rural Elec. Assoc., 1975–89; Wyo. House of Reps., 1984–89.

Committees: (1) Natural Resources; (2) Government Operations.

Election Results: 1992 Thomas 113,712 (58%); Jon Herschler (D) 77,364 (39%); Craig McCune (Libert) 5,673 (3%). 1990 Thomas (55%). 1989 (special) Thomas (61%).

Interest Group Ratings:

ADA	ACU	COPE	COC
20	79	45	88

LCV	NTLC	CFA	ASC
00	95	20	100

Office: 1019 LHOB 20505, 202-225-2311 (Liz Brimmer, AA). STATE OFFICES: 2015 Fed. Bldg., Cheyenne 82001, 307-772-2451 (Ruthann Norris, Mgr.); 4003 Fed. Bldg., 100 E. B St., Casper 82601, 307-261-5413 (Carol Leffler, Mgr.); 2632 Foothill Blvd., Rock Springs 82901, 307-362-5012 (Patti Smith, Rep.)

LOCAL GOVERNMENT
THE STATES AND THEIR PRINCIPAL CITIES

Population figures, for both states and cities, as well as each state's number of electoral votes and congressional districts, are based on the results of the 1990 census (source: Bureau of the Census, U.S. Department of Commerce). Population demographic percentages are based on the most recent data available, in almost all cases the 1990 census. Demographic percentages may add up to more than 100 percent because persons of Hispanic origin may be of any race. Since people generally classify themselves by race in the census, a percentage is given for "other." By and large, this represents persons who did not list a race. In some states this can be a sizable percentage, and is most often persons of Hispanic origin who do not list a race classification on their census questionnaire (source: Bureau of the Census, U.S. Department of Commerce). State per capita income figures are for fiscal 1991. (Source: Bureau of Economic Analysis, U.S. Department of Commerce.) Per pupil spending and state rankings are for the 1991–92 school year (source: National Education Association). Cities with populations of less than 100,000 are not ranked (NR). Per capita income figures are for 1991, the most recent year available, and are based on either metropolitan statistical areas (PMSA), consolidated metropolitan statistical areas (CMSA), or for New England cities county metropolitan areas (NECMA). In most cases these combine cities with their adjacent suburban areas (source: Bureau of Economic Analysis, U.S. Department of Commerce). The year in parentheses is the year a state entered the Union.

ALABAMA (1819)

State Capitol: Montgomery 36130
State Government Information: 501 Dexter Ave, Montgomery AL 36130 (205-261-2500)
Population & rank: 4,040,587/22
Population demographics: White—73.6%;

Black—25.3%; Hispanic—.6%; Asian—.5%; Native American—.4%
Per capita income & rank: $15,021/44
Public school per pupil spending & rank: $3,675/48
Governor: Harold Guy Hunt (R) (205-261-7100); 4-year term; elected 1986; last election (1990): Hunt 630,473 (52%) vs. Paul Hubbert (D) 585,664 (48%); next election Nov. 1994.
Lt. Governor: Jim Folsom, Jr. (D)
Secretary of State: Billy Joe Camp (D) (205-261-7200)
Attorney General: Jimmy Evans (D)
Treasurer: George Wallace, Jr. (D)
Electoral votes: 9
U.S. Congress: 7 Reps.
Legislature: (S 205-261-7800, H 205-267-7600) 35 Senate (28 D, 7 R); 105 House (82 D, 23 R). Both serve 4-year terms. Meets annually the third Tuesday in April (first year in office), first Tuesday in February (second and third years), and second Tuesday in January (fourth year).

Birmingham, Alabama

City Hall: 710 N. 20th St. 35203 (205-254-2000)
Mayor: Daniel E. Fowler; next election Nov. 1995.
Population & rank: 265,968/60
Per capita income & rank: $17,497/141
Mayor-Council form of government. The mayor and 9 council members are elected for 4-year terms. The council meets weekly.

ALASKA (1959)

State Capitol: Juneau 99811
State Government Information: 333 Willoughby Ave., Juneau AK 99801 (907-465-2111)
Population & rank: 550,043/49
Population demographics: White—75.5%; Black—4.1%; Hispanic—3.2%; Native American—15.6%; Asian—3.6%
Per capita income & rank: $21,688/7

Public school per pupil spending & rank: $9,248/2
Governor: Wally Hickel (I) (907-465-3500); 4-year term; elected 1990; last election (1990): Hickle 63,558 (39%) vs. Tony Knowles (D) 50,775 (31%) vs. Arliss Sturgulewski (R) 44,156 (27%) vs. Jim Sykes (I) 5,418 (3%); next election Nov. 1994.
Lt. Governor: John B. Coghill (I)
Attorney General: Charles E. Cole (R)
Secretary of State: None
State Treasurer: Brian Andrews
Electoral votes: 3
U.S. Congress: 1 Rep.
Legislature: (907-465-2111) 20 Senate (9 D, 10 R, 1 I) and 40 House (20 D, 18 R, 2 I). Meets annually in January for 120 days with a 10-day extension possible upon 2/3 vote. First session in odd-numbered years. Senators serve 4-year terms and Representatives serve 2-year terms.

Anchorage, Alaska

City Hall: 632 W. 6th Ave. 99519 (907-343-4431)
Mayor: Tom Fink (D); next election Sept. 1996
City Manager: Larry Crawford
Population & rank: 226,338/69
Per capita income & rank: $25,035/13
Home rule municipality which combines mayor-council (city assembly) with city manager. 11-member Assembly meets weekly on Tuesdays.

ARIZONA (1912)

State Capitol: Phoenix 85007
State Government Information: 1700 W. Washington St., Phoenix AZ 85007 (602-542-4900)
Population & rank: 3,665,288/24
Population demographics: White—80.8%; Black —3%; Hispanic—18.8%; Native American— 5.6%; Asian—1.5%; Other—9.1%
Per capita income & rank: $16,012/36
Public school per pupil spending & rank: $4,750/33
Governor: Fife Smytington (R) (602-542-4331); 4-year term; elected in runoff 1991 Smytington 492,569 (52%) Terry Goddard (D) 448,168 (48%); next election Nov. 1994.
Lt. Governor: Richard Mahoney (D)
Secretary of State: Richard Mahoney (D) (602-542-4285)
Attorney General: Grant Woods (R)

Treasurer: Tony West (R)
Electoral votes: 8
U.S. Congress: 6 Reps.
Legislature: (602-542-3032) 30 Senate (12 D and 18 R) and 60 House (25 D, 35 R). Meets annually in January.

Phoenix, Arizona

City Hall: 251 W. Washington Ave. 85003 (602-262-6011)
Mayor: Paul Johnson (D); next election Nov. 1993
City Manager: Frank Fairbanks
Population & rank: 983,403/9
Per capita income & rank: $18,042/119
Council-manager form of government. The mayor and the 8-member council are elected to 2-year terms. The mayor is a member of the council but does not have the power to veto. The council meets weekly on Wednesdays.

Tucson, Arizona

City Hall: 255 W. Alameda St. 85701 (602-791-4017)
Mayor: George Miller; next election Nov. 1995
City Manager: Ruben D. Suarez
Population & rank: 405,390/33
Per capita income & rank: 15,191/256
Council-manager form of government. The mayor and 5 at-large council members serve 4-year terms. The mayor is a member of the council but does not have veto power. The council meets the first four Mondays of every month.

ARKANSAS (1836)

State Capitol: Little Rock 72201 (501-682-3000)
State Government Information: 1 State Capitol Mall, Little Rock AR 72201 (501-371-3000)
Population & rank: 2,350,725/33
Population demographics: White—82.7%; Black —15.9%; Hispanic—.8%; Native American— .5%; Asian—.5%; Other—.3%
Per capita income & rank: $14,188/48
Public school per pupil spending & rank: $3,770/46
Governor: Jim Guy Tucker (D) (501-682-2345); 4-year term; next election Nov. 1994.
Lt. Governor: Jerry Jewell (D)
Secretary of State: Bill McCuen (D) (501-682-1010)

Attorney General: Winston Bryant (D)
Treasurer: Jimmie Lou Fisher Lumpkin (D)
Electoral votes: 6
U.S. Congress: 4 Reps.
General Assembly: (501-682-3000) 35 Senate (30 D, 5 R) and 100 House (89 D, 10 R, 1 Vac.). Senators are elected to 4-year terms; Reps to 2-year terms. Meets during odd-numbered years in January.

Little Rock, Arkansas

City Hall: 500 West Markham 72201 (501-371-4500)
Mayor: Jim Dailey; next election Nov. 1994
City Manager: Thomas D. Dalton
Population & rank: 175,795/96
Per capita income & rank: $16,949/160
Council-manager form of government. Six council members are elected to 2-year terms and appoint the mayor. Council meets twice monthly.

CALIFORNIA (1850)

State Capitol: Sacramento 95814
State Government Information: 601 Sequoia Pacific Blvd. Sacramento CA 95814 (916-332-9900)
Population & rank: 29,760,021/1
Population demographics: White—69%; Black —7.4%; Hispanic—25.8%; Native American— .8%; Asian & Pacific Islander—9.6%; Other— 13.2%
Per capita income & rank: $20,677/9
Public school per pupil spending & rank: $4,686/36
Governor: Pete Wilson (R) (916-445-2841); 4-year term; elected 1990; last election (1990): Wilson (R) 3,462,226 (49%) vs. Dianne Feinstein (D) 3,274,828 (46%) vs. three others 352,399 (5%); next election Nov. 1994.
Lt. Governor: Leo T. McCarthy (D)
Secretary of State: March Fong Eu (D) (916-445-6371)
Attorney General: Daniel E. Lungren (R)
Treasurer: Kathleen Brown (D)
Insurance Commissioner: John Garamendi (D)
Electoral votes: 54
U.S. Congress: 52 Reps.
Legislature: (916-445-4711) 40 Senate (23 D, 14 R, 2 I, 1 Vac.) and 80 Assembly (48 D, 32 R). Regular sessions begin on first Monday in December of every even-numbered year; each session lasts 2 years.

Los Angeles, California

City Hall: 200 North Spring St. 90012 (213-485-2121)
Mayor: Richard Riordan (R); next election June 1997
Population & rank: 3,485,398/2
Per capita income & rank: $20,786/44
The mayor and 15-member council are elected to 4-year terms, along with the city attorney, comptroller, and the 7-member board of education. The mayor is not a member of the city council but does have veto power. The county is run by a 5-member board of supervisors serving 4-year terms. They preside over a jurisdictional jungle of overlapping city-county agencies.

San Diego, California

City Hall: 202 C Street 92101 (619-236-6363)
Mayor: Susan Golding; next election Nov. 1995
City Manager: Jack McGrory
Population & rank: 1,110,549/6
Per capita income & rank: $19,588/63
San Diego is the largest U.S. city with a council-manager form of government. The mayor and 8 council members are elected for 4-year terms, and they appoint a city manager. The elections are nonpartisan.

San Jose, California

City Hall: 801 N. First St. 95110 (408-277-4237)
Mayor: Susan Hammer (D); next election Nov. 1994
City Manager: Leslie White
Population & rank: 782,248/11
Per capita income & rank: $25,193/12
Council-manager form of government. Mayor and 10-member council are elected to 4-year terms. Council meets weekly.

San Francisco, California

City Hall: San Francisco 94102 (415-554-4000)
Mayor: Frank Jordan; next election Nov. 1995
Population & rank: 723,959/14
Per capita income & rank: $29,942/2
Unlike any other California city, San Francisco has a consolidated city-county government. The 1932 freeholders' charter provides the mayor with strong executive powers but delegates substantial authority to a chief administrative

officer (appointed by the mayor) and a comptroller. The legislative authority is lodged with an elected 10-member board of supervisors.

Long Beach, California

City Hall: 333 W. Ocean Blvd. 90802 (213-590-6801)
Mayor: Ernie Kell (I); next election June 1994
City Manager: James Hankla
Population & rank: 429,433/32
Per capita income & rank: Combined with Los Angeles, CA
Council-manager form of government. Mayor was formerly selected by city council from among its 9 district members for a 2-year term. Now, however, the mayor is directly elected for a 4-year term, as are council members. Council meets weekly.

Oakland, California

City Hall: 1 City Hall Plaza 94612 (415-273-3611)
Mayor: Elihu Harris (D); next election Nov. 1994
City Manager: Henry L. Gardner
Population & rank: 372,242/39
Per capita income & rank: $23,452/21
Council-manager form of government. The mayor is elected by the voters to a 2-year term. The manager is elected for a 4-year term, as are eight council members, all of whom are elected at-large, with overlapping terms. City elections are nonpartisan. The mayor is a member of the council but has no power to veto. The council meets weekly.

Sacramento, California

City Hall: 915 I Street 95814 (916-449-5407)
Mayor: Joe Serna; next election Nov. 1996
City Manager: Walter J. Slipe
Population & rank: 369,365/41
Per capita income & rank: $19,180/74
Council-manager form of government. The 9-member city council includes the mayor, who hires a city manager. The council is made up of 8 district and 1 at-large member, and both the mayor and city council serve 4-year terms. The council meets weekly.

COLORADO (1876)

State Capitol: Denver 80203

State Government Information: 1525 Sherman St., Denver CO 80203 (303-866-5000)
Population & rank: 3,294,394/26
Population demographics: White—88.2%; Black—4%; Hispanic—12.9%; Asian—2.4%; Native American—.8%; Other—5.1%
Per capita income & rank: $18,890/15
Public school per pupil spending & rank: $5,259/26
Governor: Roy R. Romer (D) (303-866-2471); 4-year term; elected 1986; last election (1990): Romer 625,057 (63%) vs. John Andrews (R) 362,855 (37%); next election Nov. 1994.
Lt. Governor: C. Michael Callihan (D)
Secretary of State: Natalie Meyer (R) (303-894-2200)
Attorney General: Gail Norton (R)
Treasurer: Gail Schoettler (D)
Electoral votes: 8
U.S. Congress: 6 Reps.
General Assembly: (303-866-3521) 35 Senate (16 D, 19 R) and 65 House (31 D, 34 R). Meets annually in January.

Denver, Colorado

City Hall: 1437 Bannock Street 80202 (303-575-5555)
Mayor: Wellington Webb; next election May 1995
Population & rank: 467,610/26
Per capita income & rank: $20,885/43
The city and county government, which merged in 1912, is of the mayor-council type. 13-member council meets weekly on Mondays.

CONNECTICUT (1788)

State Capitol: Hartford 06106
State Government Information: 30 Kennedy Street 06106 (203-566-2750)
Population & rank: 3,287,116/27
Population demographics: White—87%; Black—8.3%; Asian—1.5%; Hispanic—6.5%; Native American—.2%
Per capita income & rank: $25,484/1
Public school per pupil spending & rank: $8,299/4
Governor: Lowell Weicker (I) (203-566-4840); 4-year term; elected 1990; last election (1990): Weicker 460,119 (40%) vs. John Rowland (R) 427,504 (38%) vs. Bruce Morrison (D) 232,856 (22%); next election Nov. 1994.

Lt. Governor: Eunice Groark (I)
Secretary of State: Pauline Keizer (R) (203-566-2739)
Attorney General: Richard Blumenthal (D)
Treasurer: Francisco L. Borges (D)
Electoral votes: 8
U.S Congress: 6 Reps.
General Assembly: (203-240-0100) 36 Senate (20 D, 16 R) and 151 House (87 D, 64 R). Meets annually odd-numbered years in January and even-numbered years in February.

Hartford, Connecticut

City Hall: 500 Main Street 06103 (203-722-6620)
Mayor: Carrie Saxon Perry; next election Nov. 1993
City Manager: John C. Burke
Population & rank: 139,739/127
Per capita income & rank: $24,444/16
Council-manager form of government. A mayor and 9 council members (1 at-large and 8 district) are elected to 2-year terms. The mayor is a member of the council but does not have the power to veto. The council meets second and fourth Monday of each month.

DELAWARE (1787)

State Capitol: Dover 19901
State Government Information: Legislative Hall, Dover DE 19901 (302-739-4000)
Population & rank: 666,168/46
Population demographics: White—80.3%; Black—16.9%; Hispanic—2.4%; Asian—1.4%; Native American—.3%; Other—1.1%
Per capita income & rank: $20,022/12
Public school per pupil spending & rank: $6,080/11
Governor: Tom Carper (D) (302-739-4101); 4-year term; elected 1992; last election (1992): Carper 179,268 (66%), Gary Scott (R) 90,747 (33%), Floyd McDowell (I) 3,615 (1%); next election Nov. 1996.
Lt. Governor: Ruth Ann Minner (D)
Secretary of State: William T. Quillen (302-739-4111)
Attorney General: Charles M. Oberly III (D)
Treasurer: Janet C. Rzewnicki (R)
Electoral votes: 3
U.S. Congress: 1 Rep.
General Assembly: (302-739-4114) 21 Senate (15 D, 6 R) and 41 House (18 D, 23 R). General

Assembly meets annually from second Tuesday in January to midnight June 30.

Wilmington, Delaware

City Hall: 800 French St. 19801 (302-571-4100)
Mayor: James H. Stills; next election Nov. 1996
Population & rank: 71,529/NR
Per capita income & rank: $15,778/37
Mayor-council form of government. 13-member council meets Thursdays.

DISTRICT OF COLUMBIA

City Hall: Washington, D.C. 20004 (202-727-1000)
Mayor: Sharon Pratt Kelly (D); next election Nov. 1994
Population: 606,900/8(as a city), 48 (as a state)
Population demographics: White—29.6%; Black—65.8%; Asian & Pacific Islander—1.8%; Hispanic—5.4%; Native American—.2% Other—2.5%
Per capita income & rank: $25,363/11
Public school per pupil spending & rank: $8,116/5
Washington, D.C., has a governmental structure unique among U.S. cities. It is a federal district under the control of Congress. Prior to 1964 its day to day control rested with committees in the Senate and House. Since the passage of The Limited Home Rule Act of 1964, the city has been run by a directly elected mayor and a 13-member city council. The mayor has broad organizational and appointive authority. The city council is empowered to establish and set tax rates and fees, make changes in the budget, and organize or abolish any agency of government of the District. But under Article 1 of the U.S. Constitution, Congress still has the power to veto any action of the District government that threatens the "federal interest." Thus, while the District has a recognizable municipal form of government, Congress treats it in some respects as a branch of the federal government. The city's "district attorney" is the U.S. attorney for the District of Columbia, appointed by the president. The budget, passed by the city council and approved by the mayor, is reviewed and enacted by Congress. Moreover, Congress retains the right to enact legisla-

tion on any subject for the District, whether within or outside the scope of power delegated to the city council.

FLORIDA (1845)

State Capitol: Tallahassee 32301
State Government Information: Larson Bldg., Tallahassee FL 32301 (904-488-1234)
Population & rank: 13,937,926/4
Population demographics: White—83.1%; Black—13.6%; Hispanic—12.2%; Asian—1.2%; Other—1.8%
Per capita income & rank: $18,530/20
Public school per pupil spending & rank: $5,639/15
Governor: Lawton Chiles (D) (904-488-4441); 4-year term; elected 1990; last election (1990): Chiles 1,987,863 (57%) vs. Bob Martinez (R) 1,524,313 (43%); next election Nov. 1994.
Lt. Governor: Buddy MacKay (D)
Secretary of State: Jim Smith (R) (904-488-3680)
Attorney General: Robert A. Butterworth (D)
Treasurer/Commissioner of Insurance: Tom Gallagher (R)
Electoral votes: 25
U.S. Congress: 23 Reps.
Legislature: (904-488-4371) 40 Senate (20 D, 20 R) and 120 House (71 D, 49 R). Meets annually.

Jacksonville, Florida

City Hall: 220 East Bay St. 32202 (904-630-1776)
Mayor: Ed Austin; next election May 1995
Population & rank: 672,971/15
Per capita income & rank: $17,675/134
Jacksonville city has a consolidated government with Duval County. Mayor-council form of government with council having 20 members. Meets second and fourth Tuesday of each month.

Miami, Florida

City Hall: 3500 Pan American Drive 33233 (305-579-6666)
Mayor: Xavier L. Suarez; next election Nov. 1993
City Manager: Cesar H. Odio
Population & rank: 358,548/46
Per capita income & rank: $17,823/126
Commission-manager form of government. The mayor is elected to a 2-year term, and 4 com-

missioners serve 4-year terms. The Commission meets second and fourth Tuesdays of each month. The nine-member Dade County Board of Commissioners also plays a major role in the area government. It heads a metropolitan county government, called Metro Dade, which acts to coordinate municipal activities.

Orlando, Florida

City Hall: 400 S. Orange Ave. 32801 (407-849-2221)
Mayor: Glenda E. Hood; next election Sept. 1994
Population & rank: 164,693/104
Per capita income & rank: $17,737/132
Mayor-commission form of government. Six member commission meets weekly on Mondays.

GEORGIA (1788)

State Capitol: Atlanta 30334
State Government Information: 330 Capitol Ave., S.W. Atlanta GA 30334 (404-656-2000)
Population & rank: 6,478,216/11
Population demographics: White—71%; Black—27%; Hispanic—1.7%; Asian—1.2%
Per capita income & rank: $17,049/31
Public school per pupil spending & rank: $4,720/34
Governor: Zell Miller (D) (404-656-1776); 4-year term; elected 1990; last election (1990): Miller 766,130 (53%) vs. Johnny Isakson (R) 645,649 (45%); next election Nov. 1994.
Lt. Governor: Pierre Howard (D)
Secretary of State: Max Cleland (D) (404-656-2881)
Attorney General: Michael J. Bowers (D)
State Treasurer: Steven N. McCoy
Electoral votes: 13
U.S. Congress: 11 Reps.
General Assembly: (404-656-0028) 56 Senate (41 D, 15 R) and 180 House (128 D, 52 R). Meets annually.

Atlanta, Georgia

City Hall: 68 Mitchell St. 30335 (404-658-6300)
Mayor: Maynard Jackson (D); next election Oct. 1993
Population & rank: 394,017/36
Per capita income & rank: $20,263/51

Atlanta revised its charter in 1974 to create a strong form of government that placed all administrative responsibilities under the mayor. All policy-making and legislative functions under the new charter reside within a 19-member city council, which meets on the first and third Mondays of each month.

HAWAII (1959)

State Capitol: Honolulu 96813
State Government Information: State Capitol, Honolulu HI 96813 (808-548-2211)
Population & rank: 1,108,209/40
Population demographics: White—33.4%; Black —2.5%; Hispanic—7.3%; Asian & Pacific Islander—61.8%; Native American—.5%; Other —1.9%
Per capita income & rank: $20,356/11
Public school per pupil spending & rank: $5,435/20
Governor: John D. Waihee III (D) (808-548-5420); 4-year term; elected 1986; last election (1990): Waihee 203,491 (61%) vs. Fred Hemmings (R) 131,310 (39%); next election Nov. 1994.
Lt. Governor: Benjamin J. Cayetano (D) (808-548-2544)
Attorney General: Robert A. Marks (D)
Secretary of State: None
State Treasurer: Yukio Takemoto (D)
Electoral votes: 4
U.S. Congress: 2 Reps.
Legislature: (808-548-2211) 25 Senate (22 D, 3 R) and 51 House (47 D, 4 R). Meets annually on third Wednesday in January.

Honolulu, Hawaii

City Hall: 530 S. King Street 96813 (808-523-4385)
Mayor: Frank F. Fasi (R); next election Nov. 1994
Managing Director: Jeremy Harris
Population & rank: 365,048/44
Per capita income & rank: $21,307/41
Honolulu's government is made up of a mayor and 9 district-council members who are elected directly by the voters to 4-year terms. The mayor is not a member of the council but has the power to veto. The council meets twice a month.

IDAHO (1890)

State Capitol: Boise 83720

State Government Information: 650 W. State St., Boise ID 83702 (208-334-2411)
Population & rank: 1,006,749/42
Population demographics: White—94.4%; Hispanic—5.4%; Black—.3%; Native American—1.4%; Asian—.9%
Per capita income & rank: $15,249/41
Public school per pupil spending & rank: $3,528/49
Governor: Cecil D. Andrus (D) (208-334-2100); 4-year term; elected 1986; last election (1990): Andrus 199,467 (67%) vs. Roger Fairchild 96,069 (33%); next election Nov. 1994.
Lt. Governor: C.L. "Butch" Otter (R)
Secretary of State: Pete T. Cenarrusa (R) (208-334-2300)
Attorney General: Larry EchoHawk (D)
Treasurer: Lydia Justice Edwards (R)
Electoral votes: 4
U.S. Congress: 2 Reps.
Legislature: (208-334-3175) 35 Senate (12 D, 23 R) and 70 House (20 D, 50 R). Meets annually beginning on the Monday on or nearest the ninth of January.

Boise, Idaho

City Hall: 150 N. Capital Blvd. 83701 (208-384-4000)
Mayor: Brent Coles; next election Nov. 1993
Population & rank: 125,738/145
Per capita income & rank: $18,786/88
Mayor-council form of government. 6-member council meets every Tuesday.

ILLINOIS (1818)

State Capitol: Springfield 62706
State Government Information: 501 S. 2nd Street, Rm. 176, Springfield IL 62706 (217-782-2000)
Population & rank: 11,430,602/6
Population demographics: White—78.3%; Black —14.8%; Hispanic—7.9%; Asian—2.5% Other —4.2%
Per capita income & rank: $20,419/10
Public school per pupil spending & rank: $5,248/27
Governor: Jim Edgar (R) (217-782-6830); 4-year term; elected 1990; last election (1990): Edgar 1,635,368 (52%) vs. Neil Hartigan (D) 1,538,389 (48%); next election Nov. 1994.
Lt. Governor: Bob Kustra (R)

Secretary of State: George H. Ryan (R) (217-782-2201)
Attorney General: Roland W. Burris (D)
Treasurer: Patrick Quinn (D)
Electoral votes: 22
U.S. Congress: 20 Reps.
General Assembly: (217-782-8223) 59 Senate (27 D, 32 R) and 118 House (67 D, 51 R). Meets annually in January.

Chicago, Illinois

City Hall: 121 N. La Salle St. 60602 (312-744-4000)
Mayor: Richard M. Daley; next election April 1995
Population & rank: 2,783,726/3
Per capita income & rank: $22,385/25
Chicago's unwieldy governmental structure, a mayor presiding over a 50-member Board of Aldermen, depends upon a strong mayor who can control the Board. When the late Richard J. Daley controlled the Democratic organization with an iron hand, Chicago was a model of efficiency. After his death the government disintegrated into factions, broken down in recent years along racial lines. His son, in his first term, has returned some stability to local government, although the old political machine his father commanded is now only a shell of its former self.

INDIANA (1816)

State Capitol: Indianapolis 46204
State Government Information: 100 N. Senate Ave., Indianapolis IN 46204 (317-232-1000)
Population & rank: 5,544,159/14
Population demographics: White—90.6%; Black—7.8%; Hispanic—1.8%; Asian—.7%; Native American—.2%
Per capita income & rank: $16,890/32
Public school per pupil spending & rank: $5,429/22
Governor: Evan Bayh (D) (317-232-4567); 4-year term; elected 1988; last election (1992): Bayh 1,363,630 (63%) vs. Linley E. Pearson (R) 811,530 (37%); next election Nov. 1996.
Lt. Governor: Frank O'Bannon (D)
Secretary of State: Joseph H. Hogsett (D) (317-232-6531)
Attorney General: Pamela Fanning Carter (D)
Treasurer: Marjorie H. O'Laughlin (R)

Electoral votes: 12
U.S. Congress: 10 Reps.
General Assembly: (317-232-9550) 50 Senate (22 D, 28 R) and 100 House (55 D, 45 R). Meets annually beginning in January.

Indianapolis, Indiana

City Hall: 2501 City-County Building 46204 (317-236-3600)
Mayor: Steve Goldsmith; next election Nov. 1995
Population & rank: 741,952/12
Per capita income & rank: $19,522/65
Governed by a mayor and a city council of 29 members, all elected for 4 years. The council meets once a month. The mayor is not a member of the council but may veto any measures passed by the council. The mayor also appoints members of boards and commissions.

IOWA (1846)

State Capitol: Des Moines 50319
State Government Information: E. 10th & Grand Ave. Des Moines IA 50319 (515-281-5011)
Population & rank: 2,776,755/30
Population demographics: White—96.6%; Black—1.7%; Hispanic—.2%; Asian—.9%; Native American—.3%
Per capita income & rank: $17,218/28
Public school per pupil spending & rank: $4,499/30
Governor: Terry E. Branstad (R) (515-281-5211); 4-year term; elected 1982; last election (1990): Branstad 589,035 (61%) vs. Donald Avenson (D) 377,469 (39%); next election Nov. 1994.
Lt. Governor: Joy C. Corning (R)
Secretary of State: Elaine Baxter (D) (515-281-5864)
Attorney General: Bonnie Campbell (D)
Treasurer: Michael L. Fitzgerald (D)
Electoral votes: 7
U.S. Congress: 5 Reps.
General Assembly: (515-281-5011) 50 Senate (26 D, 24 R) and 100 House (49 D, 51 R). Meets annually in January.

Des Moines, Iowa

City Hall: 400 East First St. 50309 (515-283-4500)
Mayor: John Pat Dorrian; next election Nov. 1993

City Manager: Cy Carney
Population & rank: 193,187/80
Per capita income & rank: $19,662/61
Council-manager form of government. The mayor and 6 council members are elected to 2-year terms. The mayor is a member of the council but does not have the power to veto. The council meets on the first, third and fourth Mondays of each month.

KANSAS (1861)

State Capitol: Topeka 66612
State Government Information: 915 SW Harrison St., Topeka KS 66612 (913-296-0111)
Population & rank: 2,477,574/32
Population demographics: White—90.1%; Black—5.8%; Hispanic—3.8%; Asian—1.3%; Native American—.9%; Other—2%
Per capita income & rank: $18,162/22
Public school per pupil spending & rank: $5,131/28
Governor: Joan Finney (D) (913-296-3232); 4-year term; elected 1990; last election (1990): Finney 381,446 (53%) Mike Hayden (R) 332,234 (47%); next election Nov. 1994.
Lt. Governor: James L. Francisco (D)
Secretary of State: William Graves (R) (913-296-2236)
Attorney General: Robert T. Stephan (R)
Treasurer: Sally Thompson (D)
Electoral votes: 6
U.S. Congress: 4 Reps.
Legislature: (913-296-2391) 40 Senate (14 D, 26 R) and 125 House (59 D, 66 R). Meets annually in January.

Wichita, Kansas

City Hall: 455 N. Main Street 67202 (316-268-4331)
Mayor: Elma Broadfoot; next election March 1997
City Manager: Chris Cherches
Population & rank: 304,011/51
Per capita income & rank: $18,825/87
Council-manager form of government. 5-member council meets weekly.

KENTUCKY (1792)

State Capitol: Frankfort 40601
State Government Information: Capitol An-

nex, Rm. 52, Frankfort KY 40601 (502-564-2500)
Population & rank: 3,685,296/23
Population demographics: White—92%; Black—7.1%; Hispanic—.6%; Asian—.5%; Native American—.2%
Per capita income & rank: $15,001/45
Public school per pupil spending & rank: $4,616/39
Governor: Brereton C. Jones (D) (502-564-2611); 4-year term; elected 1991; last election (1991): ; Jones 540,468 (62%) Larry J. Hopkins (R) 294,452 (34%); next election Nov. 1995.
Lt. Governor: Paul E. Patton (D)
Secretary of State: Bob Babbage (D) (502-564-3490)
Attorney General: Chris Gorman (D)
Treasurer: Frances Jones Mills (D)
Electoral votes: 8
U.S. Congress: 6 Reps.
General Assembly: (502-564-2500) 38 Senate (25D, 13 R) and 100 House (72 D, 28 R). Meets even-numbered years in January.

Louisville, Kentucky

City Hall: 601 Jefferson Street 40202 (502-625-3061)
Mayor: Jerry E. Abramson; next election November 1993
Population & rank: 269,063/58
Per capita income & rank: $18,263/111
Mayor-alderman form of government. 12-member Board of Aldermen meets on the second and fourth Tuesday of each month.

LOUISIANA (1812)

State Capitol: Baton Rouge 70804
State Government Information: 7389 Florida Blvd. Rm. 300, Baton Rouge LA 70806 (504-342-6600)
Population & rank: 4,219,973/21
Population demographics: White—67.3%; Black—30.8%; Hispanic—2.2%; Asian—1%; Native American—.4%
Per capita income & rank: $14,542/46
Public school per pupil spending & rank: $4,378/42
Governor: Edwin Edwards (D) (504-342-7015); 4-year term; elected 1991; last election (1991): Edwards 1,057,088 (61%), David Duke (R) 666,393 (37%); next election Nov. 1995.
Lt. Governor: Melinda Schwegmann (D)

Secretary of State: Fox McKeithen (D) (504-922-1000)
Attorney General: Richard P. Ieyoub (D)
Treasurer: Mary Landrieu (D)
Electoral votes: 9
U.S. Congress: 7 Reps.
Legislature: (S-504-342-2040, H-504-342-6945) 39 Senate (34 D, 5 R) and 105 House (88 D, 16 R, 1 I). Terms expire 1995. Meets annually for 60 legislative days commencing on third Monday in April.

New Orleans, Louisiana

City Hall: 1300 Perdido St. 70112 (504-586-4311)
Mayor: Sidney Barthelemy (D); next election Feb. 1994
Population & rank: 496,938/25
Per capita income & rank: $16,500/185
Mayor-council type of government. Mayor and 7-member council are directly elected (5 from districts and 2 at-large) by the voters for 4-year terms. In addition, a chief administrative officer—something like a City Manager—is appointed by the council. The mayor is the top administrator over the 13 municipal departments and oversees the affairs of various commissions and boards. The chief administrative officer is charged with supervision of city departments, preparation of the annual budget, and coordination of city relations with state and federal agencies. Although most city and parish (county) government has been consolidated in New Orleans, Orleans Parish officials continue to play an important role. These officials include the district attorney, the board of assessors, and the Orleans Parish School Board.

MAINE (1820)

State Capitol: Augusta 04333
State Government Information: 100 State St. Augusta ME 04333 (207-289-1110)
Population & rank: 1,227,928/38
Population demographics: White—98.4%; Black—.4%; Native American—.5%; Asian—.5%; Hispanic—.6%
Per capita income & rank: $17,175/30
Public school per pupil spending & rank: $5,969/14
Governor: John R. McKernan, Jr. (R) (207-289-3531); 4-year term; elected 1986; last elec-

tion (1990): McKernan 240,263 (47%) vs. Joseph Brennan (D) 227,169 (30%) vs. Andrew Adam (I) 47,672 (9%); next election Nov. 1994.
Lt. Governor: Dennis Dutremble
Secretary of State: G. William Diamond (D) (207-289-1090)
Attorney General: Michael Carpenter (D)
Treasurer: Samuel Shapiro (D)
Positions of secretary of state, attorney general and treasurer are appointed by the Legislature every two years.
Electoral votes: 4
U.S. Congress: 2 Reps.
Legislature: (207-289-1110) 35 Senate (20 D, 15 R) and 151 House (90 D, 61 R). Meets annually in December.

Portland, Maine

City Hall: 389 Congress Street 04101 (207-874-8300)
Mayor: Charles Harlow; next election May 1993
City Manager: Robert Ganley
Population & rank: 64,358/NR
Per capita income & rank: $21,362/36
Council-manager form of government. The mayor and an 8-member council are elected to 3-year staggered terms. Council meets weekly.

MARYLAND (1788)

State Capitol: Annapolis 21401 (301-974-2000)
State Government Information: 80 Calvert St., Rm. 105, Annapolis MD 21401 (301-974-3431)
Population & rank: 4,781,468/19
Population demographics: White—71%; Black—24.9%; Hispanic—2.6%; Asian—2.9%; Native American—.3%
Per capita income & rank: $21,789/6
Public school per pupil spending & rank: $6,273/10
Governor: William Donald Schaefer (D) (301-974-3901); 4-year term; elected 1986; last election (1990): Schaefer 644,528 (60%) vs. William Shepard (R) 435,361 (40%); next election Nov. 1994.
Lt. Governor: Melvin A. Steinberg, Jr. (D)
Secretary of State: Winfield Kelly, Jr. (D) (301-841-3908)
Attorney General: J. Joseph Curran, Jr. (D)
Treasurer: Lucille Maurer (D)
Electoral votes: 10

U.S. Congress: 8 Reps.
General Assembly: (301-858-3000) 47 Senate (38 D, 9 R); 141 House (116 D, 25 R). Meets 90 days annually beginning on second Wednesday in January.

Baltimore, Maryland

City Hall: 100 N. Holliday St. 21202 (301-396-3100)
Mayor: Kurt Schmoke (D); next election Nov. 1995
Population & rank: 736,014/13
Per capita income & rank: $21,461/33
Baltimore, an independent city which is not included in any county, has a mayor-council form of government. The mayor and the 19-member council (18 district and 1 at-large) are directly elected by the voters to 4-year terms. The mayor is not a member of the council, but has veto power. The council meets weekly.

MASSACHUSETTS (1788)

State Capitol: Boston 02133 (617-727-2121)
State Government Information: 1 Ashburton Pl., Boston MA 02108 (617-727-7030)
Population & rank: 6,016,425/13
Population demographics: White—89.8%; Black —5%; Hispanic—4.8%; Asian—2.4%; Other—2.6%
Per capita income & rank: $22,569/4
Public school per pupil spending & rank: $6,323/9
Governor: William Weld (R) (617-727-3600); 4-year term; elected 1990; last election (1990): Weld 1,174,916 (52%) vs. John Silber (D) 1,098,022 (48%); next election Nov. 1994.
Lt. Governor: Argeo Paul Cellucci (R)
Secretary of the Commonwealth: Michael Connelly (D) (617-727-7030)
Attorney General: L. Scott Harshbarger (D)
Treasurer: Joseph Malone (R)
Electoral votes: 12
U.S. Congress: 10 Reps.
General Court: (617-727-7030) 40 Senate (31 D, 9 R) and 160 House (124 D, 35 R, 1 I). General Assembly meets annually in January.

Boston, Massachusetts

City Hall: 1 City Hall Square 02201 (617-725-4000)

Mayor: Raymond L. Flynn (D); next election Nov. 1993
Population & rank: 574,283/20
Per capita income & rank: $24,315/18
Mayor-council type of government. Mayor and 13-member council are directly elected for 4-year terms. Council meets weekly.

MICHIGAN (1837)

State Capitol: Lansing 48913 (517-373-0183)
State Government Information: P. O. Box 30026, Lansing MI 48909 (517-373-1837)
Population & rank: 9,295,297/8
Population demographics: White—83.4%; Black —13.1%; Native American—.6%, Asian—1.1%, Hispanic—2.2%
Per capita income & rank: $18,360/21
Public school per pupil spending & rank: $5,630/16
Governor: John Engler (R) (517-373-3423); 4-year term; elected 1990; last election (1990): Engler 1,279,744 (50%) vs. James Blanchard (D) 1,260,611 (50%); next election Nov. 1994.
Lt. Governor: Connie Binsfeld (R)
Secretary of State: Richard H. Austin (D) (517-373-2510)
Attorney General: Frank J. Kelley (D)
Treasurer: Douglas B. Roberts (R)
Electoral votes: 18
U.S. Congress: 16 Reps.
Legislature: (517-373-1837) 38 Senate (18 D, 20 R) and 110 House (55 D, 55 R). Meets annually in January.

Detroit, Michigan

City Hall: 2 Woodward Ave. 48226 (313-224-3000)
Mayor: Coleman A. Young (I); next election Nov. 1993
Population & rank: 1,027,974/7
Per capita income & rank: $20,453/48
Mayor-council type of government. The mayor and 9 at-large council members are elected directly by the voters in a non-partisan contest held every 4 years, the year following the U.S. presidential election. The city clerk and treasurer are also elected on the same ballot. The council member receiving the highest vote automatically becomes the council president and acting mayor in the absense of the elected mayor. The council meets weekly.

MINNESOTA (1858)

State Capitol: St. Paul 55155
State Government Information: 50 Sherburne Ave., Rm. G18B, St. Paul MN 55155 (612-296-6013)
Population & rank: 4,375,099/20
Population demographics: White—94.4%; Black —2.2%; Hispanic—1.2%; Asian—1.8%; Native American—1.1%
Per capita income & rank: $18,731/18
Public school per pupil spending & rank: $5,510/17
Governor: Arne Carlson (R) (612-296-3391); 4-year term; elected 1990; last election (1990): Carlson 764,090 (50%) vs. Rudy Perpich (Democratic-Farmer-Labor) 750,008 (50%); next election Nov. 1994.
Lt. Governor: Joanell Dyrstad (R)
Secretary of State: Joan Anderson Growe (DFL) (612-296-3266)
Attorney General: Hubert H. Humphrey III (DFL)
Treasurer: Michael McGrath (DFL)
Electoral votes: 10
U.S. Congress: 8 Reps.
Legislature: (S-612-296-0504, H-612-296-2146) 67 Senate (45 DFL, 22 IR) and 134 House (87 DFL, 47 IR). Meets for a total of 120 days within every 2-year period.

Minneapolis, Minnesota

City Hall: 350 S. Fifth Street 55415 (612-348-3000)
Mayor: Donald M. Fraser (D); next election Nov. 1993
City Administrator: James J. Wright
Popuation & rank: 368,383/42
Per capita income & rank: $21,330/39
Mayor-council form of government. The mayor is elected by popular vote to a 4-year term. The city council is composed of 13 aldermen, 1 from each of the voting wards, who also serve 4-year terms. The council meets twice a month on second and last Fridays. The mayor is not a member of the council but does have veto power. In 1967 the state legislature created the metropolitan council to act as a planning and advisory body on matters affecting the growth of the 7-county Minneapolis-St. Paul area.

St. Paul, Minnesota

City Hall: 15 W. Kellogg Blvd. 55102 (612-298-4012)

Mayor: James Scheibel; next election Nov. 1993
Population & rank: 272,235/57
Per capita income & rank: Combined with Minneapolis ($21,330/39)
Mayor-council form of government. The mayor and 7-member council are directly elected by the voters, the mayor for a 4-year term, the council for 2-year terms. Council meets weekly.

MISSISSIPPI (1817)

State Capitol: Jackson 39201 (601-359-1000)
State Government Information: 239 N. Lamar St., Jackson MS 39201
Population & rank: 2,573,216/31
Population demographics: White—63.5%; Black —35.6%; Hispanic—.6%; Native American—.3%; Asian—.5%
Per capita income & rank: $12,823/51
Public school per pupil spending & rank: $3,344/50
Governor: Kirk Fordice (R) (601-359-3100); 4-year term; elected 1991; next election Nov. 1995.
Lt. Governor: Eddie Briggs (R)
Secretary of State: Dick Molpus (D) (601-359-1350)
Attorney General: Mike Moore (D)
Treasurer: Marshall Bennett (D)
Electoral votes: 7
U.S. Congress: 5 Reps.
Legislature: (601-948-7321) 52 Senate (39 D, 13 R) and 122 House (95 D, 27 R). Meets annually beginning in January.

Jackson, Mississippi

City Hall: 219 S. President Street 39205 (601-960-1035)
Mayor: Kane Ditto; next election June, 1993
Population & rank: 196,637/78
Per capita income & rank: $15,644/237
Mayor-council form of government. Mayor and 7-member council directly elected for 4-year terms. Council meets weekly.

MISSOURI (1821)

State Capitol: Jefferson City 65102 (314-751-3222)
State Government Information: 301 W. High Street, Jefferson City MO 65101 (314-751-2000)
Population & rank: 5,117,073/15
Population demographics: White—87.7%; Black —10.7%; Hispanic—1.2%, Asian—.8%; Native American—.4%

Per capita income & rank: $17,472/27
Public school per pupil spending & rank: $4,534/41
Governor: Mel Carnahan (D) (314-751-3222); 4-year term; elected 1992; last election (1992): Carnahan 1,374,466 (59%), William Webster (R) 967,102 (41%); next election Nov. 1996.
Lt. Governor: Roger B. Wilson (D)
Secretary of State: Judith Moriarty (D) (314-751-2379)
Attorney General: Jeremiah W. Nixon (D)
Treasurer: Bob Holden (D)
Electoral votes: 11
U.S. Congress: 9 Reps.
General Assembly: (314-751-2151) 34 Senate (20 D, 13 R, 1 Vac.) and 163 House (100 D, 63 R). Meets annually on the first Wednesday after first Monday in January; adjournment in odd-numbered years by June 30, in even-numbered years by May 15.

Kansas City, Missouri

City Hall: 414 E. 12th St. 66106 (816-274-2000)
Mayor: Emanuel Cleaver II; next election April 1995
City Manager: David H. Olson
Population & rank: 435,146/31
Per capita income & rank: $19,482/66
Under a home-rule charter adopted in 1925 and later amended, Kansas City is governed by a mayor and council elected at 4-year intervals. The 12 council members select the city manager, who is the chief administrative officer of the municipality.

St. Louis, Missouri

City Hall: 1200 Market St. 63103 (314-622-4000)
Mayor: Freeman Bosley, Jr. (D); next election April 1997
Population & rank: 396,685/34
Per capita income & rank: $20,200/53
The government structure is provided by home-rule charter, approved in 1914. The city government is a mayor-council form. The mayor and the board of aldermen are elected for 4-year terms. One alderman is elected from each of the city's 28 wards, and a president of the board is elected at-large. Except for the city comptroller, who is popularly elected, major administrative officers are appointed by the mayor.

MONTANA (1889)

State Capitol: Helena 59620 (406-444-2511)
State Government Information: Mitchell Bldg, Rm. 219, Helena, MT 59620 (406-444-2511)
Population & rank: 779,065/44
Population demographics: White—95.1%; Black —.3%; Hispanic—1.6%; Native American—6.1%; Asian—.5%
Per capita income & rank: $15,270/40
Public school per pupil spending & rank: $5,127/29
Governor: Marc Racicot (R) (406-444-3111); 4-year term; elected 1992; last election (1992): Racicot 208,841 (51%), Dorothy Bradley (D) 197,416 (49%); next election Nov. 1996.
Lt. Governor: Dennis Rehberg (R)
Secretary of State: Mike Cooney (D) (406-444-2034)
Attorney General: Joseph P. Mazurek (D)
Electoral votes: 3
U.S. Congress: 1 Rep.
Legislative Assembly: (406-444-4853) 50 Senate (30 R, 20 D) and 100 House (47 D, 53 R). Meets odd-numbered years in January.

Billings, Montana

City Hall: (mailing) P. O. Box 1178 59103 (406-657-8200)
Mayor: Richard Larsen (D); next election Nov. 1993
City Manager: Bruce McCandless
Population & rank: 81,151/NR
Per capita income & rank: $17,272/149
Council-manager form of government. Mayor and 10-member council are elected to 4-year terms. Council meets first and third Mondays of each month.

NEBRASKA (1867)

State Capitol: Lincoln 68509
State Government Information: State Capitol, Lincoln NB 68509 (402-471-2311)
Population & rank: 1,578,385/36
Population demographics: White—93.8%; Black —3.6%; Hispanic—2.3%; Asian—.8%; Native American—.8%
Per capita income & rank: $17,549/25
Public school per pupil spending & rank: $4,676/37
Governor: Ben Nelson (D) (402-471-2244); 4-year term; elected 1990; last election (1990): Nelson

286,776 (50%) vs. Kay Orr (R) 282,118 (50%); next election Nov. 1994.
Lt. Governor: Maxine Moul (D)
Secretary of State: Allen J. Beermann (R) (402-471-2554)
Attorney General: Don Stenberg (R)
Treasurer: Dawn Rockey (D)
Electoral votes: 5
U.S. Congress: 3 Reps.
Legislature: (402-471-2271) Unicameral (single chambered). All legislators, called "senators," are elected for 4-year terms and represent specific legislative districts. Although elected on a nonpartisan ballot and constitutionally mandated to be nonpartisan, they do have 'unofficial' political party affilations. Current makeup: 49 senators (22 D, 26 R, 1 I).

Omaha, Nebraska

City Hall: 1819 Farnam Street 68183 (402-444-7000)
Mayor: P. J. Morgan (D); next election May 1993
Population & rank: 335,795/48
Per capita income & rank: $18,583/96
Mayor-council form of government. The mayor and 7 district-council members are elected by the voters to 4-year terms. The mayor is not a member of the council but may veto measures passed by the council. The council meets weekly.

NEVADA (1864)

State Capitol: Carson City 89710
State Government Information: 406 E. 2nd St., Carson City NV 89710 (702-885-5000)
Population & rank: 1,201,833/39
Population demographics: White—84.3%; Black—6.6%; Hispanic—10.4%; Asian—3.2%; Native American—1.6%; Other—4.4%
Per capita income & rank: $19,035/14
Public school per pupil spending & rank: $4,910/31
Governor: Robert Miller (D) (702-885-5670); 4-year term; appointed to office January 1989; last election (1990): Miller 207,530 (66%) vs. Jim Gallaway (R) 95,619 (31%); next election Nov. 1994.
Lt. Governor: Sue Wagner (R)
Secretary of State: Cherlyn Lau (D) (702-885-5203)

Attorney General: Frankie Sue Del Papa (D)
Treasurer: Bob Seale (R)
Electoral votes: 4
U.S. Congress: 2 Reps.
Legislature: (702-687-6800) 21 Senate (10 D, 11 R) and 42 Assembly (29 D, 13 R). Meets odd-numbered years in January.

Las Vegas, Nevada

City Hall: 400 E. Stewart Ave. 89101 (702-386-6501)
Mayor: Jan Laverty Jones; next election June 1993
City Manager: William J. Noonan
Population & rank: 258,295/63
Per capita income & rank: $18,625/92
Council-manager form of government. Mayor and 9-member council are elected to 4-year terms. Council meets first and third Wednesdays of each month.

NEW HAMPSHIRE (1788)

State Capitol: Concord 03301 (603-271-1110)
State Government Information: 107 N. Main Street, Concord NH 03301 (603-271-1110)
Population & rank: 1,109,252/41
Population demographics: White—98%; Black—.6%; Hispanic—1%; Asian—.8%
Per capita income & rank: $20,872/8
Public school per pupil spending & rank: $5,500/18
Governor: Steve Merrill (R) (603-271-2121); 2-year term; elected 1992; last election (1992): Merrill 286,083 (56%), Deborah Arnie Arnesen 205,553 (40%), Miriam Luce (Libert) 20,187 (4%); next election Nov. 1994.
Lt. Governor: Ralph Hough (R)
Secretary of State: William Gardner (D) (603-271-3242)
Attorney General: Jeffery Howard (R)
Treasurer: Georgie Thomas (R)
Electoral votes: 4
U.S. Congress: 2 Reps.
General Court: (603-271-2111) 24 Senate (11 D, 13 R); 400 House (136 D, 258 R, 5 I, 1 Vac.). Meets annually beginning in January.

Manchester, New Hampshire

City Hall: 908 Elm Street 03101 (603-624-6500)
Mayor: Raymond Wieczorek; next election Nov. 1993

Population & rank: 99,567/NR
Per capita income & rank: $22,581/23
Mayor-council form of government. Mayor and 12-member Board of Aldermen are directly elected for 2-year terms. Board meets first and third Tuesdays of the month except in summer.

NEW JERSEY (1787)

State Capitol: Trenton 08625
State Government Information: John Finch Plaza, Trenton N.J. 08625 (609-292-2121)
Population & rank: 7,730,188/9
Population demographics: White—79.3%; Black —13.4%; Hispanic—9.6%; Native American— .2%; Asian—3.5%; Other—3.6%
Per capita income & rank: $24,936/2
Public school per pupil spending & rank: $10,219/1
Governor: James J. Florio (D) (609-292-6000); 4-year term; elected 1989; last election (1989): Florio 1,374,661 (61%) vs. Jim Courter (R) 835,811 (37%); next election Nov. 1993.
Senate President: Donald T. DiFrancesco (R)
Secretary of State: Daniel J. Dalton (D) (609-984-1900)
Attorney General: Robert Del Tufo (D)
Treasurer: Douglas Berman (D)
Electoral votes: 15
U.S. Congress: 13 Reps.
Legislature: (609-292-4840) 40 Senate (13 D, 27 R); 80 General Assembly (22 D, 58 R). Meets annually beginning in January.

Newark, New Jersey

City Hall: 920 Broad Street 07102 (201-733-6400)
Mayor: Sharpe James (D); next election May 1994
Population & rank: 275,221/56
Per capita income & rank: $26,600/8
Mayor-council form of government. Mayor and 9-member council (5 from wards and 4 at-large) are directly elected by voters to 4-year terms. Council meets weekly.

NEW MEXICO (1912)

State Capitol: Santa Fe 87503
State Government Information: 810 San Mateo Ave., Santa Fe NM 87503 (505-827-4011)
Population & rank: 1,515,069/37
Population demographics: White—75.6%; Black

—2%; Hispanic—38.2%; Native American—8.9%; Asian—.9%; Other—12.6%
Per capita income & rank: $14,265/47
Public school per pupil spending & rank: $4,692/35
Governor: Bruce King (D) (505-827-3000); 4-year term; elected 1990; last election (1990): King 223,526 (54%) vs. Frank Bond (R) 187,549 (46%); next election Nov. 1994.
Lt. Governor: Casey Luna (D)
Secretary of State: Stephanie Gonzales (D) (505-827-3600)
Attorney General: Tom Udall (D)
Treasurer: David King (D)
Electoral votes: 5
U.S. Congress: 3 Reps.
Legislature: (505-827-4011) 42 Senate (27 D, 15 R); 70 House (52 D, 18 R). Meets in January of odd-numbered years for 60 days, even-numbered years for 30 days.

Albuquerque, New Mexico

City Hall: 1 Civil Plaza, N.W. 87102 (505-768-3000)
Mayor: Louis E. Saanedra (D); next election Oct. 1993
Population & rank: 384,736/38
Per capita income & rank: $17,517/137
Mayor-council form of government. Mayor and 9-member council are directly elected to 4-year terms. Council meets first and third Mondays of each month.

NEW YORK (1788)

State Capitol: Albany 12224 (518-474-2121)
State Government Information: Empire State Plaza, Concourse Level, Albany NY 12224 (518-474-2121)
Population & rank: 17,990,455/2
Population demographics: White—74.4%; Black —15.9%; Hispanic—12.3%; Asian—3.9%; Native American—.3%
Per capita income & rank: $22,086/5
Public school per pupil spending & rank: $8,658/3
Governor: Mario M. Cuomo (D) (518-474-8390); 4-year term; elected 1982; last election (1990): Cuomo 2,099,539 (53%) vs. Pierre Rinfret (R) 852,077 (22%) vs. Herbert London (Cons) 815,402 (21%); next election Nov. 1994.
Lt. Governor: Stanley N. Lundine (D)

Secretary of State: Gail Schaffer (D) (518-474-4750)
Attorney General: Robert Abrams (D)
Comptroller: Edward V. Regan (R)
Electoral votes: 33
U.S. Congress: 31 Reps.
Legislature: (S-518-455-2800, A-518-455-4100) 61 Senate (27 D, 34 R); 150 Assembly (101 D, 49 R). Meets annually beginning in January.

New York, New York

City Hall: New York 10007 (212-566-1750)
Mayor: David N. Dinkins (D); next election Nov. 1993
Population & rank: 7,322,564/1
Per capita income & rank: $23,744/19
The city's governing structure has 3 major components: the mayor, the Board of Estimate, and the City Council. Elected for 4 years, the mayor appoints the deputy mayor and agency heads and prepares the budget. The City Council is made up of a president, elected on a citywide basis, and 43 members, all elected for 4-year terms. Of these, 33 are elected from districts within the five boroughs, 2 at-large (and of different parties) from each borough. The mayor has veto power over council actions. A mayoral veto may be overridden by a 2/3 vote. The Board of Estimate, whose main power is to act on the budget prepared by the mayor, is made up of the mayor, the council president, the comptroller, and the 5 borough presidents. The mayor, comptroller, and council president each have 2 votes on the board and thus can outvote the 5 borough presidents combined.

Buffalo, New York

City Hall: 30 Niagara Square 14202 (716-851-4200)
Mayor: James D. Griffin (D); next election Nov. 1993
Population & rank: 328,123/50
Per capita income & rank: $18,305/108
Mayor-council form of government. The mayor is elected directly by voters to a 4-year term and is empowered, with the consent of the city council, to appoint most administrative officials. The council has 4 members-at-large (including a president) elected for staggered 4-year terms and 9 district members elected for 2-year terms. They meet twice a month. The mayor is not a member of the council but has the power to veto.

Rochester, New York

City Hall: 30 Church St., 14614 (716-428-7000)
Mayor: Thomas P. Ryan, Jr. next election Nov. 1993
Population & rank: 231,636/66
Per capita income & rank: $20,338/50
Mayor-council form of government. Mayor and 9-member common council are directly elected by the voters for 4-year terms. Council meets weekly.

Syracuse, New York

City Hall: 233 E. Walsh Street 13202 (315-448-2489)
Mayor: Thomas G. Young; next election Nov. 1993
Population & rank: 163,860/106
Per capita income & rank: $18,211/113
Mayor-council form of government. Mayor and 10-member common council are directly elected by the voters for 4-year terms. Council meets weekly.

NORTH CAROLINA (1789)

State Capitol: Raleigh 27611
State Government Information: 116 W. Jones St., Raleigh NC 27603 (919-733-1110)
Population & rank: 6,628,637/10
Population demographics: White—75.6%; Black—22% Hispanic—1.2%; Native American—1.2%; Asian—.8%
Per capita income & rank: $16,293/35
Public school per pupil spending & rank: $4,857/32
Governor: James B. Hunt, Jr. (D) (919-733-4240); 4-year term; elected 1992; last election (1992): Hunt 1,352,637 (53%), Jim Gardner (R) 1,108,549 (43%), Scott McLaughlin (Lib) 103,316 (4%); next election Nov. 1996.
Lt. Governor: Dennis A. Wicker (D)
Secretary of State: Rufus Edmisten (D) (919-733-4161)
Attorney General: Michael F. Easley (D)
Treasurer: Harlan Boyles (D)
Electoral votes: 14
U.S. Congress: 12 Reps.

General Assembly: (919-733-1110) 50 Senate (39 D, 11 R) and 120 House (78 D, 42 R). Meets odd-numbered years in January.

Charlotte, North Carolina

City Hall: 60 E. 4th Street 28202 (704-336-2244)
Mayor: Richard Vinroot; next election Nov. 1993
City Manager: O. Wendell White
Population & rank: 395,934/35
Per capita income & rank: $18,455/104
Council-manager government. Mayor and 11-member council are directly elected by the voters to 2-year terms. The mayor is not a member of the council but has the power to veto. Council meets weekly.

NORTH DAKOTA (1889)

State Capitol: Bismarck 58505
State Government Information: State Capitol Bldg. Bismark ND 58505 (701-224-2000)
Population & rank: 638,300/47
Population demographics: White—94.6%; Black —.6%; Hispanic—.7%; Native American—4.1%; Asian—.5%
Per capita income & rank: $15,215/42
Public school per pupil spending & rank: $4,119/44
Governor: Edward T. Schafer (R) (701-224-2200); 4-year term; elected 1992; last election (1992): Schafer 175,588 (59%), Nicholas Speath (D) 123,287 (41%); next election Nov. 1996.
Lt. Governor: Rosemarie Myrdal (R)
Secretary of State: Alvin Jaeger (701-224-2900)
Attorney General: Heidi Heitkamp (D)
Treasurer: Robert Hanson (D)
Electoral votes: 3
U.S. Congress: 1 Rep.
Legislative Assembly: (701-224-2000) 49 Senate (25 D, 24 R) and 98 House (33 D, 65 R). Meets odd-numbered years in January.

Bismark, North Dakota

City Hall: (mailing) P. O. Box 5503 58502 (701-222-6471)
Mayor: Bill Sorensen; next election April, 1994
Population & rank: 49,256/NR
Per capita income & rank: $15,926/217
Mayor-council (commission) form of government. Mayor and 5-member commission elected

for 2-year terms. Commission meets second and fourth Tuesdays.

OHIO (1803)

State Capitol: Columbus 43215
State Government Information: 65 E. State Street, Columbus OH 43266 (614-466-2000)
Population & rank: 10,847,115/7
Population demographics: White—87.8%; Black —10.6%; Hispanic—1.3%; Asian—.8%
Per capita income & rank: $17,564/23
Public school per pupil spending & rank: $5,451/21
Governor: George Voinovich (R) (614-466-3555); 4-year term; elected 1990; last election (1990): Voinovich 1,924,270 (56%) vs. Anthony J. Celebrezze, Jr. (D) 1,528,244 (44%); next election Nov. 1994.
Lt. Governor: Michael DeWine (R)
Secretary of State: Robert Taft II (R) (614-466-4980)
Attorney General: Lee Fisher (D)
Treasurer: Mary Ellen Withrow (D)
Electoral votes: 21
U.S. Congress: 19 Reps.
General Assembly: (614-466-2000) 33 Senate (13 D, 20 R) and 99 House (53 D, 46 R). Meets odd-numbered years on first Monday in January for first session, and no later than March 15 of the following year for second session.

Columbus, Ohio

City Hall: 90 W. Broad St. 43215 (614-645-7671)
Mayor: Greg Lashutka; next election Nov. 1993
Population & rank: 632,910/16
Per capita income & rank: $18,319/107
Mayor-council form of government. Mayor and 7-member council elected for 4-year terms. Council meets weekly.

Cleveland, Ohio

City Hall: 601 Lakeside Ave. N.E. 44114 (216-664-2000)
Mayor: Michael R. White (R); next election Nov. 1993
Population & rank: 505,616/24
Per capita income & rank: $20,758/45
With the repeal of the manager system in 1931, Cleveland instituted a mayor-council form of government. A mayor and 21 district coun-

cilors are elected every 4 years. Council meets weekly.

Cincinnati, Ohio

City Hall: 801 Plum St. 45202 (513-352-3000)
Mayor: Dwight Tillery; next election Nov. 1993
City Manager: Gerald Newfarmer
Population & rank: 364,040/45
Per capita income & rank: $19,010/80
Council-manager form of government. 7-member council and mayor directly elected to 2-year terms. Council appoints manager. Meets weekly.

Toledo, Ohio

City Hall: One Government Center 43604 (419-245-1010)
Mayor: John McHugh (D); next election Nov. 1993
City Manager: Thomas Hoover
Population & rank: 332,943/49
Per capita income & rank: $17,697/133
Council-manager government, with a mayor and 9 at-large council members elected directly by the voters to 2-year terms. The mayor is a member of the council but does not have veto power. The council meets weekly.

OKLAHOMA (1907)

State Capitol: Oklahoma City 73105
State Government Information: 6601 N. Broadway, Oklahoma City OK 73116 (405-521-1601)
Population & rank: 3,145,585/28
Population demographics: White—82.1%; Black—7.4%; Hispanic—2.7%; Native American—8%; Asian—1.1%; Other—1.3%
Per capita income & rank: $15,457/39
Public school per pupil spending & rank: $3,939/45
Governor: David Walters (D) (405-521-2342); 4-year term; elected 1990; last election (1990): Walters 523,195 (64%) vs. Bill Price (R) 297,580 (36%); next election Nov. 1994.
Lt. Governor: Jack Mildren (D)
Secretary of State: John Kennedy (D) (405-521-3911)
Attorney General: Susan B. Loving (D)
Treasurer: Claudette Henry (R)
Electoral votes: 8
U.S. Congress: 6 Reps.

Legislature: (S-405-524-0126, H-405-521-2711) 48 Senate (37 D, 11 R) and 101 House (69 D, 32 R). Meets annually beginning in January.

Oklahoma City, Oklahoma

City Hall: 200 W. Walker Street 73102 (405-297-2424)
Mayor: N/A; next election April 1997
City Manager: Donald Brown
Population & rank: 444,719/29
Per capita income & rank: $16,501/188
Council-manager form of government. The mayor and 8 council members are elected to 4-year terms, and the city manager is appointed by the mayor. Council meets weekly on Tuesdays.

Tulsa, Oklahoma

City Hall: 200 Civic Center 74103 (918-596-7777)
Mayor: Susan Savage; next election April 1994
Population & rank: 367,302/43
Per capita income & rank: $17,782/130
Mayor-council (commission) form of government. Mayor and 5-member commission are elected for 4-year terms. Council meets twice weekly on Tuesdays and Fridays.

OREGON (1859)

State Capitol: Salem 97310
State Government Information: 1225 Ferry Street, Salem OR 97310 (503-378-3131)
Population & rank: 2,842,321/29
Population demographics: White—92.8%; Black—1.6%; Hispanic—4%; Asian—2.4%; Native American—1.4%
Per capita income & rank: $17,196/29
Public school per pupil spending & rank: $5,972/12
Governor: Barbara Roberts (D) (503-378-3111); 4-year term; elected 1990; last election (1990): Roberts 470,888 (46%) vs. David Frohnmayer (R) 403,795 (48%) vs. Al Mobley (I) 133,990 (13%); next election Nov. 1994.
Lt. Governor: None
Secretary of State: Phil Keisling (D) (503-378-4139)
Attorney General: Theodore R. Kulongoski (D)
Treasurer: Tony Meeker (R)
Electoral votes: 7

U.S. Congress: 5 Reps.
Legislative Assembly: (503-378-8511) Senate 30 (16 D, 14 R) and 60 House (28 D, 32 R). Meets odd-numbered years in January.

Portland, Oregon

City Hall: 1220 S.W. 5th Ave. 97204 (503-226-3161)
Mayor: Vera Katz; next election Nov. 1994
Population & rank: 437,319/30
Per capita income & rank: $19,352/70
Mayor-council (commission) form of government. Mayor and 5-member commission is elected on a nonpartisan ticket for 4-year terms. Each commissioner oversees a municipal department.

PENNSYLVANIA (1787)

State Capitol: Harrisburg 17120
State Government Information: 8102 Transportation Bldg., Harrisburg PA 17125 717-787-2121)
Population & rank: 11,881,643/5
Population demographics: White—88.5%; Black —9.2%; Hispanic—2%; Asian 1.2%; Other— 1%
Per capita income & rank: $18,686/19
Public school per pupil spending & rank: $6,980/7
Governor: Robert Casey (D); 4-year term; elected 1986; last election (1990): Casey 2,059,299 (68%) vs. Barbara Hafer (R) 987,649 (32%); next election Nov. 1994.
Lt. Governor: Mark A. Singel (D)
Secretary of Commonwealth: Brenda K. Mitchell (D) (717-787-7630)
Attorney General: Ernie Preate (D)
Treasurer: Catherine Baker-Knoll (D)
Electoral votes: 23
U.S. Congress: 21 Reps.
General Assembly: (717-787-2121) 50 Senate (25 D, 25 R) and 203 House (105 D, 98 R). Meets annually beginning in January.

Philadelphia, Pennsylvania

City Hall: Philadelphia 19107 (215-686-1776)
Mayor: Edward Rendell; next election Nov. 1995
Population & rank: 1,585,577/5
Per capita income & rank: $21,347/37

Until the early 1950s, the standard mayor-council government prevailed in Philadelphia. Then a new city charter effectively removed the city council from any direct administrative role and increased the powers of the mayor. A strong civil service commission improves professional employment. The council, 7 of whose members are elected by all the voters and 11 by districts, reviews and approves taxes and budgets and enacts ordinances.

Pittsburgh, Pennsylvania

City Hall: 1600 W. Carson Street 15219 (412-255-2100)
Mayor: Sophie Masloff (D); next election Nov. 1993
Population & rank: 369,879/40
Per capita income & rank: $19,159/76
Mayor-council type of government. The mayor and 9 council members are elected by popular vote for 4-year terms. The mayor is not a member of the council but may veto either ordinances or resolutions enacted by the council, the city's legislative body: a 2/3 vote of the council is required to override a veto. The council meets weekly.

RHODE ISLAND (1790)

State Capitol: Providence 02903
State Government Information: 610 Mt. Pleasant Ave., Providence RI 02908 (401-277-2000)
Population & rank: 1,003,464/43
Population demographics: White—91.4%; Black —3.9%; Hispanic—4.6%; Asian—1.8%; Native American—.4%
Per capita income & rank: $18,802/16
Public school per pupil spending & rank: $6,834/8
Governor: Bruce G. Sundlun (D) (401-277-2080); 2-year term; elected 1990; last election (1992): Sundlun 250,400 (64%) vs. Elizabeth Ann Leonard (R) 138,934 (36%); next election Nov. 1994.
Lt. Governor: Robert Weygand (D)
Secretary of State: Barbara Leonard (D) (401-277-2357)
Attorney General: Jeffrey B. Pine (R)
Treasurer: Anthony Solomon (D)
Electoral votes: 4
U.S. Congress: 2 Reps.
General Assembly: (S-401-277-6655, H-401-

277-2466) 50 Senate (39 D, 11 R) and 100 House (85 D, 15 R). Meets annually beginning in January.

Providence, Rhode Island

City Hall: 25 Dorrance St. 02903 (401-421-7740)
Mayor: Vincent A. "Buddy" Cianci, Jr.; next election Nov. 1994
Population & rank: 160,728/107
Per capita income & rank: $18,665/91
Mayor-council form of government. Mayor and 15-member council are elected to 4-year terms. The council meets weekly.

SOUTH CAROLINA (1788)

State Capitol: Columbia 29211 (803-734-1000)
State Government Information: 1026 Sumpter St. Columbia SC 29201
Population & rank: 3,505,707/25
Population Demographics: White—68.8%; Black —30.4%; Hispanic—1.1%
Per capita income & rank: $15,151/43
Public school per pupil spending & rank: $4,537/40
Governor: Carroll A. Campbell, Jr. (R) (803-734-9818); 4-year term; elected 1986; last election (1990): Campbell 522,944 (71%) vs. Theo Mitchell (D) 210,829 (29%); next election Nov. 1994.
Lt. Governor: Nick A. Theodore (D)
Secretary of State: Jim Miles (D) (803-734-2170)
Attorney General: Travis T. Medlock (D)
Treasurer: Grady L. Patterson, Jr. (D)
Electoral votes: 8
U.S. Congress: 6 Reps.
General Assembly: (803-734-2010) 46 Senate (30 D, 16 R) and 124 House (73 D, 50 R, 1 I,). Meets annually in January.

Charleston, South Carolina

City Hall: 80 Broad Street 29402 (803-577-6970)
Mayor: Joseph P. Riley, Jr.; next election Nov. 1993
Population & rank: 80,414/NR
Per capita income & rank: $14,903/268
Mayor-council form of government. Mayor and 13-member council are elected to 2-year terms. The council meets second and fourth Tuesdays of each month.

SOUTH DAKOTA (1889)

State Capitol: Pierre 57501
State Government Information: 500 E. Capitol Ave., Pierre SD 57501 (605-773-3011)
Population & rank: 696,004/45
Population demographics: White—91.6%; Black —.5%; Hispanic—.8%; Native American—7.3%; Asian—.4%; Other—.2%
Per capita income & rank: $15,797/38
Public school per pupil spending & rank: $4,255/43
Governor: Walter D. Miller (R) (605-773-3212); 4-year term; appointed, April 1993 to succeed the late George Mickelson who died in a plane crash; next election Nov. 1994.
Lt. Governor: Vacant
Secretary of State: Joyce Hazeltine (R) (605-773-3537)
Attorney General: Mark Barnett (R)
Treasurer: G. Homer Harding (R)
Electoral votes: 3
U.S. Congress: 1 Rep.
Legislature: (605-773-4498) 35 Senate (20 D, 15 R) and 70 House (29 D, 41 R). Meets annually beginning in January.

Sioux Falls, South Dakota

City Hall: 224 W. 9th Street 57102 (605-339-7200)
Mayor: Jack White; next election June, 1993
Population & rank: 100,814/194
Per capita income & rank: $18,526/98
Mayor-council form of government. Mayor and 5-member council are elected to 2-year terms. The council meets weekly.

TENNESSEE (1796)

State Capitol: Nashville 37219 (615-741-3011)
State Government Information: 334 Cordell Hall, Rm C-3, Nashville TN 37219
Population & rank: 4,877,185/17
Population demographics: White—83.7%; Black —16%; Hispanic—.7%; Asian—.7%; Native American—.2%
Per capita income & rank: $15,866/37
Public school per pupil spending & rank: $3,736/47
Governor: Ned R. McWherter (D) (615-741-2001); 4-year term; elected 1986; last election (1990): McWherter 476,996 (62%) vs. Dwight

Henry (R) 286,668 (38%); next election Nov. 1994.
Lt. Governor: John S. Wilder (D)
Secretary of State: Riley Darnell (D) (615-741-2817)
Attorney General: Charles W. Burson (D)
Treasurer: Steve Adams (D)
In one of the nation's more unusual setups, the Secretary of State and the state Treasurer are appointed for 4-year terms by the General Assembly, while the state Attorney General is appointed by the state Supreme Court.
Electoral votes: 11
U.S. Congress: 9 Reps.
General Assembly: (615-741-3511) 33 Senate (19 D, 14 R); 99 House (63 D, 36 R). Meets annually beginning in January.

Memphis, Tennessee

City Hall: 125 N. Mid America Mall 31803 (901-576-6500)
Mayor: W.W. Herenton; next election Oct. 1995
Population & rank: 610,337/18
Per capita income & rank: $17,797/129
Mayor-council form of government since 1968. The voters elect a mayor and 13 council members to 4-year terms. The mayor is not a member of the council but has veto power. The council meets weekly.

Nashville, Tennessee

City Hall: Metro Courthouse 37201 (615-862-5000)
Mayor: Philip Bredesen; next election August 1995
Population & rank: 510,748/23
Per capita income & rank: $18,339/106
Nashville was one of the first cities in the U.S. to adopt a metropolitan form of government. A mayor, a vice mayor, and a 40-member metropolitan council make up the executive and legislative branches of the government. Nonpartisan elections for those officials are held every 4 years. Voters in designated districts elect 35 of the council members. The other 5, together with the mayor and vice mayor, are chosen by the entire electorate.

TEXAS (1845)

State Capitol: Austin 78711
State Government Information: 201 E. 14th Street, Austin TX 78701 (512-463-4630)
Population & rank: 16,986,510/3
Population demographics: White—75.2%; Black —12.0%; Hispanic—26%; Asian—2%; Other— 11%
Per capita income & rank: $16,716/33
Public school per pupil spending & rank: $4,651/38
Governor: Ann Richards (D) (512-463-2000); 4-year term; elected 1990; last election (1990): Richards 1,916,673 (51%) vs. Clayton Williams (R) 1,818,281 (49%); next election Nov. 1994.
Lt. Governor: Bob Bullock (D)
Secretary of State: John Hannah, Jr. (D) (512-463-5701)
Attorney General: Dan Morales (D)
State Treasurer: Kay Bailey Hutchison (R)
Comptroller: John Sharp (D)
Agriculture Commissioner: Rick Perry (R)
Electoral votes: 32
U.S. Congress: 30 Reps.
Legislature: (512-463-4630) 31 Senate (18 D, 13 R) and 150 House (91 D, 58 R, 1 Vac.). Meets odd-numbered years in January.

Houston, Texas

City Hall: (mailing) P. O. Box 1562 77251 (713-247-1000)
Mayor: Bob Lanier; next election Nov. 1993
Population & rank: 1,630,553/4
Per capita income & rank: $19,175/75
Mayor-council government. The mayor and 15-member city council (9 district and 5 at-large) are elected to 2-year terms. The mayor is a member of the council but does not have veto power. Council meets weekly.

Dallas, Texas

City Hall: 1500 Marilla 75201 (214-670-3011)
Mayor: Steve Bartlett; next election May 1993
City Manager: Jan Hart
Population & rank: 1,006,877/8
Per capita income & rank: $20,522/46
Dallas is the largest city in the United States operating under the council-manager form of government. A mayor and 10 council members are elected directly by popular vote to 2-year terms and serve as the policy-making body for municipal business, with a city manager appointed by the council as chief administrative and executive officer. The mayor is a

member of the council but may not veto measures passed by the council. The council meets weekly.

San Antonio, Texas

City Hall: 1 Military Plaza 78283 (512-299-7011)
Mayor: Nelson Wolff; next election May 1993
City Manager: Alexander Briseno
Population & rank: 935,933/10
Per capita income & rank: $15,517/244
Council-manager form of government. The mayor and the 11 members of the city council are the only elected officials of the city government. Both serve 2-year terms. The council is made up of 10 district members and 1 at-large member, who meet once a week.

El Paso, Texas

City Hall: 2 Civic Center Plaza 79901 (915-541-4000)
Mayor: N/A; next election April 1997
Population & rank: 515,342/22
Per capita income & rank: $11,545/313
Mayor-council form of government. Mayor and 7-member council elected to 4-year terms. Council meets twice monthly.

Austin, Texas

City Hall: 124 W. 8th Street 78767 (512-499-2000)
Mayor: Bruce Todd; next election May 1994
City Manager: Camille Cates Barnett
Population & rank: 465,622/27
Per capita income & rank: $17,345/142
Since 1926 Austin has had a council-manager form of government. Voters elect the mayor directly to a 3-year term. Seven at-large city council members serve without pay, also for 3-year terms. The mayor is a member of the city council but does not have the authority to veto measures passed by the council. Council meets weekly on Thursdays.

Fort Worth, Texas

City Hall: 1000 Throckmorton 76102 (817-870-6000)
Mayor: Kay Granger; next election May 1993
City Manager: Robert Terrell
Population & rank: 447,619/28
Per capita income & rank: $18,478/102

Council-manager form of government. The mayor and 9-member city council are elected to 2-year terms. The mayor is a member of the council and may also veto any measure passed by the council. The council meets the last three Tuesdays of each month.

UTAH (1896)

State Capitol: Salt Lake City 84114
State Government Information: 1226 State Office Bldg, Salt Lake City UT 84114 (801-538-3000)
Population & rank: 1,722,850/35
Population demographics: White—93.8%; Black —.7%; Hispanic—4.9%; Asian—1.9%; Native American—1.4%
Per capita income & rank: $13,993/49
Public school per pupil spending & rank: $3,092/51
Governor: Mike Leavitt (R) (801-538-1000); 4-year term; elected 1992; last election (1992): Leavitt 320,124 (43%) vs. Merrill Cook (I) 255,159 (34%) vs. Stewart Hanson (D) (23%); next election Nov. 1996.
Lt. Governor: Olene S. Walker (R)
Attorney General: Jan Graham (D)
Treasurer: Edward T. Alter (R)
Secretary of State: None
Electoral votes: 5
U.S. Congress: 3 Reps.
Legislature: (801-538-1029) 29 Senate (11 D, 18 R) and 75 House (26 D, 49 R). Meets annually for 60 days on second Monday in January.

Salt Lake City, Utah

City Hall: 451 S. State Street 84111 (801-535-6333)
Mayor: Deedee Corradini; next election Nov. 1993
Population & rank: 159,936/108
Per capita income & rank: $15,033/261
Mayor-council form of government. The mayor and 7-member council are elected to 4-year terms. The council meets weekly.

VERMONT (1791)

State Capitol: Montpelier 05602
State Government Information: State Administration Bldg., Montpelier VT 05602 (802-828-1110)
Population & rank: 562,758/48

Population demographics: White—98.6%; Black —.3%; Hispanic—.7%; Native American—.3%; Asian—.6%; Other—.1%
Per capita income & rank: $17,511/26
Public school per pupil spending & rank: $6,992/6
Governor: Howard Dean (D) (802-828-3333); 2-year term; elected 1992; last election (1992): Dean 202,115 (75%) vs. John McClaughry (R) 62,805 (23%); next election Nov. 1994.
Lt. Governor: Barbara Snelling
Secretary of State: Don Hooper (D) (802-828-2363)
Attorney General: Jeffrey L. Amestoy (R)
Treasurer: Paul W. Ruse, Jr. (D)
Electoral votes: 3
U.S. Congress: 1 Rep.
General Assembly: (802-828-2231) 30 Senate (14 D, 16 R) and 150 House (87 D, 57 R, 6 I). Meets odd-numbered years in January.

Burlington, Vermont

City Hall: Burlington 05401 (802-658-9300)
Mayor: Peter A. Clavelle; next election May 1994
Population & rank: 37,715/NR
Per capita income & rank: $19,872/57
Mayor-council form of government. The mayor and 13-member council are elected to 2-year terms. The mayor is a member of the council but does not have the power to veto. The council meets weekly.

VIRGINIA (1788)

State Capitol: Richmond 23219
State Government Information: 109 Governor St., Richmond VA 23219 (804-786-0000)
Population & rank: 6,187,358/12
Population demographics: White—77.4%; Black —19%; Hispanic—3%; Native American—.2%; Asian—3%; Other—1%
Per capita income & rank: $19,671/13
Public school per pupil spending & rank: $5,487/19
Governor: Douglas Wilder (D) (804-786-2211); 4-year term; elected 1989; last election (1989): Wilder 896,283 (50%) vs. J. Marshall Coleman (R) 890,750 (50%); next election Nov. 1993.
Lt. Governor: David S. Beyer, Jr. (D)
Secretary of the Commonwealth: Pamela M. Womack (D) (804-786-2441)

Attorney General: Stephen Rosenthal
Treasurer: Eddie Moore, Jr. (D)
Electoral votes: 13
U.S. Congress: 11 Reps.
General Assembly: (804-786-2366) 40 Senate (22 D, 18 R) and 100 House of Delegates (58 D, 41 R, 1 I). Terms expire 1991. Meets annually beginning in January.

Virginia Beach, Virginia

City Hall: Virginia Beach 23456 (804-427-4111)
Mayor: Meyera E. Oberndorf; next election May 1994
City Manager: James K. Spore
Population & rank: 393,069/37
Per capita income & rank: $16,613/180
Council-manager form of government. The mayor is selected by the council from among its members to a 2-year term and is a member of the council but without veto power. The council is made up of 10 members, 7 elected from districts and 3 at large to 4-year terms. They meet weekly.

Richmond, Virginia

City Hall: 900 E. Broad Street 23219 (804-780-7000)
Mayor: Walter T. Kenney; next election Nov. 1993
City Manager: Robert C. Bobb
Population & rank: 203,056/76
Per capita income & rank: $21,114/42
Council-manager form of government. A mayor and 9 council members are elected to 2-year terms. The mayor is a member of the council but does not have the power to veto. The council meets weekly.

WASHINGTON (1889)

State Capitol: Olympia 98504
State Government Information: 11th Ave. & Columbia St., Olympia WA 98504 (206-753-5000)
Population & rank: 4,866,692/18
Population demographics: White—88.5%; Black —3.1%; Hispanic—4.4%; Native American— 1.7%; Asian & Pacific Islander—4.3%
Per capita income & rank: $18,775/17
Public school per pupil spending & rank: $5,331/25
Governor: Mike Lowry (D) (206-753-6780); 4-year

term; elected 1992; last election (1992): Lowry 1,030,126 (53%), Ken Eikenberry (R) 913,629 (47%); next election Nov. 1996.
Lt. Governor: Joel Pritchard (R)
Secretary of State: Ralph Munro (R) (206-753-7121)
Attorney General: Christie O. Gregoire (D)
Treasurer: Dan Grimm (D)
Electoral votes: 11
U.S. Congress: 9 Reps.
Legislature: (206-753-5000) 49 Senate (28 D, 21 R) and 98 House (66 D, 32 R). Meets annually beginning in January.

Seattle, Washington

City Hall: 600 4th Avenue 98104 (206-684-4000)
Mayor: Norman Rice (D); next election Nov. 1993
Population & rank: 516,259/21
Per capita income & rank: $22,540/24
Nonpartisan mayor-council government. The mayor and 9 at-large council members are elected for 4-year terms. The mayor is not a member of the council but may veto measures passed by the council. Council meets weekly.

WEST VIRGINIA (1863)

State Capitol: Charleston 25305
State Government Information: State Capitol Bldg., Charleston WV 25305 (304-348-3456)
Population & rank: 1,793,477/34
Population demographics: White—96.2%; Black —3.1%; Hispanic—.5%; Asian—.4%
Per capita income & rank: $13,755/50
Public school per pupil spending & rank: $5,415/23
Governor: Gaston Caperton (D) (304-348-2000); 4-year term; elected 1988; last election (1992): Caperton 365,477 (56%) vs. Cleve Benedict (R) 240,973 (37%) vs. Charlotte Jean Pritt (I) 44,560 (7%); next election Nov. 1996.
Senate President: Keith Burdette (D)
Secretary of State: Ken Hechler (D) (304-345-4000)
Attorney General: Darrell V. McGraw, Jr. (D)
Treasurer: Larrie Bailey (D)
Electoral votes: 5
U.S. Congress: 3 Reps.
Legislature: (304-348-8905) 34 Senate (32 D, 2 R) and 100 House of Delegates (79 D, 21 R). Meets annually beginning in January.

Charleston, West Virginia

City Hall: Box 2749 25330 (304-348-8000)
Mayor: Kent Hall; next election April 1995
City Manager: Curt Voth
Population & rank: 57,900/NR
Per capita income & rank: $16,615/179
Council-manager form of government. A mayor and 26 council members are elected to 2-year terms. The mayor is a member of the council but does not have the power to veto. The council meets once a week.

WISCONSIN (1848)

State Capitol: Madison 53702
State Government Information: 41 N. Mills St., Madison WI 53715 (608-266-2211)
Population & rank: 4,891,769/16
Population demographics: White—92.2%; Black —5%; Hispanic—1.9%; Native American—.8%; Asian—1.1%
Per capita income & rank: $17,560/24
Public school per pupil spending & rank: $5,972/12
Governor: Tommy G. Thompson (R) (608-266-1212); 4-year term; elected 1986; last election (1990): Thompson 802,219 (58%) vs. Tom Loftus (D) 576,292 (42%); next election Nov. 1994.
Lt. Governor: Scott McCallum (R)
Secretary of State: Douglas LaFollette (D) (608-266-5594)
Attorney General: James Doyle (R)
Treasurer: Cathy Zeuske (D)
Electoral votes: 11
U.S. Congress: 9 Reps.
Legislature: (608-266-2211) 33 Senate (18 D, 15 R) and 99 Assembly (52 D, 47 R). Meets annually beginning in January.

Milwaukee, Wisconsin

City Hall: 200 E. Wells St. 53202 (414-278-3200)
Mayor: John Norquist (D); next election April 1996
Population & rank: 628,088/17
Per capita income & rank: $19,817/58
Mayor-council form of government. The city is divided into 17 districts, each electing an alderman to a 4-year term on the common council, which is presided over by a president elected from among the aldermen. The mayor

is not a member of the council but may veto measures passed by the council.

WYOMING (1890)

State Capitol: Cheyenne 82002
State Government Information: 200 W. 24th Street, Cheyenne WY 82002 (307-777-7220)
Population & rank: 453,588/50
Population demographics: White—94.2%; Black —.8%; Hispanic—5.7%; Native American— 2.1%; Asian—.6%; Other—2.3%
Per capita income & rank: $16,314/34
Public school per pupil spending & rank: $5,333/24
Governor: Michael J. Sullivan (D) (307-777-7434); 4-year term; elected 1986; last election (1990): Sullivan 104,500 (65%) vs. Mary Mead (R) 55,426 (35%); next election Nov. 1994.
Lt. Governor: None

Secretary of State: Kathy Karpan (D) (307-777-7378)
Attorney General: Joseph Meyer (D)
Treasurer: Stanford Smith (R)
Electoral votes: 3
U.S. Congress: 1 Rep.
Legislature: (307-777-7881) 30 Senate (10 D, 20 R) and 60 House (19 D, 41 R). Meets odd-numbered years in January, even-numbered years in February.

Cheyenne, Wyoming

City Hall: 2101 O'Neil Ave. 82001 (307-637-6300)
Mayor: Gary Schaeffer; next election Nov. 1994
Population & rank: 50,008/NR
Per capita income & rank: $16,555/186
Mayor-council form of government. The 10-member council, 3 each representing 3 wards, meets each Tuesday.

States Ranked by Population, Highest to Lowest

1. California	14. Indiana	27. Connecticut	39. Nevada
2. New York	15. Missouri	28. Oklahoma	40. New Hampshire
3. Texas	16. Wisconsin	29. Oregon	41. Hawaii
4. Florida	17. Tennessee	30. Iowa	42. Idaho
5. Pennsylvania	18. Washington	31. Mississippi	43. Rhode Island
6. Illinois	19. Maryland	32. Kansas	44. Montana
7. Ohio	20. Minnesota	33. Arkansas	45. South Dakota
8. Michigan	21. Louisiana	34. West Virginia	46. Delaware
9. New Jersey	22. Alabama	35. Utah	47. North Dakota
10. North Carolina	23. Kentucky	36. Nebraska	48. Vermont
11. Georgia	24. Arizona	37. New Mexico	49. Alaska
12. Virginia	25. South Carolina	38. Maine	50. Wyoming
13. Massachusetts	26. Colorado		

States Ranked by Per Capita Income & Rank, Highest to Lowest

1. Connecticut	14. Colorado	27. Iowa	39. Montana
2. New Jersey	15. Rhode Island	28. Oregon	40. Idaho
3. Massachusetts	16. Washington	29. Maine	41. North Dakota
4. New York	17. Minnesota	30. Georgia	42. South Carolina
5. Maryland	18. Pennsylvania	31. Indiana	43. Alabama
6. Alaska	19. Florida	32. Texas	44. Kentucky
7. New Hampshire	20. Michigan	33. Wyoming	45. Louisiana
8. California	21. Kansas	34. North Carolina	46. New Mexico
9. Illinois	22. Ohio	35. Arizona	47. Arkansas
10. Hawaii	23. Wisconsin	36. Tennessee	48. Utah
11. Delaware	24. Nebraska	37. South Dakota	49. West Virginia
12. Virginia	25. Vermont	38. Oklahoma	50. Mississippi
13. Nevada	26. Missouri		

The Fifty Largest U.S. Cities Ranked by Population, Highest to Lowest

1. New York	7,322,564	26. Denver	467,610
2. Los Angeles	3,485,398	27. Austin, Tex.	465,622
3. Chicago	2,783,726	28. Fort Worth, Tex.	447,619
4. Houston	1,630,553	29. Oklahoma City	444,719
5. Philadelphia	1,585,577	30. Portland, Ore.	437,319
6. San Diego, Cal.	1,110,549	31. Kansas City, Mo.	435,146
7. Detroit	1,027,974	32. Long Beach, Cal.	429,433
8. Dallas	1,006,877	33. Tucson, Ariz.	405,390
9. Phoenix	983,403	34. St. Louis	396,685
10. San Antonio, Tex.	935,933	35. Charlotte, N.C.	395,934
11. San Jose, Cal.	782,248	36. Atlanta	394,017
12. Indianapolis	741,952	37. Virginia Beach	393,069
13. Baltimore	736,014	38. Albuquerque, N.M.	384,736
14. San Francisco	723,959	39. Oakland, Cal.	372,242
15. Jacksonville	672,971	40. Pittsburgh	369,879
16. Columbus, Ohio	632,910	41. Sacramento, Cal.	369,365
17. Milwaukee, Wis.	628,088	42. Minneapolis, Minn.	368,383
18. Memphis, Tenn.	610,337	43. Tulsa, Okla.	367,302
19. Washington, D.C.	606,900	44. Honolulu	365,048
20. Boston	574,283	45. Cincinnati, Ohio	364,040
21. Seattle	516,259	46. Miami	358,548
22. El Paso, Tex.	515,342	47. Fresno, Cal.	354,202
23. Nashville, Tenn.	510,748	48. Omaha, Neb.	335,795
24. Cleveland	505,616	49. Toledo, Ohio	332,943
25. New Orleans	496,938	50. Buffalo, N.Y.	328,123

The Fifty Wealthiest Metropolitan Areas Ranked by Per Capita Income, Highest to Lowest

1. Bridgeport-Stamford, Connecticut	26. Ft. Lauderdale-Hollywood, Florida
2. San Francisco, California	27. New Haven, Connecticut
3. Bergen-Passaic, New Jersey	28. Poughkeepsie, New York
4. Nassau County, New York	29. Santa Rosa, California
5. Middlesex-Somerset, New Jersey	30. Santa Cruz, California
6. Lake County, Illinois	31. Santa Barbara, California
7. West Palm Beach-Boca Raton, Florida	32. Aurora-Elgin, Illinois
8. Newark, New Jersey	33. Baltimore, Maryland
9. Trenton, New Jersey	34. Boulder, Colorado
10. Naples, Florida	35. Oxnard-Ventura, California
11. Washington, D.C.	36. Portland, Maine
12. San Jose, California	37. Wilmington, Delaware
13. Anchorage, Alaska	37. Philadelphia, Pennsylvania
14. Sarasota, Florida	39. Minneapolis-St. Paul, Minnesota
15. Monmouth-Ocean, New Jersey	40. Reno, Nevada
16. Hartford, Connecticut	41. Honolulu, Hawaii
17. Anaheim, California	42. Richmond, Virginia
18. Boston, Massachusetts	43. Denver, Colorado
19. New York, New York	44. Los Angeles-Long Beach, California
20. Atlantic City, New Jersey	45. Cleveland, Ohio
21. Oakland, California	46. Dallas, Texas
22. Ann Arbor, Michigan	47. Rochester, Minnesota
23. Manchester, New Hampshire	48. Detroit, Michigan
24. Seattle, Washington	49. Portsmouth-Dover, New Hampshire
25. Chicago, Illinois	50. Rochester, New York

A POLITICAL GLOSSARY

Absentee Ballot. The method of early voting by mail if a voter is not going to be able to go in person to his normal polling place on election day.

Act. Legislation passed or under consideration by a legislature. (See also *bill*.)

Advise and consent. The constitutional requirement (Art. II, Sec. 2) that the Senate vote on and approve treaties and executive branch appointments.

Affirmative action. Term used to describe plan to open jobs or to provide greater access to positions or programs to heretofore disadvantaged minorities.

Amendment. (1) A measure added to the Constitution since it was adopted in 1787. The first ten are The Bill of Rights. Sixteen others have been adopted, although one (the 21st) repealed another (the 18th which established Prohibition). (2) A measure added to a bill or already enacted law that supplements, deletes from or changes all or part of it.

Apportionment. The distribution of the 435 seats in the House of Representatives among the 50 states based on each state's population. Can also refer to the distribution of seats in a state legislature. (See also *redistricting*.)

Appropriation. Funds authorized by Congress or another legislative body for a specific purpose. Also refers to the funds themselves.

Approval rating. In a public opinion poll the percentage of respondents who say an office holder is doing a good job.

Background. Information given "on background" by a public official may be quoted as long as the individual is not identified, except as an "authoritative source." A device used frequently by staff persons speaking for their bosses.

Balanced budget amendment. In current usage an amendment to the U.S. Constitution that would require Congress to annually adopt a budget in which revenues and expenditures would be equal (in balance).

Balanced ticket. Usually used to refer to a president-vice president combination chosen to appeal to as wide a range of voters as possible with each candidate representing different geographic regions, races, genders, religions, issue positions and the like. In more general usage can refer to any slate of candidates chosen to complement one another.

Bellwether. A small sample which reflects trends or feelings from a much wider group. Often a group of voters with a history of voting the way the nation does as a whole. For instance, voters in one northwestern Iowa county voted for the winning presidential candidate in every election between 1896 and 1988 in approximately the same percentage as the candidate received nationally.

Bicameral. Used to refer to a legislature composed of two separate houses or chambers, such as the U.S. Congress and 49 of the states (only Nebraska's legislature has a single "unicameral" legislature). The practice of having two separate chambers grew out of the European tradition of having one legislative chamber representing the elite and one representing commoners.

Big government. Phrase usually used divisively by conservatives and supporters of a policy of less federal government intervention to describe centralized federal authority with its policy of heavy taxation and federal spending.

Bill. A measure proposed for action before a legislative body.

Bipartisan. When members of both political parties work together for the passage of a piece of legislation, or to resolve a problem.

Bite the bullet. To be willing to make a difficult or unpopular decision; or to commit to a difficult or unpopular course of action.

Bloc. A group of voters who vote together out of some common bond which could be ethnic, social or economic.

Block grant. Money given by the federal government which the recipient can decide how to spend within certain broad guidelines.

Boll weevil. Term to describe conservative southern Democrats in Congress who often vote with Republicans based on economic issues. Previously they were often called "dixiecrats" when their opposition was often based on racial issues.

Boondoggle. A government project or a legislative action that is generally viewed as too expensive and wasteful, but which benefits certain individuals or groups. Originally used to describe jobs programs in the Depression era.

Boss. Political party leader who often does not actually hold elective office, but who does control the party apparatus.

Boys on the bus. Term used to describe the press corps, usually in terms of the press covering a particular candidate in an election, but also the White House press corps. Reference is based on the press "bus" which follows a candidate or president everywhere. Today the bus is usually an airplane.

Bubba. In its original usage, referred to a southern rural white male. But, with the campaigning and then election of Bill Clinton, has come to mean a more upper class and urban southern white male, in effect a southern Yuppie.

Bureaucracy. Government agencies or permanent career employees protected by civil service rules who stay administration after administration. Often used in a derogatory sense to mean government complexity or "red tape."

Cabinet. Group appointed by the president or other chief executive to head executive departments and to serve as advisers. (See also *Kitchen Cabinet.*)

Captive candidate. A candidate who is dominated by others or by certain interest groups.

Caucus. (1) A meeting, often closed, of officials, legislators, or party leaders to make decisions. Originally used to describe the closed meetings of party leaders where candidates were chosen. (2) In some states such as Iowa the meetings of voters affiliated with a particular party to chose the party's candidates in a primary.

Checks and balances. Division of power among different branches and levels of government so that they act as restraints upon one another. Principle behind the Founding Fathers' structure of the new government of the United States with its co-equal executive, legislative and judicial branches.

Chilling effect. An action designed to inhibit or to intimidate, especially the exercise of a legal right. An example might be the firing of an employee by a governmental agency for talking with the press. This would naturally dissuade others from talking with the press.

Civil rights. Those rights guaranteed to all individuals for being a member of society. In common usage, especially those rights guaranteed members of minority races.

Cloakroom. Traditionally the small rooms off the House and Senate floors in the U.S. Capitol where legislators can rest, socialize, and generally meet informally out of the public eye. Now more generally used to indicate private meeting rooms in state and local legislatures.

Closed primary. See *primary, closed.*

Cloture. Process by which debate is shut off in a legislative body. In the U.S. Senate, cloture takes a 3/5 vote of members present; otherwise debate in the Senate is unlimited.

Clout. Slang for political power.

Coattails. The ability of someone heading a political ticket to attract enough votes to help elect those lower down on the ballot from the same political party. Typically a presidential candidate who is so popular he causes others from his party to be elected. "Reverse coattails" refers to the occasional situation when someone lower on the ticket is so popular he attracts voters for the person heading the ticket.

COLA. See *cost-of-living adjustment.*

Cold war. Generally a term used to describe nonmilitary conflicts. Specifically used to describe relations between the U.S. and the Soviet Union in the period 1945-88.

Committee. In Congress, the group of representatives or senators assigned to consider legislation in a specific area, (e.g., foreign relations). Bills must be approved by committee before they can be considered by the full chamber. Subcommittees are divisions of full committees. Joint committees include members of both houses.

Conference committees also include representatives and senators but are appointed specifically to reach a compromise on a specific bill. Select committees are temporary, or are named to deal with a specific issue.

Conflict-of-interest. A situation in which the personal interests of an office holder, candidate, or public employee might conflict with the more general public interest.

Conservative. In politics, traditionally someone who wishes to continue the status quo and to maintain (conserve) the existing order. In the United States, conservatives tend to believe in a powerful military, a limited role for the government in economic affairs and on social welfare issues and, recently, a strong government role to enforce "traditional" moral values. Opposite of *liberal*.

Cost-of-living adjustment (COLA). The automatic increasing of a government benefit to keep pace with increased inflation.

Cover-up. Any plan to avoid detection of wrong doing, or the act of hiding an error or mistake.

Crossover vote. When members of one party vote in the primary of another party in states that have open primaries.

Dark horse. Either a little-known candidate who is chosen to run for office, or one who is given little chance of winning.

Demagogue. An office holder, candidate or speaker who appeals to greed, hatred or fear, or to other negative emotions.

Democrat. Considered to be the more liberal of the two major parties. Although there are many exceptions, Democrats tend to believe that the federal government should be actively involved in the marketplace and in correcting social inequality. They are also less likely to favor high defense spending and U.S. military involvement abroad than Republicans. For much of the 20th century their strength lay in the older, industrial and urban areas of the country, among blacks and, to some extent, among labor union members. Their traditional strength among white Southerners and "white ethnics" has been ebbing in recent years, particularly in national elections.

Deregulation. The ending of government con-

trols on an industry. The leading recent example is the end of most government nonsafety regulation on the airlines industry during the late 1970's.

Detente. An improvement in relations between two feuding parties. Most common usage has been to describe better U.S.—Soviet relations.

District. The political subdivision the country is divided into for the purpose of representation in Congress. The country is divided into 435 districts, each of which contains about 550,000 voters.

District working period. Term now used by Congress for recesses and vacations.

Do-gooder. Derisive term used to describe a reformer or a civic minded, but nonpartisan, activist.

Double-dipping. Receiving more than one government salary or retirement benefit or a combination. An example would be the retired military officer who gets a government job and draws a salary check while also receiving military retirement pay.

Dove. A person who usually supports negotiation, as opposed to military might, to resolve global conflicts. Used, for example, to refer to opponents of the Vietnam War. Opposite of *hawk*.

Electoral college. The constitutionally mandated body that officially selects the president. It consists of electors from every state equal to the number of House members from that state plus two. This is also the number of electoral votes a state has. All electoral votes go to the candidate who wins the popular vote of that state—whether by one vote or one million. To be elected president, a candidate must win a majority of electoral votes.

Entitlement program. Any government program that pays benefits to those who meet whatever eligibility standards that are established.

Equal rights amendment. The proposed constitutional amendment, passed by Congress in 1973 but never ratified by the states, that would have forbidden any discrimination by the federal government or any state government based on gender.

Equal time. Requirement that television and

radio stations make air time available to all candidates for a particular office, or for opposing sides on an issue.

Executive branch. The part of government that carries out, or enforces, the laws. With the judicial and legislative branches, one of the three coequal branches of government.

Executive order. Generally, a rule or regulation having the force of law promulgated directly by the chief administrative office under his statutory authority. The most common usage is with the President who issues orders in his capacity as commander-in-chief.

Exit poll. See *poll, exit.*

Favorite son. A candidate at a political convention who is chosen to hold together a state's votes.

Federalism. A system of government where a strong national government shares power with lesser subgovernments (states). In the United States the system of the strong national government in Washington, and the 50 state governments.

Fence mending. To make political peace with a former opponent or opposing group.

Filibuster. Technique where a small group of legislators attempt to keep a measure from coming to a vote by talking continuously. Happens especially in the U.S. Senate which allows unlimited debate. (See also *cloture.*)

First lady. Wife of the President of the United States or of another lower-level chief executive.

Fiscal year. A 12-month accounting period with different starting and stopping dates than a calendar year. For the federal government the fiscal year begins October 1 and ends September 30 of the next year. The year's title comes from the date that it ends, thus the fiscal year beginning October 1, 1993 and ending September 30, 1994 is fiscal 1994 or FY '94 in common usage.

Foggy bottom. The U.S. State Department. Nickname given to the area of Washington where the State Department is physically located.

Free trade. The policy of eliminating any taxes, or regulatory barriers involving exports and imports between two countries. The opposite of *protectionism.*

Freedom of information act. Law passed in 1966 requiring all government agencies to turn over to citizens all information they possess unless it falls under one of a number of broad exclusionary categories such as national security or information which might violate another's right to privacy.

Front runner. In politics the candidate in an election contest who is ahead in the polls and is expected to win. The opposite of *underdog.*

GAO. The General Accounting Office, the formal investigative arm of Congress.

Gay rights. The movement to prevent discrimination against homosexuals based on their sexual preference.

Gender gap. The title given to the growing divergence in attitudes and political opinion between men and woman. In practice usually refers to the fact that a particular candidate is heavily supported by men, while his opponent has a high level of support among women.

Gerrymander. The drawing of boundaries for legislative (especially congressional) districts in such a way as to favor one political party or specific group. The term combines the names of 19th-century Massachusetts Governor Elbridge Gerry, who devised the system, and the salamander, whose shape a gerrymandered district he devised is said to have resembled.

GOP. The Republican Party (Grand Old Party).

Gramm-Rudman-Hollings act. Common usage is "Gramm-Rudman." Law passed in 1985 which mandates that the federal deficit be lowered to a certain declining ceiling annually until a balanced budget is reached. If the target deficit level is missed any year, the law acts to automatically reduce government expenditures in an across-the-board cut to reach the level. As originally enacted it called for a balanced budget by 1991. That date has now been extended to 1997.

Grassroots. Either the rank and file of a political party, or the average voter and citizen who has no history of political activism.

Hawk. In politics, a supporter of a strong military role to resolve global conflicts. Used, for example, to refer to supporters of the Vietnam War. Opposite of *dove.*

Impeachment. Method of removing public officials from office whereby the lower house of a legislature brings charges accusing an office holder or tenured judge of wrongdoing. If convicted after a trial in the upper chamber, the guilty politician is removed from office. One president, Andrew Johnson, was impeached, but the Senate failed to convict. (Richard M. Nixon was charged with impeachable offenses in the House, but his resignation stopped the process.)

Incumbent. Current office-holder or person in an appointed position. Used at election time, usually the person holding office facing a challenger.

Independent. A voter who is not allied with either major political party.

Initiative. Process whereby voters through petitioning can put measures on the ballot which if approved by a majority will then become law. The Constitution specifically forbids the process at the federal level.

Interest group. An organization of citizens who share common causes (interests) and who seek to affect government decisions in a way that is beneficial to it. In current U.S. politics it is often companies within an industry who have joined together to promote their common goals.

Isolationism. In the American context, the theory that the United States is best served by only a minimal involvement in foreign alliances.

Judicial activism. Situation whereby judges make new public policy through their broad decisions. Opposite is *judicial restraint*.

Judicial branch. The part of government that interprets the laws; the courts. With the executive and legislative branches, one of the three branches of government.

Judicial review. The power of the courts to determine whether an action of the executive or law passed by the legislative branch is constitutional. If it isn't, it's no longer valid.

Kitchen cabinet. The informal advisers of a chief executive as opposed to his regular cabinet of executive agency heads and appointed advisers.

Lame duck. Defeated office-holder whose term has not yet expired or an officeholder who cannot run for another term.

Lame duck appointment. A political or job appointment made by an elected official after he has been defeated for re-election, but before his statutory term of office has ended. In the federal government, also an appointment made by the president after Congress has adjourned. The appointee can serve until Congress comes back in session.

Landslide. An overwhelming election victory. In percentage terms usually used to indicate a victory in which a candidate receives more than 60 percent of the vote.

Leak. The deliberate disclosure of confidential information often to advance a policy or hurt an opponent.

Left (also left wing). Traditionally refers to the radical wing in a legislature (from the French National Assembly of 1789, in which radicals sat on the left). Now popularly used to refer to the more liberal end of the political spectrum. Opposite of *right wing* referring to conservatives.

Left, new. Term used to describe the antiwar protesters of the Vietnam era.

Legislation. A measure needing approval by the branch of government that makes laws. (See also *bill*.)

Legislative branch. The part of government that makes the laws. With the executive and judicial branches, one of the three branches of government.

Legislative veto. See *veto, legislative*.

Liberal. Traditionally, one who supports a political philosophy that supports the development of individual freedom. As opposed to conservatives, liberals seek to change existing order. Classic liberalism stressed individual property rights. With the development of inequities in industrial society, liberalism began to call on the government to provide a minimum standard of living. In the United States, liberals believe in a major governmental role in promoting social welfare. Opposite of *conservative*.

Libertarian. One who advocates the absolute minimum of governmental involvement in the lives of citizens.

Limited government. A governmental system in which the central government is purposely given little authority or direct power.

Line item veto. See *veto, line item.*

Lobby. (*n.*) any group, individual or organization that seeks to influence the government or the passage of legislation. (*v.*) to try to influence the government or the passage of legislation.

Logrolling. When politicians or political groups help one another, often in the context of "you vote for my bill, I'll vote for yours."

Majority leader. Generally, the ranking member and spokesman for the majority party in a legislature or legislative chamber. In the U.S. House, the head of the majority party is called the Speaker, while the majority leader is actually the number two person from the majority party.

Machine politics. The passage of legislation, the election of officials, or the governing of a municipality through the efforts of a strong political organization.

Mandate. In political terms the authority given to a candidate who wins by a large majority to implement his program.

Marital gap. Like the gender gap, the name given to the growing divergence in attitudes and political opinion between single persons and married persons. The gap is especially large between married men and single women.

Means tested. Any governmental benefit whose amount is based on the assets or income level of the recipient, or whose eligibility is dependent upon the recipient's existing income level. The food stamp program is an example of a means tested program.

Media event. An event that is organized solely to gain press coverage.

Merit system. System of governmental hiring in which only skill and not party membership plays a role. In theory the federal Civil Service system is a merit system.

Middle of the road. An expression that refers to the middle of the political spectrum, neither too liberal, nor too conservative. A comfortable spot for most politicians.

Midterm election. The election that occurs in November in the middle of the four year presidential election cycle when the presidency is not being contested.

Moderate. One whose politics are middle-of-the-road, neither left nor right wing.

Mudslinging. Issuing wild charges against a political candidate or office holder. A smear attack.

Nannygate. Term given the problem faced by a number of potential appointees of the Clinton administration involving the fact they had not paid the taxes required on domestic help in their homes or had employed undocumented workers in those positions.

Negative campaigning. The name given generally to the type of political campaigning where one candidate tells voters not so much why they should vote for him, but what is wrong with his opponent and why they should not vote for him.

Neoconservatism. A hybrid political philosophy in which the traditional liberal belief in government intervention to help individuals is combined with the conservative's traditional distrust of big government and support of free enterprise.

New left. See *left, new.*

New right. See *right, new.*

Nominate. To select a candidate to run for office in a general election, usually against a candidate from the other major party.

Open primary. See *primary, open.*

Oval office. The physical office used by the president in the west wing of the White House. Term used more generally to denote presidential authority and power.

Override. See *veto, override.*

Oversight. The power and responsibility of the Congress, through its committees and subcommittees, to oversee the operation of the executive branch and its agencies.

PAC. See *Political action committee.*

Palace guard. In medieval times the trusted guards who protected the life of a monarch. Today the most trusted advisers who surround a political figure.

Parish. Area served by a single church in some Christian religions, especially the Catholic Church. In Louisiana, term used to designate political subdivision elsewhere called a county.

Parliamentary system. That form of government where the power lies in the legislature which chooses one among its number to be prime minister and de facto head-of-state. Often found in countries with figurehead monarchs. Britain is a prime example.

Patronage. Exchange of government favors, such as contracts or jobs, for political support.

Platform. Positions taken on major issues by a politician running for office or by a political party. Used in campaigns.

Player. A political insider. Someone who has influence and power and is involved in political decision making.

Plebiscite. A direct vote by an entire population on some issue or question. See also *referendum*.

Pluralism. The theory that all groups in society participate in decision-making and that their views are used to arrive at one policy. It is considered a hallmark of democracy.

Pocket veto. See *veto, pocket*.

Point-of-order. A parliamentary objection raised that a body is violating its standing rules in the way it is conducting its business. It is a request that the presiding official rule something out of order.

Polarization. The splitting of a group or population along opposing political lines where compromise is made difficult or impossible.

Political action committee (PAC). An organization set up to raise funds and then to distribute them to candidates for elective office, or to political parties. The activities of PACs are closely regulated under law by the Federal Election Commission (FEC).

Political machine. See *machine politics*.

Poll. (1) Place where voter goes to cast his ballot. (2) A public opinion survey.

Poll, exit. Survey taken of voters as they emerge from having voted, which attempts to ascertain who they voted for and why. Election night predictions by the media as to who has won are based on exit polls.

Poll, tracking. A series of surveys taken at specified intervals (daily, weekly, etc.) asking the same questions of the same number of respondents seeking to track changes in public opinion on specific issues, or changes in attitude towards certain candidates.

Pollster. An individual or organization who does survey taking. Often a key member of a campaign organization.

Poll watcher. A volunteer or employee of a political party or a candidate who works at a polling place on election day to insure that campaign laws are being adhered to.

Populism. Movement that began in the rural South and West in the 1870s, promoting agrarian interests and suspicious of the Eastern establishment. Today, an ideology that sees many domestic conflicts as class differences and promotes the interests of the poor and working class against big business.

Pork barrel. Term meaning favoritism given in government appropriations—usually for public works projects which are often of dubious merit—that are designed to bring economic advantage to one legislative district and are allocated as a favor to a legislator.

Potomac fever. Desire by an elected or appointed official to remain in Washington after being defeated or replaced.

Power base. The voters or groups of voters who a politician can most depend on.

Power broker. A political leader who controls a block of votes and can deliver them. Someone who employs political power from behind-the-scenes.

Precinct. The lowest level of political subdivision organized to vote. Usually a neighborhood who votes at a single polling place. In a big city, can be as compact as a single large apartment building.

Precinct captain. The person given the responsibility by a political party for organizing the party's efforts in a given precinct. In some political machines, it can be a position of significant power.

Pressing the flesh. Handshaking. In politics, personal campaigning where the candidate goes out to the voter.

Pressure group. See *interest group*.

Primary. Election before an election in which a

party's candidates for the upcoming election are chosen.

Primary, closed. A primary in which a voter must have previously stated a party preference and then can vote only in that party's primary.

Primary, open. A primary in states that have no party-registration requirements. In these states a voter does not have to have previously stated a party affiliation and thus may vote in the primary of either party (but not both).

Privatization. The movement to return to the private sector functions now handled by government because of the feeling that private companies can do the job better or cheaper.

Pro choice. Those who are in favor of allowing a woman to chose whether she wants an abortion. Although not always true, in common usage, someone who generally favors abortion.

Progressivism. U.S. movement of the early 20th century promoting regulation of big business and reforms. Today, often considered synonymous with liberalism.

Progressive tax. See *tax, progressive.*

Pro life. Those who oppose abortion.

Proportional representation. The electoral system by which seats in a legislature or votes in a convention are allocated on the basis of strength in an election. For instance a party getting 45 percent of the votes would get 45 percent of the seats. It is the opposite of winner-take-all.

Protectionism. A policy of protecting domestic industries by setting up a system of taxes and restrictive regulations on imported goods which compete with those industries. The opposite of *free trade.*

Quid pro quo. A Latin phrase meaning literally something for something. In political usage meaning to do something directly in return for something or the promise of something.

Quorum. That the requisite number of a body are present in order to conduct business. In the U.S. House it is a simple majority, plus one.

Quorum call. A official head count taken to determine if a quorum is present.

Rainmaker. In a law firm, a partner who brings in new clients. In political lobbying, someone who can get results for his clients.

Rank and file. Originally a military term used to mean the common soldier in the ranks. Now used to mean the ordinary members of a group or organization.

Realignment. A reordering of political localities and alliances. Usually used in terms of political parties and voting blocs.

Reapportionment. See *apportionment.*

Reconciliation. A formal process undertaken every year by Congress to balance income against amounts authorized to be spent.

Red herring. A side issue that is brought up to deflect attention from the real issue.

Redistricting. The process whereby a state legislature redraws congressional boundaries within a state to add or subtract House seats based on a new apportionment or to reflect shifts in population within the state. Done every ten years in response to new census.

Redneck. A term for bigoted whites generally. Originally referred mainly to conservative southerners from rural areas.

Referendum. Process of submitting to the voters for their approval proposed state or local laws or constitutional amendments. Some state constitutions mandate certain matters be submitted to referendum and in other states submission of petitions with a certain number of voter signatures can force a previously passed law to be submitted for voter approval.

Regressive tax. See *tax, regressive.*

Republican. Considered to be the more conservative of the two major parties. Although there are many exceptions, Republicans tend to believe in a limited federal government role in economic policy and in correcting social inequality. They tend to believe in high defense spending, and are more likely than Democrats to favor the use of military force abroad. Recently, Republicans have also come to embrace what is called "the conservative social agenda," which opposes abortion and supports prayer in the schools. The Republicans' strength tends to lie in the West and in the more upper and middle class suburban areas. In recent years, the party has picked up strength in the South and among "white ethnics."

Recission. A bill passed by Congress canceling the spending of monies already appropriated.

Resolution (also joint resolution). A declaration submitted to Congress for adoption; usually something that expresses a sense of the Congress. When passed it does not need the president's signature, but also is not a binding act of law.

Reverse discrimination. A term used to describe the practice of discriminating against a white male in favor of a woman or a minority.

Rider. A provision added to a bill before passage that basically has no relation to the subject matter of the bill but which becomes law if the bill passes. Against House rules, a device for passing legislation in the U.S. Senate.

Right (or right wing). Derived from the French National Assembly of 1789 where the nobility sat on the right. Now used to refer to the more conservative end of the political spectrum.

Right, new. Term coined in the 1970s to describe traditional conservatives whose politics are mixed with evangelical Christian religious doctrine.

Right-to-work. Antiunion movement that allows a worker to hold a job without joining or being a member of a union.

Rubber stamp. A legislature or subordinate dominated by a political executive and who bends to his or her will.

Rule. (1) Regulation made by any duly authorized administrative body. (2) In the U.S. House, a set of regulations that accompanies any bill to the floor governing how debate over the bill will be handled and what amendments might be offered.

Running mate. A candidate running for office on the same ticket as a candidate for higher office. Most common usage is to describe a vice presidential candidate's relationship to the presidential candidate he or she is running with.

Run-off election. A second election, usually held after a primary with several candidates in which no candidate received more than a certain percentage of the vote. Used only in some states, usually those in which one party is strongly dominant or who hold nonpartisan elections.

Safe seat. Political office in which the incumbent is almost assured of reelection.

SALT. Strategic arms limitation talks. The ongoing talks between the U.S. and the Soviet Union, begun in 1969, seeking mutual arms reduction.

Seniority. Custom whereby those with the longest service in a body have the most power and authority. In Congress it determines everything from committee chairmanships to office locations and parking spaces.

Separation of powers. The division of authority among the branches of government (see also *checks and balances*).

Sign-off-on. To approve or endorse. Often used in the White House context where traditionally the President signals his assent by initialing a decision memo. Now used more generally throughout government and in the private sector.

Silent majority. Term used to describe the majority of the population who is not politically active.

Silk stocking. Term used generally to describe a wealthy area.

Slush fund. Money secretly collected or assembled and used for non public (and often illegal) reasons. From 19th century military practice of selling used oil (slush) and using the money to buy liquor and other nonauthorized goods.

Soft money. Money given by or channeled through national political parties to state parties and which is not subject to the same reporting requirements and limitations as money donated directly to candidates or officeholders.

Solid south. Term used originally to describe the Democratic electoral hold on the South beginning in the 1930s and running through the 1960s. Now used to describe the Republican hold of the same area in presidential elections.

Special session. The reconvening of a legislature outside its statutory schedule for the purpose of debating specific items.

Spin (or spin control). An attempt to cast a situation in the most favorable light. Often done by a "spin doctor."

Split ticket. A voter who votes for candidates from various parties for different offices. The opposite of a straight ticket voter.

Standard bearer. Candidate at the top of a ticket. Usually a presidential candidate, but can also refer to a gubernatorial candidate or even a mayoral candidate in a nonpresidential election.

Star chamber. Secret judicial or administrative proceedings that are biased and unfair. Named after England's secret Star Chamber Court in the 16th century.

States rights. In the Constitution those powers not specifically delegated to the federal government. In practice over much of the mid-20th century, a code word for opposition to civil rights.

Stem winder. Very emotional speech. Also an orator who can make such a speech.

Stonewall. Refusal to speak about a subject or, more generally, to refuse to give in to an opponent. From General "Stonewall" Jackson in the Civil War who got his nickname for his stubborn refusal to give ground. He was said to have "stood like a stone wall."

Straight ticket voter. A voter who votes for all the candidates of the same party.

Strict constructionist. One who interprets the Constitution very literally.

Stump. To campaign.

Suffrage. The right to vote.

Sunset law. A law or provision in a law which ends a program on a certain date unless it is specifically reauthorized.

Sunshine law. A law that requires government meetings to be open to the public.

Supply side economics. A conservative economic belief that as tax rates are lowered, the economy will grow through increased incentives to workers and tax income will actually grow even though rates have been lowered.

Swing vote. Usually used to refer to the voter or voters who do not cast their ballots along party line and who often decide the winner.

Table. To postpone a vote. Sometimes used as a tactic to kill a piece of legislation.

Tax, progressive. A tax which requires persons with higher incomes to pay a higher percentage of their incomes.

Tax, regressive. A tax which either lowers the tax rate as income increases or taxes everyone a flat amount thereby taking a higher percentage of the incomes of people earning less.

Tax revolt. The movement to cut existing taxes and to limit new taxes.

Tax, value added. One of the major sources of government revenues in many European countries. In effect, a national sales tax where all items bought or sold are taxed at every level of production or distribution. A widget, for example, would be taxed as raw steel when that steel was sold to the manufacturer. The finished widget would then be taxed when sold to the distributor, taxed again when sold to the retailer, and taxed yet again when sold to the consumer.

Teflon politician. A reference to a politician so popular that criticism, even merited, just seems to harmlessly deflect off him. Used first to describe President Ronald Reagan.

Third party. A political party other than the Democratic or Republican.

Third world. Generally underdeveloped countries not politically tied either to the west or the Soviet Union.

Ticket. Slate of political candidates.

Town meeting. A form of government, especially popular in small New England jurisdictions, where all citizens meet annually or more frequently to vote as a whole on issues.

Tracking poll. See *poll, tracking*.

Trade-off. To compromise.

Trial balloon. The leaking by the government of a potential policy or appointment to gauge public reaction.

Underdog. In politics the candidate in a race who is behind in the preelection polls or who has started a campaign as the apparent loser. Opposite of *front runner*.

Unicameral. Refers to a legislature with only a single chamber. Nebraska has the only unicameral state legislature in the United States.

User fee. An amount charged by government to the user of a public facility or service to pay for that facility or service. An example is an admission fee to a public park which would be used to maintain that park.

Value added tax. See *tax, valued added.*

Veto. Formal rejection of a legislative action or bill by the chief executive. From the Latin for "I forbid."

Veto, line item. The power by a chief executive to reject a particular item in a budget without rejecting the whole budget. it is a power held by many governors as they deal with the state budgets, but not by the president in dealing with the annual federal budget.

Veto, override. Legislature's rejection of the chief executive's veto of a given bill, which has the effect of enacting it. In Congress, a 2/3 vote of both the Senate and House is needed to override the president's veto.

Veto, legislative. A method established by law that in certain circumstances allows a president (or other political chief executive) to take some action subject to it being disallowed by Congress or other legislative body within a certain specified timeframe. For instance, the president, by law, can reorganize his cabinet subject to the reorganization being rejected by either house of Congress within 60 days.

Veto, pocket. By law when Congress is in session a bill become law unless vetoed by the President within a specified period (usually 30 days). But when Congress has adjourned at the end of a session a law that has been passed late in a session dies unless signed by the president. Thus he can kill a law by simply not signing it (putting it "in his pocket"). Can also apply to state legislatures and local government bodies.

Voter registration. Formal process whereby the official residence of a voter is established and he or she is enrolled on the voting lists in order to be eligible to cast ballots in national, state and local elections.

Walking around money. Small cash payoffs given to precinct workers to get the vote out on election day.

Ward. A political subdivision in many cities often used to determine legislative districts for the city council or assembly.

Watch list. Any group of individuals singled out for investigation. More specifically a computer list, maintained by the federal government, of foreign nationals who are prohibited from entering the United States.

Welfare state. Federal government providing social benefits to many of its citizens.

Whip. A party leader who is responsible for gathering the votes of his party members. In Congress the second in line in the political leadership of each party.

White flight. The movement of whites from the central cities as minorities move into their old neighborhoods.

White paper. Official government report or statement.

Whistle blower. Person within a governmental agency or corporation who discloses waste or misdeeds within that organization.

Wholesale politics. Campaigning directly to the voter. See also *pressing the flesh.*

Winner-take-all. The awarding of all a state's electoral votes to whomever wins the presidential election in that state, regardless of the margin of victory. See also *electoral college.*

Woman's lib. Term used to describe the movement promoting equal rights for women.

Yellow dog democrat. An expression from the south, especially Texas, meaning an unwavering party loyalist. "He would vote for a yellow dog if he ran as a Democrat."

Young turks. Any new or young members of an organization who seek to change or reform it. From the young Turkish army officers who sought to reform the Ottoman Empire.

Zero-base budgeting. Starting to calculate a new year's budget at zero, not from a base of what might have been appropriated last year.

CONGRESSIONAL DISTRICT MAPS

The following states are not included because they consist of only one district:

Alaska
Delaware
Montana
North Dakota
South Dakota
Vermont
Wyoming

ALABAMA

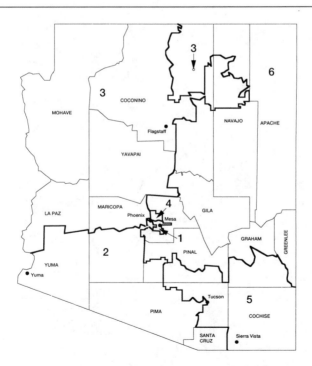

ARIZONA

ARKANSAS

CALIFORNIA

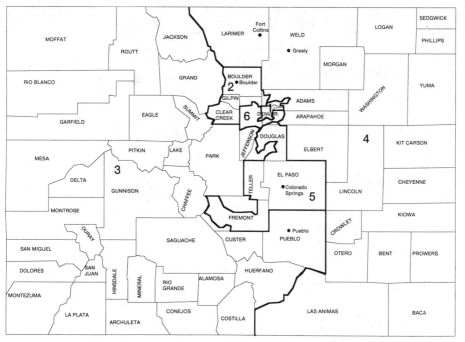

COLORADO

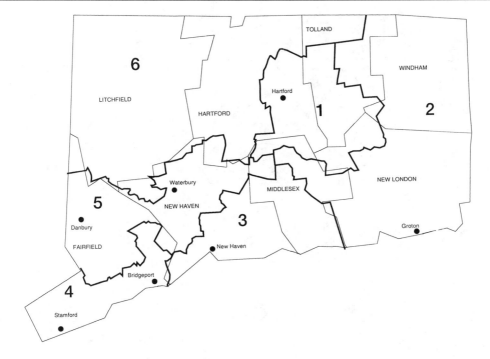

CONNECTICUT

FLORIDA

GEORGIA

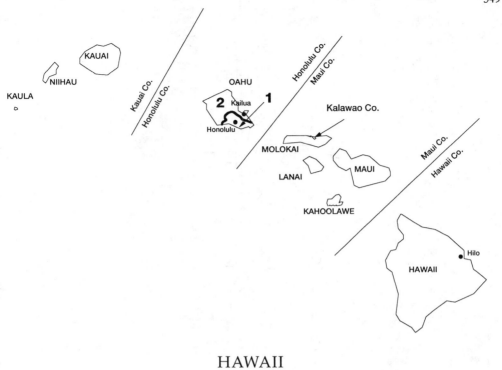

HAWAII

IDAHO

ILLINOIS

INDIANA

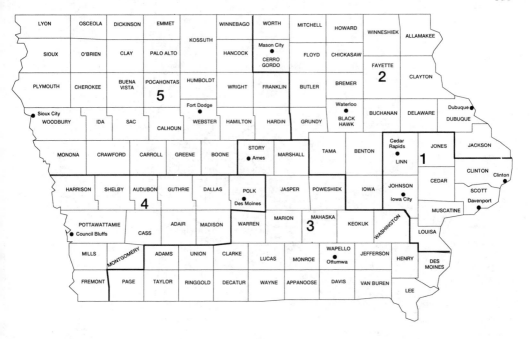

IOWA

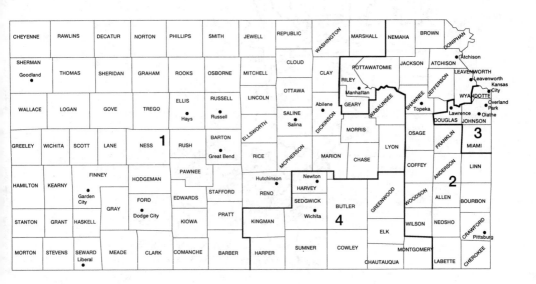

KANSAS

KENTUCKY

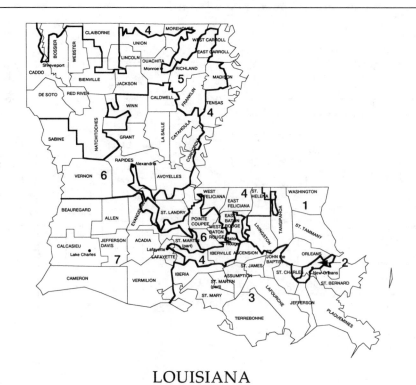

LOUISIANA

MAINE

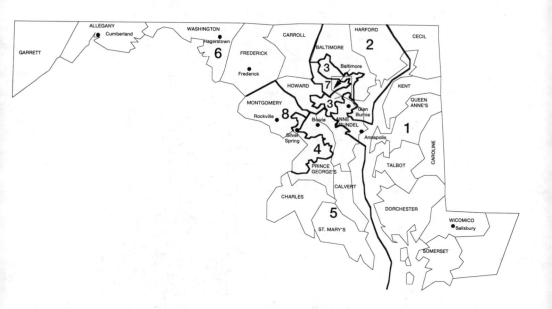

MARYLAND

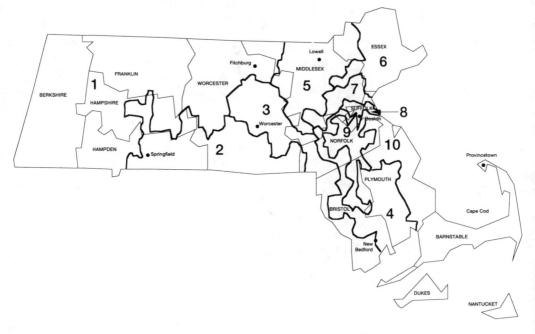

MASSACHUSETTS

MICHIGAN

MINNESOTA

MISSISSIPPI

MISSOURI

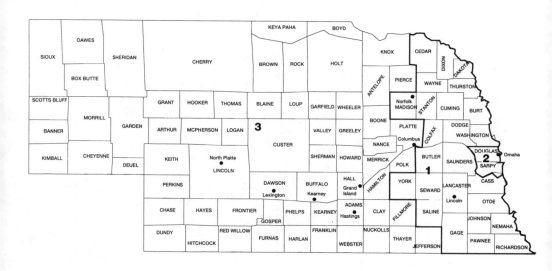

NEBRASKA

NEVADA

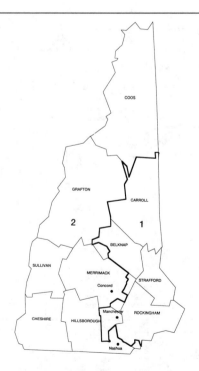

NEW HAMPSHIRE

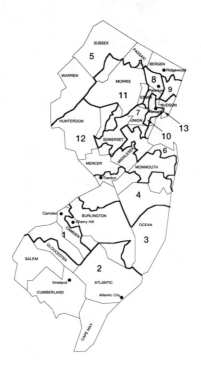

NEW JERSEY

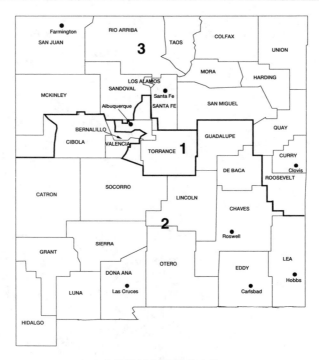

NEW MEXICO

NEW YORK

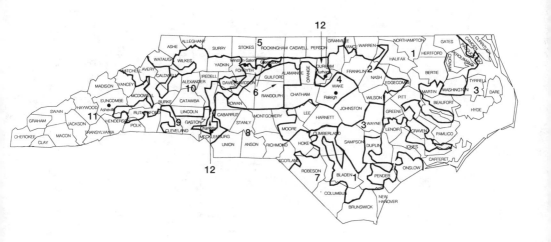

NORTH CAROLINA

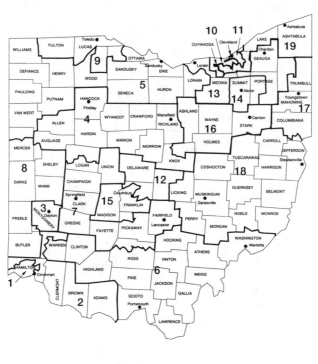

OHIO

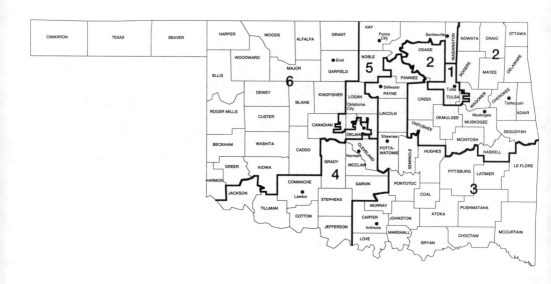

OKLAHOMA

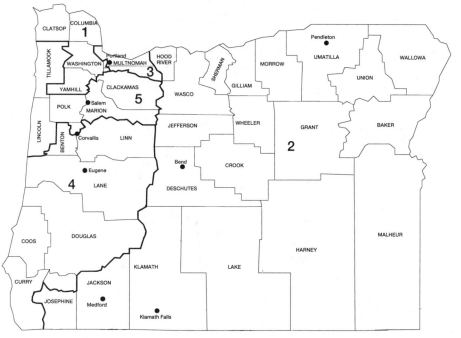

OREGON

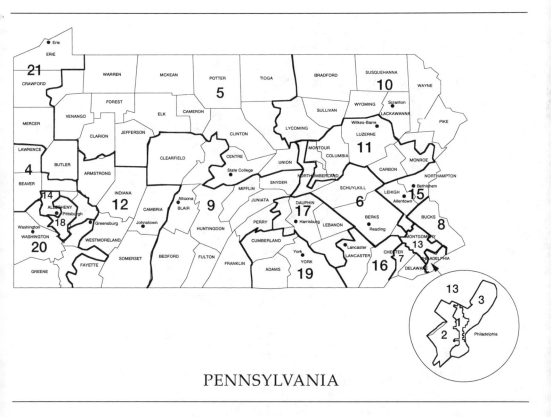

PENNSYLVANIA

RHODE ISLAND

SOUTH CAROLINA

TENNESSEE

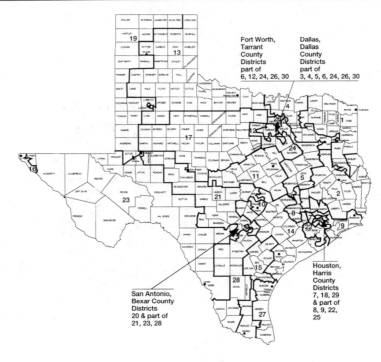

TEXAS

UTAH

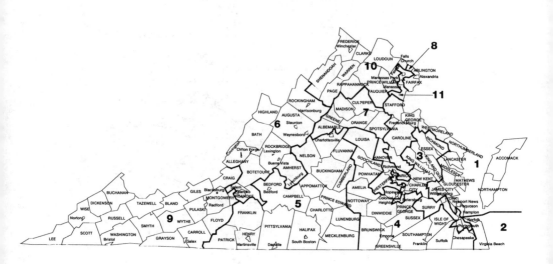

VIRGINIA

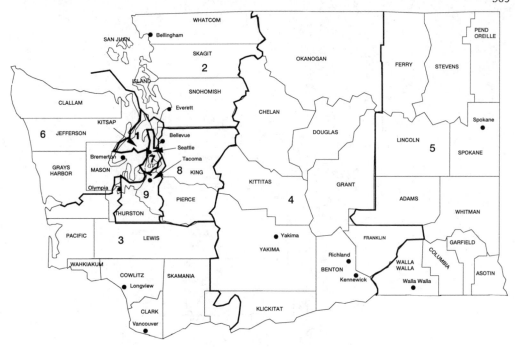

WASHINGTON

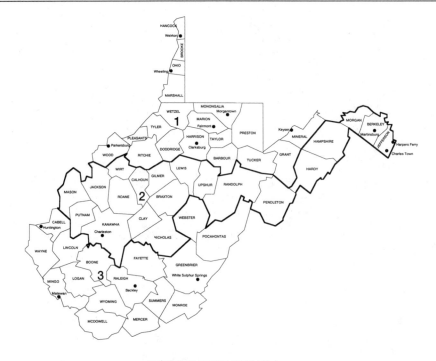

WEST VIRGINIA

WISCONSIN

SUBJECT INDEX

Abortion/reproduction rights, Supreme Court decisions, 62
Absentee ballot, defined, 332
Acquisition (Air Force), 35
Acquisition and Facilities (Veterans Affairs), 43
Act:
  defined, 332
  See also Bill; Legislation
Action (agency), 44
ACU (American Conservative Union), 103
ADA (Americans for Democratic Action), 102-3
Administrative Conference of the U.S., 44
Administration (Justice), 39
Administration and Management (Labor), 40
Administration, Office of, 31
Advise and consent, defined, 332
Advisory Commission on Intergovernmental Relations, 44
Advisory Council on Historic Preservation, 44
AFDC (Aid to Families with Dependent Children), 56-57
Affirmative action, defined, 332
African Affairs (State), 41
African Development Foundation, 44
Agency for International Development (AID), 44
Aging, National Institute on, 38
Aging, Select committee on (Senate), 85
  members, 85, 105, 111, 114, 142, 180, 184, 215, 219, 244
Agricultural Cooperative Service (Agriculture), 32
Agricultural Marketing Service (Agriculture), 32
Agricultural Research Service (Agriculture), 32
Agricultural Stabilization and Conservation Service (Agriculture), 32
Agriculture Committee (House), 87-88
  members, 87, 107, 114, 115, 118, 120, 122, 123, 130, 135, 144, 146, 147, 150, 151, 153, 157, 168, 172, 175, 176, 178, 179, 200, 201, 202, 205, 210, 212, 214, 237, 239, 247, 253, 255, 258, 270, 279, 280, 281, 291, 295, 301
  subcommittees, 87-88
Agriculture Department, 31-32, 47
  secretary, 27
Agriculture, Nutrition and Forestry Committee (Senate), 77, 105
  members, 77, 114, 150, 166, 171, 174, 177, 204, 211, 213, 237, 251, 269, 300
AID (Agency for International Development), 44
Aid to Families with Dependent Children (AFDC), 56-57
Air Force, Department of, 35
Alabama, 105-8, 306
  demographics, 306
  per capita income rank, 330
  population rank, 330
  representatives, 105-8
  senators, 105
  state officials, 306
  U.S. District Courts, 64

Alaska, 109-10, 306-7
  demographics, 306-7
  per capita income rank, 330
  population rank, 330
  representative at large, 109-10
  senators, 109
  state officials, 306-7
  U.S. District Court, 64
Albuquerque, NM, 320
  population rank, 331
Alcohol, Tobacco and Firearms, Bureau of (ATF), 43
Allergy and Infectious Diseases, National Institute on, 38
Amendment, defined, 332
American Battle Monuments Commission, 44
American Conservative Union (ACU), 103
American (Know-Nothing) Party, 11, 14
American Red Cross, 44
American Security Council (ASC), 103
Americans for Democratic Action (ADA), 102-3
AMTRAK (National Passenger Rail Corp.), 44
Anaheim, CA, per capita income, 331
Anchorage, AK, 307
  per capita income, 331
Animal and Plant Health Inspection Service (Agriculture), 32
Ann Arbor, MI, per capita income, 331
Anti-Masonic Party, 9, 13
Anti-Monopolists, 13
Antitrust Division (Justice), 39
Appalachian Regional Commission, 44
Appeals, U.S. Court of, 63
Apportionment:
  defined, 332
  See also Redistricting
Appropriation, defined, 332
Appropriations Committee (House), 88-89
  members, 88, 106, 107, 112, 113, 115, 117, 119, 127, 129, 132, 135, 138, 143, 145, 147, 152, 162, 165, 167, 169, 172, 173, 178, 179, 181, 187, 188, 191, 197, 202, 204, 215, 216, 219, 223, 224, 225, 231, 232, 234, 238, 240, 241, 246, 247, 248, 249, 253, 257, 259, 260, 276, 280, 282, 283, 292, 293, 296, 298, 302
  subcommittees, 88-89
Appropriations Committee (Senate), 77-78
  members, 77, 109, 111, 114, 116, 142, 155, 171, 177, 180, 186, 204, 207, 211, 213, 226, 251, 254, 256, 266, 275, 294, 298, 300
  subcommittees, 77-78
Approval rating, defined, 332
Arizona, 111-13, 307
  demographics, 307
  per capita income rank, 330
  population rank, 330
  representatives, 111-13
  senators, 111
  state officials, 307
  term limitation, 4

NAME INDEX

Abercrombie, Neil (HI-1), 89, 94-95, 155-56
Ackerman, Gary L. (NY-5), 92-93, 96, 228
Adams, John, 9
Adams, John Quincy, 9
Akaka, Daniel Kahikina (HI), 80-81, 83, 85, 86, 155
Albright, Madeleine, 30
Allard, Wayne (CO-4), 86, 87-88, 90, 94-95, 135-36
Anderson, John B., 15
Andrews, Michael A. (TX-25), 86, 90, 100, 283
Andrews, Robert E. (NJ-1), 91, 92-93, 219-20
Andrews, Thomas H. (ME-1), 89, 99, 185
Applegate, E. Douglas (OH-18), 97, 99-100, 249-50
Archer, Bill (TX-7), 87, 100, 277-78
Armey, Richard Keith (TX-26), 86, 91, 104, 284
Aspin, Les, 26-27

Babbitt, Bruce E., 27
Bacchus, Jim (FL-15), 90, 147
Baccus, Max (MT), 77-78, 81-82, 85, 87, 211
Bachus, Spencer (AL-6), 90, 99-100, 107
Baesler, Scotty (KY-6), 87-88, 99-100, 179
Baker, Bill (CA-10), 97, 98, 119-20
Baker, Richard Hugh (LA-6), 90, 94-95, 99, 182
Ballenger, Thomas Cass (NC-10), 91-92, 93, 240
Barca, Peter W. (WI-1), 300
Barcia, James A. (MI-5), 97, 98, 196
Barlow, Tom (KY-1), 87-88, 94-95, 96, 177-78
Barrett, Thomas M. (WI-5), 90, 93-95, 301-2
Barrett, William (NE-3), 87-88, 91-92, 94, 214
Bartlett, Roscoe (MD-6), 89, 98, 188
Barton, Joe Linus (TX-6), 92, 98, 277
Bateman, Herbert H. (VA-1), 89, 96, 289-90
Battin, James (Judge), 6
Becerra, Xavier (CA-30), 91, 98, 126
Beilenson, Anthony C. (CA-24), 90, 98, 124
Bell, John, 11
Bennett, Robert (UT), 79, 80-81, 85, 86, 286
Bentley, Helen Delich (MD-2), 88-89, 187-88
Bentsen, Lloyd, 27
Bereuter, Douglas Kent (NE-1), 93, 100-101, 213-14
Berman, Howard Lawrence (CA-26), 90, 92-93, 94-95, 125
Bevill, Tom (AL-4), 88-89, 106-7
Biden, Joseph R. Jr. (DE), 82-84, 140
Bilbray, James H. (NV-1), 89, 99, 100-101, 215-16
Bilirakis, Michael (FL-9), 92, 99-100, 145
Bingaman, Jeff (NM), 78-79, 80-81, 84, 86, 224
Birney, James G., 13
Bishop, Sanford (GA-2), 87-88, 99-100, 151
Black, Hugo, 60
Blackmun, Harry A., 59, 61
Blackwell, Lucien (PA-2), 90, 96, 97, 257
Bliley, Thomas Jerome Jr. (VA-7), 91, 92, 291-92
Blute, Peter L. (MA-3), 97, 98, 190, 191
Boehlert, Sherwood Louis (NY-23), 97, 98, 234
Boehner, John A. (OH-8), 87-88, 91, 94, 247
Bond, Christopher Samuel "Kit" (MO), 77-78, 79, 85, 207
Bonilla, Henry (TX-23), 88-89, 283

Bonior, David E., 98, 103, 197-98
Boren, David Lyle (OK), 81-82, 87-88, 251
Boren, Honest Jim, 2
Borski, Robert A. (PA-3), 92-93, 96, 257
Boucher, Rick (VA-9), 92, 95, 98, 292
Boxer, Barbara (CA), 79, 81, 116
Bradford, Drew, 2
Bradley, Bill (NJ), 80-82, 219
Brandeis, Louis, 59
Braun, Carol Moseley (IL), 79, 83-84, 85, 159
Breaux, John B. (LA), 80-81, 103, 180
Breckinridge, John C., 10, 11
Brennan, William, 58, 59
Brewster, William (OK-3), 100, 252
Brisben, J. Quinn, 2
Brooks, Jack B. (TX-9), 95, 278
Browder, Glen (AL-3), 89, 98, 106
Browner, Carol M., 29
Brown, Corrine (FL-3), 97, 99-100, 143
Brown, George E. Jr. (CA-42), 87-88, 98, 130
Brown, Hank (CO), 79, 82-84, 134
Brown, Jesse, 28
Brown, Ronald Harmon, 27
Brown, Sherrod (OH-13), 92-93, 248
Bryan, Richard H. (NV), 79, 80-81, 86, 215
Bryan, William Jennings, 10, 12, 14
Bryant, John Wiley (TX-5), 90, 92, 95, 277
Buchanan, James, 11
Bumpers, Dale (AR), 77-78, 80-81, 85, 114
Bunning, Jim (KY-4), 99, 100, 178-79
Burns, Conrad (MT), 77-78, 80-81, 85-86, 211
Burr, Aaron, 9
Burton, Dan (IN-6), 93, 96, 99-100, 168-69
Burton, Harold, 60
Burton, Phil, 5
Bush, George, 1, 10, 12, 16
Butler, Pierce, 58
Buyer, Steve (IN-5), 89, 99-100, 168
Byrd, Robert Carlyle (WV), 77-78, 84-85, 103, 298
Byrne, Leslie L. (VA-11), 96, 97, 293
Byrnes, James, 60

Callahan, Sonny (AL-1), 88-89, 105-6
Calvert, Ken (CA-43), 94-95, 98, 130
Campbell, Ben Nighthorse (CO), 79, 80-81, 85, 86, 134
Camp, David (MI-9), 87-88, 99, 196
Canady, Charles T. (FL-12), 87-88, 95, 146
Cantwell, Maria (WA-1), 92-93, 97, 294-95
Cardin, Benjamin Louis (MD-3), 94, 99, 100, 187
Carr, Robert (MI-8), 88-89, 197
Carter, Jimmy, 10, 12
Castle, Michael N. (DE), 90, 96, 140-41
Chafee, John H. (RI), 85, 86, 264
Chapman, Jim (TX-1), 88-89, 275-76
Chase, Samuel, 60
Christopher, Warren, 26
Cisneros, Henry, 27-28
Clarke, John H., 59